Strategic
Corporate Social
Responsibility

SAGE was founded in 1965 by Sara Miller McCune to support the dissemination of usable knowledge by publishing innovative and high-quality research and teaching content. Today, we publish over 900 journals, including those of more than 400 learned societies, more than 800 new books per year, and a growing range of library products including archives, data, case studies, reports, and video. SAGE remains majority-owned by our founder, and after Sara's lifetime will become owned by a charitable trust that secures our continued independence.

Los Angeles | London | New Delhi | Singapore | Washington DC | Melbourne

Strategic
Corporate Social Responsibility

Sustainable Value Creation

David Chandler

**University of Colorado Denver
Business School**

Edition 4

$SAGE

Los Angeles | London | New Delhi
Singapore | Washington DC | Melbourne

FOR INFORMATION:

SAGE Publications, Inc.
2455 Teller Road
Thousand Oaks, California 91320
E-mail: order@sagepub.com

SAGE Publications Ltd.
1 Oliver's Yard
55 City Road
London, EC1Y 1SP
United Kingdom

SAGE Publications India Pvt. Ltd.
B 1/I 1 Mohan Cooperative Industrial Area
Mathura Road, New Delhi 110 044
India

SAGE Publications Asia-Pacific Pte. Ltd.
3 Church Street
#10-04 Samsung Hub
Singapore 049483

Acquisitions Editor: Maggie Stanley
Development Editor: Abbie Rickard
eLearning Editor: Katie Ancheta
Editorial Assistant: Neda Dallal
Production Editor: Jane Haenel
Copy Editor: Paula L. Fleming
Typesetter: C&M Digitals (P) Ltd.
Proofreader: Susan Schon
Indexer: Terri Morrissey
Cover Designer: Anthony Paular
Marketing Manager: Ashlee Blunk

Printed in the United States of America

Library of Congress Cataloging-in-Publication Data

Names: Chandler, David, 1969– author.

Title: Strategic corporate social responsibility : sustainable value creation / David Chandler, University of Colorado Denver Business School.

Description: Fourth edition. | Thousand Oaks : Sage Publications, [2016] | Earlier editions authored by David Chandler and William B. Werther Jr. | Includes bibliographical references and index.

Identifiers: LCCN 2016004555 | ISBN 9781506310992 (pbk. : alk. paper)

Subjects: LCSH: Social responsibility of business. | Social responsibility of business—Case studies.

Classification: LCC HD60 .W46 2016 | DDC 658.4/08—dc23
LC record available at http://lccn.loc.gov/2016004555

This book is printed on acid-free paper.

SFI label applies to text stock

17 18 19 20 10 9 8 7 6 5 4 3 2

Brief Contents

Detailed Contents

List of Figures

Part III: An Economic Perspective

Part IV: A Strategic Perspective

Part V: A Sustainable Perspective

GLOSSARY

CSR TERMS

Consistent definitions, rhetoric, and vocabulary are the entry point to understanding any discipline, yet they remain elusive and fiercely debated within the field of CSR.[1] As such, the range of competing terminology that is used can be a source of confusion for executives, academics, journalists, and other students of CSR. Ostensibly part of the same discussion, it is common to see CSR referred to in a number of different ways:

- "Corporate responsibility" or "corporate citizenship"
- "Conscious capitalism" or "sustainable business"
- "Corporate community engagement" or "strategic philanthropy"
- "Sustainability" or "corporate environmental responsibility"
- "Corporate social performance" or "corporate social strategy"

In many cases, writers are using different terms to mean very similar things, yet heated debates can sprout from these semantic subtleties. Rather than engage in this debate, this book focuses on the term *corporate social responsibility* due to its widespread diffusion, even while recognizing that different people interpret it in different ways. In order to clarify some of the confusion and provide a consistent vocabulary with which to read this book, therefore, brief definitions of some of the many CSR concepts are detailed below. These terms are discussed in the CSR literature (some more widely than others) and referred to throughout this book.

Accountability: The extent to which a firm attends to the needs and demands of its stakeholders (see *Transparency*).

Activism: Actions (e.g., campaigns, boycotts, protest) by individuals, nonprofit organizations, or NGOs designed to further social, political, or environmental goals.

Advocacy advertising: Efforts by firms to communicate social, environmental, or political positions to stakeholders (see *Cause-related marketing*).

Badvertising: Advertising, marketing, or PR activities by a firm that promote socially irresponsible behavior, often generating a backlash by stakeholders.

B Corp: A certification awarded to firms that meet specific standards of transparency and accountability set by the nonprofit B Lab (http://www.bcorporation.net/).

Benefit corporation: A type of legal structure for businesses (http://benefit-corp.net/) that is available only in those US states that have passed benefit corporation legislation.

Business citizenship: Socially oriented actions by firms designed to demonstrate their role as constructive members of society.

Business ethics: The application of ethics and ethical theory to businesses and business decisions.

Cap-and-trade: A market established to buy and sell the right to emit carbon. It is underwritten by government-issued credits and is designed to limit the total amount of carbon in the atmosphere.

Carbon footprint: A firm's total emissions of carbon-related greenhouse gasses, often measured in terms of tons of carbon or carbon dioxide (see *Greenhouse gas*).

Carbon insetting: A firm's integration of sustainable practices directly into the supply chain to take responsibility for its carbon emissions (see *Carbon offsetting*).

Carbon intensity: A measure of a firm's environmental impact that is calculated by dividing carbon emissions by annual sales.

Carbonivore: An organization or technology that removes more carbon from the air than it emits, "either storing it, turning it into a useful product or recycling it."[2]

Carbon neutral: An effort to ensure a firm's net carbon emissions are zero (see *Net positive*).

Carbon offsetting: A firm's reduction of its carbon footprint by paying for environmentally beneficial behavior by a third party (see *Carbon insetting*).

Cash mob: A group of community residents who use social media to assemble at a given date and time to spend money in support of a local business.

Cause-related marketing: Efforts to gain or retain customers by tying purchases of the firm's goods or services to the firm's philanthropy (see *Advocacy advertising*).

Circular economy: A means to reduce waste within economies via greater efficiency or by reuse, repair, or recycling (see *Cradle-to-cradle*).

Civic engagement: Efforts by a firm to improve a local community.

Clicktivism: A form of social or environmental protest that is conducted online via social media (e.g., signing an online petition).

Climate change: The term used to describe the effect on the planet's weather systems of human economic activity.

Coalitions: Collections of organizations, stakeholders, or individuals that collaborate to achieve common goals.

Community advocacy panels (CAPS): Formal or informal groups of citizens who advise firms about areas of common interest that affect the local community.

Compliance: Actions taken by firms to conform to existing laws and regulations.

Conscious capitalism: An emerging economic system that "builds on the foundations of Capitalism—voluntary exchange, entrepreneurship, competition, freedom to trade and the rule of law. These are essential to a healthy functioning economy, as are other elements of Conscious Capitalism including trust, compassion, collaboration and value creation."[3] Synonymous with strategic CSR, it is based on four principles that encourage the development of values-based businesses: higher purpose, stakeholder interdependence, conscious leadership, and conscious culture (see *Values-based business*).

Consumer activism: Efforts by customers to have their views represented in company policies and decision making. Organized activism is more likely referred to as a "consumer movement," which can advocate for more radical changes in consumer laws.

Consumer boycott: Customers who avoid specific industries, firms, or products based on performance metrics or issues that they value.

Consumer buycott: Consumers who actively seek to support specific industries, firms, or products through their purchase decisions based on performance metrics or issues that they value. Such support is often warranted because an industry or specific firm has been marginalized by other stakeholders in society.

Corporate citizenship: See *Business citizenship*.

Corporate philanthropy: Contributions by firms that benefit stakeholders and the community, often made through financial or in-kind donations to nonprofit organizations.

Corporate responsibility: A term similar in meaning to *CSR*, but preferred by some companies because it deemphasizes the word *social*.

Corporate social opportunity: A perspective that emphasizes the benefits to firms of adopting CSR, mitigating the perception of CSR as a *cost* to business.[4]

Corporate social performance: The benefits to the firm (often measured in traditional financial or accounting metrics) gained from implementing CSR.

Corporate social responsibility (CSR): A responsibility among firms to meet the needs of their stakeholders and a responsibility among stakeholders to hold firms to account for their actions.

Corporate social responsiveness: Actions taken by a firm to achieve its CSR goals in response to demands made by specific stakeholder groups.

Corporate stakeholder responsibility: A responsibility among all of a firm's stakeholders to hold the firm to account for its actions by rewarding behavior that meets expectations and punishing behavior that does not.

Corporate sustainability: Business operations that can be continued over the long term without degrading the ecological environment (see *Sustainability*).

Cradle-to-cradle: A concept introduced by William McDonough that captures the zero-waste, closed-loop concept of the circular economy (see *Circular economy*).[5]

Downcycling: A recycling process that reduces the quality of the recycled material over time (see *Recycling* and *Upcycling*).

Eco-efficiency: An approach to business that is characterized by the need to "do more with less" and popularized by the phrase "reduce, reuse, recycle."

Ecopreneur: "Environmental and social entrepreneurs [who] lead socially committed, break-through ventures that are driven by environmental, social, and economic goals"[6] (see *Social entrepreneur*).

Ecosystem: A self-sustaining community.

Enlightened self-interest: The recognition that businesses can operate in a socially conscious manner without forsaking the economic goals that lead to financial success.

Ethics: A guide to moral behavior based on social norms and culturally embedded definitions of *right* and *wrong*.

E-waste: Toxic pollutants that are a byproduct of discarded consumer electronic goods, such as televisions, computers, and cell phones.

Externality: See *Externality* under "Strategy Terms."

Fair trade: Trade in goods at prices above what market forces would otherwise determine in order to ensure a *living wage* for the producer (see *Living wage*).

Fast money: "Money that has become so detached from people, place and the activities that it is financing that not even the experts understand it fully"[7] (see *Slow money*).

Garbology: The study of what humans throw away.[8]

Global Compact: A United Nations–backed effort to convince corporations to commit to multiple principles that address the challenges of globalization.[9]

Global Reporting Initiative (GRI): A multi-stakeholder organization designed to produce a universal measure of a firm's CSR efforts.

Global warming: See *Climate change*.

Glocalization: "Dealing with big global problems through myriad small or individual actions."[10]

Green noise: "Static caused by urgent, sometimes vexing or even contradictory information [about the environment] played at too high a volume for too long."[11]

Greenhouse gas: A gas that pollutes the atmosphere by trapping heat, causing average temperatures to rise (e.g., carbon dioxide; see *Carbon footprint*).

Greenwash: "Green-wash (green'wash', -wôsh')—verb: the act of misleading consumers regarding the environmental practices of a company or the environmental benefits of a product or service"[12] (see *Pinkwash*).

Gross national happiness: An attempt, most advanced in the Kingdom of Bhutan, to replace gross domestic product (GDP) as the primary measure of an economy's health and well-being.[13]

Human rights: Freedoms that are an integral element of what it is to be human.[14]

Impact investing: A variety of investment vehicles (e.g., mutual funds, low-interest loans, bonds, and exchange-traded funds [ETFs]) that seek to produce a financial return for investors by solving social problems that previously were not addressed by market forces (see *Social finance*).

Inclusive capitalism: The idea that "those with the power and the means have a responsibility to help make society stronger and more inclusive for those who don't."[15]

Integrated reporting: The publication of a firm's economic, environmental, and social performance in a unified document (see *Triple bottom line*).

Intrapreneurship: A combination of the terms *innovation* and *entrepreneur* to capture innovative behavior within a large, bureaucratic organization.

Iron law of social responsibility: The axiom that those who use power in ways society deems abusive will eventually lose their ability to continue acting in that way.[17]

Islamic finance: An investment philosophy guided by shariah law. "Shariah-Compliant funds are prohibited from investing in companies which derives [sic] income from the sales of alcohol, pork products, pornography, gambling, military equipment or weapons."[16]

Leanwashing: Advertising or other marketing by food- or nutrition-related companies that misleadingly suggests a product is healthy (e.g., using terms such as *natural* on labels).

Living wage: A level of pay that is designed to meet an employee's basic living standards, above subsistence levels. A *living wage*, which is culturally embedded, is usually set at a higher level than a *minimum wage*, which is legally defined. (See *Fair trade*.)

Moral hazard: To take risk in search of personal benefit where the consequences of that risk are not born by the individual. During the 2007–2008 financial crisis, this effect was captured in the finance industry by incentives that *privatized gains* but *socialized losses*.

Natural capital: The stock of all resources that exist in the natural environment.

Natural corporate management (NCM): A business philosophy "based upon genetic, evolutionary, and neuroscience components that underlie and help drive corporate management, including behavior, organizational, and eco-environmental relationships."[18]

Net positive: An effort by a firm to ensure that it draws on little or no virgin natural resources in its operational processes (see *Carbon neutral*).

Nongovernmental organizations (NGOs): Organizations that operate with a legal and accounting structure that allows them to pursue political, environmental, and/or social goals without the need to generate a profit (see *Nonprofits*).

Nonprofits: Nonprofits are similar to NGOs but often differ by having a domestic, rather than an international, focus (see *Nongovernmental organizations*).

Organic: A method of producing food without using pesticides, chemical fertilizers, or other industrial aids with the goal of promoting ecological balance and preserving biodiversity. Organic agriculture and its products are certified by the government in many countries.

Pastorpreneur: A religious figure who applies business principles to a church or related religious activity, or who applies religious principles to a business.

Philanthropreneur: An individual who targets a charitable donation (often to a socially or environmentally oriented start-up) and actively intervenes in the management of that donation (e.g., advising the organization or joining its board).

Philanthropy: A donation made, by either an individual or organization, to a charity or charitable cause.

Pinkwash: "When a company promotes pink-ribboned products and claims to care about breast cancer while also selling products linked to disease or injury"[19] (see *Greenwash*).

Public policy: Government decisions aimed at establishing rules and guidelines for action with the intent of providing benefit (or preventing harm) to society.

Recycling: A process by which resources are reclaimed from discarded materials and put to productive use (see *Downcycling* and *Upcycling*).

Renewable energy: A source of energy that is non-carbon-based (e.g., solar, wind, or tidal energy). Also referred to as *alternative energy* or *green energy*.

Shwopping: An exchange program by which consumers trade in used clothing for vouchers that can be used to purchase new clothes. Introduced in the UK by Oxfam and Marks & Spencer to support recycling within a circular economy.

Slow money: An offshoot of the "slow food" movement that, instead of focusing on local food, emphasizes impact investments in local businesses (see *Fast money*).[20]

Social entrepreneur: An entrepreneur who seeks to achieve social and environmental goals by utilizing for-profit business practices (see *Ecopreneur*).

Social finance: An approach to finance that emphasizes the social return on an investment as measured by a variety of criteria (e.g., ethical, faith based, and environmental) and that also seeks to secure financial returns for investors (see *Impact investing*).

Social innovation: An approach to business by which firms seek to meet not only the technical needs of their customers but also their broader aspirations as citizens.

Social license: The ability of a firm to continue to operate due to stakeholder approval of its activities.

Socially responsible investing (SRI): A portfolio investment strategy that seeks returns by investing in firms or projects that pursue CSR-related goals.

Social value: The benefit (or harm) of a firm's activities in terms of nonmonetary metrics, as defined by each of the firm's stakeholders.

Stakeholders: An individual or organization that is affected by a firm (either voluntarily or involuntarily) and possesses the capacity to affect the firm.

Strategic corporate social responsibility: The incorporation of a CSR perspective within a firm's strategic planning and core operations so that the firm is managed in the interests of a broad set of stakeholders to optimize value over the medium to long term.

Sustainability: "Sustainable development is development that meets the needs of the present without compromising the ability of future generations to meet their own needs"[21] (see *Corporate sustainability*).

Sweatshops: Factories that employ children or apply working standards with little, if any, respect for human rights. Conditions are deemed to be unsafe and unfair, often in comparison to minimum legal conditions established in more affluent societies.

Transparency: The extent to which a firm's decisions and operating procedures are open or visible to its external stakeholders (see *Accountability*).

Triple bottom line: An evaluation of the total business by comprehensively assessing a firm's financial, environmental, and social performance (see *Integrated reporting*).

Upcycling: A recycling process that increases the quality of the recycled material over time (see *Recycling* and *Downcycling*).

Values: Beliefs about appropriate goals, actions, and conditions.

Values-based business: A for-profit firm that is founded on a vision and mission defined by a strategic CSR perspective (see *Conscious capitalism*).

Whistle-blower: An insider who alleges organizational misconduct and communicates those allegations of wrongdoing outside the firm to the media, prosecutors, or others.

STRATEGY TERMS

In addition to the CSR terms that are used throughout this book, there are a number of specialized terms used to describe a firm's strategy or strategic decision-making processes. The intersection between CSR and corporate strategy is central to the argument presented in this textbook. As such, brief definitions of the key concepts associated with a firm's strategic planning and implementation are detailed below.

Agent: An individual appointed to act on someone else's behalf (see *Principal*).

Board of directors: The formal authority to which the CEO and executives of the firm are ultimately responsible (see *Corporate governance*).

Business: A process of economic exchange by which organizations seek to generate financial profits by satisfying stakeholder needs (see *Company*).

Business strategy: The strategy of a specific business unit within a firm that enables the firm to differentiate its products from those of other firms on the basis of low cost or another factor (e.g., superior technology, brand, customer service) in order to create a sustainable competitive advantage (see *Corporate strategy*, *Differentiation*, and *Low cost*).

Capabilities: Actions that a firm can do, such as pay its bills, in ways that add value to the production process.

Company (or corporation): A legal organizational form permitted to engage in commercial business. The name *company* comes from a combination of the Latin words *cum* and *panis,* the literal translation of which originally meant "breaking bread together."[22] (See *Business*.)

Competencies: Actions a firm can do very well.

Competitive advantage: Competencies, resources, or skills that enable the firm to differentiate itself from its competitors and succeed in the marketplace (see *Sustainable competitive advantage*).

Core competence (or capability): The processes of the firm that it not only does very well but is so superior at performing that it is difficult (or at least time-consuming) for other firms to match its performance in this area.[23]

Core resource: An asset of the firm that is unique and difficult to replicate.

Corporate governance: The structure and systems that serve to hold the firm legally accountable (see *Board of directors*).

Corporate strategy: The strategy of the firm. Strategy at this level involves decisions that allow the firm to navigate its competitive environment, identifying the businesses in which the firm will compete and whether to enter into partnerships with other firms via joint ventures, mergers, or acquisitions (see *Business strategy*).

Differentiation: A *business strategy* used by firms to distinguish their products from the products of other firms on the basis of some component other than price (see *Low cost*).

Economic value: The benefit (or harm) of a firm's activities in terms of monetary metrics, as defined by each of its stakeholders.

Externality: The effect of a transaction (either positive or negative) on a third party not involved in the primary exchange.

Fiduciary: A responsibility of one party that is a result of a formal relationship, either legal or ethical, with another party. The responsibility is founded on trust and often involves financial transactions.

Firm: A business organization that marshals scarce or valuable resources to produce a good or service that it then sells at a price that is greater than its cost of production.

Five forces: A macro-level analysis of the competitive structure of a firm's industry (see *Industry perspective*).[24]

Gig economy: An economy that is driven by "gigs"—individual tasks and short-term jobs performed by self-employed freelancers or micro-entrepreneurs and traded online.[25]

Globalization: The process (facilitated by rapidly improving communication technologies, transportation, trade, and capital flows) that allows a firm's operations to transcend national boundaries and facilitates greater interaction among people, societies, cultures, and governments worldwide.

Industry perspective: An external perspective of the firm that identifies the structure of the environment in which the firm operates (in particular, its industry) as the main determinant of its marketplace success (see *Five forces* and *Resources perspective*).

Low cost: A *business strategy* used by firms to distinguish their products from the products of other firms on the basis of more efficient operations (see *Differentiation*).

Market segmentation: A process of dividing up consumers into groups with similar characteristics (often based on demographic information).

Mission: States what the firm is going to do to achieve its vision. It addresses the types of activities the firm seeks to perform (see *Vision*).

Net present value: The value today of an investment that will mature in the future.

Offshoring: Relocating jobs to overseas countries in search of lower labor costs.

Onshoring (or reshoring): Returning jobs closer to home in order to create more flexible and responsive supply chains.

Opportunity cost: The benefit that would have been created if an alternative course of action had been chosen.

Price premium: The amount of money that consumers are willing to pay above cost (essentially, the profit on a product) for some attainable value (either perceived or real).

Principal: An individual who appoints someone to act on their behalf (see *Agent*).

Profit: The residual value (positive or negative) of a firm's transactions after subtracting costs from revenues.

Prosumer: A consumer who improves the firm's products by providing information (e.g., completing surveys) or promotion (e.g., on social media). Originated by futurist Alvin Toffler and related to the term *prosumption*, meaning "production by consumers."[26]

Resources perspective: An internal perspective of the firm that identifies its resources, capabilities, and core competencies as the main determinant of its sustainable competitive advantage (see *Industry perspective*).

Sharing economy: An economy that is driven by "shared assets"—assets that are owned by individuals, rather than companies, and rented out for short periods among an online community.[27]

Strategic planning: The process (often annual) whereby firms create or reformulate plans for future operations.

Strategy: Determines how the firm will undertake its mission. It sets forth the ways it will negotiate its competitive environment in order to attain a sustainable advantage (see *Tactics*).

Sunk cost: An investment of resources already made that cannot be reclaimed.

Supply chain (or value system): The linkages formed by relationships among organizations that provide a firm with the materials necessary to produce a product (see *Value chain*).

Sustainable competitive advantage: Competencies, resources, or skills that enable the firm to differentiate itself from its competitors and maintain its success in the marketplace over a period of time (see *Competitive advantage*).

SWOT analysis: A tool used to identify the internal Strengths and Weaknesses of the firm and the external Opportunities and Threats in the environment. The goal is to match the firm's strengths with its opportunities, understand its weaknesses, and avoid any threats.

Tactics: Day-to-day management decisions made to implement a firm's strategy (see *Strategy*).

Value chain: An analysis of the links in the production process that identifies each value-adding stage. This analysis is possible within a firm (*value chain*) or among firms (*supply chain* or *value system*).[28]

Value creation: The generation of a perceived benefit for an individual or group, as defined by that individual or group.

Vision: A statement designed to answer why the firm exists. It identifies the needs it aspires to solve (see *Mission*).

VRIO: An acronym of the four characteristics a resource must possess in order for it to be the source of a firm's sustainable competitive advantage: Is the resource **V**aluable? Is it **R**are? Is it costly to **I**mitate? Is the firm **O**rganized to capture this potential value?

PREFACE

WHY CSR MATTERS

The fourth edition of this textbook reflects the evolution that is taking place in corporate social responsibility (CSR). Increasingly, CSR is seen as more than a set of peripheral activities (such as philanthropy) and, instead, is understood as central to the firm's strategic decision making and day-to-day operations. In other words, CSR is not an option; it is what businesses do. Being able to respond efficiently and effectively to the needs and demands of stakeholders (who have increasingly powerful tools at their disposal to convey those needs and demands) is not only the key to success in today's global business environment—it is the key to survival.

To reflect the growing importance of CSR, this book is titled *Strategic Corporate Social Responsibility: Sustainable Value Creation*. Talking about CSR in terms of *value creation* means that it becomes the responsibility of the CEO and senior executives in the organization. Value creation speaks to what is core about a firm, across functional areas. While preconceived notions of *CSR* and *sustainability* may cause some CEOs to prejudge or reject these topics, *value creation* cannot be avoided. In fact, it must be embraced. In order to rebut the idea of CSR as a cost to business, therefore, supporting arguments must be embedded in operational and strategic relevance. In the process, CSR moves from an optional add-on to the center stage—it is there because it involves all of the firm's stakeholders, both internal and external. It is therefore incorrect to say that firms can chose to do CSR or chose to ignore it. On the contrary, all firms do CSR (they all seek to create value); it is just that some do it better than others.

This book exists because this argument is not yet widely accepted, by either executives or business schools. CSR is too often ignored or misunderstood partly because, on the surface at least, it is more obvious in its absence. Value can be hard to measure, while harm inflicted is only apparent after the fact. The scale of the Deepwater Horizon oil spill in the Gulf of Mexico in 2010, for example, demonstrated the consequences (for both the firm and society) when stakeholder interests are ignored. Similarly, the devastating effects of the 2007–2008 financial crisis linger and continue to define the economic policy of governments worldwide. CSR is not an abstract concept; it is real and resides at the center of almost everything we do.

CSR is pervasive because the for-profit firm is the cornerstone of a developed society. Firms are the most efficient entity we have for transforming scarce and valuable resources into the products and services on which we rely. It is important to also remember, however, that these firms are a social construction—designed as an aid to progress. As such, I believe that the most important question we face is *What is the purpose of the for-profit firm?* This question is existential. The answer will determine our collective standard of living—today, tomorrow, and for generations to come. The short answer, of course, is that firms exist to create *value*. But it is how they create value and for whom that matters. This is what makes CSR so complex and demanding; it is also what makes CSR integral to the firm's strategy and day-to-day operations.

As such, this book celebrates the positive role that for-profit firms play in our lives, while detailing a plan for how that role can be improved. This book is an endorsement of the profit motive and capitalism, but it argues that competitive forces generate the greatest welfare when embedded in a framework of values. Markets work best when all stakeholders act according to their personal ethics and morals (whether as customers, employees, journalists, regulators, or any of the other economic roles we adopt daily). As a result, this book advocates for *evolution* rather than *revolution*—it seeks to shape what is practical and realizable, not wish for what is ideal and out of reach. There is a reason why our economic system has evolved the way it has. This textbook acknowledges this and, starting with what we know about human psychology and economic exchange, builds a manifesto for change that business leaders can embrace today.

The fourth edition of *Strategic CSR*, therefore, is a road map. It provides a framework that firms can use to navigate the complex and dynamic business landscape. Increasingly, effective managers must balance the competing interests of the firm's stakeholders—understanding what they want today and, perhaps more important, what they will want tomorrow. *Strategic CSR* was written in the hope of creating a more responsive business culture in which for-profit firms take their rightful place as the primary solution to society's largest problems. But, we have a lot of work to do. What is clear is that CSR is central to the effort. It is not an optional add-on. Rather, it is an essential refinement of the market model—an operating philosophy for firms that seeks to optimize growth (and profits) over the medium to long term. It is a strategic imperative that is central to operations. It is how firms create value—the central concern that CEOs face every day. CSR is not one way of doing business among many; it is *the* way of doing business in the globalized, wired world in which we live today.

Strategic Corporate Social Responsibility

CSR matters because it encompasses all aspects of business. And, businesses matter because they create much of the wealth and well-being in society. Central to the concept of CSR, therefore, is deciding where companies fit within the social fabric. By addressing issues surrounding corporate governance, environmental pollution, corruption, and employee safety and pay—among many other issues—a firm's stakeholders define the dynamic context in which the business operates. The context is *dynamic* because the ideal mix of operational goals and stakeholder expectations is constantly evolving. Along the way, difficult questions arise: Why does a business exist? Is the goal simply to generate as much profit as possible? Who defines the boundaries between private profits and the public good? What obligations do businesses have to the societies in which they operate? Are these *obligations* voluntary, or should they be mandated by law? To whom are companies ultimately accountable? Can the interests of firms and their stakeholders be aligned, or do they conflict inherently?

While businesses are largely responsible for creating wealth and driving social progress, they do not act alone. Governments are crucial because they set the rules and parameters within which society and businesses operate. In addition, nonprofit or nongovernmental organizations (NGOs) exist to do social good without seeking profit or fulfilling the duties of a government organization—they reach into areas where politics and profit often do not go. Nevertheless, without the innovation that the market inspires, social and economic progress declines, in time reducing our standard of living to some primitive level. A simple thought experiment underscores this: Look around you and subtract everything that was produced by a business. What is left? Or, another example: What is the difference between the poorest and wealthiest nations? Is it not primarily the creativity and productivity of competitive businesses?

Businesses produce much of what is good in our society. At the same time, however, they can cause great harm, as pollution, layoffs, industrial accidents, and economic crises amply demonstrate. Yet the successful alignment of dynamic self-interest and stakeholder constraint creates optimal outcomes, as when a new lifesaving drug emerges from the profit motive. But there is tension between these two extremes, which raises questions about the ideal role of businesses in society. As a result, corporate executives face conflict and confusion about stakeholder expectations of their organizations. On the one hand, for example, Milton Friedman, the Nobel Prize–winning economist, argues:

> Few trends could so thoroughly undermine the very foundations of our free society as the acceptance by corporate officials of a social responsibility other than to make as much money for their stockholders as possible.[1]

On the other hand, firms are increasingly expected to accommodate their stakeholders' interests—embracing the needs and concerns of employees, shareholders, lenders, and customers while assuming responsibility for suppliers (throughout their extended supply chain), communities, and the natural environment. Which perspective is *ideal*? Which is *right*? Are the two positions necessarily mutually exclusive? Perhaps, more accurately, what is the best mix of the two that produces a sustainable society that optimizes societal benefit and welfare?

Studying CSR

Strategic CSR provides a framework with which readers can explore these questions. This book identifies the key issues of debate, models them around conceptual frameworks, and provides both the means and resources to investigate this intensely complex topic. What makes this exploration exciting and worthy of study is that CSR is ever present: Jobs and job losses, financial bailouts and record profits, corruption and scientific breakthroughs, pollution and technological innovations, personal greed and corporate charity—all spring from the relentless drive for innovation in the pursuit of profit that we call *business*. As such, CSR can only be studied at the heart of operations, where core competencies mold the business strategies that enable firms to compete with each other. And when they compete in the marketplace, CSR offers a sustainable path between unbridled capitalism and rigidly regulated economies. CSR helps managers optimize both the *ends* of profit and the *means* of execution by creating value for the firm's broad range of stakeholders.

Still, the question remains: What issues matter under the broad heading of corporate social responsibility? The answer depends on the industry context and the firm's strategy, or *how* it creates value for its stakeholders. Since industries and strategies vary widely, the appropriate mix of issues will differ from firm to firm and will evolve as firms adapt their strategy to their specific business environment. The result? It is impossible to prescribe the exact CSR mix to deal with any particular landscape. Instead, this book offers a strategic lens as the best perspective through which firms should approach CSR because it is through the strategic reformulation process that organizations adapt to their social, cultural, and competitive reality.

Hence, strategic CSR is best viewed from a stakeholder perspective that embraces an operating environment made up of many constituent groups (both internal and external) who have a stake in the firm's profit-seeking activities. It demonstrates the value to firms of defining CSR in relation to their operational context and then incorporating a CSR perspective into their strategic planning and throughout the organization. The situations change, but the questions remain the same: Who are the primary stakeholders? Which claims are legitimate? What do we say to those stakeholders who will disagree with the decision? What value are we creating and for whom? Is our business sustainable? These and other issues force managers to understand CSR from a stakeholder vantage point set against each firm's industry and strategy.

What makes this book a unique tool for this journey is its approach and underlying thesis: Exploration is the best method of learning. For those who like to form their own opinions, *Strategic CSR* offers a guided tour. It is designed to provoke via a series of questions, examples, and case studies that guide an online search for solutions and supporting examples. By seeking out this information online, the reader can more easily engage with the material and construct informed opinions. Using this approach, the goal is to cover all of Bloom's learning stages, from Remembering through Creating

Preface Figure 1	Bloom's Taxonomy of Learning

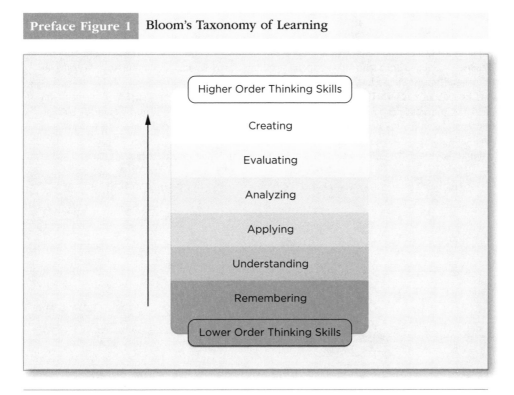

Source: Lorin W. Anderson & David R. Krathwohl (Eds.), *A Taxonomy for Learning, Teaching, and Assessing: A Revision of Bloom's Taxonomy of Educational Objectives* (New York: Longman, 2001).

(see Preface Figure 1). While every topic cannot be covered, this book provides a launching pad (via key concepts) along with the means to explore (via additional sources and references).

In my own investigation, I have found that there are no simple answers and few absolutes. Rather than provide specific answers, therefore, the goal here is to formulate the *best* questions that consider a broad range of perspectives, provoke vibrant debate, and encourage further research. The result is a book that explores the intricacies of strategic corporate social responsibility and the role of stakeholders in shaping the corporations that define the well-being of society today and tomorrow.

The journey you are about to undertake will help equip you for a career that is changing at an accelerating rate. CSR is an increasingly important component of this change. Gaining insight into the broad scope of this dynamic topic will increase your understanding and sophistication as a thinker, as a future business leader, and as an informed citizen.

Good luck!

David Chandler
March 2016

CSR Newsletters

As a result of the dynamic nature of CSR and the static nature of this textbook, I write and distribute the *CSR Newsletter* throughout the long fall and spring semesters. The *Newsletter* presents up-to-date examples taken from daily news sources that extend the case studies, questions for debate, and online references provided throughout this text. The topical themes covered in each issue of the *Newsletter*, together with access to the complete library of past issues that are archived on my blog (http://strategiccsr-sage .blogspot.com/), capture the breadth of the CSR debate and provide an added dimension to classroom discussion and student investigation into this complex subject.

To sign up to receive the *CSR Newsletter*, please email me at david.chandler@ucdenver.edu.

PLAN OF THE BOOK

S *trategic Corporate Social Responsibility* is organized into five distinct parts (each with three chapters and a case study) that, together, provide a comprehensive overview, core concepts, innovative models, and practical challenges of this complex subject. Throughout, useful teaching tools, online sources, and provocative questions for debate allow easy application in the classroom.

In Part I, the first three chapters lay the foundation for this book by defining CSR and providing a broader understanding of the context from which it emerged. In particular, Chapter 1 defines CSR, providing detail about where this subject came from and how it has evolved. In discussing this history, four arguments for CSR are presented (ethical, moral, rational, and economic), which emphasize the breadth and depth of how this subject has traditionally been taught. Chapter 2 then discusses the key drivers of CSR today—affluence, sustainability, globalization, communication, and brands. As each has become a defining characteristic of business, it increasingly alters stakeholder expectations of corporations. Finally, Chapter 3 frames the content of the rest of the book in terms of the background and evolution of corporate rights and responsibilities. By understanding the historical and legal framework in which corporations operate, we better understand their motivations and guiding principles.

Part II reflects the importance of a stakeholder perspective to the intellectual framework underpinning strategic CSR. Though firms are economic entities that exist to meet specific operational goals, the most effective way to achieve these goals today is by considering the needs and values of the broad range of groups that have a stake in the firm's pursuit of profit. Chapter 4 sets the groundwork for this argument by defining who qualifies as a *stakeholder* and by presenting the core model that describes the relationships these actors have with firms. Beyond identifying stakeholders, however, Chapter 4 presents a model that allows managers to prioritize among stakeholders, whose interests often conflict. Chapter 5 extends stakeholder theory further by arguing that, in addition to firms' duty to listen to their stakeholders, stakeholders have an equal (if not more important) responsibility to hold firms to account for their actions. Chapter 6 investigates the history of the corporation in order to challenge the myth that prevents the widespread adoption of a stakeholder perspective by firms—that the primary responsibility of managers and directors is to operate the organization in the interests of its shareholders. In the United States, at least, this widespread belief is not grounded in legal reality.

Part III presents an economic perspective on CSR. In particular, Chapter 7 discusses the motivating role of profit in the broader discussion about capitalism that emerged following the 2007–2008 financial crisis—investigating the extent to which our current economic model should be reformed. It also challenges the common refrain that firms have long focused on producing economic value and today must also produce social value. In reality, there is no *economic value* and no *social value*—there is only *value*, which the firm creates (or destroys) for each of its stakeholders. Chapter 8 introduces the concept of behavioral economics and discusses how this exciting field can advance the value creation process. This chapter also includes an extended discussion of Walmart and what the firm's ongoing success means in this context. Chapter 9 caps Part III by looking at the variety of ways in which we measure CSR, a task that is essential in order to hold firms to account for their CSR performance. Before we can develop an effective CSR measure, however, all costs need to be included in the production process. This is achieved via the concept of *lifecycle pricing*.

Part IV reflects the origins of strategic CSR. Although the ideas discussed in this book are relevant across functional areas in the business school, they find a natural home within strategic management. Chapter 10 introduces this discussion by explaining why traditional perspectives (principally, the resource-based and industry views) are insufficient tools to help firms craft strategies in today's globalized business environment. It introduces the concept of the *CSR threshold*. Chapter 11 places CSR within a competitive context, illustrating its strategic value because it serves to filter how businesses interact with their environments and implement ideas. While strategy seeks competitive success, a *CSR filter* both enables and protects the firm in its pursuit of profit and long-term viability. Chapter 12 defines the concept of strategic CSR, detailing its foundational characteristics—incorporating a holistic CSR perspective within the firm's strategic planning and core operations so that the firm is managed in the interests of a broad set of stakeholders to optimize value over the medium to long term.

Part V concludes this textbook by demonstrating how firms can embed a CSR perspective throughout the organization by building values-based businesses that serve the interests of their broad range of stakeholders. Chapter 13 leads off this section by investigating the origins of *sustainability* and its relevance to firms today, highlighting the original United Nations report that defined this term within the context of resource utilization. Chapter 14 extends the concept of *sustainable development* beyond the natural environment to encompass a values-based culture. This chapter focuses, in particular, on the implementation of a strategic CSR perspective throughout the organization. And, finally, Chapter 15 summarizes the ideas discussed in this book in terms of the ultimate outcome of strategic CSR—*sustainable value creation*.

The case studies that complete each of the five parts of *Strategic CSR* reflect the extent to which CSR affects all aspects of a firm's operations. Part I finishes with the Islamic finance case, which looks at how broad "non-business" issues such as religion are increasingly influencing corporate decisions. A case study about social impact bonds (impact investing) rounds out Part II, illustrating how any aspect of business today can be understood through the lens of a stakeholder perspective. The economic perspective in Part III is complemented with a case study that emerges from the 2007–2008 financial crisis—the implosion of the mortgage company Countrywide. Part IV is completed with a case looking at a company that implements strategic CSR effectively throughout its supply chain—Starbucks. And Part V finishes with a case study about what it means to be an employee in an economic environment that is being radically reshaped by technology (e.g., artificial intelligence) and larger structural forces (e.g., globalization and the gig economy). In particular, this case looks at firms that are owned by their employees, such as John Lewis in the UK.

While each issue is illustrated using a firm-centered case, both complementary and competing viewpoints are presented via a specific question for debate and numerous online resources. The cases and supplementary materials are all designed to stimulate further investigation and discussion, while demonstrating the productive value for firms of understanding and implementing strategic CSR.

ONLINE SUPPORT MATERIALS

As a supplement for this textbook, there is an online library of resources for instructors (password protected) and students that is hosted at the SAGE website: study.sagepub.com/chandler4e.

Instructors

Answers to in-text questions

PowerPoint slides

Test bank

Lecture notes

Sample syllabi

Issues and case studies from prior editions

Film/video resources

Students

eFlashcards

Film/video resources

Blog archive of the *CSR Newsletter* (http://strategiccsr-sage.blogspot.com/)

ACKNOWLEDGMENTS

The fourth edition of *Strategic Corporate Social Responsibility* is only the most recent iteration of what has been a long journey that began in Japan in 1995. As such, the book has benefited greatly from the advice and assistance of many friends and colleagues along the way.

Primarily, I would like to thank William B. Werther Jr. of the University of Miami, my coauthor on the first three editions of *Strategic CSR*. Quite simply, this book would not exist were it not for Bill's involvement from the beginning. When I first approached him with an 80-page Word document and an idea, he had the knowledge, contacts, and patience to help me turn it into what this project has become. I owe him a great deal more than this book, but dedicating this edition to him recognizes his influence on my work.

Similarly, I would like to acknowledge the pivotal role played by Anita Cava of the University of Miami's Business Law Department in helping to make this project possible. Both as an inspiration in the classroom and with her support as a colleague, Anita continues to embody ethics in action. The values and lessons she instills in her students are resources that they carry with them for a lifetime—I know that I certainly have.

It is important to recognize that *Strategic CSR* is possible, in large part, because of the prior and ongoing work of many leading scholars in the field of CSR. While I do not personally know many of these people, I have benefited from their research. In particular, I would like to acknowledge the pioneering work of Howard Bowen of the University of Iowa, Archie B. Carroll of the University of Georgia, Thomas Donaldson and Thomas Dunfee at the University of Pennsylvania, William C. Frederick of the University of Pittsburgh, R. Edward Freeman of Virginia University, Stuart L. Hart of Cornell University, Laura Pincus Hartman of Boston University, Andrew Hoffman of the University of Michigan, Thomas M. Jones of the University of Washington, Joshua Margolis of Harvard University, Jim Post of Boston University, C. K. Prahalad of the University of Michigan, Lynn Stout of Cornell University, and Sandra Waddock of Boston College. Their work, along with the work of many other influential scholars, provided the foundation of the field of CSR/business and society to which this text aims to contribute.

SAGE Publishing and I are also indebted to the comments and guidance offered by the many colleagues who were invited to review the third edition book and the fourth edition plan: Eshani Beddewela of the University of Huddersfield, Lars Binckebanck of the Nordakademie Graduate School, Mark A. Buchanan of Boise State University, Rod Carveth of Morgan State University, Terrence B. Dalton of the University of Akron, Danielle Dickerson of Oakton Community College, Yezdi H. Godiwalla of the University of Wisconsin–Whitewater, Tim Hart of the University of Tulsa, Sherry J. Holladay of the University of Central Florida, Epameinondas Katsikas of the University of Kent, William Patrick Leonard of Solbridge International School of Business, Debi P. Mishra of State University of New York, Don Miskiman of the University of the Fraser Valley, Sam Perez of Bunker Hill Community College, Steven N. Pyser of Rutgers University–Camden, Davar Rezania of the University of Guelph, Jose A. Sagarnaga of Oklahoma State University, Mark Suazo of Wright State University, John Tichenor of Stetson University, Brenda Wrigley of Emerson College, and Joseph Youchison of Benedictine University. The feedback of these colleagues on what worked for the third edition (and what did not) and what looked like it would work for the fourth edition plan ensured that this publication is considerably better than it otherwise would have been.

Finally, I would like to express my warm gratitude to the editorial, media, and production teams at SAGE Publishing who have all been an incredibly supportive and responsive resource, ensuring a timely update of this book. Specifically, I would like to thank Maggie Stanley, Acquisitions Editor for Business and Management textbooks, who expertly oversaw the publication of the fourth edition; Liz Thornton, Ashlee Blunk, and Georgia Mclaughlin in SAGE's marketing department; Anthony Paular, Design Director, who did such a great job converting my vague ideas into the wonderful covers of both the third and fourth editions; Gina Fenwick, who has provided excellent sales support for all four editions of the book; and Katie Ancheta and Neda Dallal, who managed the production of the Instructor and Student Resources so efficiently. I would also like to express my thanks and gratitude to the wonderful production and copyediting team of Jane Haenel at SAGE and Paula Fleming at Fleming Editorial Services, who were attentive, flexible, and extremely efficient in helping convert my unvarnished manuscript into a wonderful finished product. Finally, the vision and professionalism at different points throughout this journey of Michele Sordi, Senior Vice President of Editorial at SAGE, and Lisa Cuevas Shaw, Vice President of Publishing and Professional Learning Group at Corwin, helped ensure that this book, which is not a typical textbook, continues to be published. It is good to work with a publishing organization that not only invests in CSR but enacts the values and practices detailed in this book on a day-to-day basis.

PART I

CORPORATE SOCIAL RESPONSIBILITY

Part I of *Strategic Corporate Social Responsibility* (*Strategic CSR*) demonstrates the breadth and depth of corporate social responsibility (CSR).

Chapters 1 and 2 lay the foundation for this textbook by defining CSR and related concepts, while outlining how this subject has evolved over time. Chapter 1 provides core definitions, identifies different arguments for CSR (ethical, moral, rational, and economic), and shows why CSR is of growing importance to businesses large and small. Chapter 2 then discusses the key drivers of CSR today—affluence, sustainability, globalization, communication, and brands. As each driver has become a defining characteristic of business and life today, they alter stakeholder expectations of corporations. Though companies exist to generate a profit, they can achieve this most effectively by broadening their perspective and avoiding a self-defeating focus on the short term. Without an understanding of the broader context in which it is embedded, a firm can become exploitive, anti-social, and corrupt, losing the legitimacy and societal sanction that is necessary to remain viable over the medium to long term. Finally, Chapter 3 frames the content of the rest of the book in terms of the background and evolution of corporate rights and responsibilities. By understanding the historical and legal framework in which corporations operate, we better understand their motivations and guiding principles.[1]

Part I finishes with a case study on Islamic finance to examine how broad "non-business" factors, such as religion, are increasingly influencing corporate decisions today.

Chapter 1

WHAT IS CSR?

People create organizations to leverage their collective resources in pursuit of common goals. As organizations pursue these goals, they interact with others inside a larger context called society. Based on their purpose, organizations can be classified as for-profits, governments, or nonprofits. At a minimum, *for-profits* seek to make a profit, *governments* exist to define the rules and structures of society within which all organizations must operate,[1] and *nonprofits* (including NGOs—nongovernmental organizations) emerge to do social good when the political will or the profit motive is insufficient to address society's needs.[2] Aggregated across society, each of these different types of organizations represents a powerful mobilization of resources. In the United States alone, for example, there are currently more than 1.5 million nonprofit organizations working to fill needs not met by either government or the private sector.[3]

Within society, therefore, there is a mix of these organizational forms. Each performs different roles, but each also depends on the others to provide the complete patchwork of exchange interactions (of products and services, financial and social capital, etc.) that constitute a well-functioning society. Whether labeled corporations, companies, firms, or proprietorships, for example, for-profit businesses interact constantly with government, trade unions, suppliers, NGOs, and other groups in the communities in which they operate, in both positive and negative ways. Each of these groups or actors, therefore, can claim to have a stake in the operations of the firm. Some benefit more, some are involved more directly, and others can be harmed by the firm's actions, but all are connected in some way to what the firm does on a day-to-day basis.

Definitions of who qualifies as a firm's *stakeholders* vary (and will be discussed in more detail in Part II). For now, it is sufficient to note that a firm's stakeholders include all those who are related in some way to the firm's activities. Simply put, a firm's stakeholders include those individuals and groups that have a *stake* in the firm's operations.[4]

While stakeholders exist symbiotically with companies, the extent to which managers have paid attention to their interests has fluctuated. Depending on factors such as the level of economic and social progress, the range of stakeholders whose concerns a company seeks to address has shifted—from the earliest view of the corporation as a legal entity that exists due to government charter in the 19th century, to a narrower focus on shareholder rights at the turn of the 20th century, to the rise of managerialism by mid-century, and back again in the 1970s and 1980s to a disproportionate focus on shareholders with the rise of agency theory.[5] Today, as the full impact of business on society is becoming better understood, companies are again adopting a broader stakeholder outlook, extending their perspective to include constituents such as the communities in which they operate and, in particular, the natural environment. As a result, companies are more likely to recognize the degree of interdependence between the firm and each of these groups, leaving less room to ignore their separate and pressing concerns.

Just because an individual or organization meets the definition of an "interested constituent," however, does not compel a firm (either legally or logically) to comply with every demand from its stakeholders. Deciding which demands to prioritize and which to ignore, however, is a challenge—even more so as social media provides individuals with the power to disseminate their grievances worldwide. If ignored long enough, affected parties may take action against the firm, such as a product boycott, or turn to government for redress, or even write a song and post it to YouTube.[6] Such protests can cause significant brand damage (and even revenue loss), particularly if the grievance remains unaddressed even once it becomes widely known.

In democratic societies, laws (e.g., antidiscrimination statutes), regulations (e.g., the Internal Revenue Service's tax-exempt regulations for nonprofits), and judicial decisions (e.g., the fiduciary responsibilities of executives and board members)[7] provide a minimal framework for business operations that reflects a rough consensus of the governed. However, because (1) government cannot anticipate many issues, (2) the legislative process takes time, and (3) a general consensus is often slow to form, laws often lag behind social convention and technological change. This is particularly so in areas of high complexity and rapid innovation, such as bioethics or information technology. Thus, we arrive at the discretionary area of decision making between legal sanction and societal expectation that business leaders face every day. This area generates two questions from which the study of CSR springs:

- What is the relationship between a firm and the societies in which it operates?
- What responsibility does a firm owe society to self-regulate its actions in pursuit of profit?

CSR, therefore, is both critical and controversial. It is *critical* because the for-profit sector is the largest and most innovative part of any free society's economy. Companies intertwine with society in mutually beneficial ways, driving progress and affluence—creating most of the jobs, wealth, and innovations that enable society to prosper. They are the primary delivery system for food, housing, healthcare, and other necessities of life. Without modern corporations, the jobs, taxes, donations, and other resources that support governments and nonprofits would decline significantly, further diminishing general well-being. Businesses are the engines of society that propel us toward a better future, which suggests an interesting thought experiment: If you wanted to do the most social good in your career, would you enter public service (politics or nonprofits), or would you go into business? Fifty years ago, the best answer would have been "public service." Today, business is a more effective vehicle for social good.

At the same time, CSR remains *controversial*. People who have thought deeply about *Why does a business exist?* or *What is the purpose of the for-profit firm?* do not agree on the answers. Do companies have obligations beyond the benefits their economic success already provides? In spite of the rising importance of CSR, many still draw on the views of the Nobel Prize–winning economist Milton Friedman to argue that society benefits most when firms focus purely on their own financial success.[8] Others, in contrast, look to the views of business leaders who have argued for a broader perspective, such as David Packard (cofounder of Hewlett-Packard):

> I think many people assume, wrongly, that a company exists simply to make money. While this is an important result of a company's existence, we have to go deeper and find the real reasons for our being. . . . A group of people get together and exist as an institution that we call a company so that they are able to accomplish something collectively that they could not accomplish separately—they make a contribution to society.[9]

This textbook navigates between these perspectives to outline a view of CSR that recognizes both its strategic value to firms and the social benefit such a perspective brings to the firm's many stakeholders. The goal is to present a comprehensive assessment of corporate social responsibility that, on reflection, suggests that Friedman and Packard were not as far apart as their respective proponents assume.

A NEW DEFINITION OF CSR

The entirety of CSR can be discerned from the three words this phrase contains. CSR covers the relationship between *corporations* (or other for-profit organizations) and the *societies* with which they interact. It also includes the *responsibilities* that are inherent on both sides of these ties. CSR defines society in its widest sense, and on many levels, to include all stakeholder and constituent groups that maintain an ongoing interest in the firm's operations.

CSR

A responsibility among firms to meet the needs of their stakeholders and a responsibility among stakeholders to hold firms to account for their actions[10]

The Corporate Social Responsibility Hierarchy

Source: Archie B. Carroll, "The Pyramid of Corporate Social Responsibility: Toward the Moral Management of Organizational Stakeholders," *Business Horizons*, July–August 1991, p. 42.

Stakeholder groups range from clearly defined consumers, employees, suppliers, creditors, and regulating authorities to other, more amorphous constituents, such as the media and local communities. For the firm, tradeoffs must be made among these competing interests. Issues of legitimacy and accountability exist, such as when a nonprofit claims expertise in a particular area, even when it is unclear exactly how many people support its vision. Ultimately, each firm must identify those stakeholders that constitute its operating environment and then prioritize their strategic importance. Increasingly, companies need to incorporate the concerns of stakeholder groups within their strategic outlook or risk losing societal legitimacy. CSR provides a framework that helps firms embrace these decisions and adjust the internal strategic planning process to maximize the long-term viability of the organization.

This framework is broad, however, and definitions regarding the mix of interests and obligations have varied considerably over time. In 1979, Archie Carroll defined CSR in the following way: "The social responsibility of business encompasses the economic, legal, ethical, and discretionary expectations that society has of organizations at a given point in time."[11]

The Corporate Social Responsibility Hierarchy

Archie Carroll was one of the first academics to make a distinction between different kinds of organizational responsibilities. He referred to this distinction as a firm's "pyramid of corporate social responsibility" (see Figure 1.1):[12]

(Continued)

(Continued)

- Fundamentally, a firm's *economic responsibility* is to produce an acceptable return for investors.
- An essential component of pursuing economic gain within a law-based society, however, is a *legal responsibility* to act within the framework of laws and regulations drawn up by the government and judiciary.
- Taken one step further, a firm has an *ethical responsibility* to do no harm to its stakeholders and within its operating environment.
- Finally, firms have a *discretionary responsibility*, which represents more proactive, strategic behaviors that benefit themselves or society, or both.

As a firm progresses toward the top of Carroll's pyramid, its responsibilities become more discretionary in nature. In Carroll's vision, a *socially responsible* firm encompasses all four responsibilities within its culture, values, and day-to-day operations.

While useful, however, this typology is not rigid.[13] One of the central arguments of this textbook is that what was ethical or even discretionary in Carroll's model is becoming increasingly necessary due to the changing environment within which businesses operate. Yesterday's ethical responsibilities can quickly become today's economic and legal necessities. In order to achieve its fundamental economic obligations in today's globalized world, therefore, a firm must incorporate a stakeholder perspective within its strategic outlook. As societal expectations of the firm rise, the penalties imposed for perceived CSR lapses will become prohibitive.

Definitions, therefore, can and do evolve. It seems that, in terms of CSR, the variance is considerable with at least five dimensions identified across the many different published definitions: environmental, social, economic, stakeholder, and voluntariness.[14] And, of course, there is variance not only within countries over time but also across countries and cultures.

CSR Definitions Across Cultures

China: "The notion of companies looking beyond profits to their role in society is generally termed corporate social responsibility (CSR).... It refers to a company linking itself with ethical values, transparency, employee relations, compliance with legal requirements and overall respect for the communities in which they operate. It goes beyond the occasional community service action, however, as CSR is a corporate philosophy that drives strategic decision-making, partner selection, hiring practices and, ultimately, brand development."[15]

United Kingdom: "CSR is about businesses and other organizations going beyond the legal obligations to manage the impact they have on the environment and society. In particular, this could include how organizations interact with their employees, suppliers, customers and the communities in which they operate, as well as the extent they attempt to protect the environment."[16]

> **European Union:** CSR is a "process to integrate social, environmental, ethical and human rights concerns into their business operations and core strategy in close collaboration with their stakeholders."[17]
>
> **United Nations:** "Corporate Social Responsibility (CSR) can be understood as a management concept and a process that integrates social and environmental concerns in business operations and a company's interactions with the full range of its stakeholders."[18]

CSR, therefore, is a fluid concept. This presents the potential danger that, to the extent that CSR means different things to different people, the debate around this essential subject can descend into one over rhetoric instead of substance:

> Right now we're in a free-for-all in which "CSR" means whatever a company wants it to mean: From sending employees out in matching t-shirts to paint a wall for five hours a year, to recycling, to improving supply-chain conditions, to diversity and inclusion. This makes it difficult to have a proper conversation about what [CSR] should be.[19]

For the purposes of this textbook, it is important to emphasize that CSR is both a means and an end. It is an integral element of the firm's strategy—the way the firm goes about delivering its products or services to markets (*means*). It is also a way of maintaining the legitimacy of the firm's actions in the larger society by bringing stakeholder concerns to the foreground (*end*). Put another way, CSR is both a *process* and an *outcome*. At any given moment, CSR describes the process by which firms react to their stakeholders' collective set of needs. CSR also is the set of actions that are defined by what the stakeholders' demands require. Over time, while the process remains the same (firms should always seek to respond to the interests of their stakeholders), the actions that are required to do this will necessarily change as norms, values, and societal expectations all evolve. As such, references to "CSR" in this book will sometimes be to the process and sometimes to the set of actions (or outcomes). The underlying principles that determine the relationship between the two, however, will remain consistent.

Ultimately, a firm's success is directly related to its ability to incorporate stakeholder concerns into its business model. CSR provides a means to do this by valuing the interdependent relationships that exist among businesses, their stakeholder groups, the economic system, and the communities within which they exist. The challenges associated with managing these interdependent relationships were apparent to Peter Drucker as far back as 1974:

> The business enterprise is a creature of a society and an economy, and society or economy can put any business out of existence overnight. . . . The enterprise exists on sufferance and exists only as long as the society and the economy believe that it does a necessary, useful, and productive job.[20]

As such, CSR covers an uneven blend of different issues that rise and fall in importance from firm to firm over time. In other words, while the stakeholders stay the same, the issues that motivate them change. Whether the concern is wage levels, healthcare provision, or same-sex partner benefits, for example, a firm's employees are central to its success. A firm that consistently ignores its employees' legitimate claims is a firm that is heading for bankruptcy. CSR is a vehicle for the firm to discuss its stakeholder obligations (both internal and external), a way of developing the means to meet these obligations, as well as a tool by which the mutual benefits that result can be identified. Simply put, CSR represents a firm's best interests by managing its relationships with its stakeholders because these relations are essential to its success and, ultimately, its survival. Understanding and implementing CSR throughout operations, therefore, acknowledges:

> That markets operate successfully only when they are embedded in communities; that trust and co-operation are not antithetic to a market economy, but essential to it; that the driving force of innovation is pluralism and experiment, not greed and monopoly; that corporations acquire legitimacy only from the contribution they make to the societies in which they operate.[21]

CSR encompasses the range of economic, legal, ethical, and discretionary actions that affect a firm's economic performance. At a minimum, of course, firms should comply with the legal or regulatory requirements that relate to day-to-day operations. To break these regulations is to break the law, which does not constitute socially responsible behavior. But, legal compliance is merely a minimum condition of CSR.[22] Taking these obligations as a given, this textbook focuses on the ethical and discretionary concerns that are less precisely defined and for which there is often no clear societal consensus, but that are essential for firms to address. Firms do this (minimizing competitive risk while maximizing potential benefit) by fully embracing CSR and incorporating it within the firm's strategic planning process.

THE EVOLUTION OF CSR

The call for social responsibility among businesses is not a new concept. In short, "the pursuit of profit has been 'unloved' since Socrates declared that 'the more [men] think of making a fortune, the less they think of virtue.'"[23] As a result, ancient Chinese, Egyptian, and Sumerian writings often delineated rules for commerce to facilitate trade and ensure broader interests were considered. Ever since, public concern about the interaction between business and society has grown in proportion to the growth of economic activity:[24]

> Concerns about the excesses of the East India Company were commonly expressed in the seventeenth century. There has been a tradition of benevolent

capitalism in the UK for over 150 years. Quakers, such as Barclays and Cadbury, as well as socialists, such as Engels and Morris, experimented with socially responsible and values-based forms of business. And Victorian philanthropy could be said to be responsible for considerable portions of the urban landscape of older town centres today.[25]

Evidence of social activism in attempts to influence organizational behavior also stretches back across the centuries. Such efforts mirrored the legal and commercial development of companies as they established themselves as the driving force of market-based societies. Periodically, society stepped in when such firms were deemed to be causing more harm than good: "The first large-scale consumer boycott? England in the 1790s over slave-harvested sugar."[26] Although they were crude and lacked the efficient communication that Facebook and Twitter enable today, it is clear that these early consumer-led protests were effective—initially in terms of raising public awareness, but soon after in terms of tangible, legislative change:

> Within a few years, more than 300,000 Britons were boycotting sugar, the major product of the British West Indian slave plantations. Nearly 400,000 signed petitions to Parliament demanding an end to the slave trade. . . . In 1792, the House of Commons became the first national legislative body in the world to vote to end the slave trade.[27]

Although wealthy industrialists have long sought to balance the mercantile actions of their firms with personal or corporate philanthropy, CSR is strongest when leaders view their role as stewards of resources owned by others (e.g., broader society, the environment). The words of the late Ray Anderson, founder and chairman of Interface Carpets,[28] are instructive:

> One day . . . it dawned on me that the way I had been running Interface is the way of the plunderer, plundering something that is not mine; something that belongs to every creature on earth. And I said to myself, my goodness, the day must come when this is illegal, when plundering is not allowed [and] . . . people like me will end up in jail. The largest institution on earth, the wealthiest, most powerful, the most pervasive, the most influential, is the institution of business and industry—the corporation, which also is the current present day instrument of destruction. It must change.[29]

Leaders such as Anderson face a balancing act that addresses the tradeoffs among the firm's primary stakeholders, the society that enables the firm to prosper, and the environment that provides the raw materials to produce products and services of value. When specific elements of society view leaders and their firms as failing to meet societal needs, activism results. That was just as true of 18th-century England as it is today.

Figure 1.2 The History and Evolution of CSR

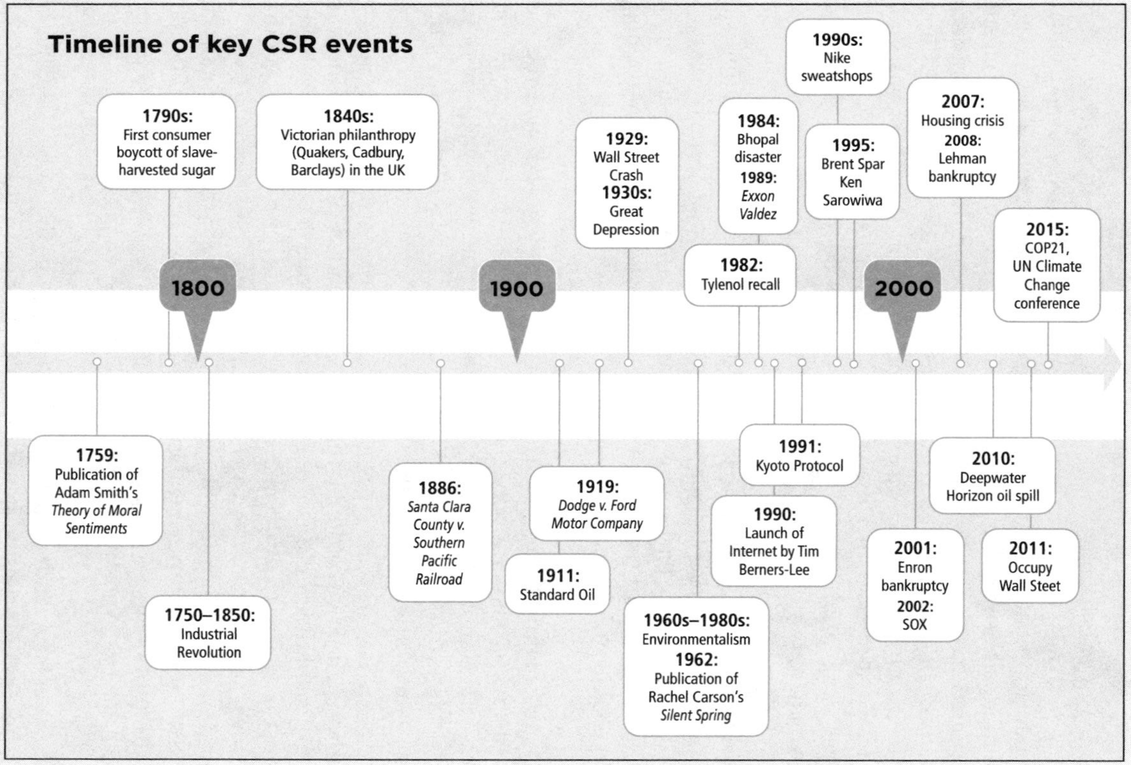

Timeline of key CSR events

1759: Publication of Adam Smith's *Theory of Moral Sentiments*

1790s: First consumer boycott of slave-harvested sugar

1800

1750–1850: Industrial Revolution

1840: Victorian philanthropy (Quakers, Cadbury, Barclays) in the UK

1886: *Santa Clara County v. Southern Pacific Railroad*

1900

1911: *Standard Oil*

1919: *Dodge v. Ford Motor Company*

1929: Wall Street Crash
1930s: Great Depression

1960s–1980s: Environmentalism
1962: Publication of Rachel Carson's *Silent Spring*

1982: Tylenol recall

1984: Bhopal disaster
1989: *Exxon Valdez*

1990: Launch of Internet by Tim Berners-Lee

1991: Kyoto Protocol

1990s: Nike sweatshops

1995: Brent Spar Ken Sarowiwa

2000

2001: Enron bankruptcy
2002: SOX

2007: Housing crisis
2008: Lehman bankruptcy

2010: Deepwater Horizon oil spill

2011: Occupy Wall Steet

2015: COP21, UN Climate Change conference

Current examples of social activism in response to organizations' perceived lack of CSR are in this morning's newspapers and on television news shows and spread online via social media, blogs, and websites. Whether the response is civil disobedience by protestors occupying Wall Street and capital cities around the world to highlight the distorted values of global finance, consumer boycotts of products that are hazardous to health, or NGO-led campaigns to eradicate sweat-shops in developing economies contracting for apparel brands, CSR has become an increasingly relevant topic in recent decades in corporate boardrooms, business school classrooms, and family living rooms. It is a subject that has evolved considerably since the beginnings of industrial society and continues to evolve today. Figure 1.2 illustrates some of the key events that have defined the history and evolution of CSR over the centuries.

This ongoing evolution ensures that CSR is not a static target. Widespread long-term industry practices, which were previously considered discretionary or ethical concerns, can be deemed illegal or socially unacceptable due to aggressive legal prosecution or novel social activism. For example, the growing criticism of investors who use high-frequency trading algorithms to gain "unfair" advantages when trading[30] indicates the danger of assuming that yesterday's accepted practices will continue to be acceptable. Firms operate against an ever-changing background of what is considered *socially responsible*. These ever-changing standards and expectations compound the complexity faced by corporate decision makers. Worse, these standards vary from society to society and even among cultures within a given society. Faced with a kaleidoscopic background of evolving standards, business managers must consider a variety of factors as they implement CSR.

Nevertheless, the pursuit of economic gain remains a necessity. CSR does not repeal the laws of economics under which for-profit firms must operate (to society's benefit). The example of Malden Mills, below, demonstrates that, unless a firm is economically viable, even the best of intentions will not enable stakeholders to achieve their goals and create social value.

Malden Mills

Aaron Feuerstein, CEO of Malden Mills (founded in 1906, family owned),[31] was an excellent employer. He operated "a unionized plant that was strike-free, a boss who saw his workers as a key to his company's success."[32] In 1995, however, a fire destroyed the firm's main textile plant that was based in Lawrence, Massachusetts, an economically deprived area in the north of the state. He then had a decision to make:

> With an insurance settlement of close to $300 million in hand, Feuerstein could have, for example, moved operations to a country with a lower wage base, or he could have retired. Instead, he rebuilt in Lawrence and continued to pay his employees while the new plant was under construction.[33]

(Continued)

(Continued)

His decision to keep the factory open and continue meeting his obligations to his employees when they needed him most was applauded in the media:

The national attention to Feuerstein's act brought more than the adulation of business ethics professors—it brought increased demand for his product, Polartec, the lightweight fleece the catalogue industry loves to sell.[34]

In addition to full pay, Feuerstein also continued all his employees on full medical benefits and guaranteed them a job when the factory was ready to restart production:

"I have a responsibility to the worker, both blue-collar and white collar," Feuerstein later said. "I have an equal responsibility to the community. It would have been unconscionable to put 3,000 people on the streets [just before Christmas] and deliver a death blow to the cities of Lawrence and Methuen. Maybe on paper our company is [now] worth less to Wall Street, but I can tell you it's [really] worth more."[35]

But the increased demand for Polartec clothing (http://www.polartec.com/) that Feuerstein's actions generated wasn't enough to offset the debt he had built up waiting for the plant to be rebuilt: $100 million.[36] This situation was compounded by a downturn in the market, as well as cheaper fleece alternatives flooding the market. Malden Mills filed for bankruptcy protection in November 2001.[37]

The Polartec example demonstrates vividly the complexity of CSR. While an imperfect measure of a firm's success, profit is clearly essential. If the goal is to create value, the firm needs to stay in business. Would Malden Mills have avoided bankruptcy if it had initially fired half its employees and relocated the factory elsewhere? What is the firm's responsibility to continue delivering a valued product to its customers, and does this outweigh the firm's duties to its employees? The answers to these questions can be debated. What is clear is that good intentions do not replace the need for an effective business model, and no company, whatever the motivation, can or should indefinitely spend money that it does not have.

Which actions should be pursued depend on many factors that are specific to the firm, its industry, and the society in which it is based. Manufacturing offshore in a low-cost environment, for example, remains a valid strategic decision, particularly in an increasingly globalized business world. This choice is strategic because it can provide a competitive advantage for some firms (such as Apple),[38] even while other firms (such as Zara)[39] see strategic value in onshoring operations due to rising costs and a shorter, more responsive supply chain:

Offshore production is increasingly moving back to rich countries not because Chinese wages are rising, but because companies now want to be closer to their customers so that they can respond more quickly to changes in demand. And some products are so sophisticated that it helps to have the people who design them and the people who make them in the same place.[40]

All business decisions have both economic and social consequences. The trick to success is managing the conflicting interests of stakeholders in order to meet their ever-evolving needs and concerns. As societies rethink the balance between societal needs and economic progress, CSR will continue to evolve in importance and complexity. And, although this complexity muddies the wealth-creating waters, an awareness of these evolving expectations holds the potential to create a competitive advantage for those firms that do it well (still a rarity).[41] The examples above indicate that the cultural context within which CSR is perceived and evaluated is crucial.

Culture and Context

A CSR perspective allows firms to manage their stakeholder interactions in a way that maintains their societal legitimacy. Yet societies differ in what their members consider acceptable. Though differences range from the anthropological and sociological to the historical and demographic, two dimensions consistently influence CSR's visibility: democracy and economics.

Different societies define the relationship between business and society in different ways. Expectations spring from many factors, with wealthy societies having greater resources and, perhaps, more demanding expectations that emerge from the greater options wealth brings. The reasoning is straightforward: In poor democracies, general well-being is focused on the necessities of life—food, shelter, transportation, education, medicine, social order, jobs, and so on. *Luxuries*, such as a living wage or environmental regulations, add costs that poor societies can ill afford. As societies advance, however, expectations change and *general well-being* is redefined. A corresponding shift in the acceptable level of response by firms quickly follows, as this example of air pollution and public transportation in Chile indicates.

Santiago, Chile

In the 1980s, air pollution in downtown Santiago, Chile, was an important issue, just as it was in Los Angeles, California. The problem, however, was addressed differently due to the differing level of economic development in these two pollution-retaining basins.

While stringent laws went into effect in Los Angeles, in Chile, necessities (including low-cost transportation) got a higher priority because of widespread poverty. After more than a decade of robust economic growth, however, Chileans used democratic processes to limit the number of cars entering Santiago and imposed increasingly stringent pollution standards. This shift in priorities reflected their changing societal needs, along with the growing wealth to afford new rules and legal actions.

Different expectations among rich and poor societies are a matter of priorities. The need for transportation, for example, evolves into a need for nonpolluting forms of transportation as society becomes more affluent. Though poor societies value clean air just as advanced ones do, there are other competing priorities (such as keeping costs low). As a society prospers, new expectations compel producers to make vehicles that pollute less—a shift in emphasis. In time, these expectations evolve from a discretionary to a mandatory (legal) requirement. What was true of transportation in the 1980s is true of issues like recycling today in São Paulo, Brazil,[42] and of social and political development in general throughout South America:

> As Latin Americans become less poor, they want better public services. Latin Americans are demanding more of their democracies, their institutions and governments; they worry about crime almost as much as about economic problems; and fewer of them think that their country is progressing.[43]

This discussion reinforces the idea that it is in the best interest of any organization (for-profit, nonprofit, or governmental) to anticipate, reflect, and strive to meet the changing needs of its stakeholders. In the case of for-profit firms, the primary stakeholder groups are its employees and customers, without whose support the business fails. Other constituents, however, from suppliers to shareholders to the local community, also matter. Businesses must satisfy these core constituents if they hope to remain viable over the long term. When the expectations of different stakeholders conflict, CSR enters a gray area, and management has to negotiate among competing interests. An important part of that conflict arises from different expectations, which, in turn, reflect different approaches to CSR.

FOUNDATIONS OF CSR

CSR represents an argument for a firm's economic interests, where satisfying stakeholder needs becomes central to retaining societal legitimacy (and, therefore, financial viability). Much debate (and criticism) in the CSR community, however, springs from well-intentioned parties who argue the same *facts* from different perspectives, breaking down along philosophical and ideological lines. Understanding these different perspectives, therefore, is an important component of understanding the breadth and depth of CSR. An introduction to the underlying ethical, moral, rational, and economic arguments for CSR follows.

An Ethical Argument for CSR

The danger of promoting a perspective of CSR that focuses primarily on its strategic value to the firm is that the ethical and moral foundations on which much of the CSR debate rests are ignored. The advantage of making the business case for CSR is that it is more convincing to those most skeptical of broadening the firm's responsibilities and, as a result, is more likely to be implemented. In other words, the business case is expedient—it offers the greatest potential gain because it will appeal to the widest possible audience. The danger in downplaying an ethical or moral component to CSR, however, is that doing so ignores an intellectual philosophical foundation that many believe is essential to fully understand CSR.

There are three essential components encapsulated within the concept of business ethics: normative, descriptive, and practical ethics. *Normative ethics* draws on moral philosophy to categorize individual actions as either *right* or *wrong* in specific situations. *Descriptive ethics* explains why individuals make these *right* or *wrong* decisions. And *practical ethics* applies ethical principles that determine *right* and *wrong* actions to day-to-day decision making.

Underpinning each of these three core components is the assumption that *right* and *wrong* can be determined. This assumption glosses over the issue of whether ethical values are relative or absolute. An ethical argument for CSR states that, rather than being relative constructs (i.e., varying from individual to individual and culture to culture), ethical values are absolute (i.e., inalienable *rights* that are consistent across cultures and applicable to all humans). Absolute values are easily definable and, as such, exist as a standard against which behavior can be assessed.

Although many discussions around CSR assume an ethical component, the precise relationship between ethics and CSR is often left unspecified. As such, the late Rushworth Kidder poses a fascinating question when he asks: "Can a socially responsible company be unethical?"[44] In constructing his answer, Kidder conceptualizes CSR as a subset of ethics:

> Responsibility . . . is one of five distinct core values that define, globally, the idea of ethics. A necessary but not sufficient condition for ethics, it needs to be fleshed out by the other four values: honesty, respect, fairness, and compassion. Ethics requires all five. So can an individual or a corporation have a strong sense of responsibility without necessarily being honest? Yes. The opposite can also arise, where a deeply honest person proves to be irresponsible. These are two big, different ideas.[45]

An ethical argument for CSR essentially rests on one of two philosophical approaches—consequentialist reasoning or categorical reasoning.[46] Consequentialist (or teleological) reasoning locates ethicality in terms of the outcomes caused by an action. This stream of thought is closely aligned with utilitarianism, which was most famously advocated by the 18th-century English political philosopher Jeremy Bentham:

> An action is considered ethical according to consequentialism when it promotes the good of society, or more specifically, when the action is intended to produce the greatest net benefit (or lowest net cost) to society when compared to all the other alternatives.[47]

In contrast, categorical (or deontological) moral reasoning "is defined as embodying those activities which reflect a consideration of one's duty or obligation."[48] As such, categorical reasoning represents more of a process orientation than the outcome-oriented focus of consequentialist reasoning. This perspective most closely maps to Immanuel Kant's categorical imperative, but it also includes guiding principles such as religious doctrine and core values such as trustworthiness, honesty, loyalty, accountability, and a broad sense of citizenship (i.e., acting out of a sense of responsibility to the common good).

An Ethical Argument for CSR

CSR is an argument based on two forms of ethical reasoning—*consequentialist* (utilitarian) and *categorical* (Kantian). Consequentialist reasoning justifies action in terms of the outcomes generated (the greatest good for the greatest number of people), while categorical reasoning justifies action in terms of the principles by which that action is carried out (the application of core ethical principles, regardless of the outcomes they generate).

In terms of application, these two ethical perspectives become realized in social norms: "those standards . . . which have been accepted by the organization, the industry, the profession, or society as necessary for the proper functioning of business." They are codified within the firm in the form of a code of conduct or code of ethics, which then acts as a point of reference or guide in determining "whether a company is acting ethically according to the conventional standard."[49]

The violation of a society's cultural heritage and ethical principles regarding issues of social justice, human rights, and environmental stewardship is deemed to be ethically wrong and socially irresponsible. This logic is the foundation of the "social contract," which is based on societal expectations that bind firms because compliance is directly related to a social license to operate. Remaining within these implicit ethical boundaries is directly related to the firm's societal legitimacy and long-term viability.

A Moral Argument for CSR

Although profits are necessary for any business to survive, firms are only able to obtain those profits because of the society in which they operate. All of the firm's stakeholders (even internal stakeholders, such as employees) exist primarily as members of a society. Without that social context, therefore, there is no marketplace in which the business can compete. CSR emerges from this interdependent relationship between business and society. It is shaped by individual and societal standards of morality that define contemporary views of *right* and *wrong*.[50] As Howard Bowen said about managers in his famous 1953 book:

> They must accept the social implications of their calling. They must recognize that ultimately business exists not for profits, for power, or for personal aggrandizement, but to serve society. . . . [The freedom and power that comes with managing a business] must be used moderately, conscientiously, and with a view to the interests of society at large.[51]

Given this, to what extent is a firm obliged to repay the debt it owes society for its opportunity to conduct business (even its continued success)? That is, what moral responsibilities do businesses face in return for the benefits society grants? And also, to what extent do the profits the business generates, the jobs it provides, and the taxes it pays already meet those obligations? As an academic study, CSR represents an organized approach to answering these questions. As an applied discipline, it represents the extent to which businesses need to deliver on their obligations as defined by evolving societal expectations.

A Moral Argument for CSR

CSR is an argument of moral reasoning that reflects the relationship between a company and the society within which it operates. It assumes businesses recognize that for-profit entities do not exist in a vacuum and that their ability to operate and achieve ongoing success comes as much from societal resources (e.g., infrastructure, rule of law) and consent (e.g., social contract) as from factors that are internal to the firm.

Peter Drucker expresses this sentiment—that there is no moral justification in pursuing profit alone—by suggesting that "profit for a company is like oxygen for a person. If you don't have enough of it, you're out of the game. But if you think your life is about breathing, you're really missing something."[52] Charles Handy similarly suggests that businesses have a moral obligation to move beyond a narrow focus on profit and the primary interests of shareholders:

> The purpose of a business . . . is not to make a profit, full stop. It is to make a profit so that the business can do something more or better. That "something" becomes the real justification for the business. . . . It is a moral issue. . . . It is salutary to ask about any organization, "If it did not exist, would we invent it?" "Only if it could do something better or more useful than anyone else" would have to be the answer, and profit would be the means to that larger end.[53]

At one level, the moral argument for CSR reflects a give-and-take approach based on a realization of the interdependent relationship between business and society. Society makes business possible and provides what firms need to succeed, ranging from educated and healthy workers to a safe and stable physical and legal infrastructure, not to mention a consumer market for their products. Because society's contributions make businesses possible, the moral argument for CSR presumes that those businesses have a reciprocal obligation to operate in ways that are deemed socially *responsible* and *beneficial*. And, because businesses operate within a social context, society has the right to define expectations for those who operate within its boundaries:

[Free-market economists] like to portray "wealth-producing" businesses as precarious affairs that bestow their gifts independently of the society in which they trade. The opposite is the case. The intellectual, human and physical infrastructure that creates successful companies . . . is a social product . . . shaped by the character of that society's public conversation and the capacity to build effective social institutions and processes.[54]

As a result, for many, a focus on money alone as the motivation for business is dispiriting—"as vital as profit is, it seems insufficient to give people the fulfillment they crave."[55] It follows from this logic that money is a social good that is accompanied by a moral obligation to return to the collective a percentage of the proceeds of economic gain earned on advantages conferred by society to the firm. As Adam Smith[56] wrote in *The Wealth of Nations*:

The subjects of every state ought to contribute towards the support of the government, as nearly as possible, in proportion to their respective abilities; that is, in proportion to the revenue which they respectively enjoy under the protection of the state. The expense of government . . . is like the expense of management to the joint tenants of a great estate, who are all obligated to contribute in proportion to their respective interests in the state.[57]

At a deeper level, societies rest upon a cultural heritage that grows out of a confluence of religion, mores, and folkways. This heritage gives rise to a belief system that defines the boundaries of socially acceptable behavior by people and organizations. All members of society have a moral responsibility to uphold these *rules* in the interests of the common good.

A Rational Argument for CSR

A loss of societal legitimacy can lead to a rise in the countervailing forces of activism, legislation, or others that place constraints on the firm's ability to act. Violations of societal expectations are not just inappropriate, therefore, but their consequences also suggest a rational argument for CSR.

Because sanctions (such as laws, fines, prohibitions, or boycotts) affect the firm's actions, efforts to comply with societal expectations are rational, regardless of ethical or moral reasoning. When compliance with societal expectations is based on highly subjective values, the rational argument rests on sanction avoidance—it may be more cost-effective, for example, to address issues voluntarily. Waiting for society to impose legally mandated requirements and only then reacting allows firms to ignore their ethical and moral obligations and concentrate on generating profits in the short term; however, it also inevitably leads to strictures being imposed that not only force compliance but often do so in ways that the firm may find neither preferable nor efficient.[58]

Worse, if the required actions are a complete surprise to the firm, or the business needs time to build a competency in the relevant area, compliance can be extremely costly in terms of both immediate investment and longer-term reputational damage. By ignoring the opportunity to influence the debate in the short term through proactive behaviors, an organization is more likely to find its business operations and strategy constrained over the long term. One need only consider the evolution of affirmative action in the United States to see this rationale in action.

Affirmative Action

Prior to the 1960s, businesses could discriminate against employees on the basis of race, sex, religion, age, national origin, veteran's status, pregnancy, disability, sexual preference, or any other non-merit-based criteria. Doing so was a discretionary right that was legal, if far from ethical. Then social activism moved these ethical and discretionary decisions into the arena of public debate and, in time, imposed legal prohibitions. The result for many businesses that were guilty of discrimination was affirmative action plans to redress racial or other imbalances in their workforce. Those organizations that lagged quickly found themselves the test case in litigation focused on institutionalizing the new legislation. As Robert Kennedy said during the civil rights movement to those firms that were reluctant to change:

> If you won't end discriminatory practices because it's the right thing to do; then do it because it's good for business.[59]

Similar resistance is apparent today in the approach of some firms to issues such as same-sex partner benefits. While there may be short-term benefit for some in holding out, the direction in which society is moving is clear. Firms that resist normative compliance will ultimately be coerced to conform to society's evolving standards against their will.

While lobbying to ensure discrimination remains legal would theoretically be an option for firms, attempts to subvert societal consensus around a particular issue represent an ethical and moral lapse that places the firm's legitimacy at risk. Instead, the rational argument advocates the benefits of avoiding the inevitable confrontation.

A Rational Argument for CSR

CSR is a rational argument that focuses on the benefits to performance of avoiding external constraints. Adopting the path of least resistance with regard to issues of concern makes common and business sense. In today's globalized world, where individuals and organizations are empowered to enact change, CSR represents a means of anticipating and reflecting societal concerns to minimize operational and financial sanctions.

The rational argument for CSR is summarized by the *Iron Law of Social Responsibility*, which states: In a free society, discretionary abuse of societal responsibilities leads, eventually, to mandated reprisals.[60] Restated: In a democratic society, power is taken away from those who abuse it. The history of social and political uprisings—from Cromwell in England, to the American and French Revolutions, to the overthrow of the shah of Iran or the Communist government of the Soviet Union—underscores the conclusion that those that abuse power or privilege sow the seeds of their own destruction. Parallels exist in the business arena. Financial scandals around the turn of this century at Enron, WorldCom, Adelphia, HealthSouth, and other icons of US business provoked discretion-limiting laws and rulings, such as the Sarbanes-Oxley Act (2002). Similarly, the financial crisis that began in 2007–2008 gave rise to the Dodd-Frank Wall Street Reform and Consumer Protection Act, passed by the US Congress in 2010.

The rational argument for CSR therefore underpins the idea that firms voluntarily seek to meet the needs and concerns of their stakeholders. Firms that wait until they are forced to comply may find that the costs of doing so quickly become prohibitive. In the finance industry today, for example, the global bank HSBC has announced that "nearly 25,000 of its 258,000 employees, almost 10%, work in compliance" and that "compliance was a major driver in the 5% increase in operating expenses reported."[61] Eventually, corporate transgressions result in heightened oversight that forces previously discretionary and ethical issues into the legal arena.

By adopting a rational argument for CSR, firms seek to interpret evolving societal values and stakeholder expectations and act to avoid future sanctions. Sensing that the tide of public opinion in the United States was moving in favor of regulating carbon emissions, for example, firms formed groups to lobby the government for change. The group BICEP (Business for Innovative Climate and Energy Policy)[62] was established by five firms with proactive CSR track records—Levi Strauss, Nike, Starbucks, Sun Microsystems, and Timberland. Perhaps more surprisingly, however, USCAP (United States Climate Action Partnership),[63] which "supports the introduction of carbon limits and trading. . . . was set up by energy companies and industrial manufacturers" who might otherwise have opposed government action in this area.[64] Implementing a rational perspective, these firms realize that it is in their interests to engage with regulators, rather than oppose legislation that they see as inevitable. As James Rogers, CEO of Duke Energy, succinctly puts it, "If you're not at the table when these negotiations are going on, you're going to be on the menu."[65] In other words, acting proactively in a socially responsible manner to avoid unwelcome intrusion or help shape prospective legislation is an act of rational business.

An Economic Argument for CSR

Building on the previous three arguments for CSR is the economic argument. In addition to avoiding ethical, moral, legal, and other societal sanctions, incorporating CSR into a firm's operations offers a potential point of differentiation and competitive market advantage upon which future success can be built.[66]

An Economic Argument for CSR

CSR is an argument of economic self-interest for business. CSR adds value because it allows companies to reflect the needs and concerns of their various stakeholder groups. By doing so, the firm is more likely to create greater value and, as a result, retain the loyalty and custom of those stakeholders. Simply put, CSR is a way of matching corporate operations with stakeholder values and expectations that are constantly evolving.

CSR influences all aspects of a business's day-to-day operations. Everything a firm does causes it to interact with one or more of its stakeholder groups. As a result, companies are best served by building positive relationships with as broad an array of stakeholders as possible. Whether the firm is acting as an employer, a producer, a buyer, a supplier, or an investment, its attractiveness and success are increasingly linked to its organizational values and culture. Concerning socially responsible investments (SRI), for example, "more than one out of every six dollars under professional management in the United States—$6.57 trillion or more—was invested according to SRI strategies."[67] Even for those who believe that the only purpose of a business is to increase the wealth of shareholders, being perceived as socially *irresponsible* risks losing access to an already significant (and growing) segment of investors and their capital:

> From 2012 to 2014, sustainable, responsible and impact investing enjoyed a growth rate of more than 76 percent, increasing from $3.74 trillion in 2012. . . . Mutual funds are one of the most dynamic segments within the ESG investing space. The number of ESG mutual funds in the United States grew from 333 to 456, and their collective assets increased from $641 billion to $1.93 trillion, an over 200 percent increase.[68]

This textbook expounds the economic argument in favor of CSR. It is the strongest of the four (ethical, moral, rational, and economic) arguments supporting CSR, due partly to its reliance on what we know about human psychology and economic theory. Rather than seeking to subvert patterns of exchange that have evolved over centuries, the economic argument for CSR operates at the intersection of the firm's self-interest and the broader well-being of society. Ultimately, indeed, there is no difference between the two. If stakeholders are willing to reward the behavior they seek from companies, then it is in firms' best interests to provide stakeholders with what they want. As long as this basic formula holds on both sides, value will be optimized and distributed broadly across society. Of course, what is simple to say is often difficult to put into practice. This book exists to build a framework that firms can use to address the complex process of listening to and seeking to meet the conflicting interests of all their stakeholders.

An important distinction that helps explain the particular value of the economic argument is between an effective *business model* and a broader, more sustainable *model for (all) businesses*. In other words, rather than focusing on what works in isolation, it is more effective to establish what works economywide. The Body Shop has implemented a successful *business model* that subscribes to a moral argument for CSR. This activist organization is able to draw on support from the small percentage of the population that is aware and sufficiently responsive to a progressive social agenda, translating this support into economic success. It is a wonderful business, but its model is not one that all businesses can emulate. Ben & Jerry's is another example, as is Patagonia. These are all great firms, but will not introduce meaningful change across the economy or globe. For that, we need to rely on corporations that operate on a sufficiently large scale to make a difference.

In contrast, therefore, an economic argument for CSR seeks to build a broad *model for businesses* that recognizes the limited application of moral activism and, instead, searches for a standard that can be applied across all large, for-profit firms. The result is an approach to business that identifies the strategic benefits of a CSR and stakeholder perspective in a way that sustains the firm and optimizes the added value of its operations.

Strategic CSR Debate

MOTION: There are no *absolute* ethical and moral standards; all values, norms, and laws in society are socially constructed and evolve over time.

QUESTIONS FOR DISCUSSION AND REVIEW

1. What is the purpose of the for-profit firm? What value does it create for society?

2. Define *corporate social responsibility*. What arguments in favor of CSR seem most important to you? How is CSR different from strategic CSR?

3. What are the four responsibilities of a firm outlined in Archie Carroll's *pyramid of CSR* model? Illustrate your definitions of each level with corporate examples.

4. Milton Friedman argued that "few trends could so thoroughly undermine the very foundations of our free society as the acceptance by corporate officials of a social responsibility other than to make as much money for their stockholders as possible."[69] What are two arguments in support of Friedman's assertion and two against?

5. What are the ethical, moral, rational, and economic arguments for CSR? Define and discuss each one briefly.

Chapter 2

THE DRIVING FORCES OF CSR

CSR is important because it influences all aspects of a company's operations. Consumers want to buy products from companies they trust; suppliers want to form business partnerships with companies on which they can rely; employees want to work for companies that make them proud; large investment funds want to support firms that they perceive to be well managed; and nonprofits and NGOs want to partner with companies seeking practical solutions to common goals. Satisfying each of these stakeholder groups (and others) allows companies to fulfill their ultimate purpose, which is to create value and contribute to society.

This is an abstract argument, however. In order for CSR to be convincing, it is necessary to place it in a contemporary context and make a practical case for this perspective today. CSR is increasingly crucial to business success because it provides firms with a mission and strategy around which its multiple stakeholders can rally. Indeed, there is a confluence of forces that make this argument particularly relevant. In particular, CSR as an integral component of strategy is increasingly relevant due to five identifiable trends—trends that will continue to grow in importance throughout the 21st century.

Any one of these drivers (affluence, sustainability, globalization, communications, and brands) might be ignored by managers unconvinced of the strategic benefits of CSR. Collectively, however, they are reshaping the business environment by empowering stakeholder groups. And because all these forces interact with each other, the interactive effects ensure that the operating context will not only continue to change but do so at an increasingly rapid rate.

AFFLUENCE

CSR issues tend to gain a foothold in societies that are more affluent—societies where people have jobs, savings, and security and can afford the luxury of choosing between, for example, low-cost cars that pollute and high-cost hybrids that do not. A poor society, in need of inward investment and economic development, is less likely to enforce strict regulations and penalize firms that might otherwise take their business and money elsewhere. Consumers in developed societies, on the other hand, have a higher standard of living and, as a consequence, expect more from the companies whose products they buy.

Affluence raises societal expectations. Firms operating in affluent societies, therefore, carry a greater burden to demonstrate they are creating value for their stakeholders. In less affluent societies, a manufacturer may be able to externalize some of its production costs to the larger society by polluting the environment. When the majority of people are desperately focused on the need for jobs to feed their families, an externality, such as pollution, is of limited concern. When most members of a society are desperately seeking food, shelter, and other basic necessities, CSR concerns appear to be a luxury.[1] As societies become increasingly affluent, however, the collective understanding of social issues like pollution grows, as does society's ability to afford effective solutions.

While affluence drives CSR, the concept of being "better off" is primarily relative. In other words, one's affluence can only be judged in relation to those who are less or more affluent. As globalization enables a greater awareness of the living standards of people elsewhere, income inequality is rising as an issue (both within and among economies) and driving action. As the UK charity Oxfam notes, by the end of 2016, "the richest 1 percent are likely to control more than half of the globe's total wealth."[2] Evidence suggests that the Internet and globalization are aggravating this social bifurcation, rather than bridging it:

> The digital revolution is opening up a great divide between a skilled and wealthy few and the rest of society. In the past new technologies have usually raised wages by boosting productivity, with the gains being split between skilled and less-skilled workers, and between owners of capital, workers and consumers. Now technology is empowering talented individuals as never before and opening up yawning gaps between the earnings of the skilled and the unskilled, capital-owners and labour.[3]

As such, it is shortsighted to assume that CSR is only applicable where there is affluence. Serious transgressions against society are always resisted by local stakeholders. Protests against international petroleum companies, for example, occur when operating standards are construed as being particularly harmful to the immediate community. In Nigeria, residents of the Niger Delta continue to attack oil workers and sabotage equipment because the Nigerian government is not distributing the wealth generated by the petroleum industry, while pollution and deforestation continue. Though Shell and other companies comply with Nigerian law, they have been attacked (both at home and in Nigeria) by those who believe the company is doing harm.

As well as reflecting local concerns, such protests demonstrate that stakeholders living in affluent societies are willing to impose their values on firms that operate overseas. As a result of such domestic pressure, for example, firms such as Nike, GAP, and Apple now require their subcontractors in developing nations to provide wages and working conditions above local norms. Even so, activists continue to advocate for higher standards, criticizing the pay and conditions of subcontractors where local standards persist well below those that prevail in more developed countries, such as the United States.[4]

Due to such activism, developed-country living standards are rapidly diffusing throughout the world, further pushing the spread of CSR. As the world's population continues to grow (projected to rise from 7.2 billion in 2015 to 9.5 billion in 2060)[5] and more people clamor to enter the middle class (estimated to increase by "two or three billion people" over the next 40 years,[6] driven primarily by economic advances in China and India),[7] ever-rising societal expectations accompany rising living standards. And, people in these rapidly developing economies understand that they cannot afford to progress along the same path as the one followed by developed economies. This applies in terms of environmental damage but also in terms of restricting economic growth:

> The Chinese Academy of Social Sciences reckons the total annual damage to China's economy from environmental degradation is the equivalent of 9% of GDP. The World Bank says bad sanitation and water pollution cost India 6% of national income.[8]

The obvious conclusion is that competitive strategies must consider the ever-shifting pattern of societal expectations fueled by the greater choices affluence affords societies. What is clear is that, as the pace of progress gets ever quicker, this task becomes ever more difficult:

> After agriculture was invented 11,000 years ago, it took 4,000 years for it to supplant hunting and gathering as mankind's main source of food, 5,000 for cities to emerge, 6,000 for writing to develop and 7,000 for the invention of mathematics. After harnesses were devised to hitch oxen to plows, it took 4,000 years to adapt harnesses to the long necks of horses. But 66 years after the Wright brothers flew a distance shorter than the wingspan of a Boeing 747, a man stood on the moon, and mankind marveled at the modern pace of change.[9]

In short, affluence leads to a more engaged civil society, which leads to more rapidly shifting public attention to issues of concern. The pace at which societal attitudes can shift on issues that previously were thought to be intractable has caught many companies unaware. To take US society as an example, on issues as diverse as "interracial marriage, prohibition, women's suffrage, abortion, same-sex marriage, and recreational marijuana," the data show that the country has moved from rejection to "widespread acceptance in a short amount of time."[10]

SUSTAINABILITY

The impact of heightened affluence and changing societal expectations is enhanced by a growing concern for the environment. When the Alaskan pipeline was built in the 1970s, crews could drive on the hardened permafrost 200 days a year. Today, climate changes leave the permafrost solid for only 100 days each year, while NASA photographs reveal that the Arctic ice cap "has shrunk more than 20 percent" since 1979,[11] a rate of decrease that is accelerating.[12]

Greater instances of extreme weather events, melting glaciers, shrinking biodiversity, and other empirical indicators all support what is intuitive—our planet has ecological limits.[13] The speed at which we are approaching those limits and the potential consequences of our actions are complicated issues about which experts do not agree. What is not in doubt, however, is that human economic activity is depleting the world's resources and causing dramatic changes to Earth's atmosphere—changes that could become irreversible in the near future. Already, the latest data indicate "that humanity has transgressed four of the nine boundaries—climate, biodiversity, deforestation and the linked nitrogen and phosphorous cycles"[14] that have been set as "red lines" that the human race crosses at its peril. Our prognosis does not look good. A fixed supply of resources (we have only one planet) faces rapidly growing demand. In the autumn of 2011, the world's population passed 7 billion people—and its growth shows no signs of letting up:

> The first billion people accumulated over a leisurely interval, from the origins of humans hundreds of thousands of years ago to the early 1800s. Adding the second took another 120 or so years. Then, in the last 50 years, humanity more than doubled, surging from three billion in 1959 to four billion in 1974, five billion in 1987 and six billion in 1998. . . . The United Nations Population Division anticipates 8 billion people by 2025, 9 billion by 2043 and 10 billion by 2083.[15]

The scale and pace of this population growth places an enormous strain on the world's resources (from freshwater, to energy provision, to affordable food, to the rare earths necessary to produce consumer electronics), causing commentators like Paul Ehrlich to predict "a collapse of global civilization."[16] This is because the world's population is not only becoming larger but is also becoming more concentrated. According to the United Nations, we recently became "a predominantly urban species. . . . Having taken around 200,000 years to get to the halfway mark, demographers reckon that three-quarters of humanity could be city-dwelling by 2050."[17]

As this concentration of humanity increases, the natural environment will bear the brunt of the associated resource depletion. In particular, climate change is an issue that has gained visibility in recent years, culminating in the first real indicator of intergovernmental commitment to act at the COP21 (21st Conference of the Parties) United Nations meeting in Paris, late in 2015.[18] As a result of this heightened awareness, *sustainability* will increasingly drive CSR. And firms that are perceived to be indifferent to their environmental responsibilities will be punished by stakeholders. The backlash against BP's Deepwater Horizon disaster in 2010 is only the latest example of the dangers firms face if they ignore the emerging consensus around the need to act.

The Argument in Favor of Action on Climate Change

The video at the website below condenses the convoluted, passionate, and often partisan debate about climate change into a straightforward argument:

http://video.stumbleupon.com/#p=p6o08udcmw[19]

The goal of the presentation is to remove the conflict over the science behind climate change and global warming from the debate and, instead, reduce the argument to one of risk management. In other words, whether you believe in the science or not, the dangers of not acting far outweigh any dangers associated with acting.

What is also clear is that internalizing the nature of the problem and the extent of action necessary to effect meaningful change has implications for our entire economic system. In particular, we need to be more efficient in our resource utilization—taking fewer resources from Earth and recycling (ideally *upcycling*) a much higher percentage of the resources we do use.[20] Because waste is inherent to GDP growth (our economic model prefers us to replace our cars every 3 years rather than 10 and buy disposable products rather than ones we can reuse) and because the supply of raw materials is finite, it is essential that we use resources more effectively.[21] Some CSR advocates see waste as a fault in our economic model and call for a *revolution*. Strategic CSR, on the other hand, seeks *evolution*—reforming the current system to create value broadly by integrating a CSR perspective into firm strategy and throughout operations. But, it is only by focusing on the system as a whole that lasting change can occur.

In response, companies as diverse as General Electric (Ecomagination program),[22] Unilever (firm-wide sustainable living program),[23] and Toyota (Prius hybrid car) increasingly recognize the advantages of innovating to meet stakeholder needs. Along similar lines, in 2015 Apple announced it would invest $850 million in "the First Solar Inc plant, . . . [which] will be used to supply electricity for Apple's new campus in Silicon Valley, and its other offices and 52 stores in the state." In making the announcement, Apple's CEO, Tim Cook, said, "We know in Apple that climate change is real. The time for talk is passed. . . . The time for action is now."[24] Further, in the buildup to the United Nations COP21 meeting, which took place in Paris in 2015, more than a dozen companies (including Alcoa, Apple, Bank of America, Berkshire Hathaway, Cargill, Coca-Cola, General Motors, Goldman Sachs, Google, Microsoft, PepsiCo, UPS, and Walmart) committed "to invest more than $140 billion in efforts to cut carbon emissions."[25]

While there is much progress still to be made, stakeholder awareness of sustainability issues will ensure that progressive firms can secure market share and competitive differentiation by integrating CSR throughout strategic planning and day-to-day operations.

GLOBALIZATION

Increasingly, corporations conduct business in a global environment. Operating in multiple countries and cultures magnifies the complexity of business exponentially. Not only are there more laws and regulations to understand, but also many more social norms and cultural subtleties to navigate. In addition, the range of stakeholder expectations to which multinational firms are held accountable increases, as does the potential for conflict among competing stakeholder demands. While globalization has increased the potential for efficiencies gained from operations across borders, therefore, it has also increased the potential to be exposed on a global stage if a firm's actions fail to meet the needs and expectations of its stakeholders.

Globalization is therefore another force propelling the strategic value of CSR. Large corporations, due to their scale and scope, are positioned better than most to take advantage of the potential that globalization offers, and they will continue to prosper as global business moves away from the United States and becomes more evenly distributed.[26] As the BRIC economies (Brazil, Russia, India, and China) continue to develop[27] and are joined by the CIVETS economies (Colombia, Indonesia, Vietnam, Egypt, Turkey, and South Africa),[28] more and more consumers will join the global middle class, the needs of which global firms are competing to meet.

While large corporations stand to gain significantly from globalization, they also present a bigger target for stakeholder concerns. The Internet, which drives this global environment, is a powerful enabling tool for communication and education, transportation, trade, and international capital flows. In the process of connecting over large distances, however, the Internet initially reduced our sense of an immediate community. This, in turn, affected business's sense of self-interest and loosened the self-regulating incentive to maintain strong local ties:

> In the capitalist utopia envisioned by Adam Smith in the 18th century, self-interest was tempered by the competing demands of the marketplace and community. But with globalization, the idea of doing business with neighbors one must face the next day is a quaint memory, and all bets are off.[29]

In Adam Smith's view of the 18th-century world,[30] all competition was local—the vast majority of products were produced and consumed within the same community. As a result, Smith reasoned, it is in producers' self-interest to be honest because to do otherwise would threaten the reputations and goodwill on which ongoing trade within their community depends. As businesses grew in size, began selling to ever more distant markets, and dividing operations across geographic locations in order to minimize costs and maximize profits, Smith's fundamental assumption broke down. Firms were free to be bad employers in Vietnam or polluters in China because they sold their products in the United States or Europe and there was no way for Western consumers to know the conditions under which the products they were buying were produced. Disgruntled employees in Vietnam and local villagers in China were no threat to this business model, especially when even the worst jobs in the factories of multinational firms were often the best source of local jobs and economic progress.

As globalization progresses, however, information is communicated more efficiently. It took "radio 38 years and television 13 years to reach audiences of 50 million people, while it took the Internet only four years, the iPod three years and Facebook two years to do the same."[31] As a result, the world grows ever smaller and societies are returning to the conditions under which Smith first suggested self-interest effectively regulates action. Once again, "all business is local,"[32] with the Internet accessible to "3.2 billion people" today, compared to only 400 million people at the turn of the century[33] and allowing any individual with a cell phone to broadcast what they witness to anyone interested worldwide.

These ideas are expressed graphically in Figure 2.1 in terms of the three phases of stakeholder access to information—from industrialization, to international trade, to globalization. Adam Smith lived in a simpler time, when all information was local and kept firms honest. While globalization initially expanded the distances over which transactions were conducted, a similar access

Figure 2.1   The Three Phases of Stakeholder Access to Information

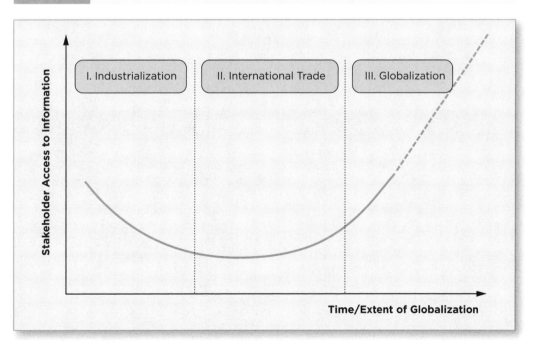

to information at a micro level is now returning. As communication technology continues to innovate and power over its control is increasingly devolved to individuals, the ability of firms to manipulate stakeholder perceptions of their activities will decrease. As GE's vice president of corporate communications reports, "Every three seconds we see something posted online about GE—not all of it good—and so, if you're not out there engaging with people in discussion authentically, you're losing out."[34]

Globalization, therefore, transforms the CSR debate because a domestic context is no longer the only lens through which the issue of CSR should be viewed. Today, no multinational company can afford to ignore its broad range of stakeholders, wherever they may be. European consumers, for example, are just as likely to look to a company's operations elsewhere in the world when judging whether they are going to buy its products. This is a lesson the British bank, Barclays, learned when it continued to do business in apartheid-plagued South Africa in the 1980s;[35] the oil multinational Shell learned a similar lesson from its involvement with the Nigerian regime that executed writer and activist Ken Saro-Wiwa in the 1990s;[36] and it was a lesson that Nike learned when the wages of its employees in Southeast Asia were compared to the endorsement contract of its star spokesperson at the time:

> [In 1992] *Harper's* magazine . . . published an annotated pay-stub from an Indonesian factory, making the soon-to-be famous comparison between workers' wages and Michael Jordan's endorsement contract. [The article] noted that at the wage rates shown on the pay stub, it would take an Indonesian worker 44,492 years to make the equivalent of Jordan's endorsement contract.[37]

Globalization enables stakeholders across different cultures to express their concerns directly. Actions that are acceptable, even required, in one culture may be prohibited in another. Fairly or not, firms will increasingly be expected to meet these varying standards.

Discrimination

Discrimination based on gender is generally prohibited in developed societies, albeit with varying degrees of enforcement; however, in some cultures, like Saudi Arabia, women are segregated from male workers and encounter gender-based limitations on the type of work available to them. A firm operating in Europe and Saudi Arabia may well be considered socially irresponsible and culturally insensitive if it applies the same human resource policies across all operating locations. Yet, if women are treated differently in Saudi Arabia, criticisms may arise in Europe or elsewhere. The Swedish furniture giant IKEA learned this lesson when it airbrushed women out of photos in the Saudi version of its catalog out of respect for local cultural sensitivities.[38] Ignoring inconsistencies in company practices can place multinational firms in awkward positions. On the one hand, they must adapt their strategies to local expectations; on the other hand, strategies based on varying standards can leave the firm open to negative publicity, lawsuits, or other harmful outcomes at home.

This process of globalization can be visualized as progressing through two phases, as suggested by Figure 2.2. Phase I greatly empowered corporations, enabling them to expand operations on a worldwide basis, shift manufacturing offshore, reform supply chain management, and develop powerful global brands. Merger and acquisition activity blossomed (because it was a quick way for companies to grow) and, as firms grew, their power increased significantly. As globalization transcends national boundaries, the power of global firms expands further. They are free to incorporate offshore or relocate their official headquarters through accounting *inversions*—both methods to avoid paying higher tax rates in their home country.

Globalization, however, eventually created countervailing forces that are curtailing corporations' power (Phase II of Figure 2.2). Corporations are gradually losing control over the flow of information that empowers stakeholders to communicate and mobilize. A growing list of examples suggests that companies are no longer able to dictate the quality and quantity of information about their

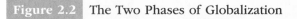

Figure 2.2 The Two Phases of Globalization

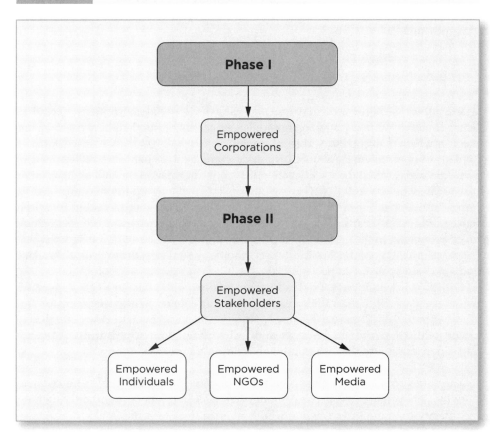

company and how that information affects the social debate. Nike,[39] GAP,[40] Coca-Cola,[41] and Google[42] are just a few examples of companies that have been damaged at some point by global information flows. Such companies may be well advised to communicate more effectively with their stakeholders to better understand and anticipate their needs, before they find themselves fighting against the free flow of information:

> Transparency [among firms] is on the rise, not just for legal or purely ethical reasons but increasingly because it makes economic sense. Firms that exhibit openness and candor have discovered that they can better compete and profit.[43]

This self-feeding cycle of globalization suggests that CSR will increasingly become a mainstay of strategic thinking for businesses, especially global corporations:

> In a world where our demand for Chinese-made sneakers produces pollution that melts South America's glaciers, in a world where Greek tax-evasion can weaken the euro, threaten the stability of Spanish banks and tank the Dow, our values and ethical systems eventually have to be harmonized as much as our markets. To put it differently, as it becomes harder to shield yourself from the other guy's irresponsibility, both he and you had better become more responsible.[44]

COMMUNICATIONS

Globalization demonstrates that the pace at which social innovations spread is heightened by communication technologies, which increasingly define the environment in which firms operate. This information exchange has risen to a level that is difficult to comprehend. As noted by Eric Schmidt (chairman of Google), on any given day today, "modern society generates more information than all of civilization had created before 2003."[45] This revolution is driven by communication that is instant and global. It has ramifications not only for the latest fashions but for social movements, as popular unrest can be spread just as easily as new products. In such an environment, to the extent that a company appears to be out of touch with local concerns, it will face a backlash from stakeholders. Similarly, those firms that adapt and appear responsive to societal claims will be ever more successful.

The growing influence of the Internet makes sure that any CSR lapses by companies are brought rapidly, often instantaneously, to the attention of the worldwide public. Scandal is news, and yesterday's eyewitnesses are today armed with GoPro video cameras and cell phones with sophisticated cameras and video capability that was unimaginable only a decade ago:

> The transformative power of smartphones comes from their size and connectivity. . . . Even the most basic model has access to more number-crunching capacity than NASA had when it put men on the Moon in 1969.[46]

This technology enables communication among activist groups and like-minded individuals, empowering them to spread their message and providing the means to coordinate collective action. Such technologies are decentralizing power in a way that allows individuals to mobilize and protest. Thomas Friedman, for example, explains how this communication revolution is affecting the relationship between the government and people of Iran:

> What is fascinating to me is the degree to which in Iran today—and in Lebanon—the more secular forces of moderation have used technologies like Facebook, Flickr, Twitter, blogging and text-messaging as their virtual mosque, as the place they can now gather, mobilize, plan, inform and energize their supporters, outside the grip of the state.[47]

As presented in Figure 2.2, Phase II of globalization suggests a shift in the balance of power concerning control over the flow of information back toward stakeholders in general and three important constituent groups in particular. First, the Internet has greatly empowered individuals because of the access it provides to greater amounts of information, particularly when an issue achieves a critical mass in the media. In every minute we spend online, it is estimated that we generate "100,555,555 emails; 72 hours of YouTube video; 138,889 tweets; 34,722 App Store downloads; 53,819 new Tumblr posts; [and] every two minutes, we snap as many photos as the whole of humanity took during the 1800s."[48] Today, the Internet has "as many hyperlinks as the brain has synapses. . . . It is already virtually impossible to turn the Internet off."[49]

Second, globalization has increased the influence of NGOs and other activist groups because they, too, are benefiting from easily accessible and affordable communications technologies. These tools empower NGOs by enabling them to inform, attract, and mobilize geographically dispersed individuals and consumer segments, helping to ensure that socially nefarious corporate activities achieve visibility worldwide.

The CNN Test

Simply put, "The Internet makes it possible to organize a global community around a certain issue in a split second."[50] As such, the influence of a few giant media companies that control much of the information we receive extends far beyond the watching public:

> The CNN test has been a criterion that causes CSR sensitive decision makers to ask, "How will this be viewed by watchers of CNN when broadcast around the world?" Even U.S. military commanders used this test to select bombing targets during the second Iraq war in 2003. This test shows the influence of the media in shaping government policy as well as public opinion today and why the CNN test is part of the CSR Filter for some organizations.[51]

And third, new technology and the demand for instantaneous information have enhanced the power of media conglomerates. Media companies have responded by increasing both their size and scope of operations. The combination of empowering these three groups ensures that corporations today are unable to hide behind the fig leaves of superficial public relations campaigns:

> We are approaching a theoretical state of absolute informational transparency. . . . As individuals steadily lose degrees of privacy, so, too, do corporations and states. . . . It is becoming unprecedentedly difficult for anyone, anyone at all, to keep a secret. . . . Truths will either out or be outed. This is something I would bring to the attention of every diplomat, politician and corporate leader: the future, eventually, will find you out. . . . In the end, you will be seen to have done that which you did.[52]

It is increasingly apparent that two trends will dominate future Internet growth: First, people will access the Internet via mobile devices (primarily cell phones and tablet computers), and second, they will share information via social media sites (such as Facebook and Twitter).

Mobile Devices

Cell phones and other mobile devices are now ubiquitous in most countries. They are proliferating because they provide people with their preferred means of accessing the Internet: wireless technology (cell phones, text messaging, blogs, and social media sites).[53] For example, "only 4% of households in Africa have Internet access, but more than 50% have cell phones"[54] and "In some African markets you can buy a daily dose of internet on a mobile phone for about the cost of a banana (i.e., less than ten American cents)."[55]

While a number of social ills have become associated with the use of mobile devices, such as texting while driving[56] and an increase in emergency room visits among children of distracted parents,[57] it is also apparent that they are very attractive because they make life so convenient. Increasingly, mobile devices are becoming the primary way we get our news, access the Internet, and run many aspects of our lives.[58]

The use of mobile devices spread so quickly not only because it is convenient for the customer but also because the infrastructure necessary to support it (wireless antennas) is much cheaper than the desktop computers and land telephone lines that were the foundation of the Internet in developed economies.[59] Developing countries that struggle to provide the basic infrastructure of society, therefore, nevertheless see the rapid diffusion of mobile devices—India, for example, "has more mobile phones than toilets."[60]

Social Media

As people access the Internet via their mobile devices, they are using social media to exchange information. Social media is perhaps more accurately described as "social technologies," of which there are two types—websites that "allow people to broadcast their ideas" (e.g., Twitter and its Chinese equivalent, Sina Weibo) and websites that allow people to "form connections" (e.g., Facebook and its corporate equivalent, LinkedIn).[61] The amount of data these platforms distribute is staggering, with Facebook registering well over 1.5 billion active users and the number of tweets sent each day now exceeding 500 million.[62] While much of this information is trite, some of it has the power to drive revolutions.

The Twitter Revolution

Social media in general, and Twitter in particular, has played an important role in almost all of the popular insurrections in the 21st century. Whether Twitter continues this trend or a competing platform replaces it, what is clear from the tweets quoted below[63] is that social media provides a way for dissatisfaction to spread and protesters to mobilize:

--

June 2009: Iran's Green Movement
"#iranelection #Neda // You saw the pain in her eyes. Don't let her die in vain."
HY @niphette

--

January 2011: Tunisia's Jasmine Revolution
"Tunisia is entering a critical stage in fight for freedom. This is no time to stop. No settlement only **#jasminerevolution #tunisia #sidibouzid**"
Voice of Tunisia **@Voiceoftunisia**

--

February 2011: Tahrir Square, Egypt
"Despite the blood and the pain, spirits here are sky-high. People singing the anthem & waving flags while throwing stones **#Jan25 #Tahrir**"
Mosa'ab Elshamy **@mosaaberizing**

--

September 2011: Occupy Wall Street
"If you haven't heard already, the People are taking over NYC **#occupywallstreet**"
Terrestria Movement **@UCEarth**

--

August 2014: Ferguson Missouri
"**#Ferguson** residents, start uploading pictures and video, NOW."
Tammi LaTela **@TLaTela**

As the above examples indicate, it is in the interaction of these two technologies (mobile devices and social media) where the potential for revolution is most apparent. Whether it is using Facebook and Twitter to overturn decades of totalitarianism in the Middle East or simply using GPS technology to play Pac-Man in the streets of New York ("Pac-Manhattan"),[64] the power of technology to mobilize strangers and unite them in pursuit of a common agenda is growing daily:

> Tick off the protests that characterized 2011, and you'll find that every one of them featured cell-phones, tweets, texts, Facebook, and YouTube. The immediacy and accuracy of information ramped up the speed of these activities and the intensity of the results. It you doubt that, here's this week's essay question: Comment on how the U.S. civil rights movement might have developed if the marchers in Alabama had used today's communications systems.[65]

The result, as suggested by Figure 2.3, is an ever-widening, free flow of information in a globalizing world that portends danger for entrenched interests everywhere. As firms scramble to formulate a "social media policy," they are being forced to react to rumors and complaints that can quickly escalate beyond their control:[66]

> In the two weeks after the 1989 Exxon Valdez oil spill in Prince William Sound, in Alaska, Exxon's shares dropped 3.9% but quickly rebounded. In the two months after the Gulf of Mexico oil spill in 2010, BP's shares fell by half.[67]

Figure 2.3   The Free Flow of Information in a Globalizing World

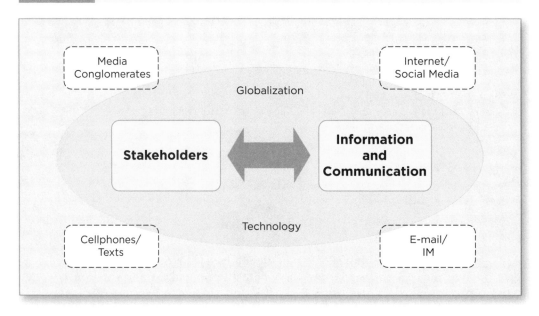

Harnessing this power and directing it at a corporate target has the potential to inflict significant damage to any firm's product, brand, or reputation. It does not stretch the imagination too far to see how Copwatch (http://www.copwatch .com/, which monitors police activity and posts videos online to guard against abusive behavior)[68] easily becomes *Corpwatch* (http://www.corpwatch.org/), using the same technology and community motivation to build campaigns against specific firms. The danger no longer lies in insufficient information but in being able to detect "whispers of useful information in a howling hurricane of noise."[69]

The relationship between stakeholders and the growing pool of information is iterative. As stakeholders gain access to larger amounts of information and communicate among each other, they build support for issues and disseminate their opinions to other stakeholders.[70] This trend is already reflected in the rapid growth of websites with user-generated content, such as YouTube and Flickr. It is taken a step further with the development of the sharing economy (think Uber, Airbnb, or BlaBlaCar), which allows users to rate and review the products and services provided, even as governments struggle to understand and regulate these new kinds of economic exchanges.[71]

The result is that more and more consumers are interacting with firms in real time in ways that shape purchase decisions. Consumers are informed and, just as they are willing to spread good news, they are also willing to share their horror stories with millions of others.[72] Consequently, firms have an even more precarious hold on their reputations and need to be more responsive to stakeholders' concerns in order to protect them: "The conventional wisdom is that a satisfied customer will tell one person and an unhappy person will tell 10. . . . That's now been upped by orders of magnitude."[73]

While this growth in information and communication is clearly "shifting power from a few Goliaths to many Davids,"[74] it is less clear how fully stakeholders will take advantage of these capabilities. For example, while Change.org "is the web's leading platform for social change, empowering anyone, anywhere to start petitions that make a difference," it is hard to know how firms should respond to the stakeholder concerns that are registered there. If 5,000 people sign an online petition, what does that mean? Will they refuse to buy from that company anymore? Will they protest at stores? And, if so, so what? For a large brand, 5,000 people widely diffused is a small percentage of the firm's customers, and clicking a mouse is hardly an indication of personal conviction or willingness to sacrifice on behalf of a cause.

Nevertheless, it is a brave manager who ignores the dramatic shift in online engagement that has emerged in the last few years. Going forward, those firms that can respond to external pressure for more responsible behavior, ethics, transparency, and social involvement by rethinking their strategic approach to business will be best placed to operate in a business context in which they no longer control the flow of information. In short, for companies to enjoy sustained success, CSR will increasingly form a central component of strategy and operations, particularly in relation to a firm's reputation and brand management.

BRANDS

All of these drivers of CSR overlap in terms of the importance of a firm's reputation and brand. Brands are a focal point of corporate success. Companies try to establish popular brands in consumers' minds because doing so increases their competitive advantage, which results in higher sales and revenue—consumers are more likely to pay a premium for a brand they know and trust. However, due to growing societal expectations, combined with the increased complexity of business in a global environment and the ability of stakeholders to spread missteps instantaneously to a global audience, today, more than ever before, a firm's reputation is precarious—hard to establish and easy to lose. Brands therefore drive CSR because they raise the stakes of business. All things equal, brands that are trusted by stakeholders will be more successful in the market than those that are not trusted.

The value of brands to firms is quantified by *Interbrand* in its annual brand survey, which reveals that brands are more valuable than ever. Apple's brand, for example, is estimated to be worth as much as $170,000 million (Interbrand's No. 1 global brand).[75] Coca-Cola's brand is worth close to half of the company's total market capitalization—in other words, the value of the intangible brand is almost equal to the value of the firm's tangible assets. As a result, firms need to take ever greater steps to protect an investment that is central to their continued success. The best way to protect a brand is for the firm to integrate a CSR perspective throughout operations. Doing so can help firms build their brand,[76] insure their brand,[77] and repair their brand in the event of a crisis.[78]

CSR is important to brands within a globalizing world because of the way brands are built: based on perceptions, ideals, and concepts that usually appeal to stakeholders' values. In particular, lifestyle brands (which base more of their appeal to consumers on aspirational values) need to live the ideals they convey to their consumers. CSR is a means of matching corporate operations with stakeholder values at a time when these values are constantly evolving. In particular, brands are a way for a company to communicate directly with its stakeholders in general, but its consumers in particular. Of course, this only works if the narrative the firm seeks to build matches the mood of customers, which can shift quickly. Nevertheless, one of the companies that has done this most effectively is Starbucks, driven by the values of its founder and CEO, Howard Schultz:

> Promoting civic harmony represents a way for Starbucks to define itself without reference to its coffee or tea—and, let's face it, there was nothing particularly virtuous about a $5 Frappuccino in the first place. Rather, the company is encouraging consumers to focus on its ethos—its good intentions. That is the brand, not the flavoured water in the paper cup with the plastic top.[79]

Businesses today need to build a watertight brand with respect to all stakeholders. The attractiveness of a company—whether as an employer, producer, supplier, or investment—is directly linked to the strength of its brand. CSR affects all aspects of operations within a corporation because of the need to consider the needs of constituent groups. Each area builds on all the others to create a composite image of the firm and its brand in the eyes of its stakeholder groups. Given the large amount of time, money, and effort companies invest in creating brands, a good CSR policy has become a vital component of generating a return on that investment—an effective means of maximizing market appeal over the long term.

Strategic CSR Debate

MOTION: Social media does not represent progress for society. It reduces attention spans, dumbs down debate, and minimizes human interaction.

QUESTIONS FOR DISCUSSION AND REVIEW

1. What are the five driving forces that make CSR more relevant for firms today?

2. Of these five forces, is there one that you feel is more important than the others? Defend your choice with examples from your own experience and knowledge.

3. For each of the five forces, can you think of a firm that is strategically well positioned to take advantage of the changes being propelled by that force?

4. For each of the five forces, can you think of a firm that is vulnerable to these shifting dynamics?

5. Ten years from now, do you think these five forces will still be driving ever-greater CSR? Do you see any other emerging forces (e.g., religion, big data)[80] that might reshape CSR in the future to the same extent as the five forces discussed in this chapter?

Chapter 3

CORPORATE RIGHTS AND RESPONSIBILITIES

I n order to understand the social *responsibilities* of the corporation, it is also important to understand the corporation's *rights*. Another key component of the CSR debate is the corporation's *self-interest*. To the extent that the responsibilities expected of it do not infringe upon its rights and also align with its self-interest (see Figure 3.1), the chance of introducing meaningful change and building a more sustainable economic model increases.

Figure 3.1 The Corporation's Rights, Responsibilities, and Self-Interest

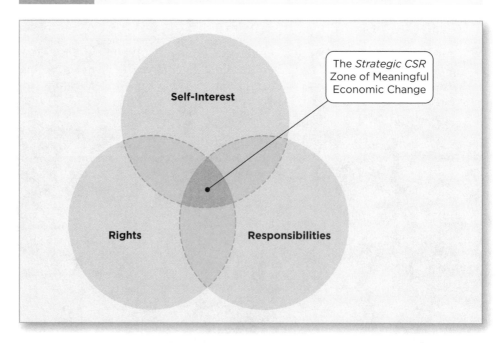

One aspect of the ideas discussed in this textbook that differentiates it from related conversations around CSR, business ethics, and sustainability is an underlying faith in the market to solve some of the largest challenges we face. While for-profit firms have clearly been part of the problem in the past, they are also central to any viable solution. Unless we can harness the creative power of the corporation to further society's interests in a way that optimizes value creation, broadly defined, the problems of social inequity and environmental degradation will only worsen. But for change to occur, we have to understand how economies work and what motivates human interaction within this framework. It is only then that we can have a coherent conversation about how companies can meet our needs, rather than frustrate them.

In other words, it is important to understand what we mean when we discuss *corporate social responsibility*. When we ask the question *What are the social responsibilities of the firm?* what I believe we are really asking is *How can a firm create the most value for the broadest section of society?* It is only society that can decide what is in society's best interest, and society does that every day when we all interact with the firm as stakeholders.

To put that another way, when Greenpeace demands that a firm decrease its pollution of carbon emissions, it is really asking the firm to create value in the way that Greenpeace defines value (i.e., less environmental destruction). Similarly, when consumers demand safer products or when employees demand better working conditions or when suppliers demand quicker payment cycles or when the government demands compliance with a law, each stakeholder is asking the organization to operate in a way that they define as "value creating." If a consumer values a safe product, then the firm meets their needs when it delivers that product. Equally, if an employee values better working conditions, then the firm creates value for them when it provides that workplace, and so on. In each case, it is the stakeholder that defines what "value creation" looks like. When the stakeholder actively seeks that value from the firm, then it is the firm's decision as to whether to meet the need. Thus, society determines the extent to which any one firm is useful, because it has the power to decide whether the firm remains profitable.

By asking the wrong questions (or, at least, framing the right questions incorrectly), the traditional CSR debate focuses on *objective outcomes* that particular individuals or groups believe should be achieved (e.g., Walmart *must* pay its employees a living wage). This is essentially a *normative* approach—one that starts with a predetermined outcome and then works out how to achieve it. When the focus is instead on the *fluid process* by which value is created for multiple stakeholders, however, outcomes are not dogmatic—they are defined as different stakeholders bring their interests to bear in a complex process of negotiation. This is essentially a *descriptive* approach—one that allows the outcome to emerge (depending on what stakeholders value at any given time), rather than imposing a fixed view about what should or should not happen.

This textbook adopts this descriptive approach. It argues that capitalism works best when stakeholders represent their interests to demand the results from firms that provide value for them, not when those outcomes are predetermined by a vocal minority. In other words, the discussion in these pages does not encourage absolute positions: It does not advocate in favor of outsourcing or in favor of domestic production; similarly, it does not advocate in favor of a living wage or a minimum wage. What it seeks instead is to describe how stakeholder actions translate into signals about how those stakeholders want the firm to act. To put it bluntly, consumers should understand that, when they shop at Walmart, they are endorsing a business model of outsourcing. If they support outsourcing, they should carry on shopping at Walmart. But, if they would prefer to support companies that employ Americans by manufacturing domestically, then they should not shop at Walmart. At present, Walmart is only doing what its stakeholders tell it they want it to do.

For-profit firms are the most efficient tools we have to deliver the social progress that we seek. As such, understanding the framework of rights and responsibilities within which these firms operate is central to understanding CSR. In particular, in contrast to much of the CSR debate, which highlights the corporation's *responsibilities*, it is worth asking: What *rights* does the corporation have?

CORPORATE RIGHTS

The corporation is the focus of much of the critical attention of CSR advocates. It is the organization blamed for many of the ills created by globalization and free trade. The attention reflects the high profile of the corporation in modern society:

> Hegel predicted that the basic unit of modern society would be the state, Marx that it would be the commune, Lenin and Hitler that it would be the political party. Before that, a succession of saints and sages claimed the same for the parish church, the feudal manor, and the monarchy. . . . They have all been proved wrong. The most important organization in the world is the company: the basis of the prosperity of the West and the best hope for the future of the rest of the world. Indeed, for most of us, the company's only real rival for our time and energy is the one that is taken for granted—the family.[1]

When we discuss a corporation's social responsibilities, it is important to remember that, merely by existing—by providing jobs for employees and suppliers, by providing value to customers, by providing a return on investment to shareholders, and by paying taxes to governments—the corporation benefits society. If you add to that mix the constant innovation necessary to maintain sales and profits (as a general rule, only products that are in demand are purchased), then the corporation should be considered an extremely positive and productive component of a healthy society. As Todd Stitzer, past CEO of Cadbury Schweppes, proclaimed:

Remember Adam Smith's invisible hand? It is one of the most repeated phrases in the business world. But business has allowed society to forget a very simple fact: the hand that connects markets and balances supply and demand is ours. We are the people who put food on plates, books on shelves, music in people's ears and information online. We are the distributors and we are the creators of wealth.[2]

The corporation, however, can also do harm to the societies in which it operates. Doing all of the above does not ensure a firm's long-term viability and does not replace the need for an effective CSR policy implemented throughout the organization. Walmart exists as prima facie evidence that a company that is successful and producing products in demand can still be accused of behavior that is harmful to society as a whole. As a result, the positive aspects of Walmart's operations[3] are often lost among the negative publicity the company receives.[4]

Given all of this, to what extent is the corporation a positive factor in the CSR debate? To what extent is business essential to achieve the social agenda sought by CSR advocates? And, how can a corporation's contribution to the wider good be measured and evaluated?

In addressing the *value* of the corporation to society, we are inherently determining what position it deserves in the social strata. Given that the ability to incorporate is a privilege bestowed by society, what rights should accompany the legal status of corporation? If we are going to argue that a corporation has *responsibilities* that we would like it to fulfill, we also need to grant *rights* that protect its ability to exist and do what is it designed to do—make money.

Citizens United

A *corporation* is a fictitious legal person that is endowed with many of the characteristics of a human being. It can possess property; it can incur debts; it can sue and be sued; and it can be criminally prosecuted, fined, and, in theory, dissolved by the federal government. Under US law, the Supreme Court has extended portions of the Bill of Rights to corporations, even while it has been less stringent in imposing many of the responsibilities of citizenship.

The basis of these rights rests in the concept of *corporate personhood*—which has become an essential component of US society because "the constitution is so specific about the rights it bestows on people."[5] The idea is traced to an 1819 Supreme Court case, *Trustees of Dartmouth College v. Woodward* (17 U.S. 518, 1819). This case centered on a dispute between the college and the New Hampshire legislature's attempts to force it to become a public institution. In deciding in favor of the organization, the Court distinguished between public and private charters and, in the process, reinforced the rights of a private organization to remain private (and, by definition, outside the control of the state). In keeping with this precedent, the Court continued to understand corporations as legal individuals, gradually increasing the rights bestowed on them in line with constitutionally protected individual rights:

While corporations had been afforded limited rights, such as property ownership or contract-making, . . . the idea that an inanimate entity was eligible for rights of personhood sprang from the 1886 case of Santa Clara County v. Southern Pacific Railroad. The corporation in this case was able to wield the newly minted 14th Amendment to argue that [it] was entitled to the same tax benefits as individuals.[6]

As noted, *Santa Clara County v. Southern Pacific Railroad* (118 U.S. 394, 1886) is often cited as the cornerstone of modern corporate rights in the United States. It dealt with the issue of states' taxation of railroad properties. Southern Pacific Railroad had refused to pay these taxes because the rules under which they were levied were more stringent than the rules for personal taxation. Rather than the Court specifically deciding that corporations were individuals, however, that assumption was the starting point for the Justices' deliberations. In other words, this position was stated, rather than decided, which leaves its status as legal precedent somewhat precarious. This ambiguity is the source of much of the debate around the legal rights of corporations today, even while corporations quickly took the opportunity offered by the decision:

Although the [14th Amendment to the Constitution] had been added to protect the rights of African Americans after the Civil War, only 19 individuals invoked it for protection between 1890 and 1910. Businesses, on the other hand, claimed 14th Amendment protection 288 times during that period.[7]

The concept of corporate personhood was extended more recently as a result of a 1976 Supreme Court case, *Buckley v. Valeo* (424 U.S. 1, 1976), which bolstered one of the most contentious corporate rights, freedom of speech.[8] In this case, the Court ruled explicitly that political donations were free speech and, as such, were constitutionally protected behavior. This applied whether the donations were made by individuals or by organizations. This decision was followed shortly after in 1978 by *First National Bank of Boston v. Bellotti* (435 U.S. 765, 1978), which granted firms the right to donate money to political campaigns.[9] It is these decisions that laid the foundation many years later for the controversial *Citizens United v. Federal Election Commission* (558 U.S. 310) decision, which the Court decided in 2010.

While the particulars of the case focused on a narrow component of campaign finance regulation ("involving whether *Citizens United*, a nonprofit corporation, had the right to air a slashing movie about Hillary Rodham Clinton during the Democratic primary season"),[10] the Court decided to expand the parameters of the case to consider its broader implications for the legal doctrine of "corporate personhood." *The New York Times* argued in advance of the decision that doing so represented a significant overreach by the Justices and that "corporations cannot and should not be allowed to vote, run for office or bear arms."[11] Moreover, such critics of the case point out that a narrow interpretation of a corporation's rights (as opposed to the expansion represented by *Citizens United*) is a purer interpretation of the Constitution's original intent, which was detailed in the 1819 *Dartmouth College* case (17 U.S. 518) by Chief Justice John Marshall:

A corporation is an artificial being, invisible, intangible, and existing only in contemplation of law. Being the mere creature of law, it possesses only those properties which the charter of its creation confers upon it. . . . Among the most important are immortality, and . . . individuality; properties by which a perpetual succession of many persons are considered as the same, and may act as a single individual.[12]

Citizens United was important because it decided (apparently definitively) that corporations enjoy the same First Amendment rights to free speech as individuals. Although the majority in the Supreme Court decision used well-established legal precedent to support this interpretation of the Constitution, debate continues about the case's potential consequences. As with most rulings, there is the theory that justifies it (which may be defendable) and the reality in implementation (which may be subject to abuse). This decision allows corporations greater freedom to finance political ads and individual candidates. The consequences of the decision are projected to alter the face of political campaigns; it is thought that increasing the amount of money in politics will have direct consequences for the number of attack ads and favor those candidates who support corporations. As such, it is clear that a number of stakeholders, including shareholders, are equally concerned about the uncertainty the case creates. From 2010 to 2014, for example, "more than 430 shareholder proposals on the topic of corporate political activity [were] filed at Russell 3000 companies," while in 2014 alone, "88.9% of the political spending proposals filed requested the disclosure of corporate political contributions and/or the company's lobbying related activities."[13] Moreover, firms "donated $1.68 billion to candidates and political groups [in 2014] and $2.71 billion in 2012, the most recent presidential-election year."[14]

While commentators continue to disagree about the case's effect on political elections,[15] it is important to see *Citizens United* in the broader context of the Court's evolving position on which rights should be ascribed to corporations. Even though the range of rights has been steadily increasing over time, progress is neither linear nor necessarily logical. Such inconsistency is evident in a 2011 decision that focused on a corporation's right to privacy in which the Court "ruled unanimously that corporations have no personal privacy rights for purposes of the Freedom of Information Act."[16] While the intricacies of the arguments are fascinating, it is not clear why the same arguments were not used to deny corporations the right to free speech in *Citizens United*. If the Court is going to decide that a firm has the right to free speech, surely it must also decide that firms also have other rights that we attribute to individuals, such as the right to privacy.

A central component of the argument presented in this textbook is that corporations exist because their products are in demand and that, in general, it is in society's best interests to encourage healthy and wealthy corporations because they bring many benefits. Equally important, however, is that demand for a product is a necessary but insufficient condition for survival over the medium to long term. On top of a healthy foundation of an efficient organization and a profitable product, managers must construct an integrated CSR policy that seeks to create value for a broad range of stakeholders. The concept of corporate personhood enables this goal and is essential for the fluid operation of a market economy (firms need to be able to enter into contracts, to be able to sue and be sued, etc.). It is an essential complement to the concept of limited liability. Together, these two innovations (personhood and limited liability) have laid the foundation for an explosion in growth and prosperity among developed economies:

> Until the mid-19th century companies . . . were regulated by corporate charters which laid down tight rules about what they could do. But reformers used the idea that companies, like people, should be captains of their own souls, to free them from these restrictions. The result of this liberation was an explosion of energy: Western companies turbocharged the industrial revolution and laid the foundations for mass prosperity.[17]

In spite of this, the Supreme Court's inconsistent logic is in danger of getting itself in a mess. It is difficult for the Justices to continue to extend certain individual rights to corporations (like free speech) but not others (like privacy), unless the Court has a clear rationale for why it is drawing the distinction. At present, this rationale has not been made clear, but it could be with the intention of providing constitutional support only for those rights that are essential "for the efficient functioning of business."[18]

The danger for corporations is that, if the logic of personhood is extrapolated, the rights that are granted should be accompanied with "onerous responsibilities."[19] Already many in the business community would point out that government regulation of business today is much stricter than it has been historically.[20] While many note that corporations have no one to blame but themselves for this, in the absence of matching obligations, the privileges afforded to corporations will continue to be questioned. The inconsistency in the Court's decisions aggravates perceptions of bias and divides activists on where the boundary between corporate rights and societal responsibilities should lie. Many activist organizations, such as Move to Amend (https://movetoamend.org/) and Reclaim Democracy (http://reclaimdemocracy.org/), campaign in the United States for a constitutional amendment to redress this imbalance. Some among the Justices might be sympathetic. In his dissent to *Citizens United*, Justice John Paul Stevens argues that "because companies are without feelings, consciences or desires, they shouldn't benefit from laws that protect ordinary citizens."[21] Others see the value in affording corporations rights but would like to see some corresponding responsibilities enforced with equal enthusiasm.

CORPORATE RESPONSIBILITIES

In contrast to a corporation's legal rights, what is its *public purpose*—its responsibilities and obligations as determined by corporate law and founding corporate charters? On this issue, there is apparently a strong consensus:

The corporation, as created by law, . . . compels executives to prioritize the interests of their companies and shareholders above all others and forbids them from being socially responsible—at least genuinely so.[22]

This shareholder perspective is popularly believed to have become enshrined in popular perception as a result of a Michigan Supreme Court case, *Dodge vs. Ford Motor Company*.[23] In deciding in the Dodge brothers' favor, the judge in the case

> reinstated the dividend and rebuked Ford . . . for forgetting that "a business corporation is organized and carried on primarily for the profit of the stockholders"; it could not be run "for the merely incidental benefit of shareholders and for the primary purpose of benefiting others." *Dodge v. Ford* still stands for the legal principle that managers and directors have a legal duty to put shareholders' interests above all others and no legal authority to serve any other interests—what has come to be known as "the best interests of the corporation" principle.[24]

The legal foundation for this idea of shareholder primacy, however, is disputed (as discussed in detail in Chapter 6). Rather than unambiguous corporate law, this perspective has evolved in accordance with the values we choose to espouse as a society. As Lynn Stout explains in her analysis of corporate legal precedent in the United States, contrary to widespread perception, executives and directors have no legal obligation to focus the firm's efforts on shareholder value:

> Shareholder value ideology is just that—an ideology, not a legal requirement or a practical necessity of modern business life. United States corporate law does not, and never has, required directors of public corporations to maximize either share price or shareholder wealth. To the contrary, as long as boards do not use their power to enrich themselves, the law gives them a wide range of discretion to run public corporations with other goals in mind, including growing the firm, creating quality products, protecting employees, and serving the public interest.[25]

In spite of the dispute over its legal foundation, the myth of maximizing shareholder value is firmly entrenched in today's executive suite and boardroom. This position is very different from how corporations were initially envisaged, with *public purpose* as a founding requirement. Early corporate charters were granted by legislative bodies under strict rules—they were issued only for a limited period of time (the corporation would be wound up after this period ended) and only for a specific task that was sanctioned by societal need (e.g., build a bridge over a river or construct a railroad):

> The early American states used chartered corporations, endowed with special monopoly rights, to build some of the vital infrastructure of the new country—universities (like America's oldest corporation, Harvard University, chartered in 1636), banks, churches, canals, municipalities, and roads.[26]

Today, in contrast, politicians give corporate leaders significantly greater flexibility to meet shareholders' expectations. The legislation that removed the public purpose provision of a corporation's charter (or, its articles of incorporation) was designed to root out the corruption that had become inherent in the political process to award charters:

> The earliest, recognisably modern business corporation was the famous—or infamous—East India Company. Chartered on 31 December, 1600, its public purpose—"the advancement of trade"—was in fact nothing more glorious than the making of money for its proprietors.[27]

In working to treat "the corporation as simply another business form, available to all—just as a partnership or an unincorporated company" in the first half of the nineteenth century, President Andrew Jackson deliberately eliminated "determinations of a 'public purpose' that warranted granting special privileges to a particular business organization. Theoretically, all corporations would receive the same privileges and immunities."[28] As such, while early corporations and business leaders would have accepted a *social responsibility* as an implicit contract with society in return for the right to operate, today's corporate executives understand incorporation as a right, rather than a privilege. This reinforces the idea that the firm contributes to society simply by its continued existence, rather than the idea that the firm exists at the behest of society, to which something is owed in return.[29] Rather than *fact*, however, this *belief* is a social construction. As such, it can be changed if, as a society, we decide it should be different.

To this end, the state government in Vermont is famous for creating the "Ben & Jerry's law" that was passed by the legislature in the run-up to Unilever's acquisition of the firm. The law allowed the boards of directors of Vermont firms to consider factors in addition to shareholder value when deciding whether to accept a takeover offer:

> [The law] permitted a company's directors to reject a takeover bid if "they deem it to be not in the best interests of employees, suppliers, and the economy of the state." Thus, even when a company was offered a financial premium in a buyout situation, its directors where permitted to reject the offer based on the best interests of the State of Vermont.[30]

From a CSR perspective, how should we determine what responsibilities should be placed on corporations? What prevents a firm from operating in the best interests of a broad array of stakeholders, rather than having a narrow focus on shareholders?

> Shareholders provide capital to the business and acquire a right to a percentage of the profits of the business. They should get a fair return. But capital is not the only asset the business should value—it must protect its staff, its reputation and the continued favor of its customers.[31]

The firm has a responsibility to its shareholders, but they are only one of many stakeholders. Their interests are important, but there are many instances in which those interests are likely to be (or even *should* be) subservient to the interests of other stakeholders:

> People forgot (or never realized) that shareholders do not actually own the company; they own only its stock. This entitles them to get the residual assets of the company upon its breakup and to vote on resolutions at annual meetings and on the appointment of directors, but not to tell the firm what to do. A company is in law an independent person, and its directors have a fiduciary duty to the company as a whole—that is, to its workers and customers as well as its investors.[32]

What *should* a corporate charter look like, and what is the most appropriate authority (federal vs. state government) to regulate this area of corporate law? What should the responsibilities of the firm be, and what structure is best suited to achieve these outcomes?

Benefit Corporations

Issues of corporate governance in the United States are currently regulated under state, rather than federal, law. Those who support this system argue that it encourages competition between states (to entice businesses to incorporate within their state) and, therefore, produces effective and efficient legislation. Critics rebut the benefits of interstate competition, suggesting that the result is a race to the bottom as states craft legislation to appease corporations. States want firms to incorporate within their jurisdiction because of the lucrative fees and taxes they receive for each company registration, wherever the company is actually headquartered or employs the most people. Instead, "managers can go jurisdiction-shopping, looking for the most advantageous set of laws, since getting a corporate charter is easier than getting a driver's license."[33]

In terms of oversight, liability, responsibility, and regulation, Delaware is considered the friendliest place to do business in the United States. It has judges who are more knowledgeable than those in other states about business law and who have "long been reluctant to disturb the decisions of corporate boards."[34] Delaware has been developing this reputation since 1792, when it established its Court of Chancery to deal with corporations: "By the early 20th century, the state was writing friendly corporate and tax laws to lure companies from New York, New Jersey and elsewhere."[35] As a result, firms seeking to incorporate in the United States tend to choose Delaware. This is confirmed by the Delaware State government website, which claims:

> The State of Delaware is a leading domicile for U.S. and international corporations. More than 1,000,000 business entities have made Delaware their legal home. More than 50% of all publicly-traded companies in the United States including 64% of the Fortune 500 have chosen Delaware as their legal home.[36]

Delaware is perceived to have the most advantageous system of company regulation, which translates to having the least regulation. Moreover, the state (whose 1,000,000 registered companies exceeds its population of approximately 936,000 people) advertises benefits to incorporation such as "allowing even greater secrecy than offshore tax havens."[37] As a result of its efforts, "corporate fees paid to the state are projected to total more than $1 billion for [FY2015]— that is 26% of Delaware's budget, up from $665 million, or 21%, a decade ago."[38] Due to these benefits, "most states end up mimicking Delaware law,"[39] if for no other reason than to keep companies currently headquartered there from moving to Delaware.

The problem with this competition to see which state can provide the most accommodating business environment, of course, is that it encourages firms to neglect CSR. With fewer legal constraints, governments essentially are surrendering their oversight of companies—an essential stakeholder function. As such, one possible area for reform advocated by activists is for the federal government to take control of the incorporation process. The authority to do so is invested in the federal government under the Commerce Clause of the Constitution.[40] Doing so would allow either Congress or the Securities and Exchange Commission (SEC) to raise the bar for all corporations without having to worry that companies would simply flee in protest to the state with the weakest rules.[41]

A starting point for the federal government would be a law stating that corporations have to incorporate where they have the largest presence—that is, where their true headquarters are, where they employ the most people, or where they have the greatest percentage of operations. This would make corporations more directly accountable for their actions to the community within which they actually operate. By introducing these changes, the government would also go a long way toward closing the loophole in the tax code that allows corporations to incorporate offshore to avoid[42] paying the higher rates of corporation tax levied in the United States:

> Just £349 ($560) buys you a company in the Seychelles, with no local taxation, no public disclosure of directors or shareholders and no requirement to file accounts.[43]

As a first step in this campaign toward federalization, various attempts have been made to introduce a *Code for Corporate Responsibility* at the state level, which would reform the law with regard to broadening the focus of executives and directors. This simple but far-reaching change could have a significant impact. In particular, the new law would give stakeholders a tool by which to hold corporations accountable for their actions and policies. Forcing US firms to adopt this multiconstituency approach would encourage behavior more similar to that of European firms, as well as those in Asian countries such as Japan, which tend to define their stakeholders more broadly and actively:

The Code requires directors to ensure that profits do not come at the expense of five elements of the public interest: 1) the environment; 2) human rights; 3) public health and safety; 4) the welfare of communities; and 5) employee dignity.[44]

There are legitimate concerns regarding the implementation of a law such as this. In particular, it is not clear how firms are supposed to prioritize among their stakeholders' interests. For example, what happens if a company moves a plant to a more environmentally friendly facility but, in the process, makes a number of workers in an economically deprived area of the country unemployed? What would the consequences be if investors began to sell their stock under these *anti-investor* policies in favor of firms in more *investor-friendly* states or countries? Also, what would be the proposed penalties for directors who fail the new test? Would they be individually liable for any damage or stakeholder complaint that ensued? Nevertheless, the idea that modern corporations should be compelled to register a *public purpose* that reflects a broader set of social responsibilities is receiving growing support.

These issues have given rise in recent years to a variety of proposed new corporate structures in different economies. In Europe, for example, the Economy for the Common Good (http://www.ecogood.org/) seeks to solve the problems it sees in modern-day capitalism by building "an economic system that 'places human beings and all living entities at the center of economic activity.'"[45] More specifically, in The Netherlands, there are laws protecting stakeholder-based companies, which are "run not solely for the benefit of shareholders but for all people, . . . including the world at large."[46] And in the UK since 2005, Community Interest Companies (http://www.cicassociation.org.uk/) dedicate all profits "for community benefit rather than private advantage."[47] In the United States, the idea of the *benefit corporation* is gaining popularity. Becoming a benefit corporation expands the fiduciary responsibilities of the firm's executives and directors by committing the organization to meet the needs of a broad range of stakeholders:

> A benefit corporation is a new class of corporation that voluntarily meets different standards of corporate purpose, accountability, and transparency.
>
> Benefit Corporations: 1) have a corporate purpose to create a material positive impact on society and the environment; 2) are required to consider the impact of their decisions not only on shareholders but also on workers, community, and the environment; and 3) are required to make available to the public, except in Delaware, an annual benefit report that assesses their overall social and environmental performance against a third party standard.[48]

Although the idea of the benefit corporation was only recently established (Maryland was the first state to pass the necessary legislation in 2010), it has already made an impact. By early 2016, 31 US states had passed legislation permitting the establishment of benefit corporations and another 5 were considering doing so.[49] Once a state has passed the new law, a firm can restructure itself, imposing a legal requirement to implement a stakeholder model and ensuring "its board commits to considering environmental and social factors every time it makes a decision and has to hit specific social and environmental performance targets."[50] In 2012, Patagonia became the first company in California to become a benefit corporation. According to Patagonia's founder, Yvon Chouínard, the primary motivation for doing so was to create "the legal framework to enable mission-driven companies like Patagonia to stay mission-driven through succession, capital raises, and even changes in ownership, by institutionalizing the values, culture, processes, and high standards put in place by founding entrepreneurs."[51]

While the need for the change in law to establish a new type of organization (the benefit corporation) is disputed, there are clear advantages for firms that want to signal more clearly to stakeholders that they seek to manage the firm in their broader interests. In essence, doing so establishes new operating standards for transparency and accountability that become embedded throughout the organization. The firm builds this broader stakeholder perspective by instituting a structure that formalizes the mission in quantifiable goals. As such, that mission is more protected should the founder retire or the firm is bought by another firm. This succession challenge tends to surface whenever a social enterprise is taken over by a multinational, such as when Green & Black's was sold to Cadbury (now Kraft)[52] and The Body Shop sold to L'Oreal.[53] As noted above, one of the primary benefits to Yvon Chouínard of converting Patagonia into a benefit corporation is "that making a firm's social mission explicit in its legal structure makes it harder for a new boss or owner to abandon it."[54] This asset would have been valuable for Ben & Jerry's (which announced its B Corp certification in 2012) during its sale to Unilever in 2000, which occurred "despite the objections of co-founder Ben Cohen and some directors."[55]

Whether it is headquartered in a state that permits firms to become benefit corporations, any firm, anywhere

What Is the Difference Between a Benefit Corporation and a B Corp?

While organized by the same nonprofit (B Lab), a benefit corporation (http://benefitcorp.net/) and a B Corp (http://www.bcorporation.net/) should not be confused. One is a different legal entity (a new kind of corporation) and only companies in certain states are eligible, while the other is a certification process that any company can go through (whether it is a corporation or not):

Benefit corporation status is a type of legal structure for businesses. It is not a certification, and it is available to firms only in those states which have passed benefit corporation legislation. To become a benefit corporation, a company must incorporate as one in one of the states where it is available.

To be a Certified B Corp, a company must meet high standards of performance, transparency, and accountability as set by the non-profit B Lab, including meeting a certain score on the B Impact Assessment, which measures a company's impact on its workers, community, and environment. Companies of any size, structure, or location may be certified as B Corporations.[57]

in the world, can become *B Corp* certified. This status is awarded by the non-profit B Lab to firms that undergo a rigorous self-examination and pass specific performance criteria, including reporting requirements to ensure the results are disseminated to stakeholders. The result is designed to ensure "individuals will have greater economic opportunity, society will move closer to achieving a positive environmental footprint, more people will be employed in great places to work, and we will have built stronger communities at home and across the world."[56] In this way, B Lab certifies companies in a similar way that coffee and bananas are certified Fairtrade and buildings are certified LEED (Leadership in Energy and Environmental Design).

As of early 2016, B Lab had certified over 1,600 firms in 43 countries and 130 industries as B Corps.[58] And interest in the certification is growing as the benefits of undergoing the process become apparent in terms of understanding the firm's operations from a holistic perspective. As indicated by Ben & Jerry's full B Impact Assessment, which was released in 2012:

> Highlights show that 45% of the cost of goods sold go toward investing in and supporting small scale suppliers through the Caring Dairy program; its lowest paid hourly worker receives 46% above the living wage, and between half and three quarters of staff took part in an organised community programme in the last year. Between 65%-80% of its staff are "satisfied" or "engaged" at work, and the highest paid individual earns between 16 and 20 times more than the lowest paid full time worker. . . . In terms of overall performance, Ben & Jerry's scored 93% of available points for its governance structure, 55% for environment and 45% for community.[59]

The growing number of firms seeking to become certified as a B Corp reflects the interest in reforming the status quo and encouraging firms to become more socially responsible. B Lab's timeliness is reflected in the rise of other legal alternatives for corporate structures that are based on similar goals:

> California's B Corp legislation took effect alongside a new law creating the "flexible purpose company" (FlexC), which allows a firm to adopt a specific social or environmental goal, rather than the broader obligations of a B Corp. Another option in America is the low-profit limited-liability (LC3) company, which can raise money for socially beneficial purposes while making little or no profit.[60]

The extent to which fiduciary responsibilities can include an expanded set of stakeholder interests was considered comprehensively in the important *Freshfields Report* of 2005.[61] The report concluded that, while there appears to be relative flexibility across many jurisdictions for the inclusion of a broader set of stakeholder interests in management decisions, there is also considerable scope for legal challenges to those actions, particularly where they can be considered to have diminished firm profits. While establishing the firm as a benefit corporation must mitigate such challenges to a degree, it is not clear where that leaves regular corporations that have received B Corp certification. As such, it will be interesting to see what happens when this new organizational structure and expanded focus are challenged in court.

In the broader picture, B Lab's goal is for this corporate structure to become a legitimate alternative to the current narrow focus on shareholder value. As corporate charters are reformed, so it is hoped that the changes will initiate widespread reform of the market economy:

> The key question to address is whether social entrepreneurs, B corporations and community interest companies can be managed in a way that enables them to reach scale. And how should they do so—is it best for each one to become big, or for small organisations to be replicated by the dozen?[62]

An equally important question, however, is this: Do we need to invent new organizational forms, ones more effectively grounded in CSR principles, or can we fix the model that already has scale—our current corporate structure and small and medium-size businesses? Given the work of our law school colleagues (discussed briefly above and in detail in Chapter 6), it is not clear that there is strong precedent within corporate law for shareholders to sue firms on the basis that their value has not been maximized. If true, the benefit corporation structure, while useful in focusing debate on the responsibilities of the firm and institutionalizing CSR principles throughout operations, is essentially redundant in a conceptual sense. Benefit corporations promise to act in the interests of a broad range of stakeholders, but that is also a promise that regular corporations can (and should) make within current legal and governance structures. In other words, it is not the organizational form that is preventing firms pledging to be more socially responsible, but the willingness of executives to make such commitments. The benefit corporation is a solution to a problem that may not exist.[63]

That benefit corporations are perceived to be an innovation, however, indicates how far the incorporation process has moved from its original focus on public purpose. It does not necessarily follow that the underlying structure is in need of reform but rather that our current interpretation of those structures reflects skewed priorities. B Lab will only effect meaningful change through benefit corporations if it is able to persuade CEOs and executives not already predisposed to CSR to change their organizational focus. Convincing firms like Patagonia and Ben & Jerry's (which are already examples of CSR best practice) to become benefit corporations will not save the planet! We will know benefit corporations are here to stay when more intransigent firms decide there is value in altering their foundational charter documents.

Strategic CSR Debate

MOTION: The corporation, as a legal person, should be extended the same individual rights as all other citizens.

QUESTIONS FOR DISCUSSION AND REVIEW

1. Make a list of the *rights* of a corporation and a separate list of its *responsibilities*. Which is longer? Why do you think this is?

2. Can you imagine a world without corporations? What would we lose? What would we gain?

3. What is your opinion about *Citizens United*? Was it the correct decision by the Court? Do you think the US Constitution should be amended to read that "money is not speech, and that human beings, not corporations, are persons entitled to constitutional rights"?[64]

4. What are the arguments for having corporate governance issues regulated at the federal rather than state level? Do you support these arguments?

5. What are the advantages and disadvantages of a firm incorporating as a benefit corporation? Is this new organizational form necessary? If you were starting a firm and you were in a state that allowed it, would you consider incorporating your firm as a benefit corporation?

Part I Case Study

RELIGION

A good illustration of the range of stakeholder interests that encompass CSR is the role of religion in the workplace. To what extent is religion a unifying (versus a divisive) force for firms? How can firms incorporate religion into their operating and strategic outlook? What does it mean for a firm to be socially responsible with respect to religion? Beyond tolerance, how can a firm respond to its stakeholders' religious needs without shifting its position from issue to issue or seeming to favor one constituency over another? Where people disagree about religion, how can firms respect that diversity to the advantage of all?

In the United States, it is hard to collect definitive statistics about the nation's religious profile. Religion is a sensitive subject. Federal law, for example, prohibits the Census from asking about someone's religious affiliation on anything other than a voluntary basis.[1] As such, what data there are tend to be self-reports, which are unreliable indicators of actual behavior.[2] There are interesting statistics available from other sources, however, which can be used to piece together a religious profile of the United States.[3]

The data presented in Figure I.1 can be compared to numbers produced more recently by Gallup, which reports:

> About three in four Americans . . . name a Christian faith when asked for their religious preference, including 50% who are Protestants or another non-Catholic Christian religion, 24% who are Catholic and 2% who are Mormon. . . .
>
> About 6% of Americans identify with a non-Christian religion, including 2% who are Jewish, less than 1% who are Muslim and 3% who identify with other non-Christian religions. This leaves 16% who say they don't have a religious preference, along with another 3% who don't answer the question.[4]

Although some have suggested the strength of Americans' religious affiliation has waned in recent years,[5] in general religion plays a larger role in public life in the United States than in many other developed countries. In a country where "over one-third of Americans, more than 100m, can be considered evangelical,"[6] religion is deeply embedded in the social fabric:

Figure I.1 Religion in the United States (% of adult population, 2001–2008)

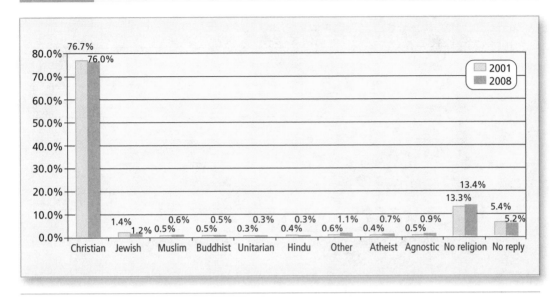

Source: US Census Bureau, *Statistical Abstract of the United States: 2012*, January 2013, Table 75: Self-Described Religious Identification of Adult Population: 1990, 2001, and 2008, p. 61, https://www.census.gov/prod/2011pubs/12statab/pop.pdf.

The number of Americans with faith in a spiritual being—nearly nine in 10—has not changed much over the past two decades, according to historical polling. . . . Eighty-five percent said religion is "very important" or "fairly important" in their own lives—a number that hasn't changed much since 1992.[7]

While numbers tell the story in the abstract, a comparative view of the role of religion in other countries can paint a more interesting picture. In the UK, for example, the census includes questions about religious affiliation. As such, an accurate profile of the religious affiliation of the population is more readily available—and it does not make easy reading for the Church of England:

Around 3% of English people attend an Anglican service at least once a month. Perhaps more significantly, according to the 2011 census, only 59% call themselves Christian, representing a drop of 13 points in a decade. . . . The concept of Christendom, a Christian realm that has endured since the time of Constantine the Great, is dying in Britain. In the most godless continent, it is one of the most secular countries.[8]

As the most recent census data in Figure I.2 indicate, a significant number of people in the UK identify themselves as having no religion (25.1%). In the United States, by comparison, the number of people claiming no religion, plus

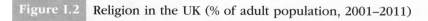

Figure I.2 Religion in the UK (% of adult population, 2001–2011)

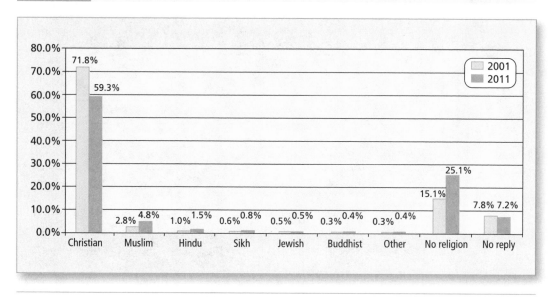

Source: Office for National Statistics (UK), Census 2011, December 11, 2012, http://www.ons.gov.uk/ons/rel/census/2011-census/key-statistics-for-local-authorities-in-england-and-wales/rpt-religion.html.

the very few willing to label themselves atheists or agnostics, does not exceed 15%. In a *Newsweek* poll in the United States, for example, "Only 9 percent [of respondents] said they were neither religious nor spiritual."[9] This difference is reflected in everyday life, where religion plays a role in the United States to a degree that many British people find difficult to understand:

> A plaque at Chick-fil-A's headquarters in Atlanta says the company's mission is to "glorify God," which it does by serving chickenburgers and closing its 1,600 outlets on Sundays. The founder, Truett Cathy, once said that while "you don't have to be a Christian to work at Chick-fil-A . . . we ask you to base your business on Biblical principles because they work."[10]

As the firm's current CEO, Dan Cathy,[11] remarked in answer to a question about Chick-fil-A's "closed-on-Sunday" policy:[12]

> It was not an issue in 1946 when we opened up our first restaurant. But as living standards changed and lifestyles changed, people came to be more active on Sundays. . . . We've had a track record that we were generating more business in six days than the other tenants were generating in seven [days]. . . . We intend to stay the course. . . . We know that it might not be popular with everyone, but thank the Lord, we live in a country where we can share our values and operate on biblical principles.[13]

Ironically, it is the United States (with its constitutionally defined separation of church and state) that is overtly religious, while the UK (where the head of state, the queen, is also the head of the Church of England) is more agnostic and atheist.[14] In spite of this, religion causes as many issues in the UK as the United States; the issues just tend to be of a different nature. In the UK, for example, religion is detrimental to a successful political career. As Alastair Campbell, Tony Blair's press secretary, famously intervened when the prime minister was asked a question about his Christianity, "We don't do religion!"[15] By contrast in the United States, it is hard to imagine a candidate being elected president unless that person is willing to state publicly (and often) a belief in God. After all, "over 40% of Americans say they would never vote for an atheist presidential candidate," and "several states still ban atheists from holding public office."[16]

The fervor with which many people welcome a strong role for religion in everyday life naturally extends into controversial political and social debates. As such, when the government oversteps the bounds of religious liberty, the courts can intervene to reinstate religious rights. A high-profile example occurred in the Supreme Court case *Burwell v. Hobby Lobby* (573 U.S., 2014) in which the Court allowed closely held companies based on religious convictions to exclude contraception from employee health plans.[17]

> [There is] a battle in the United States over religious freedom, a series of skirmishes that include a Kentucky clerk's refusal to issue marriage licenses to same-sex couples and a Muslim woman's being passed over for a job at Abercrombie & Fitch because she wore a headscarf.[18]

While in the United States the sensitive nature of the religious debate means that even a minor slight can have major ramifications, in the UK it is a lack of sensitivity to issues surrounding religion that tend to be the problem. In 2006, for example, British Airways found itself in the media spotlight for suspending an employee for wearing "a small crucifix." In defense of its actions, and in the face of strong public criticism and accusations of "religious discrimination," BA parroted its "uniform policy," looking somewhat ridiculous in the process:

> BA says that, under its uniform policy, employees may wear jewelry—including religious symbols—but it must be concealed underneath the uniform. However, the airline says that items such as turbans, hijabs and bangles can be worn "as it is not practical for staff to conceal them beneath their uniforms."[19]

At around the same time, a government minister drew attention to the secular nature of British society by criticizing a Muslim teacher who wore a veil during school lessons.[20] The minister suggested the veil helped create "parallel communities" within Britain[21] and that if he could choose, "he would prefer Muslim women not to wear veils which cover the face."[22] Similar debates over religions symbols have emerged more recently in Quebec in Canada,[23] Russia,[24] and Switzerland.[25]

The ensuing confrontations are reflected in record numbers of discrimination complaints to bodies such as the Employment Opportunity Commission (US) and the Equality and Human Rights Commission (UK).[26]

Part of the explanation for the lack of religious sensitivity in the UK is the large (and growing) percentage of the population who do not believe in God. In 2009, for example, the Atheist Bus Campaign launched a series of advertisements on London's famous red buses to promote atheism. Gaining the support of high-profile atheists, such as Richard Dawkins (*The God Delusion*),[27] the text of the ads read, "There's probably no God. Now stop worrying and enjoy your life."[28] In contrast, when issues arise in the United States, they tend to concern the overbearing influence of religion rather than a lack of sensitivity to the issue. The political influence of the Christian Right, for example, is well reported. What is less well-known is the influence this same lobby has over corporate policy:

> Wal-Mart and Lands' End have been forced to apologize for slighting Christmas. And the [American Family Association] has boasted that its complaints led to Ford yanking ads for Jaguar and Land Rover from gay publications.[29]

In the United States, however, religion also has its lighter side, with commentators using humor to convey their message. The "What Would Jesus Drive?" (http://www.whatwouldjesusdrive.info/) campaign, for example, is organized and sponsored by the Evangelical Environmental Network, a biblically orthodox Christian environmental organization. The campaign seeks to reduce the numbers of SUVs, vans, and pickups on US roads because of the environmental damage these vehicles cause. And, extending the transportation theme, the Atheist Bus Campaign reached across the Atlantic in 2010 in an attempt to influence Americans during the run-up to Christmas:

> In New York City, a large billboard promoting atheism at the entrance of the Lincoln Tunnel, which a local affiliate of American Atheists paid for, has generated controversy. (The message: "You know it's a myth. This season, celebrate reason!").[30]

RELIGION AND CAPITALISM

Whether strongly embedded or culturally agnostic, religion is an issue that firms find hard to ignore because it matters to so many of their stakeholders. In terms of the CSR debate, therefore, an important question is this: *To what extent are religion and business compatible?*

Pope Francis has inserted himself into this debate with his first Apostolic Exhortation, *Evangelii Gaudium* ("The Joy of the Gospel," 2013)[31] and his encyclical on the environment, *Laudato Si* ("Be Praised," 2015)[32] in which he was critical of what he sees as the exploitative effects of capitalism. This continues a tradition within the Catholic Church that stretches back to Pope Leo XIII's encyclical *Rerum Novarum* ("The Rights and Duties of Capital and Labor," 1891),[33] which stated that "To misuse men as though they were things in the pursuit of gain, or to value them solely for their physical powers—that is truly shameful and inhuman."[34]

Others are more willing to see the potential overlap between the consequences of market economies and the goals of the majority of the world's religions. Responding to Pope Francis's *Laudato Si*, David Brooks of *The New York Times* offers a more inspiring view of the power of capitalism to deliver social progress:

> Hardest to accept . . . is the moral premise implied throughout the encyclical: that the only legitimate human relationships are based on compassion, harmony and love, and that arrangements based on self-interest and competition are inherently destructive. . . . You would never know from the encyclical that we are living through the greatest reduction in poverty in human history. A raw and rugged capitalism in Asia has led, ironically, to a great expansion of the middle class and great gains in human dignity. You would never know that in many parts of the world, like the United States, the rivers and skies are getting cleaner. The race for riches, ironically, produces the wealth that can be used to clean the environment.[35]

In practice, religion has had a long and contentious association with business. A good example in the UK is the Quakers, who were

> banned from careers in government, the church or law and with their pacifism barring a military career, they were forced into commerce. . . .
>
> Their high ethical standards meant they couldn't be involved with alcohol, gambling or making armaments. The grocery trade became a natural outlet for their energies. All the great English chocolate dynasties: Cadbury, Fry, and Rowntree were Quakers. Their belief in the brotherhood of man led to paternalistic employment practices. They built garden towns for their employees with crèches, sporting facilities and healthcare. . . . They believed that cooperation and social provision were a necessary and natural adjunct to making money.[36]

In the United States, "New England's Puritan settlers brought with them two ideas that have driven American society ever since: Calvinism and capitalism." As a result, many people believe that businesses are entitled to the "same religious protections as people."[37]

> [Today] religious faith is on display in American business as perhaps never before. . . . "Corporations like Ford and Xerox sponsor spiritual retreats to spark creativity." Even companies with no overt religious or spiritual interests may be the site of spiritual expression, whether that means a Bible study in a conference room or a weekly meeting hosted by the Spiritual Unfoldment Society at the World Bank.[38]

Tom Chappell, the CEO of Tom's of Maine, presents a good example of how to incorporate religion into everyday working life.[39] In his case, the time he spent at Harvard Divinity School during a break from running his company provided him with

> "a worldview that I could use everywhere in life." More important, he says, he no longer felt he had to apologize for wanting to incorporate values more thoroughly into his business. After Harvard, he says, "I could argue quite confidently that a holistic view of what's good for society or nature was also good for consumers and shareholders."[40]

This debate over whether there is a conflict between capitalism and religion, in general, extends into specific areas of business that raise moral challenges for religious believers. Some commentators, for example, suggest finance is a particularly challenging industry in which to work and be successful, yet remain true to a strong moral and religious compass. The experiences of people such as Ken Costa,[41] a vice chairman of UBS, support such arguments:

> During the last 30 years, being a Christian at work has, if anything, become more difficult. . . . Financial markets have become more volatile, decisions more complex. . . . The work place is the coal-face where faith is tested and sharpened by day-to-day encounters with ambiguities and stresses of modern commerce.[42]

As noted by the Right Reverend Justin Welby, bishop of Durham at the time (and, since 2013, the archbishop of Canterbury), while chairing a government inquiry into UK banking standards, "Coming from a Christian point of view on human sinfulness and failure, the efficient market system doesn't work. . . . People don't make rational decisions in markets more than anywhere else."[43] Rather than finding evidence that these challenges make religion and finance incompatible, however, Costa of UBS finds plenty of support for his career choice in the Bible:

> [In the] parable of the talents (Luke 19: 11–27) it is the two servants who put the master's money to work who are rewarded, while the one who preserved the capital and took no risks is punished. And he quotes the great Methodist John Wesley, who told his followers: "Gain all you can, without hurting either yourself or your neighbor."[44]

More broadly, Dave Evans, cofounder of the videogame company Electronic Arts, believes that "all of work—not just church work—is holy. . . . Work itself has value. It is a huge countercultural behavior to train yourself to value work for its own sake and to see it as a service to God."[45] But, it is in finance where different religions have strived most overtly to overcome any religious hurdles to participation and incorporate an industry-wide social responsibility.

ISLAMIC FINANCE

Evidence that the worlds of religion and finance are compatible (or, at least, that the market is capable of adapting to religious needs when there is sufficient potential profit at stake) can be seen in the rapid growth and acceptance of faith-based mutual funds:

> Faith-based mutual funds typically screen out stocks of companies that violate the tenets of a given religion or religious denomination. A Muslim fund is likely to screen out companies related to pork production, for example, while a Catholic fund can avoid a maker of contraceptives.[46]

In some ways, religion and capitalism are well matched. This is particularly true in the United States, where capitalism is framed within a Judeo-Christian ethos and considered to be "a moral endeavor."[47] In addition, there is always the money:

> Religions rarely praise consumerism. But 2.2 billion Christians and 1.6 billion Muslims are a big market. Sales of books on the world's two biggest faiths are soaring, with interactive Korans and Bibles among the innovative products.[48]

Religion and finance, however, have not always happily coexisted. Usury (the charging of excessive interest) has traditionally been rejected by the major religions. The early Christian church, for example, banned the collection of interest, on punishment of excommunication and condemnation to hell,[49] with Dante's third rung of hell reserving a special distaste for the work of usurers.[50] By charging others for borrowing money over a defined period, it was felt that lenders "were not trading in goods but in time, and this was God's":[51]

> Based on biblical passages—fallen man must live "by the sweat of his brow" (Genesis 3:19), Jesus' appeal to his followers to "lend, expecting nothing in return" (Luke 6:35)—medieval theologians considered the lending of money at interest to be sinful. Thomas Aquinas, based on Aristotle, considered usury—like sodomy—to be contrary to nature because "it is in accordance with nature that money should increase from natural goods and not from money itself."[52]

How much interest is too much, of course, is open to debate—a debate that has been occurring for a long time:

> Hammurabi, a ruler of ancient Babylon, set an annual limit of 33.5%. Brutus, Julius Caesar's assassin, was rebuked for charging a rate of 48% when the legal limit was 12%. Aristotle argued that since coins do not "bear fruit," unlike cattle, which might bear calves while on loan to a neighbour, no interest should be paid at all when borrowing money.[53]

The corrupting influence, of course, is money (or, the pursuit of it), which serves three essential purposes—it must be exchangeable, it must be stable (retaining value over time), and it must be a measure of worth. In different forms ("Tea, salt and cattle have all been used as money"),[54] money has been used by human societies for millennia. While societies in what is now western Turkey used gold and silver as a means of exchange as far back as 650 BCE, paper money only began circulating in China around 1000 CE.[55] As long as money has existed, however, there has been antipathy toward those who control access to it:

> Jesus expelled the moneychangers from the Temple. Timothy tells us that "the love of money is the root of all evil." Muhammad banned usury. The Jews referred to interest as *neshek*—a bite. The Catholic church banned it in 1311. Dante consigned moneylenders to the seventh circle of hell—the one also populated by the inhabitants of Sodom and "other practisers of unnatural vice."[56]

The partner of *interest* is *credit*. Interest, today, is charged on loans that are made on the basis of credit, which is extended on the understanding that the borrower undertakes a future obligation to repay the loan. While Jesus might have appealed "to his followers to 'lend, expecting nothing in return' (Luke 6:35),"[57] financiers today are not so altruistic. In addition to their commitment to repay the debt, borrowers agree to pay a fee to the lender for the service that reflects the level of *risk* the lender is accepting in agreeing to loan the money to the borrower. This risk fluctuates based on variables such as the size of the loan, the likelihood of repayment, and competing demands for the funds. In addition, however, there is an unspoken element of mutual *trust*—I lend money to you because I trust that you will pay it back; I pay you with this banknote because you trust that the Treasury will honor its face value.

Without trust, our economic system breaks down, as the financial crisis of 2007–2008 demonstrated only too clearly. Today, the global economic system is underpinned by an interlocking financial system founded on credit. While trust underpins this model, however, it is also true that the profit incentive has distorted the relationship between lender and borrower. Some commentators have gone as far as to argue that it was "the

Financial Etymology

Company: The word *company* comes from a combination of the Latin words *cum* and *panis*, the literal translation of which originally meant "breaking bread together."[58]

Credit: "The root of [the word] credit is *credo*, the Latin for 'I believe.'"[59]

Money: From the Latin *moneta* meaning "place for coining money, mint; coined money, money, coinage," from *Moneta*, a title or surname of the Roman goddess Juno, in or near whose temple money was coined.[60]

Risk: "Derives from Tuscan *rischio*, the amount considered necessary to cover costs when lending money, i.e., a euphemism for interest.[61]

legalization of usury" that was the cause of the financial crisis.[62] The root of the problem, according to this argument, is a 1978 US Supreme Court case that prevented Minnesota from enforcing strict limits on the amount of interest charged on a credit card loan by an out-of-state bank.[63] In response to the case, other states quickly repealed similar laws in an attempt to prevent national banks from relocating elsewhere, which led to the situation today where banks and credit card companies have an incentive to offer unlimited credit and charge high interest rates to customers who are unable to repay the total amount:

> You know, if you are Mr. Potter in *It's a Wonderful Life* and can only get six percent, seven percent on your loan, you want the loan to be repaid. Moral character is important. You want to scrutinize everybody very carefully. But if you're able to charge 30 percent or, in a payday lender case, 200 or 300 percent, you don't care so much. . . . In fact, you actually want the loan not to be repaid. You want people to go into debt.[64]

In contrast to modern-day Western finance, Islamic (or *sharia*, literally, "the way" and also known as *shariah* or *shari'a*)[65] law forbids the charging of interest (or *riba*).[66] Money should only be used as a facilitator of business and the trade of goods; it cannot be used as a commodity to be traded or a tool for speculation. In other words, money should be used to create *things*, not just to create more *money* because "the Prophet Mohammed said debts must be repaid in the amount that was loaned. Money proffered must be backed by collateral, and if financial instruments are traded, they generally have to sell for face value, which deters banks from repackaging debt."[67] As a result, with a global population of 1.9 billion believers in 112 countries[68] and a total halal market reported to be worth $2.1 trillion,[69] there is a significant market of devout Muslim investors who previously were forced either to compromise their principles or avoid modern finance because of its conflict with their beliefs. This has not only had personal limitations; some also believe it has affected the Muslim world as a whole:

> While ignored by many secular Muslims and the conventional banks that operate in most Muslim nations today, this ban [on usury] has long denied the benefits of modern banking to strict believers—contributing, some way, to the Muslim world's relative decline after interest-based bonds and loans powered the West's industrial revolution.[70]

Islamic finance provides a way for Muslims to participate in modern finance while staying true to their religious principles.[71] Banks enable this by developing sharia-compliant instruments that, although based on alternatives to interest, aim to deliver similar returns. These alternatives "are technically based on profit-sharing, leasing or trading—all activities permissible in Islam because they involve entrepreneurial work rather than simply moneylending."[72] To determine whether an investment is sharia compliant, banks appoint boards of sharia scholars (Muslim clerics) who help develop these products and certify them as compliant when issued:

At present, devout Muslims will only buy such instruments if a recognized sharia scholar, such as a mullah, has issued a *fatwa* to approve it.[73]

Like all financial products, sharia-compliant investments run the spectrum from mortgages, to bonds (*sukuk*), to mutual funds and stocks, each with their own set of rules that enable them to remain compliant with Islamic law. A common method for devout Muslims to take out a sharia-compliant mortgage, for example, is *ijara*. With *ijara*, instead of the bank lending the home buyer the money to buy the property and charging a fee (interest) until the loan is repaid, a bank buys the property on behalf of the home buyer, who then pays back the principal over time, while also paying a "lease payment" to use the property in the meantime.[74] Similarly, in order for Islamic bonds (*sukuk*)[75] to be sharia compliant, it is essential that they "don't pay interest, but instead give investors profits from an underlying business that backs a bond."[76] For stocks, Muslim investors can only invest in firms (directly or indirectly through mutual funds) that are considered to be sharia compliant:

> To be sharia-compliant, companies can't run casinos or sell tobacco, alcohol, pork, or pornography, and debt can't exceed 30% of equity. Such rules leave more than half the companies in the Standard & Poor's 500-stock index— including Microsoft, Southwest Airlines, and Nike—in compliance.[77]

Even though the principles underpinning Islamic finance are drawn from the seventh century, contemporary Sharia-compliant instruments were first developed in the 1960s.[78] Since then, the size of the Islamic finance market has grown exponentially, with "total assets of around $2 trillion," an amount that is predicted to "grow by an average of 19.7% a year to 2018."[79] One reason why growth projections are so strong is because "only a small percentage of Muslims, estimated at about 12 per cent, . . . [currently] use Islamic finance."[80]

The rapid growth of the Islamic finance industry was initially fueled with money from the expanding oil countries of the Persian Gulf,[81] with Western banks (such as Citigroup, HSBC, and Goldman Sachs) only becoming interested once the potential market became apparent and growing awareness prompted Muslim communities in the West to push for change. Among Muslim countries, however, even though the Dubai Islamic Bank was established in 1975 ("the world's first Islamic bank"),[82] it is Malaysia that is credited with being the leading source of expansion and product innovation.[83] In 1983, the Malaysian government passed an Islamic banking law and established Bank Islam, "which gave out the nation's first Islamic loans. . . . more than a decade before Saudi clerics followed suit."[84] In many ways,

> [Malaysia] is the world's most important Islamic-finance centre. Just over a fifth of the country's banking system, by assets, is *sharia*-compliant; the average for Muslim countries is more like 12%, and often a lot less. Malaysia dominates the global market for *sukuk*, or Islamic bonds. The country issued the world's first sovereign *sukuk* in 2002; in the first three quarters of 2012 it was responsible

for almost three-quarters of total global issuance. Malaysia is also home to the Islamic Financial Services Board, an international standard-setting body.[85]

In the West, Britain has worked hard to market itself as the "world centre for the Islamic finance industry."[86] The UK, which has been completing Sharia-compliant transactions since the 1980s, "was the first European Union member to adapt its fiscal legislation to place conventional and Islamic finance on a level playing field," opened "the first 100% Sharia-compliant retail bank in a non-Muslim country, . . . the Islamic Bank of Britain (IBB),"[87] and, in 2014, became the first country outside the Muslim world to issue an Islamic bond.[88]

Along with a rapidly growing market for Islamic finance is a corresponding growth in organizations seeking to cater to an Islamic clientele. This growth extends from Citigroup (which "operates what is effectively the world's largest Islamic bank in terms of transactions. Some $6 billion of Citibank deals now have been structured and marketed in conformance with Islamic laws since starting out in 1996")[89] to the FTSE (which launched a series of Sharia-compliant indices that "has been fully certified as Shariah-compliant").[90]

In the aftermath of the financial crisis, Islamic finance was heralded by advocates as offering a way forward for those wishing to remodel a global financial system founded on credit and the collection of interest.[91] Although Islamic banks, like the financial industry worldwide, have been negatively affected by the global recession, "no Islamic bank has failed during the [financial] crisis."[92] Others contend that the Islamic finance industry is really no different from Western finance and merely subverts the rules in search of profit.[93] Critics suggest that Muslim clerics who certify products as Sharia compliant are acting in line with steps taken throughout the ages to subvert the inherent tension between religion and capitalism:

> In about 1220 a canonist named Hispanus proposed that, although usury was prohibited, a lender could charge a fee if his borrower was late in making repayment. The period between the date on which the borrower should have repaid and the date on which he did repay, Hispanus termed *interesse*, literally that which "in between is."[94]

The accusation is leveled that the Islamic finance industry is merely the latest evolution of financial products that are designed to conform to strict limitations on the surface, but, in fact, generate "window-dressing pseudo-Islamic financial instruments that [are] mathematically equivalent to conventional debt and mortgage contracts."[95] This critique suggests that, rather than remaining true to the principles of Islamic finance, the industry today is "dominated by conventional bankers . . . focused on 'reverse engineering' of conventional financial products into their sharia-compliant counterparts."[96]

> The gestation of products within this very un-Islamic framework has resulted in the ultimate mutant, an Islamic personal loan at 7.9 per cent annual percent rate courtesy of the Islamic Bank of Britain. How different this is from the original vision of Muslim economists.[97]

Strategic CSR Debate

MOTION: Religion is a private matter that does not belong in the workplace.

QUESTIONS FOR DISCUSSION AND REVIEW

1. What role does religion play in your life? Do you feel the society in which you live is becoming more or less religious? Is this *good* or *bad*? Does it matter?

2. Have a look at photos of the Atheist Bus Campaign's advertisements on London buses at https://humanism.org.uk/about/atheist-bus-campaign/. What is your reaction? Do you find them provocative? Why or why not?

3. Are you interested in a career in finance? Would you have any religious or moral concerns about working in the finance industry? Are there any jobs or industries that you would avoid based on your moral or religious values?

4. What is your reaction to the accusation that the Islamic finance industry is generating "interest-bearing loan[s] in all but name"? From what you have learned in this case study, do you agree that Islamic financial products are sharia compliant?

5. Have a look at the website for the campaign "What Would Jesus Drive?" (http://www.whatwouldjesusdrive.info/). What car would Jesus drive? Why?

NEXT STEPS

Beyond defining CSR and identifying the five driving forces that demonstrate its importance to firms, it is necessary to demonstrate that CSR can work in practice. It must allow firms to prosper, as well as act as a conduit for stakeholder concerns. But, how are firms supposed to identify key stakeholders and prioritize among their competing interests? Under what circumstances are stakeholders willing to engage and impose their views on corporations? In other words, to what extent are stakeholders responsible for shaping corporate actions? And, how should firms begin to integrate a CSR perspective into their strategic planning and day-to-day operations? The importance of stakeholder theory to the arguments presented in this textbook is explored in detail in Part II.

An economic perspective on CSR will be explored in Part III (including a discussion of important concepts such as behavioral economics and lifecycle pricing), while Part IV puts CSR into a strategic perspective and expands on the growing importance of CSR and its impact on corporate strategy. Finally, Part V explores how firms can integrate CSR into day-to-day operations and begin to build a business model of *sustainable value creation*—the ultimate goal of strategic CSR.

PART II

A STAKEHOLDER PERSPECTIVE

Part II reflects the importance of a stakeholder perspective to the intellectual framework underpinning *Strategic Corporate Social Responsibility (Strategic CSR)*.[1]

Though firms are economic entities that exist to meet specific operational goals, the most effective way to achieve these goals today is by considering the needs and values of the broad range of actors who have a stake in the firm's pursuit of profit. Chapter 4 lays the groundwork for this argument by defining who qualifies as a *stakeholder* and by detailing a model that describes the relationships such individuals and groups have with firms. Beyond identifying stakeholders, however, Chapter 4 also develops a framework that allows managers to prioritize among stakeholders, whose interests often conflict. Chapter 5 extends stakeholder theory further by developing the idea of corporate *stakeholder* responsibility. This suggests that, in addition to firms' duty to listen to their stakeholders, stakeholders have an equal (if not more important) responsibility to hold firms to account for their actions. Chapter 6 investigates the history of the corporation in order to challenge the myth that prevents the widespread adoption of a stakeholder perspective—that shareholders *own* the corporation and, as such, that managers and directors have a fiduciary responsibility to operate the organization in its shareholders' interests. In the United States at least, this widespread belief is not grounded in legal reality.

A case about impact investing rounds out Part II, emphasizing how all aspects of business today relate to the interests of the firm's broad range of stakeholders.

Chapter 4

STAKEHOLDER THEORY

Throughout this century, as businesses worldwide evolve to account for the dynamic environment in which they operate, CSR will occupy an increasingly core component of the strategic planning process. As such, CSR finds a natural home within corporate strategy.[1] The ideal vehicle for the integration of CSR and strategy is a multi-stakeholder perspective that enables firms to respond to the varied interests of all the individuals and groups that have a stake in the firm's pursuit of profit. It is this broad range of interests that underpins the idea that CSR relates to all aspects of the firm's day-to-day operations. CSR is not a peripheral exercise—it is central to being a successful business. Adopting a stakeholder perspective allows the firm to predict and respond to the ever-changing demands of its stakeholders, who together constitute the environment in which the firm operates.

While stakeholder theory constitutes an important way to understand the complex series of relationships that make up an organization, two questions are fundamental to understanding what stakeholder theory means for managers in practice: *Who is a stakeholder?* and, when interests conflict, *Which stakeholders should be prioritized?*

WHO IS A STAKEHOLDER?

While different definitions of what constitutes a stakeholder differ in emphasis, they largely agree in terms of sentiment. Here are three foundational examples:

Definitions of a Stakeholder

Stakeholders in an organization are the individuals and groups who are depending on the firm in order to achieve their personal goals and on whom the firm is depending for its existence.

Eric Rhenman (1964)[2]

> A stakeholder in an organization is (by definition) any group or individual who can affect or is affected by the achievement of the organization's objectives.
>
> *R. Edward Freeman (1984)*[3]
>
> The stakeholders in a firm are individuals and constituencies that contribute, either voluntarily or involuntarily, to its wealth-creating capacity and activities, and who are therefore its potential beneficiaries and/or risk bearers.
>
> *Post, Preston, and Sachs (2002)*[4]

Among these three definitions, contemporary stakeholder theory is usually credited to the work of Ed Freeman.[5] While Freeman's inspirational ideas led directly to the prominence enjoyed by stakeholder theory within the field of management today, the notion that the manager has responsibilities to a broad range of constituents has its foundations in the middle of the 20th century. In 1945, for example, Frank Pierce, a director of the Standard Oil Company (New Jersey) argued that a firm's managers have a duty "to act as a balance wheel in relation to three groups of interests—the interests of owners, of employees, and of the public, all of whom have a *stake* in the output of industry" (emphasis added).[6] In 1951, Frank Abrams, the CEO of the Standard Oil Company (New Jersey), stated:

> Business firms are man-made instruments of society. They can be made to achieve their greatest social usefulness . . . when management succeeds in finding a harmonious balance among the claims of the various interested groups: the stockholders, employees, customers, and the public at large.[7]

Similarly, in 1953, Howard Bowen discussed the idea of the "participation of workers, consumers, and possibly of other groups in business decisions."[8] And as noted above, in 1964, Eric Rhenman defined the *stakeholders* in an organization as "the individuals and groups who are depending on the firm in order to achieve their personal goals and on whom the firm is depending for its existence."[9]

Although the idea of the stakeholder has therefore been around for a while, Freeman's contribution has been pivotal for two main reasons: First, he rendered the concept pragmatic in meaning and action for business practitioners, and second, he promoted the concept within the academic community in general and the field of management in particular. As a result, a *stakeholder* is today widely understood to be a group or individual with a self-defined interest in the activities of the firm.[10] In line with this, a core component of the intellectual argument driving strategic CSR is that it is in a firm's best interests to meet the needs and expectations of as broad an array of its stakeholders as possible.

A New Stakeholder Definition

Although a general understanding of *Who is a stakeholder?* is now well established in the academic field of management, the idea that "anyone who wants to be" should be considered a stakeholder is less than helpful from a manager's perspective. In other words, while Freeman's definition of a stakeholder is still the "most widely adopted of all definitions within high quality management journals,"[11] it is sufficiently broad to encompass anyone who self-appoints themselves into the role. While expedient, this loose definition is unlikely to reflect a firm's priorities and, more importantly, offers little guidance to managers who are trying to determine how to allocate their attention and the firm's scarce resources.

In this sense, asking the manager to focus on "everyone," since everyone is a potential stakeholder, runs the risk of decision-making paralysis. The resulting danger, as Freeman himself recognizes, is that "the notion of stakeholder risks becoming a meaningless designation."[12] In essence, if everyone is a stakeholder, then no one is a stakeholder. In an attempt to move past this impasse, I propose a narrower definition:

Stakeholder

Any entity who is affected by the organization (either voluntarily or involuntarily) and possesses the capacity to affect the organization.

In short, a stakeholder is any group or individual who has a stake (similar to Freeman), but also who has the capacity to act in order to promote their interests (more specific than Freeman). This definition does not exclude non-acting entities (such as the environment or young children) from the firm's concerns. It merely focuses the firm's attention on the individuals and groups who have the capacity to affect the firm's operations (in essence, the firm's meaningful stakeholders) and who will act on the behalf of those who are unable to defend their own interests. As such, while this means that the environment itself is *not* a stakeholder, any actor who seeks to represent the environment (e.g., Greenpeace) is included.

The Environment as a Stakeholder

It is interesting to debate whether the natural environment, as a non-independent actor, should be included as an identifiable stakeholder of the firm. Many argue that it should and that, in fact, the environment has rights that should be protected by law.[13]

Others argue that it should not be included because the environment itself does not speak or feel or act; rather, the degradation of the environment affects other stakeholder groups (e.g., NGOs or the government), who then advocate on its behalf.

An argument for including the environment as one of the firm's societal stakeholders is to reinforce the importance of sustainability within the CSR debate, while recognizing that the environment requires actors to speak and act on its behalf in order to be protected.

In Figure 4.1, however, the environment is excluded due to its lack of agency. Since the environment is unable to speak for itself, the manager's priority (in relation to sustainability issues) should be to attend to those stakeholders who speak most vigorously (and knowledgeably) on the environment's behalf.

This imperfect proxy relationship helps explain why problems such as pollution and the abuse of children's rights persist. Without the ability to advocate directly in their defense, such groups are more susceptible to abuse. To put it bluntly, the reason the environment has been polluted for so long is that the environment is unable to state what it wants. It has no "self-interest" as such. Similarly, young children, who undoubtedly do have rights and interests but are less able to articulate them, are forced to rely on others to interpret and act on those interests.[14]

For any group in society to be disenfranchised (whether it is children, the environment, or "the poorest of the poor")[15] is for that group to lack representation. While usually employed in discussions related to democracy, the same principle holds for general societal engagement. Society fails these groups if no advocate steps forward to represent them, and we are all worse off as a result. In such cases, therefore, the agents for these interests (e.g., parents, Greenpeace, the government, the media, etc.) have an elevated role in ensuring the groups are represented and their concerns addressed. This is true in general, but also specifically in terms of the actions firms may take to protect the interests of groups who cannot represent themselves. It is these agents who have the ability to influence the firm who should be considered *stakeholders*.

With this general definition in place, the firm needs to sort these groups. To do so and begin to understand the interests of its core stakeholders, the firm may find it helpful to divide its constituents into three categories: *organizational* stakeholders (internal to the firm) and *economic* and *societal* stakeholders (external to the firm). Together, these three kinds of stakeholders form a metaphorical concentric set of circles, with the firm and its organizational stakeholders at the center of a larger circle that signifies the firm's economic stakeholders. Both of these circles sit within the largest circle, which represents society and the firm's societal stakeholders. This model is presented in Figure 4.1 as a framework that firms can use to identify their key stakeholders and demonstrates the broad spectrum of issues that affect corporate behavior and are related to CSR.

As indicated in Figure 4.1, a firm's stakeholders can be divided into three categories: organizational stakeholders (internal to the firm) and economic and societal stakeholders (external to the firm). First, stakeholders exist within the organization. Examples of such groups include employees, managers, and directors. Taken

Figure 4.1   A Stakeholder Model

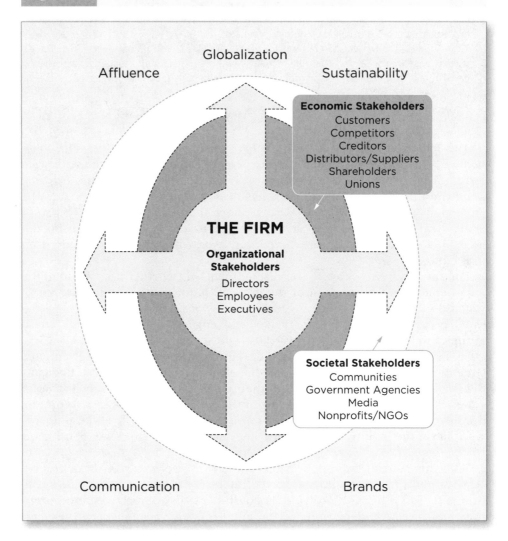

together, these internal stakeholders constitute the organization as a whole—they are most directly involved in producing the products and services the firm offers and, therefore, should be its primary concern.

Second are economic stakeholders, examples of which include consumers, shareholders, and competitors. The interactions that these stakeholders have with the firm are driven primarily by economic concerns. As such, these stakeholders fulfill an important role as the interface between the organization and its larger social environment. Not only do these groups affect the financial/economic aspects of the organization, but they also create bonds of accountability between the firm and its operating context.

Third are those stakeholders that constitute the broader business and social environment in which the firm operates. Examples of societal stakeholders include the media, government agencies and regulators, and local communities. These societal stakeholders are essential for the organization in terms of providing the legitimacy necessary for it to survive over the medium to long term. Without the general consensus that it is *valued* by its broader society, no organization can expect to survive indefinitely.

Finally, the three layers of stakeholders all sit within the larger business context that is shaped by the five driving forces of CSR (affluence, sustainability, globalization, communication, and brands), which frame this model of concentric circles. A central argument of this textbook is that the emergence of these forces in recent years has changed the rules of the game for firms, leading directly to a shift in control over the free flow of information from firms to their stakeholders (see Chapter 2) and, together, enhancing the importance of CSR for businesses today.

Within this overall classification, all possible actors fit primarily into one of the three stakeholder groups, although almost all stakeholders exist simultaneously as multiple stakeholder types with network ties among each of them, as well as with the firm.[16] A company's employees, for example, are primarily organizational stakeholders. They are also, however, occasional customers of the company, as well as being members of the society in which the business operates. The government that regulates the firm's industry, however, is only a societal stakeholder and has no economic relationship with the company (beyond the taxes it levies), nor is it a formal part of the organization. Similarly, a firm's customers are, first and foremost, economic stakeholders of the firm. They are not organizational (internal) stakeholders, but they are part of the society within which the firm operates. They are also one of the primary means by which the firm delivers its product and interacts with its society. Without the economic interface, an organization loses its mechanism of accountability and, therefore, its legitimacy over the long term. This is true whether the organization is a business, government, or nonprofit.

It is important to understand the symbiotic relationship a firm has with its shareholders. The firm cannot act alone. It is not a sentient actor but is a bundle of contracts (formal and informal) that reflect the aggregated interests of all its stakeholders. If we agree that employees are stakeholders, as well as executives, directors, shareholders, consumers, the government, suppliers, distributors, and so on, then we understand that the firm does not exist independently of these groups. If you take away all the firms' stakeholders (the executives, directors, and employees, in particular), there is nobody left to act—the firm's substance is derived from those who constitute it. This substance comes from the actions initiated by stakeholders pursuing their specific interests (sometimes competing, sometimes complementary) that intersect in the firm's day-to-day operations. This is why stakeholder theory is central to any CSR perspective (really, to any view of the firm). It is also why it is so important for managers to be able to manage these different interests. To make decisions that can sustain the firm, managers need to be able to prioritize among the many different groups who have a stake in the outcomes of those decisions.

WHICH STAKEHOLDERS SHOULD BE PRIORITIZED?

An effective stakeholder model must do more than merely identify a firm's stakeholders. Equally important, if the model is to be of practical use, is the ability to prioritize among these stakeholders. In other words, in addition to answering the question *Who is a stakeholder?* another challenge for managers in implementing stakeholder theory arises when faced with this question: *When interests conflict, which stakeholders should be prioritized?*

Stakeholder theory can only be of true value to the firm's managers when it accounts fully for the dynamic environment in which business is conducted. To this end, stakeholder theory has not been very useful in providing a road map to navigate among the interests of the firm's stakeholders, especially when they conflict. There is a reason for this—while accounting for a broader range of interests is a valuable perspective for a modern-day corporation, it often complicates decisions:

> A single goal, such as maximum profit, is simple and reasonably concrete. But when several goals are introduced and businessmen must sometimes choose from among them (e.g., greater immediate profit vs. greater company security, or good labor relations vs. low-cost production, or higher dividends vs. higher wages), then confusion and divided counsel are sometimes inevitable.[17]

In short, while identifying stakeholders is easy, prioritizing among stakeholder interests is extremely difficult, and stakeholder theory has been largely silent on this essential issue. Partly this is because the process is idiosyncratic (different firms have different stakeholders with different issues), but mostly it is because the interests are so compelling and so often conflict. What is required is a framework that provides guidance to managers on how and when to prioritize.

For managers to make these determinations, it is essential for firms to define their environments in terms of issues that evolve and stakeholders that compete. Accounting for this dynamic context within the firm's strategic framework helps managers decide how to prioritize among stakeholders, depending on the issue at hand. This is essential because stakeholders have claims on activities that range across all aspects of a firm's operations. For stakeholder theory to account for this level of complexity and become more than an interesting intellectual exercise, it must tease apart what John Mackey (the founder and co-CEO of Whole Foods Market) describes as the incessant claims stakeholders place on his company:

> Customers want lower prices and higher quality; employees want higher wages and better benefits and better working conditions; suppliers want to give fewer discounts and want you to pick up more of their products; communities want more donations; governments want higher taxes; investors want higher dividends and higher stock prices—every one of the stakeholders wants more, they always want more.[18]

In other words, being able to prioritize among stakeholder groups is important because their interests often conflict. As Mackey continues, each stakeholder group "will define the purpose of the business in terms of its own needs and desires, and each perspective is valid and legitimate."[19] Each stakeholder understandably has a relatively narrow perspective on the firm's operations that revolves around their specific interests. This creates opportunities for those firms willing to form lasting relationships with their stakeholders. Similarly, it creates potential threats for those firms that are unwilling to form such ties or accommodate such interests:

> Some industries . . . have long had to contend with well-organized pressure groups. . . . Many of the world's major pharmaceutical companies have been pushed to sell low-cost drugs to developing countries. Gap and Nike had been attacked for exploiting child labour in the Indian sub-continent. Coca-Cola, Kraft and other food and beverage companies have been accused of contributing to child obesity in the developed world. . . . Companies that do not acknowledge such claims run risks of reputational damage.[20]

The businesses most likely to succeed in today's rapidly evolving global environment will be those best able to adapt to their environment by balancing the conflicting interests of multiple stakeholders. While this is true of firms, it is doubly true for managers. It can even be argued that the fundamental "job of management is to maintain an equitable and working balance among the claims of the various . . . interest groups" that are directly affected by the firm's operations.[21] Increasingly, managers who understand the firm as a series of ties with its various stakeholders will be better able to identify and take advantage of potential opportunities (while mitigating or avoiding potential threats) than those managers who see the firm more narrowly.

Having said this, just because an individual or organization merits inclusion in a firm's list of relevant stakeholders does not compel the firm (either legally or logically) to comply with every demand that stakeholder makes. This would be counterproductive, as the business would spend all its time chasing different demands and negotiating among stakeholders with diametrically opposed requests. Integrating a stakeholder perspective into a strategic framework allows firms to respond to stakeholder demands in ways that maximize both economic and social value. A central component of this strategic framework is the ability to prioritize among stakeholders—both in absolute terms and on an issue-by-issue basis.

Organizational, Economic, and Societal Stakeholders

The concentric circles of organizational, economic, and societal stakeholders presented in Figure 4.1 provide a rough guide to prioritization. By identifying the firm's key stakeholders *within* each of the three categories, executives can prioritize the needs and interests of certain groups over others. In addition, it is important to note that *among* categories, stakeholders generally decrease in importance to the firm the further they are removed from core operations. Implicit in Figure 4.1, therefore, is the idea that organizational stakeholders are a firm's most important set of constituents. These stakeholders are followed in importance by economic stakeholders, who provide the firm with its economic capital. Finally, societal stakeholders deliver the firm with the social capital that is central to its legitimacy and long term validity, but is less immediately needed for day-to-day operations.

In seeking to prioritize the firm's stakeholders, however, managers need to keep two points in mind: First, no organization can afford to ignore consistently the interests of a powerful stakeholder, even if the group to which the stakeholder belongs is lower in the firm's relative hierarchy of stakeholders or is relatively removed from the firm's day-to-day operations. A good example of this is the government, which is a societal stakeholder in the model and therefore, in theory, less important to the firm than its organizational or economic stakeholders. It would be unwise, however, for a firm to ignore the government repeatedly in relation to an issue that enjoys broad societal support. Given that the government has the power to constrain industries dramatically via legislation, it is only rational that firms should adhere to the government's basic needs and requests.[22] This logic applies on an ongoing basis; it applies even more so when a specific issue spikes the attention of politicians who feel pressured by their constituents to act.

Second, it is vital to remember that the relative importance of stakeholders will inevitably differ from firm to firm, from issue to issue, and from time to time. And, depending on these factors, the change in relative ordering can be dramatic. As such, addressing the fluctuating needs of stakeholders and meeting those needs wherever possible (ideally proactively, but also reactively) is essential for firms to survive. In order to do this, it is important that executives have a framework that will enable them to prioritize stakeholder interests for a given issue and account for those expectations in formulating a strategic response.

Evolving Issues

Simon Zadek, founder and CEO of AccountAbility,[23] has developed a powerful tool that firms can use to evaluate which issues pose the greatest potential opportunity and threat.[24] First, Zadek identified the five stages of learning that organizations go through "when it comes to developing a sense of corporate responsibility":[25] *defensive* (to deny responsibility), *compliance* (to do the minimum required), *managerial* (to begin integrating CSR into management practices), *strategic* (to embed CSR within the strategy-planning process), and *civil* (to promote CSR practices industry-wide). Zadek combines these five stages of learning with four stages of intensity "to measure the maturity of societal issues and the public's expectations around the issues":[26] *latent* (awareness among activists only), *emerging* (awareness seeps into the political and media communities), *consolidating* (much broader awareness is established), and *institutionalized* (tangible reaction from powerful stakeholders). The range of possible interactions of these different stages is presented in Figure 4.2.

Figure 4.2 Prioritizing Issues

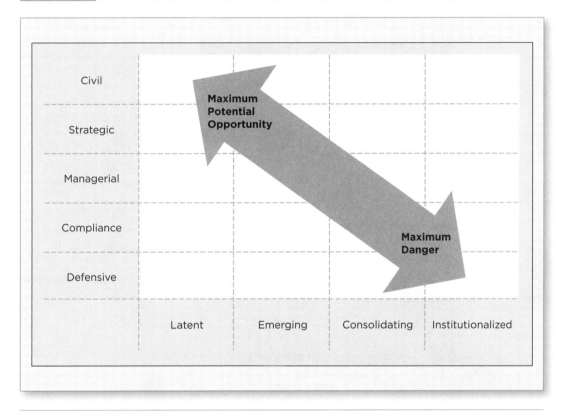

Source: Simon Zadek, "The Path to Corporate Responsibility," *Harvard Business Review*, December 2004, p. 129.

The maximum danger, Zadek argues, is for a company that is in defensive mode when facing an institutionalized issue, as it will be resisting an issue that has sufficient public support to pose a threat to its business. A firm that continues to deny publicly the existence of climate change, for example, falls into this category. In contrast, those businesses that are promoting industry-wide adoption of standard practices in relation to a newly emerging issue stand to gain the maximum *potential* opportunity. A firm that introduces a standardized process to measure carbon footprint and report this information on product labels in the retail industry, for example, falls into this category. Such a company stands to gain the maximum economic and social value for its effort. It is important to note, however, that being an early adopter of a controversial idea or practice that has yet to be widely accepted is only a *potential* opportunity. Due to its controversial nature, early action also poses potential danger. Moreover, if the idea never institutionalizes, the firm may expose itself to the danger of being out of touch with its stakeholders.

A Model of Stakeholder Prioritization

While it is essential for firms to understand that issues vary along metrics such as their intensity and level of widespread acceptance, a limitation of Zadek's model is that it focuses on the firm's interaction with a particular issue, without including the firm's interactions with its various stakeholders. In reality, a firm cannot consider its environment without also considering its wide variety of stakeholders, for whom certain issues are more or less important.

The model presented in Figure 4.3 addresses this complexity. It does so by focusing on the three core components that define the firm–environment relationship in any given context: the firm, the issue, and the stakeholder. The goal is to build a multistep process by which managers can account for variance in (1) the strategic interests of the *firm*, (2) the evolution of the *issue*, and (3) the motivation to act of the *stakeholder(s)*. The resulting tool provides managers with the framework they need in deciding how to prioritize stakeholder concerns and when to act.

The Firm. Any for-profit firm has strategic goals that determine the industries in which it operates and the products it produces. In addition, the firm has

Figure 4.3 Prioritizing Stakeholder Interests

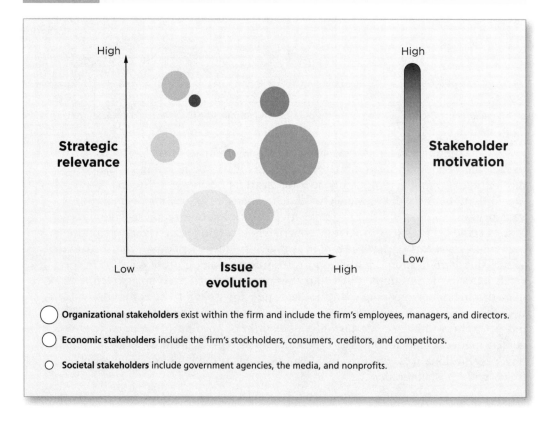

Organizational stakeholders exist within the firm and include the firm's employees, managers, and directors.

Economic stakeholders include the firm's stockholders, consumers, creditors, and competitors.

Societal stakeholders include government agencies, the media, and nonprofits.

performance targets it deems both attainable and desirable (such as percentage market share or a particular level of sales). Together, these strategic goals and performance targets determine the operational priorities of the firm. With this benchmark in mind, managers are able to gauge the relevance of any issue that arises.

The Issue. The key factor that arises with any issue is the extent to which it has become established. As Zadek notes, the maximum risk arises when a firm is defensive in relation to an issue that is institutionalized, because it will be resisting a potential threat (or opportunity) to its business. A good example of this is a firm that continues to deny publicly the existence of climate change, even while its operations contribute to and are affected by this phenomenon. In contrast, those firms that promote industry-wide adoption of standardized practices in relation to an issue that is emerging (but not yet formalized in law) stand to gain the maximum economic and social value for their efforts. Even better, firms willing to take a bold stand on a contentious issue differentiate themselves in the eyes of those stakeholders for whom the issue is important.

The Stakeholder. Once a manager has established that an issue is important and relevant to the firm, the next step is to identify those stakeholders who are most affected. It is these stakeholders who will likely demand action from the firm in relation to this issue. But different issues will resonate with different stakeholders at different times. Rather than launch a prosocial campaign after the fact designed to dilute media attention and mitigate potential stakeholder threats, such as a consumer boycott, effective prioritization allows firms to intervene sufficiently early to avoid some problems and solve others, before confrontation occurs. The goal should be to "quantify how big an issue it is and how rapidly it's spreading and how influential the people hollering are,"[27] while allowing for the degree of consensus within the stakeholder group regarding the issue. The firm can then prioritize and formulate a proactive response.

Once these three dimensions have been defined independently, it is necessary for the manager to consider them in combination to determine how the firm should proceed. This is achieved by considering the three factors in terms of three dimensions on the same matrix—strategic relevance, issue evolution, and stakeholder motivation. *Strategic relevance* captures how important the issue is to the firm—in other words, how proximal it is to the firm's core competency or source of competitive advantage. This dimension is plotted along the *y*-axis of Figure 4.3. *Issue evolution* captures the extent to which an issue has become institutionalized—in other words, the extent to which the issue has become accepted business practice. This dimension is plotted along the *x*-axis of Figure 4.3. Finally, *stakeholder motivation* captures how important the issue is to each stakeholder—in other words, how likely that group is to act. This dimension is captured in terms of degree of intensity—the more motivated the stakeholder is to act, the darker the color of the circle that represents that stakeholder. These three dimensions form the dominant variables that help managers react to stakeholder demands. Additional prioritization is achieved by plotting each of the stakeholders on Figure 4.3 according to whether they are organizational (the largest circles), economic (the medium circles), or societal (the smallest circles).

The extent to which a firm should respond to a stakeholder demand for change with substantial action is determined at the intersection of these three dimensions. Importantly, this framework should be embedded within a culture of outreach to stakeholders that allows firms to understand their evolving concerns and assess the level of importance of each issue to each stakeholder on an ongoing basis. Ultimately, when strategic relevance, issue evolution, and stakeholder motivation are all high (i.e., a dark circle is located in the upper righthand corner of Figure 4.3), the firm is compelled to act, and act quickly, in order to protect its self-interest (in terms of either avoiding a potential threat or taking advantage of a potential opportunity).[28]

Prioritizing Stakeholders

The combination of these three factors (the firm, the issue, and the stakeholder) determines the extent to which any particular issue or stakeholder is central to the firm's interests and which stakeholder demands the firm should prioritize in response. Implementing this framework arms managers with a five-step process-oriented model that empowers them to analyze and respond to the firm's dynamic operating environment on an ongoing basis:

The Five Steps of Stakeholder Prioritization

1. **Identify** and engage the set of stakeholders that are relevant to the firm (Figure 4.1).

2. **Analyze** the nature of the issue to see how it relates to firm operations and what stage it is at in its evolution (Figure 4.2).

3. **Prioritize** among any competing stakeholder interests and demands in relation to the issue at hand (Figure 4.3).

4. **Act** as quickly as is prudent, attempting to satisfy as many stakeholders as possible, in order of priority (while avoiding excessive harm to any one stakeholder).

5. **Evaluate** the effect of the action to optimize the outcomes for the firm and its stakeholders. When necessary, repeat the process (Figure 4.4).

Utilizing these five steps optimizes the practical value of a stakeholder perspective for the firm. The resulting managerial stakeholder model is presented in Figure 4.4.[29]

The primary value of this model is that it allows the firm to analyze the interests of its broad set of stakeholders issue by issue (i.e., a single issue and multiple stakeholders), but it can also be adapted to analyze how any one stakeholder's interests vary across issues (i.e., a single stakeholder and multiple issues). For

Figure 4.4 The Five Steps of Stakeholder Prioritization

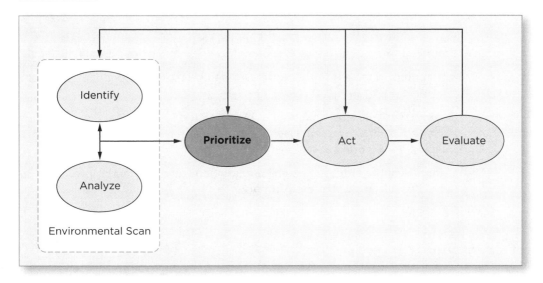

example, while the issue of Exxon's stance on climate change is one that a large number of its stakeholders will feel is relevant to them, it is particularly relevant to Greenpeace. Having said this, Greenpeace has a number of issues that it thinks are important, one of which is Exxon's stance on climate change. While Exxon can analyze the issue of climate change in relation to all of its stakeholders using the frameworks in Figure 4.3 and Figure 4.4, it can also use the same frameworks to analyze Greenpeace in terms of the many issues that are important to the NGO and that affect its relationship with Exxon.

In addition, it is important to emphasize that this model is both proactive and reactive—it constitutes a tool that firms can use either to anticipate or to respond to stakeholder concerns in relation to both opportunities and threats. As such, it allows managers both to add value by identifying potential opportunities and to avoid harm to operations by identifying potential threats.

In essence, this model of stakeholder prioritization allows the manager to take stakeholder theory (a relatively abstract concept) and apply it to the decisions they make on a day-to-day basis. Increasingly, a manager's job will be dominated by the difficult task of managing the complex and often competing interests of the firm's wide range of stakeholders. In order to do so, it is essential not only to identify these constituent groups but also to determine which among them are of primary strategic importance to the firm.

Strategic CSR Debate

MOTION: The natural environment is a stakeholder of the firm.

QUESTIONS FOR DISCUSSION AND REVIEW

1.   What is your definition of a *stakeholder*?

2.   Can an individual or a group self-appoint itself as a stakeholder, or does the firm need to recognize it as a stakeholder in order for it to qualify as such?

3.   What criteria do you think should be used to prioritize competing stakeholder interests?

4.   Of the "five steps of stakeholder prioritization," which step, if missed, is likely to have the most adverse effect on the firm's ability to build effective stakeholder relationships?

5.   Using a real-life firm, list its stakeholders and use the model presented in the chapter to prioritize their importance.

Chapter 5

CORPORATE *STAKEHOLDER* RESPONSIBILITY

Whose responsibility is CSR? The term *corporate social responsibility* suggests that such behavior is the responsibility of corporations—that the corporation has a responsibility to society. Is this the best way to think about CSR? Does it produce optimal outcomes? In reality, where does the motivation for socially responsible behavior come from?

More specifically, should corporations act *responsibly* because they are convinced of the moral argument for doing so (irrespective of the financial implications of their actions) or should they act responsibly because it is in their self-interest? What is the point of a firm acting responsibly if its key stakeholders do not care sufficiently to pay the price premium that is often associated with such actions? As the Malden Mills example in Chapter 1 illustrates, in which employees remained on the firm's payroll while the factory was rebuilt, the best intentions do not help a firm's stakeholders if the firm is bankrupt.

The economic argument for CSR assumes that firms act most effectively when they are incentivized to do so. It assumes that for-profit firms are conservative—that they are more responsive to economic stimuli and are less willing to initiate change proactively when there is little evidence that their actions will be rewarded in the marketplace. Importantly, it assumes that CSR optimizes value creation when the firm's goals and society's expectations are aligned.

Core to the argument advanced in this textbook is that firms should integrate a CSR perspective throughout operations. Nevertheless, unprincipled behavior—even outright disregard for CSR—does not always have a direct and immediate impact. Sometimes stakeholders are willing to overlook socially *irresponsible* behavior because other issues are more pressing. A firm with unacceptable employment practices that are despised by employees, for example, may not reap the negative consequences of its actions if the jobs are vital to the well-being of the local community and there are no good alternatives. Should firms interpret the lack of pushback against their actions as an invitation to uphold the status quo without consideration for any broader concerns about their operations?

A more difficult question arises when a CSR perspective fails to align the firm's interests with those of its stakeholders—that is, when stakeholder interests conflict. What happens when some stakeholders demand socially *irresponsible* behavior? What happens if consumers want to purchase a product that is not only bad for them (e.g., tobacco, alcohol, or fast food) but is also bad for society (e.g., higher healthcare costs or resource utilization)? What happens when consumers' primary concern is the lowest price to the exclusion of all other concerns, such as conditions in the factories where the product is made or the environmental consequences of consumption? If firms can be successful without a CSR perspective, does this mean that CSR does not matter or, at least, does not matter all of the time?

The focus of much of the CSR debate has been to urge firms to act proactively out of a social or moral duty. The label *CSR* itself talks about the *social responsibility* of corporations, without understanding that, often, there are no meaningful consequences for firms that do not act responsibly. In contrast, it is possible that firms are rewarded for *not* pursuing CSR. Unless a firm's business suffers as a result of its actions, should it be expected to change? More specifically, who decides what is responsible behavior and what is not?

Discussion around the issue of CSR focuses almost exclusively on the responsibilities of business, while ignoring the responsibilities of stakeholders for corporate behavior. Think of it as a chicken-and-egg problem: Should the firm alter its behavior to act more responsibly in the hope it will be rewarded for its actions, or should stakeholders demonstrate the behavior they want through a commitment to reward the firm if it meets those expectations? Anecdotal evidence suggests, for example, that consumers want the highest quality products at the lowest possible prices. If those products happen to coincide with an ethical message, that is great, but consumers (on the whole) are willing to plead ignorance if it means getting their sneakers for $10 less:

> In the United Kingdom, ethical consumerism data show that although most consumers are concerned about environmental or social issues, with 83 percent of consumers *intending* to act ethically on a regular basis, only 18 percent of people act ethically occasionally, while fewer than 5 percent of consumers show consistent ethical and green purchasing behaviors.[1]

Given this, whose fault is it if firms do not act responsibly? Alternatively, what would our economy look like if governments started passing meaningful legislation and then enforcing it, or consumers began demanding minimum standards from firms and took their custom elsewhere if the firms failed to comply? It is likely that firms would change their practices and change them quickly, or else they would go out of business. In the absence of such active stakeholder action, how can we expect businesses to introduce CSR when doing so means they have to interpret what stakeholders say they want—opinions that often contradict the criteria those same stakeholders use in their interactions with the firm?

To complicate things further, there is no statute of limitations on stakeholder reactions. Socially irresponsible behavior without immediate market consequences does not mean that the behavior is, or should be, condoned (or that there will not be other, non-market consequences for their actions). Business practices that are profitable today may not necessarily be profitable (or even legal) tomorrow. Short-term success simply means that other issues take precedence . . . for now. As circumstances or expectations evolve, the lack of CSR may alter the firm's prospects.

The Financial Crisis

In pursuit of process fees, brokers sold adjustable mortgages to those who could not afford them. These loans were then packaged and sold by financiers (in pursuit of annual bonuses) to investors, who didn't understand them or appreciate the associated risks. Given the AAA rating these securities were assigned by the credit-rating agencies (in pursuit of corporate fees), the industry continued to sell these mortgages to a growing percentage of the population. With insufficient oversight by regulators, these irresponsible actions continued for years. When housing prices declined and mortgage defaults soared, the consequence of actions by brokers, bankers, credit-rating agencies, and Wall Street was widespread bankruptcies:

> The finance sector is, by its nature, an intermediary. . . . This agent-principal relationship has to rely on trust if it is to work. The subprime mortgage debacle of 2007 showed the problems that arise from a long chain of intermediaries who cared little about the credit quality of the loans they were passing on. . . . Smarter people have been employed in finance in recent decades, using more sophisticated technology, but the quality of intermediation has got worse.[2]

As a result of this chain of corporate actions and stakeholder reactions, the finance industry today is one of the most regulated, with senior executives routinely complaining about the constraints imposed by excessive government oversight.[3] In reality, these executives have few people to blame but themselves.

The question that opened this chapter, *Whose responsibility is CSR?*, therefore reflects an important debate within the CSR community: Can firms safely ignore calls for reform as long as they are profitable? By definition, do profitable operations indicate that a firm is adding sufficient value (perceived or real) for key stakeholder groups, even if those needs have broader negative consequences? What is the role of stakeholders in prompting firms to change, and what is the role of firms to initiate change? This chapter addresses these questions within the larger framework of strategic CSR. The answer proposed is that, by definition, a *social responsibility* is a responsibility that is defined by society, and *society* consists of all of the firm's stakeholders. In other words, the actions that stakeholders reward are, essentially, the actions that they value. The challenge for firms is, first of all, to understand and meet those expectations but, second, to know when these expectations will change. The danger is that a failure to be perceived as socially responsible will, if not now then at some point, carry repercussions—as the 2007–2008 financial crisis revealed.

CSR: A CORPORATE RESPONSIBILITY?

The focus of much of the CSR debate (captured by the term *corporate social responsibility*) is the assumption that firms have a responsibility to pursue goals other than profit. This chapter explores this assumption in more detail. In particular, it suggests that the CSR community expects too much of firms—that firms *react* to change better than they *initiate* change and that, if society decides it wants greater social responsibility from firms, then perhaps it is a firm's stakeholders that have an equal, if not greater, responsibility to demand this behavior. More importantly, stakeholders need to demonstrate that they will support such behavior, thus providing the economic rationale for firms to respond. By definition, firms that provide products and services not supported by stakeholders (and, in particular, demanded by consumers) will quickly go out of business. With CSR, as with many aspects of business, it does not pay firms to be too far ahead of the curve. If consumers, for example, demonstrate that they are willing to pay a price premium for CSR behavior (rather than reporting in surveys that they think firms should be more responsible, but basing their purchase decisions mainly on price), firms will quickly adapt. If consumers are not willing to pay this premium, however, is it in society's best interests for firms to bear the burden of producing such products at the risk of going bankrupt?

Milton Friedman Versus Charles Handy

Two important articles on CSR frame this debate about the responsibility that a firm has to be socially responsible. The first article, by Nobel Prize–winning economist Milton Friedman, was published in *The New York Times Magazine* in 1970: "The Social Responsibility of Business Is to Increase Its Profits."[4] In the article, Friedman argues that profit, as a result of the actions of the firm, is an end in itself. He believes strongly that a firm need not have any additional justification for existing and that, in fact, value for society is maximized when a firm focuses solely on pursuing its self-interest by seeking to maximize profit:

> I share Adam Smith's skepticism about the benefits that can be expected from "those who affected to trade for the public good." . . . In a free society, . . . "there is one and only one social responsibility of business—to use its resources and engage in activities designed to increase its profits."[5]

The second article, written by the influential British management author and commentator Charles Handy, appeared in *Harvard Business Review* in 2002.[6] In contrast to Friedman, Handy presents a much broader view of the role of business in society, arguing that it is not sufficient to think of a firm's profit as an end in itself. For Handy, a business has to have a motivation other than merely making a profit in order to justify its existence—profit is merely a means to achieve a larger end. A firm should not remain in existence just because it is profitable but because it is meeting a need that society *as a whole* values:

It is salutary to ask about any organization, "If it did not exist, would we invent it? Only if it could do something better or more useful than anyone else" would have to be the answer, and profit would be the means to that larger end.[7]

On the surface, the positions taken by Friedman and Handy appear irreconcilable. Indeed, Friedman seems to go out of his way to antagonize CSR advocates by arguing that socially responsible behavior is a waste of the firm's resources, which "is why, in my book *Capitalism and Freedom*, I have called [social responsibility] a 'fundamentally subversive doctrine' in a free society."[8] But, on closer analysis, how different are the arguments really? Incorporating a strategic CSR perspective narrows the gap between these two commentators considerably, as indicated by a comparison of these two questions.

CSR: Fundamentally Subversive?

- Does it make sense for a large financial firm to donate money to a group researching the effects of climate change because the CEO believes this is an important issue?
- Does it make sense for an oil firm to donate money to the same group because it perceives climate change as a threat to its business model and wants to mitigate that threat by investigating possible alternatives?

In both cases, the action—a large for-profit firm donating money to a non-profit group—is the same. The difference is in the relevance of the nonprofit's activities to the firm's core operations. Most level-headed CSR advocates would acknowledge that the first action is less prudent (incorporating Friedman's argument that the actions represent an inefficient allocation of resources in an area in which the firm has no expertise), while the second action is strategic for the firm because it involves an issue that relates directly to operations and is important for a key stakeholder group.

Rather than take the positions of Friedman and Handy at face value, therefore, a more insightful interpretation of their arguments suggests that, to the extent that it is in a firm's interests to create value for its key stakeholders, it should do so. From Handy's perspective, this point is easy to argue, but Friedman also recognizes this. He qualifies his statement that a manager's primary responsibility is to the shareholders, who seek "to make as much money as possible," by noting that this pursuit must be tempered "while conforming to the basic rules of the society, *both those embodied in law and those embodied in ethical custom*." In addition, a firm's actions are acceptable only as long as it "engages in open and free competition *without deception or fraud*"[9] [emphasis added]. Both points acknowledge that a firm cannot ignore the consequences of its actions for a wider set of stakeholders. It is worth quoting Archie Carroll at length addressing this same issue in his foundational *Business Horizons* article:

Economist Milton Friedman . . . has argued that social matters are not the concern of business people and that these problems should be resolved by the unfettered workings of the free market system. Friedman's argument loses some of its punch, however, when you consider his assertion in its totality. . . . Most people focus on the first part of Friedman's quote but not the second part. It seems clear from this statement that profits, conformity to the law, and ethical custom embrace three components of the CSR pyramid—economic, legal, and ethical. That only leaves the philanthropic component for Friedman to reject. Although it may be appropriate for an economist to take this view, one would not encounter many business executives today who exclude philanthropic programs from their firms' range of activities.[10]

The CSR debate is often characterized as a battle between supporters of Friedman on one side and the supporters of Handy on the other—as if these two positions are mutually exclusive. Instead, I suggest they are much closer than most people think. Moreover, I argue that Friedman's views and strategic CSR are compatible approaches to business—that the way to be successful in business today is for firms to implement a long-term, progressive, stakeholder perspective. To what extent this is true in practice, however, depends on how CSR is defined and implemented by management. In essence, the progressive manager is one who understands that "social issues are not so much tangential to the business of business as fundamental to it."[11]

But then, if Friedman and Handy are, in essence, not that far apart in terms of the purpose of the firm, *Whose responsibility is CSR?* More specifically, what is the role of stakeholders in ensuring the firm acts in a way that is consistent with their aggregate expectations?

CSR: A STAKEHOLDER RESPONSIBILITY?

The question at the beginning of this chapter (*Whose responsibility is CSR?*) challenges stakeholders, collectively, to demand the behavior they want to see from businesses. In other words, it suggests that stakeholders have an obligation to help shape the behavior they want from businesses. Should regulators, for example, demand greater care in the issuing of loans from the finance industry? Should employees demand higher wages from their employers in the fast-food industry? Should consumers expect more responsible television advertising by firms that make children's products? Should firms expect overseas contractors to sign codes of conduct to ensure more responsible behavior throughout the supply chain?

More specifically, while it is easy for stakeholders to demand better conditions, to what extent are they willing to sacrifice in order to achieve those goals? The reason that fast-food companies pay the low wages that they do, for example, is that they are able to staff all of their open positions at that rate with employees who have the skill set needed to do the job. In other words, employees value those jobs either because they have no alternative or because any alternative pays at a lower rate. For McDonald's to be forced to pay its employees the arbitrary wage of $15 an hour, as some activists suggest, would most likely be economic suicide in an industry where the firm's competitors pay significantly lower wages.[12] For this to change, a stakeholder needs to act—either by the government increasing the minimum wage, or employees refusing to work at that wage rate, or consumers refusing to shop at McDonald's because they are unhappy with the wages the company is paying its employees. Until one of its key stakeholders sends a serious message to McDonald's that its current wages are unacceptable, then McDonald's will (and should) continue doing exactly what it is doing.

The point is that, ultimately, firms do not define our societal values; instead they reflect them. Firms are very good at providing us with what we actually want (rather than what we say we want). As such, *all stakeholders* have an obligation to help design the society in which they want to live and work. If society decides that financial bubbles and crises should be avoided, then it is fair to acknowledge the role of stakeholders in realizing this outcome. Similarly, if society decides that it does not want all of its jobs outsourced to low-cost environments, then stakeholders need to be willing to pay the higher costs that will result from keeping those jobs at home. The responsibility is not solely with one group or another; it is important to acknowledge that "we live in the house we all build."[13]

EarthShare

Consider a full-page advertisement that appeared in *The New York Times* for the environmental activist group EarthShare (http://www.earthshare.org/):[14]

> Every decision we make has consequences. We choose what we put into our lakes and rivers. We choose what we release into the air we breathe. We choose what we put into our bodies, and where we let our children run and play. We choose the world we live in, so make the right choices. Learn what you can do to care for our water, our air, our land and yourself at earthshare.org.

What is attractive about the ad is the emphasis it places on individual responsibility, rather than merely haranguing firms for polluting too much. The headline of the ad (including capital letters and bold) captures the tone exactly:

WE **LIVE** IN THE HOUSE WE ALL **BUILD**.

This emphasis on individual action is often absent from the CSR debate. Firms act much more quickly in response to key stakeholder demands (those of consumers, in particular) than when expected to initiate action that has no demonstrated support in the marketplace. If consumers stop buying a certain product because they disapprove of the way it was produced or some other action by the firm that produced it, that firm will quickly adapt or fail. In other words, stakeholders are as responsible for the firms that survive and thrive in our society as the organizations themselves. Stakeholder action is not a perfect solution for the problems in our capitalist system, and firms are not absolved of all responsibility (and those firms that are able to differentiate themselves in relation to CSR will be more successful in the long term); it is just that more would be achieved that much faster in terms of CSR advocacy if emphasis were placed equally on *stakeholder responsibility* and *corporate responsibility*.[15]

This idea is expressed in the concept of corporate *stakeholder* responsibility.[16] If we are going to advocate for a *corporate* social responsibility (the responsibility of firms to act in accordance with stakeholder needs) and, in particular, if we are going to build the business case for CSR, we also need to advocate for a corporate *stakeholder* responsibility (the responsibility of a firm's stakeholders to hold that firm to account).[17] Both elements are essential to the extent that, without one, we are unlikely to see enough of the other. Similarly, the more the latter happens, the more it is in the firm's interests to do the former.[18]

> ### Corporate *Stakeholder* Responsibility
>
> A responsibility among all of a firm's stakeholders to hold the firm to account for its actions by rewarding behavior that meets expectations and punishing behavior that does not

Consistently, for-profit firms have demonstrated that they are very good at reacting to market forces and economic incentives, and that they are *not* very good at either predicting consumer trends or shifting markets in ways that counter demonstrated demand. An alternative focus for the CSR community, therefore, is to shift attention from firms to their stakeholders.

In Chapter 1, CSR was defined as "a responsibility among firms to meet the needs of their stakeholders and a responsibility among stakeholders to hold firms to account for their actions." In other words, there is a responsibility of stakeholders to hold firms to account that is *equal* (if not more important) to the responsibility of firms to act according to those expectations. This more balanced approach is essential to generate meaningful change:

> We get more of what we signal we want through our dollars, clicks and votes. If our politics are too often poisonous, it is because, as a society, we are demanding too much poison. If we want to grow in virtue, and experience a healthier, more productive political environment, each of us must demand more virtue.[19]

The primary purpose of a business is to create *value* for its stakeholders, but it is its stakeholders who define what that value looks like in practice. For the market system to work at its optimal potential capacity, therefore, stakeholders need to translate their values, needs, and concerns into action that punishes firms that fail to meet their criteria and rewards those that exceed it (i.e., governments start regulating effectively, suppliers start choosing business partners that treat them fairly, consumers start discriminating among firms based on their ability to deliver the products they seek, etc.). Given such incentives, firms have shown they are capable of rapidly and efficiently altering the way they operate in order to meet expectations.

But, it is important to reinforce that *all* stakeholders, not only consumers, have leverage over the firm and need to act. For example, the media plays an important oversight role. This was demonstrated perfectly in the United States in 2015 when the CBS program *60 Minutes* exposed the mislabeling of products by the flooring company Lumber Liquidators.[20] Similarly, action by US regulators that revealed the efforts by Volkswagen to deceive emissions-testing equipment demonstrates what is possible when stakeholders act to shape the behavior they want from corporations.[21] VW executives had told Environmental Protection Agency officials "for more than a year" that the company's cars passed emissions tests, but polluted while being driven, due to a "technical error" rather than any intention to deceive. They only admitted the truth "when the [EPA] took the extraordinary action of threatening to withhold approval for the company's 2016 Volkswagen and Audi diesel models."[22] In both cases, the firms' share prices dropped precipitously following the exposure of the disputed behavior.

The full implications of the idea of corporate *stakeholder* responsibility make apparent the difference between mainstream CSR and the new definition of CSR presented in Chapter 1. The accompanying shift is presented graphically in Figures 5.1a and 5.1b. CSR is often discussed in terms of understanding how stakeholders react to firm actions. In other words, the firm acts and its stakeholders react. You only have to think for a few minutes about the stakeholder model, however, to understand this does not represent reality. Because managers, employees, and directors are all stakeholders, the firm cannot be thought of as a separate thing. It is not that the firm acts and then its stakeholders react, but that the firm's actions represent the aggregated effect of all its stakeholder actions. The firm is constituted by its stakeholders and, as such, they are one and the same.

Figure 5.1a   The Firm and Stakeholders as Independent Actors

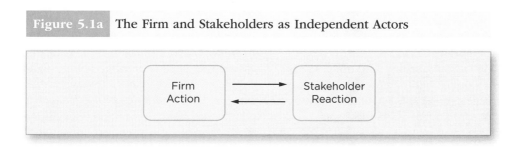

Figure 5.1b   The Firm and Stakeholders as Integrated Actors

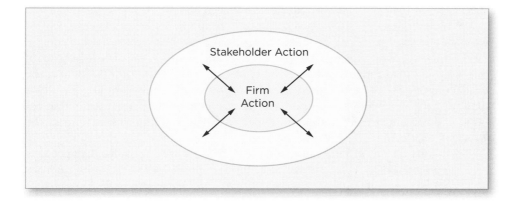

Put another way, it is the environment in which the firm operates that creates the boundary conditions that define what the *pursuit of profit* means at any given point. The *rules of the game* determine what is acceptable and unacceptable in the way that any single business conducts operations. *It is the collective set of values of all of the firm's stakeholders that make these rules.* The firm's goal continues to be profit and has always been so, back to the earliest markets on the Silk Road; it is the rules that evolve over time and vary from culture to culture. And, it is the more astute managers who understand current conditions and when the rules (both written and unwritten) have shifted who can guide their firms to greater economic success. They understand that abiding by those rules provides the firm with the license that it requires in order to operate.[23] But, for this relationship to work, it is essential that the rules be enforced by stakeholders. If the rules are enforced, they will determine the outcome.

Firms are designed to make a profit. It is up to a firm's stakeholders to define the parameters of which actions are profitable and which are not. It would advance the CSR cause considerably, therefore, if stakeholders were caring, informed, transparent, and educated.

Caring Stakeholders

In order for CSR to be a stakeholder responsibility, stakeholders need to care sufficiently to warrant corporate action. The argument in favor of CSR presupposes that there are benefits for a company being perceived as a net contributor to the society in which it is based. At the very least, there should be economic penalties for firms that act contrary to stakeholder expectations. Managers already understand the benefits of being perceived as an important and positive influence within a local community, as suggested by advertising campaigns that highlight examples of corporate philanthropy. The extent to which that perceived image differs from societal expectations represents the potential for either an economic or social deficit, as depicted in Figure 5.2. These deficits suggest misalignment between the expectations of the firm's stakeholders (both internal and external) and what the firm delivers.

A firm that is successfully implementing a strategic CSR perspective (represented by the 45° line in Figure 5.2) is able to align the value its internal stakeholders seek with the broader value that is sought by its various external stakeholders. Typically, the value sought internally focuses on growing profits, which benefit organizational stakeholders such as employees. To be considered legitimate over the medium to long term, however, the firm's pursuit of profit should also provide value to the firm's external stakeholders, such as the local community in the form of preserving local jobs or producing products that are safe to consume. The range of firm behavior that generates value for both internal and external stakeholders in sufficient quantities is termed the *strategic CSR window of opportunity*.

This model is important because it emphasizes the need for balance. An unchecked, unbridled pursuit of profit, without regard to the social consequences (e.g., such as a manufacturing process that generates excessive pollution), creates

Figure 5.2 The Strategic CSR Window of Opportunity

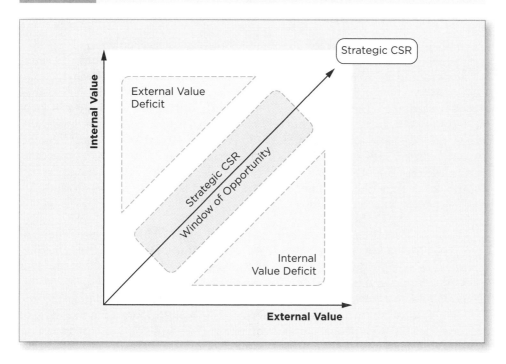

a deficit for the society in which the firm operates. Likewise, a firm that pursues external value too aggressively (e.g., Malden Mills in Chapter 1) may diminish its ability to generate profits—causing a deficit in the form of slowed economic activity. While actions that focus solely on profit maximization (internal) or philanthropic activity unrelated to the firm's core operations (external) add value, they do so in ways that fail to support a strategic CSR perspective. Simply put, when either internal or external value is deficient to some degree, stakeholders have a basis upon which to question the legitimacy of the firm as a valued member of society.

The alignment of value across stakeholder groups represents the implementation of a strategic approach to CSR throughout the organization. Restated, firms must act in ways that are valued by their multiple stakeholders—not just their directors, employees, or any other single constituent. For the *strategic CSR window of opportunity* to apply in practice, however, it is important that stakeholders evaluate firm actions and act to correct any deficit when they perceive one. In the same way that activist shareholders protect their investments by holding firms to account, we need *activist stakeholders* that will act to hold the firm to account in order to protect the interests they have in the firm's ongoing operations. At present, however,[24]

a whopping majority of American shoppers may consider themselves environmentalists, but . . . only 10% to 12% "actually go out of their way to purchase environmentally sound products." Similarly, . . . even among consumers who called themselves "environmentally conscious," more than half could not name a single green brand.[25]

Although it appears that the number of the socially concerned is growing, a large component of consumer-driven economic pressure still indicates that companies should compete in terms of price or other, more traditional, characteristics, such as quality. In spite of a rise in the availability of ethical products and producers willing to sell them, "[for] the majority of consumers, cheap products of decent quality remain the popular choice." If this is true, then "what incentives do businesses have in maintaining responsible or ethical standards?"[26] As the *Financial Times* notes, even though it has increased since 1999, ethical spending in the UK still represents only "9 percent of the British public's spending, up from 3 per cent in 1999."[27] Similarly in the United States, one report showed that safe and fair working conditions

> would add less than one dollar to the price of a pair of blue jeans. But despite responding to surveys that they care about ethics, shoppers refuse to pay more. In one study, only half of customers chose a pair of socks marked "Good Working Conditions" even when they were the same price as an unmarked pair; only one quarter of customers paid for the socks when they cost 50 percent more. Until the general public acknowledges the true cost of consumption, the people inside companies fighting for more responsible practices will be waging an uphill battle.[28]

To what extent, therefore, are investors, suppliers, and other stakeholders willing to sacrifice some short-term value in the name of longer-term sustainable value?[29] Are employees, creditors, regulators, and other key stakeholders willing to exert influence when they enjoy some degree of leverage? Thomas Friedman of *The New York Times* captures this argument in a column about citizens demanding change from politicians: "So what do we do? The standard answer is that we need better leaders. The real answer is that we need better citizens."[30] The same is true for business and CSR. We do not need more responsible companies; we need more responsible stakeholders.

Globalization provides powerful tools that stakeholders can use to represent their best interests, but only if they are willing to take advantage of the opportunity and demand change.

Informed Stakeholders

Stakeholders encourage socially responsible behavior when they represent rational or economic motives for the firm. Although this advocacy often comes from customers, investors, or other external activists, internal advocates (including founders, leaders, and employees) can also push a CSR agenda. At issue is the willingness to become informed and act.

The revolution in communications technology, which fueled the growth of the Internet and global media industry, has presented stakeholders with the opportunity to mobilize and convey their collective message. They now have previously unimaginable abilities to monitor corporate operations and quickly disseminate any actions or information they feel do not represent their best interests. In this manner, the communications revolution has been a great leveler of corporate power. Examples include Change.org (https://www.change.org/),[31] Purpose.com (http://www.purpose.com/), and even Tumblr (https://www.tumblr .com/),[32] which act as platforms to mobilize and act, while BuyPartisan (http:// buypartisan.com/) reveals the nature of corporate political donations (Republican or Democrat) on a product-by-product basis.

As Figure 2.2 (Chapter 2) illustrates, globalization has facilitated a great expansion in corporate influence. Today, global companies span national boundaries, outsourcing large elements of operations offshore, incorporating supply chain efficiencies, cutting costs, and growing their brands into cultural icons that span the globe; think of Coke, Nike, or McDonald's as examples of massive global corporations, all of which regularly feature in surveys of the world's most powerful brands.[33] Phase II of globalization, however, has been marked by countervailing pressures from stakeholders with access to increased sources of information and to increased means of acting on that information. Thomas Friedman, with greater historical perspective, refers to this as the era of

"Globalization 3.0," following Globalization 1.0, which ran from 1492 until 1800 and was driven by countries' sheer brawn, and Globalization 2.0, in which "the key agent of change, the dynamic force of driving global integration, was multinational companies' driven to look abroad for markets and labor. . . . That epoch ended around 2000, replaced by one in which individuals are the main agents doing the globalizing, pushed by . . . "software [and a] global fiber-optic network that has made us all next-door neighbors."[34]

As a collective and armed with the tools to communicate and mobilize, stakeholders have the power to shape the society they say they want. This is particularly true for a group of consumers that is as large as those that shop at Walmart every week:

Does [Walmart's operating practices] matter? Only if consumers say it does; . . . Wal-Mart listens to "voters." If shoppers say they won't buy [a product] until Wal-Mart insists on higher standards from suppliers, then Wal-Mart will meet those demands.[35]

Many CSR advocates have relied on the moral argument for their cause, which boils down to the notion that businesses *should* act in a socially responsible manner because it is the *right* thing to do. Values (such as judgments of right and wrong) are subjective, however, and can be subordinated within organizations to profit, sales, or other bottom-line considerations. Companies may wish or intend to act in a socially responsible manner for a variety of reasons, but they are more likely to commit consistently and wholeheartedly to CSR business practices if they are convinced of the rational or economic benefits of doing so. The evidence suggests that the dangers of not doing so for large corporations are growing exponentially, with one study finding that "the five-year risk of such a disaster for companies owning the most prestigious global brands has risen in the past two decades from 20 percent to 82 percent."[36]

The importance of being able to prioritize stakeholder concerns in relation to a given issue is illustrated in Figure 5.3.[37] The *CSR sweet spot* is maintained when the firm is able to stay within the shaded area where opportunity is maximized and risk minimized. The tradeoff between opportunity and risk demonstrates the extent to which any given issue has been institutionalized within society. As a result, the *CSR danger zone* occurs where risk outweighs

Figure 5.3   The CSR Sweet Spot Versus Danger Zone

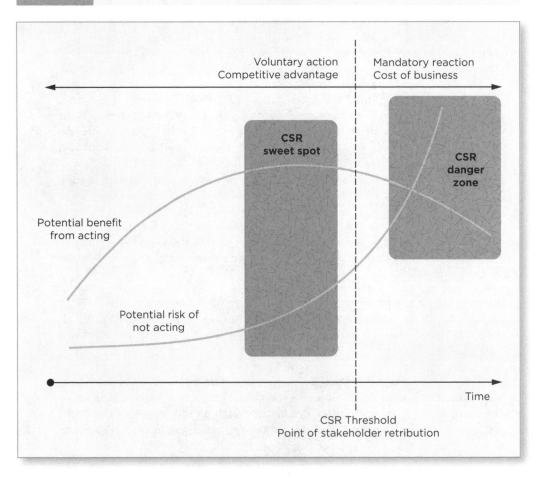

opportunity in relation to an issue that has become taken for granted among the firm's key stakeholders. The *CSR threshold*[38] (the dotted line) occurs when stakeholders act to punish the firm for not meeting their expectations in relation to that issue.

As Figure 5.3 illustrates, there is an advantage to acting on CSR, and there is a danger to waiting too long. Once stakeholder impatience passes the point of retribution, the firm can be heavily penalized for not responding to expressed concerns. Examples of such stakeholder retaliation can include regulation by the government, boycotts by consumers, investigations by the media, and strikes by employees. In order for firms to act, however, stakeholders need to convey their concerns clearly with action that punishes firms that do not listen or respond. Stakeholder concerns become more evident and measurable when key groups are willing to support their words with informed action and communicate that intent clearly to firms.[39]

Transparent Stakeholders

To the extent that they reveal which issues are on the minds of stakeholders, opinion surveys can serve as a useful tool. The message polls send, however, may not always be clear. The Gallup "Annual Honesty and Ethics poll," which rates

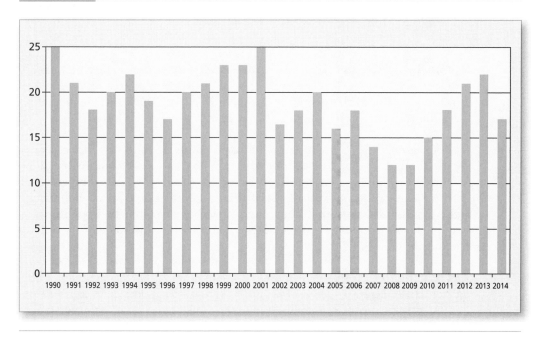

Figure 5.4 The Honesty and Ethics of Business Executives (1990–2014)

Source: Based on data from Gallup, http://www.gallup.com/poll/1654/honesty-ethics-professions.aspx.

"the honesty and ethics of workers in 21 different professions," for example, reveals that the public does not hold business executives in very high esteem. Figure 5.4 indicates that a review of the results from 1990 to 2014 shows the percentage of the US public surveyed who rated business executives' ethics as "high" or "very high" never rose above 25%.[40]

A similar poll of the public's confidence in "American institutions" revealed that business "came second to bottom, just above Congress, with only 21% expressing 'a great deal' or 'quite a lot' of confidence in it."[41] Even more indicative of the low esteem in which many business leaders are held, "another poll . . . found that 35% of American employees would forgo a substantial pay rise if they could see their direct supervisors fired."[42] The implicit accusation is that the current performance of executives is unacceptable. Yet, politicians keep getting elected and businesses keep generating large profits, even if there is now greater turnover at the top:

> The average time a company spends on the *Fortune* 500 list has fallen from 70 years in the 1930s to about 15 years today; and the average job tenure of a *Fortune* 500 CEO has gone from ten years in 2000 to five years today.[43]

While people say they disapprove of unethical behavior, there appears to be a disconnect between perception and practice. Although public opinion is commonly gauged about issues such as CSR via surveys,[44] it is unclear the extent to which people tell pollsters their true feelings rather than merely what they think they should say or what they think the pollster wants to hear. What many suspect is this: "The trouble with market research is that people don't think how they feel, they don't say what they think and they don't do what they say."[45]

> Unfortunately, we now have over two decades of evidence that this survey research on sustainability is flawed. "Social desirability" biases lead people to avoid saying things that would make them look bad (such as that they don't care about the environment or workers rights) when interviewed.[46]

Various surveys and reports over the years continue to tell us that consumers care about CSR and are willing to pay more for more responsible business practices. This sentiment is supported by the survey data presented in Figure 5.5 (an online survey of more than 30,000 people in 60 countries), which suggests not only that consumers *care* but also that their willingness to pay more is increasing. Unfortunately, many CEOs now suspect these data are misleading:

> CEOs don't believe consumer-stated commitments to sustainability. This makes sense. There is a massive gap between what consumers say and do. Which is why most companies don't ask consumers what they believe or value; they study their actual behaviours (and increasingly their brain waves).

| Figure 5.5 | Consumers' Willingness to Pay for CSR (2011–2014) |

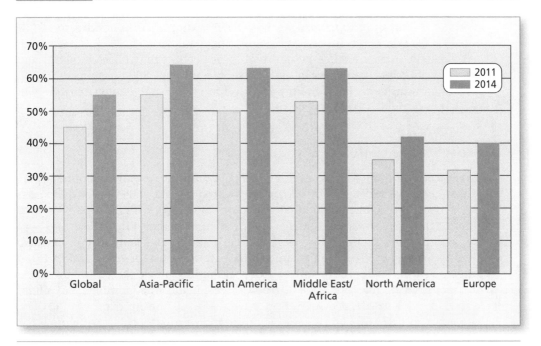

Source: "How Much Do Consumers Care?" *The Wall Street Journal Report: Business & Environment*, March 31, 2015, p. R6.

Brands, retailers, and market researchers assert that the newest behavioural tracking and neuroscience tools are designed to help them learn what consumers want and need.[47]

In order for companies do be able to respond to their stakeholders' needs, it is essential that those stakeholders convey their concerns clearly and act in ways that are consistent with those beliefs. Otherwise, firms are left to try to interpret the mixed messages they are currently receiving, where people say they want one thing but reward something else.

It is important to understand that being *socially responsible* is not a set of abstract standards (don't pollute, don't outsource, pay your employees $15 an hour, etc.) but is defined by the values of the firm's collective set of stakeholders (which, on aggregate, equals *society*). In other words, for a firm to be socially responsible means doing what society wants the firm to do. Within this view of CSR, if society wants to destroy the planet, then firms are being socially responsible if they give society what it wants. Equally, if society wants firms to be environmentally conscious, then protecting the planet is being socially responsible. The definition of what is and what is not socially responsible is not fixed but is changing all the time and up to stakeholders to determine. For example, 50 years ago wearing a fur coat was socially acceptable, but today it is not. There is nothing absolutely *right* or *wrong* about wearing a fur coat—what has changed is our attitude toward it. As a result, what is considered *responsible* behavior (in relation to fur coats) has also changed.

Ultimately, firms are value-neutral tools. They reflect the collective needs and concerns of their stakeholders in order to serve a very specific economic purpose. If we want firms to act in a certain way, therefore, we have to demonstrate the will needed to bring that behavior about.

Educated Stakeholders

An indicator of hope for a future in which CSR becomes a more prominent part of business (both in terms of managers' awareness and stakeholder demands) is the degree to which individual and corporate responsibility is an integral component of business education. To what extent, therefore, are ethics and CSR classes entering the business school curriculum? This is important because every year, "more than 366,000 undergraduate business degrees and 191,000 graduate business degrees were awarded in the U.S., more than any other type of undergrad or masters-level degree."[48] Worldwide, the numbers are much larger. In other words, it matters how we educate our future corporate leaders. The concern is that business schools are not currently teaching students what they need to know:

> Business is *the* cultural, organizational, and economic superforce in human development.
>
> And yet the current state of this social institution is fundamentally flawed: It falls short in its potential to serve our global society. Today's predominant business models drive public companies, for instance, to focus on predictable, short-term shareholder returns that may be detrimental to employees, communities, or the broader social good. They also fail to motivate industries to reduce their environmental impact.[49]

Ethics in Practice

Ethics is complex and difficult to teach. The example below reveals its complexity.[50] Not only does it convey the irrationality and inconsistency of humans but also how thinking of anyone as ethical (or not) misses the point. As is often the case with complex issues, the answer is that "it depends."

If you're shopping for a used car—or deposing a witness—try to do it in the morning. That's the implication of new research . . . [that] found that people are quite a bit more honest in the morning than in the afternoon.

This conclusion emerged from a series of scientific experiments on university students in which participants were given a financial incentive to cheat:

Sure enough, afternoon participants cheated 20% more than did their morning counterparts. In a second trial, afternoon volunteers not only cheated more on the perception task but showed lower moral awareness. Given four word fragments to complete, including "_ _ R A L" and "E_ _ _ C_ _," morning participants were nearly three times likelier to complete the words as "moral" and "ethical" (versus "coral" and "effects").

These findings match earlier research that reported prison parole boards are more likely to grant parole to a prisoner if the request is considered immediately after a break (e.g., lunch or a coffee break). The explanation is that, as the board members became tired or hungry (and more irritable), their ability to evaluate objectively is compromised. It turns out that humans are frustratingly inconsistent when applying their ethical and moral values:

As the day wears on, mental fatigue sets in from hours of decision-making and self-regulation.... "Unremarkable daily activities," the researchers write, can produce depletion that leads [individuals] "to act in ethically questionable ways."

The *Beyond Grey Pinstripes* biennial survey by the Aspen Institute[51] was designed to measure progress in this area: "Our mission is to spotlight innovative full-time MBA programs that are integrating issues of social and environmental stewardship into curricula and research." The organization's final MBA ranking assessed schools in four areas: relevant coursework, student exposure, business impact, and faculty research, reporting that "the percentage of schools surveyed that require students to take a course dedicated to business and society issues has increased dramatically," from 34% in 2001 to 79% in the final ranking in 2011.[52]

Net Impact provides another example of progress. Its data suggest that "65% of MBAs surveyed say they want to make a social or environmental difference through their jobs."[53] Similarly, "according to a Deloitte survey, . . . 70% of young Millennials, those ages 18 to 26, say a company's commitment to the community has an influence on their decision to work there."[54] In support of this growing sentiment, Net Impact, originally founded as Students for Responsible Business in 1993, boasts a growing membership:

At the heart of our community are over 80,000 student and professional leaders from over 300 volunteer-led chapters across the globe working for a sustainable future. Together, we make a net impact that transforms our lives, our organizations, and the world.[55]

One factor fueling the rise in CSR courses at universities (reflected in the Aspen Institute's rankings) and the growth in activist organizations (such as

Net Impact) is PRME—the United Nations' six Principles of Responsible Management Education.[56] PRME's signatories now number over 500 "leading business schools and management-related academic institutions from over 80 countries across the world. More than a third of the Financial Times' top 100 business schools are signatories to PRME."[57] By committing to the principles, schools agree that

> as institutions of higher education involved in the development of current and future managers we declare our willingness to progress in the implementation, within our institution, of the following Principles, starting with those that are more relevant to our capacities and mission. We will report on progress to all our stakeholders and exchange effective practices related to these principles with other academic institutions.[58]

The PRME Six Principles[59]

Principle 1 | Purpose: We will develop the capabilities of students to be future generators of sustainable value for business and society at large and to work for an inclusive and sustainable global economy.

Principle 2 | Values: We will incorporate into our academic activities and curricula the values of global social responsibility as portrayed in international initiatives such as the United Nations Global Compact.

Principle 3 | Method: We will create educational frameworks, materials, processes and environments that enable effective learning experiences for responsible leadership.

Principle 4 | Research: We will engage in conceptual and empirical research that advances our understanding about the role, dynamics, and impact of corporations in the creation of sustainable social, environmental and economic value.

Principle 5 | Partnership: We will interact with managers of business corporations to extend our knowledge of their challenges in meeting social and environmental responsibilities and to explore jointly effective approaches to meeting these challenges.

Principle 6 | Dialog: We will facilitate and support dialog and debate among educators, students, business, government, consumers, media, civil society organisations and other interested groups and stakeholders on critical issues related to global social responsibility and sustainability.

A growing awareness and acceptance of CSR is a necessary component of meaningful change. As future business leaders become more aware of the importance of CSR, the likelihood of its acceptance in a corporate setting will increase. More important from a societal perspective, however, is the extent to which a growing awareness of CSR motivates stakeholders to hold firms to account. If the market rewards CSR-sensitive companies and punishes CSR-insensitive companies, then business leaders will be incentivized to integrate CSR policies into the firm's strategic perspective and day-to-day operations.

ENGAGED STAKEHOLDERS

The result of stakeholders that care, are more informed, are transparent, and are better educated is that they are more fully engaged with their society. An essential aspect of this engagement is a belief in something larger than the *self*. A willingness to shape society (rather than be shaped by it) by definition entails that we believe, at some level, that the group (society) is more important than the individual. Unfortunately, in recent decades, the trend has been in the opposite direction:

> The proportion of American teenagers who believe themselves to be "very important" jumped from 12% in 1950 to 80% in 2005. On a test that asks subjects to agree or disagree with statements such as "I like to look at my body" and "Somebody should write a biography about me," 93% of young Americans emerge as being more narcissistic than the average of 20 years ago. With the rise in self-regard has come an unprecedented yearning for fame. In a survey in 1976, people ranked being famous 15th out of 16 possible life goals. By 2007, 51% of young people said it was one of their principal ambitions. On a recent . . . quiz, nearly twice as many middle-school girls said they would rather be a celebrity's personal assistant than the president of Harvard University.[60]

The role of materialism in our society and the way we identify with consumption are both strongly connected with this sense of self-worth:

> Set-piece social psychology experiments have shown that even a few words that prime people to think of themselves as Consumers, result in more selfish behaviour and attitudes and lower social and ecological motivation levels. Consumer is an inherently narrow, selfish view of the individual. What effect does that have? The best guess is that at the same moment these communications promote a "good" thing to us as Consumers, by the very act of reinforcing that mode of being they're actually undermining the extent to which we feel we have a genuine responsibility to anyone apart from ourselves.[61]

Untrammeled consumption has damaging consequences—environmental, sociological, and psychological. If we see ourselves in society primarily as individuals who exist solely to gain material advantage for ourselves, we are all worse off. Instead, if we are *engaged stakeholders*, we are able to shape the society that we say we seek.

A holistic view of the organization and its interests (only possible with a stakeholder perspective combined with the goal of medium- to long-term viability) dictates that CSR should be central to a firm's strategic planning and implemented throughout operations. A commonsense view of stakeholder interests, however, suggests an equal investment in deciding what behavior is responsible and seeking to encourage more of that behavior by ensuring it is rewarded. In other words, there is a synergistic relationship between a firm and its range

| Figure 5.6 | A Stakeholder's Responsibilities |

Stakeholder		Responsibilities
Organizational	Directors	Exercise vigilance in monitoring executives to make sure the interests of the organization are protected.
	Employees	Be productive and maintain an ethical workplace.
	Executives	Develop and execute strategies that create long-term value for all stakeholders, not just short-term value for shareholders.
Economic	Customers	Purchase products and services that are produced and delivered in ways that reflect their personal values and ethics.
	Competitors	Ensure the marketplace is defined by competition that occurs within local legal and ethical norms.
	Creditors	Lend or invest capital in ways that reinforce the lending organization's best-practice expectations.
	Distributors/Suppliers	Maintain awareness of the business practices of partners throughout the supply chain and ensure they conform to legal, ethical, and best-practice expectations.
	Shareholders	Invest in companies that reflect the investor's personal values and ethics.
	Unions	Represent their members' interests and negotiate in good-faith with management.
Societal	Communities	Be vigilant of local companies and exert pressure on those that fail to conform to local ethical and social norms.
	Educators	Educate beyond traditional concepts of business practice in ways that demonstrate the long-term value of stakeholder management.
	Government agencies	Act impartially and without corruption to enforce the laws and regulations for which they are responsible.
	Media	Conduct investigative journalism to highlight transgressions committed by companies against the best-interests of society.
	Nonprofits/NGOs	Pressure companies to adopt policies and practices that reflect the interests of their members.

of stakeholders, which is reflected in terms of CSR by a joint responsibility to maximize favorable outcomes. Whether those outcomes are tangible or intangible, economic or social, responsibility is shared. CSR is not only a *corporate* responsibility; it is also a *stakeholder* responsibility. The responsibilities of each of a firm's stakeholders are outlined in Figure 5.6.[62]

Strategic CSR Debate

MOTION: A stakeholder's responsibility to hold the firm to account is more important than the firm's responsibility to meet the needs and concerns of that stakeholder.

QUESTIONS FOR DISCUSSION AND REVIEW

1.   Who is *responsible* for CSR—firms or their stakeholders? Why?

2.   List three points in favor of both Friedman's and Handy's view of the firm and its responsibilities? Which position to you agree with? Why?

3. Would you report a classmate you suspected of cheating at school? Why or why not?

4. Think about a recent example of a firm that changed its behavior in response to the demands of a stakeholder. Was this an example of corporate *stakeholder* responsibility?

5. If a firm's stakeholders condone the irresponsible behavior of a firm, should the firm keep acting this way or should it change? Why?

Chapter 6

WHO OWNS
THE CORPORATION?

Who owns the publicly traded, limited liability corporation? Who owns Microsoft? Who owns Walmart? And who owns McDonald's? The question of ownership is central to the CSR debate because, at present, most executives and directors (and, for that matter, most business journalists and business school professors) believe that the shareholders are the owners. Influenced by agency theory, these officers of the firm believe that they have a fiduciary responsibility to operate the firm in the best interests of its shareholders. Moreover, they believe that if they adopt a different focus, they will be failing in their responsibilities and, perhaps equally importantly, are likely to be sued.

But, what if this belief is just that: a *belief* rather than a legal *fact*? If that were true, then the belief could be changed to a different belief—a more accurate interpretation of the law based on actual legislation and legal precedent. If that were to happen, then executives would be freed of the *responsibility* to operate the firm in the narrow interest of its shareholders and, instead, would be able to make decisions in the interests of the firm's wider set of stakeholders. Because the consequences of this question (*Who owns the corporation?*) are so dramatic, it is worth dedicating a chapter of this book to addressing them. The answer might surprise you.[1]

The purpose of this chapter, therefore, is to challenge a claim that the business community takes for granted but that, I believe, does not stand up to rigorous analysis.

HISTORY OF THE CORPORATION

As argued in Part I, for-profit firms are the most effective means we have devised to advance social well-being. And as argued so far in Part II, because firms are part of society and society is constructed of multiple components (including firms), the interests of the firm and society are inextricably interwoven. In other words, business is not a zero-sum exchange but an ongoing, reciprocal relationship between the for-profit firm and its various invested stakeholders. Together, all of these actors form the broader entity that we refer to as *society*. An answer to the fundamental question that we face (*What is the role of the for-profit firm in society?*), therefore, is best achieved when the interests of the firm and its stakeholders are aligned.

This iterative relationship stems from the origins of the corporation and the evolution of this organizational form throughout history. In particular, it relates directly to the introduction of the concept of *limited liability* in the mid-19th century.[2] Prior to this point, corporate charters were granted by the state as a privilege (rather than a right) under strict conditions in terms of the projects that were to be completed (e.g., building a bridge or a railroad) and the length of time the corporation was allowed to exist. Importantly, these projects were determined on the basis of perceived societal need, rather than the ability of the firm to make a profit:

> In the legal environment of the 1800s, the state in the initial formulation of corporate law could revoke the charter of a corporation if it failed to act in the public good, and routinely did so. For instance, banks lost their charters in Mississippi, Ohio, and Pennsylvania for "committing serious violations that were likely to leave them in an insolvent or financially unsound condition." In Massachusetts and New York, charters of turnpike corporations were revoked for "not keeping their roads in repair."[3]

And when the specified project was completed, the corporation ceased to exist. In short, the corporation existed at the pleasure of the state:[4]

> In 1848, Pennsylvania's General Manufacturing Act set a twenty-year limit on manufacturing corporations. As late as 1903, almost half the states limited the duration of corporate charters to between twenty and fifty years. Throughout the nineteenth century, legislatures revoked charters when the corporation wasn't deemed to be fulfilling its responsibilities.[5]

It is because the fundamental legitimacy of the corporation is grounded in these societal origins (i.e., invented to serve society's needs) that, ultimately, *business* is a social exercise. The introduction of limited liability, however, led directly to a shift in the operating principles of the firm. As profit became the primary purpose, rather than the outcome of a socially sanctioned project, the parameters by which the firm's success is measured changed. While this shift initially generated many benefits, its value has waned over time. Specifically, executives today operate under the assumption that the firm's primary obligation is no longer to the state or society, but instead that it has a legal responsibility to operate in the interests of its owners—its shareholders. While this *belief* that shareholders own the firm is widely shared, there is compelling evidence to suggest it is a social construction rather than a legally defined *fact*:[6]

Conceiving of public shareholders as "owners" may in some instances be a helpful metaphor, but it is never an accurate description of their rights under corporate law. Shareholders possess none of the incidents of ownership of a corporation—neither the right of possession, nor the right of control, nor the right of exclusion—and thus "have no more claim to intrinsic ownership and control of the corporation's assets than do other stakeholders."[7]

Understanding the true nature of the relationship between the firm and its investors is therefore necessary to reorient firms to act in the interests of society as a whole. In short, it is essential in order to adopt strategic CSR as the managing philosophy of a firm.

Shareholders

The great value of limited liability is that it enabled corporations to raise the capital that was needed to finance the infrastructure that fueled the Industrial Revolution. In particular, limited liability allowed firms to build the railways, canals, and bridges that were central to economic development in the West during the 19th century (particularly in the UK and United States). As such, at least in its original formulation, the idea of shareholders as a firm's owners had some validity because, while stocks were still traded, the primary purpose of shares was to raise capital and provide a return on that investment from the firm to its investors. Over time, however, the shareholder's role and value to the firm have evolved.

Today, on the surface, the relationship between the firm and its shareholders appears unchanged. Many people believe that the primary function of the stock market is for firms to raise the capital they need to finance their business, and, indeed, when firms initially list their shares, this transfer of funds from investor to entrepreneur occurs. In reality, however, this transaction is only a minor part of the stock market's function, which has evolved primarily into a forum for the subsequent trading of those shares rather than for their initial offering. This shift represents the difference between a trade for which the firm receives money (the initial listing) to one where it receives no money (a subsequent trade between third-party investors). The differences between the primary (IPO) and secondary (stock market) markets for capital are explained in Figure 6.1.

As a firm's shares continue to trade and a track record of performance is established, the share price essentially becomes a vote of confidence in the firm's current management team and its future potential. In other words, when I buy a share in Apple, I almost certainly buy it not from the company but from another investor who is seeking to sell that share. The price on which we agree reflects our respective bets on the future success of the company. I buy at a price that I believe is lower than it will be in the future, while the seller sells at a price they believe is higher than it will be in the future. So, we place our respective bets and the trade is made. This exchange reflects an important shift in the purpose of the stock market and of investors, who buy and sell shares today not because they expect to influence a firm's strategic direction but

Figure 6.1   Primary Versus Secondary Markets for Securities

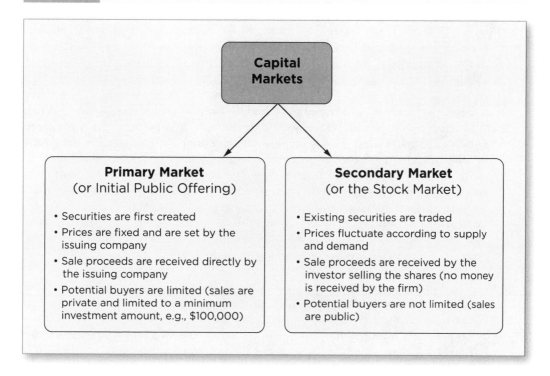

because they hope to profit from the strategic direction that has already been determined by management. Although activist investors occasionally win seats on a board by amassing significant share holdings, these investors are a minority. In reality, most shareholders can only express their opinions about a firm's management by holding, buying, or selling shares.

The consequences of this shift in the underlying relationship between the firm and its shareholders were identified long ago as a central tenet of the agency theory of the firm:[8]

> In the late 19th century industry had a voracious need for capital; it found it by listing shares publicly on exchanges. The problem with this . . . was that over time big successful corporations would come to finance themselves out of retained earnings and have little need for investor-supplied capital. So while the ownership structure provided liquidity for shareholders—they could easily exchange rights for cash—it did not give them the authority tied to conventional ownership, because the company did not need it to maintain their support.[9]

Stock markets are neither efficient (in terms of money flows being dictated by complete and freely available information) nor public (in terms of access being equally and evenly distributed). Stock markets have benefits (in terms of liquidity and providing tools to save for retirement), but it is legitimate to question the overall value they provide. This is especially true today as the majority of trades on any of the major exchanges are made by high-frequency algorithms—computers running programs and holding positions for microseconds.[10]

One characteristic of high-frequency trading, therefore, is the sheer volume of activity. While high-frequency trades can constitute "as much as two-thirds of all trades in American shares,"[11] they "submit almost 99% of the orders."[12] Partly this is because the algorithms are able to handle the associated complexity and can arbitrage value in small increments; partly, though, it is because placing a large number of small orders allows high-frequency traders to discover the intentions of other traders in the market and trade advantageously on that information.[13]

In addition to volume, another characteristic of high-frequency trading is speed. By positioning themselves between buyer and seller, high-frequency traders can generate massive profits on small margins and extremely large volume. Central to this advantage is being the first to market—the value of which is indicated by the extent to which high-frequency traders are willing to invest in order to gain the slightest of edges over the competition:

> [One] group spent $300m to lay a cable in the straightest possible line from Chicago to New York, cutting through mountains and under car parks, just so the time taken to send a signal back and forth could be cut from 17 milliseconds to 13. In return, the group could charge traders $14m a year to use the line. Traders were willing to shell out those fees because those fractions of a second might generate annual profits of $20 billion.[14]

Almost all of these trades are third-party transactions in which the firm receives no capital directly. The overall effect is to drive a wedge between the interests of the shareholder (return on investment) and the managers of the firm (sustainable competitive advantage). As pools of assets are increasingly managed by a concentrated number of massive investment firms, this wedge grows larger. Take BlackRock, for example, the "biggest shareholder in half of the world's 30 largest companies" with managed investments totaling $4.72 trillion, "making it bigger than any bank, insurance company, government fund or rival asset-management firm."[15] Firms such as BlackRock specialize in what are known as "*passive* investment products," such as exchange-traded funds (ETFs), which attempt to mirror (rather than outperform) the performance of the markets while minimizing fees to their clients.[16] The traders who work for firms like BlackRock have little direct interest in the day-to-day management of the firms in which they invest. By definition, traders that seek to mirror market performance invest in proportion to the size of each firm in the market, rather than caring necessarily whether Firm A performs better or worse than Firm B. In other words, these traders care about the overall performance of the market (since that is the benchmark they are trying to mimic), but whether they hold positions in Firm A or Firm B is less important—they simply move assets from one to the other in response to macro movements in the market as a whole.

The combination of high-frequency traders holding positions for microseconds and massive investment funds holding large but passive positions is redefining what it means to be a *shareholder*. In essence, John Maynard Keynes's characterization of financial speculation as "anticipating what average opinion expects the average opinion to be"[17] is truer today than ever before. And, when traders act on behalf of investors, "they're actually in the business of convincing other people that they can anticipate average opinion about average opinion."[18] The cumulative effect is for an individual investor to surrender any claim of *ownership* in favor of managerial control. This trend has been apparent for at least half a century:

> Under modern conditions of large-scale production great power over the lives of people is centered in the relatively few men who preside over our great corporations. Though the stock ownership of these corporations may be diffused, effective ownership in terms of control resides in management.[19]

In response, some concede that, while shareholders do not control the firm, they still own it. But, does ownership not encompass the ability to control? It is very difficult to think of a definition of *ownership* that does not also include aspects of control or authority over the thing that is owned. In the Merriam-Webster online dictionary, for example, *ownership* is defined as "the state, relation, or fact of being an owner," with *own* defined as "to legally possess something," and *possess* defined as "to seize and take control of." Similarly, the *Oxford English Dictionary* defines *ownership* as the "legal right of possession," with *possession* defined as "the action or fact of holding something (material or immaterial) as one's own or in one's control."[20] Clearly, shareholders do not control the firm.

SHAREHOLDERS OWN STOCK

Irrespective of dictionary or intuitive definitions of ownership, what does the law say about the relationship between the firm and its shareholders? Given the extent to which the idea that shareholders are the "legally defined" owners of the firm permeates society, it would follow that such a fact is unambiguously stated in law and demonstrated via legal precedent.[21] In the place of clarity, however, the evidence suggests there is ambiguity:

> This argument [that shareholders own the firm] is based on a misinterpretation of the legal position on the issue of share ownership. . . . Once shareholders subscribe to shares in the corporation, payment made in consideration for the shares is considered property of the corporation, and the shareholders are not free to withdraw the sum invested except for payments through dividends, selling their shares, and other permitted means.[22]

Shareholders own shares. A share is a legal contract between the investor and the firm in the same way that employees, suppliers, and other stakeholders hold legal contracts with the firm. What is becoming increasingly clear is that, while stockholders invest capital in companies (in the same way that employees invest time, effort, and skills), they have no greater claim to ownership of those companies than other stakeholders.[23] And, a growing number of commentators, such as Martin Wolf in the *Financial Times*, believe their claim is significantly less than that of other stakeholders:

> The economic purpose of property ownership is to align rights to control with risk-bearing. The owner of a corner shop should control the business because she is also its chief risk-bearer. Risk, reward and control are aligned. Is it true that the chief risk-bearer in [a publicly traded corporation] is the shareholder? Obviously not. All those who have stakes in the company that they are unable to hedge bear risks. The most obvious such risk-bearers are employees with firm-specific skills. . . . Shareholders, in contrast, can easily hedge their risks by purchasing a diversified portfolio.[24]

Essentially, being a shareholder entitles the owner of that share to a few specific and highly limited rights, such as the *right* to vote at the company's annual general meeting (AGM). In reality, however, the practical application of shareholder democracy is weak and narrow. Although shareholders nominally have the right to vote for directors, nominating candidates is extremely difficult and, once elected, directors can ignore shareholder interests.[25] In one year's worth of director elections, for example, the "Institutional Shareholder Services, a proxy advisory firm, says only 14 out of 14,000 board candidates were rejected by a majority of votes cast in elections."[26] In reality, management's slate of directors is almost always elected. And although shareholders can protest in terms of resolutions at AGMs, "only certain kinds of shareholder votes—such as for mergers or dissolutions—are typically binding. Most are purely advisory."[27] In addition, shareholders have the *right* to receive dividends, but only as long as management is willing to issue them. In essence, the only meaningful right that shareholders appear to have is the *right* to sell their share to a third party at a time of their choosing (although this is also dependent on there being a willing buyer at that time). These actual shareholder rights are summarized (in comparison to the widely held beliefs about those rights) in Figure 6.2.

These *rights* constitute a contractual relationship between the firm and the shareholder, but they do not constitute *ownership*. As noted by Eugene Fama, one of the originators of the agency theory of the firm, "Ownership of capital should not be confused with ownership of the firm."[28]

A Legal Person

One of the great advantages of the LLC (limited liability company) form is that the organization is recognized as an independent entity in the eyes of the law (i.e., as a legal person). As such, the firm, as an artificial person, has many of the rights (although, it seems, fewer of the responsibilities) of a human being, or natural person. It can own assets; it can sue and be sued; it can enter into contracts; and, in the United States, it has the right to freedom of speech (which

Figure 6.2 Shareholder Rights in the United States

Popular Belief	Legal Reality
• A claim on the firm's assets.	• Non-existent while the firm is ongoing; limited in the event of bankruptcy, when all other claims and debts are given priority over shareholders.
• A right to the firm's profits (via a dividend).	• Only as long as the firm is willing to issue them. If the firm chooses to allocate its resources to other stakeholders (e.g., higher pay for employees), shareholders have no right to demand a dividend.
• A right to vote at the Annual General Meeting (AGM).	• In practice, shareholder democracy is weak and narrow. Many votes are non-binding and the ability to nominate directors to the board is limited. Shareholders have the right to abstain.
• A right to sell their share to a third-party at a time of their choosing.	• Yes, but only if there is a willing buyer.

it exercises by spending money). It is these rights (the right to be sued, in particular) that allow the investors in a firm to have their legal liability limited to the extent of their financial investment. In short, the firm is a legal creation that exists, by design, independently of all other actors "and it is the corporation not the individual shareholders, that is liable for its debts."[29]

This concept of the firm as a legal person is established in the subconscious of society in the same way that the idea that firms are owned by their shareholders is established. The difference between the two is that the idea of the corporation as a person is legally defined, while the idea of shareholders as owners is not. In fact, the unique legal status of corporations is constitutionally protected. Following the Civil War, the Fourteenth Amendment was passed to protect the rights of recently freed African American slaves. In particular, it stipulates that the states cannot "deprive any person of life, liberty, or property without due process of law." It is via the Fourteenth Amendment that corporations appropriated those rights for themselves.[30] In other words, the US Supreme Court has agreed with the argument that corporations are legally similar to real people and, as such, enjoy similar constitutionally protected rights. Appropriating the precedent that individuals have a constitutional right to "due process," corporate lawyers argued over decades of case law that corporations, as legal individuals, have that same right. The fact that the root of this legal status lies in the Fourteenth Amendment, which was passed to prevent the ownership of individuals by others, reinforces the idea that the corporation is an independent legal entity.[31]

As *The Economist* puts it, "the shareholder-value model has conceptual as well as practical problems. Its proponents argue that companies are owned by shareholders, when in fact they are 'legal persons' that own themselves."[32]

Business Judgment Rule

A similar legal foundation for the idea that shareholders own the firm does not exist, in spite of the popular perception that it is true. In other words, as even supporters of the notion of shareholder primacy note, "shareholder wealth maximization is widely accepted at the level of rhetoric but largely ignored as a matter of policy implementation."[33] The reason for this is that, even if it was an ideal, "the rule of wealth maximization for shareholders is virtually impossible to enforce as a practical matter."[34] As a direct result, under US corporate law, courts are reluctant to intervene in the business decisions of a firm unless there is evidence of fraud, misappropriation of funds, or some other illegal activity. The law is clear that corporations are managed by the board of directors, who have "broad latitude to run companies as they see fit":[35]

> The principle that a company's directors should have a free hand to manage its affairs can be traced at least as far back as an 1880 New Hampshire Supreme Court decision. In *Charlestown Boot & Shoe Co. vs. Dunsmore*, directors won a ruling that shareholders couldn't second guess their decisions, including one to skip insurance on a plant that later burned down. The principle has been adopted by many states, including Delaware, where many large companies are organized.[36]

This *business judgment rule* is similar to common law in the United Kingdom, which refers to the board and senior executives as the "controlling mind and will" of the company. This finding can be traced back to a 1957 Court of Appeal decision by Lord Denning, in which the judge made a distinction between the hands and brains of a company:

> A company [is like] the human body. It has a brain and nerve centre which controls what it does. It also has hands which hold the tools and act in accordance with directions from the centre. Some of the people in the company are mere servants and agents who are nothing more than hands to do the work. . . . Others are directors and managers who represent the directing mind and will of the company and control what it does. The state of mind of those managers is the state of mind of the company.[37]

As noted above, in theory shareholders have a claim to the future earned profits of the firm.[38] In reality, that claim is weak, with no right to demand the firm issue dividends or buy back shares if it does not wish to do so. Even in one of the most famous corporate law cases, in which the Dodge brothers sued Henry Ford to increase the proportion of profits that were distributed to shareholders in the form of dividends,[39] the Michigan Supreme Court was reluctant to interfere:

> It is recognized that plans must often be made for a long future, for expected competition, for a continuing as well as an immediately profitable venture. . . . We are not satisfied that the alleged motives of the directors, in so far as they are reflected in the conduct of the business, menace the interests of shareholders.[40]

In essence, the reason limited liability is so important (because it enables investors to limit their risk while allowing firms to raise capital from multiple sources) also explains why the shareholder is legally impotent in terms of ownership:[41]

Corporations are universally treated by the legal system as "legal persons" that exist separately and independently of their directors, officers, shareholders, or other human persons with whom the legal entity interacts. . . .

Shareholders do not own corporations; nor do they own the assets of corporations.[42]

As John Kay from the *Financial Times* wrote in a column titled "Shareholders think they own the company—they are wrong," in the UK there is a clear duty of a director

to promote the success of the company for the benefit of the members. The company comes first, the benefit to the members follows from its success. And English shareholders are definitely not owners. The Court of Appeal declared in 1948 that "shareholders are not, in the eyes of the law, part owners of the company." In 2003, the House of Lords reaffirmed that ruling, in unequivocal terms.[43]

Beyond legal precedent, however, in practical terms, it does not make sense that we would think of shareholders as owners:

If I own an object I can use it, or not use it, sell it, rent it, give it to others, throw it away and appeal to the police if a thief misappropriates it. And I must accept responsibility for its misuse and admit the right of my creditors to take a lien on it. But shares give their holders no right of possession and no right of use. . . . They have no more right than other customers to the services of the business they "own." The company's actions are not their responsibility, and corporate assets cannot be used to satisfy their debts. Shareholders do not have the right to manage the company in which they hold an interest, and even their right to appoint the people who do is largely theoretical. They are entitled only to such part of the income as the directors declare as dividends, and have no right to the proceeds of the sale of corporate assets—except in the event of the liquidation of the entire company, in which case they will get what is left; not much, as a rule.[44]

Contrary to popular myth, as well as widespread belief among executives and directors,[45] therefore, shareholders do not *own* the corporation.[46] Instead, they *own* a type of security (a legal contract) that is commonly referred to as *stock*. The rights associated with this stock are highly limited; in reality, the value of a share lies largely in its resale price, achieved via a transaction on a stock exchange based on third-party perceptions of the firm's future performance potential. As acknowledged, even by shareholder advocates, "today, . . . there seems to be substantial agreement among legal scholars and others in the academy that shareholders do not own corporations."[47]

FIDUCIARY DUTIES

This challenge to the idea of shareholders as the legal owners of the firm is gradually being recognized. Perhaps more importantly, however, there is weak legal precedent, in the United States or elsewhere,[48] for the idea that managers and directors have a fiduciary responsibility to place shareholder interests over the interests of other stakeholders:[49]

> Contrary to widespread belief, corporate directors generally are not under a legal obligation to maximise profits for their shareholders. This is reflected in the acceptance in nearly all jurisdictions of some version of the business judgment rule, under which disinterested and informed directors have the discretion to act in what they believe to be in the best long term interests of the company as a separate entity, even if this does not entail seeking to maximise short-term shareholder value. Where directors pursue the latter goal, it is usually a product not of legal obligation, but of the pressures imposed on them by financial markets, activist shareholders, the threat of a hostile takeover and/or stock-based compensation schemes.[50]

As discussed above, this core concept within corporate law of deference to directors concerning operational decisions (the *business judgment rule*) is embedded firmly in the United States, as well as other countries, such as the UK:

> Courts in the United States have on several occasions clearly stated that directors are not agents of the shareholders but fiduciaries of the corporation. Section 172 of the U.K. Companies Act 2006, moreover, requires directors to act in the way they consider, in good faith, would be most likely to promote the long-term success of the company for the benefits of its members as a whole, heeding the likely consequences of their decisions on stakeholders such as customers, suppliers, and community, not simply shareholders. The Law even allows the board to put the interests of other stakeholders over and above those of shareholders.[51]

If all of this is true, where did the idea that shareholders do own the firm and that managers and directors have a legal obligation to operate it in shareholders' interests come from?

Dodge v. Ford

The legal foundation for the belief in the primacy of shareholder interests rests largely on a single case decided in 1919 by the Michigan Supreme Court—*Dodge v. Ford Motor Co.*[52]

In the case, two brothers, John Francis Dodge and Horace Elgin Dodge (who, together, owned 10% of Ford's shares), sued Henry Ford because of his decision to distribute surplus profit to customers in the form of lower prices for his cars, rather than to shareholders in the form of a dividend. As noted above, however, the value of this case as legal precedent for the idea that the firm must operate in the interests of its shareholders is disputed. As Lynn Stout explains in her detailed analysis, contrary to widespread perceptions, this case constitutes no legal precedent for the idea that managers or directors have a duty to manage the organization in the interests of its shareholders:

> *Dodge v. Ford* is . . . bad law, at least when cited for the proposition that the corporate purpose is, or should be, maximizing shareholder wealth. *Dodge v. Ford* is a mistake, . . . a doctrinal oddity largely irrelevant to corporate law and corporate practice. What is more, courts and legislatures alike treat it as irrelevant. In the past thirty years, the Delaware courts have cited *Dodge v. Ford* as authority in only one unpublished case, and then not on the subject of corporate purpose, but on another legal question entirely.[53]

More specifically, Stout's empirical analysis of historical case law provides compelling evidence to support her arguments. Not only was the case decided by the Michigan Supreme Court and essentially ignored in Delaware (where the most important points of US corporate law are established), but the legal precedent it represents is more properly understood as a question of the relative responsibilities of majority shareholders (in this case, Ford) toward minority shareholders (in this case, the Dodge brothers).[54] As a result, Stout argues that "we should stop teaching *Dodge v. Ford*"[55] in our universities and business schools as support for a perceived obligation that is neither legally required nor operationally necessary:

> U.S. corporate law does not, and never has, required directors of public corporations to maximize either share price or shareholder wealth. To the contrary, as long as boards do not use their power to enrich themselves, the law gives them a wide range of discretion to run public corporations with other goals in mind, including growing the firm, creating quality products, protecting employees, and serving the public interest.[56]

Even among those who argue that *Dodge v. Ford* is a more meaningful statement of legal precedent,[57] there is a recognition of the absence of support for a relationship that most people assume is *legally defined* and, as such, compels a fiduciary responsibility:

> The goal of profit maximization is to corporate law what observations about the weather are in ordinary conversation. Everybody talks about it, including judges, but with the lone exception of *Dodge v. Ford*, nobody actually does anything about it.[58]

There is even precedent to suggest that courts will favor the firm's directors over shareholders when the investors were deceived, basing investment decisions on the firm's publicly stated goals, even if those statements later turn out to be false.[59] A lack of competence or an honest mistake is not sufficient to override the courts' reluctance to interfere with the running of the firm. Unless it can be proved that the directors acted dishonestly or with the intention to deceive, the business will be allowed to rise or fall on the basis of its managerial decisions. Although this issue has been studied and debated by corporate legal scholars, however, it is less well-known in business schools. This is important and should change:

> Oddly, no previous management research has looked at what the legal literature says about [shareholder control of the firm], so we conducted a systematic analysis of a century's worth of legal theory and precedent. It turns out that the law provides a surprisingly clear answer: Shareholders do not own the corporation, which is an autonomous legal person. What's more, when directors go against shareholder wishes—even when a loss in value is documented—courts side with directors the vast majority of the time. Shareholders seem to get this. They've tried to unseat directors through lawsuits just 24 times in large corporations over the past 20 years; they've succeeded only eight times. In short, directors are to a great extent autonomous.[60]

In short, therefore, the history of the corporation, together with existing legislation and legal precedent suggest strongly that *shareholders do not own the firm*. In reality, no single group *owns* a large, publicly traded corporation and, as a result, managers and directors do not have a fiduciary responsibility to manage the firm primarily in the interests of shareholders. Legally, the corporation is an independent entity (a legal person) with contractual interests. Philosophically, it is the collective effort of the actions and interests of multiple parties, all of whom have a stake in the value creation process. An important step managers can take to reinforce this reality is to resist pressures for short-term performance and, instead, make decisions that are in the medium- to long-term interests of all the firm's stakeholders.

SHAREHOLDERS VERSUS STAKEHOLDERS

Contrary to popular myth, therefore, shareholders do not own the firm and directors do not have a fiduciary responsibility to act primarily in their interests. This is both a descriptive statement of US corporate law and a normative statement of ideal corporate strategy. The counterproductive results of operating the firm disproportionately in the interests of its shareholders are increasingly being recognized by the CEOs of some of the largest companies.

CEOs on Shareholders

"If you want me to do things only for ROI reasons, you should get out of this stock."[61]

Tim Cook, Apple CEO, March 2014

"Unilever has been around for 100-plus years. We want to be around for several hundred more years. So if you buy into this long-term value-creation model, which is equitable, which is shared, which is sustainable, then come and invest with us. If you don't buy into this, I respect you as a human being, but don't put your money in our company."[62]

Paul Polman, Unilever CEO, November 2010

"On the face of it, shareholder value is the dumbest idea in the world. . . . Your main constituencies are your employees, your customers and your products."[63]

"Shareholder value is an outcome—not a strategy."[64]

Jack Welch, former CEO of General Electric, March 2009

Instead, this textbook argues for a return to the understanding that the driving purpose of a firm is to meet the needs of society, broadly defined. Central to this argument is the idea that firms should seek to create value over the medium to long term for all of their stakeholders, avoiding the recent trend of focusing disproportionately on short-term returns to shareholders. The reason such a narrow focus is counterproductive is that it privileges the interests of a minority (shareholders) over the majority (everyone else)[65] in ways that often do not even benefit the organization.

Pressures from shareholders to maximize results in the short term can be expressed internally within the firm in many ways,[66] "including lower expenditures on research and development, an excessive focus on acquisitions rather than organic growth, underinvestment in long-term projects, and the adoption of executive remuneration structures that reward short rather than long-term performance."[67] The counterproductive effects of running the firm in the best interests of shareholders are apparent from the recent spike in share buybacks that have occurred in the United States, which are "done at the expense of investing in 'innovation, skilled work forces or essential capital expenditures necessary to sustain long-term growth'" (according to the CEO of BlackRock).[68] As such, share buybacks create "the sense that executives are more interested in short-term share-price performance than in the company's long-term health."[69]

The overall effect is to skew the firm's priorities in all aspects of decision making. Why invest for the long term, for example, when doing so will diminish the chance of achieving the more immediate priority—short-term profits? Cutting long-term costs, such as R&D or safety and preventative measures, has the desired effect of increasing profits, which is then reflected in a higher share price.[70] While this immediate accounting profit pleases those investors who have a short-term outlook, such actions constrain the firm's medium- to long-term operations.

In order to manage the firm based on a more sustainable business model, one of the most important changes managers must make is to adopt a broader stakeholder perspective. The difference from the CEO's perspective centers on whether the goal is to maximize performance in the short term (the average tenure for a Fortune 500 CEO is about 5 years)[71] or to preserve the organization for the foreseeable future (10, 15, 20 or more years from now). The focus should be on what Gus Levy, former senior partner of Goldman Sachs, characterized as being "long-term greedy"[72]—the willingness to privilege long-term value over short-term profits.

To achieve this, an important step is for firms to adopt policies that better align executive remuneration with long-term performance drivers (including CSR and sustainability-related metrics).[73] In addition, firms can deemphasize short-term results by refusing to issue quarterly earnings reports to shareholders: "Over three quarters of companies still issue such [earnings] guidance."[74] Above and beyond specific policy solutions, however, the key is to deconstruct the idea that there is a legal compulsion to operate the firm in the interests of its shareholders. Once this is achieved, the justification for favoring them over other stakeholders is removed (and, with it, the cause of much of the short-term focus of our economic system):

> As a theoretical matter, the issue of ownership is necessary to a proper understanding of the nature of the corporation and corporate law. As a practical matter, it is an important consideration in the allocation of rights in the corporation: if shareholders are owners, then the balance of rights will tip more heavily in their favor, and against others, than if they are not. . . . Because the issue of ownership has the potential to shape all of corporate law and direct the very purpose of corporations, it is of utmost importance.[75]

The value to the firm in understanding this (removing a short-term focus on shareholder interests and, instead, seeking constructive, trust-based relations with all stakeholders) is that it immediately alters the nature of the decision-making process. If, as a CEO, I see interactions with my stakeholders as one-off exchanges (i.e., a short-term perspective), for example, I am likely to prioritize my own interests during negotiations. If I perceive all my interactions as repeat transactions (i.e., I want to build long-lasting relationships), however, then I am more likely to also care about my partners' interests because, if my partners do not value the exchange, it is less likely that they will do business with me again in the future.[76]

In other words, the key focus for debate is temporal. Attempts to maximize profits over the *short term* lead to all the problems that are evident with a narrow focus on shareholder value. If a firm seeks to optimize value over the *long term*, however, many of those problems dissolve, and the process of building meaningful, lasting relations with all stakeholders becomes central to the mission. Firms like Unilever, which stopped issuing quarterly earnings guidance in 2009,[77] understand this and encourage long-term thinking across all aspects of operations.[78] Amazon is another firm that is altering our understanding of what constitutes a return on investment:

> Amazon seems to have put the "long term" back into Anglo-Saxon capitalism. At a time when Wall Street is obsessed by quarterly results and share buybacks, Amazon has made it clear to shareholders that, given a choice between making a profit and investing in new areas, it will always choose the latter.[79]

It is fundamental to the idea of strategic CSR that, by seeking to meet the needs of as broad an array of stakeholders as possible, a firm holds a competitive advantage in creating value over the medium to long term. Central to achieving this, however, is understanding the true nature of the relationship between the firm and its shareholders and removing the misplaced and inaccurate belief that executives and directors have a legal obligation to make decisions in the interests of shareholders, who are only one of the firm's many stakeholders.[80]

Once managers understand they are free of this mythical obligation, they can take a more expansive (and, in terms of the health of the organization, more sustainable) approach to building relations with a much broader range of stakeholders.[81]

Strategic CSR Debate

MOTION: The shareholders are the firm's most important stakeholder group.

QUESTIONS FOR DISCUSSION AND REVIEW

1.   Who owns the publicly traded, limited liability corporation?

2.   Why was the concept of limited liability introduced? What are its main advantages? Does it have any disadvantages?

3.   When you own a share, what are the main rights that accompany that legal contract with the firm?

4.   Why is it important for advocates of CSR that the belief that shareholders own the firm is undermined?

5.   If the idea that shareholders do not own the publicly traded corporation became widely accepted, what consequences do you think this would have for the stock market? Would this be a good thing or a bad thing?

Part II Case Study

IMPACT INVESTING

This case highlights the rise in impact investing in recent years.[1] It is a growing, if controversial, area within CSR to which firms will face increasing pressure to respond. The exact nature of this response will depend on the extent to which activist investors are willing to discriminate among companies in order to pursue socially responsible investing strategies.

At the end of 2014, $60 billion was committed to impact investments worldwide, up 25% from year-end 2013, a study by JPMorgan and the Global Impact Investing Network finds. It predicts 16% growth in 2015. Geographically, the most impact money is invested in North America and Sub-Saharan Africa; everything from an Uber-like app for auto rickshaws in India to early childhood education in Utah has attracted impact dollars.[2]

While, from a CSR perspective, social activists have typically been considered the more relevant group of activist investors, as risk management becomes a more mainstream area of concern for firms and socially responsible mutual funds grow in number and size, the distinction between the two groups has blurred. On specific issues, both groups can easily find themselves seeking the same change in firm behavior. It is easy to imagine a scenario, for example, where these two groups see overlapping interests in demands for greater transparency and accountability (on issues such as corporate governance, executive pay, or even greenhouse gas emissions). Increasingly, shareholders in both groups are seeking to support behavior that protects their investment and is consistent with their values, and they are becoming more vocal in their criticism of executives who make decisions that do not meet these expectations.[3]

A good example of this increased activity is the volume and subject of shareholder resolutions that are being tabled at firms' annual general meetings (AGMs):

[In 2015] shareholder advocacy organization As You Sow released its 10th annual *Proxy Preview* report, detailing the record-breaking 433 social and environmental shareholder resolutions filed so far this proxy season, with political spending and climate change driving most of the activity.[4]

Not only is the number of filed resolutions increasing, however, but so is the amount of shareholder support each resolution is receiving. It is a trend that is prevalent across a broad range of issues and is becoming harder and harder for firms to dismiss:

> Investor support for environmental and social resolutions had been growing steadily over the past decade, from an average of 9 percent in 2001 to 18 percent in 2010. [In 2011] 82 resolutions were supported by votes of 20 per cent or more. "[Companies] cannot ignore it if a quarter or a third of their shareholders are asking for something."[7]

As this engagement continues to gather strength ("In 2014 73% of so-called proxy votes were won by dissidents"),[8] it signals what the *Financial Times* refers to as "the trend towards investor activism amid a crisis of confidence in corporate America."[9] That crisis is driven by many factors, not least of which is the desire to increase returns, but it also appears to be more than purely a financial phenomenon. More and more investors today "are no longer content merely to make money, but want to ensure they are doing so responsibly:"[10]

> While proxy season has long been the domain of labor unions and activist investors with large personalities and forceful demands, increasingly it is mutual funds and other more tempered institutional shareholders who are criticizing lavish pay packages and questioning corporate governance. Emboldened by new regulations—and angered by laggard stock performance and recent scandals—this new crop of activists is voting down company policies and backing proposals to reform corporate boards.[11]

The SEC stipulates a threshold of only 3% of shareholder votes at an annual general meeting for a proposition to be deemed to have sufficient support for it to be resubmitted the following year. This threshold rises to 6% for the proposal to be carried over for a second year, and 10% for a third year.[12] The reason this threshold is low is the dispersed nature of shares (with any one shareholder unlikely to hold a significant stake in the enterprise) and the

Activist Investors

In general, there are two types of *activist investors*:

- *Professional activists*—Institutional investors who manage large blocks of a firm's shares (such as hedge, pension, or mutual funds) and who are driven largely by concerns of maximizing shareholder price. A good example of an institutional investor is Carl Icahn, whose battles with the management of firms such as Netflix and, more recently, Apple routinely make front-page news.[5]
- *Social activists*—NGOs, other socially concerned groups, and individual investors who usually hold smaller blocks of a firm's shares but attempt to influence firm action on specific issues that reflect social values that are important to them and their members. Examples of such groups include teachers' and college professors' pension fund TIAA-CREF (http://www.tiaa-cref.org/) and the Interfaith Center on Corporate Responsibility (http://www.iccr.org/) but also include groups such as Investors Against Genocide (http://www.investorsagainstgenocide.org/).[6]

historical reluctance of institutional investors (who hold more than 50% of all listed corporate stock in the United States and about 60% in the largest 1,000 corporations) to vote for change:

> In most cases, an investor with 3% ownership in a company would be one of the top shareholders and thus even single digit votes may gain considerable attention from a company. Social proposal votes more than 10% are difficult to ignore and often result in some action by the company to address the shareholders' area of concern. Votes that receive 20–30% or more have garnered strong support from mainstream institutional investors and send a clear cut signal to management. Only the least responsive of companies is willing to ignore one out of every three or four of its shareholders.[13]

As individual shareholders become increasingly strident in protesting failed executive performance, institutional investors are taking more of an interest in protecting their holdings. Resolutions that seek directly to challenge board recommendations are increasingly common. And, as pressure continues on institutional investors to ensure that corporate governance minimizes risk and reflects societal values, the number of votes approaching 50% will increase.[14]

In response, firms are increasingly realizing that reaching out to concerned shareholders (one of the firm's most important stakeholders) represents the path of least resistance regarding sensitive issues. Moreover, such action may help businesses interact with multiple stakeholder groups as managers begin to understand issues of concern. One way in which investors can hold management to account is by investing in tailored funds that reflect the interests they value—socially responsible investments (SRI).

SOCIALLY RESPONSIBLE INVESTING

To what extent are investors supporting companies deemed to be operating in an ethical and socially responsible manner by investing in SRI funds?

> An investment is considered socially responsible because of the nature of the business the company conducts. Common themes for socially responsible investments include avoiding investment in companies that produce or sell addictive substances (like alcohol, gambling and tobacco) and seeking out companies engaged in environmental sustainability and alternative energy/clean technology efforts. Socially responsible investments can be made in individual companies or through a socially conscious mutual fund or exchange-traded fund (ETF).[15]

A debate that speaks to the potential for SRI funds to influence firm behavior is whether such funds offer returns that are any better than those of regular investment funds. If SRI funds' returns are better, it would suggest a connection between

CSR and superior firm performance, which should encourage a virtuous circle of investor support and firm responses:

> Nearly two-thirds of 160 socially responsible mutual funds offered by member companies of the Social Investment Forum outperformed their benchmark indexes and beat the Standard & Poor's 500-stock index in 2009 by significant margins.[16]

Critics challenge this connection, however, claiming that SRI funds are ineffective and that ethical or virtuous stocks do not outperform either regular mutual funds or so-called "sin stocks":

> U.S. stock SRI funds have returned 4.24% [in 2015], compared with 4.31% for the S&P 500, according to data from investment research firm Morningstar. Over the past decade, the SRI funds have returned 7.38% compared with 7.88% for the S&P 500.[17]

Socially responsible investing is not a new idea, but it is becoming increasingly common as societal pressures on firms for more socially responsible behavior grow and investors apply these same values to their financial portfolio. While the mutual fund industry began offering SRI products in the 1970s,[18] today it is estimated that there are 456 environmental, social, and corporate governance (ESG) mutual funds in the United States, with collective assets at $1.93 trillion:[19]

> From 2012 to 2014, sustainable, responsible and impact investing enjoyed a growth rate of more than 76 percent, increasing from $3.74 trillion in 2012. More than one out of every six dollars under professional management in the United States today—18% of the $36.8 trillion in total assets under management . . . —is involved in SRI.[20]

Figure II.1 indicates that the number of ESG funds in the United States "has grown by nearly 1,600% from just 55 in 1995 to 925 in 2014," while total assets invested have "increased by nearly 36,000% from $12 billion in 1995 to $4,306 billion" over the same period.[21]

Outside the United States, the SRI industry is also growing. In the UK, SRI has both a long history (which "can be traced back to two Quakers who started the Friends Provident Institution on a mutual basis in 1834") and strong growth ("The UK is Europe's largest [SRI] market with at least £1.4 trillion worth of assets under management").[22] More broadly, SRI is spreading into Europe[23] and Asia,[24] and, worldwide, "assets under management incorporating sustainability investment strategies reached $21.1 trillion globally as of the beginning of 2014, up 61% from the onset of 2012, . . . [accounting] for 30.2% of all assets under management."[25]

One of the underlying drivers of this growth is the professionalization of the SRI industry, which, in turn, is driven by two factors. First, is the publication in 2015 of the United Nations' Principles for Responsible Investment (UNPRI, http://www.unpri.org/).

| Figure II.1 | Growth of ESG Funds in the United States (1995–2014) |

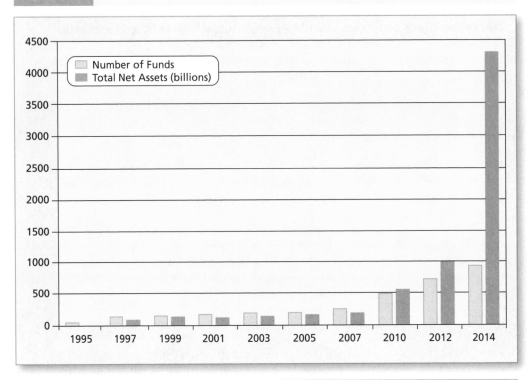

Source: The Forum for Sustainable and Responsible Investment, quoted in Kevin Mahn, "Modern Sustainable Responsible Impact Investing Versus Traditional Socially Responsible Investing," *Forbes*, April 16, 2015, http://www.forbes.com/sites/advisor/2015/04/16/modern-sustainable-responsible-impact-investing-versus-traditional-socially-responsible-investing/.

The United Nations' Principles for Responsible Investment

The UNPRI were developed in order to solidify and guide the rapidly emerging field of responsible investing. The UNPRI consist of six principles that "better align investors with broader objectives of society" and that signatories pledge to uphold:

- **Principle 1:** We will incorporate ESG issues into investment analysis and decision-making processes.
- **Principle 2:** We will be active owners and incorporate ESG issues into our ownership policies and practices.
- **Principle 3:** We will seek appropriate disclosure on ESG issues by the entities in which we invest.
- **Principle 4:** We will promote acceptance and implementation of the Principles within the investment industry.
- **Principle 5:** We will work together to enhance our effectiveness in implementing the Principles.
- **Principle 6:** We will each report on our activities and progress towards implementing the Principles.

As of early 2016, the UNPRI website (http://www.unpri.org/) reports 1,446 signatories (asset owners, investment managers, and service providers) who, together, manage $59 trillion.

The second factor driving the professionalization of the industry is a commitment to a market return on investment. Increasingly, fund managers

> "go out of their way to make clear that they are no longer willing to sacrifice returns for social considerations." . . . A requirement that an investment yield a "market rate of return" is a feature of nearly every definition of social investing.[26]

While the publication of the UNPRI is a welcome step for the industry, however, the danger of committing to performance that mimics the broader market is that it forces a relaxation in terms of which companies are included. In other words, it is difficult to have it both ways—either the makeup of firms in SRI funds is distinctive (and therefore, by definition, will have returns that are different from those of the market) or the makeup of companies mirrors the overall market (with a correspondingly similar rate of return). The more the SRI industry claims to match the broader market's performance, therefore, the greater the suspicion that the filters being used are not sufficient to generate the socially optimal outcomes that SRI investors are seeking.

While there is much debate over the performance of funds that employ some kind of SRI filter, objective research suggests that, at the very least, while there may not be a significantly advantageous return from such funds, there is no disadvantage and, "in the long run, there's no statistical difference in performance between SRI and non-SRI funds."[27] Other commentators, however, argue that the level of return is not the issue. What is more misleading is the idea that investing in an SRI fund advances the causes in which the investors believe:

> Socially responsible investing oversimplifies the world, and in doing so distorts reality. It allows investors to believe that their money is only being invested in "good companies," and they take foolish comfort in that belief. Rare is the company, after all, that is either all good or all bad. To put it another way, socially responsible investing creates the illusion that the world is black and white, when its real color is gray.[28]

A common theme underpinning these issues is that definitions of *socially responsible investing* vary considerably across funds. In the same way that CSR is criticized for not developing a unified definition, SRI can mean whatever someone wants it to mean:

> The absence of a standard definition . . . has been cited as a reason for the proliferation of funds and other vehicles that are labelled as socially responsible but which employ a wide variety of investment strategies.[29]

In response, funds are beginning to develop more sophisticated vehicles for investors to invest according to their values. Rather than blunt filters, funds are being created that target specific goals, and in ways other than just investing in stocks (e.g., they provide loans or seed capital to startups or fund public policy initiatives). This latest evolution ensures a more direct link between the investor's values and the available investment options.

Another recent innovation has been to move beyond *investing* in funds that reflect specific values to start *divesting* the stocks of specific companies that do not reflect SRI values. The campaign to divest fossil fuel stocks (which is organized by groups such as 350.org, the Responsible Endowment Coalition, and the Natural Resources Defense Council) is the most well-known of such efforts.[30] While the stated goal of such campaigns is "the idea that socially responsible groups should not profit from companies that directly exacerbate global warming,"[31] it is difficult to know how anyone could invest in any stock without somehow indirectly supporting fossil fuel energy, without which no company could operate.

VALUES-BASED FUNDS

Values-based investing, which in its broadest definition includes investments that align with religious faiths and beliefs, has existed since the 1500s. In its modern form, it was introduced by The Pioneer Fund, set up "to avoid companies involved in gambling, tobacco and alcohol."[32] Values-based funds can take many forms but are advertised as a more focused form of impact investing than SRI. While there is still considerable debate about the performance of these funds, what is clear is that they are becoming increasingly popular with investors seeking more innovative investing opportunities that meet their social objectives:

> In its 2012 review, the Global Sustainable Investment Alliance estimated the size of the [values-based] investing markets at $13.6 trillion globally, which represents more than 20% of assets under management in the regions surveyed.[33]

Large amounts of money equals competition among firms seeking to attract that money. The result is a wide range of different investment opportunities, such as "green bonds," tailored to individual investors' financial goals, as well as their personal values and beliefs. Although demand has not matched the most optimistic projections, these bonds, which are designed to finance environmentally beneficial projects (such as renewable energy) and are "mostly issued by the World Bank and other multilateral lenders,"[34] still involve large sums of money:

> The Climate Bonds Initiative . . . forecast $100 billion in new green bonds in 2015 after sales roughly tripled [in 2014]. But green bond sales are about in line with [2014] pace, with $18.3 billion sold [by June], compared with $20 billion in the first half of [2014]. About $37 billion of green bonds were sold [in 2014] in total.[35]

Another environment-related investment screen is water conservation.[36] There is evidence to suggest investors are willing to accept a lower yield on such investments in order to ensure they are investing in line with their values.[37]

Gender-lens investing is also a dynamic area of values-based investing. Here, tools are emerging that provide three broad options for investors seeking to support female entrepreneurs and women in work: "They can make money available to enterprises owned by women, focus on employment for women or invest in companies that provide products and services that help women."[38] A typical fund is Barclays' Women in Leadership Total Return Index, which is "made up of U.S. companies with a female chief executive or at least a 25% female board." According to research that supports the foundation of such tailored funds, "from 2004 to 2008, Fortune 500 firms with three or more female directors had an 84% better return on sales and a 46% better return on equity."[39] Research by MSCI reveals similar results:

Companies with more women on their boards have delivered a 36 per cent better return on equity since 2010 than those groups lacking board diversity.[40]

Another example of values-based investments is faith-based funds, such as the Stoxx Europe Christian Index, which was launched in the aftermath of the 2007–2008 financial crisis.[41] Today, this faith-based segment of values-based investing has broadened into a sector labeled "biblically responsible investing" (BRI), a term that is defined by the Christian Investment Forum:

BRI is an investment decision making process that applies Christian values to issues facing shareholders and stakeholders regarding moral and social principles. This coupled with traditional financial analysis provides a platform for investment decisions that allows us to be faithful stewards of God's gifts and respect the foundational beliefs of our shared Christian faith.[42]

Along with other values-based funds, BRI has enjoyed rapid growth in recent years:

15 years ago there were no more than 5 mutual funds that described themselves as BRI focused. Today, there are at least 100 different mutual funds across 28 . . . categories that explicitly incorporate Christian faith values as one part of their investment process.[43]

It is worth noting that these funds (whether utilizing an environmental, gender, or faith-based lens) come with two caveats. The first is the need to put their performance in the correct context. Some commentators, for example, have noted that "female leaders are often appointed in times of poor company performance, so their posts may be precarious."[44] If such a firm performs badly in the future, it may have nothing to do with the female CEO and everything to do with the poorly performing firm she inherited.[45] Second, there is still considerable debate about the value of mutual funds with higher-than-average management fees, such as SRI, ESG, or values-based funds. If we can agree that such funds "typically produce performance that's on par with the market; typically not better, but not worse,"[46] then higher management fees could result in an inferior overall return to the investor.

Reasons to Invest

There are three kinds of benefits that investors can receive from their investments and that, as a result, motivate their decisions (either consciously or subconsciously):[47]

- *Utilitarian benefits*—The ability of the investment to provide a return (e.g., does an SRI fund generate larger or smaller returns than a sin fund).
- *Expressive benefits*—The ability of the investment to convey an image of the investor to others (e.g., a Toyota Prius demonstrates concern for the environment).
- *Emotional benefits*—The ability of the investment to affect the investor's feelings (e.g., SRI allows us to feel good about ourselves).

In reaction to the growth of SRI and ESG funds and the doubt that they make a difference, some analysts have begun a backlash against values-based investing. One manifestation of this is the emergence of *sin funds* (which invest in companies normally excluded by funds with ethical filters) that aim to provide superior returns to investors. A prime example of this type of anti-values-based investing is USA Mutuals' Vice Fund (ticker VICEX, now called the Barrier Fund, http://www.usamutuals.com/products/), which first went on sale to the public in 2002 and today advertises itself as a "socially irresponsible fund"[48] that invests in "industries with significant barriers to entry, including the tobacco, alcoholic beverage, gaming and defense/aerospace."[49] More recently, Freedom Capital (http://freedomcapitalfunds.com/) has spearheaded what has become known as

> antisocial investing[,] . . . backing industries such as fossil fuels and armaments, hoping to counterbalance the rising influence of socially responsible funds that swear off those sectors for environmental or ethical reasons.[50]

Anecdotal evidence suggests that there is reason to invest in sin stocks. Partly the better returns are because these industries tend to be mature and do not have large costs associated with growth, but returns may also be better because many of these products satisfy basic human needs ("When the going gets tough, the tough go eating, smoking and drinking"[51]) that will always be in demand:

> A dollar invested in US tobacco companies in 1900, with dividends prudently reinvested, would have turned into $6.28m [today]. . . . [Similarly] brewers and distillers were the best-performing British shares of the past 115 years, turning £1 into £243,152, including dividends.[52]

The fact that shares of these companies have outperformed those of their more virtuous competitors suggests that "the wages of sin is exorbitant profit. . . . Over the very long term . . . nothing beats tobacco and alcohol stocks." As a result, the Vice/Barrier Fund has grown into a serious attempt to rival the reach and impact of values-based funds. According to USA Mutuals, since its inception, VICEX has outperformed the S&P 500 Index, generating $33,472 from a $10,000 investment compared to $29,189 for the same amount invested in the S&P.[53]

SOCIAL IMPACT BONDS

Beyond the ability of values-based investing to affect corporations (by encouraging more socially responsible behavior), the advent of social impact bonds (SIBs) demonstrates the ability of values-based investing to influence public policy:

> Pioneered by Social Finance U.K. in 2010, [an SIB] draws on private investment capital to fund prevention and early intervention programs that, if successful, reduce the need for expensive crisis-driven services. The SIB structure enables the government (or other payers) to shift program risk to private investors who finance the service delivery upfront, with ultimate payment to the investors based on the achievement of predefined outcomes. If the outcomes are not achieved, the government is not required to repay investors.[54]

In short, "private investors—typically foundations—pay the costs of a new program in its early years, and the government later repays the investors, often with a bonus, as long as the program meets its goals. If it fails, taxpayers pay nothing."[55] SIBs are exciting because they channel the consequences of impact investing more directly toward social progress with quantifiable outcomes. Programs that are a good fit for SIBs include welfare provision, education, healthcare, employment policies, and goals like reducing recidivism rates among prisoners, which in the UK in 2010 were as high as 60% for short-term prisoners:[56]

> Peterborough Prison in the United Kingdom issued one of the first social impact bonds anywhere in the world. The bond raised £5 million from 17 social investors to fund a pilot project with the objective of reducing re-offending rates of short-term prisoners. The relapse or re-conviction rates of prisoners released from Peterborough will be compared with the relapse rates of a control group of prisoners over six years. If Peterborough's re-conviction rates are at least 7.5% below the rates of the control group, investors receive an increasing return that is directly proportional to the difference in relapse rates between the two groups and is capped at 13% annually over an eight-year period.[57]

In addition to the interest SIBs are generating in the UK,[58] they are growing in countries like Australia,[59] as well as in the United States where, in 2011, "President Obama earmarked $100 million for various pilot programs involving SIBs in his 2012 budget proposal."[60]

In Massachusetts, work is under way to use SIBs to address recidivism rates among young people as well as the chronically homeless. And in New York City, Goldman Sachs is putting up $9.6 million for a SIB aimed at reducing recidivism rates among young inmates at Rikers Island prison.[61]

The Goldman Sachs project in New York, in coordination with Bloomberg Philanthropies (which underwrote the project with a $6 million guarantee against Goldman Sachs' potential losses), was the first SIB project to be implemented in the United States.[62] Similar to the UK project, the focus was on prisoner rehabilitation. But, in spite of the involvement of Goldman Sachs and the firm's statement that its investment "is not a charitable donation,"[63] the results of the public policy experiment were disappointing:

> Aimed at reducing teenage recidivism by 10 percent, the Adolescent Behavioral Learning Experience was found . . . not to keep teenagers from being sent back to Rikers at all.[64]

In spite of this initial failure, SIB advocates are encouraged by success elsewhere (primarily in the UK). There is also the benefit of trying an innovative experiment with no cost to the taxpayer. Most encouraging, however, is that rigorous quantitative evaluation was introduced to assess the success of a social program. Without the influence of private capital, a program such as the one tried at Rikers and funded via public money could have continued for years without anyone bothering to see whether it was working. Thus, even when ideas fail, there is the potential for impact investing to generate positive social outcomes via SIBs:

> To date, seven [SIBs] have been set up in the United States. Starting at Rikers, Goldman has been involved in four, including a $17 million pre-K program for disadvantaged children in Chicago, which will return $9,100 a child for each year he or she avoids special education, . . . $2,900 for each child deemed prepared for kindergarten and $750 for each student who scores above the national average on the third-grade reading test.[65]

And, although Goldman's first investment in prisoner recidivism failed, it is beginning to have reported success elsewhere. In addition to its Chicago preK program, for example, Goldman has invested in a similar program in Utah in which it funded early education costs for children who were expected to require special education when they entered formal schooling:

> When the students were tested . . . after a year in preschool—and found not to need extra help, the State of Utah paid Goldman most of the money it would have spent on special education for the children. The payment represented the first time a so-called social impact bond paid off for investors in the United States.[66]

Since the first SIB was launched in the UK in 2010, there have now been a total of 45 introduced around the world (as indicated in Figure II.2). Most of these are in the UK, and most are focused in social welfare and employment programs (with four criminal justice, three education, and two health-related programs making up the rest).

Figure II.2 Growth of SIBs Worldwide (2010–2015)

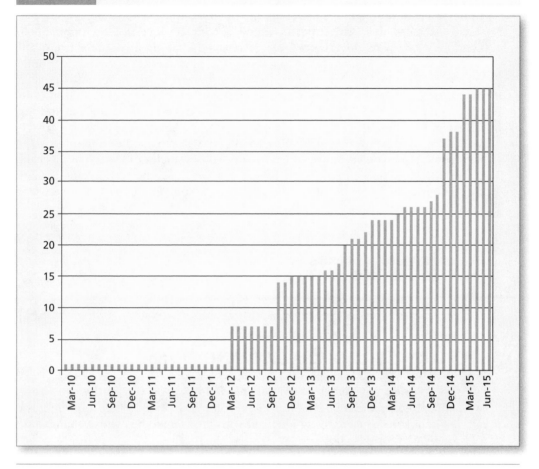

Source: Eduardo Porter, "Wall St. Cash Meets Social Policy in City Jail," *The New York Times*, July 29, 2015, p. B1.

In spite of the growing popularity of SIBs, a number of challenges remain in order for these "pay for success" programs to realize their hoped-for potential. First is the issue of identifying which programs are suited to this sort of financing. Second is the issue of how best to measure success. Many of the lead times on these sorts of projects are long (which will not fit some investors' time frames for a meaningful return), but they also deal with intractable social problems that do not always lend themselves to easy measurement. This issue arose in the Utah experiment, with Goldman's claims to success having since been questioned due to misleading measurements.[67] Third is the issue of the higher costs caused by the third-party assessment, which is essential to add rigor but is more costly "when compared to simply delivering the services directly."[68] And fourth is the general concern that introducing financial incentives into the public policy arena will distort behavior, with individuals motivated to produce specific outcomes and held accountable for doing so. In areas where quantifiable metrics may need to be newly developed, this increases the potential for abuse.

Nevertheless, this is an innovative time for impact investing as foundations, charities, NGOs, and governments are increasingly "taking [their] cues from Wall Street and Silicon Valley," adopting venture capital tactics to invest in public policy projects and social enterprises that promise "both social and financial benefits."[69] Not every SIB will work, but for their champions, that is OK. Although the above SIB with Goldman failed to reduce youth recidivism and the investors lost their money, for example, "the city declared the effort a success. It was: New York got to run a valuable experiment without shouldering the cost."[70] Ultimately, the complete range of impact-investing vehicles discussed in this case (from SRI, ESG, and values-based funds to, more recently, SIBs) demonstrates the potential social value of the finance sector, something that has been less evident in recent years.

Strategic CSR Debate

MOTION: Impact investing is an effective means of solving social problems.

QUESTIONS FOR DISCUSSION AND REVIEW

1.   Do you own any shares of a company? If so, do you vote at the company's annual general meeting (either in person or by proxy)? Is it important for shareholders to be actively involved with the companies whose shares they own? Why, or why not?

2.   What are your thoughts about increasing demands for firms to hold "say-on-pay" votes on executive compensation packages? Is it a good idea or unnecessary interference in the day-to-day management of the firm? Should the votes be binding?

3.   When considering an investment in a mutual fund, would you consider the CSR profiles of the companies in which the fund invested? What about SRI funds? Why, or why not?

4.   Would you think twice about investing in a sin fund if historical returns showed greater growth potential than SRI funds? What is the justification for your decision?

5.   Conduct an online search of "social investment fund companies." What is your opinion of the websites of some of these companies and their stated mission and values? Are these funds a force for good, or are they merely lulling gullible investors into a false sense of security by allowing them to think they are investing with a conscience?

NEXT STEPS

The concept of strategic CSR represents a unique approach to the dynamic topic of CSR because it seeks to understand the purpose of the firm based on what we know about human psychology and economic theory, rather than try to overturn what centuries of economic and human exchange have taught us about how society operates. As such, beyond the stakeholder model that is detailed here in Part II and forms the intellectual foundation of strategic CSR, Part III of this text explores the economic perspective, including concepts such as behavioral economics and *lifecycle pricing*, which are essential to understand the full implications of the ideas discussed in this book.

Following that, Part IV approaches CSR from a strategic perspective, emphasizing the importance of integrating these ideas throughout all aspects of strategic planning and day-to-day operations. Finally, Part V presents a sustainable perspective of the firm based on values that reflect the needs and concerns of key stakeholders—the ultimate goal of strategic CSR.

PART III

AN ECONOMIC PERSPECTIVE

Part III of *Strategic Corporate Social Responsibility* (*Strategic CSR*) presents an economic perspective. One of the unique aspects of strategic CSR is that it is based on what we know of economic theory and human psychology (a *realistic* rather than *idealistic* depiction of human behavior). Part III includes three chapters at the intersection of these two crucial disciplines.

Specifically, Chapter 7 discusses the motivating role of profit in the broader discussion about capitalism that emerged following the 2007–2008 financial crisis and investigates the extent to which our current economic model should be reformed. It also challenges the common refrain that firms have long focused on producing economic value and today must also produce social value. In reality, there is no *economic value* and no *social value*; there is only *value*, which the firm creates (or destroys) for each of its stakeholders. Chapter 8 introduces the concept of behavioral economics and discusses how this exciting field can advance the value creation process. This chapter also includes an extended discussion of Walmart and what the firm's ongoing success means in this context. Chapter 9 caps Part III by looking at the variety of ways in which we measure CSR, a task that is essential in order to hold firms to account for their CSR performance. Before we can develop an effective CSR measure, however, all costs need to be included in the production process. This is achieved via the concept of *lifecycle pricing*.

The economic perspective in Part III is completed with a case study that emerged out of the financial crisis—the implosion of the mortgage company Countrywide.

Chapter 7

THE PURSUIT OF PROFIT

By definition, profit is what drives all *for-profit* organizations. The pursuit of profit underwrites market-based economies and forces companies constantly to innovate and improve by meeting society's developmental needs. Profit is also cited by business leaders as a reason for *not* being able to pursue CSR. In this perspective, CSR represents a short-term cost that the firm has a duty to minimize in order to be as profitable as possible and maximize returns to investors. One of the goals of strategic CSR is to overcome this perceived divide between profit and CSR.

The argument for CSR as an essential component of a firm's strategic planning and day-to-day operations assumes that CSR and profit are not mutually exclusive goals. On the contrary, given today's globalized, online world, this book argues that CSR is the most effective means to ensure the firm's long-term viability via the support of its stakeholders. After all, the best of intentions aside, a bankrupt company does not benefit anyone. On the contrary, a bankrupt company hurts its stakeholders—its employees who lose a job, its customers who do not get a beneficial product, the government who does not receive the firm's taxes, and so on.

On the flip side, however, a profitable company creates value for all of those stakeholders and many more. It is the source of great wealth and social progress from which we all benefit. This link between for-profit business and social progress is one that should not be in doubt. As John Mackey, CEO of Whole Foods Market, notes:

> In 1800, 85% of everyone alive lived on less than $1 per day (in 2000 dollars). Today only 17% do. If current long-term trend lines of economic growth continue, we will see abject poverty almost completely eradicated in the 21st century. Business is not a zero-sum game struggling over a fixed pie. Instead it grows and makes the total pie larger, creating value for all of its major stakeholders—customers, employees, suppliers, investors and communities.[1]

The perceived gap between a firm's pursuit of profit and its social responsibility is bridged by strategic CSR. By seeking to create value across their broad range of stakeholders, profitable firms will also be optimizing their contribution to societal well-being. Market capitalism is the ideal framework for this complex economic progress.

MARKETS[2]

In reality, the way we differentiate between private sector motivations and public sector demands is through the pursuit of profit. But are these behaviors really all that different? Another way to express the balancing act between conflicting stakeholder interests is as a push and pull of market forces. While markets are normally thought of in terms of exchanges quantified in monetary value, the process of valuation can be expanded to include a firm's relationships with all its stakeholders, but measured in different ways. Each stakeholder brings different resources to the exchange in ways that can be expressed as opportunities or threats to the firm. As the firm responds, different outcomes are shaped that, ultimately, match the desires of all parties involved. A good example of a company that actively institutionalizes this mutually dependent relationship is Patagonia, whose Product Lifecycle Initiative represents

> a unique effort to include consumers in Patagonia's vision of environmental responsibility. An internal document articulated that reducing Patagonia's environmental footprint required a pledge from both the company and its customers. The initiative thus consisted of a mutual contract between the company and its customers to "reduce, repair, reuse, and recycle" the apparel that they consumed.[3]

As discussed in Chapter 6, the history of the modern-day company is embedded in its foundation as a tool to serve society's purposes. Although the emphasis in the company–society relationship has shifted over time, the idea that the corporation is a tool that serves society's interests remains fundamentally intact. In short, if capitalism is no longer serving our interests well, it is because we are not using it correctly. More specifically, we are sending firms the wrong signals, and those signals relate directly to our collective values.

Take the advent of the $5 T-shirt. This is a product that is readily available today, but it did not occur by accident. More importantly, its existence has profound implications for the type of society in which we live. The idea that firms are imposing $5 T-shirts on us, for example, greatly misrepresents the way markets operate. If we tell firms with our purchase decisions (and materialistic values) that with our $30, we want to buy six T-shirts at $5 each rather than two T-shirts at $15 each, then that is what the market will provide. This is not merely an economic decision, however, but one that is laden with values that have monumental consequences for the kind of society in which we live—one that values quantity over quality, one that values material goods over holistic well-being, one that values short-term comfort over long-term sustainability.[4]

If, in contrast, we were willing to buy two T-shirts at $15 each, that choice would have radical consequences that would revolutionize our economy (fewer workers in the global apparel industry, but better conditions and higher quality T-shirts, for example). Just because we can make T-shirts for $5 each does not mean that we have to—it is a choice that we make. And, when that choice is repeated for each of the "150bn pieces of clothing [that] are made every year,"[5] the consequences quickly add up. It is essential to the ideas underpinning strategic CSR that we understand that our consumption decisions (as all stakeholder relations with the firm) represent our values in action. In supplying us with $5 T-shirts, firms are merely responding to our demand for such products.[6] If we want the market to change, therefore, we are likely to be more successful if we change the collective set of values that the market reflects, rather than trying to change the centuries-old principles on which the market and for-profit firms operate.

In other words, the argument constructed in this book (and detailed in Part II) is not an absolution of the manager's ethical responsibilities but is instead a call for those responsibilities to be enforced by the firm's stakeholders who, collectively, have the power to shape the corporate behavior they wish to see. The result of a system that is characterized by tension among competing interests, with give and take on both sides, is a more democratic distribution of the overall *wealth* embedded within that system. As Howard Bowen noted back in 1953:

> In a rapidly growing society, even if industry is predominantly competitive, there is nothing to prevent the society from receiving part of its increasing product in the form of better working conditions, shorter hours, greater security, greater freedom, better products, etc. Gains need not be realized solely in the form of a greater flow of final goods and services. The rising standard of living may consist not alone in an increasing physical quantity of goods and services, but also in improved conditions under which these goods and services are produced.[7]

Increasingly, tools are becoming available that enable stakeholders to adopt this proactive role. Another way of saying this is that we no longer have an excuse for failing to act. The Internet provides access to the information we need to make value-based judgments about the policies and operating procedures of the firms with which we interact. Moreover, the price of communication has been lowered essentially to zero, which enables us to mobilize in ways that counteract the power previously held only by governments or corporations.

The overall effect of the encroachment of the Internet and social media into every aspect of our lives is to cause companies to lose control over the flow of information. The rise of social media has broken down barriers in ways that are changing how stakeholders interact with firms. At the same time as firms benefit from increased communication and data (to increase efficiencies and market-test products, for example), this technology also hands stakeholders a tool they can use to take direct action and hold firms to account. When we demand more *and* demonstrate a willingness to sacrifice in order to obtain it, the corporation is the most rapid and efficient mechanism to meet that demand. There is a large body of evidence that demonstrates stakeholder activism is effective. Strategic CSR calls for an expanded sense of responsibility among all stakeholders to ensure such activism becomes the norm, rather than the exception. And when it is in place, the best way for a firm to make a profit will be to meet the needs of its stakeholders.

Stakeholders as Market Makers

The ideal ecosystem in which business and society coexist consists of a constant back-and-forth between the self-interest of the business minority and the collective interest of the majority. As society's interests evolve, the resulting external pressures on firms increasingly reflect this change. As these pressures rise, it becomes apparent to the manager that the firm's self-interest lies in conforming to these external expectations. Similarly, as businesses innovate and introduce new products and services to society that shape how we live and interact with each other, so these changes challenge existing norms and expectations in ways that alter how we live our lives. Understanding that all parties in our economic system help identify this point of balance is essential to create an economic system that optimizes total value.

Within this framework, an ethics or CSR transgression committed by a firm represents a failure of stakeholder oversight—a breakdown in collective vigilance. Whether as a result of lapsed government or media oversight, consumer ignorance, employee silence, or supplier deceit, a *transgression* (which, by definition, is a socially constructed assessment of *right* and *wrong*) reflects the stakeholders' failure to hold the firm to account. In other words, the firm violates our collective determination of what constitutes *responsible* behavior.

As a mirror to the collective set of values that make up society, however, firms react to the signals their stakeholders send. It is when those signals become mixed or we fail to enforce the behavior we have previously said we want that problems can emerge. The temptation to trade short-term profits for necessary safety precautions, for example, led to a change in culture at BP and a series of serious accidents from Alaska to Texas to the Gulf of Mexico. If the firm's stakeholders had enforced their oversight (e.g., government inspections, partner operating procedures, employee whistle-blowers, etc.), these hugely consequential accidents might have been prevented. Even viable companies that produce legal products (such as the tobacco and gun industries often vilified by CSR advocates) exist only as a result of stakeholder support. If we feel these companies do more harm than good, then it is the responsibility of government to make their products illegal or consumers to boycott them. Stakeholders have it in their collective power to shape the firms we want to populate our economies. Companies are not to blame for profiting by selling products that the firm's collective set of stakeholders have said they value.

Rather than favoring a form of unregulated capitalism, which has been roundly (and correctly) criticized for causing economic mayhem in recent decades, the core argument in this book calls for an expanded form of regulation, by *stakeholders*. Rather than rely on legislatures to constrain business via restrictive laws (a necessary but insufficient stakeholder action), an effective and comprehensive form of corporate *stakeholder* responsibility (Chapter 5), in which all stakeholders act to hold firms to account, will generate a market-based system of checks and balances formed around multiple interests. This complex web acts as a curb on unlimited power; it also provides unbounded opportunity for the firm that is sufficiently progressive to meet and exceed its stakeholders' expectations. The ultimate effect will be to ensure capitalism is tailored toward broader societal interests rather than narrow individual or corporate interests.

In this sense, strategic CSR is not a passive doctrine; it is highly empowering and potentially revolutionary. True, it is working within the current system, utilizing a firm's pursuit of profit and individuals' self-interest to achieve its goals, but the subtle shifts that it advocates seek to generate very different outcomes throughout society. The potential benefits are demonstrated in the way that firms are beginning to pursue profit in the developing world.

PROFIT

A significant reason for the supremacy of market forces is the pivotal role of profit:

> The existence of a profit is an indication *prima facie* that the business has succeeded in producing something which consumers want and value.... A business that fails to make an adequate profit is a house of cards. It cannot grow or provide more jobs or pay higher wages. In the long run, it cannot even survive. It offers no stability or security or opportunity for its workers and investors. It cannot meet its broader obligations to society. It is a failure from all points of view.[8]

I would amend that quote only to replace the narrow stakeholder group, *consumers*, with the much broader concept of *society*. If a society (the collective group of all stakeholders) permits a firm to continue operations, then it is essentially acknowledging that the organization adds value—that society is better off than if the organization did not exist. At present, the best method we have of measuring that value is the profit the firm generates.

A firm's profit represents the ability to sell a good or service at a higher price than it costs to produce. Production and consumption, however, are more than technical decisions. They encapsulate the total value added by the firm. This statement is core to the idea of strategic CSR, but exists in contrast to the way that profit is discussed within the CSR community—as a narrow measure of economic value and something that can detract from social value. This representation of *economic value* and *social value* as independent constructs demonstrates a misunderstanding of what profit represents. In reality, economic value and social value are highly correlated.

Economic Value + Social Value

The profit motive is closely linked in business to the price mechanism, which is an assessment of the cost of bringing a product or service to market, plus a margin that provides sufficient incentive for the business to operate. In the marketplace, *price* is the best way we have developed to measure the value added in an exchange. In terms of firm performance, a profit or loss is the aggregate outcome of multiple production and consumption decisions. These decisions are arrived at through individual evaluations of cost and benefit along many, many dimensions and expressed in the consumer's willingness to pay the price that is being charged. If the value I obtain from a product exceeds the costs involved in earning sufficient money to pay the price, then I should be willing to buy it. In other words, when I buy a product, I am signaling to the firm that I value it. When this transaction is repeated on a society-wide basis within a competitive market system, this signal amounts to a social sanction of the underlying business:

> When businessmen follow the profit motive they are merely following social valuations as expressed in the prices at which they can sell their products and the prices at which they can buy productive services, materials, supplies, and their other requirements. . . . When the businessman follows this signal, he is following not only his own interest but that of society as well. . . . The practical and the democratic thing for him to do is to rely primarily on profit as his guide in deciding his business actions.[9]

Conceptually, therefore, while it can be helpful to think of *economic value* and *social value* as separate constructs, in reality, they are not independent. On the contrary, they are highly correlated and are infused in the firm's decisions regarding production (Do we pollute the local river, or not? Do we hire at the minimum wage or a living wage?) and the consumer's decisions regarding consumption (Do I buy from the firm that produces domestically or the one that outsources? Do I pay the premium associated with a more environmentally friendly product or purchase the cheaper, disposable product?). All of these production and consumption decisions contain value-laden consequences that, ultimately, determine the economic success of the firm:

> 200 years' worth of work in economics and finance indicate that social welfare is maximized when all firms in an economy maximize total firm value. The intuition behind this criterion is simply that (social) value is created when a firm produces an output or set of outputs that are valued by its customers at more than the value of the inputs it consumes (as valued by their suppliers) in such production. Firm value is simply the long-term market value of this stream of benefits.[10]

To put this in more concrete terms: When I buy a product, I am not just purchasing something to fulfill a technical function—I am buying something that makes me happy, that conveys my status, that boosts my self-esteem, and, yes, something that is *socially responsible* (depending on the values I hold and the criteria I prioritize). This is something we all know intuitively to be true. It is why car companies like BMW and Mercedes exist—they produce a product that does much more for the consumer than provide transport from point A to point B.

In addition to this private, nontechnical value that is built into the price the consumer pays for a good, there is also a component that relates to the level of social value generated. If I buy a Toyota Prius, for example, I pay a price premium over similar, nonhybrid cars because of the superior technology built into the Prius's engine and battery. While I get a private benefit from this purchase in that I can now demonstrate to everyone how environmentally conscious I am,[11] there is also a significant public benefit in the reduced pollution that my car emits. The price premium I am paying therefore represents a subsidy to society in that I am covering the cost of improving the air quality—a positive externality from which everyone benefits but is built into the price that I pay. More specifically, by providing this product that reduces environmental pollution, is Toyota engaged in solving an economic problem (the demand for cars) or a social problem (the need to transport people in a way that minimizes damage to the environment)? The answer, of course, is "both." And these different types of value are captured in the profit (or loss) that Toyota reports at the end of the year.

CSR advocates talk about the need for "compassion in organizations" that allows them also to "focus on social problems and social welfare concerns,"[12] as if economic problems and social problems are separate things. Again, a simple thought experiment highlights the overly simplistic nature of this forced dichotomy. Is feeding people a social problem or an economic problem? Of course, there are hundreds of for-profit food manufacturers (not to mention the hundreds of thousands of restaurants) that produce food and distribute it widely (and efficiently). What about clothing people—a social problem or an economic problem? A visit to the mall will quickly reveal how efficiently for-profit firms have essentially eradicated the supply of clothes as a challenge for all but the most deprived societies. Or, what about providing Internet access to every household—economic or social? Certainly, you could argue today that a family is excluded from many aspects of society if it cannot get online ("what many people consider as basic a utility as water and electricity"),[13] yet Internet provision in most developed economies is the sole responsibility of the private sector (as is the provision of nutrition and clothing for the food and apparel industries).

So, how is it that for-profit firms are not already intricately involved in addressing social problems? In fact, you could argue that, essentially, every company uses economic means to solve social problems. Now, you may challenge the business models of some of these firms, or the quality of the final product they produce, but I believe there is no one who can say these for-profit firms are not involved in addressing complex problems that have intertwined economic and social components. In essence, there are no economic problems or social problems; there are just problems that have both social and economic consequences.

As the above examples indicate, much of what is referred to as *social value* (the value that is derived above and beyond the functional purpose of a product or service) is captured in a willingness among consumers to part with their disposable income. Given that, for most of us, our disposable income is a scarce resource, how we decide to spend it reflects our values in action. That is not to say that market forces are perfect.[14] Negative externalities are a good example of how imperfect the market can be. An example is the pollution that is generated in either the production (e.g., factory emissions) or the consumption (e.g., driving a car) of a product, but not accounted for. Both are examples of how a firm's profits do not reflect perfectly the public costs incurred by society at some later date, but it is important to remember that "it is the *abuse* of the profit motive, not the motive itself" that is the problem.[15]

In other words, given what we know, a firm's profit is the best way we have of capturing overall value creation. It incorporates a significant amount of all aspects of the value (economic, social, moral, etc.) that is encapsulated in market transactions. But it is not perfect. An example of how to overcome this is to ensure all costs are included in the price that is charged. This will be discussed in detail in Chapter 9. Before we turn to that discussion, however, it is necessary to complete our consideration of the role played by profit in terms of overall value creation.

Profit Optimization

In the process of delivering value to its broad range of stakeholders, it is essential that the firm generates a profit. Profit generation is, therefore, also central to the concept of strategic CSR. Rather than challenge *what* the firm does (make money), strategic CSR focuses more specifically on *how* the firm does it (the hundreds and thousands of operational decisions made every day). In the process, one of the goals of this book is to change the debate around the role of the for-profit firm in society. By challenging taken-for-granted assumptions about business and the value it delivers, reform that will build a more sustainable economic system becomes possible. One of the assumptions that must be challenged is that firms pursue policies and practices in order to *maximize profit*. First, this concept is not possible; second, it is unhelpful.

First, this concept is impossible to prove as a firm can never know whether the profit generated was in fact *maximized* or what effect alternative decisions would have had instead:

> A simple statement that managers try to maximize corporate profits, as is frequently assumed in economic theory, is almost meaningless. The concept of profit is a highly tenuous one in that it involves the valuation of assets, the allocation of joint costs, the treatment of developmental expenses [etc.]. . . . The idea of profit maximization raises the troublesome question of the time period over which profits are to be maximized, and it is difficult for either managers or observers to calculate the effect on profits of given actions which may affect the business indefinitely in the future. . . . It may be more realistic to describe the quest for profit as a seeking for "satisfactory profits" rather than maximum profits ("satisfactory" defined in relation to the profit experience of other firms).[16]

Second, the idea of profit maximization is unhelpful because it distorts decision making within the firm. The only way that we could know whether a particular set of decisions maximized profits would be to rerun the time period, under exactly the same conditions, and investigate the effects of all possible decisions. In reality, the decisions that guide the firm constitute a debate among philosophies (e.g., Do you believe paying a minimum wage to employees will generate larger profits than paying a living wage?). Any executive that claims their decisions will *maximize* profits for the firm is, therefore, being disingenuous at best; most likely, they do not fully understand the nature of the statement and certainly cannot in any way prove the claim.

As a result of being both impossible to achieve and unhelpful because it distorts decision making, the goal of profit *maximization* is a distraction, In its place, strategic CSR calls for a focus on profit *optimization*. Although equally impossible to prove definitively, profit optimization better approximates the subjective nature of the decision-making process—different people will use different values to determine what they consider to be *optimal*. In other words, while the idea of a maximum suggests an absolute point (a definitive amount), an optimum suggests a more relative state of existence. What is optimal for me may not be optimal for you, but you cannot say the values by which I determine my optimum are *wrong*—just that they differ from the values you use to determine your optimum. As such, this rhetorical shift helps encourage a balance among short-, medium-, and long-term decisions that create value across the firm's range of stakeholders.

Production Value and Consumption Value

As the discussion above indicates, while defining social value and economic value and understanding how they relate to each other appears superficially straightforward, these are highly complex processes. As such, an alternative conceptualization is to think of the value added by a firm during production and the value added by a product or service during consumption. At either stage, the assessment of the value added would be either neutral, net positive, or net negative. In this alternative conceptualization, employees' wages would be included as part of the calculation of total value added (or subtracted) during *production*, as would any pollution emitted during manufacturing. In contrast, the emissions caused by driving a car or the e-waste from discarding a phone, TV, or MP3 player would be accounted for as part of the value added (or subtracted) during *consumption*. The net effect, in theory, would define our collective quality of life, which would in turn help determine necessary reforms:

> An improvement in the conditions of production—resulting in a better working environment or better functioning of the economy—may frequently be entirely justified even if achieved at a sacrifice in output of final goods and services.[17]

The challenge we face as a society, therefore, is to strike a balance between the part of our standard of living that is formed from the production of goods and services and the part that is formed from the consumption of goods and services.

The *production* component includes incorporating costs that firms currently seek to externalize, such as the pollution emitted during manufacturing, while the *consumption* component includes incorporating costs that consumers currently seek to avoid, such as the pollution emitted during consumption (e.g., driving a car) and recycling (e.g., e-waste). If a marginal $1 spent on production yields greater returns than the same $1 spent on consumption, it is in our collective best interests to spend the $1 on improving aspects of production (and vice versa).

In this sense, understanding the true nature of what profit represents, while conceptually important, is helpful only up to a point. If we accept that long-term profit is a good (if imperfect) measure of total value added, we must also recognize that it is just that—a measure of performance that still does not help us understand how the firm should add that value:

> Defining what it means to score a goal in football or soccer, for example, tells the players nothing about how to win the game. It just tells them how the score will be kept. That is the role of value maximization in organizational life.[18]

In other words, profit is the outcome of a highly complex process that, more accurately, determines whether the firm is being *socially responsible*. Understanding how firms can balance the pursuit of profit with the need to create value for their stakeholders is therefore essential. One way to establish this is in terms of the level of social progress that a firm delivers.

SOCIAL PROGRESS

The merging of the pursuit of profit and integration of CSR within corporate strategy renders a *short*-term, profit-only approach increasingly untenable. Combined with the increasing pressure placed on companies today to perform consistently over the *medium* to *longer* term, managers need to be as innovative and progressive as possible in creating value for stakeholders. Understanding the firm's potential customers is central to this task. The firms that are being most innovative in this respect cast a broader net in search of customers to serve:

> There is a huge neglected market in the billions of poor in the developing world. Companies like Unilever and Citicorp are beginning to adapt their technologies to enter this market. Unilever can now deliver ice cream in India for just two cents a portion because it has rethought the technology of refrigeration. Citicorp can now provide financial services to people, also in India, who have only $25 to invest, again through rethinking technology. In both cases the companies make money, but the driving force is the need to serve neglected consumers. Profit often comes from progress.[19]

Is it OK for firms to profit from poverty? Where is the dividing line between fulfilling a social mission and pursuing a valid market opportunity in an emerging market? Is there any advantage in drawing such a distinction? Today, is it more helpful to think of all firms as having a social mission but delivering varying degrees of added value?

Bottom of the Pyramid

It is estimated that, by 2016, the richest

> 1% of the world's population will own more wealth than the other 99%. . . . [Research] shows that the share of the world's wealth owned by the best-off 1% has increased from 44% in 2009 to 48% in 2014, while the least well-off 80% currently own just 5.5%.[20]

This means, as indicated in Figure 7.1, that 65% of the world's population, or 4 billion people, exist on less than $2,000 per year.[21] This section of the world comprises Tier 4—the largest and lowest portion of the four-tier pyramid that represents the world's population. These people at the bottom of the pyramid (BOP) represent a huge market segment that needs the help of the developed world. They can pay their way in terms of buying essential and reasonably priced products—as long as firms are creative in bringing to market products that are in demand and deliver social progress:

> To be profitable, firms cannot simply edge down market, fine-tuning the products they already sell to rich customers. Instead, they must thoroughly re-engineer products to reflect the very different economics of BOP: small unit packages, low margin per unit, high volume. Big business needs to swap its usual incremental approach for an entrepreneurial mindset, because BOP markets need to be built not simply entered.[22]

While this market is already impressive,[23] with estimates of its annual worth ranging from "as much as $5 trillion"[24] to "$13 trillion,"[25] it is the future that offers the greatest potential:

> [It is estimated that] almost 3 billion people will enter the ranks of the middle classes by 2050—nearly all in emerging economies. That would create a seismic shift in the world economy: Consumption in emerging countries could account for almost two-thirds of the global total in 2050, a significant increase from only about one-third today.[26]

For C. K. Prahalad ("perhaps the most visible proponent of the view that the globe's poor are a huge—and hugely untapped—market"),[27] the business opportunity is clear.[28] It requires effort and commitment on the part of multinational corporations to "stop thinking of the poor as victims or as a burden and start recognizing them as resilient and creative entrepreneurs and value-conscious consumers."[29] Once this occurs, there are benefits in terms of top-line growth,

Figure 7.1 Income Distribution Throughout the World (income, population)

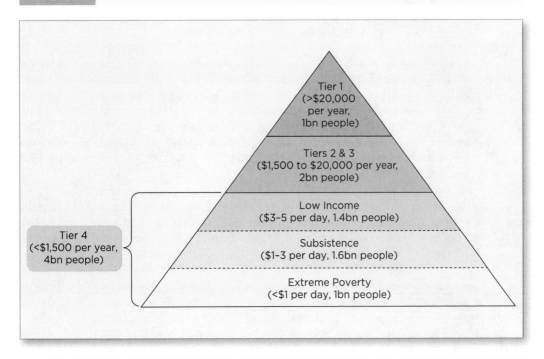

Source: The concept of a "world economic pyramid" is based on data from the United Nations World Development Report and cited in C. K. Prahalad & Stuart L. Hart, "The Fortune at the Bottom of the Pyramid," *strategy+business,* January 10, 2002, No. 26, http://www.strategy-business.com/article/11518/. The idea of segmenting the bottom tier of the pyramid into different groups with different characteristics and needs was developed by V. Kasturi Rangan, Michael Chu, and Djordjija Petkoski, "The Globe: Segmenting the Base of the Pyramid," *Harvard Business Review,* June 2011, https://hbr.org/2011/06/the-globe-segmenting-the-base-of-the-pyramid/.

reduced costs, and inspired innovation. For example, a company that is moving to take advantage of this potential market is the chocolate maker Cadbury's, which has been expanding its presence in the Indian confectionary market to reach the bottom of the pyramid:

> The candy maker's latest product for the low end of the Indian market is Cadbury Dairy Milk Shots. The pea-sized chocolate balls . . . are sold for just two rupees, or about four U.S. cents, for a packet of two, which weighs five grams—a fraction of an ounce. They have a sugar shell to protect them from the heat.[30]

It is important to note that Prahalad, who died in 2010, has his critics[31] who question the size of the BOP market, as well as the ability (and willingness) of multinational corporations to provide products that add significant social value. In the case of Cadbury's, for example, given some of the more fundamental problems that face the poorest sections of India's society, it is hard to see how bringing chocolate to the masses constitutes *progress*:

> Much of the profitable business with lower-income markets involves products such as mobile phones, not the provision of basic nutrition, sanitation, education and shelter. . . . In addition, . . . claims about empowering people by providing means for them to consume cannot be taken at face value. The environmental impacts of changing consumption patterns also need to be looked at. . . . And we need to assess, if more foreign companies do come to serve lower income markets, might they not displace local companies and increase the resource drain from local economies?[32]

Nevertheless, it is also clear that Prahalad has had a significant influence on how firms perceive the developing world and that this has had a material impact (for better or worse) on the lives of people there.[33] Rather than focus on whether chocolate or mobile phones are what the firms of the developed world think the consumers of the developing world want, it is the principle that matters—the greater the opportunity for the private sector to cater to the needs of consumers in developing economies, the greater the chance for the social progress that the private sector has instigated elsewhere. The market is a powerful means to incentivize the production of goods and services that people demand. Prahalad's role was to help envision a different perception of the developing world and how the developed world can and should interact with it:

> For decades, the main model of Third World aid has been the obvious: Give stuff to poor people—be it hydroelectric dams, surplus food or medical equipment. But Western countries have poured some $1.5 trillion into such efforts over the last 60 years, and more than 1 billion people worldwide still live on less than a dollar a day. . . . [Alternatively,] if you design a useful product for a market . . . the target population is more likely to actually want it and use it. If businesses can turn a profit making that product, it not only creates jobs but will keep getting made even if Western donors lose interest.[34]

A company that is working hard to deliver products that are both in demand and are essential to societal progress and human well-being is Unilever.

Unilever

For-profit firms are the best hope for social progress because the products businesses produce enable people to pursue dreams and better their lives. A good example is mobile phones, which are becoming increasingly important in developing countries without the necessary infrastructure (such as fixed land-lines) because they enable people to communicate and conduct business. Because these phones are so important, "people will skip a meal or choose to walk instead of paying for a bus fare so that they can keep their phone in credit."[35] For-profit firms produce products that fulfill peoples' aspirations, which is why economic development, rather than international aid, offers the best means for rapid social progress in the developing world.[36] And, nowhere is this more important than in the area of personal hygiene:

> Hindustan Lever, the Indian consumer goods company 51% owned by Unilever, for example, knew that many Indians could not afford to buy a big bottle of shampoo. . . . So it created single-use packets (in three sizes, according to hair length) that go for a few cents—and now sells 4.5 billion of them a year.[37]

Unilever, in particular, has committed itself to implementing CSR as a core component of strategy and operations and has moved quickly to adapt its products for BOP consumers. As part of this process, Unilever is increasingly exploring the tension between for-profit goals and nonprofit priorities in the developing world. Unilever's involvement in a campaign to increase hand washing in Uganda, for example, rests on its branded soap (Lifebuoy) becoming associated in the public's mind with hand washing. The firm's NGO partner, UNICEF, has a different goal, however—just to get people to wash their hands. UNICEF does not care which soap people use, but its goal benefits from the marketing and distribution expertise that Unilever offers.[38] Campaigns such as this are part of a long history at Unilever that places the company within its broader social context:

> Outdoing even the Cadburys of Birmingham and the Rowntrees of York, [Unilever founder, William] Lever had pioneered the Victorian model of paternalistic business. At a time when disease and malnutrition were widespread in Britain, his products were marketed for their health benefits. His employees were decently housed in a purpose-built company town. . . . Lever campaigned for state pensions for the elderly and even provided schooling, health care and good wages at palm-oil plantations in the Congo.[39]

More recently, under current CEO Paul Polman, that business model has evolved into what Unilever calls its *Sustainable Living Plan*. The Plan, which was launched in 2010, commits Unilever to achieve specific, measurable targets by 2020, such as "help more than a billion people improve their health and well-being, . . . halve the environmental footprint of the making and use of our products, . . . [and] source 100% of our agricultural raw materials sustainably":[40]

> Unilever has a long history of doing well by doing good. William Lever, one of its founders, created Lifebuoy soap to encourage cleanliness and reduce infectious diseases in Victorian Britain. Today, in the developing world, 3.5m children under five die from diarrhea and respiratory infections. Teaching children to wash their hands is a way of reducing this toll. The company sees opportunities to save lives and sell soap.[41]

Figure 7.2 Unilever—The Sustainability Leader (2015)

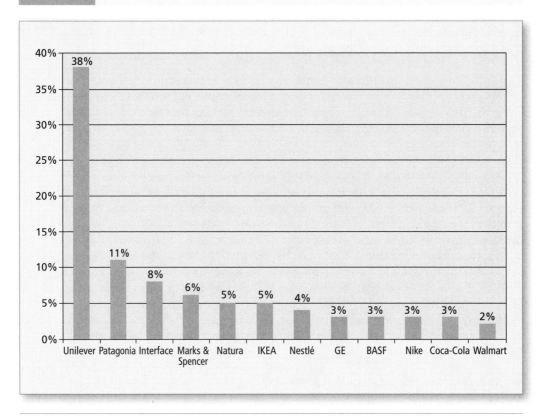

Source: "The 2015 Sustainability Leaders," *GlobeScan/SustainAbility*, May 28, 2015, slide 13 of 24, http://www.globescan.com/component/edocman/?view=document&id=179&Itemid=591.

Unilever sees the Plan as integral to its business model and the source of a competitive advantage in the marketplace. In particular, due largely to its values-based approach, the firm is recognized as having "the most comprehensive strategy of enlightened capitalism of any global firm."[42] As Polman notes, the firm is particularly popular among Millennials, who have helped make it "the third-most-looked-up company after Google and Apple" on LinkedIn.[43] And as Figure 7.2 indicates, this attention translates into a reputation as *the* sustainable company.[44]

While the attention is welcome, it is also hard-earned. Unilever's work in BOP countries has taught it that there are unique challenges to accessing these markets and adapting to new cultural and economic environments. These challenges range from product packaging (single portions rather than family-size packets), to shop design and layout (smaller outlets), to different shopping habits (daily rather than weekly trips):

In emerging markets, P&G estimates that 80% of people buy their wares from mom-and-pop stores no bigger than a closet. . . . Rather than stock up on full-size goods, which cost more per item, they buy small portions of soap, laundry detergent, and single diapers as they need them—even though the smaller sizes are usually sold at a premium.[45]

These adaptations reflect an approach that demands businesses understand their stakeholders in the markets they are attempting to enter. And it is because firms are willing to undertake this effort, of course, that value is created in those markets. But success requires them to listen rather than instruct and conform to existing norms rather than try to change them. In order to do this, Unilever Pakistan "segments the market not by income, but by 20 different spending profiles—carefully measuring everything from how many fans, or scooters or cars people own to how often they replace their toothbrushes."[46] This complements the firm's improvements in logistics, creating "a 45,000-strong army of female entrepreneurs who sell its products in 100,000 villages in 15 Indian states,"[47] who are also essential to success.

BOP consumers have the same aspirations as consumers everywhere, but they have different expectations and needs that firms must respect if they are to be successful.[48] Unilever's goal by 2020 is "for developing markets to account for 70% of total sales."[49] If the company, which is described as "the bottom-of-the-pyramid market leader,"[50] is able to achieve this, it will be due to the innovation that flowed from the pursuit of profit. Unilever is unique in embracing a **strategic CSR** perspective more thoroughly than virtually any other company. Central to that achievement is an understanding that the most socially responsible firms are those that are profitable as a result of creating value across their broad range of stakeholders.

Strategic CSR Debate

MOTION: A company cannot be socially responsible unless it is profitable.

QUESTIONS FOR DISCUSSION AND REVIEW

1. How do you respond to the assertion that "the most important organization in the world is the company: [It is] the basis of the prosperity of the West and the best hope for the future of the rest of the world"?[51]

2. Is it OK for a for-profit company to profit from poverty?

3. Outline the opportunity that exists at the bottom of the pyramid. Can you think of a firm or existing product that can be modified to become profitable in the developing world?

4.   Assuming a company found a profitable niche in serving the fourth tier (the 4 billion people at the bottom of the economic pyramid), how might such a breakthrough help the firm sell to the top of the economic pyramid?

5.   Have a look at Unilever's Sustainable Living Plan (http://www.unilever.com/ sustainable-living/). Before reading this chapter, were you aware of this initiative? Does it change your impression of Unilever at all? Is this plan CSR, or strategy, or both? Why?

Chapter 8

INCENTIVES AND COMPLIANCE

In general, it is recognized that firms seek to pursue their best interests, which are narrowly defined around increasing profits. What is debated within the CSR community, however, is the extent to which this focus on profit is too narrow, benefitting only a few stakeholders rather than the broad range of stakeholders that every firm has and, together, constitute society as a whole. Assuming that the most value is created when the largest segment of society benefits from a firm's operations, how should that outcome be achieved? Should firms be free to pursue their self-interest and let the market determine their actions (via interactions with consumers and competitors, for example), or should one particularly strong stakeholder (e.g., the government) intervene to impose specific constraints designed to achieve specific goals (such as via legislation and regulation)? In short, should CSR be voluntary or mandatory?

VOLUNTARY VERSUS MANDATORY

Those who support the *mandatory* enforcement of society's interests believe that coercion is the only way to ensure firms will behave in a way that is socially acceptable. As evidence, they offer the argument that "every example of major environmental progress—reducing acid rain, improving air quality, restoring the ozone layer—has been the result of national legislation or a global treaty."[1] Similarly, where governments have introduced a tax on sugary drinks (as they have done in Hungary since 2011, France since 2012, and Mexico since 2014), the data suggest that producers pass the higher costs on to customers and the demand for such drinks decreases, while demand for healthier alternatives (such as bottled water) increases.[2] And in terms of punishment, advocates of mandatory measures suggest that, for executives and other corporate employees, "fines are meaningless. Only prison can change behavior."[3]

In contrast, those who support allowing firms to define for themselves (*voluntarily*) how best to serve their stakeholders believe that excessive regulation is a distraction and an added cost to business that generates less optimal social outcomes. In the US healthcare industry, for example, proponents of voluntary action note that due to excessive regulation, for every hour spent treating a patient, there is a corresponding increase in paperwork of at least the same amount. In 2015, "the number of federally mandated categories of illness and injury for which hospitals may claim reimbursement [rose] from 18,000 to 140,000. There are nine codes relating to injuries caused by parrots, and three relating to burns from flaming water-skis."[4] And, in order to cover all eventualities, there are codes that enable doctors to record "whether the patient was crushed by a crocodile or sucked into a jet engine."[5] These people suggest that only when an organization genuinely believes that a specific action is in its best interests will it commit sufficient resources to achieving that goal. Moreover, they argue that coercion cannot work because modern society is simply too complex; the state does not have sufficient resources to control every aspect of our lives. In the United States, for example,

> The Occupational Safety and Health Administration has authority over more than eight million workplaces. But it can call upon only one inspector for about every 3,700 of those workplaces. The Environmental Protection Agency has authority not just over workplaces but over every piece of property in the nation. It conducted about 18,000 inspections in 2013—a tiny number in proportion to its mandate.[6]

In short, this argument suggests that governments have neither the resources nor capabilities to create value. Regulatory overkill results in complexity, which generates additional compliance costs without necessarily any improvement in outcomes. In terms of healthcare, the more resources that are devoted to paperwork, the fewer resources that can be devoted to patient care. This leads to resistance and, in extreme cases, actions designed to avoid the rules altogether ("Time and again, financial innovation finds a lucrative path around regulation").[7] While laws and rules designed to prevent excesses may avoid disasters, they also constrain the huge benefits that result from the freedom to innovate. At a minimum, "legislation is designed to enforce minimum standards. CSR is about best practice. . . . A government can no more legislate for best practice than it can repeal the laws of gravity."[8] Or, as Milton Friedman puts it, "If you put the federal government in charge of the Sahara Desert, in five years there'd be a shortage of sand."[9]

Voluntary Versus Mandatory

At one end of the spectrum is an argument in favor of enacting and enforcing laws and rules that seek to control the worst excesses of firms:

Existing laws do not compel a high enough standard of social behavior. Companies will never do more than is required of them if the action is considered a cost to business. Therefore, new and stricter legislation is required to compel more responsible corporate behavior.

At the other end of the spectrum is an argument in favor of incentivizing action by demonstrating the value of compliance:

Companies should realize it is in their best interests to make sure the communities in which they do business accept them. It is those communities' expectations and shifting standards that will define what is and what is not acceptable behavior. Best practice cannot easily be defined or mandated. If CSR behavior is tied to success, then the profit motive will provide the ideal incentive for the necessary innovation.

Needless to say, there are also several shades of gray between these two points of view at the extremes.

Compliance with stakeholder expectations goes to the heart of CSR because it largely dictates the degree to which a company is accepted by society. Those companies that add value will be welcomed, and those that are perceived to be detracting from the general well-being will be criticized and eventually rejected. As such, there is a strong case for the strict regulation of a company's actions when they come into (potentially negative) contact with society. Left to its own devices and if it felt it could get away with it, for example, a firm transporting nuclear waste might be tempted to avoid undertaking all the costly precautions necessary to ensure a safe journey. As the discussion above suggests, however, there is an equally strong case to be made that a company has to be genuinely committed to implementing CSR in order for it to be effective and that no amount of regulation can dictate such commitment.

Alan Greenspan and the Financial Crisis

Alan Greenspan (chairman of the US Federal Reserve from 1987 to 2006) has long been an advocate of self-regulation (voluntary compliance) within the financial industry:

"It is in the self-interest of every businessman to have a reputation for honest dealings and a quality product," he wrote ... in 1963. Regulation, he said, undermines this "superlatively moral system" by replacing competition for reputation with force.[10]

Government regulatory interventions—such as producing a national currency and guaranteeing individual savings deposits—Greenspan argues, reduces "the incentive for bankers and businessmen to act prudently...[and makes] depositors less concerned about the reputation of the bank to which they entrusted their money."[11]

Needless to say, the 2007–2008 financial crisis shook Greenspan's unwavering faith in the self-correcting power of the market. Appearing before the House Committee on Oversight and Government Reform to give testimony on the crisis, Greenspan declared, "Those of us who have looked to the self-interest of lending institutions to protect shareholders' equity, myself included, are in a state of shocked disbelief."[12]

Many CSR advocates believe that voluntary change is central to an understanding of CSR as the "integration of environmental and social considerations into core business operations over and above legal obligations, and is based on dialogue with stakeholders."[13] It is also easy to imagine, however, that a system in which companies determined their own operational costs and guidelines would be ripe for abuse. It is not challenging to find examples of companies that have sought to deceive their external stakeholders for private gain:

> Enron, for example, proudly presented its CSR credentials as a giant PR exercise while internally betraying them. Unless companies really own CSR it is only window-dressing, argue the voluntarists. . . . The best instrument is to show business that behaving well is good business, so that it adopts CSR willingly and internalizes it.[14]

In general, people have argued for a place for regulation in areas of greatest concern to the largest number of people. In France, for example, "all public companies [are] required to report social and environmental information as part of the annual report";[15] in 2011, "Ecuador and Bolivia [both] passed a law . . . granting all nature equal rights to humans";[16] and in Mexico in 2013, the government passed a soda tax that "prompted a substantial increase in prices and a resulting drop in the sales of drinks sweetened with sugar."[17] As noted above, however, the trouble with well-intentioned regulation is that compliance can be costly. Where costs become too high, the advantages of remaining public are reduced and the dangers to society increase as firms shrink from the glare of public oversight: "The number of public companies has fallen dramatically over the past decade—by 38% in America since 1997 and 48% in Britain."[18]

While too much regulation stifles entrepreneurship and encourages inefficiency, firms' best interests require an understanding that stakeholder definitions of acceptable behavior are dynamic. If firms ignore stakeholder interests as they evolve, a potentially more damaging backlash of widespread, punitive regulation may stifle the business environment for all. Ironically, it is often those firms that have felt the brunt of the stakeholder attention in the past that are subsequently the most proactive regarding CSR. These companies understand more completely how reacting positively to societal concerns serves their self-interest.

Given the very real concerns that drive advocates to support mandatory government intervention, together with the acknowledged potential costs that result from such constraints, an interesting alternative draws on economic theory and human psychology to deliver more socially optimal outcomes without discarding the freedom to choose among different options.

BEHAVIORAL ECONOMICS

What is the most effective way to encourage recycling? Is it better to appeal to people's self-interest, arguing the importance of creating a sustainable economic model that minimizes the impact on the world's resources so that their children and their children's children can have a planet to inherit? Or, is it better to mandate specific actions that seek to alter behavior? Much of the argument presented in this textbook is based on the assumption that it is only when firms become convinced of the self-interest inherent in socially responsible behavior that meaningful change will occur. In terms of individual consumer behavior in relation to recycling, however, there is evidence to suggest that mandated action is effective. There is also evidence to suggest that, if a shift in consumer behavior occurs, then firms will quickly adapt.

In the case of recycling by companies, some understand the value of voluntary action—that they can reduce costs and, therefore, increase efficiency by recycling. As highlighted below, Walmart's work in this area is now considered best practice. This is partly to do with the scale on which Walmart operates, but it is also clear that the firm genuinely sees sustainability as a means to become more efficient and pass those lower costs on to customers as ever-lower prices. Anheuser-Busch is another firm that has long been recognized as following recycling best practice. By 2013, the firm was recycling "99.8 percent of the solid waste generated in the brewing and packaging process, including beechwood chips, aluminum, glass, brewers' grain, scrap metal, cardboard and many other items."[19]

In spite of this, the overall recycling rate in the United States, particularly in relation to plastics, is not encouraging, with only 1.44 of the 5.15 billion pounds of plastic bottles used every year recycled.[20] In total, almost 600 billion pounds of single-use plastic (plastic that is used once and disposed) are produced every year. While many of these products are essential, such as disposable syringes, the vast majority of them, "like the bags, drinking straws, packaging and lighters commonly found in beach clean-ups, are essentially prefab litter with a heavy environmental cost."[21] In terms of individual consumers, therefore, it would help if we recycled a lot more of the plastic we use. A good place to start would be the plastic bag:

> After the plastic water bottle, you couldn't do much better than the plastic shopping bag as a symbol of American consumerism run amok. We go through 380 billion a year. An estimated 5.2% get recycled; in landfills, they could last 1,000 years. Bags are made from oil, and our bag habit costs us 1.6 billion gallons each year.[22]

Plastic Bags

Two interesting social experiments indicate that legislation mandating specific action carries the potential to produce much greater and quicker change than appealing to consumers' greener instincts. First, IKEA introduced a policy to charge consumers for any plastic bags they use and donate the money generated to a nonprofit organization. Within six months, the policy "cut bag consumption in the United States by more than 50%. . . . In the United Kingdom, the policy . . . cut bag use by 95%."[23]

With the introduction of its leadership "bag the plastic bag" program . . . , IKEA set a goal of reducing its US stores' plastic bag consumption by 50%; from 70 million to 35 million plastic bags in the first year. . . . Now it is one year since the program began and . . . more than 92% of their customers said no more plastic bags![24]

As a result of the policy's success, the firm decided to make it permanent so that "IKEA will no longer offer plastic bags, and paper bags are not available in IKEA stores either."[25]

The second experiment was conducted by the Irish government, which passed the equivalent of a 33 cent tax on every plastic bag used.[26] Similar to the results seen by IKEA, the tax had a dramatic and immediate impact on consumer behavior:

Within weeks, plastic bag use dropped 94 percent. Within a year, nearly everyone had bought reusable cloth bags, keeping them in offices and in the backs of cars. Plastic bags were not outlawed, but carrying them became socially unacceptable—on a par with wearing a fur coat or not cleaning up after one's dog.[27]

It is estimated that, every month worldwide, as many as "42 billion plastic bags [are] used"[28]—that is in only one month! Every year, major supermarkets in England go through "roughly 7.6 billion single-use plastic bags, about 140 per person."[29] The IKEA and Ireland experiments show that dramatic change is possible, given the political will. Having noted the rapid change in behavior, the government of Wales put a 5 pence per bag charge in place and quickly recorded that "usage of plastic bags has dropped 79 percent."[30] Ireland is planning to build on its success, "proposing similar taxes on customers for A.T.M. receipts and chewing gum."[31] The real lesson from the IKEA and Irish government's success, however, is not that coercion works but that well-designed policies can incentivize humans to change their behavior radically and quickly. We will make good decisions when offered good choices:

Ever since Aristotle defined man as a rational animal, that has been seen as the very essence of our species. But the philosopher left a little room for interpretation. Did he mean man to be perennially rational, constantly raising himself above the beasts, or rather merely capable of such rationality, but infrequently demonstrating it? The latter is the more plausible.[32]

Nudges

While proponents of mandatory regulation to encourage CSR have always focused on a mix of coercive incentives and strict punishments to achieve the goals they seek, the pathway toward encouraging voluntary behavior has been less clear. Recent research in this area suggests that using a mix of economic and psychological tools is effective. While financial incentives (economics) have always played a role, more recent behavioral research suggests that peer group pressure (social psychology) can also help generate socially optimal outcomes.

Economics is all about how people make choices; sociology is all about how they don't have any choices to make.

James Duesenberry[33]

As the quote above suggests, economists and social scientists have traditionally disagreed vehemently about what drives human behavior. The emergence of *behavioral economics* as a field of research offers a bridge between the two disciplines and, more importantly for strategic CSR, offers a promising solution to the mandatory versus voluntary debate. This exciting area of study combines economic theory and human psychology to account for the irrational nature of our decision making—it deals with the "frailties of the human mind":[34]

[Behavioral economists] predict and explain how people use faulty logic in building a framework for making decisions. Then they figure out how to make people behave properly by inserting new triggers for better behavior.[35]

The application of this work to public policy suggests that subtle *nudges* to human behavior can have dramatic effects. Nudges incorporate the biases that inform our decisions into policies that encourage *optimal* social outcomes, while still retaining the *illusion* of choice:

Behavioural economists have found that all sorts of psychological or neurological biases cause people to make choices that seem contrary to their best interests. The idea of nudging is based on research that shows it is possible to steer people towards better decisions by presenting choices in different ways.[36]

When deployed intelligently, the results can be powerful. In one experiment in the UK, different versions of a letter were sent to people who had not paid their vehicle taxes:[37]

[For some recipients, the letter] was changed to use plainer English, along the lines of "pay your tax or lose your car." In some cases the letter was further personalised by including a photo of the car in question. The rewritten letter alone doubled the number of people paying the tax; the rewrite with the photo tripled it. . . . A study into the teaching of technical drawing in French schools found that if the subject was called "geometry" boys did better, but if it was called "drawing" girls did equally well or better.[38]

There are vast areas of public policy for which nudges would help achieve the intended goals. In spite of the perception that most people in developed economies pay their personal income taxes, for example, the reality is that many do not. In the United States alone, "the gap between what is owed and what is paid is nearly $400 billion a year . . . and about £40 billion ($70 billion) in Britain."[39] The key to improving compliance lies in the way choices are presented. The crucial question is always *What is the most effective way to produce the desired outcome?* Take the healthcare issue of obesity. Sometimes the best approach is a consumption tax (e.g., "a per ounce tax on beverages with added sugar"),[40] sometimes a ban on certain foods (such as excessive serving sizes[41] or those containing high levels of trans fat[42]), but sometimes motivating people to make different choices can be as simple as improving access and choice.

In order to understand how children choose which foods to eat for their school lunches, for example, researchers studied selection behavior in school cafeterias. What they found was that, simply by placing the lower nutrition foods in harder-to-reach places (e.g., placing fresh milk at the front of the counter and chocolate milk toward the back), they were able to alter the selections made. Placing broccoli at the beginning of the food line, for example, "increased the amount students purchased by 10 percent to 15 percent," while encouraging the use of trays resulted in higher vegetable consumption ("students without trays eat 21 percent less salad but no less ice-cream").[43] A similar benefit was achieved by researchers who used shopping carts in supermarkets that were marked with separate labeled sections for fruits, vegetables, and other groceries. What they found was that by making the sections marked for fruits and vegetables larger (by moving the demarcation lines in the cart), people bought more of those healthier foods.[44] Of course, the reverse psychology is employed by supermarkets that place chocolate and candy near the checkouts so that children will pester their parents to buy these items when they are most distracted and, therefore, least likely to resist.[45]

The goal of behavioral economics, therefore, is to explain human action in terms of empirical examination rather than theoretical assumptions. Its value for public policy lies in the ability to shape human action to achieve socially beneficial outcomes, while retaining the individual choice that is an essential component of an open society:

> When you renew your driver's license, you have a chance to enroll in an organ donation program. In countries like Germany and the U.S., you have to check a box if you want to opt in. Roughly 14 percent of people do. But . . . how you set the defaults is really important. So in other countries, like Poland or France, you have to check a box if you want to opt out. In these countries, more than 90 percent of people participate.[46]

The extent to which nudge economics is now influencing public policy is demonstrated by the establishment of a Social and Behavioral Sciences Team (https://sbst.gov/) in the United States that seeks to "use what research tells us about how people make decisions to better serve Americans and improve government efficiency." This unit was designed to emulate the Behavioral Insights Team in the UK (BIT, http://www.behaviouralinsights.co.uk/), which was set up by the government in 2010 to make policy recommendations. While the unit has been a success, it has been constrained by the scale on which it has operated, saving the British government "only £300m ($457m), a negligible proportion of GDP" over a 2-year period.[47]

Faced with alternatives, people choose what they perceive to be in their best interests. An understanding of behavioral economics helps us shape those decisions in ways that can promote socially beneficial outcomes. But, there is danger in governments deciding what is *socially beneficial*. And when this approach is used in the private sector, there is the danger that some companies will use it to mislead consumers. As Richard Thaler lays out in an article, three principles should inform the ethical use of nudges:

1. "All nudging should be transparent and never misleading."

2. "It should be as easy as possible to opt out of the nudge."

3. "There should be good reason to believe that the behavior being encouraged will improve the welfare of those being nudged."[48]

When these principles are followed, nudges provide a powerful tool to further individual and societal well-being. Of course, the debate over what exactly is in our *best interest* is fierce. Ultimately, we live in a free society, and it is our collective decisions that determine what society needs and wants. A company that sits at the center of this debate is Walmart.

WALMART

As the largest for-profit firm in the world, Walmart embodies the full range of CSR concerns as it engages with stakeholders and continues to expand. As such, this extended example illustrates the interconnections between corporate actions and consequences (from the perspective of Walmart's stakeholders) that can release a cascade of effects tempered by economic, cultural, and other realities. The intent is not to praise or condemn but merely to highlight the breadth and depth of CSR, as seen from the perspective of this important firm.

The Walmart Paradox

Walmart is the world's largest company and, as such, is a test case for CSR. Walmart is clearly an extremely successful company. It has become so because it delivers a great deal of value to the tens of millions of customers who shop at its stores every week.

Walmart

Some facts about the world's largest private-sector firm:[49]

- Each week, Walmart serves more than 200 million customers at more than 10,400 stores in 27 countries.
- Walmart has more employees worldwide than the population of Houston. The firm employs 1.4 million people in the U.S. alone.
- 90% of all Americans live within 15 miles of a Walmart.
- In 2012, Walmart registered $444 billion in sales. . . . If Walmart were a country, it would be the 26th largest economy in the world.
- It is bigger than Home Depot, Kroger, Target, Sears, Costco, and K-Mart, combined.
- China's exports to Walmart accounted for 11% of the growth of the total U.S. trade deficit with China between 2001 and 2006.
- In 2010, [Walmart CEO's] annual salary of $35 million earned him more in an hour than a full-time employee makes in an entire year.
- In 2000, Walmart was sued 4,851 times—about once every 2 hours.

Some things you didn't know about the food sold at Walmart:[50]

- It is the biggest seller of organic milk (and buyer of organic cotton) in the world.
- Its zero-waste-to-landfill program donated 571 million pounds of food in 2013.
- Walmart sources $4 billion annually from approximately 1.4 million small and medium-sized farmers.
- One out of every four grocery dollars is spent at Walmart (the average family spends more than $4,000 a year at the store).

In spite of this success, to Google "Walmart" is to reveal the extent to which many of its stakeholders are dissatisfied with the firm. This is partly because of its business strategy of minimizing costs, which relies on policies and decisions that affect stakeholders in different ways (often perceived as negative). *Employees* of Walmart, for example, complain that their wages are too low (even though the firm routinely has more job applicants than openings available).[51] *Suppliers* to Walmart complain that their margins are continually squeezed by the firm's unrelenting focus on cost reduction (even while they compete fiercely to supply the firm). *Regulators* complain that the state has to subsidize the low wages and benefits Walmart pays its employees (even as they welcome the jobs the company provides). And, the steady flow of litigation against the firm attests to the wide range of additional stakeholders (from female employees to the local communities in which Walmart has announced a new store) who object to some aspect of Walmart's business.

In pursuit of its self-interest, it appears that Walmart is constrained on all sides by its stakeholders. Even while today "Walmart operates over 11,500 retail units under 65 banners in 28 countries [and employs] 2.2 million associates around the world—1.3 million in the U.S. alone,"[52] as one writer observed,

"Wal-Mart might well be both America's most admired and most hated company."[53] And, the controversy its ongoing success generates follows it around the world as it continues to expand at an ever-increasing rate (as indicated by Figure 8.1).

As a result of its size and success ("Ninety-six percent of Americans live within 20 miles of a Walmart")[54] and, in particular, the perception that the firm does as much harm as good, the argument *against* CSR offers up Walmart as its main case in point. Does the fact that consumers continue to shop at the store (on average, almost 30 million customers pass through Walmart's doors every day)[55] critically undermine the argument in favor of strategic CSR as the pursuit of self-interest? If the criticisms of the firm are true, what role do Walmart's stakeholders have in producing more socially responsible behavior? The paradox that surrounds Walmart and the controversy its success generates explain why the firm is a case study across the business disciplines. Ultimately, *Is Walmart good for society?*

| Figure 8.1 | Walmart Stores Worldwide: Total Number of Retail Stores per Country, by Region (July 2015) |

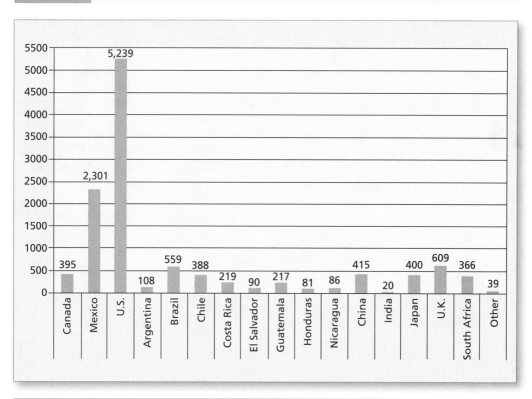

Source: http://corporate.walmart.com/our-story/locations/ (accessed September 2015).

IS WALMART GOOD FOR SOCIETY?

Is it healthy for an economy to have companies with the size and power of Walmart? Proponents of the pro-Walmart case credit the company with directly saving US consumers billions of dollars because of the downward pressure it exerts on its own prices and the prices of its competitors.[56] As a result, it is credited with holding down inflation and driving economic growth to the extent that "about 12% of the economy's productivity gains in the second half of the 1990s could be traced to Wal-Mart alone."[57]

Walmart gives consumers what they indicate (with their shopping practices) they want—reasonable quality at low prices. Yet the methods by which Walmart achieves these cost savings and low prices are also having a lasting impact, often negative, in the eyes of other stakeholders:

> Wal-Mart is a double-edged sword, and both edges are quite sharp. . . . On the price side, consumers wouldn't flood Wal-Mart if there wasn't something there they liked, the low prices. On the other hand, by sticking solidly to the low-wage path, they create tons of low-quality jobs that dampen wage and income growth, not just for those who work in Wal-Mart but for surrounding communities as well.[58]

There are many potential dangers of this business model. Even if consumers are content with low prices today, what if they start to worry more about the impact the company is having on the wider society? Communities that worry about a megastore's impact on rural downtowns have already restricted Walmart's growth.[59] Will employees continue to apply for positions at Walmart if better paid alternatives exist? As the company continues to expand, will the government begin to fear the monopolistic characteristics of a firm with such a huge presence in the market? Suppliers are stakeholders who relish Walmart's market scale and scope, yet fear the firm's pricing pressures. How will these various stakeholder reactions affect Walmart's business strategy over the longer term? What is the outlook for the company from a CSR perspective?

Is Walmart Good for Society? Yes!

- ☺ Reasonable quality and low prices for consumers (lower inflation)
- ☺ Good jobs in economically deprived regions
- ☺ Wide range of products
- ☺ Redefinition of supply chain management (SCM) through technological efficiencies
- ☺ Increased productivity

Is Walmart Good for Society? No!

- ☹ Loss of domestic jobs to overseas suppliers
- ☹ Strong opposition to collective representation of workforce

⊗ Relatively low employee wages and benefits
⊗ Competitors (and sometimes suppliers) go out of business, reducing competition and, ultimately, consumer choice
⊗ Litigation against the company brought by many stakeholder groups

In 2002, Walmart became the number one firm in the Fortune 500[60] and has remained either number one or number two ever since.[61] In 2003 and 2004, Walmart also was named Fortune's Most Admired Company in America[62] and has routinely placed in the top 50 firms on that list ever since.[63] It is the largest for-profit organization in the world and, as the discussion above indicates, continues to generate both passion and loathing.

None of the issues discussed so far, however, solves the paradox that Walmart's promise to produce low prices and "Save money. Live better." appeals to the very workers who cannot afford to pay more. Many of these workers have had their wages driven down and their job security threatened because of Walmart's pursuit of ever-lower costs, whether they work for the company itself, a supplier, a competitor, or another company in the affected labor pool.

A CSR perspective argues that Walmart's business model will only remain viable as long as the firm's attractions offset any negative consequences of its actions. Ultimately, a strategy of low prices that alienates some stakeholders (even while satisfying others) could erode the innovation, choice, and societal support necessary to operate. CSR is an argument about business today, together with an understanding of what business will be about tomorrow. In order for Walmart to sustain its dominant market position, stakeholder theory suggests that a CSR perspective should be embedded throughout the firm. Absent this shift, Walmart is endangering its societal legitimacy, particularly among the key constituents (such as employees and local community zoning boards) that are crucial to its growth mandate. Mounting evidence suggests that Walmart understands this and has moved to change its perception among specific stakeholder groups, at least in terms of sustainability.

Walmart and Sustainability

If CSR is central to a firm's competitiveness in a global business environment, how is it that a firm like Walmart can apparently ignore calls for greater CSR from key stakeholders? The answer is that perhaps it cannot. Walmart's position regarding CSR has evolved drastically in the last decade, a transition it has been forced to make because the "'constant barrage of negatives' in the US over everything from Wal-Mart's low wage business model to alleged discrimination against women [threatened] the company's ability to grow":[64]

Walmart adopted sustainability as a corporate strategy in 2005. It was struggling mightily at the time. Bad headlines stalked the chain, as its history of mistreating workers and suppliers finally caught up with it. One analysis found that as many as 8 percent of Walmart's customers had stopped shopping at its stores. Grassroots groups were blocking or delaying one-third of its development projects. Stockholders were growing nervous. Between 2000 and 2005, Walmart's share price fell 20 percent.[65]

In contrast, Walmart is today considered to be a market leader in sustainability.[66] An early indication of the firm's dramatic shift occurred when Walmart announced a $35 million campaign in partnership with the National Fish and Wildlife Foundation "to offset the amount of land [Walmart] develops to use for its stores and other facilities" by purchasing 138,000 acres "of land in sensitive habitats" for conservation.[67] But, the real shift came in a speech given by then CEO Lee Scott ("Wal-Mart: Twenty First Century Leadership")[68] shortly after the devastation of Hurricane Katrina in the United States in August 2005. In the immediate aftermath of the storm, Walmart was the first source of relief for residents. The firm had the distribution network to restock its stores with those supplies that were in demand with an efficiency that the federal and state governments were unable to match.[69] The experience was reported to have been a personal revelation for Scott. This sense of "a key personal moment"[70] was conveyed in the speech he subsequently delivered a couple of months later in October 2005:[71]

> To better understand our critics and Wal-Mart's impact on the world and society, [our top executives] spent a year meeting with and listening to customers, Associates, citizen groups, government leaders, non-profits and non-government organizations, and other individuals. . . . Most of our vocal critics do not want us to stop doing business, but they feel business needs to change, not just our company, but all companies.[72]

In particular, Scott used the speech to commit Walmart to an overarching framework of three environmental goals.

Walmart's Environmental Goals[73]

1. To be supplied 100 percent by renewable energy
2. To create zero waste
3. To sell products that sustain our resources and environment

As an initial step toward these goals, Scott announced a number of quantifiable policy targets, such as "reducing greenhouse gases at our existing [stores] . . . by 20 percent over the next 7 years"; "increasing our fleet efficiency by 25 percent in the next 3 years"; "reducing our solid waste from U.S. [stores] by 25 percent in the next 3 years"; and "working with suppliers to create less packaging overall, increase product packaging recycling and increase use of post-consumer material."[74] Taken together, these commitments built a comprehensive sustainability policy about which Walmart appears to be both serious and sincere:

> [Hurricane] Katrina asked this critical question, and I want to ask it of you: What would it take for Wal-Mart to be that company, at our best, all the time? What if we used our size and resources to make this country and this earth an even better place for all of us: customers, Associates, our children, and generations unborn?[75]

In essence, Walmart's consumers make short-term purchase decisions based on price, placing less emphasis on the longer-term societal consequences of those decisions. Implementing a stakeholder perspective reveals to Walmart that there is a broader set of stakeholders to which the firm must pay attention if it wants to remain viable over the long term. Importantly, as Walmart exposes itself to different ideas, it is discovering that responding to its stakeholders' demands need not diminish the firm's business model and may even enhance it:

> At today's prices, if we improve our fleet fuel mileage by just one mile per gallon, we can save over 52 million dollars a year. We will increase our fleet efficiency by 25% over the next 3 years and double it within 10 years. If implemented across our entire fleet by 2015, this would amount to savings of more than $310mn a year.[76]

Walmart's decisions affect not only its own operations but also those of all of its stakeholders. For example, its 2006 decision "to stock only double concentrate liquid laundry detergent led to the entire US detergent industry shifting to smaller, lighter bottlers by the start of [2008], saving millions of dollars in fuel costs."[77] The same year, the firm announced a goal to sell 100 million compact fluorescent lightbulbs (CFLs) by the end of 2007, an achievement that "would save consumers $3 billion in electricity costs and cut U.S. power needs by the equivalent of 450,000 homes." In the end, Walmart easily exceeded its goal:

> In 2007, it sold 162 million CFLs. Shipments of the bulbs surged across the U.S., surpassing 400 million—more than double the 2006 total. Walmart's massive purchase of CFLs allowed it to dictate specs to its suppliers. It required Energy Star–rated bulbs . . . and got manufacturers to reduce the amount of mercury in CFLs. Walmart's actions also helped secure passage of the Energy Independence Act of 2007, which ordered the gradual phase-out of inefficient incandescent bulls by 2015.[78]

Literally, Walmart has the ability to change the world.[79] And as it realizes the benefits that accrue from a more progressive approach, its ambition also grows. In 2009, for example, Walmart's CEO announced a commitment "to create a global, industry-wide sustainable product index. The ambitious plan . . . aims to establish a sustainability rating system for each item on Wal-Mart's shelves."[80] It is worth emphasizing the enormity of this task: "to track the life cycle of every product it sells, measuring it on water use, greenhouse-gas emissions, and fair labor practices."[81] The complexity of the goal is astounding. Given Walmart's size and influence, however, it demands to be taken seriously. The subsequent "Sustainability Index"[82] has evolved into a consortium of firms, activists, and governmental agencies that "has attracted everyone from Monsanto to Disney, Seventh Generation to the EPA"[83] and "drives scientific research and the development of standards and IT tools, through a collaborative process, to enhance the ability to understand and address the environmental, social, and economic implications of products."[84]

So, is Walmart promoting sustainability this aggressively because of a belief in the ethical, moral, rational, or economic arguments for CSR? Walmart would be wise if it is acting for all four reasons. The firm appears to realize that, even if specific stakeholders do not care or think about CSR in the short term, there are *ethical* and *moral* arguments for actions that win it support with other important groups. In addition, there are very *rational* arguments for pursuing a course of action that limits potential future constraints on the firm's business interests. Finally, Walmart also undoubtedly recognizes that implementing a CSR perspective assists the firm in its overall *economic* goal of providing goods to consumers as efficiently as possible.

One of the benefits Walmart hopes to accrue from its work with the Sustainability Index, for example, is to better understand the processes by which the products it sells are made and distributed so it can extend its efficiencies (and cut costs) throughout the supply chain. In short, it is the combination of all four arguments for CSR that has resulted in Walmart's current sustainability vision, which appears genuine.[85] Nevertheless, the firm's approach is still being met with skepticism by some. Due to the firm's narrow focus on sustainability (where it can cut costs) and a reluctance to adopt a broader CSR perspective (which sometimes involves higher costs), Walmart's overall CSR performance remains open to challenge.

Walmart and Greenwash

In 2015, Walmart celebrated the 10th anniversary of Lee Scott's pivotal 2005 speech. The firm has come a long way in the subsequent decade, during which total revenue has "grown by just over 50 percent . . . from about $315 billion to $485 billion" and its stores (both Walmart and Sam's Club) have grown "from about 6,500 . . . to more than 11,000":[86]

> Already famously efficient, [Walmart] has become more so, driving efficiency and sustainable practices deeper into its supply chain so that food is grown with less fertilizer, stuff arrives with less packaging, trucks use less fuel and fisheries are better managed.[87]

Walmart has "reduced its energy costs per square foot of retail floor space by 9%."[88] Moreover, it "has installed 105 megawatts of solar panels—enough to power about 20,000 houses—on the roofs of 327 stores and distribution centers."[89] The firm is already the largest commercial solar generator in the country but intends to double its efforts by 2020.

But, judged by the standard Lee Scott set for the firm back in 2005, there is still much work to be done. For example, while the firm's total emissions peaked in 2012, "holding emissions steady, or driving them down, while adding stores is hard to do." Further, "Walmart has failed to set science-based targets for its climate emissions," an essential step. And in terms of renewable energy, "progress towards the goal of buying 100% renewable energy has been slow. Globally, about 26% of its energy comes from renewable sources; in the US, it's about 13%."[90] As a result, even as Walmart continues to implement its sustainability program and proclaims progress,[91] accusations of "greenwash" continue.[92] It is estimated, for example, that at its current pace, it will take Walmart 300 years to reach its goal of 100% renewable energy:[93]

This criticism arises partly due to Walmart's size and reach (its rural stores "contributed heavily to the more than 40 per cent increase in the amount of vehicle miles American households travel for shopping purposes since 1990"),[95] partly due to its employment policies ("Wal-Mart Lowers Benefits for Employee Health Care"),[96] and partly due to its continued success ("If Walmart continues to add stores at its current growth rate, its new stores alone will use significantly more energy than any of its energy-saving measures will save").[97] But more than this, the trouble with Walmart's approach to sustainability is that it is only willing to improve when it knows it can reduce costs. It is much less willing to take the risks that might advance the firm that much quicker. Unfortunately, the planet might be on a different schedule.

Greenwash

Greenwash (green'wash', -wôsh')—*verb*: the act of misleading consumers regarding the environmental practices of a company or the environmental benefits of a product or service[94]

Beyond sustainability, there is evidence to suggest that other aspects of operations have not changed and continue to pose a threat to the firm. The "bribery in Mexico" scandal that was unearthed in 2012 by *The New York Times*,[98] for example, damages Walmart because it details a pattern of corruption and suppression of information (which the firm was legally obligated to report to the US federal government) that continued for a number of years:[99]

Walmart's Mexican arm, Walmex, stands accused of greasing local officials' palms over several years to speed the granting of permits to open new stores. Managers at group headquarters in Bentonville, Arkansas, were apparently informed about the payments . . . in 2005. They launched a probe, but wound it down without disciplining anyone. They did not disclose any of this to the authorities until [December 2011].[100]

The scandal is revealing due to the importance of Mexico to Walmart's worldwide operations (see Figure 8.1): "Today, one in five Wal-Mart stores is in Mexico, . . . where Wal-Mart now employs 209,000 people, making it the country's largest private employer."[101] The result of the bribery probe? In addition to legal challenges from pension funds[102] and protests at its 2012 annual meeting for endangering shareholder value,[103] Walmart faced stock market sanctions that wiped almost 5% off its market capitalization when "jittery investors cut $10 billion from the value of [Walmart's] shares"[104] in the week following *The New York Times* article. And in its 2013 fiscal year, "Walmart took a $157 million charge" against its internal investigation into the scandal.[105]

More important than any specific incident, however, is what the collective pattern of behavior says about Walmart's business model. While the firm attracts a lot of attention purely because it is so large and influential, its shift toward sustainability is remarkable. Even so, it is unlikely that Walmart's business model is sustainable. The firm still relies entirely on growth through expansion—mass consumption in a disposal-oriented society. As it grows, although its commitment to sustainability ensures it consumes fewer resources than it otherwise would, Walmart's carbon footprint continues to expand and its CSR profile continues to draw criticism.

Walmart and Strategic CSR

The central issue of this chapter is to understand how best to achieve *socially responsible* behavior. Is it as a result of firms pursuing their best interests, or is it the result of external stakeholders (such as the government) imposing their will on the firm to force the behavior they seek? A philosophy of strategic CSR suggests that, ultimately, these two things are the same.

In order to understand why this is so, it is essential to understand stakeholder attitudes to CSR and to what extent these attitudes determine company action. Do firms have a responsibility to use their market position to educate stakeholders about CSR and create a point of competitive differentiation? Or, do stakeholders have a responsibility to educate themselves and demand change from firms in order to shape the society in which they wish to live? These are not easy questions, but they are central to the CSR debate. This extended discussion highlights the complexity involved; it also provides an intuitive answer. Walmart is an essential part of the global economy. Whether you love the store or refuse to shop there, understanding what Walmart does and why it does it is integral to understanding the role of CSR in business today.

What should have been apparent from the discussion above is that different stakeholders have different perspectives and that these different perspectives often lead to conflict. In other examples, corporate actions may be less ambiguous with more direct consequences—think of Bhopal, India, where a Union Carbide plant accident killed thousands;[106] Enron's self-destruction due to the irresponsible behavior of its leaders that resulted in lost jobs and shareholder value (as well as criminal indictments); or the 2007–2008 financial crisis that was fueled by the selling of subprime mortgages to people with little chance of repaying the loans, resulting in record foreclosures and evictions. In these examples, and others presented in this book, a lack of basic (let alone *strategic*) CSR led to condemnation, along with significant legal and market penalties.

In most cases, however, the consequences of firms' actions are more ambiguous. In general, firms that ignore stakeholder tradeoffs face limits, as suggested by the "iron law of social responsibility" (Chapter 1). The backlash to a firm's indifference, however, is not necessarily felt immediately—the tobacco and fast-food industries stand as prime examples. Nevertheless, a firm that fails to reflect the evolving interests of its stakeholders is risking its future. Walmart appreciates this sentiment more today than previously. The firm exists because, ultimately, it provides value to its stakeholders. Accusations that the firm underpays its employees and puts "mom-and-pop" stores out of business represent a fundamental misunderstanding of basic economics. Firms that underpay their employees do not have applications that far outweigh vacancies. And Walmart does not put anyone out of business—while the firm obviously competes fiercely, it is customers who decide not to shop at mom-and-pop stores and do so because, for them, Walmart is a better proposition.

What is increasingly evident, however, is that in the past, Walmart had offended some stakeholders and, as a result, its reputation was beginning to hurt its ability to operate. When stakeholders convey a clear message to a firm and then follow up by punishing the behavior they do not want and rewarding the behavior they do, firms react. And Walmart has demonstrated a capacity to adapt. The firm has made great strides in the last decade (even raising wages in response to market forces),[107] but it still retains a relatively narrow CSR perspective. Walmart focuses its efforts almost exclusively on environmental sustainability as a means of doing what it does best—reducing costs and passing those savings on to customers in the form of lower prices. Until its stakeholders enforce other changes they wish to see, Walmart will have some work to do to reach its CSR potential. Because of its continued selectivity in relation to the larger issues of social responsibility, Walmart will remain subject to stakeholder scrutiny and criticism.

Financial success for firms in the 21st century will increasingly be defined by those organizations that can foster the most symbiotic relationships with their stakeholders. In order to achieve this, firms need to work proactively and not merely react to what their stakeholders are telling them today. Stakeholder and broader societal concerns are fluid. What is *acceptable* today can become *unacceptable* very quickly. To some extent, therefore, while firms need to understand their stakeholders' needs today and meet those needs, they should also seek to exceed those needs by anticipating how they will evolve tomorrow. Certainly, the benefits to Walmart of its sustainability efforts so far indicate the value of fully committing to a CSR perspective. As the employee charged with working with Walmart at the Environmental Defense Fund put it, "It is getting harder and harder to hate Walmart."[108]

What this relationship also reveals, however, is that a firm's stakeholders have a great deal of influence in shaping corporate actions. As such, stakeholders have an incentive to use that influence to help shape the society in which they want to live. Just as we get the politicians we vote for, we get the businesses we patronize (customers), supply (suppliers), and regulate (government). Stakeholders need to use their influence and purchasing power to reward the behavior they support and punish the behavior they consider *irresponsible* (however that is defined today). If we do not demand change, we should not be surprised when firms do not deliver it. Firms are incentivized to generate profits, so it is up to a firm's stakeholders to ensure that the best way to achieve those profits is to act in a socially responsible manner.

Strategic CSR Debate

MOTION: Nudge economics is a tool for progressive change in the hands of government, but it is potentially dangerous in the hands of firms.

QUESTIONS FOR DISCUSSION AND REVIEW

1.   Should companies be persuaded to incorporate a CSR perspective voluntarily or forced to do so? Why? Which of these two approaches is ideal? Which is more realistic?

2.   Google the terms *csr, mandatory,* and *voluntary.* What is your reaction to how this debate is unfolding in the business world? Where do you think most firms would like the balance between coercion and incentives to fall?

3.   In 2003, the Norwegian government passed a law that was designed to force public companies to have 40% female directors on their boards. At the time "only 6 per cent of directors were female." The law came into effect in 2008, and as a result, today Norway "has the world's highest proportion of female board members. . . . 44 per cent of directors are women."[109] This compares, in 2015, to "only 15 percent of seats on the boards of the S&P 1500."[110] How well do you feel women are represented as executives and directors in your country? Do you think a law similar to Norway's would improve things?

4.   Walmart argues that it provides valuable jobs to small communities and should be allowed to grow. Critics argue that these jobs are often low-paying, with few benefits. What is your position? Is a low-paying job better than no job at all?

5.   Compare Walmart's current and previous logos:

Which do you prefer? Why? Do you believe that Walmart is sincere in its commitment to sustainability issues, or is its public stance just an example of corporate *greenwash*?

Chapter 9

ACCOUNTABILITY

Do you think of corporate social responsibility in terms of a dichotomy (i.e., a firm is either socially responsible or not)? Or, do you think of CSR in terms of a continuum (i.e., all firms are either more or less socially responsible, depending on a number of factors and the context in which they occur)? If it is the former, then CSR is relatively easy to measure and there are plenty of options out there that claim to capture the CSR profile of firms. If it is the latter, however, then CSR is very difficult even to conceptualize fully in all its many dimensions, let alone measure accurately.

In general, dichotomous measures of CSR are unhelpful to those who advocate for greater CSR for two reasons: (1) They contain the biases of the measuring organization (e.g., excluding specific industries, such as tobacco or firearms), and (2) CSR is more complicated than a simple *yes* or *no*. All firms contain good *and* bad; the goal is to be able to capture accurately the *net effect*—on balance, is a firm better or worse than other firms? The difficulty lies in equating these effects across the spectrum of firm activities. Is a *responsible* firm in the pharmaceuticals industry, for example, equivalent to a *responsible* firm in the airlines industry? It is impossible to answer this question meaningfully unless you use a standard evaluation system that captures all dimensions of action across all firms and industries. As such, any attempt to use dichotomous ratings to measure a causal relationship between CSR and overall firm performance (the foundation of a business argument for CSR) is unlikely to generate reliable or valid results. In terms of strategic CSR, therefore, it is essential to think of firm performance as a continuum, rather than a dichotomy.

Once CSR is thought of in terms of a continuum, what is the best way to measure it? Is a tobacco firm that employs tens of thousands of people and pays significant taxes a *better* or *worse* firm (in terms of CSR performance) than a supermarket that sells food but pays its employees low wages? Is a firearms manufacturer, whose products are used to defend national security, *better* or *worse* than a pharmaceutical firm that produces lifesaving drugs but refuses to make them affordable in developing countries? In adding up the *good* and the *bad*, it is firms that have a *net positive effect* that are incorporating social responsibility into everyday operations. Capturing all possible metrics in a way that is objective and permits comparability across firms and industries, however, is incredibly complex. As a result, *How do we measure CSR?* is one of the most pressing and contentious areas of the CSR debate today.

DEFINING CSR

In order to measure CSR, we first need to define it. But, as with many things related to CSR, this is easier said than done. As noted in the glossary at the front of this book, consistent definitions, rhetoric, and vocabulary remain elusive and fiercely debated within the field of CSR:

> Right now we're in a free-for-all in which "CSR" means whatever a company wants it to mean: From sending employees out in matching t-shirts to paint a wall for five hours a year, to recycling, to improving supply-chain conditions, to diversity and inclusion. This makes it difficult to have a proper conversation about what corporate responsibilities are and should be.[1]

In other words, in spite of a large and growing body of work that seeks to understand a firm's *social responsibility*, there remains great confusion and inconsistency. Far from the absence of possible definitions, however, as the above quote implies, "the problem is rather that there is an abundance of definitions, which are . . . often biased toward specific interests and thus prevent the development and implementations of the concept."[2] As a result, "the CSR literature remains highly fragmented."[3] While there is broad agreement that firms have a social responsibility, there is little agreement on what that responsibility looks like in practice:

> There is . . . considerable debate as to whether [society] requires more of the corporation than the obvious: enhancing the society by creating and delivering products and services consumers want, providing employment and career opportunities for employees, developing markets for suppliers, and paying taxes to governments and returns to shareholders and other claimants on the rents generated by the corporation.[4]

How can we argue that CSR is important if we cannot agree what CSR is, or at least narrow it down to a reasonable set of definitions?[5] If CSR remains idiosyncratic (different things to different people), then it loses its essential meaning and ability to influence the way we structure the economic order. This confusion suggests the need for additional clarification, and hopefully some agreement, before we can begin to measure this complex concept.

MEASURING CSR

Unfortunately, because we have had difficulty defining CSR, we have also not done a very good job of measuring CSR. As a result, we do not have a good sense of what a firm's holistic CSR profile looks like. Although we have some intuitive sense of which firms are *good* and which firms are *bad* (based on our individual assumptions and values), we are presently unable to compare one firm to another reliably across all aspects of operations (particularly if the firms operate in different industries). The reason we are not able to do these things, of course, is that they are incredibly difficult. The challenges involved in defining societal expectations and then quantifying those expectations holistically in terms of firm performance quickly become apparent with a simple thought experiment. Consider the complexities inherent in any attempt to quantify the impact an individual firm's operations has on the environment:

> Let's suppose changes in average world temperature lead to the extinction of, let's say Blue Whales, and an obscure currently undiscovered insect in the Amazon. What valuation would we place on the Blue Whale, and how would we calculate it? On the potential economic value of products that might be extracted from it? On the basis of what someone would be prepared to pay for its existence to be preserved? And what about the insect we never even heard of? Suppose it might hold the secret of a new pharmaceutical discovery? Or then again, it might not.[6]

While we may be able to agree that in the aggregate, economic activity is contributing to climate change,[7] the degree to which it is doing so and what we might do about it remains unclear. In essence, calculating the present-day value of that cost and determining what percentage an individual firm might be expected to pay is extremely challenging.

Should a firm be responsible only for the costs incurred during the production of its products, for example, or also for those incurred during their consumption? Should automobile companies be held responsible for the pollution caused by people driving cars or only for the pollution involved in actually making the cars? What about cell phone companies, where there is little cost to the environment during consumption of the product but the potential for significant damage during disposal? And, what about a firm's supply chain—where does one firm's responsibility begin and another's end? Should a sports shoe company be responsible for the costs incurred during the manufacture of the shoe (even though that process is completed by an independent contractor)? What about the rubber that is used to make the soles of the shoes—is that also the sports shoe company's responsibility, or the responsibility of the contractor who purchases the raw material, or of the plantation where the rubber was initially harvested? There are no easy answers to these questions, which relate only to the *costs* incurred by a firm. What about quantifying the *benefits* the firm and its products provide, which raises a whole new set of challenges? And, perhaps most importantly, how should the net effect of these benefits and costs be calculated?

In spite of these complexities (and many more), the idea that firms have a *social responsibility* remains a pressing question.[8] We remain convinced that CSR matters for a firm to be a success. One way in which this is apparent is our ongoing effort to address the question *What are the effects of CSR on firm per-formance?* Because we are as yet unable to measure CSR accurately, however, the vast majority of studies tend to capture only a narrow slice of a firm's CSR profile (e.g., pollution levels, litigation against the firm, philanthropic donations, etc.). While all of these are important, none of them captures the totality of CSR—a broad construct that encompasses all aspects of operations. The result is more confusion, with some results showing that CSR helps performance, some showing it has no effect, and some that it hurts performance. In short, "the empirical literature on the relationship between CSR and performance is mixed and fraught with empirical question marks around not just how performance is measured but what it means to 'do good.'"[9]

Yet, we continue to believe that CSR matters. It must matter, right? Being *responsible* is better than being *irresponsible*. And it is important for our sense of justice that those firms that are more responsible be rewarded in some way, while those firms that are less responsible are punished. But, what if the reverse is true and it is those firms that make the most effort to be socially responsible that are penalized for doing so by stakeholders who fail to reward the behavior they claim to want from firms?[10] Ultimately, if we cannot come up with consistent definitions of *good* and *bad*, and then construct a set of measures that capture the extent to which these ideas are implemented in practice, how can we determine whether CSR actually matters?

We need to get this right because erroneous correlations cause deterministic judgments to be made about these essential ideas. If we are honest with our-selves, we would understand that, in spite of large numbers of studies on this topic,[11] we do not yet have adequate data to measure the all-encompassing nature of CSR. On the contrary, there is good reason to believe that not only are we unable to measure CSR but the measures we have are gravely misleading. That would explain why firms like Enron and BP win CSR, sustainability, and business ethics awards shortly before they commit devastating ethics and envi-ronmental transgressions. It is also why companies like Kellogg's and PepsiCo are criticized by Oxfam for "ethical shortfalls, scoring low on commitment to improving the rights of women and farmers . . . [and on] transparency," yet "the following month, they were listed as two of the world's most ethical companies by the Ethisphere Institute and awarded at a gala dinner in New York."[12] As Mallen Baker argues:

> One of the most common questions I still get asked by managers and journal-ists alike is for figures to show that "doing CSR" has a measurable and inevi-table positive impact on a company's share price, or on its bottom line. It is a mirage, a distraction. Such figures that do exist are based on a fundamen-tally flawed premise. . . . Not only is there no agreement about what consti-tutes a good, or a sustainable, company, but there is also no agreement even on how you would measure the achievement of these criteria.[13]

Given the apparent futility involved in measuring a firm's CSR profile, must we throw up our hands and surrender, relying instead on subjective moral and ethical arguments to persuade managers to *do the right thing*? To the extent that we can arrive at a standardized way of measuring what we agree should be measured, then we will be able to compare one firm's activity with another's.[14] Whether those numbers are 100% accurate is less important than whether any biases are known and applied equally across all firms. So many of our measurements involve subjective interpretations and assumptions, but are widely perceived as objective statements of fact (e.g., think about how accountants measure brand value or goodwill). Placing relative values on the extinction of the blue whale and the potential damage of an unrealized pharmaceutical discovery will always involve some element of subjectivity and debate. Nevertheless, there is a great deal of benefit in being able to construct a relative and standardized measure of which firms add more or less value. Doing so will help us define CSR accurately and in a way that encourages the reforms in our corporations that are essential to building a more sustainable, value-adding economic system.

This pursuit of defining and measuring CSR is essential because the question *What is the role of the for-profit firm in society?* is highly consequential. Whether we are talking about environmental degradation or social cohesion, wealth distribution or global free trade, the answer to this question defines our immediate and future quality of existence. It determines the society we live in and will pass on to future generations. While some people believe it is impossible to conclude whether a firm is *socially responsible*,[15] the more essential question is relative. In other words, it is important to identify the firms that are more or less responsible than others, without needing to make definitive claims about whether they are absolutely responsible or irresponsible. While recognizing the difficulty in doing so, being able to identify the business models that produce more responsible behavior is a challenge that is inherently worth tackling. Yet, the confusion that is sown by inconsistent definitions, partial measures, and the multitude of labels and rating systems that purport to reveal which products and which firms are *green*, or *ethical*, or *socially responsible* serves only to undermine the good intentions of all involved.

We need to agree on a definition of CSR, and we need to recognize that, until we can measure this complex construct, we should be careful about drawing definitive conclusions based on unrepresentative empirical studies. The challenge of answering the question *What is the business case for CSR?* is related directly to our ability to agree on what we want firms to do and to know whether they are actually doing it. Regarding a definition of CSR, this book is dedicated to refining our understanding of this complex topic in realistic terms, based on what we know about economics and human psychology. In terms of measuring CSR, there are many organizations that are striving toward this very difficult task. In essence, therefore, when we talk about a firm being *accountable* and measuring CSR as a means to that end, we are really talking about three separate steps, each of which needs to be clear and transparent if the system as a whole is to be effective: CSR standards, certification, and product labels.[16]

CSR Standards

The modern corporation is complex. As such, any attempt to summarize its overall effect on society is difficult. No firm is either all good or all bad, and any means of measuring CSR that suggests otherwise is insufficiently nuanced to be of value. It is the broader issue, however, that is stimulating. Taking aim at the superficial nature of much of the work firms refer to as CSR is important because doing so also questions the ability of the CSR community to validate that work. Most attempts to do so reveal a tendency toward some degree of obfuscation or distortion.

Greenwashing is a label that is too easily thrown around, but it speaks to a core problem within CSR—the inability of stakeholders to measure responsible behavior in a way that allows comparisons across firms. To capture such behavior, we need first to find a way to assess accurately those firms that are genuinely conducting business in a way that is qualitatively different from the actions of those firms that are simply using CSR to sell more products. Second, we need to educate stakeholders to discriminate among these firms in ways that reward those that most constructively contribute to social value, broadly defined. Both steps are essential to ensure sufficient, meaningful change.

But, how can a company be held accountable for its CSR actions in a way that is objectively measurable, yet financially feasible? How can we develop an accurate and consistent measure of CSR that allows stakeholders to evaluate the social and environmental impact of different products and firms, then compare them to other products and firms (i.e., compare apples to oranges along common metrics)? And, if we can't measure CSR, how can we tell whether and when it matters? A *CSR report* by a firm provides some answers. A *CSR audit*, containing objective standards developed by an independent third party, provides additional information.

CSR reports are increasingly recognized as a critical tool for firms seeking to incorporate CSR into everyday operations and strategic outlook. They allow firms to set CSR goals (thus, helping establish expectations and minimum operating standards internally), measure progress in relation to those goals, and remain accountable to stakeholders by communicating progress. Important advances in CSR reporting include Gap's 2003 Social Responsibility Report, which disclosed vendor violations of the firm's code of conduct; Nike's 2004 Corporate Responsibility Report, which identified its complete list of worldwide supplier factories; Timberland's 2006 Our Footprint labeling scheme, which clearly listed the environmental and social impact of the production process for each of its products; Stonyfield Farm's 2008 partnership with Climate Counts to measure carbon emissions; and Patagonia's 2009 Footprint Chronicles, which combines elements of all of the above.[17]

As firms increasingly accept the idea of internal monitoring beyond financial metrics and engage with external audit and evaluation organizations, the field is beginning to converge on a universal standard—the Global Reporting Initiative (GRI), which "is referenced by 95% of the DJSI Super Sector leaders, 78% of the

FTSE4Good Global 100, and 70% of the Global 100 Most Sustainable Corporations."[18] In total, "more than 4,000 organizations report their sustainability performance and impacts using GRI guidelines."[19]

Multi-Stakeholder CSR Reporting Frameworks

Over the last two decades, a variety of organizations have emerged to help promote more transparent relations among firms and their stakeholders via CSR reports and audits:

AccountAbility (http://www.accountability.org/), a British organization founded in 1995, has been at the forefront of the push to establish a credible, objective means by which the CSR performance of companies can be evaluated. Its AA1000 series of principle-based standards is "the assurance standard of choice. [The 1000AS] is used by 26% of the Global 100 Most Sustainable Corporations and also 26% of the DJSI Super Sector Leaders."[20]

The *B Impact Assessment* (http://www.bcorporation.net/) was introduced in 2006 by the nonprofit B Lab to assess companies along metrics that set "rigorous standards of social and environmental performance, accountability, and transparency."[21]

The *Carbon Disclosure Project* (https://www.cdp.net/), founded in 2000, is a nonprofit organization with the primary mission of reducing greenhouse gases. To this end, it provides a "global system [so that] companies, investors and cities are better able to mitigate risk, capitalize on opportunities and make investment decisions that drive action towards a more sustainable world."[22]

The *Ceres Principles* (http://www.ceres.org/) were created in 1989. The Principles is a 10-point code of environmental conduct that is to be "publicly endorsed by companies as an environmental mission statement or ethic. Embedded in that code of conduct was the mandate to report periodically on environmental management structures and results."[23]

The *Fair Labor Association* (http://www.fairlabor.org/), founded in 1999, encourages multinational firms to allow their overseas factories to be audited by the FLA. Significantly, the FLA pushes to allow the final reports to be made public, something often resisted by corporations in the past.

The *Global Impact Investing Rating System* (http://b-analytics.net/giirs-ratings/) was introduced by the nonprofit B Lab in 2011. GIIRS uses data derived from B Lab's B Impact Assessment to generate ratings about the social and environmental impact of a specific company or investment fund.[24]

Global Reporting Initiative (http://www.globalreporting.org/) is the leading light in the field. Founded in 1997, GRI works with the United Nations to realize its vision "to create a future where sustainability is integral to every organization's decision making process."[25]

The *Greenhouse Gas Protocol* (http://www.ghgprotocol.org/) was launched in 2001 out of a partnership between the World Resources Institute and the World Business Council for Sustainable Development. The Protocol claims to be "the most widely used international accounting tool for government and business leaders to understand, quantify, and manage greenhouse gas emissions."[26]

The *International Labour Organization (ILO) Labour Standards* (http://www.ilo.org/) were introduced in 1919 with the goal of "promoting opportunities for women and men to obtain decent and productive work, in conditions of freedom, equity, security and dignity."[27] Today, they represent "a comprehensive system of instruments on work and social policy, backed by a supervisory system designed to address all sorts of problems in their application at the national level."[28]

The ***International Integrated Reporting Council*** (http://integratedreporting.org/) aims to "create a framework for integrated reporting that brings together financial, environmental, social and governance information in a consistent and comparable format."[29]

ISO 26000 (http://www.iso.org/iso/iso26000/). Launched in 2010, the standard is intended to act as a guide for *appropriate* behavior and is not available as a certification process (unlike other ISO standards). The ISO 26000, however, is recognized as "the leading global multi-stakeholder forum for debate on what is meant by social responsibility and how it should be applied to organizations on a day-to-day basis."[30]

The ***Organisation for Economic Co-operation and Development (OECD) Guidelines for Multinational Enterprises*** (http://mneguidelines.oecd.org/), were first adopted in 1976. They "provide voluntary principles and standards for responsible business conduct in areas such as employment and industrial relations, human rights, environment, information disclosure, combating bribery, consumer interests, science and technology, competition, and taxation."[31]

Social Accountability International (http://www.sa-intl.org/), founded in 1997, was one of the eight founding members of the auditing and accreditation alliance ISEAL (International Social and Environmental Accreditation and Labeling). ISEAL has an international focus and shows the willingness among accreditation organizations to move toward a set of internationally recognized standards. SA 8000, in particular, is "a global and verifiable standard designed to make workplaces more humane."[32]

The ***Sustainability Accounting Standards Board*** (http://www.sasb.org/) was established in 2011. "SASB's mission is to develop and disseminate sustainability accounting standards that help public corporations disclose material, decision-useful information to investors."[33] SASB develops standards specific to different industries. The first standard was released for the healthcare industry in 2013.

The ***Sustainable Development Goals*** (https://sustainabledevelopment.un.org/) were adopted by the member nations of the United Nations in September 2015. The Sustainable Development Goals (SDGs) replaced the ***Millennium Development Goals***, which were adopted in 2000 but expired in 2015. The 17 SDGs and 169 targets are designed to be "a plan of action for people, planet and prosperity.... They are integrated and indivisible and balance the three dimensions of sustainable development: the economic, social and environmental."[34]

The ***United Nations Global Compact*** (http://www.unglobalcompact.org/), launched in 2000, is a global initiative designed to encourage firms to align their policies with 10 principles in areas such as human rights, anticorruption, and the environment.[35] Since 2000, it has grown to include "12,000+ signatories in 170 countries," including over 8,000 companies.[36]

The ***United Nations Guiding Principles on Business and Human Rights*** (http://business-human-rights.org/en/un-guiding-principles/), also known as the Ruggie Principles, were endorsed by the UN Human Rights Council in 2011. The Guiding Principles "recommend how governments should provide greater clarity of expectations and consistency of rule for business in relation to human rights."[37]

The ***Universal Declaration of Human Rights*** (http://www.un.org/en/documents/udhr/) was adopted by the UN General Assembly in 1948. The Declaration defines "the concept of human rights broadly, to include not only political rights but also social and economic rights. Universally accepted, the UDHR has formed the basis of many constitutions around the world. Moreover, the UDHR is cited in many corporate responsibility codes and principles."[38]

Verité (http://www.verite.org/), founded in 1995, is a major influence in the social auditing field as a nonprofit organization that works with firms, through factory inspections, to improve working conditions throughout the supply chain.

Among the many different multi-stakeholder platforms and measurement tools, GRI is preeminent. It is successful because it is indicator based and thus has the potential to track progress more effectively and produce reports that are comparable across organizations and industries. GRI also claims that revisions to its framework "take place through an exhaustive set of committees and sub-committees, ensuring the credibility and trust needed to make a global frame-work successful."[39] At present, GRI has diffused to the point where "many countries now require [it], either by law or as a condition of stock exchange listing."[40] And, while earlier drafts of the framework were criticized for being a box-ticking exercise that conveyed much data but little meaning, the most recently published version (G4) represents significant progress.[41]

Nevertheless, GRI is still criticized for creating "a model of reporting which was over-complicated and based on the conceit that a single document could effectively communicate with all stakeholders."[42] While GRI now appears to be moving away from a simple count of how many companies use its framework and toward an assessment of the quality of their reporting, it is still true that "the majority of [GRI] reports . . . are little read and drive little change."[43] This dissatisfaction has created an opening for competing organi-zations such as B Lab and its B Impact Assessment (see Chapter 3), a different tool that firms can use to assess their performance and communicate the results to stakeholders. At present, however, the industry-specific metrics being developed by the Sustainability Accounting Standards Board (SASB) offer the most exciting and competitive alternative to GRI. Possibly this is because SASB is an accounting standards board, which suggests a greater potential for acceptance by firms that already place a high importance on the formal auditing process:

> SASB is busy devising sustainability accounting standards for 88 different industries—a mammoth task it hopes to complete by 2015. These standards are designed expressly to be used when US-listed companies complete their 10-K and 20-F forms required by the US Securities and Exchange Commission (SEC).[44]

CSR Certification

When a firm's CSR reporting is both transparent and honest, it allows external observers to evaluate all aspects of the organization, its managers, and policies. The reporting of a firm's activities in a misleading way, however, if discovered, can have a negative impact on external stakeholders' perception of that orga-nization. The different perceptions of BP and Exxon in the oil industry are instructive—while BP had spent a lot of money rebranding itself as "beyond petroleum," Exxon drew criticism from the CSR community due to its CEO's long-standing denial of climate change.[45] Nevertheless, as we discovered with the 2010 Deepwater Horizon oil spill, performance outweighs branding in terms of environmental impact:

Between 1997 and 1998 alone, . . . BP was responsible for 104 oil spills in the Arctic. And in 2008, BP received the largest fine in the history of the U.S. Chemical Safety and Hazard Investigation Board: $87 million for failing to correct safety hazards revealed in the 2005 Texas City explosion. As of June 2010, BP has had 760 such OSHA fines for "egregious, willful" safety violations. Meanwhile Exxon Mobil has had just one.[46]

In other words, although CSR reporting has come a long way in recent years, it still suffers from the potential for *greenwash* and the lack of authenticity that only an independent audit can provide. As such, as CSR measures move beyond the "triple bottom line" (which measures firm performance on various financial, environmental, and social metrics)[47] into the search for detailed, objective, and verifiable standards that allow comparisons among organizations, the field of CSR auditing/certification is also evolving, with new tools constantly being developed to help observers certify different firms' operations from a CSR perspective.

Ideally, this process consists of specific independent actors (such as the NGOs Rainforest Alliance Network, Greenpeace, or Forest Stewardship Council) auditing and then certifying that particular products are being produced and sourced in ways that meet established criteria.[48] Where the process is not too costly or time-consuming, firms are well aware of the legitimacy benefits such certifications offer. That is why McDonald's announced in 2013 that it would partner with the Marine Stewardship Council (MSC) "to show that the fish it serves is caught in an environmentally sustainable manner"[49] and Sainsbury's supermarket in the UK "is the largest retailer of MSC certified fish in the UK and . . . the UK's largest retailer of RSPCA Freedom Food approved salmon."[50]

One of the most heralded developments in recent years has been the negotiation of a voluntary standard for CSR by the International Organization for Standardization (ISO). The consultation phase for the Corporate Social Responsibility standard, ISO 26000, was initiated in 2005, with the standard launched worldwide in 2010.[51] The evolution of ISO 26000 represents both the political and practical challenges in attempting to measure and verify CSR. Some commentators, for example, while supporting ISO 26000, caution against its being held up as the gold standard of CSR behavior. They argue that CSR is not like *quality* or *environmental performance*, which can be measured, but contains important qualitative components that are not easily quantified. This is the primary reason why ISO 26000 was developed as a *guide*, rather than as a *standard*:

Fundamentally, CSR is about relationships. Stakeholders change their minds. They can punish you today for doing what they demanded yesterday. Building those relationships—and resolving the dilemmas that present themselves along the way is really more of an art than a science. It's not something that easily lends itself to a standards-based approach.[52]

As a result of this qualitative component of CSR, and notwithstanding the diffusion of GRI and the emerging SASB and B Lab standards, progress toward a universally accepted CSR certification remains incremental. More than 2 years after the launch of ISO 26000, for example, its value remains dubious, with some dismissing the guide as a political process that lacks the rigor normally associated with ISO standards. The accusation remains that the process produced a "limp noodle . . . [that consists of] little more than high-minded rhetoric."[53] Others complain that ISO 26000 is not nearly ambitious enough—that it is good as a basic outline or checklist and helps identify and define stakeholders, but is less effective in terms of how to implement the ideas. Most importantly, perhaps, there is next to no enforcement.

In the absence of a universal standard that can measure performance, CSR reports remain focused on processes rather than focusing on outcomes:

> [Today CSR reports talk] about whether the company sets targets, . . . about whether the report follows the GRI guidelines, . . . about whether the report is assured by an independent third party. The only thing [they do not] talk about is how that company is actually performing on a social, environmental or economic scale. . . . By and large, CSR reports—whether GRI, independently assured, or printed on hemp with biodegradable ink, are not being accepted as providing useful evidence.[54]

CSR Labels

Beyond standards and certifications, the third step in the reporting process concerns the disclosure of goals and progress to external stakeholders (in particular, consumers). This usually involves a product label of some sort, ideally accompanied by the logo of a respected certifying auditor, which is either attached to the product or advertised at the point of sale. The goal is to convey some sense of the standards passed in order to earn the gold star, letter grade A, score of 5 out of 5, or whatever method is used to convey CSR quality. Whole Foods supermarket, for example, uses a color-coded rating program to assess and support sustainable seafood products:

> Similar to a stoplight, seafood is given a green, yellow or red rating. A green rating indicates the species is relatively abundant and is caught in environmentally friendly ways. Yellow means some concerns exist with the species' status or the methods by which it was caught. And a red rating means the species is suffering from overfishing, or the methods used to catch it harm other marine life or habitats. . . . Whole Foods also announced Monday that it will end sales of red-rated species by Earth Day 2013.[55]

As this example indicates, often these labels are instigated at the initiative of a particular company and may or may not conform with industry standards (even if such standards exist). As such, the main problem with these labels is not the absence of such measures but their proliferation. In terms of *ecolabels* (labels designed to measure environmental impact), for example, there are currently estimated to be "400 and counting—and the move to mainstream for many (thus removing their value as a differentiator) is significantly reducing their value."[56] In North America alone, there are 88 such eco-labels.[57] Food products are a particular area of confusion, with labels such as "natural" or "chemical-free" open to abuse because they are unregulated, while specific foods, such as fish, are subject to inaccurate descriptions[58] designed either to obscure illegal fishing or justify a higher price for a lower quality fish.[59]

This proliferation is a problem not only for consumers (who quickly become confused) but also for companies, which are increasingly expected to be more transparent in their messaging. Another constraint is that there is only so much room on a product label. So, for example, in response to a question about why Marks & Spencer is not advertising its use of certified sustainable palm oil to consumers, the firm's sustainable development manager replied, "We could also list the dairy, cocoa, nutrition, soy, UK sourcing, factory standards, water-use, forestry, pesticides, gluten-free, fairtrade. . . . You have to decide what is most important to customers."[60] The result is chaos, rather than clarity. As a result, the Federal Trade Commission has produced guidelines designed to increase the value of such certifications:

> The commission's revised "Green Guides" . . . warn marketers against using labels that make broad claims that cannot be substantiated, like "eco-friendly." Marketers must qualify their claims on the product packaging and limit them to a specific benefit, such as how much of the product is recycled. [61]

Of course, if all firms were socially responsible and worked to eradicate unsustainable or harmful practices from their supply chains, none of this would be necessary. In the absence of an overnight conversion by all firms, economics provides us with a market-based approach to achieving these outcomes by accounting for all costs in the pricing of products.

PRICING CSR

The value for firms of being able to define and measure CSR is threefold: It allows them to set goals, it allows them to measure progress, and it allows them to communicate that progress to their various stakeholders. A perfect example of both the complexity of measurement and the benefits of communication is the work that is being done by Walmart (and other retailers, including "Gap, JC Penney, Levi Strauss, Nike, Marks and Spencer, Adidas, H&M," and many more)[62] to create a standardized *eco-label* for all products.[63] The ultimate goal is to have a unified evaluation metric that captures environmental impact ("from the greenhouse-gas emissions of an Xbox to the water used to produce your Sunday bacon")[64] and a label that conveys this measurement effectively on every one of the 100,000+ products in every Walmart Superstore (and every other store):

More than 200 clothing manufacturers and retailers have joined together to create an industry-wide sustainability rating, the Eco Index, which will assess the environmental impact of products along their entire life-cycle chain. . . . The Eco Index . . . provides three types of tools—guidelines, indicators and metrics . . . [that] enable any company to participate, whether seasoned in sustainability or not. Each tool assesses a product's impact within six life-cycle stages: materials; packaging; product manufacturing and assembly; transport and distribution; use and service; and end of life.[65]

The goal of the group (the Sustainable Apparel Coalition, http://apparel coalition.org/) is to connect the consumer with every stage of the production process ("giving them a much more detailed view into the supply of fabrics, zippers, dyes, threads, buttons and grommets that come together to form the clothing they buy, as well as what impact the creation of that clothing has on both people and the planet"),[66] while also giving firms more knowledge about the supply chain:

The coalition's tool is meant to be a database of scores assigned to all the players in the life cycle of a garment—cotton growers, synthetic fabric makers, dye suppliers, textile mill owners, as well as packagers, shippers, retailers and consumers—based on a variety of social and environmental measures like water and land use, energy efficiency, waste production, chemical use, greenhouse gases and labor practices.[67]

Lifecycle Pricing

In order for this effort to be effective, the Eco Label (launched as the Higg Index in 2012)[68] has to grapple with the idea of *lifecycle pricing*. The goal is to capture all of the impacts of the production process, at each step in the supply chain, and assign a quantitative value to every step. Although it is a lot more complicated than this (simply trying to avoid double-counting is, in itself, highly complex), in essence the Sustainable Apparel Coalition seeks to add up the positive and negative values to arrive at a net impact score for each product. In short, the group is trying to measure externalities—costs that firms previously have often pushed onto others.

Lifecycle pricing, therefore, attempts to eradicate the idea of an *externality* by incorporating (or internalizing) *all* costs within the final price of the product. This is important because "if prices reflected all the costs, including ecological costs spread across generations, the world would not face sustainability challenges, at least in theory."[70]

Externality

The *Oxford English Dictionary* defines an *externality* as:

A side-effect or consequence (of an industrial or commercial activity) which affects other parties without this being reflected in the cost of the goods or services involved; a social cost or benefit.[69]

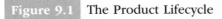 The Product Lifecycle

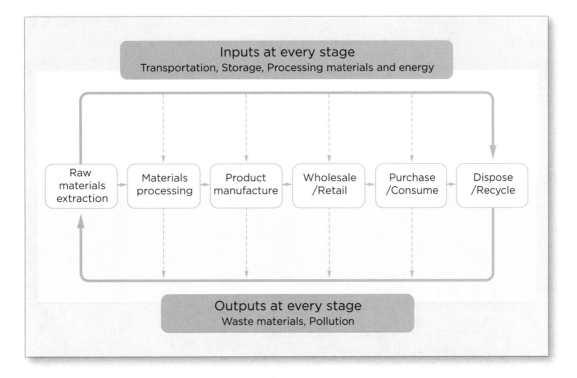

Figure 9.1 presents the six stages of the lifecycle framework: Extraction → Processing → Manufacture → Wholesale/Retail → Purchase/Consume → Dispose/Recycle. Between each stage there are transportation and storage, as well as inputs of energy, materials, and other resources used in the processing that occurs before and after the transition. Each stage also generates outputs, such as waste materials and other forms of pollution.

As such, lifecycle pricing supports the development of an economic model that is no longer founded on waste by including the costs at each stage in the price that is charged to the consumer (i.e., similar to the idea of Pigovian taxes— "When an activity imposes costs on society, economists have long said that the activity should be taxed").[71] In other words, the price of a product should include not only the cost of production (with no externalities) but also the costs associated with replenishing the raw materials used and disposing of or recycling the waste after consumption. Attempts to put a price on carbon reflect this process (either through a carbon tax or cap-and-trade program),[72] while firms' efforts to develop product-specific carbon footprints[73] provide a possible means of implementation. This analysis ensures that each stage can be quantified and included as a separate line item in an integrated report to stakeholders. Done comprehensively, the report accounts for the total value created by the firm (positive or negative).

Circular Economy Versus Lifecycle Pricing

It is useful to draw a distinction between the *circular economy*[74] and the concept of *lifecycle pricing*.

While the circular economy normally focuses on resource utilization and waste reduction (either via greater efficiency or reuse, repair, and recycling), lifecycle pricing is an attempt to incorporate all costs into the final price that is charged for a product. In other words, while the circular economy relies on persuasion within the confines of the existing distorted market to encourage reform, lifecycle pricing seeks to correct existing distortions via a more direct intervention (often a tax) to account for costs that the market otherwise ignores. Once these costs are included, a more free market exists.

In this sense, lifecycle pricing is the more important initiative because it seeks a more direct way to allow market forces to increase efficiency and reduce waste. Waste occurs at the moment because it is economically efficient (or not too inefficient) to produce it. By incorporating all costs, lifecycle pricing makes waste prohibitively expensive, which incentivizes the creation of more resource-efficient alternatives.

A number of firms incorporate lifecycle pricing into their core business model. Nike is a good example, with its GreenXchange initiative,[75] "which open sources life cycle design methods."[76] But, perhaps the best example of a firm that has comprehensively attempted to integrate a lifecycle approach throughout operations is Interface, a carpet manufacturer, whose inspirational founder and CEO, the late Ray Anderson, explained his journey in terms of the seven (plus one) faces of "Mount Sustainability": (1) waste, (2) emissions, (3) energy, (4) materials, (5) transportation, (6) culture, (7) market, and (8) social equity.[77] In Anderson's vision, the peak of the mountain represents *sustainability*, which he defined as "take nothing, do no harm." The natural conclusion of such a *cradle-to-cradle*, closed-loop system throughout a firm's value chain is zero waste. Anderson expanded on his vision of the business logic of sustainability ("Project Zero," to be reached by 2020) at the TED conference in 2009.[78]

Puma has also advanced this debate by introducing the idea of an environmental profit and loss (EP&L) accounting statement. This is an attempt to put a price on natural capital—loosely defined as "everything that nature gives us for free":[79]

Forests, fisheries, water, soil, clean air, the ability of the atmosphere and the oceans to absorb CO_2, minerals, biodiversity, pollination, even scenic landscapes upon which tourism may depend: all these are forms of natural capital.[80]

Instead of valuing natural capital, however, current financial and accounting models "value essential natural components such as water and air quality at zero or 'free,' when accounting for profits and losses."[81] As a result, resources such as freshwater are exploited by companies like Coca-Cola without any attempt to price the cost of their replacement:

[Coke sells] more than 1.8 billion servings a day. . . . Over 79 billion gallons of water are required annually to dilute Coke syrup, and an additional eight trillion gallons are needed for other aspects of production, including the manufacturing of bottles. [Every year, Coke uses] more water than close to a quarter of the world's population.[82]

If we were to start pricing the cost of replenishing the freshwater supplies that Coke currently utilizes at close to zero cost, the price of a can of Coke would rise significantly. The same is true for a plain cotton T-shirt, which "can take 2,700 liters" of water to make.[83] The same again goes for a tax on carbon; at present, "the nations that consume the most energy impose little cost for the damage from burning fossil fuels."[84] These natural resources are currently not included in the prices we pay for products.

The challenge, of course, is to value something for which there is currently no market—a form of *contingent valuation*. In terms of the environment, "assigning a monetary value . . . is notoriously tricky. There is, after all, no market value for intact ecosystems or endangered species."[85] Although this approach is therefore yet to be perfected, it is clear that the effects would be dramatic. The real cost of a gallon of gasoline, after accounting for all costs and removing all existing subsidies, for example, is estimated to be US$12–$20.[86] Similarly,

> some years ago, Indian researchers attempted to quantify the environmental costs linked to a $4 hamburger (for example, loss of rainforests, loss of ecosystems provided by the rainforest, loss of carbon, loss of biodiversity, etc.) and concluded that the price of a burger should be nearer $200. . . . In 2007, the National Audit Office estimated the value of bees' service to the British economy at £200m. The retail value of what the bees pollinate was estimated to be closer to £1bn.[87]

It is only by developing industry-wide standards within a lifecycle pricing model that we will move closer to understanding the holistic impact of our current economic system and business practices. What is not clear is the extent to which consumers want this information and will act on it. What is without doubt is that, as a society, we need to act and act quickly. We have created an economic system based on convenience and waste—we spend money we do not have, on things we do not want, for purposes that are unimportant.[88] As a result, "the typical person discards 4.5 pounds of stuff per day, [only] 1.5 pounds of which are recycled."[89] Even recycling is an insufficient goal within a lifecycle framework. Instead, we need to move toward "upcycling" because "almost all products can be recycled only as low-grade reclaimed basic substances, and the recycling process itself consumes a great deal of energy and labor."[90] In short, we need to find a way to decrease our unsustainable exploitation of virgin resources.

Free Markets

What should be clear from the above discussion is that, as currently constituted, "markets fail to price the true costs of goods."[91] The reasons for this are twofold: First, the market, if left to its own devices, tends toward abusive practices (a tendency we have long known about); and second, in an attempt to regulate these abuses, the markets we have created are riddled with inefficiencies (what politicians call subsidies, tax breaks, loopholes, etc.). Both the abusive practices and the inefficiencies introduce costs that prevent the final price from reflecting a product's true value (i.e., its total costs). As such, the market system needs reform.

An economy where negative externalities are internalized and embedded within a moral framework moves us closer to the economy Adam Smith envisioned and wrote about in *The Theory of Moral Sentiments* (1759) and *The Wealth of Nations* (1776)—truly free markets filled with values-based businesses and vigilant stakeholders. Smith used these two great works to detail the intellectual foundation establishing the market as the mechanism by which values are converted into productive actions, well-being, and social progress. It is worth revisiting his words about the role of the invisible hand in the market and the productive powers it unleashes:

> Every individual necessarily labours to render the annual revenue of the society as great as he can. He generally, indeed, neither intends to promote the public interest, nor knows how much he is promoting it. By . . . directing that industry in such a manner as its produce may be of the greatest value, he intends only his own gain, and he is in this, as in many other cases, led by an invisible hand to promote an end which was no part of his intention. Nor is it always the worse for the society that it was no part of it. By pursuing his own interest he frequently promotes that of the society more effectually than when he really intends to promote it. I have never known much good done by those who affected to trade for the public good. It is an affectation, indeed, not very common among merchants, and very few words need be employed in dissuading them from it.[92]

Smith was clear that, as a result of imperfections in the market, there are two prices—a "natural price" that reflects the costs involved in bringing a product to market and a "market price," which results from the market's tendency toward monopoly. In response, he saw the purpose "of the sovereign state to restore, free play." In essence, Smith believed in free markets; "he just thought that you needed the oversight of the sovereign to make them free."[93] As such, the first response of many who perceive abuses by firms in the marketplace is to call on the government to correct the action by constraining the freedoms that produced the abuse.

Instead of this ideal, however, we have a very different reality where government subsidies distort markets worldwide, from energy to basic foods:

> [As a result of] tariffs, quotas, floor prices, ceiling prices, producer subsidies, consumer subsidies, state monopolies, . . . the market for rice is more distorted than that for any other staple. Rice growers pocketed at least $60 billion in subsidies [in 2014], according to the OECD, twice as much as maize (corn) farmers, the second-most coddled lot.[94]

In terms of energy subsidies (which include tax allowances to firms for things like R&D expenses and price reductions for consumers), governments spend $550 billion a year on fossil fuels ("on everything from holding down the price of petrol in poor countries to encouraging companies to search for oil"),[95] while also spending "$140 billion a year on subsidizing renewable energy."[96] The International Monetary Fund calculates that, if the harm done during consumption is included, "fossil fuels are being subsidized to the tune of $5.3 trillion, or 6.5 percent of global gross domestic product."[97] These payments constitute gross market distortions.

As noted above, if companies were forced to price finished products accurately, many of the disproportionately cheap items in our disposable economy (such as oil or products made from oil, such as plastics) would become significantly more expensive, and firms would be incentivized to produce sustainable alternatives. The market remains the most effective means we know of to allocate scarce and valuable resources in ways that optimize social outcomes. Rather than subsidizing specific firms and industries, pricing the *true* cost of a product leads to less distorted competition in the marketplace, which then should generate more socially responsible outcomes.

The Conditions for a Free Market

A number of conditions are necessary to satisfy the textbook definition of a *free market*:

- Multiple actors on both the demand and supply sides of the market
- Perfect information held by all parties
- The absence of externalities
- The absence of the distorted incentives posed by moral hazard

When these conditions are not met, which is to say in virtually all competitive markets, we have *competitive markets*, rather than free markets.[98]

It is the combination of reduced government intervention (i.e., the removal of subsidies, quotas, tax breaks, etc.) *plus* the internalization of all externalities in pricing (i.e., lifecycle pricing) that allows a truly free market to emerge. One without the other is not *free*; at present, we have neither. In this light, a government tax on carbon is simply a means of accounting for the full environmental costs of oil/gas extraction, processing, and consumption—a policy that enjoys "overwhelming support" among economists.[99] In other words, it is a means of creating the conditions for a free market. Once the level playing field has been created (with more accurate prices for all forms of energy—traditional and alternative), then the market will determine which energy sources should drive our future economies. Ultimately, "markets are truly free only when everyone pays the full price for his or her actions. . . . That's the most fundamental of economics lessons and one any serious environmentalist ought to heed."[100]

Strategic CSR Debate

MOTION: A carbon tax is the most effective way to combat climate change.

QUESTIONS FOR DISCUSSION AND REVIEW

1. Do you think of CSR in terms of a dichotomy, or do you think of CSR in terms of a continuum? If it is the former, what advantages does this approach provide? If it is the latter, what implications does this have for those seeking to measure CSR?

2. Is a tobacco firm that employs tens of thousands of people and pays significant taxes a *better* or *worse* firm (in terms of CSR performance) than a supermarket that sells food but pays its employees low wages?

3. Who benefits most from the publication of a CSR report—the firm or its stakeholders? What are the dangers of *greenwashing*, marketing statements that are intended to inflate or misrepresent a firm's CSR achievements in the hope of enhancing its reputation?

4. Why is it important that an audit of a company's operations be conducted by an independent organization? How could a firm benefit from working with NGOs to conduct a social audit of operations? What are the dangers of doing this? Which approach would you use if a major client wanted you to demonstrate your CSR commitment?

5. Have a look at the following certification logos. Do you recognize any of them? Do you know what they measure? If you wanted to buy a product and one brand had one of these logos attached and another didn't, would it affect your purchase decision?

Part III Case Study

FINANCIAL CRISIS

This case views the global economic system through the prism of the 2007–2008 financial crisis (referred to here as the Financial Crisis). What challenges does the crisis present for the global economy and capitalist system today? What has been the role of CSR throughout? And, moving forward, what changes does a strategic CSR perspective suggest?

THE GREAT RECESSION

In many ways, the dramatic economic events that began toward the end of 2007,[1] which have widely been reported as, alternatively "the most serious financial crisis since the Great Crash of 1929"[2] or the "Great Recession,"[3] brought into focus the comprehensive nature of CSR. From individual greed and the abdication of responsibility, to organizational fraud and the mismanagement of resources, to governmental failure to monitor and adequately regulate the financial system, the crisis emphasized the many interlocking factors that make CSR such a complex issue. At the same time, however, and with the benefit of hindsight, these events also demonstrate how straightforward CSR can be. At its simplest, CSR is not rocket science. It is often common sense combined with an enlightened approach to management and decision making. To look back at some of the decisions that contributed to the economic crisis and try to rationalize why they were taken, however, represents an exercise in exasperation:

> What do you call giving a worker who makes only $14,000 a year a nothing-down and nothing-to-pay-for-two-years mortgage to buy a $750,000 home, and then bundling that mortgage with 100 others into bonds—which Moody's or Standard & Poor's rate[s] AAA—and then selling them to banks and pension funds the world over?[4]

Essentially, the crisis resulted from the cumulative effects of multiple bad decisions by many individuals who had lost their sense of perspective:[5]

... how so many people could be so stupid ... and self-destructive all at once.[6]

The scale of stupidity and greed at the big banks defies belief.[7]

How could the people who sold these [products] have been so short-sightedly greedy? ... how could the people who bought them have been so foolish?[8]

... a near total breakdown of responsibility at every link in our financial chain, and now we either bail out the people who brought us here or risk a total systemic crash.[9]

At various stages, key actors suspected the *system* was unsustainable, but had no self-interest in advocating for change. As Citibank's Chuck Prince said in 2007, shortly before his ouster as CEO later that year, "As long as the music is playing, you've got to get up and dance. We're still dancing."[10]

MORAL HAZARD

In general, the Financial Crisis was driven by three main factors: (1) the housing market bubble, which was fueled by low interest rates and easy access to mortgages (so-called "liar loans");[11] (2) the underpricing of risk, particularly by investors on Wall Street; and (3) the failure (or inability) of the regulatory infrastructure to police the increasingly liquid global financial market. As such, blame for the crisis can be shared widely—from the individuals who sold mortgages that had attractive commissions but were unlikely to be repaid, to the organizations that allowed these sales to continue because they were passing on the risk, to the regulators who failed to oversee the markets it was their responsibility to monitor, to the investors who developed complex securities and other financial instruments that they knew no one fully understood. This culpability extends to the people who failed to question whether it was wise to apply for 100% mortgages on hugely inflated home prices with little or nothing down, purely on the belief that house prices would continue to rise and that, anyway, they would be able to refinance in a couple of years. All of these decisions were made within an atmosphere of overdependence on the *market* as the ultimate arbiter that relieved individual actors of personal responsibility for many of their day-to-day decisions.

Primary among these reasons, however, was *moral hazard*—the finance industry was essentially rigged to fail. Over time, a system of incentives had been put in place whereby the rewards to business were privatized (accrued directly to individuals) while the risk was socialized (borne by the system through financial institutions that were deemed too big and important to fail) represents, according to George Soros, the failure of a pure market ideology:

[Market] fundamentalists believe that markets tend towards equilibrium and the common interest is best served by allowing participants to pursue their self-interest. It is an obvious misconception, because it was the intervention of the authorities that prevented financial markets from breaking down, not the markets themselves.[12]

Western governments have essentially created a system that is unsustainable. As Soros notes, in order to avoid the damage to the broader economy that would result from undermining the positions of global financial traders, governments and central banks have averted their eyes from the moral hazard that is an inherent part of the financial system. The result was "a system of asymmetric incentives" backed by a federal agreement that "every time the credit expansion ran into trouble the financial authorities intervened, injecting liquidity and finding other ways to stimulate the economy."[13]

Martin Wolf in the *Financial Times*[14] paints an equally complicated interaction of causes, which include a "fundamentally defective financial system," "rational responses to incentives," "the short-sightedness of human beings," overly loose US monetary policy, and "the massive flows of surplus capital" around the globe. He highlights the role of governments in sustaining a system that has become too important to the economy to be allowed to fail:[15]

> Those who emphasise rationality can readily point to the incentives for the financial sector to take undue risk. This is the result of the interaction of "asymmetric information"—the fact that insiders know more than anybody else what is going on—with "moral hazard"—the perception that the government will rescue financial institutions if enough of them fall into difficulty at the same time. There is evident truth in both propositions: if, for example, the UK government feels obliged to rescue a modest-sized mortgage bank, such as Northern Rock, moral hazard is rife.[16]

GLOBAL CAPITALISM

While the crisis was inherently an invention of the US financial markets and regulators, for it to have the global reach that it did required the buy-in of the rest of the world. Everyone was happy to play along while the market was going up. The resulting backlash against the status quo following the crash, therefore, represents a challenge to the spread of globalization shaped largely by US liberal capitalism (e.g., deregulation, free international money flows, self-correcting markets, and the efficient pursuit of profit in the form of shareholder returns):

> This suspicion of Anglo-Saxon economic liberalism cut across the usual political boundaries. Right-wing industrialists disliked it, but so did left-wing labor unions. Chinese communists felt threatened, but so did Green Party activists in Germany. . . . The critique of U.S. liberalism . . . is shared by a diverse group that includes French President Nicolas Sarkozy, German Chancellor Angela Merkel, Chinese Prime Minister Wen Jibao and Russian President Dmitry Medvedev.[17]

What is not clear is how effective or self-sustaining this critique will be and whether, in conjunction with any shift in economic ideology, there will be a corresponding shift in global political power. The dominant feature of the US economic model prior to the crisis was an inherently unstable combination of excessively low savings and excessively high borrowing. This surplus of credit was being used to finance an unsustainable level of consumption—unsustainable because the United States was consistently spending more than it saved. That money had to come from somewhere, and most of it came from China. As such, the only real, long-term solution to the crisis is a rebalancing of demand and supply within the global economy, which represents a shift in influence from the borrower to the lender:[18]

> [The crisis] is not only a crisis of capitalism or of a particular form of capitalism after all; it's one of U.S. economic and global power as well. . . . The fact that [the meeting to discuss a global response to the crisis] is one of the G-20 rather than the Group of Seven . . . is a symbol of the decline of U.S. economic power exposed by the crisis.[19]

The sense is that the times have changed and US capitalism, as the driving force behind globalization, will have to change with them:

> Even a newspaper as inherently pro-business as [*The Economist*] has to admit that there was something rotten in finance. The basic capitalist bargain, under which genuine risktakers are allowed to garner huge rewards, seems a poor one if taxpayers are landed with a huge bill for it.[20]

And change is what we need, and quickly. In the decade since Lehman Brothers filed for bankruptcy protection and signaled "the moment when everything changed,"[21] we have had some time to reflect:

> Prior to Lehman, it was easy to believe that housing prices could only go up and that we could always rely on debt to maintain our standard of living. We shrugged as manufacturing jobs disappeared . . . and good middle-class jobs became harder to find. We didn't talk much about income inequality. Nor did we care much that Wall Street had developed a mercenary trading culture, which had little to do with providing capital for companies, ostensibly its reason for being. Post-Lehman, economic reality set in.[22]

The debate that has emerged within the CSR community regarding the future shape of capitalism reflects this shift in the content and tone of discussions about the global economic system. Thomas Friedman in *The New York Times*, for example, highlights the intersection of the economic and environmental crises:

> What if the crisis of 2008 represents something much more fundamental than a deep recession? What if it's telling us that the whole growth model we created over the last 50 years is simply unsustainable economically and ecologically and that 2008 was when we hit the wall—when Mother Nature and the market both said: "No more"?[23]

In early 2009, articles with titles such as "Is Capitalism Working?"[24] "The End,"[25] and "The End of the Financial World as We Know It"[26] began to appear.

This sense of seismic change was reinforced by a major series of articles in the *Financial Times* about the crisis and its consequences for the global economic order. The goal of the series, which was titled the "Future of Capitalism" and had contributions from the newspaper's top economic columnists as well as invited articles by experts such as Paul Kennedy, Nigel Lawson, and Amartya Sen, was to assess the consequences of the crisis, given that "assumptions that prevailed since the 1980s embrace of the market now lie in shreds." Representative of the debate was this comment by Martin Wolf in the opening article in the series:

> It is impossible at such a turning point to know where we are going. . . . Yet the combination of a financial collapse with a huge recession, if not something worse, will surely change the world. The legitimacy of the market will weaken. The credibility of the US will be damaged. The authority of China will rise. Globalisation itself may founder.[27]

Combined with Bill Gates's call for "creative capitalism"[28] (2008) and Muhammad Yunus's book *Creating a World Without Poverty*[29] (2009), the sense at the time was that we were at a point of "inflection"[30] in the economic history of our planet. While we might not notice measurable change immediately, the intellectual shift indicates that, whatever the shape globalization takes moving forward, it will be different than it was prior to the crisis.[31]

OCCUPY WALL STREET

The resulting economic reality led initially to various forms of protest, most notably the Occupy Wall Street movement (http://occupywallst.org/), which initially started with a tweet by Adbusters (#occupywallstreet).[32] It took root in Zuccotti Park in Lower Manhattan but soon spread worldwide. The failure of this movement to organize and sustain its momentum does not diminish the foundation on which it was founded. An important indicator of change, therefore, will be whether the intellectual driving force behind Occupy Wall Street that challenged the legitimacy of the *efficient market* can be corralled into a meaningful platform for reform.

Along these lines, the evolving thoughts of Alan Greenspan, chair of the US Federal Reserve from 1987 to 2006, on the policing role of market forces is instructive. In 1963, Greenspan wrote that it would be self-defeating (and, therefore, highly unlikely) for firms "to sell unsafe food and drugs, fraudulent securities, and shoddy buildings. It is in the self-interest of every businessman to have a reputation for honest dealings and a quality product." By 2008, in testimony to the House Committee on Oversight and Government Reform, however, Greenspan admitted the error in this line of thought:

> Those of us who have looked to the self-interest of lending institutions to protect shareholders' equity, myself included, are in a state of shocked disbelief. . . . This modern [free market] paradigm held sway for decades. The whole intellectual edifice, however, collapsed in the summer of last year.[33]

Greenspan's shift demonstrates the limits of the unregulated market (the "efficient market hypothesis")[34] in the face of incentives that significantly distort the checks and balances that are theoretically in place. As summarized in a *Financial Times* editorial, "The intellectual impact of the crisis has already been colossal. The 'Greenspanist' doctrine in monetary policy is in retreat. . . . Finance has already changed irrevocably."[35] The extent of public anger towards the finance industry was demonstrated over time in terms of regulatory action to hold banks to account for their wrongdoing. While very few individuals were ever indicted (let alone sent to jail)[36] for their roles in bringing about the worst crisis of confidence in capitalism since the Great Depression, the organizations they worked for were penalized heavily:

> The six biggest U.S. banks, led by JPMorgan Chase & Co. (JPM) and Bank of America Corp., have piled up $103 billion in legal costs since the financial crisis, more than all dividends paid to shareholders in the past five years.

Figure III.1   Fines Paid by the Six Largest US Banks (2010–2013, billions of $)

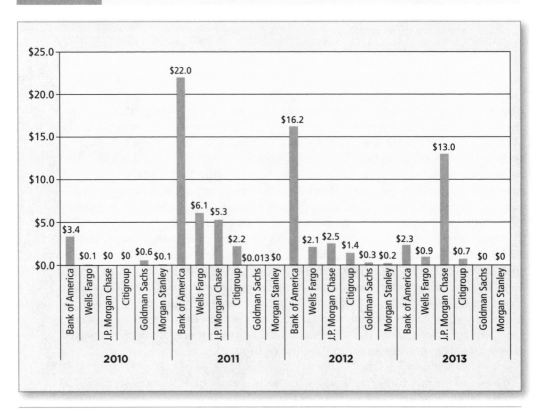

Source: Saabira Chaudhuri, "U.S. Banks' Legal Tab Is Poised to Rise," *The Wall Street Journal*, October 28, 2013, http://www.wsj.com/articles/SB10001424052702304470504579163810113326856/.

That's the amount allotted to lawyers and litigation, as well as for settling claims about shoddy mortgages and foreclosures, according to data compiled by Bloomberg. The sum, equivalent to spending $51 million a day, is enough to erase everything the banks earned for 2012.[37]

While the legal costs associated with the Financial Crisis for the world's 16 largest banks have been estimated to top £200 billion (perhaps hitting $306 billion),[38] Figure III.1 illustrates the extent of the fines paid annually by the 6 largest US banks, from 2010 to 2013.

As such, the Financial Crisis refocuses the debate on the personal ethics of decision makers and the wisdom of fostering leaders willing to make the best decisions in the long-term interests of their organizations and stakeholders. Together with the debate about the implications of the crisis for the global political power balance and the form of capitalism that will drive globalization forward, the crisis injects an element of urgency to achieving cross-cultural understanding in an increasingly online and interconnected global business environment, where decisions taken by firms in one country have implications that can reverberate around the world. In the process, this crisis crystallizes a number of questions that highlight the importance of CSR: What does it mean for society when widespread business failure results in broad social and economic harm? How will this affect the environment in which we seek jobs and launch the firms of the future? How will societal expectations of these firms change (if at all), and how should the business community respond? And essentially, what obligations do we have as individuals, organizations, governments, or societies to avert similar crises in the future?

COUNTRYWIDE

Countrywide (a company that "has become synonymous with the excesses that led to the housing bubble")[39] is a good example of how bad things had become within the financial industry, in terms of corporate irresponsibility, prior to the downturn.

Countrywide,[40] founded in 1969 by Angelo Mozilo and David Loeb, was a mortgage lender that aggressively sought to expand its market share by "promoting homeownership for as many Americans as possible."[41] As the firm became more successful, however, particularly in the early 1990s, external pressures to maintain its growth led to the search for more and more customers and increasing amounts of money to loan them. Initially, the growth continued and, by 2006, "Countrywide had 800 consumer branches, 54,000 employees and about $200 billion in assets."[42] But as expansion became more difficult, the temptation to compromise loan qualification standards became too great. It proved to be a short step from granting mortgages to customers who met standard qualifications, to a more liberal interpretation of those standards, to the development of riskier financial products that would expand the potential pool of applicants:

When the great refinancing wave of 2003 came to a close, [Countrywide] scrambled to maintain volume by offering riskier types of loans and encouraging Americans to pull the equity out of their house and spend the proceeds.[43]

At the height of the boom, the subprime mortgage industry in the United States had clearly lost all sense of proportion, such that "in Bakersfield, Calif., a Mexican strawberry picker with an income of $14,000 and no English was lent every penny he needed to buy a house for $720,000."[44] The result was higher default rates and, as a consequence, higher rates of home repossessions:

> Between 2005 and 2007, which was the peak of sub-prime lending, the top 25 subprime originators made almost $1,000bn in loans to more than 5m borrowers, many of whom have [since] had their homes repossessed.[45]

In Countrywide's case, the pursuit of profit without consideration for the consequences led to a rapid growth in Alt-A (Alternative A-paper) and subprime mortgages (mortgages given to underqualified homeowners), which would eventually trigger the Financial Crisis. The blame should be spread far and wide ("Some commentators pointed to the SEC changing a rule in 2004 to expand the amount of debt that banks could carry. Others cited Congress's 1999 repeal of the Glass-Steagall Act, which threw open banks' doors to investment banking"),[46] but ultimately the system was at fault. Individual mortgage brokers were only responding to incentives that had been devised to encourage short-term revenue growth, rather than a longer-term focus on the sustainable expansion of the housing market:

> Countrywide, determined to gain market share, kept making high-risk loans well into 2007 as the housing market began to crumble. . . . The managers also believed that their bonuses would rise indefinitely, or at least as long as the company continued to expand. . . . Greed and wishful thinking prevailed.[47]

The result of this short-term focus and rapid expansion of the mortgage market was a service that undermined trust and proved very costly for Countrywide. More importantly, it became disastrous when extrapolated to the level of the national and global economic system:

> It took Fannie [Mae] and Freddie [Mac] over three decades to acquire $2 trillion in mortgages and mortgage-backed securities. Together, they held $2.1 trillion in 2000. By 2005, the two [government-sponsored enterprises] held $4 trillion, up 92% in just five years. By 2008, they'd grown another 24%, to nearly $5 trillion. . . . [Critics estimate] $1 trillion of this debt was subprime, . . . almost all bought between 2005 and 2007.[48]

While Countrywide became the face of the mortgage-fueled asset bubble in the United States, it was by no means the only transgressor. In addition to the role played by Fannie Mae and Freddie Mac (who, in 2008, owned "almost half of all American mortgages"),[49] Washington Mutual (WaMu) faced similar accusations of improper lending practices, with equally devastating consequences:

> At WaMu, getting the job done meant lending money to nearly anyone who asked for it—the force behind the bank's meteoric rise and its precipitous collapse [in 2008] in the biggest bank failure in American history. On a financial landscape littered with wreckage, WaMu . . . stands out as a singularly brazen case of lax lending. By the first half of [2008], the value of its bad loans had reached $11.5 billion, nearly tripling from $4.2 billion a year earlier.[50]

A similar fate occurred at the mortgage lender Northern Rock, which became the face of the financial crisis in the UK. The mortgage lender's collapse and eventual nationalization in February 2008[51] prompted the first run on a British bank since 1866, but the damage in the UK was not limited to Northern Rock. Ultimately, the "losses that UK banks suffered in 2008–2009 wiped out roughly half of the economic value added—wages, salaries, and gross profits—that the banking sector generated between 2001 and 2007."[52] All of this occurred, in spite of warning signs by prominent, independent observers such as the Interfaith Center on Corporate Responsibility, which, as early as 1993, "was filing shareholder resolutions raising red flags on predatory subprime lending."[53]

The industry, as a whole, experienced all the signs of a bubble, the aftermath of which generated dramatic headlines such as "Sex, Lies, and Mortgage Deals."[54] As a society, we should have picked this up earlier and acted to diffuse it. As such, the Financial Crisis highlights the central role of CSR in today's global business environment. It is a lens through which excesses can be minimized, risk can be mitigated, and value can be optimized. When firms lack a CSR perspective, they not only endanger themselves but also can cause great harm to society.

Countrywide and Merrill Lynch, for example, formerly the biggest firms in their market, have disappeared as independent entities due to the *irresponsible* manner in which they were run. A short-term profit maximization mindset, without constraint or guiding principles (i.e., without CSR), is a moral issue for individual employees and an issue of survival for the firm. On June 25, 2008, California attorney Jerry Brown Jr. sued Countrywide Financial CEO Angelo Mozilo and president David Sambol for "engaging in deceptive advertising and unfair competition by pushing homeowners into mass-produced, risky loans for the sole purpose of reselling the mortgages on the secondary market"[55] and scheming to "deceive consumers into taking out dangerous mortgages.[56]

BANK OF AMERICA

After increasing an amazing 25,000% from 1982 to August 2007, Countrywide's share price "plummeted more than 90 percent, to around $4, in February 2008.

At the insistence of government officials, Bank of America bought the lender for $4 billion, or roughly $4.25 a share, in July 2008.[57] In order to purchase Countrywide, Bank of America received approval from the Federal Reserve's board of directors, and the purchase was officially completed in July 2008.

Why Bank of America purchased Countrywide (beyond being forced to by the US government) is not clear. The acquisition, together with the assumption of responsibility for Countrywide's bad debts, contributed to a $1.79 billion loss in the fourth quarter of 2008—the bank's first quarterly loss in 17 years.[58] It also added $20 billion to the $25 billion in bailout money the firm had already received from the US government (which had to be repaid).[59] On April 27, 2009, Bank of America "quietly retired" the Countrywide brand, "renaming Countrywide's operations as part of Bank of America Home Loans."[60]

In June 2009, the US Securities and Exchange Commission charged Mozilo and his top two executives with fraud, "alleging that they misled investors about the financial condition of the mortgage company in the months leading up to its sale to Bank of America":[61]

In October 2010, Mr. Mozilo agreed to pay $22.5 million to settle federal charges that he misled investors about Countrywide's risky loan portfolio. The settlement was the largest penalty levied by the Securities and Exchange Commission against a senior executive of a public company. As part of the deal, Mr. Mozilo, who did not admit or deny wrongdoing, also agreed to forfeit $45 million in "ill-gotten gains."[62]

In terms of Countrywide's legacy for Bank of America, the acquisition continues to be a drain on profits as the bank winds down its involvement in the mortgage market:[63]

Bank of America's $4 billion purchase [of Countrywide] may go down as one of the worst deals in American corporate history. . . . Since 2008, Bank of America has paid monetary and non-monetary fines and penalties of more than $91 billion . . . in some 51 settlements, including a record $16.65 billion to the Justice Department and several states in August 2014.[64]

In the end, as demonstrated in Figure III.1, "JPMorgan and Bank of America bore about 75 percent of the total costs" of the billions of dollars in fines levied against the banks in the aftermath of the Financial Crisis.[65] In Bank of America's case, much of this total can be attributed to its purchase of Countrywide. In short, buying Countrywide "'turned out to be the worst decision we ever made,' said one Bank of America director who had voted for the Countrywide deal."[66]

Angelo Mozilo, needless to say, had a different take on the legacy of Countrywide. In deposition to a congressional inquiry in September 2010, with the benefit of hindsight and full awareness of the damage that had been caused by the Financial Crisis, he declared:

Countrywide was one of the greatest companies in the history of this country. . . . [I am] proud of what we accomplished. . . . [Countrywide's stock grew] 25,000 percent over 25 years—a much better performance than Warren Buffett at Berkshire Hathaway.[67]

Bank of America is still trying to recover. As an indication of its further fall from grace, in 2013 the bank was removed from the Dow Jones Industrial Average index along with Alcoa and Hewlett-Packard, to be replaced by Goldman Sachs, Visa, and Nike.[68]

Strategic CSR Debate

Motion: The Occupy Wall Street campaign (http://occupywallst.org/) was a success.

QUESTIONS FOR DISCUSSION AND REVIEW

1. In your view, what were the main causes of the Financial Crisis?

2. Given your answer to question 1, what are the main solutions? What form of global economic system should we be striving to create?

3. What was the role of CSR in the Financial Crisis, and how can it help us find a solution? What do you think of Bill Gates's speech at 2008 World Economic Forum at Davos, Switzerland (http://www.youtube.com/watch?v=Ql-Mtlx31e8)?

4. How would you recommend a mortgage lender reform its employee incentives to ensure it avoids Countrywide's mistakes? In general, how can a firm motivate salespeople who work on commission (as many mortgage brokers did in the run-up to the Financial Crisis) to sell products that are in their customers' interests rather than their own?

5. How many credit cards do you carry? What loans have you taken out? Do you think that reform of the credit-fueled economic model in the West is essential for a more equitable global economy? In general, to what extent is it *fair* to ask the West to make any sacrifices in its standard of living for the benefit of the rest of the world?

NEXT STEPS

art III of *Strategic CSR* demonstrated that an economic perspective is central to an understanding of how firms and markets work to create value and societal progress. As such, this perspective complements the ideas of corporate *stakeholder* responsibility detailed in Part II. For-profit firms and capitalist markets are only tools that need to serve society's best interests. The primary way to achieve this is through stakeholders holding firms to account—rewarding the behavior they seek and punishing the behavior that creates value only for a narrow section of society. If this system is implemented effectively, it quickly becomes in firms' best interests to meet their stakeholders' needs—if they don't, they will go out of business.

But, how do firms predict and respond to those needs? Primarily by incorporating a CSR perspective throughout all aspects of operations and strategic planning. This strategic perspective will be tackled in Part IV, where tools such as the *CSR filter* and concepts such as the *CSR threshold* will be introduced. Part IV also defines strategic CSR in detail, allowing a clearer understanding of the factors that indicate which firms fundamentally understand this complex construct. Building on Part IV, Part V completes the book by building a sustainable perspective of the firm based around values that reflect the needs and concerns of key stakeholders—the ultimate goal of strategic CSR.

PART IV

A STRATEGIC PERSPECTIVE

Part IV reflects the foundations of *Strategic Corporate Social Responsibility* (*Strategic CSR*). Although the ideas discussed in this book are relevant across functional areas in the business school, they find a natural home within corporate strategy.

Chapter 10 introduces the discussion of integrating strategy and CSR by explaining why traditional perspectives (principally, the resource-based and industry views) are insufficient tools to help firms craft strategies in today's globalized business environment. It introduces the concept of the *CSR threshold* in order to emphasize how important it is for firms to be attuned to the dynamics of the environments in which they operate. Chapter 11 places CSR within a competitive context, illustrating its strategic value to the firm because it serves to filter how businesses interact with their environments and implement ideas. While strategy seeks competitive success, a *CSR filter* both enables and protects the firm in its pursuit of profit and long-term viability. Chapter 12 is the central chapter of Part IV, defining the concept of strategic CSR by detailing its foundational characteristics—incorporating a holistic CSR perspective within the firm's strategic planning and core operations so that the firm is managed in the interests of a broad set of stakeholders to optimize value over the medium to long term.

Part IV is completed with a detailed case study of a company implementing strategic CSR throughout its operations—Starbucks.

Chapter 10

STRATEGY + CSR

All organizations survive or perish depending on how they adapt to their environment. As discussed throughout this book, a firm's stakeholders are key elements of that environment—they constitute the firm and largely determine its ability to exist. While stakeholders depend on the value that firms create, firms depend on their stakeholders for the resources that enable them to deliver that value, not least of which is the societal legitimacy necessary to remain in business. Given this symbiotic relationship, how the firm is evaluated by its stakeholders depends not only on *what* the firm does but on *how* it does it. For the firm, strategy constitutes the *how*.

Strategy seeks a sustainable competitive advantage. Its success rests on matching the organization's internal competencies with the demands of its external competitive environment. Central to both sides of that equation are the firm's internal and external stakeholders. As such, while traditional strategy perspectives contain important insights into a firm's ability to build a competitive advantage, this textbook argues that a stakeholder perspective is better suited for firms navigating today's global business environment. Such a perspective enables managers to identify the multiple constituents that can affect operations, while providing a means to prioritize among those stakeholders' often competing demands. The goal is not to replace existing strategy perspectives, however, but to complement and extend them in a single, comprehensive framework.

In short, by integrating a CSR perspective within strategic planning and day-to-day operations, firms are better prepared to respond and adapt to their dynamic environment, helping to ensure the firm's strategy is effective and durable. Conversely, in today's increasingly interconnected world, if key constituents are ignored, the firm's strategy risks a lack of support—even active resistance—with potentially negative consequences for performance and, eventually, organizational survival.

WHAT IS STRATEGY?

Although businesses exist for many reasons, survival depends on success, and *success*, in business, equals profits. At its simplest, profits are determined by the extent to which the firm's revenues exceed the costs incurred during the value creation process. The firm generates revenues from its customers, who are satisfied with the value the firm offers through the goods and services produced by its employees.[1]

The pursuit of profit, however, is so broad a mandate that it offers little guidance about where to begin or what to do. Instead, insight comes from understanding the need in society that the business seeks to meet. That need, toward which the organization strives, forms the basis of its aspirations or *vision*. Ideally, a firm's vision is an ennobling, articulated statement of what it seeks to do and become. A vision that ignores the broader context in which the firm operates will be neither noble nor sustainable. Vision statements must appeal to multiple stakeholders, including members of the organization (employees), its investors (shareholders), its economic partners (customers and suppliers), and the larger community in which the firm operates (society, broadly defined). But, to do so, these statements also must be genuine.

From these aspirations, the firm's *mission* identifies what the organization is going to do in order to attain its vision. A food bank, for example, may have a vision of "ending hunger in the community" and a mission to "feed the poor." An automobile company may have a vision of "providing the best personal transportation vehicles to a broad section of society" and a mission of "making affordable, efficient cars." But, here again, the mission must balance both the methods and the results to be considered socially responsible. The vision identifies what the organization is striving toward, while the mission tells us what the organization is going to do to get there. Both these statements are constrained by what the firm's stakeholders (both internal and external) are capable of doing and are willing to tolerate.

A firm's *strategy* explains how the organization intends to achieve its vision and mission. It defines the organization's response to its competitive environment. At the corporate level, a firm's strategy determines the businesses and industries in which the firm will operate and whether it will enter into partnerships with other firms (via joint ventures, mergers, or acquisitions). Thus, a food bank may have a corporate-level strategy of partnering with a government agency to enhance its access and distribution capabilities, whereas a car manufacturer may have a corporate-level strategy of securing multiple brands to gain exposure to different market segments and minimize risk. At the level of the business unit, a firm's strategy determines how the firm will compete by differentiating its products from those of its competitors. Thus, the food bank may have

A Firm's Vision, Mission, Strategy, and Tactics

- The *vision* answers why the organization exists. It identifies the needs the firm aspires to solve for others.
- The *mission* states what the organization is going to do to achieve its vision. It addresses the types of activities the firm seeks to perform.
- The *strategy* determines how the organization is going to undertake its mission. It sets forth the ways it will negotiate its competitive environment in order to attain a sustainable advantage.
- The *tactics* are the day-to-day management decisions made to implement the firm's strategy.

a strategy of using a mobile soup kitchen that can transport food to where the poor live, whereas the car manufacturer may have a strategy of producing cars with specific technical advantages over competitors' products.

A firm's *tactics* are the day-to-day management decisions that implement the strategy. Tactics are the actions people in the organization take every day. As a result, tactics are flexible and can be altered more easily to reflect changes in the firm's operational context. Ultimately, however, the purpose of these day-to-day tactical actions is to realize the firm's strategy.

Aligning its vision, mission, strategy, and tactics gives direction to the firm and focus to its employees. As important as giving direction to the firm, this chain also determines what it will *not* do. An accounting firm, for example, will not build airplanes without a major revision of its vision, mission, strategy, and tactics. Ultimately, this set of aspirations and policies provides managers with a template against which decisions can be made and evaluated. The overall goal is to ensure that the strategy and tactics achieve the organization's guiding vision and mission.

COMPETING STRATEGY PERSPECTIVES

Given that its focus is to explain how firms build a competitive advantage and sustain that advantage over time, the field of strategy embraces a complex set of tools and concepts. While many of these ideas complement each other, they also compete for the limited attention of a firm's executives. Often, the strategy planning process begins with a SWOT analysis.

SWOT Analysis

A SWOT analysis is a tool that allows a firm to identify its internal *strengths* and *weaknesses*, while also analyzing the external *opportunities* and *threats*. The goal of a firm's strategy, therefore, is to recognize its strengths and align them with the opportunities that are present in the environment, ensuring that the strategy and tactics remain consistent with its vision and mission. Weaknesses are addressed to the extent that they impair the strategy's effectiveness, while threats in the environment are monitored and evaluated for their disruptive potential.

Building on the foundation of the SWOT analysis, *strategy* is traditionally viewed from two competing perspectives—the resources perspective and the industry perspective.[2] Although the extent to which these perspectives enjoy empirical support is not clear, they are well established and commonly taught. These competing perspectives draw on the two sides of the SWOT analysis—the *internal* strengths and weaknesses and the *external* opportunities and threats.

The *resources perspective* is an internal view of the firm that identifies its unique resources (e.g., highly skilled employees or monopoly access to valuable raw materials) and capabilities (e.g., effective research and development or efficient production processes) as the main determinant of a competitive advantage. Those firms that have the most valuable resources or most innovative capabilities (collectively called *competencies*) will likely produce the most valued products and services in the most efficient manner. As a result, these firms are able to build and sustain a competitive advantage over the competition.

An alternative view is the *industry perspective*, which focuses on the firm's immediate operational context. This external perspective identifies the structure of the environment in which the firm operates (in particular, its industry) as the main determinant of its competitive advantage. Success in the market, this perspective argues, has less to do with individual differences among firms and more to do with the competitive structure of the industry. To the extent that an industry is structured favorably, the companies operating in that industry will enjoy greater profit potential than those that operate in a more constrained industry.

The tensions between these two perspectives form a central theoretical component of strategy thinking and, as such, merit further elaboration.

The Resources Perspective

The resources perspective is detailed in a 1990 *Harvard Business Review* article by C. K. Prahalad and Gary Hamel,[3] who then expanded on their ideas in a 1994 book.[4] The core idea that Prahalad and Hamel convey is the distinction between a firm that is built around a portfolio of business units and a firm that is built around a portfolio of *core competencies*. While separate business units encourage functional replication and inefficiencies, core competencies develop efficient systems that can be applied in multiple settings across business units and throughout the firm. Walmart's core competency of efficient distribution, for example, can be applied at all stages of its retail operations. Equally, Google's core competency of writing sophisticated algorithms, which allows it to pursue its mission to "organize the world's information,"[5] can be applied to searching for products, images, academic papers, and many other topics. Moreover, core competencies can be built, given the ideal circumstances. The resulting skills differentiate the firm from its competition and allow it to sustain a competitive advantage:

> In the long run, competitiveness derives from an ability to build, at lower cost and more speedily than competitors, the core competencies that spawn unanticipated products. The real sources of advantage are to be found in management's ability to consolidate corporatewide technologies and production skills into competencies that empower individual businesses to adapt quickly to changing opportunities.[6]

Prahalad and Hamel apply three tests to define a core competency: It should be applicable to multiple markets, it should be valued by the consumer, and it should be difficult for a competitor to imitate. Importantly, the resources perspective argues that, while firms have different valuable resources and unique capabilities, it is the combination of the two that leads to a core competency and a sustainable competitive advantage. Southwest Airlines, for example, has a valuable resource in its corporate culture and a unique capability in its ticketing and boarding technologies (in particular, its airplane turnaround times). But, it is the combination of culture and technology that builds Southwest's sustained competitive advantage. As a result, the firm's record of profitability is "unmatched by any airline in the world."[7]

VRIO

VRIO, which represents a subtle twist on the resources perspective, stems from work by Jay Barney.[8] The acronym VRIO stands for the four questions that must be answered affirmatively for a resource to be the source of a firm's sustained competitive advantage:

- Is the resource Valuable?
- Is the resource Rare?
- Is the resource costly to Imitate?
- Is the firm Organized to capture this potential value?

If the resource is not valuable, then the firm has no competitive advantage. If the resource is not rare, then the firm is merely competitive, at best. If the resource is not costly to imitate or the firm is not organized sufficiently to capitalize on the potential, then the firm may have a competitive advantage, but it is likely temporary. According to Barney, it is only when all four conditions apply that the firm has a competitive advantage that can be sustained over time.

Limitations of the Resources Perspective

In spite of its intuitive value, there are two main limitations of the resources perspective. First, by focusing primarily on the internal characteristics of the firm as the source of competitive advantage, the resources perspective de-emphasizes the external context in which the firm operates. While the value of a resource or capability is, by definition, partly defined by its ability "to neutralize its external threats or exploit its external opportunities," it is the resource/capability itself (an internal characteristic of the firm) that is deemed to be the source of profitability.[9] It is highly likely, however, that the external context will influence directly the firm's ability to build core competencies and also contribute to the firm's ability to take advantage of that resource. As Southwest experienced in the aftermath of the 9/11 terrorist attacks on America, the federal government has an important voice in the airline's ability to operate in the way it wants.[10] By not including context in the model and recognizing the potential constraints it presents, therefore, the resources perspective provides an incomplete description of the processes that generate the phenomenon (core competencies) that it is seeking to explain.

Second, the resources perspective provides a description of the firm that is very deliberate and rational. The suggestion is that firms are quite capable of identifying potential core competencies and then proceeding to gather the necessary resources, break down barriers among business units, and design the necessary processes to allow them to flourish. Decades of research on organizations, however, tells us that, even if managers are able to act rationally (which is far from clear), there is a whole host of other factors (ranging from political infighting to events beyond managers' control) that intervene to prevent the intended goal from being realized.

These two limitations suggest that, while valuable, the resources perspective alone provides an incomplete understanding of firm strategy.

The Industry Perspective

The industry perspective is grounded theoretically in industrial economics. Its main proponent in the management literature is Michael Porter, whose five forces model is a staple component of strategic management courses in business schools around the world. Porter first outlined his ideas in a 1979 *Harvard Business Review* article.[11] He later published two books that expanded on his

---

Figure 10.1 Porter's Five Competitive Forces

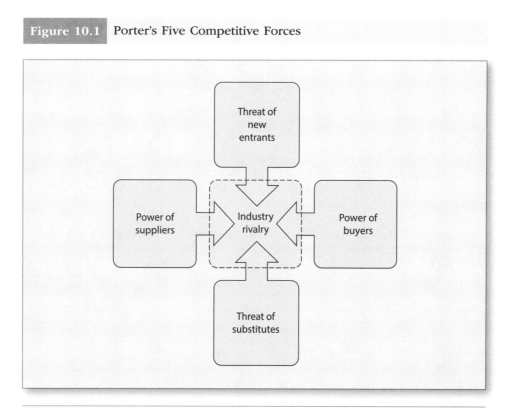

Source: Michael E. Porter, "How Competitive Forces Shape Strategy," *Harvard Business Review,* March/April 1979, p. 141.

initial ideas by introducing a distinction between business- and corporate-level strategies[12] and the value chain.[13] More recently, in a 2008 *Harvard Business Review* article, Porter updated his five forces model to address criticisms since its initial publication.[14]

The industry perspective focuses on the firm's operating environment (in particular, its industry structure) as the most important determinant of competitive advantage. There are five competitive forces in Porter's model (adapted in Figure 10.1): suppliers, buyers, new entrants, substitutes, and industry rivalry. These five forces compete for a fixed pool of resources, and it is this competition that determines the ability of any individual firm to profit in the industry. As such, Porter envisions competition as a zero-sum game among these five forces and the focal firm. The strength of each force is measured relative to the strength of the focal firm. In other words, to the extent that any of the five forces grows in strength, this occurs to the detriment of the focal firm, which becomes relatively weaker. The application of this model can be illustrated effectively by looking at the competitive structure of two related industries—aircraft manufacturing and passenger airlines.

Porter's Industry Analysis

The value of Porter's model in analyzing a firm's competitive environment is illustrated using the examples of two related industries.

Industry 1: Aircraft Manufacturing

This industry is dominated by two firms—Boeing and Airbus:

Power of suppliers: Medium. In this industry, the power of suppliers is medium because the inputs needed to make planes vary in their rarity. While there are only a few jet engine makers, for example, and the computer systems that fly planes are specialized, other raw materials, such as steel or aluminum, are cheap and readily available.

Power of buyers: Weak. The buyers in this industry are not the end consumers (the passengers) but the passenger airline companies. These airlines essentially have little choice but to acquire the planes they need from Boeing and Airbus.[15]

Threat of new entrants: Low. The barriers to entry in terms of expertise, government contracts, global distribution networks, and brand recognition suggest that Boeing and Airbus are not likely to see any serious competitors in this industry anytime soon.

Threat of substitutes: Low. While in theory, if costs rise too far, passengers will seek alternatives to plane travel (e.g., cars, Skype business calls), in reality, the number of airline passengers keeps increasing (projected by the International Air Travel Association to reach 7.3 billion by 2034).[16] Thus, there will always be a demand for planes to carry them.

Industry rivalry: Medium. While there is some competition among Boeing and Airbus for airline contracts, most of the competitive burden (in terms of profits) is borne by the airlines themselves. Also, due to the support they receive from their national governments (the United States and European Union, respectively), both companies will continue to earn sufficient profits to remain in business. The main costs incurred as a result of competition are those related to future aircraft model research and development.

As a result of this competitive structure, the aircraft-manufacturing industry is extremely favorable for Boeing and Airbus. Although both firms have had problems in the past with bribery allegations, inefficiencies, and government interference, the industry remains stable and highly profitable for these two companies.

Industry 2: Passenger Airlines

In contrast to the airline-manufacturing industry, the passenger airline industry is populated by a large number of firms that compete furiously:[17]

Power of suppliers: High. There is considerable consolidation in the aircraft-manufacturing industry, which consists of two major firms, Boeing and Airbus. As a result, there are not many alternative sources of the airline industry's main input—large airplanes.

Power of buyers: Low. This is one factor that works in the airlines' favor. Buyers (i.e., airline passengers) are diffuse, and invariably there are great discrepancies in the amounts of money passengers are willing to pay for comparable seats on the same flight. The rise in online websites that allow passengers to compare prices, however, has reduced the advantage the airlines hold in this area.

Threat of new entrants: High. In spite of low profits, it is relatively common for new airlines to enter this industry. There is added danger because new airlines are immediately competitive due to the absence of the legacy costs (e.g., pension and health benefits) and inefficiencies that diminish profitability for the more established airlines.

Threat of substitutes: Low. In the United States, alternative forms of public travel for long distances (such as train) are not well established. As a result, people have little choice but to purchase the services that many airlines offer.

Industry rivalry: High. Evidence of the high level of competition among airlines lies in the fact that Southwest Airlines' consistent profitability in the industry is the exception, rather than the norm.[18]

As a result of this industry structure, the competitive environment is unfavorable for the numerous passenger airlines, which operate in an industry with high demand and few alternatives but seem unable to make sustained profits.

Limitations of the Industry Perspective

There are three main limitations inherent to the industry perspective. First is the presentation of business as a combative pursuit—a zero-sum game of survival.

This model teaches firms that their relations with different stakeholders are confrontational and that, in order to survive, a firm needs to beat its stakeholders in a battle for relative supremacy. In other words, if its customers or suppliers gain an advantage, it is to the detriment of the focal firm.

Second, the industry perspective presents a narrow view of the firm's operating environment. Only five forces are included, which cover only three stakeholders—the firm's buyers, suppliers, and competitors. This picture omits numerous stakeholders that have the potential to alter dramatically a company's competitive environment and profitability—such as the local community, the government, and the media.[19]

Third, the industry perspective fails to give sufficient recognition to differences in characteristics among companies, which likely predict a firm's competitive success. A holistic model of the firm in its environment that also recognizes the value of the firm's resources and capabilities would provide a more comprehensive tool that firms could use to analyze their operating context (both internal and external conditions) and plan their strategy accordingly.

THE INTEGRATION OF STRATEGY AND CSR

While the resources and industry perspectives are valuable conceptual tools that provide insight into the actions of businesses, the situations in which they operate, and the potential to build a sustainable competitive advantage, it is clear that these two perspectives have their limits. Both are narrow in application and exclude factors that intuitively contribute to a firm's strategy and, therefore, its success. In contrast, this textbook suggests that a broader stakeholder perspective, which incorporates the total mix of influences, expectations, and responsibilities firms face in their day-to-day operations, better approximates the realities of business today for most companies.

That the key proponents of both the resources and industry perspectives implicitly recognize the limitations of their earlier work can be deduced from their more recent publications. In two important respects, both Prahalad and Porter have since published work that constitutes an evolution of their original positions—first, to integrate both the internal (resources) and external (industry) perspectives into one comprehensive vision and, second, to incorporate components of CSR and, implicitly, a broader stakeholder perspective.

Combining the Resources and Industry Perspectives

This evolution of their ideas is apparent in the late Prahalad's most recent work detailing the business opportunity for multinational firms in serving the estimated 4 billion people (65% of the world's population) who live on less than $2,000 per year.[20] This group of people forms the largest and bottom tier of the four-tier pyramid that comprises the world's population—the bottom of the pyramid (BOP), as discussed in Chapter 7.[21] Prahalad views these people as potential consumers who, at present, are largely ignored by multinational firms, which tend instead to focus on developed-economy consumers:

> It is simply good business strategy to be involved in large, untapped markets that offer new customers, cost-saving opportunities, and access to radical innovation. The business opportunities at the bottom of the pyramid are real, and they are open to any MNC willing to engage and learn.[22]

In Porter's case, the evolution of his ideas is apparent in three *Harvard Business Review* articles that he wrote with Mark Kramer in 2002 ("The Competitive Advantage of Corporate Philanthropy"),[23] 2006 ("Strategy & Society"),[24] and 2011 ("Creating Shared Value"):[25]

> For any company, strategy must go beyond best practices. It is about choosing a unique position—doing things differently from competitors in a way that lowers costs or better serves a particular set of customer needs. These principles apply to a company's relationship to society as readily as to its relationship to its customers and rivals.[26]

Both Prahalad and Porter, therefore, talk more expansively in their recent work and, in the process, come much closer to combining the resources and industry perspectives. Prahalad, in discussing the potential opportunity for firms at the BOP, recognizes that a change in environmental context alters the potential of a fixed set of resources and capabilities. In addition, Porter and Kramer incorporate both "inside-out linkages" (a firm-level perspective) and "outside-in linkages" (an environmental-level perspective) within one view of the firm and its strategic environment that emphasizes "the interdependence between a company and society."[27]

Integrating CSR

The integration of CSR represents a strong theme running through all of Prahalad and Porter's most recent work. In addition to identifying new markets for multinational corporations, Prahalad is clearly concerned with the value that the efficient delivery of products and services can provide to the developing world. In addition, Porter writes about the potential social and economic value to the strategic decision-making process in firms:

> Efforts to find shared value in operating practices and in the social dimensions of competitive context have the potential not only to foster economic and social development but to change the way companies and society think about each other.[28]

On the one hand, it is clear that CSR can be thought of as a firm's core competence. In order to integrate CSR effectively throughout operations, a manager needs to draw on resources and capabilities that are valuable, rare, difficult to imitate, and non-substitutable.[29] Doing so raises the potential for the firm to differentiate itself from its competitors and build a sustainable competitive advantage.[30] On the other hand, however, CSR is also clearly a means to evaluate a firm's environment in terms of its primary stakeholder groups—identifying the structural components that present the firm with a favorable opportunity to succeed.

An important question remains, however: *How do companies define socially responsible action that is strategic?* In their work, both Prahalad and Porter are correct to focus on areas of expertise and relevance to firms. There is a strong connection between economic competence and the potential for social progress. An important distinction of strategic CSR, however, is the premise that actions that are strategic and socially responsible are defined for the firm by its stakeholders. It is *society* that determines what is *socially* responsible. As such, an increasingly important predictor of success for managers is the ability to be attuned to the firm's stakeholders' needs and concerns and respond accordingly.

THE CSR THRESHOLD

The decision of *what* strategic behavior is socially responsible is compounded by *where* and *how* it should be implemented, not to mention *who* should oversee the process. The culture, resources, and capabilities of the firm are a constraint. The industry context complicates things further due to the varied stages of acceptance of CSR by different competitors. Another level of complexity is differences among countries and cultures, which ensure that firms will approach CSR in vastly different ways. Although the value of CSR within specific industries and firms is becoming increasingly accepted, the point at which such a policy becomes ripe for implementation (or unavoidable for those unconvinced of the benefits) varies. Thus, *when* depends on many factors that include the CEO's attitude toward CSR, the firm's industry and actions of competitors, and the cultural environment in which the firm is operating.

Companies can pursue an effective CSR policy of either offense ("corporate social opportunity")[31] or defense (CSR as "brand insurance").[32] The innovative, proactive CEO who is convinced of the intrinsic value of CSR sees it as an opportunity to utilize core competencies and identify new competitive advantages. Examples abound: From Nike's FlyKnit Racer (a shoe with an upper made from a single thread that reduces weight and waste),[33] to Anheuser-Busch's comprehensive recycling policies,[34] to Coca-Cola's preservation of water,[35] firms implementing a CSR perspective innovate in ways that make them more competitive. Companies with a progressive and innovative mind-set see benefits that range from being an attractive employer (helping retention and recruitment), to greater acceptance among government agencies (facilitating needed zoning and tax relief), to better relations with social activists (such as Greenpeace). Timberland, for example, believes that its Path of Service program, which grants "full-time staff an annual benefit of (up to) 40 paid hours and part-time staff an annual benefit of (up to) 20 paid hours for community service," raises morale and increases retention, thereby lowering training costs while inducing new skills and stoking corporate pride.[36]

In terms of defense, CSR still has value by protecting the firm's reputation— avoiding criticism and implementing effective crisis management. In this instance, CSR is a rational choice that acts like a brand insurance policy, minimizing stake-holder disillusionment in response to perceived CSR transgressions. A good example of this approach is USCAP (United States Climate Action Partnership, http://www.us-cap.org/), formed by a group of energy and manufacturing firms, which "supports the introduction of carbon limits and trading" as a means of miti-gating federal legislation designed to control carbon emissions:[37]

> Executives find it difficult to apply cost-benefit analysis to avoid future prob-lems of uncertain likelihood. But, these are the ideal conditions for insurance— not an insurance that pays off after a crisis, but more like traditional boiler insurance, one that focuses on preventative protection. The reason why firms need CSR is not because they necessarily have a pressing problem at the moment, but so that they can avoid (or, at least, lessen) problems that under-mine their brand going forward.[38]

Either approach (offense or defense) assumes an up-front investment of some kind. *When* to introduce CSR into the strategic process, however, depends on the driving force behind its implementation. For those managers convinced of CSR's strategic potential, there is no time like the present. Innovative ideas and policies that create market opportunities, minimize costs, and increase productivity can produce immediate benefits. For managers yet to be persuaded by the argument for CSR, however, the temptation exists to delay as long as possible. Worse, cyni-cal managers might see CSR as a public relations exercise, assuming they can postpone hard CSR choices and avoid the expense altogether. Perhaps this is analogous to someone who imagines that, as long as they remain healthy, they will be able to avoid outlays for health insurance.

Nevertheless, a crisis point can arise. Once stakeholder backlash becomes sufficient to warrant a genuine reaction, however, it may be too late. In 2011, for example, Walmart announced it would create "new programs aimed at helping women-owned businesses and women workers."[39] Though commendable, this announcement was made within three months of the US Supreme Court's deci-sion on the decade-long class-action lawsuit filed against Walmart claiming sex discrimination in its employment practices. As such, the announcement, which amounted to commitments totaling only "a small percentage of Wal-Mart's overall budget," served primarily to remind stakeholders of the alleged discrimination and failed to persuade anyone who was already skeptical that the firm had intro-duced a meaningful new approach to supporting female business owners.[40]

In short, firms introduce CSR for different reasons. Implementing CSR proac-tively throughout the firm can generate efficiencies and new opportunities, as well as potential legitimacy benefits associated with first-mover status. Further, the genuine implementation of CSR, whether for offensive or defensive reasons, generates insurance-like benefits that can reduce the impact of subsequent transgressions. Whatever the motivation, there is a *CSR threshold* that varies for each *firm* (depending on whether it is the market leader or a smaller player), *industry* (some industries are more susceptible to stakeholder backlash than others), and *culture* (different societies place different expectations on corporations). The variable nature of this threshold (which can also ebb and flow with changes in public perception and the media news cycle) suggests why some companies perceive CSR to be of greater importance at different points in time. Still, why do different thresholds exist? An important part of the answer lies in the firm's business-level strategy.

Variation Among Companies

Analyzing a company's business-level strategy reveals how it distinguishes its products in the marketplace. Its value proposition is captured in its strategy and attracts stakeholder groups, particularly customers. In turn, the firm's strategy has a direct impact on the CSR threshold for that company within its industry.

Consider these comparisons in light of Figure 10.2. Walmart's strategy probably raises its CSR threshold; that is, the firm has more CSR leeway and can

Figure 10.2   The Business-Level CSR Threshold

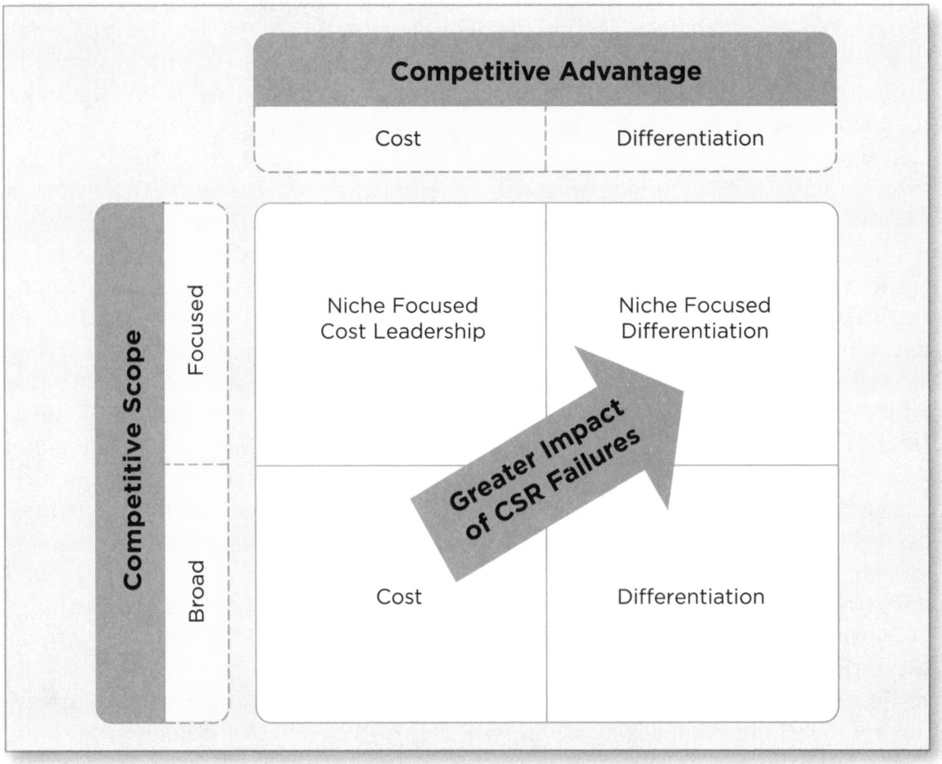

"get away with" more because its value proposition is based on a business-level strategy of low cost. A Walmart shopper, for example, is unlikely to be surprised to discover that the company favors products manufactured overseas in low-cost environments rather than higher cost products made by US employees. For a company like The Body Shop, however, which has built its reputation and customer base largely on the social justice issues it advocates (such as no animal testing and fair trade), the CSR threshold at which customers, media, and society react may have a much lower tipping point. Thus, The Body Shop's stakeholders are more likely to have a lower tolerance for perceived CSR violations. Restated, a Body Shop customer would expect the company to live up to the values that attracted them to the store in the first place, which translates into a lower CSR threshold for the firm. One CSR error by The Body Shop, for example, may well be equal, in terms of stakeholder perception, to multiple CSR oversights by Walmart.

A low-cost business-level strategy suggests an ability to deliver products or services more efficiently than competitors (often resulting in a lower price to the consumer). The products that Walmart sells, for example, are not fundamentally different from those of its competitors. Instead, the firm gains its competitive advantage from its "everyday low prices," which enable its customers to "Save money. Live better." Walmart is able to generate its low prices as a result of a laser-like focus on minimizing costs throughout the value chain. In contrast, a differentiation strategy offers the customer something unique, such as a luxury car from Rolls Royce, for which there is an associated price premium.

These low-cost and differentiation strategies can be further categorized as either broad (e.g., targeting a large market segment, such as the automobile market) or narrow (e.g., targeting only consumers seeking to purchase luxury cars). As a result, Walmart has a scope of business that can be labeled *broad,* while Rolls Royce's products are *focused.* Overall, therefore, Rolls Royce's business strategy offers a *differentiated* product, focused on the *niche* market of luxury cars, whereas Walmart's strategy pursues *cost leadership* (low costs) across a *broad* base of customers. An alternative strategy is pursued by a firm like McDonald's, which seeks a focused strategy of low cost (cheap food) *and* differentiation (fast, convenient service).[41]

Business-Level Strategies

Firms' business level strategies can be divided into those that pursue low costs and those that pursue differentiation:[42]

- *Low cost:* A business strategy used by firms to distinguish their products from the products of other firms on the basis of more efficient operations. Companies like Walmart and Exxon pursue business-level strategies of low cost.

(Continued)

(Continued)

- *Differentiation:* A business strategy used by firms to distinguish their products from the products of other firms on the basis of some component other than price. Companies like Apple and Whole Foods Supermarket pursue business-level strategies of differentiation.

While traditionally these two business-level strategies have been taught as separate alternatives that should not be confused, in reality, most companies employ a mix of activities that focus on *operational effectiveness* and *strategic positioning* in order to gain a competitive advantage. As such, a more effective way to understand how firms compete at the product level is to see them as using a combination of low cost and differentiation, with most companies tending toward one or the other depending on their competitive context:

Ultimately, all differences between companies in cost or price derive from the hundreds of activities required to create, produce, sell, and deliver their products or services. . . . Cost is generated by performing activities, and cost advantage arises from performing particular activities more efficiently than competitors. Similarly, differentiation arises from both the choice of activities and how they are performed. Activities, then are the basic units of competitive advantage. Overall advantage or disadvantage results from all the company's activities, not only a few.[43]

In drawing these distinctions among firms, it is important to stress that the distinction between low cost and differentiation, and between broad and narrow, refers to a firm's *business-level* strategies. As such, it is possible for a firm to have different strategies across its business units. Apple's range of computers, for example, targets a narrower segment of the total computer market (and the firm willingly exchanges high margins for continued low market share), while its iPhones and iPads have a broader scope.

As reflected in Figure 10.2, whether a company pursues a cost- or differentiation-based strategy shapes the firm's CSR threshold—the point at which CSR becomes a necessary component of strategic success. The most vulnerable strategy is focused differentiation, particularly for those products dependent on lifestyle segmentation—products targeted at specific customers based on aspirational values. Nike, for example, makes a determined effort to associate its products (athletic apparel and shoes) with people who have a positive, outgoing, and physically active lifestyle. If, however, Nike is seen as socially irresponsible by its target customers, they are less likely to identify with the firm's products.

Products targeted at market segments or niches, such as lifestyle brands, are especially valuable to a company because they often rest more heavily on subjective impressions tied up within shifting social trends, rather than objective price and quality comparisons. Such customers are often willing to pay a greater premium for the product. Yet, paradoxically, those able to pay this premium are precisely those with the widest range of alternatives, backed by the resources to make different choices. The subjective base on which lifestyle brand allegiance lies, therefore, also presents a danger to these firms.

A CSR-related transgression that might inflict limited harm on a firm relying on a broad, cost-based strategy could prove significantly damaging to one reliant on a strategy of focused differentiation.

As different companies move across the chart in Figure 10.2 (in the direction of the arrow) from cost- to differentiation-based strategies, the CSR threshold they face is likely to fall. That is, a business-level strategy of differentiation is likely to make those firms more susceptible to stakeholder backlash. This increases the importance of an effective and well-implemented CSR perspective throughout the firm. A similar tendency is visible when analyzing the industries within which these firms operate.

Variation Among Industries

Different industries also evoke different stakeholder emotions. Although there are likely to be differences within the apparel industry, for example, between a firm that sells unbranded clothing based on low costs (a higher threshold) and a firm using a focused differentiation strategy to offer a lifestyle brand (a lower threshold), the industry as a whole may have a lower threshold than industries where the connections among product, brand, and customer aspirations are weaker. As Nike found out to its detriment, a reputation for sweatshop labor throughout the apparel industry does not sit well with an aspirational brand.

In the financial or banking industry, for example, the CSR threshold is relatively higher than for apparel. Here, it is harder for consumers to identify a victim or accurately quantify the degree of harm caused by any CSR violation. While firms benefit from striving to meet the needs and demands of their stakeholders, in general, and their customers, in particular, this relationship is more easily open to abuse by those firms that sell products their consumers do not fully understand. In other words, for finance and banking, "the logic of the industry rewards complexity."[44] And even when they perceive a bank to be acting in a way they do not support, consumers are sometimes relatively powerlessness to act. When the First National Bank of Chicago decided to charge all customers $3 for every transaction they conducted that was not online, for example, there was significant stakeholder backlash. The result?

> The bank lost a percentage of its customers, but its profits went up by 28 per cent. Why? There was indeed a big move to cheaper electronic transactions, and the customers they lost were generally the unprofitable ones they were only too happy to gift to their competitors. So what about the right of those customers to get a decent service? What about the social role that banking provides and their public duty?[45]

This perception has been changing, however, due to the 2007–2008 financial crisis, which resulted in generous government-backed bailout payments for financial firms. In spite of these publicly financed payments, these firms retained excessive compensation levels for a sizeable proportion of employees. In spite of the traditionally lower threshold than in other industries, therefore, the financial crisis (and the public reaction to the financial industry's behavior throughout) suggests that this industry has moved significantly closer to its CSR threshold.

The issues that determine the CSR threshold for an industry are more complicated than those for individual companies, with specific industries being more vulnerable than others. Indeed, a number of industries have already passed through their CSR threshold, causing companies that operate within them to take corrective action. One example is the fast-food industry and its relatively recent conversion to healthier foods.[46] Another example, the tobacco industry, passed through its CSR threshold long ago. To see Philip Morris's (Altria's) website warning against the dangers of smoking, listing the health consequences of consuming the firm's products, and recommending tips on how to give up smoking[47] is to know that the industry has long since passed the point of no return in terms of its CSR threshold.

Variation Among Cultures

CSR thresholds driven by different cultural expectations further complicate firms' operating environment. Even among developed economies, there are stark differences. For example, it was legal action in the United States that determined the CSR thresholds for the tobacco, fast-food, and asbestos industries. In Europe, instead of litigation-driven activism, NGO and nonprofit activism has largely driven the CSR agenda. Again, examples abound and include Greenpeace's campaigns against Shell's operations in Nigeria,[48] Friends of the Earth's campaigns against Monsanto and genetically modified foods,[49] and Oxfam's work (both with and against) Starbucks and its fair trade coffee program.[50]

In much of the developing world, however, the perception of CSR has traditionally revolved around issues of corporate philanthropy, an issue that consumes only a fraction of the CSR debate in developed economies. This is changing, however, with the work being done at the bottom of the pyramid[51] and by Grameen Bank (established by Muhammad Yunus, who won the Nobel Peace Prize for his efforts), which has transformed perceptions of developing economies among multinational firms, as well as perceptions of CSR within those economies.[52] In addition to CSR evolving in different ways in each area, it also developed at different speeds, with European firms adapting to increased societal expectations before most other regions, followed by North America, and then developing countries.

Newsweek's Green Rankings, designed to evaluate "the world's largest companies on corporate sustainability and environmental impact,"[53] begins to demonstrate this phenomenon empirically: "Is the same value assigned to being 'green' in Europe, North America, and Asia-Pacific?"[54] The article accompanying the 2011 list compares the performance of European, US, and Asian companies along the rankings' different metrics, with a clear pattern emerging:

> First and foremost is the issue of disclosure, where Europe takes the clear lead. Of the top 100 global disclosure scores featured in the 2011 Green Rankings, Europe accounts for 65% (though it only represents one-third of

the companies ranked), compared to 19% for North America and 10% for Asia-Pacific. . . . European companies, most notably Northern European companies, have also taken the lead in environmental management, though the regional discrepancy is much narrower in this category.[55]

Where the United States has taken the lead in terms of "environmental impact," the report argues that the driver is a greater propensity for environmental crises, which likely prompt litigation, forcing US firms to take more drastic action in response. It is ironic that "some of the most innovative environmental initiatives to date have been launched in reaction to controversies."[56]

Another factor contributing to this difference in approach to the environment is resource dependency. The United States is self-sufficient in natural resources in a way that Europe is not. Since the United States has more resources, it has less perceived need to preserve them. Given an ingrained way of life that has not prioritized resource preservation, Americans are finding it more difficult to adapt to the consolidating global view that resources are not unlimited and must be preserved.

Although these historical differences among cultures are real and have consequences for firms, globalization and the free flow of information help drive down CSR thresholds across the board (reducing stakeholder tolerance and increasing the chance of backlash). As the news media and blogosphere continue to expose corporate CSR transgressions and people are better able to compare conditions across cultures, societal tolerance for irresponsible behavior is lowered.

This greater availability of information helps forge a stronger link between stakeholders and a specific company or product. Furthermore, as levels of affluence and living standards rise generally and problems like climate change are recognized as transnational, the CSR threshold is likely to become lower still as issues of societal necessity evolve into greater social choice and demands for change. Reporting on relative levels of corruption among countries, for example, highlights environments where CSR transgressions are more likely and suggests areas where even greater controls are needed. Transparency International's annual Corruption Perceptions Index, which was first published in 1995 and ranks "countries on how corrupt their public sectors are seen to be"[57] is the best guide to how different countries perform on this issue:

> Not one single country gets a perfect score and more than two-thirds score below 50, on a scale from 0 (highly corrupt) to 100 (very clean). Corruption is a problem for all countries. . . . Leading financial centres in the EU and US need to join with fast-growing economies to stop the corrupt from getting away with it.[58]

The combination of globalization, rising living standards, and an increasingly free flow of information suggests that a CSR perspective is necessary for all firms and will only grow in importance as these trends continue. The *CSR threshold* model presented here argues that the different points at which CSR jumps onto the radar screens of leaders in different firms, industries, and cultures varies as a function of a host of strategic factors. Best practice in response to this uncertainty is a proactive approach that provides economic benefit to the firm, as well as a means of avoiding, or at least minimizing, negative publicity and societal backlash.

Central to the argument presented in this textbook is the idea that, when short-term perspectives result in behavior that is not supported by key stakeholders and those stakeholders are willing to hold the firm to account for its actions, the consequences will eventually catch up with the perpetrators. But as the examples of the tobacco and fast-food companies illustrate, firms in certain industries can delay the day of reckoning significantly. This is because the threshold of concern varies across stakeholders, industries, and cultures. Stakeholders' concerns depend on a unique mix of individual priorities and available options, both of which continuously evolve. They also reflect a dynamic battle among conflicting interests. In the short run, even a flagrant disregard for CSR may be ignored by some, or even all, stakeholders. On the other hand, reaction may be swift and unequivocal. Mostly, however, reactions will be mixed. It is clear, however, that firms eventually suffer the consequences of stakeholder disillusionment for a perceived lack of commitment to CSR.

Strategic CSR Debate

MOTION: The fast-food industry has passed its CSR threshold.

QUESTIONS FOR DISCUSSION AND REVIEW

1. Define each of these terms: *vision*, *mission*, *strategy*, and *tactics*. What is the relationship among them in relation to a firm's strategy-planning process?

2. Outline the resources perspective. Identify a firm and its core competency: How does that competency meet the three tests proposed by Prahalad and Hamel that define it as a source of sustainable competitive advantage for the firm?

3. Outline the industry perspective. Choose an example industry and conduct an analysis of its competitive structure using Porter's five forces model. Is that industry a good industry in which to do business?

4. What is meant by the phrase "CSR as brand insurance"? Can you think of a firm that has benefited from CSR in this way?

5. What is the difference between a business-level strategy based on low cost and a business-level strategy based on differentiation? How do these different strategies affect a firm's CSR threshold?

Chapter 11

CSR as a Strategic Filter

There are three kinds of organizations: nonprofit, governmental, and for-profit. Each exists to meet different needs in society. Those needs may be altruistic in the case of a nonprofit (e.g., feeding the poor), they may be civic in the case of government agencies (e.g., providing for the safety and security of the public), or they may be primarily economic in the case of businesses (e.g., combining resources to yield a profit). In a free society, all organizations exist to meet societal needs in some form, or they eventually go away. Restated, no publicly traded company, government, or nonprofit initially sets out to do harm. Yet, as demonstrated through numerous examples in this book, harm is certainly one possible outcome of day-to-day actions. In the case of for-profit firms, these often unintended consequences spring not from the firm's goals themselves but from the methods or strategies deployed to pursue those goals. As a result, it is important to understand the strategic context of CSR.

In fulfilling their mission and vision, organizations face constraints on their methods and results. The economics of survival, for example, require each entity to produce the *results* that generate the income it requires to operate—donations for nonprofits, taxes for governments, or profits for firms. At the same time, these results must be attained by *methods* that are acceptable to stakeholders, broadly defined. Leaders of all organizations constantly grapple with the trade-offs between methods and results. When these issues involve for-profits, a CSR perspective helps balance the methods used with the results sought. It does this by ensuring that profit-seeking businesses plan and operate in the interests of multiple stakeholders.

The problem that decision makers face is straightforward: Which stakeholders and what issues *matter* under the broad heading of corporate social responsibility as it pertains to our organization? The simple answer is, *It depends on the firm's strategy.* And because these strategies vary widely, the ideal mix differs from firm to firm and from industry to industry. It will also evolve over time as firms adapt both their strategy and execution to increasingly turbulent operational environments. As a result, the exact issues that any firm is likely to face at any given time are impossible to predict. What is constant and can be applied to any firm in any situation, however, is that a strategic lens offers the best tool to view CSR.

THE CSR FILTER

Effective strategy results in providing businesses with a competitive advantage. For this to be sustained, however, the tactics used to implement the strategy must be acceptable to the firm's collective set of stakeholders. If they are not acceptable, any stakeholder can bring reprisals against the firm that threaten its ability to operate, such as when the government levies legal and regulatory sanctions for polluting the air and water or the firm's employees strike in order to achieve better pay and working conditions.

Both CSR and strategy, therefore, are concerned primarily with the firm and the context in which it operates. Whereas *strategy* addresses how the firm competes in the marketplace, *CSR* considers the firm's impact on relevant stakeholders. Strategic CSR represents the intersection of the two. Thus, in order to implement a strategic CSR perspective throughout operations, it is essential that executives understand the interdependent relationships among a firm, its strategy, and its stakeholders that define the firm's environment and constrain its capacity to act.

As illustrated in Figure 11.1, a firm's vision, mission, strategy, and tactics are broadly constrained in three ways—*resource constraints*, *policy constraints*, and *environmental constraints*.[1] First, a significant limitation on the firm's capacity to act is its access to resources and capabilities—the human, social, and financial

Figure 11.1   Strategic Constraints and the CSR Filter

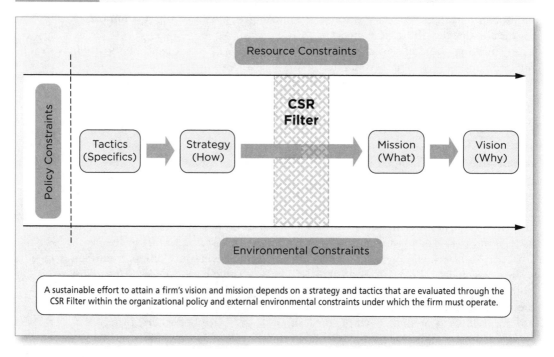

A sustainable effort to attain a firm's vision and mission depends on a strategy and tactics that are evaluated through the CSR Filter within the organizational policy and external environmental constraints under which the firm must operate.

capital that determine the firm's productive parameters. A second constraint is the firm's internal policies, which shape its culture by requiring and forbidding specific actions. Because these policies are internally enforced, however, they can be changed relatively easily by management (a flexibility that is indicated in Figure 11.1 by the dashed line). Finally, a firm's external environmental constraints are generated by a complex interaction of sociocultural, legal, and other external factors, such as the influence of markets and technology. These factors further limit the firm's freedom to act by shaping the context in which it implements tactics to pursue its strategic goals, which, in turn, enable it to perform its mission and strive toward its vision. Compounding the complexity of integrating CSR into the vision–mission–strategy–tactics linkages, therefore, are the ever-changing expectations of society.

As a result of this complexity, a sole focus on the linkage among vision, mission, strategy, and tactics is insufficient to achieve the firm's goals. Not only is such a narrow focus insufficient, but it also represents potential danger. Given the stakes, any tactical and strategic actions necessary to achieve the mission (and, thus, the vision) must first be passed through a *CSR filter*. The CSR filter assesses management's planned actions by considering their impact on the firm's broad range of constituents. A tactical or strategic decision that runs counter to stakeholder interests can undermine the firm's sustainable competitive advantage. At the extreme, such violations may force the firm into bankruptcy (as happened to Malden Mills and Enron) or threaten its existence (as happened to BP and VW).

Strategy formulation links the firm's strengths with opportunities in its environment. The strategic decision-making process faces limitations, however. While these appear in Figure 11.1, they do so as broad categories. In detail, the formulation of firm strategy occurs most effectively when it is run through a CSR filter.

First, a feasible strategy is limited by the firm's vision and mission, which are determined by the leadership. A plane manufacturer, such as Boeing or Airbus, is unlikely to make cars and trucks because these activities do not achieve its vision and mission, which is to make jet-powered airplanes. Second, the strategy is further limited by a firm's structure and competencies—organizational characteristics and competitive actions that aid the firm and set it apart from competitors. Boeing and Airbus, for example, which undoubtedly could make cars and trucks if they wanted, lack other resources, such as the network of dealerships necessary to sell cars and trucks nationwide. Third, whatever strategy the firm develops, it is enhanced by the CSR filter, which assesses the impact of the firm's activities on its various constituents. Above all, Boeing and Airbus must make planes in ways that do not harm their key stakeholders—their regulators, employees, passengers, and others. In other words, before a competency-based strategy can be deployed, it must be developed within constraints and evaluated through a CSR filter to assess its impact on those groups that are essential for the strategy to be a success.

There is an iterative relationship between the resulting strategy and organizational design. While strategy shapes design, it is also true that the firm's structure, roles, and reporting relationships should be configured to facilitate strategy. The *ideal* organizational structure is a design that best supports effective execution of the strategy. For many firms, that means a departmental hierarchy organized around business units. In terms of embedding a CSR perspective throughout strategy and operations, therefore, the structure presents an additional opportunity to disseminate decisions made at the top (with a CSR filter) throughout the organization.

The connection between a firm's internal strengths and its external opportunities is driven by the strategic axiom that success depends on competing from a position of strength. For the strategist to connect strengths with opportunities requires an intimate understanding of both internal and external factors. In order to remain competitive, therefore, it is essential for firms to employ a CSR filter in formulating and implementing their strategies. Figure 11.1 demonstrates how this process unfolds. In order to better understand the role of the CSR filter in a firm's success, however, we must investigate the complex interplay among a firm's structure, competencies, and strategy in relation to the CSR filter and operating environment.

Structure

The structure (the organizational design) exists to support the strategy. What architects say of a building, organization designers say of the firm's structure— form follows function. Thus, the *right* structure is the one that best supports the strategy. Because the optimal design is firm specific, therefore, structure varies from industry to industry, as well as from company to company within an industry. When low-cost strategies are pursued, for example, expertise is often concentrated in a *functional* organization design in which site location, construction oversight, information systems, warehousing, distribution, store operations, and other similar activities are grouped together by their common functions into specialized departments. This functional design seeks to enhance specific areas of expertise and is scalable as the firm grows.

In the case of Walmart, different parts of the company might pursue different structural designs. Support activities like accounting or finance, for example, may be grouped by function at corporate headquarters. At the same time, because Walmart is spread across a wide geographical area, the management oversight and distribution systems may be similarly organized, such as a northeastern warehouse division. At Nike, CSR is such an important element of strategy that it is built into the firm's structure in the form of a separate Corporate Responsibility department, headed by a vice president.[2]

Competencies

To facilitate an understanding of the firm's ability to build a sustainable competitive advantage, a clear distinction among *capabilities, competencies, core resources,* and *core competencies* is required.

Capabilities, Competencies, Core Resources, and Core Competencies

- *Capabilities* are actions that a firm can do, such as pay its bills, in ways that add value to the production process.[3]
- *Competencies* are actions a firm can do very well.
- *Core resources* are the assets of the firm that are unique and difficult to replicate.
- *Core competencies* are the processes that the firm not only does very well, but is so superior at performing that it is difficult for other firms to match its performance.

It is the combination of a firm's core competencies (valuable *processes*, such as an efficient logistics operation) with its core resources (valuable *assets*, such as people, capital, or technology) that form the foundation for a firm's long-term, sustainable competitive advantage. The source of Southwest's long-running success in the passenger airline industry, when most other airlines were losing significant amounts of money, for example, is the combination of its organizational culture (a core resource) with its ability to operate its planes on a significantly more cost-effective basis due to innovations such as its rapid turnaround time (a core competency). Similarly, consider how Walmart is able to manage the flow of goods from suppliers, through its stores, and on to its customers—often referred to as *supply chain management.*

Walmart's Supply Chain Management

Walmart has a *capability* of hiring employees; it has a *competency* to locate stores where they will be successful; it has a *core resource* in its distribution system, including the world's largest private satellite network; and it has a *core competency* of maintaining and distributing its inventory throughout the supply chain. In fact, Walmart is so very good at managing its supply chain that it minimizes both the amount of inventory it carries and the number of times items are out of stock in its stores. Other firms have the capability to maintain their inventory; some even have a competency at doing that. However, none of Walmart's competitors are able to match its combination of core resources and core competencies that align in the firm's masterful supply chain management.

Strategy

Walmart's *vision* is to offer the best customer value in retailing, which gives rise to a *mission* of delivering groceries and other consumer products efficiently. That vision and mission are attained by a *strategy* of passing on cost savings to customers by continually seeking to roll back the firm's "everyday low prices." In turn, that strategy is built upon *core resources* and *core competencies,* which are the competitive weapons with which Walmart competes. Ultimately, how Walmart folds its resources and competencies into a strategy determines the extent to which stakeholders view the firm as a valued partner and a socially responsible company.

Certainly, a firm like Walmart must advertise and do hundreds, even thousands, of other activities. But its competitive advantage comes from its network of store locations, backed by an unmatched ability to manage and deliver its inventory in optimal ways. To this end, the firm's resources and competencies interact, reinforcing each other over time as experience enables the firm to refine its day-to-day operations. Without its exceptionally efficient and effective supply chain management, Walmart would not be a low-cost provider of groceries and other goods. But with these resources and competencies supporting its strategy, it creates a *virtuous cycle* in which the firm's lower prices attract more customers. More customers, in turn, mean greater volumes, which lead to increased economies of scale in operations and greater power to demand price reductions from suppliers. The result is even lower costs, which Walmart passes on in the form of lower prices, which then continue the virtuous cycle by attracting still more customers. Like all firms, therefore, Walmart's business level strategy rests upon combining core resources and competencies in ways that support its mission and vision.

As noted in Chapter 10, Walmart employs a *low-cost* business strategy in order to compete. Mercedes-Benz, on the other hand, does not seek to produce the lowest priced cars. Instead, it competes based on a *differentiation* business strategy. By making its products superior along the lines of safety, prestige, and durability, Mercedes-Benz (and other luxury goods producers) can charge a premium for the differentiation (real or perceived) that consumers value. Apple is another firm that seeks to differentiate its products on the basis of factors other than price—product design and technological innovation. For The Body Shop, the point of differentiation is not product quality so much as the social agenda and campaigns that the firm pursues. Consumers of The Body Shop's products gain value from this social agenda, which enables them to support causes that match the values to which they aspire, in addition to the functional value they gain from the firm's products (personal cosmetics and toiletries).

Firms that are able to establish a point of differentiation can then build a brand. Brands are valuable because they instill customer loyalty and enable the firm to charge a premium for its product. Whether that point of distinction is fashion, lifestyle, design, technical quality, product functionality, or social responsibility, a business-level strategy of differentiation can be valuable as it increases the firm's potential profits.

Whether businesses compete on cost or differentiation (or a combination of the two), strategy seeks to add value to customers in order to build a sustainable competitive advantage.

CSR Filter

Competencies molded into a strategy and supported by an efficient structure are a necessary minimum for success—but, increasingly, more is required. It is vital that firms also consider the stakeholder implications of their strategy and operations. The *CSR filter* is a conceptual screen through which strategic and tactical decisions are evaluated for their impact on the firm's various stakeholders. Here, the intent is to take a viable strategy and make it *optimal* for the environment in which the strategy must be executed—even clever strategies can fail if they do not meet stakeholder expectations. Together, these stakeholders form the larger context in which the firm operates and seeks to implement its tactics, strategy, mission, and vision.

The CSR Filter: Nike

Nike is a well-managed firm with an extremely valuable brand. Nike exploits its brand value to great effect in selling its lines of shoes, apparel, and other products. Each of its product lines, however, faces strong competition from companies such as Adidas, Puma, and New Balance. If Nike's strategy of offshore contract production leads to employer abuse in sweatshop factories (perceived or actual), consumers may shift their buying preferences to the firm's competitors. Even if Nike does not own or manage its overseas contract factories, any negative publicity represents danger to Nike's otherwise effective business strategy of product differentiation.

Thus, Nike's offshore sourcing strategy must be constantly scrutinized using a CSR filter. Doing so enables the firm to retain sight of what is core to its brand. Although manufacturing is a peripheral function for Nike, its brand value lies in the lifestyles it appeals to among the people who consume its products. Newspaper reports about human rights abuses, for example, undermine the aspirational values of Nike's consumers and, as such, represent a direct threat. Nike's strategy before the mid-1990s was constructed without a CSR filter. Today, the firm employs a CSR filter at the core of its strategy.

The examples presented throughout this textbook illustrate the many issues encapsulated in the CSR filter. Together, these issues provide insight into the dynamic operating environment that firms face today that is driven by ever-changing societal expectations. Although not all firms are able to create a business model that is as valuable as the models of Walmart and Nike, ultimately, all successful strategies rest on a firm's ability to construct a sustainable competitive advantage within its operating environment. Today, a CSR filter is central to that effort.

Environment

Customers, competitors, economics, technology, government, sociocultural factors, and other forces all shape the firm's operating environment. Together, this mix determines what strategies and actions are deemed to be both effective and socially acceptable. When the environment demands a change in strategy, the existing resources and competencies of the firm may no longer be sufficient. If Walmart is seen as exploiting its low-paid workers, for example, the accompanying negative publicity may harm its image. This can cause stakeholders to withdraw their support. As such, a dynamic environment requires constant innovation of the firm's core resources and competencies in areas such as public relations, advertising, and human resource management to minimize the gap between actions and expectations.

When change is necessary, leaders face a *make-or-buy* decision. Should the needed competencies be developed internally (*make*) or acquired from others outside the firm (*buy*)? Historically, large businesses have had the resources to develop the needed competencies internally through hiring and training. Today, the external environment is changing so rapidly that firms often buy the needed skills from others because the speed of execution is critical. If managers decide to buy the necessary resources or competencies, they face a second decision—whether to bring the needed skills within the organizational structure or outsource them via contractual relationships with suppliers. When the activity is seen as a core resource or competency (e.g., managing inventory at Walmart or designing products at firms like Apple or Nike), most companies retain control over that activity within the structure of the firm. If the activity is seen as peripheral, such as manufacturing apparel or processing payroll checks, the firm will often outsource it for convenience or efficiency. Either way, firms must adapt in the face of a dynamic environment that is driven by constantly evolving societal expectations.

Equal Pay

Over time, actions that were previously considered discretionary or ethical can be codified as laws or regulations and, finally, as economic necessities to which a firm must adhere in order to remain competitive.[4] Many firms in the United States, for example, once blatantly paid women less than men for the same work (a discrepancy that persists to different degrees in different industries). In spite of whatever justifications were applied, this behavior was at the discretion of the firm. Gradually, however, such discrimination came to be seen as unfair, even unethical. In response to shifting values, the federal government enacted the Equal Pay Act in 1963, outlawing discrimination in pay based on an employee's gender. This legislation immediately served to limit this once discretionary area of management decision making. Today, diversity in the workplace is viewed as an economic imperative that enables firms to better reflect their stakeholders' expectations.

Once society determines that a particular form of behavior has become unacceptable, the perceived abuse can lead to a legally mandated correction, such as the Equal Pay Act. This forces change among the range of socially acceptable employment policies used to facilitate firms' competitive strategies. Similar changes can be identified with regard to environmental pollution, product safety standards, financial record keeping, and scores of other previously discretionary behaviors. Once discretionary issues evolve into legal constraints, meeting societal expectations becomes an absolute requirement that is enforced by criminal or civil sanctions.

More difficult to identify are issues that are not yet subject to legal mandates but may still affect the firm. If leaders exercise discretionary authority to attain economic ends, but the actions are perceived to be socially irresponsible (even though they are legally permissible), the consequences may damage the firm.[5] Such damage can become evident in terms of lower sales, diminished employee recruitment and retention, evaporating financial support from investors and markets, and adverse effects on a host of other important relationships. What should a company do?

Strategic CSR bridges all aspects of the firm's value-creating process. Ultimately, stakeholders have the power to determine what is *acceptable* corporate behavior. While societies benefit greatly from the innovation that businesses create in pursuit of profits, businesses are expected to pursue their strategies in ways that, at a minimum, do not harm others and, increasingly, are expected to address and solve social problems. What makes this calculation so difficult is that the definition of *social harm* changes constantly. As such, the argument underpinning strategic CSR assumes that very little is discretionary anymore. Instead, the firm's stakeholders will determine what is considered *responsible* behavior. Past perspectives of firms as profit engines for a narrow slice of society have been altered by globalization and growing affluence—interconnected societies have more knowledge and more choice, while wealthier societies have the resources to demand more. The way stakeholders convey what they value is through their interactions with the firm.

Stakeholder Value: Walmart

Walmart is a well-managed firm with complex stakeholder relations. Contrary to the general notion that the firm destroys value, however, there is considerable evidence that Walmart creates a great deal of value for its stakeholders. When "one out of every four grocery dollars" in the United States is spent at Walmart,[6] you know the firm is adding value—not only for its customers, but also for its employees.

Walmart vehemently denies that it only creates low-paying jobs.[7] The firm notes that it pays above average wages for its industry and that its "average hourly wages exceed state minimums, sometimes by a considerable amount."[8] Walmart is known for promoting from within and emphasizes the high percentage of senior managers who have risen through the ranks. Moreover, if Walmart is as unattractive an employment option as it is reported to be, it is difficult to believe it would attract so much interest from job seekers—when the firm opened a store in Chicago, for example, "25,000 people applied for 325 jobs."[9]

Walmart is often criticized for competing with other firms (as if that were a bad thing). The impact of a Walmart Supercenter on existing local businesses is often cited in protests opposing the opening of a new store. While a new Walmart undoubtedly causes some small firms to go out of business, this has to be weighed against the jobs that become available at the new store, which offer better potential for promotion and a stable career. It is also true that, while some businesses close, they create space for other businesses to open.

It is worth keeping in mind that Walmart is successful only because consumers choose to shop there. Ultimately, "critics are wrong when they say that Wal-Mart puts little people out of business. We (consumers) put little people out of business. . . . We vote with our wallets, and we're the ones who choose Wal-Mart over local stores."[10] Walmart is a large and complex organization that consists of millions of people making decisions every day (many good, some bad). If we define *social responsibility* as something society values, however, there are not many firms that serve society more effectively than Walmart.

In today's globalizing world, *shareholder* value can only be created over the long term if a firm attends to the needs of its *stakeholders*, broadly defined. Satisfying stakeholders is most efficiently achieved by integrating a CSR filter as part of the firm's structure, competencies, and strategy in a way that matches the values and expectations of its operating environment.

THE MARKET FOR CSR

Central to the strategic argument for CSR is the notion that firms that best reflect the current needs of their stakeholders and anticipate how those needs will evolve over time will be more successful in the marketplace over the medium to long term. This principle, however, rests on the assumption that there is a market for CSR. That is, it assumes the firm's stakeholders are willing to reward the behavior they want to see from the firm (the *CSR price premium*) and punish non-CSR behavior when it is exposed (*CSR market abuse*).

CSR Price Premium

As demonstrated in Chapter 8, Walmart has found that adopting specific aspects of CSR (sustainability, in particular) need not undermine the firm's business model and can in fact enhance it. What Chapter 8 also demonstrates, however, is that Walmart is still taking the path of least resistance in the early stages of CSR implementation:

> "There is a substantial opportunity to make green pay," [Rand Waddoups, Wal-Mart's senior director of corporate strategy and sustainability] said. "We haven't even gotten to the low-hanging fruit yet. We are still picking up $1,000 bills off the floor."[11]

Walmart's business strategy relies on a core competence of minimizing costs and passing those savings on to customers. As such, there is little evidence to suggest Walmart would choose the socially responsible long-term option when that decision would lead to a short-term increase in costs. Doing so would threaten the laser-like focus on costs that Walmart executives have spent decades instilling in the firm's employees. What happens, therefore, when CSR increases costs and firms are forced to pass those increases on to their customers in the form of higher prices?

As indicated earlier, firms that seek to differentiate their products on some feature other than low cost often charge a price premium for that product. What is also clear (as with most differentiated products), however, is that the market for these offerings is limited. A quick scan of public opinion polls and media articles about consumers' willingness to pay for products differentiated on an ethical or environmental basis reveals that, in the United States, "35 percent said they are willing to pay extra for a green product."[12] Reports elsewhere, however, suggest such results are inflated. A report in the UK, for example, notes that "only 22 percent of consumers around the world will pay more for 'eco-friendly' products even though 83 percent believe it is 'important for a company to have environmental programs.'"[13] Increasingly, consumers say they expect firms to be socially responsible, but "they don't expect to pay for it. They are, however, more than willing to punish if it's not there."[14]

Firms should take two things away from this shift in market expectations regarding CSR. First, firms should ensure they understand the operational value that CSR offers. An important distinction, therefore, is between those firms that perceive CSR to be a cost and those that perceive it to be an opportunity.[15] Until firms understand CSR as an opportunity to add operational value above and beyond any potential short-term increase in sales, they will have little chance of successfully implementing CSR throughout operations.

Second, part of the reason for consumer skepticism about the value of CSR is firms' record in marketing prior CSR activities. A combination of promises that have subsequently been revealed to be misleading with a proliferation of product labels and ratings designed to *educate* consumers about the CSR credentials of various firms and products (but more often just confusing them) has made people reluctant to pay the associated bill.

CSR Market Abuse

The market for CSR is complicated by the potential for abuse. Stakeholders, in general, and consumers, in particular, need to be vigilant. There is a gap between the information about a product that is known to the firm and the information that the consumer is willing and able to access—in other words, "the information asymmetry between manufacturers and the buying public about the real social, health, and environmental impacts of consumer goods."[16]

As the number of groups and individuals interested in CSR grows, so too does the amount of information that is distributed by firms seeking to take advantage of consumer trends and sympathies. Some of this information will be accurate, while some will be misleading; some of the misleading information will be mistakenly so, while some will be deliberately deceptive. Either way, the proliferation of information is confusing for the firm's stakeholders. In the face of such a barrage, most consumers disengage.[17] Whether deliberate or accidental, therefore, the effect is negative. As CSR becomes more profitable, the potential for *greenwash* increases.[18]

Greenwash measures the extent to which firms are willing to jump on the CSR bandwagon and mislead consumers in the hope of financial gain. Research suggests that a significant percentage of CSR product-marketing claims are false or misleading. In 2010, for example, the environmental marketing organization Terrachoice tested the veracity of the 12,061 environmental claims made on the labels of 5,296 consumer products and found that "more than 95% of consumer products claiming to be green were found to commit at least one of the 'Sins of Greenwashing.'"[19] In total, there are "seven sins"[20] that firms engage in when marketing the CSR components of their products: the *Sin of the Hidden Trade-off*, the *Sin of No Proof*, the *Sin of Vagueness*, the *Sin of Irrelevance*, the *Sin of*

Lesser of Two Evils, the *Sin of Fibbing*, and the *Sin of Worshipping False Labels*. Taken together, they indicate "both that the individual consumer has been misled and that the potential environmental benefit of his or her purchase has been squandered."[21] The accusation is that firms say the *correct* things but do not necessarily alter the way they do business. As Terrachoice's report indicates, there are many examples to choose from, ranging from toilet paper[22] to hybrid cars[23] to the Olympics:[24]

> McDonald's may support sustainable fisheries, but its core business is still selling Big Macs. Big oil companies can talk all they want about reducing greenhouse emissions, but they are still drilling for hydrocarbons.[25]

Moreover, as different groups seek to establish their CSR ranking, certification, or policy as the standard, CSR comes to mean different things to different people. And because it takes time for information and practices to emerge as the standard, the potential for confusion grows. Consumers, in particular, stand to lose as different self-proclaimed experts bombard them with more information, leading to the growth of *green noise*, "static caused by urgent, sometimes vexing or even contradictory information [about the environment] played at too high a volume for too long":[26]

> An environmentally conscientious consumer is left to wonder: Are low-energy compact fluorescent bulbs better than standard incandescents, even if they contain traces of mercury? Which salad is more earth-friendly, the one made with organic mixed greens trucked from thousands of miles away, or the one with lettuce raised on nearby industrial farms? Should they support nuclear power as a clean alternative to coal?

The effect of this information overload on consumer behavior is to reduce consumer confidence in companies and arouse suspicion about CSR claims. While, to an extent, this confusion is unavoidable (CSR is complex), the result of too much information is paralysis—ineffective, bad, or non decisions. Here, CSR is a victim of its own success. Without its growing popularity and acceptance, the issue of growing and contradictory information would neither exist nor matter. Nevertheless, the goal for any firm serious about CSR should be to have an honest and genuine conversation with its stakeholders about its efforts—a conversation that Unilever is seeking through "five simple levers": Make it understood, Make it easy, Make it desirable, Make it rewarding, and Make it a habit. [27]

A strategic CSR perspective demands "solutions where you can take your customers with you. You can be one step ahead of them and take them with you. But if you're three steps ahead, you'll lose them."[28] Understanding the market for CSR (i.e., when stakeholders are willing to pay a CSR premium while punishing greenwash) ensures that executives are much better equipped to deal with the complex environment in which business is conducted today. This understanding is gained by applying a CSR filter to the firm's strategic planning and day-to-day operations.

THE CSR FILTER IN ACTION

The model of strategy formulation presented in Figure 11.2 summarizes the relationship between CSR and strategy. Corporate success assumes that *strategy* matches *internal competencies* with the *external environment*, within the constraints of *mission* and *vision*. The implementation of strategy, however, rests upon *corporate operations* being successful. Finance, accounting, human resources, and other functional areas must be executed effectively if the strategy is to be successful at matching competencies to market opportunities. To improve overall performance, therefore, leaders create *strategic objectives* that aim to strengthen these corporate operations. To ensure sufficient financial resources, for example, a strategic objective may be set for the accounting department to accelerate the collection of accounts receivable. Or, marketing might be tasked with the strategic objective of gaining 5% market share. These strategic objectives, however, must be viewed as *strategic imperatives* that enhance the firm's CSR goals; otherwise, the tactics and strategies may cause resistance among stakeholders. To achieve these strategic objectives that meet the firm's strategic imperatives, key players must undertake strategic initiatives in the form of *action-oriented projects*. The head of accounting, for example, might create a task force charged with a project that identifies and tracks clients who are slow to pay their bills. A similar action-oriented task force might also be created in marketing to evaluate the firm's advertising as a first step to gaining market share. However these actor-oriented projects perform, they must do so by achieving strategic objectives in ways that are consistent with the firm's strategic imperatives; otherwise, larger threats to the firm's viability arise. As such, the firm's strategic perspective is surrounded by a *CSR filter*.

Companies understand the value of being perceived as good corporate citizens. Until now, however, managers have largely confined this concern to public relations departments because they were able to control the information that shaped the public face of the corporation. Figures 2.1, 2.2, and 2.3 in Chapter 2 illustrate why this situation is changing as power swings away from companies and toward their various constituent groups. As globalization progresses, communication technologies will continue to democratize and fuel the exchange of information in all free societies. The CSR filter enables firms to capture these trends within their strategic planning in a way that better reflects stakeholder priorities and, as a result, increases the likelihood of success in the marketplace.

Importantly, however, firms must reflect stakeholder concerns via genuine engagement. Ideally, progressive companies seek to stay ahead of these evolving values and meet new demands as they arise. In order for this to happen, business leaders must be persuaded that CSR offers strategic value to the firm. Strategic CSR, powered by stakeholder theory, delivers these results. It is a means of allowing firms to analyze the total business environment and formulate the appropriate strategic response. It can protect the firm and its assets, while also offering a point of competitive differentiation—it is the route to success in business today.

Figure 11.2   Strategy Formulation Using the CSR Filter

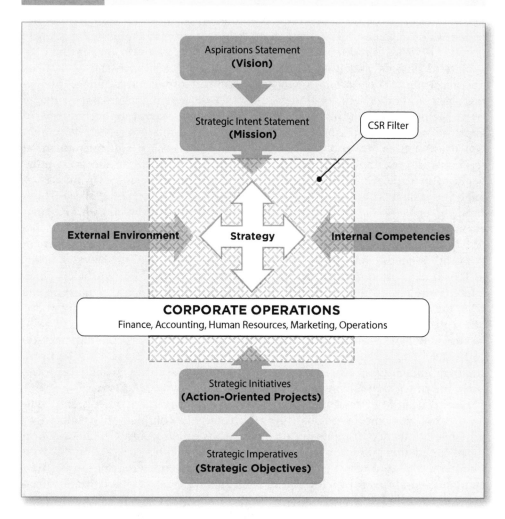

Motion: Customers should be willing to pay a CSR price premium.

QUESTIONS FOR DISCUSSION AND REVIEW

1. Why is it important to view CSR from a strategic context?

2. Why are large, multinational firms more likely to be concerned about CSR? Why are lifestyle brands more susceptible to CSR than companies that seek to compete with a business-level strategy of low cost?

3. How do structure, competencies, strategy, and the environment combine with the *CSR filter* to create a successful organization?

4. If you were CEO of a firm, how would you apply a *CSR filter*—what form might it take? Can you think of a company that is successfully utilizing a *CSR filter* today?

5. Why does *greenwash* present a danger to CSR? Have a look at Terrachoice's report "The Sins of Greenwashing" (http://sinsofgreenwashing.com/ind ex35c6.pdf). Which of the seven sins (p. 10) do you think is the most important? Think of a firm that is committing that sin—what is misleading about the firm's actions?

Chapter 12

STRATEGIC CSR

The firm and its stakeholders are synonymous. The firm does not exist independently of its stakeholders, who benefit tremendously from the economic power of the for-profit firm to deliver societal progress. Firms do this by solving problems—problems that have economic, social, moral, and ethical components. By enforcing their expectations, stakeholders ensure it is in a firm's best interests to meet the behavior that is expected of it. That is how profit, the purpose of the firm, is generated.

This synergistic relationship between the firm and its stakeholders is why CSR is a key element of business strategy. In the words of *The Economist*, CSR is "just good business."[1] It is how the firm becomes profitable; it is how society progresses. In contrast, CSR implemented superficially—or, worse, completely ignored—may threaten whatever comparative advantage the firm holds in its industry. At the beginning of the 20th century, for example, Standard Oil pressured industry suppliers to treat its competitors unfairly in the eyes of society. The result was a 1911 US Supreme Court case (221 U.S. 1, 1911) that found the company in breach of the Sherman antitrust laws, forcing Standard Oil to break into separate companies.[2] Today, activist organizations such as Greenpeace and the Rainforest Action Network (RAN) target corporate actions they deem socially irresponsible. The result of these protests can be dramatic shifts in corporate policies and damage to the brand, such as when Shell changed course regarding the breakup of the *Brent Spar* oil platform (Greenpeace) or Citigroup adopted wide-ranging environmental metrics in the criteria it uses to grant loans (RAN).

As these examples demonstrate, CSR is not only about avoiding potential threats to the brand. There is also great potential for firms that embrace CSR.[3] For example, in part, Citigroup's reaction to RAN's campaign helped encourage the firm to play a leading role in the creation of the Equator Principles.[4] Similarly, Unilever's adoption of its "sustainable living plan"[5] and GE's commitment to "ecoimagination"[6] demonstrate the competitive advantage that CSR can deliver to firms that embrace it as a basis for differentiation in the market.

In other words, CSR allows executives to address stakeholder concerns in ways that carry strategic benefit for the firm. CSR is not about saving the whales or ending poverty or other worthwhile goals that are unrelated to a firm's operations and are better left to government or nonprofits. Instead, CSR is about the economic, legal, ethical, and discretionary issues that stakeholders view as directly related to the firm's plans and actions. The solutions to these issues, the overlap where economic and social value intersect, lie at the heart of any successful CSR policy. This approach is illustrated in the concept of "strategic corporate philanthropy," but the same approach can be applied to the wider issue of CSR:

> The acid test of good corporate philanthropy is whether the desired social change is so beneficial to the company that the organization would pursue the change even if no one ever knew about it.[7]

Beyond the desired outcomes, however, are the approaches employed to achieve those changes. Too often, the end (profit maximization and share price growth) has been used to justify the means (operations that ignore the firm's broader stakeholder obligations). In contrast, a firm that seeks to implement a CSR policy that carries strategic benefits is concerned with both the ends of economic profitability and, more importantly, the means by which those profits are achieved. As such, the connection between these means and ends, the processes by which the firm operates, is central to the concept of strategic CSR and something that sets it apart from other discussions of corporate social responsibility.

This distinction becomes apparent when discussing an issue such as ethics, which is concerned about the honesty, judgment, and integrity with which various stakeholders are treated. There is no debate—ethical behavior is a prerequisite assumption for strategic CSR. Ethics, however, are not absolute but vary from stakeholder to stakeholder. As such, *ethics* is not the central focus of this textbook, except insofar as stakeholders can define a firm's actions as unethical, thus harming its legitimacy and profit potential. Likewise, other social issues exist outside the direct focus of strategic CSR. Domestic and international income disparity, gender discrimination, spirituality and workplace religiosity, technological impacts on indigenous populations, and other issues all affect societal well-being. Unless firm operations directly affect stakeholders in these areas, however, the study of these topics might better fall under ethics, public policy, sociology, or developmental economics courses.

All of these issues only encroach upon strategic CSR to the extent that they influence relations between the firm and its stakeholders—the means by which firms create value.

DEFINING *STRATEGIC CSR*

The goal of this book has been to frame strategic CSR in terms of a set of principles that differentiate it from related concepts, such as sustainability and business ethics. While sustainability relates to issues of ecological preservation and business ethics seeks to construct normative prescriptions of *right* and *wrong*,

Strategic CSR

The incorporation of a holistic *CSR perspective* within a firm's strategic planning and *core operations* so that the firm is managed in the interests of a broad set of *stakeholders* to *optimize value* over the *medium to long term*

strategic CSR is a pragmatic philosophy that is grounded, first and foremost, in the day-to-day operations of the firm. As such, *strategic CSR* is central to the firm's value-creating activities and, ultimately, its success in the market.

In constructing a working definition of *strategic CSR*, five components are essential: (1) that firms incorporate a CSR perspective within their culture and strategic planning process; (2) that any actions taken are directly related to core operations; (3) that firms seek to understand and respond to the needs of their stakeholders; (4) that they aim to optimize value created; and (5) that they shift from a short-term perspective to managing their resources and relations with key stakeholders over the medium to long term.

It is the combination of these five pillars that ensures the integration of CSR within the strategic planning and day-to-day operations of the organization.

CSR Perspective

Essential to any definition of *strategic CSR* is that firms incorporate a CSR perspective within their organizational culture and strategic planning process.

This presupposes an iterative relationship between the firm and its stakeholders, with equal responsibilities to both convey needs and respond to those needs whenever possible. An important tool that helps the firm do this is a *CSR filter* that is integrated throughout the firm's decision-making processes. The CSR filter is defined as a conceptual screen through which strategic and tactical decisions are evaluated for their impact on the firm's various stakeholders. Embedding the profit incentive within a framework of guiding values that set the parameters of decisions and guide employees in relation to the firm's strategy helps managers implement *strategic CSR* throughout all aspects of day-to-day operations.[8]

In outlining their ideas about how firms can incorporate a social dimension in their strategic decision making, Porter and Kramer provide a three-tiered framework that forms a guide to how organizations can assess and prioritize the range of social issues they encounter.[9] The interaction between firms and stakeholder issues of concern are divided into three levels:

- "Generic social issues" (not directly related to a firm's operations)
- "Value chain social impacts" (the extent to which a firm's operations affect society)
- "Social dimensions of competitive context" (the extent to which the environment constrains a firm's operations)

In the case of a retail clothing company that outsources production overseas, for example, the issue of a livable wage (as opposed to a minimum wage) in the United States is a *generic social issue*—an issue that is important and something

| Figure 12.1 | Porter & Kramer's Strategy and Society Model |

Social Issues

Firm
Operations

Environmental
Constraints

Strategic CSR

Responsive CSR

Source: Michael E. Porter & Mark R. Kramer, "Strategy & Society," *Harvard Business Review,* December 2006, p. 89.

on which the firm might take a position, but that is not directly relevant to operations. The issue of a livable wage in a country in which the firm's products are made, however, is a clear example of a *value chain social impact*, an issue in which its operations directly affect the local community. The prospect of government legislation on this issue represents a *social dimension of competitive context* for the organization, as it has the potential to constrain operations.

Figure 12.1 illustrates how Porter and Kramer use the interactions among social issues, firm operations, and environmental constraints to distinguish between "responsive CSR" and "strategic CSR." *Responsive CSR* occurs when the firm becomes involved in a generic social issue that is not related to operations or structures its value chain to avoid any negative social impacts. Strategic CSR, however, occurs when the organization seeks actively to benefit society as a consequence of its value chain or influence its competitive context through activities such as "strategic philanthropy."[10] In Porter and Kramer's framing, strategic CSR occurs where there is a direct effect of a firm's operations on society and vice versa, allowing the firm to identify the issues and stakeholders it can influence.

Core Operations

The second component of strategic CSR states that any action a firm takes should be directly related to its day-to-day operations.

As a result of this defining characteristic, the same action will differ from firm to firm in terms of whether it can be classified as strategic CSR, depending on the firm's expertise and the relevance of the issue to the organization's vision and mission. This logic is motivated by an appreciation that firms create value as a direct result of their unique mix of resources and capabilities. For-profit firms are the most efficient way we have developed to convert scarce and valuable resources into products and services that are in demand because they meet a societal need. Firms vary in their areas of expertise and the market segments they target (and many other dimensions)—they have become experts in those areas because that is how they define their niche and survive in a competitive environment. As a result, the firm creates the most value when it focuses on what it does best, which is defined by its core operations.

For example, it makes a great deal of sense for a computer company like Dell to offer a computer-recycling program as part of its product awareness throughout the lifecycle.[11] It makes much less sense, however, for Dell to offer a "Plant a Tree for Me" program as a way for consumers to offset greenhouse gas emissions produced as a result of the production of their new computer.[12] Dell knows about computers and should be responsible for its products throughout the value system. Less obvious is Dell's expertise in tree planting (what trees to plant, where to plant them, or which trees are most effective in combating climate change). Even though Dell outsources these responsibilities to its program partners (The Conservation Fund, http://www.conservationfund.org/), it is not clear how well qualified Dell is to select partners in this area or how able the firm is to monitor the behavior of those partners.

Strategic CSR is not about activities that are peripheral to the firm; it is also not about reinventing capitalism. It is about the operational decisions the firm makes day in and day out. All aspects of business involve economic, social, moral, and ethical considerations, and the primary role of the manager when making decisions is to balance these considerations in prioritizing the diverse interests that have a stake in the firm's operations.

Stakeholder Perspective

The third component of strategic CSR is that firms incorporate a stakeholder perspective throughout the firm.

A barrier to the implementation of a stakeholder perspective, however, is the primary emphasis currently given by many corporations to the interests of shareholders. Instead, firms need to expand their view to include all stakeholders who, collectively, define the operating environment. In doing so, the firm has an interest not only in responding to stakeholder concerns but also in anticipating these concerns whenever possible. For their part, stakeholders should be willing to incentivize firms to meet their needs by actively discriminating in favor of those businesses that best match expectations. By making decisions that are in the interests of the firm's broad range of stakeholders, managers increase the chances of building a sustainable competitive advantage.

An essential aspect of this shift to a stakeholder model is the issue of prioritization (see Chapter 4). While it is important for an organization to be able to identify its different stakeholders and their different interests and demands, the real difficulty comes when those interests and expectations conflict, which they often do. Given limited resources, the most effective means to deal with stakeholder conflict is prioritization. If a firm has two stakeholder groups whose demands conflict (i.e., the firm is unable to satisfy fully both stakeholders), it makes sense for it to respond more wholeheartedly to the more important of the two, while attempting not to offend the other.

Critics might point out that this is what firms have been doing all along—it is just that they always give top priority to their shareholders. In reality, however, the choice is not between either a shareholder or stakeholder perspective. A firm's shareholders are one of its stakeholders and, as such, have an interest. It is not the case, however, that this automatically ensures their demands deserve top priority. In reality, different stakeholders should be prioritized for different issues. What is counterproductive is a blind loyalty to any one stakeholder group over the others.[13] This especially applies to the firm's shareholders, who do not have the same risk exposure to the firm's performance as other stakeholders, such as employees:

> The claim of shareholders is solely on the residual income of the company. But . . . their exposure to the risks generated by an individual company is far less than the exposure of workers with firm-specific knowledge and skills.[14]

Sumantra Ghoshal, the late strategy professor at London Business School, agrees, suggesting that the pursuit of shareholder value fails to reflect the relative contributions of different stakeholders to the success of the organization:

> Most shareholders can sell their stocks far more easily than most employees can find another job. In every substantive sense, employees of a company carry more risks than do the shareholders. Also, their contributions of knowledge, skills, and entrepreneurship are typically more important than the contributions of capital by shareholders, a pure commodity that is perhaps in excess supply.[15]

Johnson & Johnson is an excellent example of a company that has formally prioritized its stakeholders in its famous Credo.[16] Importantly, the Credo places customers first and shareholders (stockholders) last as a "final responsibility." The firm rationalizes that, as long as "we operate according to these principles," with its customers (health practitioners), suppliers and distributors, employees, and communities in which it operates being given a higher priority than its shareholders, then "the stockholders should realize a fair return."[17]

Although their firms have not formalized this prioritization to the same extent as Johnson & Johnson, business leaders as diverse as Herb Kelleher and Colleen Barrett at Southwest,[18] Howard Schulz at Starbucks,[19] Sam Walton at Walmart,[20] and Yvon Chouínard at Patagonia[21] have all recognized that shareholders are best served when stakeholders that are more immediate to operations (in particular, employees) are motivated, loyal, and committed to serving customers. Amazon has a similar "customers first" approach to business.[22] In addition, Costco routinely rejects investors' calls to reduce the pay and benefits they provide to their employees. In spite of investors' resistance, Costco's share price has greatly outperformed the share price of its main competitor, Walmart, in recent years.

None of this, of course, is to suggest that shareholder interests do not matter or that they should never be placed above the interests of other stakeholders. In reality, a flexible approach is best. While there is a general ordering of stakeholders (organizational, economic, and societal—see Chapter 4), the specific ordering on any given issue will vary depending on the situation. The main point for managers to remember, therefore, is that shareholders should not automatically be their primary concern in those instances when the consideration of the interests of a broader set of stakeholders will better serve the overall interests of the organization.

Optimize Value

The fourth component of strategic CSR is the drive to *optimize* (as opposed to *maximize*) value, broadly defined.

In essence, the goal is to seek a balance between the production and consumption activities in society in order to build a standard of living that meets the needs of the collective. The production component includes incorporating costs that firms currently seek to externalize, while the consumption component includes incorporating costs that society currently seeks to avoid. If we can achieve this balance, and spread both the benefits and the costs over a wide range of stakeholders, we will be significantly closer to optimizing value throughout society.

As a result of being both impossible to achieve and unhelpful because it distorts decision making, a more valuable focus for firms to adopt than profit *maximization* is the goal of profit *optimization*. A focus on optimization automatically reorients the manager toward the interests of a broader collection of constituent interests. It speaks to compromise and mediation, rather than tradeoffs among winners and losers. While the idea of a maximum suggests an absolute point (a definitive maximum amount), an optimum suggests a more relative state of existence. There is not right and wrong so much as more or less ideal, given the circumstances. Such a distinction is not merely rhetorical, however; it helps encourage a balance among short-, medium-, and long-term decisions that create value across the firm's stakeholders.

Medium to Long Term

The final, and perhaps most important, component of strategic CSR is the shift from a short-term perspective when managing the firm's resources and stakeholder relations to a medium- or long-term perspective.

If managers alter their horizons from the next quarter or next season to the next decade or beyond, they immediately alter the priorities by which they manage and, as a result, automatically change the nature of the decisions they make today.[23] If a CEO is only interested in the next quarter, it is difficult to make the case for strategic CSR. But, if the CEO is concerned with the continued existence of the firm 5, 10, or 20 years from now, the value of building lasting, trust-based relationships with key stakeholders increases exponentially.

As discussed throughout this book, firms must satisfy key groups among their various constituents if they hope to remain viable in today's business context. When the expectations of different stakeholders conflict, firms need to be able to balance the competing interests. Not only are these competing interests apparent *among* stakeholders, however, but also *within* stakeholder groups. As an example of such conflict, consider a firm's investors who might have different expectations of what constitutes a reasonable return on their investment.

The Shareholder Shift—From Investor to Speculator

The evolving role of shareholders has greatly strengthened the case for firms to adopt a broader stakeholder approach. In particular, shares today are perceived less and less as a long-term investment in a company and more and more as a stand-alone, short-term speculation for personal benefit. A distinction can be drawn, therefore, between *investors*, who seek firms with a share price that reflects sound economic fundamentals, and *speculators*, who gamble on firms based on whether they think the share price will rise, irrespective of whether it deserves to go up or is valued at a fair price.

This shift is indicated by the fact that "the average holding period for shares in America and Britain has dropped from six years in 1950 to less than six months today."[24] As John Bogle, founder of Vanguard, puts it in his book *The Clash of Cultures: Investment vs. Speculation*, "A culture of short-term speculation has run rampant."[25] The result is a huge increase in both volume and turnover, an effect that has been termed the "three-million-shares-per-second casino of Wall Street."[26]

Too much money is aimed at short-term speculation—the seeking of quick profit with little concern for the future. The financial system has been wounded by a flood of so-called innovations that merely promote hyper-rapid trading, market timing, and shortsighted corporate maneuvering.[27]

When a computer program is triaging miniscule differences in share prices across trading exchanges, holding individual positions for microseconds, how should we think about the relationship between that "shareholder" and the company? The focus is increasingly away from the overall health of the organization and toward protecting the dollar investment of the individual. As *The Economist* puts it, "high-frequency traders are not making decisions based on a company's future prospects; they are seeking to profit from tiny changes in price. They might as well be trading baseball cards."[28]

Shareholders today have risen to a position of influence that is distracting for businesses. Managers now have to concentrate a disproportionate amount of their time on the short-term considerations of quarterly results, dividend levels, and share price in order to keep demanding shareholders happy. This short-term perspective comes at the cost of long-term strategic considerations of the company and its business interests.[29]

Increasingly, the idea that shareholders have the best interests of the firm at heart is hard to defend. In today's business environment, a broader stakeholder perspective provides the stability necessary for managers to chart the best course for the organization so that it remains a viable entity over the medium to long term. This is in the interests of a company's *investors*, rather than those of its *speculators*.

The development of stock options and other compensation tools designed to solve the principal–agent conflict and align the interests of shareholders and managers has exacerbated this trend. The short-term nature of shareholder investments in firms, plus executives' financial incentives to develop personal wealth, combine to distort the conditions under which organizational decisions are made.[30] The effect influences behavior as executives (consciously or subconsciously) accommodate the demands of the firm's short-term investors. In the United States, for example, research has found

> a persistent rise in unorthodox reporting. In 2003, 22 percent of the [earnings announcements filed with the SEC] featured "pro forma," non-GAAP measures of financial performance. By 2013, 49 percent did. Rising share prices create a demand for the earnings with which to rationalize them.[31]

More specifically, evidence suggests directors are willing to sacrifice the organization's future in favor of raising the stock price in the short-term:

> A frequently cited study by two Duke University professors found that 80 percent of chief financial officers were willing to cut spending on research, development and marketing to hit short-term financial targets.[32]

Altering this dynamic, however, is extremely complicated because "it turns out that nearly everyone in the investment world plays a role in creating the challenges companies face in setting their sights on the far horizon."[33] The focus is less and less on the underlying value of a business and more and more on the pursuit of shareholder returns. John Maynard Keynes perceived this distorting influence of stock exchanges, comparing the process of stock picking to a beauty contest: The object is not to choose the most beautiful face but merely the one that the investor thinks others will find the most beautiful. In other words, for the investor, "it is better . . . to be conventionally wrong than unconventionally right."[34]

> It is not a case of choosing those [faces] that, to the best of one's judgment, are really the prettiest, nor even those that average opinion genuinely thinks the prettiest. We have reached the third degree where we devote our intelligences to anticipating what average opinion expects the average opinion to be. And there are some, I believe, who practice the fourth, fifth and higher degrees.[35]

In response, some CEOs are seeking a longer-term approach. Wendelin Wiedeking, the CEO of Porsche from 1993 to 2009, for example, consistently argued for a broader perspective to strategic planning that shifts executives' attention beyond the demands of shareholders—they "give their money just once, whereas the employees work every day."[36] Similarly, firms such as Unilever, Coca-Cola, McDonald's, and AT&T have stopped releasing such quarterly earnings reports, "stating that they detract from creating a sustainable company for the long term":[37]

London-based consumer company Unilever PLC doesn't give out annual earnings or sales guidance, aside from saying it wants to grow consistently ahead of markets. Colgate-Palmolive Co. provides annual sales and earnings guidance . . . but it doesn't provide quarterly forecasts. Coca-Cola Co. generally refrains from providing specific annual guidance. Instead it guides investors to long-term targets for increases in sales volume, revenue, operating income and per-share earnings.[38]

In the UK, the government "recently eliminated mandatory quarterly reports with the goal of lengthening the time horizon for corporate business decision-making." As a result, there are calls in the United States to allow boards "to choose semiannual instead of quarterly reporting."[39] Beyond changing the firm's reporting patterns, other CEOs are going to greater lengths, delisting their firms and "avoiding the stock market so they can be free of the short-term pressure that can undermine corporate performance over time."[40]

A Truly Long-Term Perspective

The Long Now Foundation (http://longnow.org/) focuses on combating the "here and now" culture in which we live and trying to get people to think in terms of a longer time frame. To reinforce this perspective, all the years on the website are written in terms of 10,000 years, rather than 1,000 years (e.g., 02017 = 2017):

> The Long Now Foundation was established in 01996 to creatively foster long-term thinking and responsibility in the framework of the next 10,000 years.

The organization's major project is the 10,000 Year Clock, which was first proposed by computer scientist Daniel Hillis:

> When I was a child, people used to talk about what would happen by the year 02000. For the next thirty years they kept talking about what would happen by the year 02000, and now no one mentions a future date at all. The future has been shrinking by one year per year for my entire life. I think it is time for us to start a long-term project that gets people thinking past the mental barrier of an ever-shortening future. I would like to propose a large (think Stonehenge) mechanical clock, powered by seasonal temperature changes. It ticks once a year, bongs once a century, and the cuckoo comes out every millennium.

In essence, strategic CSR represents an enlightened approach to management that retains the focus on creating value that is emphasized by a traditional bottom-line business model, but does so over a much broader base of the firm's stakeholders than do traditional economic models. In order to implement strategic CSR in a meaningful way, therefore, the firm's focus has to be on optimizing value over the long term in areas of expertise (related to core operations). A short-term focus, driven by quarterly earnings guidelines for investors with little at stake in the firm, has no value (and is likely detrimental)[41] to firms committed to implementing strategic CSR.

STRATEGIC CSR IS NOT AN OPTION

As detailed above, strategic CSR is a philosophy of management that infuses the firm. It is not a peripheral activity; it is central to everything the firm does. All business decisions have economic, social, moral, and ethical dimensions. As such, all firms do strategic CSR, whether they realize it or not; it is just that some firms do it better than others.

Not Philanthropy

Strategic CSR is not about *philanthropy*;[42] it is about day-to-day *operations*.[43] If any money is being spent by the firm on areas not directly related to core competencies, it is likely not the most efficient use of that money. If, however, the main justification for an expenditure is brand awareness and the firm feels there is value in being associated with a particular charity or good cause (in other words, if the values underpinning the cause align with those of the firm's stakeholders), then that investment should be made, but responsibility for it should be placed where it belongs, in the marketing department. The marketing department contains experts who know best how to manage the brand. If, however, there are other business-related reasons for the firm to donate money to a specific cause, then responsibility for that decision should lie with the relevant functional area—it should be part of the firm's core functions so that the relevant expertise can be applied for optimal effect.

The connection between CSR and philanthropy is tangential, at best. Although there are specific tax advantages associated with donations, the main reason for making the payment is the potential marketing-related benefits, if employed strategically. Unless there is a direct connection to business operations, the argument for firms donating large sums in areas in which they have low levels of expertise is difficult to make. This is true not only because corporate philanthropy is massively inefficient if it is unrelated to core operations, but also because it can often go largely unrewarded (or even unrecognized) by the stakeholders it is designed to placate:

> Walmart is extremely generous, giving away over $1bn in cash and product annually—but it's still viewed by the public as one of the least responsible companies on the planet, and is a continual target of boycotts and protests. Wells Fargo donated over $315m in 2012, the most cash of any company in the nation, and even did so in a thoughtful manner, focusing on low-income housing and first-time homebuyer support—yet it still ranked as one of the 10 most disliked companies in America in 2013.[44]

What if corporate America were willing to take the more than $18 billion it donates annually[45] and, instead, invest it in what it does best—operating its businesses?

> Imagine that [Walmart] didn't give away a billion dollars this year—and instead took that money, combined it with a negligible price increase, and

paid all of its workers a living wage of $12 per hour. . . . The effort would improve the lives of its employees and families, save the economy hundreds of millions of dollars annually, and potentially change the way the public perceives Walmart.[46]

For-profit firms should focus on identifying problems for which there is a clear market-based solution and then deliver that solution in an efficient and socially responsible manner. The idea of strategic CSR as a managing philosophy focuses on firms' areas of operational expertise and de-emphasizes actions for which either there is no market solution or the firm is not well-suited to deliver that solution. That is how value is optimized over the medium to long term—by operating in a way that meets the needs and demands of the firm's stakeholders, broadly defined. In other words, the focus of business remains the same; it is the way the organization goes about achieving it that is different with a strategic CSR perspective.

Not *Caring* Capitalism

Strategic CSR is not *caring* capitalism but *market* capitalism. In recent years, and particularly since the 2007–2008 financial crisis, there have been various attempts to reinvent capitalism. High-profile actors, such as Bill Gates of Microsoft ("caring capitalism") and Muhammad Yunus of Grameen Bank ("social business"), have sought to reform the underlying principles of capitalist ideology by urging firms to adopt goals beyond a focus on profit. More recently, work has begun to develop the concept of "inclusive capitalism, which is the idea that those with the power and the means have a responsibility to help make society stronger and more inclusive for those who don't."[47]

As discussed throughout this book, strategic CSR rejects these attempts as not only futile but quite possibly counterproductive. It is not the ends of capitalism that matters so much as the means by which those ends are pursued.[48] Although efforts to alter the ends of capitalism are delivered with the best of intentions, the difficulties in implementation quickly become apparent when these ideas are investigated in a little more detail. Bill Gates, for example, launched his manifesto for a "new system" of capitalism in a speech at the World Economic Forum at Davos: "an approach where governments, businesses, and nonprofits work together to stretch the reach of market forces so that more people can make a profit, or gain recognition, doing work that eases the world's inequities."[49] While appealing at first glance, it is not clear what Gates actually means by "creative capitalism" and how it is to be realized. For example, it is easy to say:

I hope corporations will consider dedicating a percentage of your top innovators' time to issues that could help people left out of the global economy. . . . It is a great form of creative capitalism, because it takes the brainpower that makes life better for the richest, and dedicates it to improving the lives of everyone else.[50]

But, in reality, how is a firm to decide which issue it should prioritize and devote its most valuable resources to if that decision is not based on market forces? How much value is compromised because these "top innovators" are working on a philanthropic problem (that may or may not be suited to their particular set of skills) instead of one based on supply and demand? Do firms need to calculate a certain level of potential "social goodness" in advance? How would they do that? What if it is not realized? None of these questions are addressed sufficiently, with Gates weaving back and forth between an argument based on market forces and one based on an appeal to the altruistic side of firms and their stakeholders without offering any clear guidance as to how priorities among competing claims should be set. As one supportive commentator noted:

> In Gates' vision, private companies should be encouraged to tweak their structure slightly to free up their innovative thinkers to work on solutions to problems in the developing world. It's gung-ho, rather than hairshirt, philanthropy. . . . While companies or individuals may ultimately profit from this work in developing nations, the reward primarily comes in the form of recognition and enjoyment.[51]

On an individual/micro level, such arguments are appealing—romantic even. But at a macro level, they quickly fall apart. The market, while imperfect, remains the best means society has for allocating scarce resources. As noted by a critic of caring capitalism:

> There is a stronger argument to be made against "creative capitalism," and it is that profits come from serving society. The larger the profits, the better job the company tends to have done. Profit maximization is a worthy goal by itself.[52]

Put more bluntly, strategic CSR, implemented throughout the firm via a stakeholder perspective and a focus on medium- to long-term value creation, optimizes performance:

> Sure, let those who have become rich under capitalism try to do good things for those who are still poor, as Mr. Gates has admirably chosen to do. But a New-Age blend of market incentives and feel-good recognition will not end poverty. History has shown that profit-motivated capitalism is still the best hope for the poor.[53]

Similar criticisms can be leveled against Muhammad Yunus, the 2006 winner of the Nobel Peace Prize, whose concept of "social business" touches on ideas similar to those of Gates.[54] In reality, what both men are expressing is a form of social entrepreneurship, which demands that firms replace profit seeking with something that amounts to altruism:

> "Social business" . . . [envisages] a new sector of the economy made up of companies run as private businesses but making no profits. These would

focus on products and services that conventional companies do not find profitable, such as healthcare, nutrition, housing and sanitation for the poor. It is predicated on the view that investors will be happy to get zero return as long as they can see returns in social benefits.[55]

Such business models have limited market appeal—while some consumers are willing to pay the associated price premiums, the evidence suggests strongly that these same values cannot be assumed market-wide. In advocating such a philosophy, Yunus is turning his back on the sound business model for which he won his Nobel Prize. Microfinance (and Grameen Bank, the organization founded by Yunus to deliver microloans to individuals who could not secure them from mainstream financial institutions) is effective because it extends the market to consumers whose demand was thought to be insufficient for traditional finance models. All it took was a product tailored to the specific needs of a specific segment of the market. While the microfinance industry is grounded in business fundamentals, however, it is not clear how Yunus expects altruism to constitute sufficient incentive to mobilize the private sector as a whole:

> The genius of microfinance was in getting the profit motive to work for the very poorest. The drawback of social business is that it depends on the kindness of strangers.[56]

Not *Sharing* Value

Strategic CSR is also not about *sharing* value—it is about *creating* value. The ideas of "caring capitalism" and "social business" present leaps of faith and logic that are similar to those generated by the idea of "shared value." Like Gates and Yunus, Michael Porter and Mark Kramer have enjoyed a significant amount of publicity for their idea, which also attempts to overturn centuries of economic theory and practice to reinvent the purpose of the firm "as creating shared value, not just profit per se."[57]

On the surface, Porter's shared value and strategic CSR can appear to produce similar behavior. The motivating force is different, however, and this is important because it will lead to different outcomes in terms of the venture's ultimate success or failure. The difference comes down to the focus of the firm and the relevance to core operations of the issue at hand. Starbucks, for example, should not form partnerships with shade-grown coffee farmers in Guatemala because it recognizes those farmers face an uncertain future with an insufficient welfare net to support them if their businesses fail (a nonoperational goal). Instead, Starbucks should do so because it needs to secure a stable supply of high-quality coffee beans and supporting these farmers in a sustainable manner is the best way to guarantee that supply (an operational goal). In other words, Starbucks should form stable, lasting partnerships with these key suppliers not because it is seeking to fill a charitable need but because these farmers produce a raw material that is essential to its business. This incentivizes

Starbucks to protect the raw material in a sustainable way rather than ruthlessly exploit it. If those Guatemalan farmers are not producing a product that is in demand (i.e., if the business logic for a relationship is not there), the argument that Starbucks should get involved is difficult to make.

Ultimately, although for-profit firms can help with the first perspective (caring capitalism), they are much better suited to the second perspective (market capitalism). Ideally, the governmental and nonprofit sectors focus on those problems that the market ignores or cannot solve. In contrast, Porter and Kramer argue that charitable goals should be considered equally with operational goals and firms should then utilize their market-based skills and expertise to solve both kinds of problem—in other words, that they should become less like for-profit firms and more like social entrepreneurs, government agencies, or nonprofit organizations. While well-intentioned, this is not an effective plan for "how to fix capitalism," but is a misunderstanding of the purpose of for-profit firms in our society (and of the role that a strategic CSR perspective brings in optimizing that purpose). As suggested by other critics of these attempts to reinvent capitalism:[58]

> [In her book *SuperCorp*,] Rosabeth Moss Kanter warned of the pitfalls for companies that make "social commitments that do not have an economic logic that sustains the enterprise by attracting resources." More companies are learning to reap commercial benefits from strategies that have a wider social value. That's great. But the basic job of coaxing capitalism in the right direction is the same as it always has been: find ways to harness society's needs to companies' self-interest and hope the two stay together.[59]

While there is certainly an important role for social entrepreneurs in CSR, it is naive to suggest all companies should exist primarily to solve problems motivated by altruism. Business is the solution to market problems/opportunities that create value as a direct consequence. Firms optimize value, broadly defined, by combining scarce and valuable resources to meet market needs, while considering the interests of a broad range of stakeholders and seeking to provide sustainable shareholder returns over the medium to long term. Firms can often use their expertise to assist in meeting nonoperational goals, but this should not be their primary concern. Governments and nonprofits also play important social roles where gaps in the market occur.

The difference between a firm with strategic CSR integrated fully throughout the organization (encompassing strategic decision making and all aspects of day-to-day operations) and a firm that ignores the ideas discussed in this book is not in whether its CEO donates to charity but is reflected in the way the firm operates the core aspects of its business. There is a more socially responsible way to treat your suppliers, to pay your employees, to comply with laws, for example, and there is a less responsible way of doing all these things. Those firms that seek to carry out their day-to-day operations in a *responsible* and *sustainable* manner are creating more value than any amount of philanthropy can achieve.

STRATEGIC CSR IS BUSINESS

The consequence of internalizing the discussion above is the realization that *CSR is not an option*. It is not an option because CSR, or at least strategic CSR, is not about philanthropy and is more than brand insurance;[60] it is not about "caring capitalism" and is not about "sharing value." Strategic CSR is about *business*—creating value for stakeholders, broadly defined, by focusing on the firm's areas of expertise to solve market-based problems.

Because the scale and scope of strategic CSR are so thoroughly embedded within core operations and everyday decisions, it is not something the firm can choose to do; it is the way business is conducted. When a firm hires an employee, engages with a supplier, responds to a regulator, sells a product, or does any one of the many hundreds of things it does every day, it is engaging in strategic CSR. All of these business decisions have economic, social, moral, and ethical dimensions. As such, strategic CSR is not something that can be ignored or relegated in importance—it is what firms do. It is just that some firms do it better and more deliberately than others. Vigilant and informed stakeholders who incentivize organizations to pay attention to their values will ensure that this measure of performance (the extent to which the firm performs better at strategic CSR) will increasingly become a predictor of market success.

Once firms understand that they are embedded in a network of complex stakeholder relations and that they need to manage these relations effectively if they are to survive and thrive over the medium to long term, then strategic planning and daily operations represent the most effective means to manage the messy trade-offs and priority setting. Certainly, firms are either better or worse at managing these relationships, and they draw the lines of key stakeholders narrowly (at shareholders alone) or more broadly (in terms of a wider group of constituents). Either way, however, CSR is not an option, it is *the* way that business is conducted in the 21st century. Understanding and applying the principles

Figure 12.2 The Difference Between CSR and *Strategic CSR*

	CSR	*Strategic* CSR
The corporation	The problem	The solution
The profit motive	Value-destroying	Value-creating
The functional location	Philanthropy	Core operations
***Responsible* behavior**	Top-down, objective	Bottom-up, subjective
Motivation to act	Mandatory (coercion)	Voluntary (self-interest)

detailed in this book will help firms be more effective at implementing strategic CSR and building a sustainable organization.

This discussion establishing the essence of strategic CSR sets it apart from other discussions and definitions of CSR. The differences between strategic CSR and regular CSR are summarized in Figure 12.2.

Strategic CSR Debate

MOTION: Unless tied directly to operations, corporate philanthropy is a waste of money.

QUESTIONS FOR DISCUSSION AND REVIEW

1.   Define *strategic CSR* in your own words. What are the signs you would look for to indicate that a firm has implemented a strategic CSR perspective?

2.   What are the five key components of the definition of strategic CSR? Which of these do you think will generate the greatest resistance or difficulty for managers?

3.   Are shareholders *investors* or are they *speculators*? Does your answer to this question affect how you think about the stock market?

4.   Why is strategic CSR not a choice for companies?

5.   Are there any firms that you can think of that are currently practicing strategic CSR as defined in this chapter? If so, what is it that they are doing differently? If not, which firm is closest, and what does it need to do to fully implement strategic CSR?

Part IV Case Study

SUPPLY CHAIN

To what extent do business practices contribute to the community in which the firm is based and operating? Increasingly, business is global, with markets in many different countries and cultures. The resulting complexity represents the operating reality for multinationals such as Unilever, which "has a solid claim to the biggest supply network, with 160,000 companies providing it with goods and services."[1] One consequence is that companies are increasingly relocating operations offshore, which often means that jobs are lost at home and gained by the countries to which the companies relocate. Whether this represents an overall gain or loss for society in terms of CSR, however, is not clear.

The upside of this aspect of globalization is that firms are able to locate operations in the region of the world that make the most business sense. These decisions can be justified in terms of distribution logistics (proximity to market) or simply in terms of efficiencies (lower costs and fewer regulations). This mix of determining factors can generate unusual situations in which a Ford Mustang is assembled using parts largely manufactured outside the United States, while a Toyota Sienna is assembled in Indiana with 90% of its parts originating in the United States and Canada.[2] And, the longer a supply chain becomes, the more complex it becomes—to the point where "a shirt imported to the US from Hong Kong includes tasks of workers from as many as 10 countries":[3]

> It is why . . . terms like "made in America" or "made in China" are phasing out. The proper term . . . is "made in the world." More products are designed everywhere, made everywhere and sold everywhere.[4]

The downside of increasingly complex global supply chains is most dramatic for the component of production that is the least mobile—a firm's employees. As a result of more blue-collar factory jobs in China and Southeast Asia, and more white-collar call-center and computer-programming jobs in India, many workers in the West are experiencing globalization up close and personal. Specifically, "in the 10 years ending in 2009, . . . roughly one out of every three manufacturing jobs [in the United States]—about 6 million in total—disappeared."[5] And by the end of this decade, it is estimated "a total of 2.3 million jobs in finance, IT, procurement, and HR will have moved offshore . . . about one third of all jobs in these areas."[6] But the downside of global supply chains is not experienced solely by employees in the West. Reports of poor working conditions and human rights abuses in overseas sweatshops appear regularly in the media.[7] And the worst abuses seem to fall disproportionately on those least able to defend themselves: "The International Labour Organization (ILO) estimates that there are 122m economically active five to 14-year-olds in the Asia-Pacific region, with 44m of them in India, giving it the largest child workforce in the world."[8]

As such, while advocates of offshoring or outsourcing point to its value for the workers in developing countries who gain a job, ultimately it is not clear whether these employees benefit (from the jobs created)[9] or suffer (from the conditions in which they are forced to work).[10] This shift in the global economic system has occurred in a relatively short period of time, with dramatic effects. The United States, for example, now "makes 3% of the clothing its consumers purchase, down from about 50% in 1990."[11] Some of these jobs would have been lost anyway to automation, as a result of technological progress, but offshoring has also been a significant driver of change.

What effects have these rapid changes had on firms from a CSR perspective? To what extent does operating in a foreign environment, with different values and norms, render the corporation vulnerable to cultural conflict?[12] How does outsourcing affect firms that are seeking to implement CSR throughout the supply chain? To what extent can an *ethical* supply chain, "from ethical purchasing through to proper disposal of the end product,"[13] be an asset for the firm and a force for positive societal change?[14] Similarly, to what extent is an *unethical* supply chain punished by stakeholders who are based in a firm's home market and so judge news stories by local values and expectations, rather than those of the foreign culture?[15] Integrating CSR throughout the supply chain is particularly challenging for multinational corporations, which source their products in many countries but need to satisfy all stakeholders.

AN *ETHICAL* SUPPLY CHAIN

Although much of CSR is just good management that enables firms to operate more efficiently and reduce costs,[16] other aspects of CSR cost money, at least in the short term. To operate in a socially responsible manner means to operate *ethically* (as defined by stakeholders), which is not always the easiest or the cheapest option. Unfortunately, while consumers often say they want to purchase from firms that are ethical and socially responsible,[17] it is not always clear that they are willing to pay the associated price premium.

Naturally, this uncertainty influences the extent to which firms have an interest in operating an *ethical* supply chain. Is there any additional value if the firm secures products from suppliers at prices that are *fair*, rather than at prices dictated by the market? What is the extent of the market in developed economies for products with ingredients that have been purchased in this way from developing economies? More specifically, what exactly is *fair* trade?[18]

Fair Trade

The fair trade movement began "in the Netherlands in the late 1980s as a way to organize small farmers producing various commodities into cooperatives and to improve their incomes by pressuring buyers to pay guaranteed minimum prices":[19]

> Fairtrade is about better prices, decent working conditions, local sustainability, and fair terms of trade for farmers and workers in the developing world. By requiring companies to pay sustainable prices, . . . Fairtrade addresses the injustices of conventional trade, which traditionally discriminates against the poorest, weakest producers.[20]

Price guarantees help small farmers overcome the instability that is characteristic of the global market trade in *commodities*, a term that covers a wide range of raw materials. One product that is *protected* in this way is coffee, which was the first consumer product to be certified using the *Fairtrade* label.[21] Sales have grown, year over year, ever since:

> Sales of Fairtrade coffee alone increased by 8% in the year 2013–14. This is consistent with a longer term trend that has seen Fairtrade retail sales of coffee

Figure IV.1a   Retail Sales of Fair Trade Products in the UK (£ million, 2001–2011)

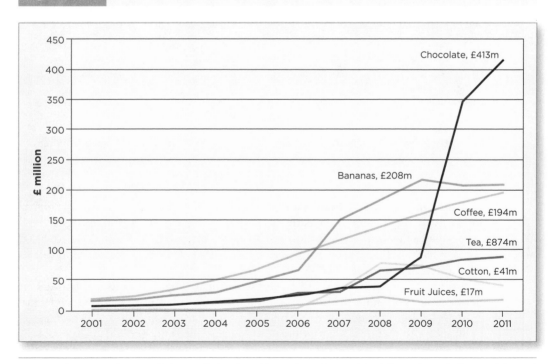

Source: The Fairtrade Foundation website, http://www.fairtrade.org.uk/en/what-is-fairtrade/facts-and-figures/ (accessed January 2013).

Figure IV.1b | Imports of Fairtrade Coffee to the United States (volume in millions of pounds, 1998–2013)*

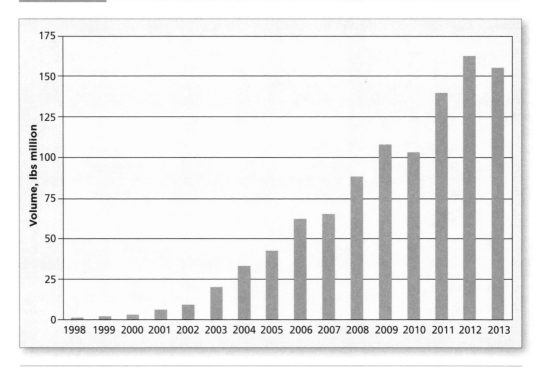

Source: Fairtrade USA *2013 Almanac*, September 2015, p. 5, http://fairtradeusa.org/sites/default/files/2013-Fair_Trade_USA-Almanac.pdf.

*Approximate numbers.

beans grow by 250% in the [past] decade. . . . Nine out of 10 tea brands carry some kind of ethical accreditation, while seven out of 13 brands of coffee bean are ethically accredited.[22]

Although fair trade began with coffee, it rapidly expanded to include many foods, with retail sales increasing dramatically. Figure IV.1a, for example, presents retail sales in the UK for a range of fair trade products, from 2001 to 2011, while Figure IV.1b presents the volume of certified Fairtrade coffee imported to the United States from 1998 to 2013.

Although primarily intended to improve the living standards of workers in developing economies, an important additional goal of fair trade is to educate "developed-world consumers to gain a greater awareness of those on the far end of the supply chain."[23] This education enables firms to explain the price gap between fair trade and "regular" products and is essential in order to convey the additional value to consumers firms hope such products bring. Market sales indicate there is clearly a percentage of consumers willing to pay "above market prices for commodities such as coffee, bananas and chocolate, if he knows that this premium will be spent on higher wages for those who did the planting, picking and packing."[24] As a result, the global market for Fairtrade-certified products is expanding rapidly:

> Global retail sales of Fairtrade products such as coffee, sugar and bananas soared by 15% [in 2013] to reach £4.4bn, mirrored by strong growth of 14% in the largest international market—the UK—to £1.8bn. . . . The number of Fairtrade producer countries has reached 74, while more than 30,000 Fairtrade products are on sale in 125 countries across the world, . . . [a supply chain that now consists of] more than 1.4 million farmers and workers, belonging to 1,210 producer organisations, including local co-operatives.[25]

Fairtrade, therefore, is becoming big business with a wide range of products that are being driven by market forces. In the UK alone, since the introduction of Fairtrade in 1994, the industry has expanded to "over 4,500 Fairtrade products including tea, coffee, cocoa, chocolate, bananas, sugar, cotton, gold, cut flowers, wine and cosmetics."[26] In spite of the speed at which the fair trade market has grown, however, it is important to remember that the overall market segment to which such goods appeal is limited. To what extent fair trade has mass market appeal, therefore, remains an open question. In general, "Purchasing levels of green and ethically-produced goods are linked to levels of affluence. For the majority of consumers, price overrides ethical considerations as the key factor in their decision-making."[27]

Beyond limited consumer support, there are four main criticisms of fair trade. The first is that, as a pricing mechanism, fair trade distorts the market by encouraging the overproduction of goods that are economically unsustainable. This argument ignores the choice being exercised by the willing consumers to whom such products are being sold:

> Buying Fairtrade chocolate no more distorts the chocolate market than buying a Louis Vuitton handbag distorts the handbag market. In both cases buyers are sending signals: that they are prepared to spend more on a bag with a prestigious label, or on chocolate that provides cocoa growers with a better life.[28]

As discussed in Part III, there are many distortions in our market economies, not least of which are government quotas and subsidies to favored industries, which greatly distort the market for cotton in West Africa, for example. As a result,

> millions of black farmers are undercut by the 35,000-or-so mainly white farmers in the former slave states of Texas and the American south. Some $4bn dollars a year in federal government handouts encourages high-cost American farmers to dump subsidized cotton on the world market, depressing its price.[29]

As such, the ultimate argument advanced by economists against *fair* trade is, in fact, an argument in favor of *free* trade. Many supporters of fair trade would prefer to see *free trade*, which they believe would have a wider, quicker, and longer-lasting impact in favor of farmers worldwide than any artificial designation of what may or may not constitute *fair trade*.

The second criticism of fair trade relates to the certification process—who gets to decide what is fair and what is not and the process by which this certification occurs and is publicized to consumers. A particular problem is the proliferation of product labels from competing organizations that consumers have to decipher:

> There are over 600 labels in Britain alone. This has blurred the definition of what qualifies as fair trade. Worse, there is little evidence that fair trade has lifted many producers out of poverty, not least because most of the organisations that are certified tend to come from richer, more diversified developing countries, such as Mexico and South Africa, rather than the poorer ones that are mostly dependent on exporting one crop. And why the focus on agricultural produce, when a booming fair-trade manufacturing sector potentially would help far more countries? Moreover, most of the benefit from fair-trade produce seems to stay where it is consumed. . . . For each dollar paid by an American consumer for a fair-trade product, only three cents more are transferred to the country it came from than for the unlabelled alternative. [30]

Related to this point, the third criticism of fair trade suggests that, because it appeals to consumers' better instincts and makes "shoppers feel good about themselves and the food they are buying,"[31] it is open to abuse by firms that want to appear more socially responsible than they actually are.[32] The accusation is that supermarkets and other retailers use fair trade to generate additional revenue, while passing on only a small amount of the profit to the farmers who produced the raw materials. There is some validity to this argument, with studies indicating that "between 10 per cent and 25 per cent" of the price premium of an average fair trade product reaches the farmer who produced the raw product,[33] and this amount may be so low that "only about 9 cents of the $3.10 cost of an average fairly traded 100g bar of chocolate goes to Africa or a poor country."[34] In response, while committing not to be "Fairtrade profiteers,"[35] firms note that one cause of the higher prices of fair trade products is the initial costs involved in establishing a fair trade supply chain. The idea of *equitrade* has also been floated as a way to offer a more equitable distribution of the economic benefits of ethical retailing:

> Whereas Fairtrade provides help [only to the] farmers, Equitrade tries to raise the quality of life for the majority of poor people by carrying out the processing operations, where most of the profits are made, in the poor countries themselves.[36]

Finally, the fourth criticism of fair trade is that, for consumers who want to support CSR companies and causes, and for whom issues such as "food miles"[37] are important, buying a local product is more ethical and sustainable than sourcing one from thousands of miles away. While there is some truth to this point, making the *best* choice becomes a matter of prioritization. Whether, for example, a consumer's support for local farmers in the West adds more or less social value than the same support for poor farmers in Africa is a personal judgment.

In spite of these criticisms, an increasing number of firms see fair trade as good business rather than an act of charity. Beyond improving its reputation among consumers, fair trade allows a firm to build long-term relationships with suppliers and guarantee a more stable supply of higher quality products that is essential to its business. In 2009, for example, the UK chocolate company Cadbury, in partnership with the Fairtrade Foundation, announced its decision to supply all its cocoa beans from Fairtrade sources.[38] Similarly in 2012, Hershey's committed to source 100% certified cocoa by 2020, ensuring the crop is grown to "the highest internationally recognized standards for labor, environment and better farming practices."[39] The advantages of such moves not only extend to the specific company but also ripple out to other producers and consumers throughout the industry.

Ultimately, firms like Cadbury and Hershey's have determined that their best interests lie in forming long-term ties to the suppliers who produce the quality inputs on which they rely for a core part of their business. This is a message that continues to resonate as fair trade becomes an established way to source ethically and consumers increasingly demand fair trade products.

AN *UNETHICAL* SUPPLY CHAIN

While there are advantages associated with an *ethical* supply chain, an *unethical* supply chain poses dangers to firms, such as intermittent supply or low-quality products. More likely, however, a business risks reputational threats generated by partner firms that are perceived to be operating unethically, as determined by stakeholders in the firm's home country.

In many cases, these perceptions are driven by cultural and economic differences. Such differences mean that people "in the West mostly despise sweatshops as exploiters of the poor, while the poor themselves tend to see sweatshops as opportunities."[40] The argument in favor of sweatshops is that, in comparison to the alternatives facing many people in the developing world, a factory job for a supplier of a Western multinational presents the opportunity for advancement:

> While it shocks [Westerners] to hear it, the central challenge in the poorest countries is not that sweatshops exploit too many people, but that they don't exploit enough. Talk to those families [who live and scavenge in a garbage] dump, and a job in a sweatshop is a cherished dream, an escalator out of poverty, the kind of gauzy if probably unrealistic ambition that parents everywhere often have for their children.[41]

An important aspect of this debate, therefore, is the idea of *cultural relativism*: To what extent should actions overseas be judged by the home country's moral, ethical, and religious standards, rather than in terms of the context in which they occur? Western NGOs, in particular, are accused of actively campaigning against the opening of multinational operations in developing countries based on Western notions of *acceptable* work conditions, but these organization are not in a position to provide alternative sources of investment if the company is forced to withdraw:

> Notoriously, Nike, by running its Southeast Asian athletic footwear plants and paying its workers in accordance with local customs and practices, opened itself to charges of operating sweatshops. In essence, it was accused of averaging down its level of corporate responsibility. Although the company protested that its conduct was virtuous by local standards, angry U.S. consumers made it clear that they expected Nike to conform to [the standards of] the U.S. civil foundation.[42]

The example of Nike is instructive because it demonstrates how far Western corporations have come in overcoming the perception that their supply chains are unethical. Nike has long been plagued by allegations that it profits from sweatshop conditions in its factories abroad—allegations that were made irrespective of whether the factories were Nike owned and operated or merely contractors producing shoes and clothing on the firm's behalf.[43] Of course, the people leveling these accusations often forget that, 150 years ago, the working conditions we see today in much of the developing world were commonplace in the industrializing world (i.e., the UK, Europe, and the United States). In fact, although the delay was partly to allow for child actors,

> the United States outlawed child labor only in 1938 when . . . passage of the Fair Labor Standards Act allowed the federal government for the first time to regulate minimum ages of employment and hours of work for children.[44]

Similarly, "nearly half of the workforce in British cotton mills in the early 19th century consisted of children."[45]

Of course, that is not to suggest that we should ignore abuses when they arise (and, in order to address concerns about human rights abuses and promote transparency throughout the supply chain, in 2015 the UK government passed the Modern Slavery Act).[46] But it is instructive to ask whether these conditions are a necessary stage that economies progress through in order to reach a more *developed* state. Critics say essentially that, because we know better today, those economies should be able to skip those stages (and it is incumbent upon us to help them do that). While developing countries will undoubtedly take less time to reach living standards comparable to those of the developed world today, I doubt the process is as simple as just willing ourselves there. The ineffectiveness of much overseas aid indicates the challenges faced in building modern institutions rapidly in underdeveloped societies. As such, if those countries take another 50 years to evolve beyond today's standard of living, it will be an amazing achievement in a relatively short period of time. But that is a difficult argument to convey to those who demand reform today, even given the powerful inertial forces in place:

In 2013 more than 1,100 people were crushed when a factory complex collapsed in Bangladesh. The victims included workers stitching clothes for [the British retailer] Primark. The company has paid $14m to victims' families. It is one of many firms to have signed an agreement to promote safety at textile factories. The sad truth, however, is that most consumers soon forgot about the tragedy. In 2014, . . . Primark's sales jumped by more than 20%. [Employee abuse in the supply chain] will take some stopping.[47]

Nevertheless, Nike today is one of the most progressive global corporations in terms of its ability to balance the various competing pressures up and down the supply chain.[48] As a direct result of the firm's past mistakes and attacks by NGOs (which continue to this day)[49] and in spite of an initial reluctance to reform,[50] Nike understands the strategic value in seeking to eradicate abuses from its operations and products worldwide. The ongoing program of repositioning its brand on issues of social responsibility appears to be paying off as Nike once again dominates the US running-shoe market with 55% market share.[51] The firm is now recognized as "a standard-setter for efforts to improve supply chain conditions and other companies have followed its lead on corporate responsibility."[52] For example, in 2005,

Nike surprised the business community by . . . releasing its global database of nearly 750 factories worldwide. No laws presently require a company to disclose the identity of its factories or suppliers within global supply chains. Yet, between the early 1990s and 2005, Nike went from denying responsibility for inhumane conditions in its factories to leading other companies in full disclosure—a strategic shift that illustrates how a firm can leverage increased transparency to mitigate risk and add value to the business.[53]

This shift in approach to supply chain management is occurring as there is an ongoing reassessment of the value of outsourcing everything that is not tied down. This is partly due to rising labor costs overseas, which "in China have recently been growing by around 20% a year,"[54] but also because executives are taking a broader perspective on this business decision. Firms are increasingly questioning whether it makes sense to achieve short-term cost savings at the expense of exposing themselves to the danger of longer-term threats to reputation and other problems associated with logistics, customer service, and market flexibility.[55] Executives are becoming increasingly aware that the firm's supply chain is central to its strategic planning.

The effort in the United States to rid the supply chains of multinational companies of conflict minerals demonstrates both how central this issue has become and how difficult building an *ethical* supply chain can be. In 2010, the Dodd-Frank Wall Street Reform and Consumer Protection Act was passed in the United States. Although the law was designed as a legislative response to the 2007–2008 financial crisis and focused on issues such as regulating the trade of complex financial derivatives, it also contained an important clause that related to conflict minerals (i.e., precious metals and other naturally occurring substances that, when traded, generate funds used to sustain conflicts in war-torn areas of the world).

In particular, the clause required "issuers with conflict minerals that are necessary to the functionality or production of a product manufactured by such person to disclose annually whether any of those minerals originated in the Democratic Republic of the Congo or an adjoining country."[56] The rule was due to be implemented on January 1, 2013, with first reports due to the Securities and Exchange Commission (SEC) by May 31, 2014:

> Conflict minerals include coltan, cassiterite, gold and wolframite, and while you may not be familiar with some of these, they are widely used in electronics. Your cellphone may very well contain them.[57]

In essence, the rule was designed to force firms to account for all aspects of their supply chain to identify which products contain conflict minerals (i.e., certain raw materials that were mined in the Congo or nearby countries). By requiring firms to report this information to the SEC, the regulatory agency was also beginning a process whereby consumers also become aware of the origins of key components in products that they purchase on a regular basis.

In response, many companies have criticized the legislation as being costly to implement and impossible to enforce. Even those firms that do not have these minerals in their products have to confirm that is the case. Multinational companies have complex supply chains that can involve tens of thousands of independent firms across their complete range of products. When you realize, for example, that a company like Caterpillar has "identified 38,700 suppliers who might potentially provide components containing conflict minerals,"[58] the level of complexity and expense involved becomes clear. As a result, the majority of firms that reported essentially said they "couldn't be certain if these metals and minerals were used by their suppliers."[59] One company that has made more progress than most on this issue, however, is Apple, "surveying more than 400 suppliers" and "identifying 205 smelters and refiners of conflict minerals."[60]

Apple

Although some firms are reconsidering the value to their business of outsourcing, for others, outsourcing makes clear business sense. Apple is one of these companies. One reason for this is that, today, the best electronics in the world are made most efficiently in Asia. One company in particular does it bigger and better than anyone else:

> Foxconn (also known by its parent company's name, Hon Hai) is the world's largest contract manufacturer. . . . Across China, it employs 1.4m on 28 campuses. . . . In the past decade it has gone from being one of many invisible firms in the electronics supply chain to the world champion of flexible manufacturing.[61]

Apple, along with many other major consumer electronics firms, is highly reliant on Foxconn. According to some reports, "about half of all consumer electronics sold in the world today are produced at [Foxconn's] mammoth factory campus in Shenzhen, China."[62] As such, the firm makes a large percentage of Apple's iPhones and iPads. Not only is Foxconn able to make those products well, but it is also able to make them extremely efficiently:

> Apple had redesigned the iPhone's screen at the last minute, forcing an assembly-line overhaul. New screens began arriving at the [Chinese] plant near midnight. A foreman immediately roused 8,000 workers inside the company's dormitories, according to the executive. Each employee was given a biscuit and a cup of tea, guided to a workstation and within half an hour started a 12-hour shift fitting glass screens into beveled frames. Within 96 hours, the plant was producing over 10,000 iPhones a day.[63]

In spite of the remarkable economic value that Foxconn delivers, like Nike before it, Apple has received some negative press for its extended supply chain in Asia. In particular, as its biggest supplier, conditions at Foxconn's factories have drawn the greatest media attention[64] that has covered a range of issues related to employees striking,[65] rioting,[66] committing suicide,[67] being underage and underpaid,[68] and being poisoned.[69]

As a result of the press coverage, Apple under Tim Cook has moved to alter stakeholder perceptions of its commitment to an ethical supply chain by taking a number of steps to improve conditions at Foxconn's factories. First, Apple released a report that comprehensively assessed working conditions in firms "that represent 97% of its materials, manufacturing and procurement spending"—the most detailed report on its supply chain that Apple has released. Second, Foxconn announced it will increase wages, reduce overtime, and generally improve working conditions for all its employees.[70] Third, Apple committed to have all its supplier factories audited by the third-party organization Fair Labor Association (FLA), along with a promise to stop working with those suppliers that "do not measure up to its labor and human rights standards."[71] Finally, following the FLA's audit, Apple and Foxconn agreed to implement the changes recommended, in particular in relation to pay and overtime—recommendations that "included reducing work hours to a maximum of 40 hours a week and limiting overtime to a maximum of 36 hours a month—the legal maximum in China."[72]

In spite of all the negative stories that have emerged in the Western press about Foxconn's oppressive factory conditions and its relationship with Apple, two points are worth keeping in mind. The first point concerns the effect these stories have had on public perceptions of Apple—arguably, "they have not impacted Apple's reputation one jot,"[73] which suggests they are not an issue for most of the firm's many stakeholders. The second point is the position of Foxconn's employees, many of whom moved from the countryside in China to its big cities in pursuit of economic progress. In response to Foxconn's commitment to bring its overtime rules in line with Chinese laws, "allowing workers to work no more than nine hours of overtime a week," and improve health and safety conditions (which some fear will reduce margins and threaten jobs), employees are beginning to push back. Interviews with workers at Foxconn's Shenzhen campus revealed

> that they work more than the legal limit of nine overtime hours a week. A majority said they work 10 to 15 overtime hours and would prefer more, having left their distant homes to make money in this southern Chinese boomtown.[74]

In acting to protect its reputation, Apple is merely the latest firm to learn from the trial and error of earlier pioneers, such as Nike. For these firms, their reputations and the values around which their brands are built are core strategic assets. And in some respects, the supply chain is more of a strategic issue for Apple, given that supplier contracts are usually longer in the consumer electronics industry than "the three-month terms common in the apparel business." This necessarily "gives Apple a much bigger stake in the long-term success of Foxconn as a supplier, and makes it less attractive to cut and run to a cheaper option."[75]

In general, factory audits conducted by independent third parties serve to guard against these reputation threats. In spite of the challenges ("At HP, for example, only seven of the 276 factories in its supply chain fully complied with its code of conduct at the last audit"),[76] audits are seen as a solution whereby Western firms can continue to operate in low-cost environments, local employees can continue to benefit from their presence, and NGOs can receive some assurance that the local employees are not being abused.[77] Best practice, pushed by firms such as Nike and GAP (and now Apple), dictates that firms should work with contractors to improve conditions when violations occur and should sever ties only in persistent cases.[78]

A *STRATEGIC* SUPPLY CHAIN

In spite of the admirable efforts of these firms and those of many others, reports of worker abuse throughout the supply chain continue—so much so that it raises a difficult question for CSR advocates: *How far does a firm's responsibility extend across the supply chain?*[79]

If we are to hold firms to account for their supply chains, we need to understand the effects (and associated costs) of what we are asking. As can be seen in Figure IV.2, the distance between the firm and its many suppliers can quickly grow. In other words, while we might be able to agree that a firm is responsible for its immediate suppliers, how far does responsibility extend beyond this first level? A company like Walmart, for example, has "more than 100,000 suppliers around the world."[80] Conservatively, if each of those firms has 10 suppliers and Walmart is expected to be responsible for both its immediate and intermediate suppliers, then the firm will need to keep track of the operations of 1,000,000 companies. It is arguable that this can only be done with reasonably regular audits. If best practice dictates that suppliers should be inspected at least once

Figure IV.2 Ripples of Responsibility Across the Supply Chain

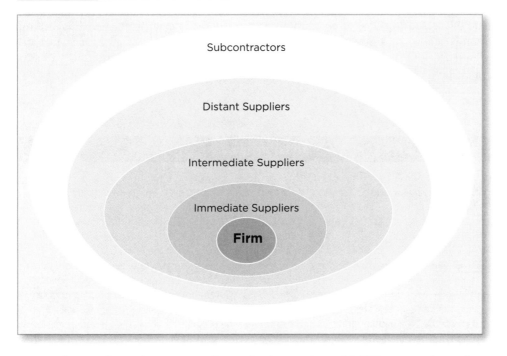

a year, then Walmart has to coordinate the inspection of 2,750 companies a day, 7 days a week, 365 days a year. And, if we believe Walmart's responsibility should extend beyond its intermediate suppliers to include its distant suppliers and their occasional subcontractors, this number grows exponentially.

A related issue arose for GAP when a piece of investigative journalism by the UK newspaper *The Observer* uncovered evidence of underage children making the firm's clothes.[81] While the speed and extent of GAP's response appeared genuine, the more interesting question was the extent to which it could (or should) have been expected to avoid this problem. It appears that GAP's vendor had subcontracted embroidery work to a rural community center that had, in turn, subcontracted the work to a smaller workshop in Delhi. "While auditing in factories is relatively straightforward, checking conditions in the informal work-shops where hand embroidery is done is harder because large contracts are often divided up among dozens of small workshops."[82]

This is not an argument in favor of absolving firms from all responsibility for their supply chain; it is only a recognition that, if we are going to expect firms to take such responsibility, we need to be aware of the costs that are generated as a result. It is one thing for a firm to be held responsible for the business practices of an immediate supplier. It seems to be another thing altogether to expect a firm like GAP to know about a subcontractor (a rural community cen-ter) that had again contracted out this order to a Delhi factory—three steps removed from the initial order. And what about the factories that process the cotton that is used by GAP's suppliers? What about the farmers who grow the cotton and the numerous hands through which the cotton passes before it even reaches a factory that subcontracts to GAP? The extent to which a firm is responsible for the actions of its suppliers throughout its supply chain (including enforcement) is an issue on which CSR advocates have yet to agree. As Paul Polman, CEO of Unilever, puts it, "We have 200,000 suppliers and audit 20,000 suppliers, probably more than any other company, but there's a capacity to that, otherwise you go bankrupt."[83]

Distributors

While the issue of firms' responsibilities for their suppliers is well-established in the CSR community, the opposite responsibility (of supplier firms for their distributors) is not discussed. But if we are going to say a firm is responsible for actions taken by firms that precede it in the supply chain, why are we not willing to say the same about actions taken by firms that come after it? This does not diminish the good work done in terms of lifecycle pricing and the post-consumption obligations of the business to consumer relationship. In fact, it is all part of the same discussion—it is all a matter of where to put the emphasis.

Take the mining industry: Why are extraction firms not held to account for the subsequent uses of the raw materials they take out of the ground? While there has been some discussion of conflict diamonds/minerals, responsibility for the supply chain appears to rest with the firm that sells the finished product, rather than the firm that sold the component parts. In terms of e-waste, however: Why are we willing to hold a firm like Dell responsible for recycling those parts of the computer that are toxic (precious metals and minerals), but not the firm that was responsible for extracting those metals and minerals and selling them to Dell (and others)?

This is an issue that has yet to emerge for extraction companies, but it is not difficult to imagine a day when we will begin holding extraction firms responsible for the actions of the firms that are their consumers. Given this, the progressive extraction company that is sensitive to the relationships it has with its stakeholders should act now to understand this issue and prevent any future risk to its business.

Ultimately, firms have to do a better job of communicating these complexities because outsourcing is not going away. Establishing an efficient and effective supply chain is essential to firms seeking to reach markets worldwide. As their supply chains become longer, however, firms run into increasingly complex stakeholder conflicts. As such, there is a clear strategic imperative for multinational firms to respond to those concerns about the sustainability of their supply chains in ways that are transparent and acceptable, both at home and overseas.

A strategic CSR lens provides a means to navigate these complexities as firms seek to operate in the region that offers the best mix of geographic location, employee skills, and costs. The ideal situation occurs when ethical behavior in the supply chain coincides with strategic value to the firm. No firm illustrates this more effectively than Starbucks, whose CEO, Howard Schultz, is on record as saying that companies should have a broad view of the pursuit of profit: "There needs to be a balance between commerce and social responsibility. . . .

The companies that are authentic about it will wind up as the companies that make more money."[84]

Starbucks

As one of the top five coffee buyers in the world,[85] Starbucks has significant influence over its industry, but its actions have also been a source of negative publicity. Among other things, Starbucks has been accused of profiting at the expense of coffee growers, whose livelihoods rise and fall in line with the widely fluctuating global market price for coffee; indeed, the market price of coffee can fall below the cost of production.[86] As a result, while "25 million smallholder farmers produce 80% of the world's coffee. . . . many of them fail to earn a reliable living from coffee."[87] This is surprising because coffee is in high demand. It was not only the first consumer product to be widely available as a Fairtrade-certified product, but it is also one of the most popular. Today, fair trade coffee makes up "20 per cent of the UK retail sales of ground coffee"[88] and "70% of the [products sold in the] US fair trade market."[89] As a result of the combination of growing awareness of fair trade in general and the growing popularity of fair trade coffee in particular, Starbucks has attracted a lot of attention from campaigners seeking to increase the amount of fair trade coffee the firm buys.

In response, Starbucks has been at the vanguard of improving the sustainable nature of the coffee supply chain.[90] Today, the company works closely with suppliers to help them convert to best practices and offers long-term purchasing contracts as an incentive to do so. This approach helps Starbucks meet the needs of the fair trade industry, as well as increase the quality of the product it buys and then resells in its stores. It does this by developing its own quality standards because the Fairtrade certification does not include all of the metrics that are important to Starbucks. In particular, in 2004, Starbucks launched the Coffee Agronomy Company,[91] which is based in Costa Rica and positioned as "the flagship vehicle for Starbucks' sustainable supply chain commitment." Soon after, the company launched its Coffee and Farmer Equity (C.A.F.E.) Practices guidelines, which "spell out Starbucks' expectations for its suppliers on economic, social and environmental issues."[92]

Starbucks' C.A.F.E. Practices

Starbucks C.A.F.E. Practices include guidelines for farmers in four areas:[93]

Product Quality: All coffee must meet our standards for high quality.

Economic Accountability and Transparency: Economic transparency is required. Suppliers must submit evidence of payments made throughout the coffee supply chain to demonstrate how much of the price that we pay for green coffee gets to the farmer.

(Continued)

(Continued)

Social Responsibility: Measures evaluated by third-party verifiers help protect the rights of workers and ensure safe, fair and humane working and living conditions. Compliance with minimum-wage requirements and prohibition of child and forced labor is mandatory.

Environmental Leadership: Measures evaluated by third-party verifiers help manage waste, protect water quality, conserve water and energy, preserve biodiversity and reduce agrochemical use.

Starbucks developed C.A.F.E. in conjunction with the environmental charity Conservation International (http://www.conservation.org/).[94] The goal for suppliers in conforming to the guidelines is to be certified as a Starbucks *preferred supplier* and thus benefit from specific price guarantees by Starbucks over and above current market prices.[95] Rather than being primarily motivated out of sympathy for the coffee farmer, however, this decision recognizes the strategic value to Starbucks that these growers represent:[96]

> To support [its] high growth rate, it was clear that an integral part of the company's future success would come from meeting increased demand through a secure supply of high-quality coffee beans. Coffee beans constituted the bread and butter of Starbucks' business—the company had to ensure a sustainable supply of this key commodity.[97]

As a result of the rapid increase in demand for coffee worldwide in recent years, Starbucks has faced the combination of a rapidly evolving competitive market and wildly fluctuating commodity prices.[98] Starbucks has always faced competition on *price* (people could always buy coffee cheaper elsewhere), but now the firm is also facing real competition on *quality* as fast-food firms such as McDonald's and Dunkin' Donuts seek to eat into Starbucks' core target market at home, as well as abroad.[99] In the United States, for example, Dunkin' Donuts has been serving fair trade–only coffee in its stores since 2003, and McDonald's is also looking to expand the amount of fair trade coffee that it serves.[100] Similarly, in the UK, Marks & Spencer has been sourcing all of the coffee it serves in its coffee shops from fair trade sources since 2006, while McDonald's began sourcing all its coffee served in the UK from fair trade and sustainable sources in 2007.

This growing competition strikes at the heart of Starbucks' business model. Ultimately, what is Starbucks' product? Is it *quality coffee*; or is it the *coffeehouse experience* that Howard Schultz tried to bring back to the United States from a 1983 trip to Milan, Italy; or is it the location—a *third place* between home and work? When there is deterioration in the economy, can Starbucks justify the price premium it charges based on customer experience alone (if competitors are catching up in terms of quality yet offering products at a cheaper price)? Either way, the company is increasingly being pushed to innovate, and the supply chain is an area where Starbucks can continue to push industry best practice.[101] Today for example, Starbucks' website tracks the firm's progress regarding its ethical sourcing practices, which allowed it to claim in 2015 that "99% of its coffee is now ethically sourced."[102]

So, what is the strategic CSR argument for the attention Starbucks pays to its supply chain? Does the firm pay its suppliers of high-quality, shade-grown Arabica beans an above-market price because it feels morally or ethically responsible for farmers who do not earn sufficient wages in a country with an inadequate welfare safety net, or does it pay those prices because it needs to secure a guaranteed supply of its most essential raw material? Remember that, for Starbucks, cheap coffee prices represent a threat to its business—not because the firm enjoys paying higher prices for its raw materials but because, if coffee prices dip below their cost of production, the small farmers who produce the high-quality beans Starbucks needs are more likely to go out of business. It is essential for Starbucks' business model that this does not happen.

Whether you think of Starbucks as a café or as a "third place" between home and work, the firm risks its core business if it loses access to high-quality coffee beans. As such, paying close attention to its supply chain is a straightforward business decision for Starbucks. It enables the firm to deflect criticism, helps win those customers who are willing to pay for the value added by the Fairtrade certification label, and, most importantly, helps secure supplies of the high-quality coffee beans that are central to Starbucks' business. In short, a *fair* supply chain is a source of competitive advantage for Starbucks that helps it expand further into those markets where it is not yet established and retain market share where it is already dominant. As such, it is in Starbucks' best strategic interest to ensure that the producers of its most highly prized raw material are incentivized to remain in business and continue to supply the firm over the long term.

Strategic CSR Debate

Motion: Working in a sweatshop is preferable to being unemployed in a country with no welfare safety net.

QUESTIONS FOR DISCUSSION AND REVIEW

1. Do you believe in the idea of *fair trade*? Why, or why not? What does *fair* mean? Are you happy to pay a premium for fair trade products?

2. Do you know what the Fairtrade symbol looks like? Can you name a Fairtrade product that you have bought recently? Why did you buy that product?

3. Is Apple a *good* company? Why or why not?

4. Did you know about Starbucks' C.A.F.E. Practices and the Fairtrade products the company sells? Does knowing about these products make you more likely to shop there? Do you think this effort is something the company should publicize? Would there be any downside to doing so?

5. Should a firm's operations abroad be judged by the standards (legal, economic, cultural, and moral) of the country in which it is operating or by the standards of its domestic market? Is a firm responsible for its supply chain? If so, how far does that responsibility extend—to immediate suppliers, the suppliers' suppliers, or beyond?

NEXT STEPS

Part IV of this textbook details the relationship between strategy and CSR. Constructing strategy using a *CSR filter* and integrating it throughout operations offer firms the most effective means of navigating an increasingly complex, global business environment. In order for firms to receive the benefit of a CSR perspective, however, there also needs to be a focus on implementation. Without comprehensive and effective implementation, combined with support from the highest levels of the organization, the best laid plans will fall short of their potential.

As such, the remaining chapters (Part V) detail how firms integrate CSR into day-to-day operations and begin to build a business model of *sustainable value creation*. In other words, these chapters address the question *How does strategic CSR function in practice?* Chapter 13 focuses on the essential issue of sustainability and waste reduction; Chapter 14 discusses the issues that influence the implementation of CSR within a strategic decision-making framework over the short, medium, and long term; while the final chapter of the book, Chapter 15, presents a model of the values-based business.

Encouraging more values-based businesses is the purpose of this book. By integrating the strategic CSR concepts that have been detailed here into its strategic planning, a firm is positioned to build a sustainable competitive advantage based on creating value for its broad range of stakeholders. It is these firms that are best placed to compete and succeed in the 21st-century global business marketplace.

PART V

A SUSTAINABLE PERSPECTIVE

P art V concludes *Strategic Corporate Social Responsibility* (*Strategic CSR*) by demonstrating how firms can embed a CSR perspective throughout the organization by building values-based businesses that serve their stakeholders, broadly defined.

Chapter 13 leads off this section by investigating the origins of *sustainability* and its relevance to firms today, highlighting the original United Nations report that defined this term within the context of resource utilization. It also investigates the inherent dangers of our current, unsustainable economic model through the issue of waste. While we currently face many ecological challenges, the amount of waste that our economies generate illustrates the extent of the problem in a way to which we can all relate. Chapter 14 extends the concept of *sustainable development* beyond the natural environment to encompass the challenges associated with building a values-based culture. This chapter focuses, in particular, on implementing a CSR perspective throughout the organization. Finally, Chapter 15 summarizes the ideas discussed in this book in terms of the ultimate outcome of strategic CSR—*sustainable value creation*. Encouraging a business model that focuses on the firm's complete set of stakeholders is the most effective way for a firm to be competitive in today's global business environment, while working within the resource constraints our planet faces.

Part V finishes with a case study about firms that are owned by their employees, demonstrating the productive value of strategic CSR in action.

Chapter 13

SUSTAINABILITY

The issue of *sustainability* raises a number of questions that business and society are in the process of addressing: What is the extent of firms' responsibility for the environment? Beyond legal requirements, should firms internalize the environmental costs of operations (e.g., clean up the pollution their operations produce)? Should governments help with these costs? Should firms pay to deplete Earth's resources during production (i.e., remove more than they replenish)? Should firms support government-led efforts to place a minimum price (a tax)[1] or a market price (a cap-and-trade scheme) on carbon?[2] Should the price of a product, such as a car, contain the costs to the environment incurred during consumption (i.e., as it is being driven)? *Should* consumers be expected to pay a premium to ensure products are produced in a way that protects the environment? *Will* they pay this premium or continue to reward firms that find ways to avoid the full costs of production? In other words, *What does sustainability mean in practice?*

SUSTAINABLE DEVELOPMENT

The term *sustainability* was popularized by the 1987 Brundtland Report, published by the United Nations (UN). Though officially named "Our Common Future,"[3] the report became known as the Bruntland Report after its main author, Gro Harlem Brundtland—Norwegian prime minister and chair of the UN's World Commission on Environment and Development.

One of the report's key contributions was to define the term *sustainable development* and identify the importance of sustainability for firms.[4] It also inspired the UN's 1992 Framework Convention on Climate Change, signed by "more than 190 countries"[5] in Rio de Janeiro. This was notably followed by the Kyoto Protocol in 1997 and, in 2015, by COP21 in Paris—the 21st UN Conference on Climate Change since Rio. The Brundtland Report was also prescient in framing the business case to protect the environment. It therefore constituted a pivotal point in the debate that has emerged around CSR and sustainability, in particular regarding the role that society demands of for-profit organizations:

Many "of the development paths of the industrialized nations are clearly unsustainable." However, it held fast to its embrace of development toward industrialized nation living standards as part of the solution, not part of the problem. "If large parts of countries of the global South are to avert economic, social, and environmental catastrophes, it is essential that global economic growth be revitalized," the report stated.[6]

In essence, the Brundtland Report popularized the term *sustainability*,[7] and its definition has become the essential definition. While some people use the term to capture broader issues related to CSR, the discussion about sustainability originated in response to issues of resource utilization and the unsustainable rate of extraction. As such, today, most people understand the term *sustainability* to mean issues related to the natural environment.

One of the reasons this definition has become so widely accepted is that it is extremely broad. This has the advantage of making it applicable to all organizations, which can interpret it to suit their circumstances, in turn leading to varying levels of responses. A reluctance to act has not just characterized firms' responses to climate change, however, but has been most evident among national governments. Even though the COP21 agreement (http://www.cop21paris.org/), which took almost 4 years to negotiate, at least recognizes the extent of the problem, it is far from clear that it contains action that is sufficient to remedy the problem that we face.

> **Sustainability**
>
> "Sustainable development is development that meets the needs of the present without compromising the ability of future generations to meet their own needs."[8]

COP21

On the plus side, unlike the UN climate agreements in Rio and Kyoto, COP21 covers all countries (both rich and poor). While Kyoto "was ratified by 35 countries covering just 12% of global emissions, 167 governments, responsible for some 94% of emissions, . . . submitted national targets to cut emissions in the run-up to Paris."[9] In addition, COP21 incorporated the more ambitious target of keeping global temperature increases below 1.5°C (2.7°F), reducing emissions to "essentially zero by the latter half of this century."[10] In order to achieve this, individual countries made specific commitments. The United States, for example, has pledged to reduce greenhouse gas emissions "26%–28% below 2005 levels by 2025"; the EU has committed to reduce emissions "40% below 1990 levels by 2030"; Mexico "has put in place the strongest climate legislation of any developing country, . . . 40% below the current trend line by 2030"; and China "has promised by 2030 to reduce its carbon-dioxide emissions, per unit of GDP, to at least 60% below 2005."[11]

While presenting an opportunity (in that the whole planet is now engaged), the Paris agreement also raises a number of challenges: First, it has to be ratified by "at least 55 countries representing at least 55 percent of global emissions" before it can take effect,[12] and, second, it has to be implemented.[13] Unfortunately, the commitments made are not legally binding and are a patchwork of promises, rather than "one single, internationally agreed policy such as a global carbon price,"[14] making enforcement much more difficult. The greatest concern about COP21, however, is that it is too little, too late:

> If all the pledges are implemented, it would mean global emissions rise to the equivalent of 56.7bn tonnes of CO_2 by 2030. . . . [This is] nearly 4bn tonnes less than it would have been without the pledges. But the trouble is, it is still well over 10bn tonnes more than what the latest scientific report from the UN's [IPCC] suggests is needed to have a reasonable chance of avoiding 2C of global warming from pre-industrial times.[15]

In order to meet the UN's estimate of the planet's carbon budget that limits the global temperature increase to 2°C (3.6°F)—the amount of carbon we can emit before climate change spirals out of control[16]—it is calculated that carbon emissions "have to peak well before 2030 and should be eliminated as soon as possible after 2050."[17] Instead, if the commitments agreed to in Paris are implemented, "humanity will outspend its carbon budget by 2040 at the latest."[18] Given this, an important component of the Paris agreement is 5-year reviews, when countries are expected to assess their progress and the changing global climate and revise their targets accordingly. The success of COP21 relies on this occurring.

Given that nothing will change until substantive action is taken, what does *sustainability* mean in practice for firms today—why should they care? There are four main reasons why businesses should care: climate change, resilience, natural capital, and stakeholders.

Climate Change

The first reason why sustainability is such an important issue for firms today is that the climate is changing, fast. While for-profit firms are a large driver of these changes, they are also uniquely positioned to do something about it, both in terms of the scale on which change is needed and the speed with which we need to bring it about. If businesses do not change the way they interact with the natural environment, however, we will soon push Earth past its known limits. As Thomas Friedman puts it, "The Earth Is Full": "We are currently growing at a rate that is using up the Earth's resources far faster than they can be sustainably replenished. . . . Right now, global growth is using about 1.5 Earths."[19] This carrying capacity is directly related to the strain we are placing on the available resources—all 7 billion of us. This strain will likely worsen before it improves because "the United Nations estimates that by the end of the century we could number as many as 15.8 billion."[20] More than the size of our population, however, it is our collective rate of consumption that is the problem:

If everyone on Earth lived the lifestyle of a traditional Indian villager, it is arguable that even 12 billion would be a sustainable world population. If everyone lives like an upper-middle-class North American (a status to which much of the world seems to aspire), then even two billion is unsustainable.[21]

If we do not act and act quickly, we will face a change in the planet's climate patterns that may well be irreversible. In that instance, we would rather not find out whether the worst predictions by scientists are likely to come true:

Global warming isn't a prediction. It is happening. . . . If [we continue to exploit all known oil reserves], it will be game over for the climate. . . . Concentrations of carbon dioxide in the atmosphere eventually would reach levels higher than in the Pliocene era, more than 2.5 million years ago, when sea level was at least 50 feet higher than it is now. That level of heat-trapping gases would assure

Figure 13.1a Total Carbon Emissions by Country (percent, 2015)

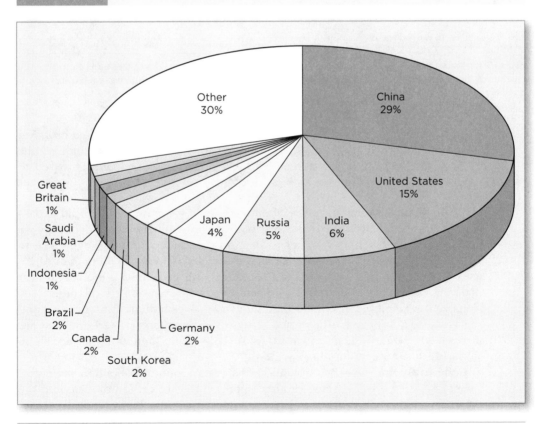

Source: "Hotter than August," *The Economist*, August 8, 2015, p. 22.

Figure 13.1b Per Capita CO$_2$ Emissions Among the G20 Countries (metric tons, 2011)

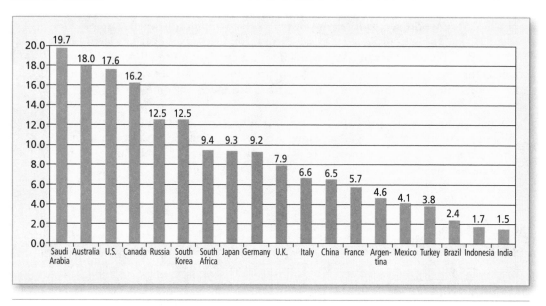

Source: US Energy Information Administration, cited in Rob Taylor & Rhiannon Hoyle, "Australia Becomes First Developed Nation to Repeal Carbon Tax," *The Wall Street Journal*, July 17, 2014, http://www.wsj.com/articles/australia-repeals-carbon-tax-1405560964/.

that the disintegration of the ice sheets would accelerate out of control. Sea levels would rise and destroy coastal cities. Global temperatures would become intolerable. Twenty to 50 percent of the planet's species would be driven to extinction. Civilization would be at risk.[22]

Given the unsustainable nature of our economic systems and the rapid expansion of living standards, it is easy to appreciate how the individual decisions we make every day (such as whether to turn on the air-conditioning) aggregate to a planetary-wide problem: "America uses more electricity for cooling than Africa uses for everything,"[23] with 40% of that energy still generated using coal power plants.[24] Figures 13.1a and 13.1b present the cumulative effects of these decisions across countries. It is clear that, while countries like the United States and regions like Europe were previously the primary emitters of carbon, they are increasingly being joined by countries such as China and India as access to "luxuries" like air-conditioning spreads.

Collectively, the world's population "harvests around 100 billion megawatt hours of energy each year and dumps 36 billion tons of carbon dioxide into the planetary system."[25] As a result, "every single year so far this decade has been hotter than every single year before 1998."[26] Amazingly, "No one under 30 has ever lived through a month of global temperatures below the 20th-century average,"[27] a reflection of the damage we are doing to our planet.

If emissions continue unchecked, [scientists] say the global warming could ultimately exceed 8 degrees Fahrenheit, which would transform the planet and undermine its capacity to support a large human population. . . . The risks are much greater over the long run . . . but the emissions that create those risks are happening now.[28]

But the extent of the problem, in terms of unsustainable resource utilization, goes well beyond climate change to include

ocean acidification; the thinning of the ozone layer; intervention in the nitrogen and phosphate cycles (crucial to plant growth); the conversion of wilderness to farms and cities; extinctions; the buildup of chemical pollutants; and the level of particulate pollutants in the atmosphere.[29]

To be clear, the science on climate change is not disputed. What is disputed are the consequences of climate change, the potential to pass a point of no return, and how best to avoid the worst-case scenarios that climate models predict. In deciding how best to respond, the challenge lies in valuing future benefit against present-day cost. One effort to tackle the associated tradeoffs inherent in this choice is the Stern report on climate change,[30] which argued that society must "value the welfare of all present and future citizens equally and give no special preference to current voters."[31] The difficulty, however, is how to account for the possibility of unknowns such as the technical innovation and greater wealth of future generations and, as a result, avoid exaggerating the immediate cost implications of climate change, which would cause unnecessary present-day sacrifices. In essence, "the problem of weighting the present and the future equally is that there is a lot of future. The number of future generations is potentially so large that small but permanent benefit to them would justify great sacrifice now."[32] Getting the balance between current and future obligations *correct* is crucial if we are to mount an effective response to this hugely important issue.

Resilience

While it appears that our capacity for altruism toward future generations is limited, perhaps we can act to save ourselves. The speed at which climate change is occurring suggests that we will see dramatic changes to the environment in our lifetime. If so, sustainability increasingly represents a present-day imperative. This raises the second reason why firms should be concerned about sustainability: Climate change dramatically influences operations today, so some form of adaptation will be essential.

On the country level, China, which "accounts for two-thirds of the world's increase in the carbon dioxide emitted since 2000," recognizes the need to adapt, including "a blueprint for the Communist Party's intentions" in its latest 5-year plan.[33] In terms of firms, you do not have to be an oil company to understand that a changing climate shifts the parameters within which you currently operate.

Resilience

"Resilience: how to help vulnerable people, organizations and systems persist, perhaps even thrive, amid unforeseeable disruptions. Where sustainability aims to put the world back into balance, resilience looks for ways to manage in an imbalanced world."[35]

Reports suggest there is a growing financial risk for any corporation not conducting business in what contemporary society considers an appropriate manner:

> Munich Re, a large German insurance company, estimates that the effects of climate change could cost companies $300 billion annually by 2050 in weather damage, pollution, industrial and agricultural losses. . . . Companies may also face unexpected expenses resulting from future taxes, regulations, fines, and caps on products that produce greenhouse gases.[34]

Even though it amounts to admitting defeat, the scale of the environmental challenge we face suggests that adaptation (*resilience*)[36] will be an essential part of our future existence:

> Energy demand, which is strongly correlated with rising incomes and living standards, is expected to grow by some 50 percent by midcentury, driven by economic progress in developing countries and by population growth. . . . Improvements in energy efficiency can help, but even if today's annual per capita emissions of three tons in the developing world grew by midcentury to only five tons (about 70 percent of Europe's per capita emissions today), annual global emissions would *increase* by about 60 percent.[37]

Cities recognize this and are acting without waiting for direction from national governments. Plans are afoot to place chief resilience officers in 100 cities throughout the United States,[38] and these officials have already been appointed in cities such as Boulder, Colorado.[39] One way to frame climate change from a business perspective, therefore, is in terms of managing risk. As awareness about the extent of climate change and the need to act spreads, business success will increasingly require accounting for a rapidly changing ecological context and adapting operations accordingly.

Natural Capital

While accounting for sustainability and adapting operations accordingly is a means of managing risk, there are also many positive reasons for firms to act. Primary among these is the value of acting voluntarily before you are forced to change (recall "A Rational Argument for CSR" in Chapter 1). Doing so positions the firm to reap any benefits associated with being an early mover on an issue that will increasingly be central to the survival of our species. Rather than wait for the government to impose restrictions on how they operate, many firms are choosing to act now, devising ways to account for the *natural capital* that they consume during production:

Natural capital is simple. The value of well-functioning natural systems is clearly manifest to all people and companies—in the form of clean air, reliable availability of freshwater and productive topsoil in which to grow food, among other benefits. Yet, the way that finance works—from GDP calculations through corporate to accounting—it is as if reliable flows from well-functioning natural systems have no value.[40]

Calculating the value of natural capital (the resources that exist naturally and are often exploited for free) and incorporating these costs into planning therefore constitutes the third reason for firms to care about sustainability. It is important (and will only become more so) because, as discussed in Chapter 9, "if prices reflected all the costs, including ecological costs spread across generations, the world would not face sustainability challenges, at least in theory."[41]

One of the earliest firms to adopt this concept of "environmental profit and loss accounting"[42] (EP&L) was Puma. The firm developed and first published an EP&L statement in 2011 in which it concluded its operations had an "impact of €51 million resulting from land use, air pollution and waste along the value chain added to previously announced €94 million for GHG emissions and water consumption."[43] For those firms not willing to undertake the same firm-wide process as Puma, calculating a price for carbon is an important first step.[44] According to the Carbon Disclosure Project (https://www.cdp.net/), at present "437 companies are calculating an internal price on carbon. . . . An additional 583 big companies [said] they planned to start carbon pricing within two years":[45]

> Disney and Microsoft [now] attach a "shadow price" to their carbon emissions; Colgate Palmolive and EcoLab . . . are trying to measure the true cost of water; and Interface . . . puts a price on the natural capital consumed by its carpet tiles.[46]

Similarly, Pepsi, in association with the Carbon Trust,[47] was an early adopter of the carbon footprint, calculating the impact of a half-gallon carton of its Tropicana orange juice:

> The equivalent of 3.75 pounds of carbon dioxide are emitted to the atmosphere for each half-gallon carton of orange juice. . . . PepsiCo is among the first [firms in the United States] that will provide consumers with an absolute number for a product's carbon footprint.[48]

Pepsi's attempt to measure the carbon footprint of its Tropicana orange juice (see Figure 13.2) is instructive—the majority of emissions (60%) occur during production. The value for firms in conducting these exercises is therefore two-fold—not only do they prepare for the day when there is a price placed on carbon (either by a tax or a cap-and-trade market), but they are also compiling the information they need to better understand their value chains. These data

| Figure 13.2 | The Carbon Footprint of Tropicana Orange Juice (0.5 gallons = 3.75 lbs [1.7 kg] of CO_2) |

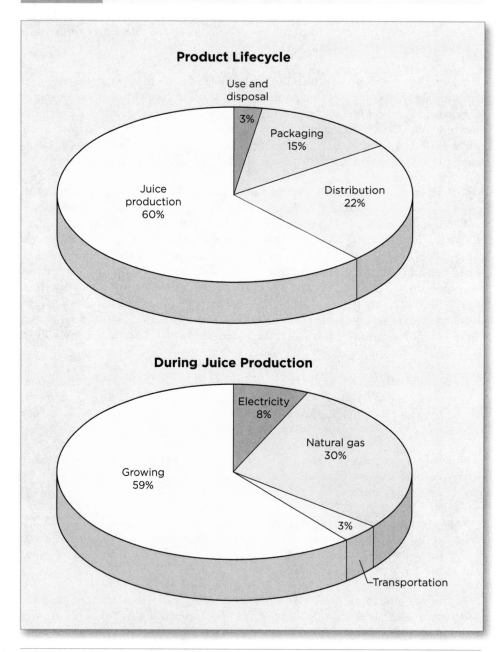

Product Lifecycle

Use and disposal 3%

Packaging 15%

Distribution 22%

Juice production 60%

During Juice Production

Electricity 8%

Natural gas 30%

Growing 59%

3%

Transportation

Source: Adapted from Andrew Martin, "How Green Is My Orange," *The New York Times*, January 22, 2009, p. B1.

allow them to identify inefficiencies and communicate that information to stake-holders. Other firms taking progressive action on this issue include Walkers and Cadbury in the UK.[49] Like Pepsi, for example, Cadbury has found that "the famous glass and a half of milk that goes into a Cadbury milk chocolate bar is responsible for 60% of the product's greenhouse gas emissions."[50]

Stakeholders

Understanding the need to price natural capital is the first action step,[51] which brings us to the fourth reason for firms to care about sustainability: the likeli-hood that stakeholder perceptions will change as the consensus about the need to do something coalesces. Consumer behavior, in particular, is a strong driver of corporate action and will have to change in order to make any meaningful dent in our carbon emissions. As Goodyear discovered, for example, 87% of the total CO_2 emitted during the life of one of its tires can be attributed to after-sales use by customers (in particular, each tire's "rolling resistance").[52] Similarly, as Unilever discovered as it worked to implement its *Sustainable Living Plan*:[53]

> Three years ago the company measured the carbon footprint of 2,000 prod-ucts and found that on average 68% of greenhouse-gas emissions in their life cycles occurred only after they got into the hands of consumers, mostly through the energy-intensive process of heating water (e.g., for tea bags or washing powder).[54]

As such, firms are beginning to anticipate the day when consumers will demand greater accountability from businesses for their environmental perfor-mance. In the United States, for example, GE acted early to stake its claim to a significant share of the sustainability market, appointing its first VP for corporate citizenship in 2002. It then launched its drive to capitalize on the shifting busi-ness context with its Ecomagination program in 2005 because, as CEO Jeff Immelt put it, "not only is it a nice thing to do, it's a business imperative."[55] As GE realizes and Walmart has demonstrated, an effective sustainability program *saves*, rather than *costs*, money[56] and, in the most progressive firms, is "a key component of long-term strategy."[57] General Motors has gone "landfill-free,"[58] and Samsung has announced plans to invest $20 billion by 2020 because, "just as electronics defined swathes of the 20th century, the company believes that green technology . . . will be central to the 21st."[59] For firms like Unilever, "sus-tainability is now the key driver of innovation"—a strategic imperative and "innovation's new frontier":[60]

> [In 2015,] Unilever's factories are emitting 37 percent less emissions than in 2008, even while producing more goods. Waste going to landfills is down 85 percent. Those things please environmentalists, while shareholders are happy that revenue is up 22 percent since Mr. Polman took over, though profits are up less.[61]

Reasons for Firms to Care About Sustainability

There are four main reasons why firms should care about *sustainability*:

- **Climate change:** Climate change is real. For-profit firms are both the main cause of this problem and the main hope for a solution. Our planet will be destroyed unless firms alter their operating practices.
- **Resilience:** A changing climate will affect business operations. Managing risk and adapting to the new environment will increasingly be an aspect of business success.
- **Natural capital:** Acting proactively on an important social issue arises from the *rational argument for CSR*. It is in firms' best interests to act before they are forced to do so.
- **Stakeholders:** As the need to act becomes apparent, stakeholders will increasingly demand change. Those firms that move first will be best placed to succeed in a more environmentally aware world.

Taking into account these four drivers of action on sustainability, no firms demonstrate as progressive an approach to transforming operations (or the financial benefits of doing so) as do Interface, the world's largest carpet-tile maker, and the UK retailer Marks & Spencer (M&S).

Interface and M&S

Interface's founder, the late Ray Anderson, launched his attack on Mount Sustainability in the mid-1990s, measuring progress using Eco-Metrics[62] and developing processes such as "plant-based carpeting."[63] The value for the firm quickly became self-evident:

> By 2007 the company was, he reckoned, about halfway up "Mount Sustainability." Greenhouse-gas emissions by absolute tonnage were down 92% since 1995, water usage down 75%, and 74,000 tonnes of used carpet had been recovered from landfills. The $400m he was saving each year by making no scrap and no off-quality tiles more than paid for the R&D and the process changes. As much as 25% of the company's new material came from "post-consumer recycling." . . . Most satisfying of all, sales had increased by two-thirds since his conversion, and profits had doubled.[64]

Ray Anderson was prompted to reimagine Interface's operations in response to the harm he realized industrial firms such as his were doing to the planet. After reading Paul Hawken's 1993 book *The Ecology of Commerce*,[65] Anderson understood the extent of the problem but also that, unless something changed, businesspeople like him would be judged by future generations as "thieves and plunderers of the planet."[66]

A similar approach is being adopted by Marks & Spencer, the UK retailer, which launched its Plan A in 2007.[67] M&S named its response *Plan A* because the firm believes there is no Plan B—that is, no alternative to implementing a sustainable business model throughout operations: "We believe it's now the only way to do business."[68] Plan A consists of a 100-point plan, spread over five commitment areas that the firm has pledged will "'change beyond recognition' the way M&S operates."[69] In spite of an initial plan to spend £200 million over the 5 years of Plan A,[70] by the first half of 2009, M&S claimed Plan A was "cost-neutral."[71] More importantly, based on progress during the first half of the plan, three trends were apparent:

> Corporate responsibility guidance and the Plan A commitment have systematically embedded themselves into the company's management platform; clear package labels and effective outreach to third-party stakeholders are changing consumer behavior; and steady progress is being made towards fulfilling Plan A's five commitment areas of carbon emissions, waste, sustainable sourcing, ethical trading, and healthy lifestyles.[72]

In 2012, on the fifth anniversary of Plan A's launch, M&S announced, "Already 138 commitments have been achieved, with a further 30 on course. Of all M&S products, 31% adhere to a Plan A commitment and a total of £185m in net benefits has been delivered."[73] By the middle of 2014, M&S had achieved all of Plan A's goals. Building on this success, the firm has now used this platform to launch a more ambitious initiative:

> Plan A . . . was launched in 2007 as a 100 point, 5 year plan. Having achieved our major aim of making our UK business carbon neutral, we've now introduced Plan A 2020, which consists of 100 new, revised and existing commitments, with the ultimate goal of becoming the world's most sustainable major retailer.[74]

WASTE

A central goal of this textbook is to restore faith in the corporation. For all its faults, the corporation is best placed to deliver the goals that CSR advocates support. While the government and nonprofits fill valuable non-market roles, it is the corporation that has the ability to allocate valuable and scarce resources in ways that encourage innovation and optimize total value. Those corporations that embrace CSR at all levels of operation, seeking to engage stakeholders to meet their needs and expectations, will be much better placed to survive and thrive over the medium to long term. In terms of sustainable resource utilization, in the absence of dramatic political action on a global basis, for-profit companies are, quite possibly, our only hope:

> Ready or not, we are moving to a world of scarce resources, in which companies will . . . have to monitor how much water, soil, and other natural resources they consume, as well as the payback they get from them. Companies that fail to calculate this equation will find themselves at the mercy of price increases and volatility, regulation, and social pressures, while those that master it will enjoy competitive advantage and gain market share.[75]

If for-profit firms are going to lead the reform of our economic model, a good place to start is the amount of waste that we generate—a central driver of the global economy. For firms, the more you buy of their products, the better they perform and the faster the economy grows. In other words, mass consumption and quick turnover are essential. Whether we *need* a product is less important than whether we *want* it. And, if we buy a product, the quicker we throw it away and buy another one, the faster GDP rises. Restraint and conservation are not the point. When you realize that Starbucks goes through "approximately 4 billion cups globally each year,"[76] you understand that resolving to bring a reusable cup to the store (even if you get all of your friends to do the same) pales in comparison to the scale of the action required to make a difference.

A huge assumption of this economic model is that the world's resources are infinite. When a company extracts a raw material and converts it into something that consumers want to buy, the consumer pays only for the costs the firm incurred during the extraction and conversion. For the most part, there is no charge associated with the replenishment of the resource (e.g., the cost of losing forever the precious metals used in cell phones that are not recycled) or the environmental costs incurred during consumption (e.g., the pollution emitted when driving a car). In short, our economy is founded on *waste*—the more that is wasted, the *stronger* the economy becomes. The numbers are staggering:

> According to the OECD, the average person creates 3.3lb (1.5kg) of rubbish a day in France, 2.7lb in Canada and no more than 2.3lb in Japan. By the OECD's reckoning, the average American produces 4.5lb a day, and more recent accounting puts the figure at over 7lb a day, less than a quarter of which is recycled.[77]

As economies across the world evolve and people in less developed countries seek the lifestyle long enjoyed by people in developed economies, the total amount of trash continues to build:

> China has surpassed the U.S. to become the world's largest trash producer, churning out more than 260 million tons a year. Beijing's 20 million residents generate about 18,000 tons a day, most of which goes to landfills.[78]

In terms of per capita trash, however, the United States is still far ahead: "At 7.1 pounds of trash a day, each of us is on track to produce a staggering 102 tons of waste in an average lifetime."[79] As such although it is central to economic growth, this level of waste creates inefficiencies:

> American communities on average spend more money on waste management than on fire protection, parks and recreation, libraries or school-books. . . . [Estimates suggest] there is at least $20 billion in valuable resources locked inside the materials buried in U.S. landfills each year, if only we had the technology to recover it cost effectively.[80]

While we bury a great deal of our waste, a lot of it is shipped overseas to be processed in countries with less strict environmental regulations. In fact, waste is one of the developed economies' largest exports. While "China's No.1 export to the U.S. is computers. . . . the United States' No.1 export to China, by number of cargo containers, is scrap."[81] A large proportion of this export to China (and countries in Africa, such as Nigeria)[82] is electronic waste, or *e-waste*—the waste associated with consumer electronics products such as computers and cell phones.[83]

e-Waste

Within the casing that surrounds most consumer electronics products, the metals, chemicals, and soldering that make up the components are toxic.[84] Many are also valuable, but the cost and effort of separating and recovering that value often means it is more effective either to throw the products away or get someone else to recycle them for us:

> Each phone contains about 300mg of silver and 30mg of gold. Between now and the end of 2020, 10m tonnes of electronic products will be purchased in the UK. This will include silver, gold and platinum group metals with an estimated total market value of £1.5bn.[85]

As these consumer electronic devices become more central to our lives, the amount of e-waste we produce is growing rapidly, to the point where "electronics make up the fastest-growing waste stream on the planet."[86] Our consumer-oriented economic model dictates that we trade in our fully functioning old phone and buy a new model whenever one comes out, without thinking through the consequences of that exchange. Every time Apple launches a new iPhone, for example, it replaces "tens of millions of cell phones . . . in more than 100 countries."[87] According to the Environmental Protection Agency's latest figures (2010), when these products are discarded,[88] there is a significant environmental cost. In the United States alone,

- 142,000 computers and over 416,000 mobile devices are thrown away every day;
- in total, 2.4 million tons (384 million units) of e-waste are discarded annually; and
- only 27% (of total weight) and 19% (of total units) of e-waste are recycled.[89]

As a result, the total amount of e-waste keeps piling up.[90] Figure 13.3 indicates the scale of discarded e-waste for different consumer electronics products in the United States in terms of both weight (in tons) and total units.[91] But this is not just a problem for consumers. A company like IBM, for example, has to process 38,000 electronic devices *a day* and maintains a staff of 250 people and "thousands of additional contractors" who are solely dedicated to e-waste disposal at the firm's 22 recycling plants worldwide.[92] The amount of heavy metals contained in all this waste presents a serious problem for whoever has to clean it up. A

Figure 13.3   Total e-Waste in the United States (2010)

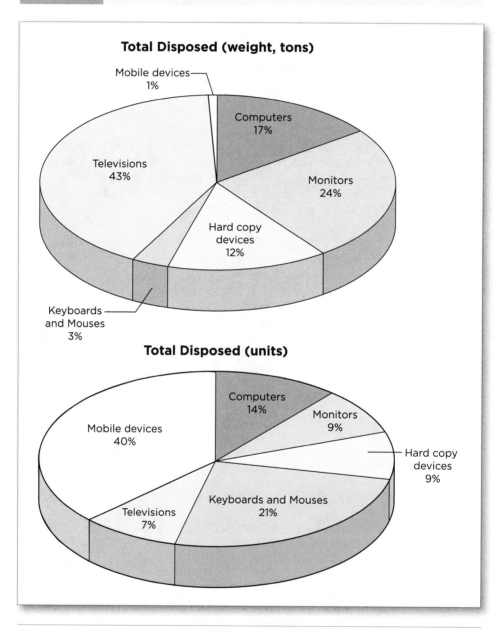

Source: EPA data, quoted in Electronics TakeBack Coalition, "Fact and Figures on E-Waste and Recycling," June 25, 2014, p. 2.

television or computer, for example, "can contain as much as eight pounds of lead, as well as mercury, cadmium and other substances that are harmless when part of a piece of equipment but a health risk when they reach a landfill."[93]

At present, much of the West's recycling is outsourced to China, where it is often dismantled by hand by poorly paid women and children with little or no protective clothing or equipment. Consumers who want to dispose of products responsibly are left with few good options—"noxious chemicals in the soil versus the health of Chinese workers."[94] As a result, specific areas in China have become "wastelands"[95] as Chinese workers save us the cost and effort of recycling our own e-waste. With little more than hand tools, workers "take apart old computers, monitors, printers, video and DVD players, photocopying machines, telephones and phone chargers, music speakers, car batteries and microwave ovens."[96] In Guiyu, China, where it is estimated 150,000 people, "including large numbers of children," work in e-waste recycling,[97]

> standard practice is to separate the plastic by boiling circuit boards on stoves, and then leach the metals with acid. Workers risk burns, inhaling fumes and poisoning from lead and other carcinogens. A study found high miscarriage rates in local women.[98]

What is being done to regulate the movement of e-waste from country to country? The UN's Basel Convention and the EU legislation on waste electrical and electronic equipment are two important government-level initiatives to regulate e-waste. These international regulatory efforts are extensive and offer workers significant protection, but enforcement is problematic in many developing countries. In Guiyu, for example,

> recycling e-waste is apparently free of any environmental or health and safety regulation. . . . Chinese law forbids the importation of electronic waste and Beijing is also a signatory to the Basel agreement. . . . But so far, official prohibitions have been about as effective as the official banners urging environmental protection that flap in the breeze above the trash-congested streets of Guiyu.[99]

As landfills reach their limits and the dangers of e-waste become more apparent, local and state governments in the United States are pursuing policies designed to change consumer behavior and limit the amount we throw away (or at least have it correctly recycled). By 2015, laws mandating e-waste recycling had been passed in 25 states, with many more pending in 31 states:

> All laws except [those in] California and Utah use the Producer Responsibility approach, where the manufacturers must pay for recycling. This means that 65% of the population of the U.S. is now covered by a state e-waste recycling law.[100]

In spite of the apparent common sense of this legislation, implementation can be problematic. In particular, there is debate over whether pollution costs should be borne by the individual (based on the amount disposed), the company (based on the revenue the products produce), or society (based on the idea that comprehensive waste disposal is a public good). A deposit on consumer electronic products collected at the point of sale, with part of the cost passed on to customers (higher prices), part borne by firms (lower profits), and part passed on to the state (tax revenue), would at least ensure the burden is shared. It would help reinforce the message that the environmental problems we face will only be solved when we all contribute.

BEYOND SUSTAINABILITY

Beyond solutions to specific problems, such as e-waste, this textbook argues for system-wide change fueled by the value-creating capacity of for-profit firms. It recognizes that the status quo is unstable, but also recognizes the power of the market to innovate and overcome the most intractable human problems. In short, we need a comprehensive reassessment of our capitalist model, but one in which we retain what is most effective about market forces to mobilize and allocate valuable and scarce resources in ways that optimize total value. Firms like TerraCycle, through its pledge to "eliminate the idea of waste," demonstrate the power of innovation and entrepreneurial spirit to generate change along these lines.[101] TerraCycle is successful because it adopts a stakeholder perspective and implements it comprehensively throughout all aspects of operations and strategic planning.

Where the market fails to provide an adequate solution (e.g., dealing with waste and recycling), firms must work in tandem with government agencies and NGOs to incentivize efforts and identify best-practice solutions. A point-of-sale tax, if applied equally across firms, would incentivize the creation of either more sustainable products or more efficient recycling processes (e.g., mobile phones containing dissolving circuit boards).[102] It is this concept of *system-wide* sustainability that is essential—only by focusing on the system as a whole can meaningful and *sustainable* change occur. And it is only the largest corporations that can provide the scale we need, given the extent of the changes in behavior that will be required by people worldwide in order to tackle climate change:

> Here's a question. Which trio of companies has done more for the environment . . . Patagonia, Starbucks and Chipotle? Or Walmart, Coca-Cola and McDonald's? . . . Patagonia, Starbucks and Chipotle have been path-breaking companies when it comes to sustainability, but Walmart, Coca-Cola and McDonald's are so much bigger that, despite their glaring flaws, . . . they will have a greater impact as they get serious about curbing their environmental footprint, and that of their suppliers.[103]

While provocative, the answer to the question is intuitive. That is not to say that the question isn't an important one to ask. Perhaps, for the CSR/sustainability community, it is the only one worth asking. Ultimately, the core of the issue is this: Are we interested in *ideal possibilities* or *meaningful change*? If *change* is what we want, then Walmart, Coca-Cola, and McDonald's need to be the source. That is not to diminish the wonderful business models of companies such as Patagonia, Starbucks, and Chipotle. If anything, they are the road map for what larger firms also need to accomplish. But, unless the largest companies are fully invested in strategic CSR, we will only be scratching the surface of the progress that needs to be made.

Massive firms have a disproportionate impact on our lives. The market capitalization of the top 10 global firms alone is $1.5 trillion.[104] What these large firms do in the near future, therefore, will do more to influence our standard of living and future security than all of the smaller firms combined. As Jason Clay states in his TED talk on how big brands can save biodiversity, "100 companies control 25% of the trade of all 15 of the most significant commodities on the planet. . . . Why is 25% important? Because if these companies demand sustainable products they will pull 40–50% of production."[105] According to Clay, it is all about the supply chain. Suppliers are as important a stakeholder to the firm as the customer. Large companies pushing other large companies to improve will achieve change much faster and on a scale that actually matters. Contrast this with waiting for consumers, one by one, to wake up to the global consequences of their consumption decisions.

Climate change has reached a point where only substantial action will produce meaningful effects and help avert the catastrophic outcome we are otherwise hurtling toward. In this light, while for-profit firms are the main cause of the environmental mess we face, they are also the main hope for a solution, and stakeholder pressure is the way to encourage the necessary change. There is much work to do—both in terms of production and consumption—in order to create a truly *sustainable* economic system.

Strategic CSR Debate

Motion: We should levy a tax on computers and smartphones to pay to recycle the e-waste that these products generate.

QUESTIONS FOR DISCUSSION AND REVIEW

1. Is sustainability an issue you consider in your purchase decisions? Why or why not?

2. Have a look at this video: http://www.storyofstuff.org/movies-all/story-of-stuff/. Does it change your answer to Question 1? How do you answer the main question posed in the video: *How can we make a linear economic system more sustainable?*

3. What is your image of the NGO Greenpeace? Do you trust the organization to provide accurate and objective assessments of the environmental impact

of business? Visit the organization's website (http://www.greenpeace.org/). Is sustainability given a high enough priority in business, politics, and society today? Why, or why not?

4. What are your impressions of Marks & Spencer's Plan A website (http://corporate.marksandspencer.com/plan-a/)? Do you get the sense that this is a genuine effort, or is it window dressing? More importantly, is it enough?

5. How can you minimize the amount of e-waste you produce? How often do you upgrade your cell phone or computer? Is it *fair* that workers in developing countries (including children) clean up our e-waste?

Chapter 14

IMPLEMENTING CSR

The first four parts of this book laid out the case for firms to integrate CSR into their strategic planning and throughout all aspects of operations. But making the case for why strategic CSR is important is separate from understanding how firms might actually go about implementing this management philosophy. That is, *How does a company become more socially responsible?* This chapter tackles this question by detailing the design and implementation of strategic CSR, introducing the major structural components, together with the key policies, practices, and norms that are necessary to support a comprehensive plan of action.

STRATEGIC PLANNING

The business case for CSR originates inside the firm. It is a process by which leaders take stock of past performance, interpret the shifting demands of stakeholders (both internal and external), and prepare a plan to meet those expectations moving forward. Once devised, this plan needs to be executed, which speaks directly to the issue of implementation. In other words, however good the plan, it is useless if implemented poorly. Similarly, whatever the intentions of the firm's leaders, unless a strategic CSR perspective is able to align stakeholders in support of the firm's vision and mission, the result will be less than optimal. The key question for the firm's leaders is, broadly speaking, *How do we create value?* The more specific question in terms of implementing strategic CSR, however, is this: *Who do we create value for?* Does the firm create value for a narrow segment of its stakeholders, or does it create value more broadly?

As such, the implementation of CSR begins with strategic planning, which is designed to build and sustain a competitive advantage for the firm. This process includes identifying the firm's goals, analyzing its competitive environment, reassessing its capabilities, and allocating the resources necessary to achieve its goals. Typically, planning covers both the short and long term, perspectives that can have very different meanings among industries. For electric utilities, for example, the planning horizon might stretch 10, 15, or more years into the future (given the complexity of estimating future electricity demand and designing, permitting, and building the capacity to produce and distribute electricity in a highly regulated environment). In a consumer products firm, however, the long term might be measured in months, from design to release and obsolescence. A firm like Zara, the Spanish clothes retailer, for example, has constructed a value chain that allows it to move from design to production to display "in as little as two weeks."[1] The firm's production cycle is significantly faster than the industry average of several "months to bring new merchandise to market"[2] and has created a new industry of "Fast Fashion."[3]

The process of planning formulates the firm's future objectives. For this, big-picture business goals (growth rates, market share, etc.) must be set. These broad, overarching targets form the basis for specific strategies, which must be infused with a stakeholder perspective. These longer-term strategies must then be translated into realizable objectives for each business unit and within these units for operating and support groups—from production to finance to human resources. These specific, shorter-term objectives must be both attainable and verifiable. Then, the resources necessary to implement the objectives are allocated. The unifying approach to resource allocation is the budget process, which is usually done near the end of the fiscal or calendar year.

Implementing CSR Throughout the Value Chain

The implementation of strategic CSR can be divided into three focal areas:

1. Supply chain: Prefirm production, such as raw materials extraction, supplier manufacturing, and outsourcing

2. Operations: Internal production, including all aspects of the value chain, such as transportation, logistics, and design

3. Consumption: Postfirm production, such as consumption and recycling

Because the strategic planning process traditionally focuses on goals and decisions selected on some objective basis (such as net present value or return on investment), goals that are difficult to quantify (such as stakeholder value) can be marginalized. The ease with which this can happen in the planning process only serves to emphasize the importance of adopting a methodical approach to ensuring uniform implementation throughout the firm. The whole process, which covers the three broad areas of *supply chain*, *operations*, and *consumption*, can be broken down into two broad implementation stages: short- to medium-term and medium- to long-term.

SHORT- TO MEDIUM-TERM IMPLEMENTATION

The urgency with which CSR policies are implemented depends on the perceived *CSR threshold* (Chapter 10) and the priorities of the firm's leaders. The implementation process itself is a commonsense approach to aligning stakeholder interests. The ultimate goal should be for CSR to form an integral component of the firm's culture, as reflected in day-to-day operations. The challenge is to move to a position in which all employees approach their work using a *CSR filter* (Chapter 11). The following steps offer an overview of how any firm can further the integration of CSR into its policies, practices, and culture over the short to medium term.

Executive Investment

For implementation to be successful, the CEO must actively sponsor CSR. Executive ownership is central to ensuring that a stakeholder perspective is institutionalized as a core component of day-to-day operations. Ideally, the CEO will consider himself or herself the chief CSR officer.[4] At a minimum, the CEO must remain in touch with the company's CSR performance by receiving regular updates, while granting a clear line of access to the top for the CSR officer. This commitment from senior management is crucial for effective implementation. Executives must exhibit leadership to infuse a stakeholder perspective. Otherwise, any CSR policy or statement will quickly become a hollow gesture.

Language is important, and its ability to shape behavior should not be underestimated. Clearly, however, a well-crafted position statement is not enough. Not only must the move to inject a CSR perspective be supported by executives, but that commitment must be genuine and reinforced on a day-to-day basis to avoid accusations of "empty rhetoric."[5] Consider:

> A well-led organisation will always seek to create the optimal value in all its relationships. In a way, that is simply good leadership. The most impressive corporate leaders have always been those whose vision of a successful business stretches beyond the product and the profits to their positive impact on the world around them.[6]

Tim Cook's commitment to understanding Apple's supply chain indicates that he is more engaged on this issue than his predecessor:

> Mr. Cook's appearance at a facility where Apple devices are made was an illustration of how differently Apple's new chief relates to [issues in Apple's supply chain]. Since Mr. Cook became chief executive . . . shortly before the death of Mr. Jobs, Apple has taken a number of significant steps to address concerns about how Apple products are made.[7]

Contrast this support for CSR with comments by Jeffrey Hollender (founder of Seventh Generation) on Walmart's commitment to CSR while Mike Duke was CEO (2009–2013):

In October 2005, Walmart announced plans to transform itself into one of the greenest corporations in the world. Then-CEO Lee Scott called sustainability "essential to our future success as a retailer." . . . Several years after Scott's departure as CEO, something has gone seriously wrong. . . . Michael Duke became CEO in February 2009. . . . I believe that, from the day Duke started, the initiatives that Lee Scott championed, but never saw come to fruition, stalled and then slowly unraveled.[8]

The contrast between the two CEOs identifies the importance of executive investment in a firm's CSR. This is important not only for current CEOs but also during the transition between CEOs. While changing from a disengaged CEO to an engaged CEO (i.e., the shift from Steve Jobs to Tim Cook at Apple) can improve a firm's CSR profile, the reverse shift (i.e., the change from Lee Scott to Mike Duke at Walmart) can undermine a lot of good work.[9] Today, progressive CEOs, such as Paul Polman of Unilever, Howard Schultz of Starbucks, and Yvon Chouínard of Patagonia, all understand that there is not only a legal imperative to be *responsible* but also ethical, moral, rational, and economic motivations. Sustainable businesses are operated over long-term horizons; anything less will jeopardize operations.

It used to be said that the problem with business is that it only thinks two quarters ahead. That is no longer the case—companies are having to think decades ahead, to plan for resource scarcity and climate volatility and to lock in supply chain resilience.[10]

CEO: Chief Ethics Officer

In order to embed this concept of the CEO as the ultimate *chief ethics officer*, some have suggested that a firm's senior executives should take an oath of office, swearing to do the following:

- "Protect the interests of all stakeholders of the company: customers, employees, suppliers, regulators, communities and creditors as well as shareholders.
- See business in today's rapidly evolving and increasingly diverse environment as both an economic and social institution.
- Analyze a wide variety of quantitative and qualitative metrics, and tie executive compensation to both sets of metrics to balance economics and ethics."[11]

While the investment of the CEO and the executive team is essential, they are not the firm's only leaders. The board of directors also has a vital role to play in supporting the firm's CSR goals, along with those charged with implementing them. The heads of all divisions within the company are also crucial to the success of any policies. And for multinational companies that have to manage cultural tensions, the managers in each country in which the firm operates are central in deciding which policies are based on core principles (standardized throughout the organization) and which policies can be subject to local interpretation. In short, leadership from the middle is almost as important as tone from the top. As one employee puts it,

> The CEO can be trumpeting ethics all he or she wants, but if it's not being manifested by the middle managers that's where the breakdown occurs. It's the middle manager asking me to do something unethical, not the CEO. It's the middle manager who decides what my compensation is based on and who may punish me or not promote me if I'm not doing what they are asking me to do, although I may feel uncomfortable about ethical issues surrounding that situation.[12]

CSR Officer

Top management support must translate into tangible action. As *The Economist* notes, "It has become almost obligatory for executives to claim that CSR is 'connected to the core' of corporate strategy, or that is has become 'part of the DNA.'"[13] To be effective, however, CSR needs both visibility and sponsorship. Backing by the CEO equals sponsorship, and the creation of a CSR officer[14] position, staffed by an executive with a direct reporting relationship to the CEO and/or board of directors, creates visibility. Influencing the organizational culture toward greater CSR requires time and effort. Given other demands, CEOs are forced to delegate their efforts to a CSR officer who formulates the firm's CSR policy. Thus, this position must have access to the highest levels of decision making to ensure a CSR perspective is part of the firm's strategic direction. Starbucks[15] and Nike provide good examples of this approach:

> [Nike's VP for Sustainable Business and Innovation has] overall responsibility for managing Nike's global corporate responsibility function, including labor compliance, global community affairs, stakeholder engagement and corporate responsibility strategic planning and business integration. She will report to Nike's Brand President.[16]

While compliance officer positions are "booming"[17] and "about 50% of chief compliance officers report directly to their company's chief executive or board,"[18] it is essential that this reporting relationship is genuine. There is only value in reporting to the boss if the boss is willing to listen and, even better, seek your counsel on a regular basis. Similarly, it is important that a company does not give the impression that it is only creating such a position in response to external pressure. This happened to Amazon when, following a detailed report by *The New York Times* that identified high levels of bullying and stress among its employees, the firm announced that it would hire a director of social responsibility:

Though Amazon has donated millions of dollars to disaster relief efforts and has been praised for environmentally-conscious buildings and packaging efforts, it is under fire for turning a blind eye to its own corporate culture and mistreating workers.[19]

The CSR officer defines, implements, and audits the firm's CSR policies across functional boundaries and throughout the supply chain. This includes assisting with legal and regulatory compliance, as well as compliance with discretionary certifications, such as the ISO 26000 guidelines for social responsibility.[20] The CSR officer also is responsible for responding to requests to complete surveys tied to "the proliferation of non-financial performance metrics,"[21] such as CSR and sustainability rankings.[22] As activist NGOs increasingly hold firms accountable for their operations, "managers at major U.S. employers receive literally thousands of pages of surveys each year on their social, environmental, governance, and ethics policies."[23]

Perhaps the most famous of these is *Fortune*'s Most Admired Firm rankings,[24] although there are many others such as *Newsweek*'s Green Rankings,[25] the Global Reporting Initiative,[26] and indexes produced by social responsibility research firms such as MSCI.[27] The rankings constitute signals to external constituents about the work that the firm is doing in relation to CSR. Although completing such surveys, "all seeking information tailored to the needs of their specific ratings framework,"[28] is no doubt tedious and time-consuming, performing well in these rankings may well be of strategic advantage to the firm.

In addition, a CSR officer should innovate—such as by introducing a *Stakeholder Relations Department* in place of the existing Investor Relations Department (see below) or creating a CSR subcommittee of the board on which both the CEO and president sit—to ensure the organizational design reinforces the firm's CSR commitments. Most importantly, the position should contribute to strategy formulation. The most effective way to do this is to appoint the CSR officer to a key operations committee. For example, at Nike, the vice president for sustainable business and innovation works with buying departments to ensure products are not only high quality and on time (traditional operations metrics) but also are produced in line with the firm's CSR criteria.[29] Operations is where the CSR officer can hope to make the most progress in terms of fully integrating CSR throughout all aspects of the business.

All these policies need a firm-wide perspective to ensure effective implementation and dissemination of benefits and goals. Ideally, the CSR officer must create awareness by using a blend of rewards and penalties to incentivize employees to make high-quality decisions. Thus, the CSR position is all-encompassing—the CSR officer should be part risk manager, part ethics officer, part compliance and crisis manager, part brand builder and insurer, and part beacon bearer.[30] Also included in the job description is developing contingency plans for unexpected crises.

Ideally, the long term goal for all departments is to grow a CSR perspective. In the short term, however, this effort must begin with an officer whose contribution to the strategic decision-making process starts from a CSR perspective.

Over time, CSR will become more integrated throughout the firm, with managers at all levels in the organization reinforcing CSR norms and practices.[31] But initially at least, focused leadership by the CSR officer, supported by the CEO, senior executives, and the board, is vital to strengthening the firm's CSR perspective.

CSR Vision

Equally important for the firm's CSR direction is a position statement. Cadbury's CSR vision statement, for example, is displayed prominently on its website and in its CSR reports:

> Cadbury Schweppes is committed to growing responsibly. We believe responsible business comes from listening and learning, and having in place a clear CSR vision and strategy. It also comes from having the processes and systems to follow through and an embedded commitment to living our values.[32]

The CSR Vision Statement

An effective CSR position statement does the following:

- *Engages* the organization's key stakeholders to determine their perspectives
- *Maps out* a conflict resolution process that seeks mutually beneficial solutions
- *Involves* the CEO's necessary endorsement and active support
- *Reinforces* the importance of CSR through rewards and sanctions
- *Provides* policies for how CSR is to be implemented on a day-to-day basis

All stakeholders (internal and external) need to understand the firm's set of values and how that affects them. The value of a statement outlining the vision and mission for the firm is part of this awareness process, as detailed in Chapter 10. Ideally, CSR or sustainability will feature prominently, as it does for Toyota:

> Vision: Toyota aims to achieve long-term, stable growth in harmony with the environment, the global economy, the local communities it serves, and its stakeholders.[33]

At present, there is much more that firms can do to embed CSR and sustainability throughout the organization. Few companies rise to the level of commitment that Unilever has demonstrated in this respect by pledging to "help a billion people take steps to improve their health and well-being."[34] Nevertheless, for stakeholders to take a firm's commitment seriously, it should have a CSR mission and vision statement and an effective plan of implementation—all essential components of firm-wide CSR.

Performance Metrics

Collectively, top management support, the creation of a senior executive CSR position, and the elaboration of the firm's CSR vision in a position statement all address a critical element in implementing CSR—awareness. Although the intent of CSR may be noble, however, people tend to focus on "what is inspected, not expected." As such, aligning the firm's incentives with its CSR goals is essential. The goal is to find the CSR champion at all levels within the firm, then empower and incentivize that employee to succeed. To measure performance, of course, firms must be able to monitor their employees. The emergence of *big data* makes this easier for the firm, but it also raises ethical issues of privacy, not to mention the demotivating consequences of the lack of trust that can be fostered in environments where "Big Brother" is always watching:

> Companies are using everything from biometrics to keep track of when employees clock in to work, to cameras tracking workers as they do their jobs and GPS systems for out-of-office workers that monitor where they are.[35]

Ideally, data collection is minimal and restricted to the metrics necessary to incentivize performance. These metrics should be embedded throughout the value chain, in terms of both individual compensation packages and firm-wide operations:

> Florida Ice & Farm, a Costa Rican food and drink company, has adopted exacting standards for the amount of water it can consume in producing drinks. [The firm also] links 60% of its boss's pay to the triple bottom line of "people, planet and profit." The sustainability champions also encourage their workers to come up with green ideas. Natura, a Brazilian cosmetics company, gives bonuses to staff who find ways to reduce the firm's impact on the environment.[36]

A danger of economic incentives, however, is that they can lead to unintended consequences. This is one of the most important issues for the CSR community to face.

The Unintended Consequences of Economic Incentives

In introducing economic incentives to encourage CSR behavior, it is important to ensure that the behavior being incentivized is what was intended. For example, during the 18th century, when the British government was still shipping its criminals to Australia, sea captains were paid based on the number of people they carried on their ships. What the government found, however, was that many inmates were dying during the journey—up to one third in some instances. Neither taking a doctor onboard for the journey nor raising the captains' pay increased the number of passengers who survived the trip. It wasn't until the government began paying captains based on the number of people who arrived in Australia (rather than the number of people who left the UK) that behavior changed and the survival rate greatly increased—to as high as 99%.[37] A similar effect was evident in another example from India:

During the time of British rule in colonial India, in order to free Delhi from a plague of snakes, the City's governor put an incentive scheme in place for their capture by introducing a bounty on cobra skins. The bounty was quite high as cobras are tricky to catch. And so, instead of the snakes being caught in the city, it became a sound business idea to start farming them. All of a sudden, the number of bounty claims increased disproportionately. The local authority realised what was going on and responded by abandoning the incentive scheme. And as they were no longer profitable, the cobras were released from the farms into the city, exacerbating the original problem.[38]

While the desired outcome was a reduction of the number of snakes, the action that was incentivized was killing snakes, so people responded by raising *more* snakes so they could kill them. The exact opposite of the intended goal was achieved by poorly directed economic incentives. The dangers of unintended consequences are very real.

Many CSR violations come about because decision makers at different levels of the organization are sincerely trying to make good decisions but have not been given the tools or incentives to make the most appropriate decision. Faced with a choice between committing a minor violation of company rules about pollution, for example, or meeting a key performance deadline, a decision maker at any level of the firm might make a tradeoff that results ultimately in stakeholder backlash. Why? Because in most firms, rewards (pay, promotions, and bonuses) are based on short-term economic performance, not CSR compliance. A survey of the member organizations of the Ethics & Compliance Officers Association (now the Ethics & Compliance Initiative), for example, revealed that, while 54.3% of firms included some ethics and compliance benchmarks as part of CEO performance evaluation and 58.2% did so for managers, only 14.0% of firms did the same for board members.[39] If an incentive is tied to meeting a goal and CSR is neither measured nor rewarded, reasonable people inside the firm may conclude that CSR is in fact of secondary importance.[40]

Nike's Subcontractors

Today, subcontractors to Nike must comply with company employment standards that dictate pay, rest breaks, overtime, and other working conditions. These standards are enforced by inspections. Those subcontractors who perpetuate sweatshop conditions contrary to Nike's requirements risk losing their production contracts, even if these firms are in full compliance with local human resource laws and practices.

For a long time, however, Nike's production demands contradicted the employment conditions outlined in its code of conduct for suppliers. It is ineffective to stipulate specific low-cost and high-production targets if, at the same time, a firm is asking its suppliers to restrict employee overtime and pay living wages. Given such a choice, many suppliers decided to meet Nike's production demands in order to keep their contracts with the firm at the expense of working conditions in their factories.

Once Nike realized the counterproductive effects of these competing demands, it worked to ensure its incentives for subcontractors accurately supported its CSR goals.[41]

Economic incentives tied to specific performance metrics serve a fundamental role in shaping organizational culture. Applying this same philosophy to CSR increases awareness and reinforces the idea that CSR is something the firm values as an integral part of its strategy. An added benefit is that these measures can form the basis for auditing the firm's CSR performance.

Integrated Reporting

A genuine organization-wide CSR audit with published results, integrated with the firm's financial documents, furthers awareness among stakeholders of the firm's CSR activities. Environmental audits, for example, are now widely documented in annual reports because stakeholders have begun to demand greater accountability for the sustainability of firms' actions. Indeed, these audits can be a legal requirement where climate change constitutes a material business risk.[42] The value of communicating this information to investors is that they understand the rationale for the firm's actions. Past surveys suggest that "few business leaders believed that their company's share price reflected its responsible business initiatives."[43] Better communication with all stakeholders (investors, in particular) improves this situation.

Ideally, integration should be extended to all nonfinancial measures and supported by regular firm-wide risk assessment updates, as is increasingly happening in both the UK (as far back as 2008, "81 per cent of FTSE 100 companies [were] producing stand-alone reports on corporate responsibility, sustainability, environment or similar")[44] and the United States (in 2013, "a record 72% of companies in the [S&P 500] index filed sustainability reports, . . . up significantly from 53% in 2012 and 20% in 2011").[45] Further evidence suggests this trend is growing worldwide: An "analysis of 3,400 companies across 34 countries and 15 industry sectors concluded that nearly every Global Fortune 250 (G250) company now reports its CR activity."[46] Reporting requirements will only become more stringent as governments increasingly recognize that (a) companies incur a number of costs that are currently externalized and (b) firms are reluctant to publish this information voluntarily:

> [The SEC] says all firms that file standardised annual reports must include details of climate-change risks that are "material" to earnings. The British government requires large quoted companies based in Britain to disclose their carbon-dioxide emissions to shareholders. And the European Union plans to make firms with more than 500 employees publish environmental and social data in their management accounts.[47]

As a result of the EU's move to make CSR reporting mandatory, "some 6,000 large companies will be required to report on their policies on diversity, social issues and on corruption, as well as the risks they pose to human rights and to the environment, including through their supply chains."[48] As these processes become more normalized, at least in terms of sustainability reporting, it is not hard to imagine the emergence of "generally accepted accounting principles for the environment" in the not too distant future:

The basic framework would not be hard to set: companies should publish assessments of climate risks and opportunities (Exxon is doing that); disclose their greenhouse-gas emissions; and explain how they are seeking to cut them.[49]

The key is the degree to which such reports are genuine. Even where metrics are established, firms can be reluctant to report their progress (either because they feel the information is proprietary or, perhaps, because their performance is less than ideal):

Only 128 of the 4,609 largest companies listed on the world's stock exchanges disclose the most basic information on how they meet their responsibilities to society. . . . 97% of companies are failing to provide data on the full set of "first-generation" sustainability indicators—employee turnover, energy, greenhouse gas emissions (GHGs), injury rate, pay equity, waste and water. . . . More than 60% of the world's largest listed companies currently fail to disclose their GHGs, three quarters are not transparent about their water consumption and 88% do not divulge their employee turnover rate.[50]

Figure 14.1 The Triple Bottom Line

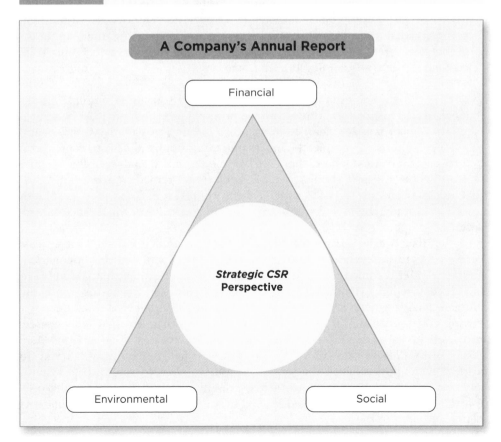

Figure 14.1 presents a minimum requirement for any company serious about reporting its CSR activities to stakeholders. A firm that wants to be considered *transparent* and *accountable* should expand the scope of its annual report to incorporate the "triple bottom line,"[51] which measures performance across various financial, environmental, and social metrics. Such reports provide benchmarks to *internal* constituents that encourage further efficiency improvements; they also serve as a basis for communication with *external* constituents, providing feedback on prior commitments and statements of future intentions.

A company that led the way in CSR auditing and reports is Shell, which was prompted to reanalyze its business practices in 1995 following two separate NGO-orchestrated campaigns. The first attacked the company's decision to sink the *Brent Spar* oil platform in the ocean, while the second attacked the firm's failure to prevent the execution by the Nigerian government of an environmental activist, Ken Saro-Wiwa, who had been campaigning against Shell's operations in Nigeria. The stakeholder backlash over these two issues threatened Shell's underlying business model.[52] In response, the firm moved to change its culture—the result was the *Shell Report*,

> disclosing Shell's successes and failures in human rights and environmentalism, including oil spills and community protests, as well as the profits and losses of its multibillion-dollar business. . . . "I don't know any [other] oil company that produces anything as comprehensive and candid about its global social responsibility programs as the Shell Report," said Frank Vogl, co-founder of Transparency International.[53]

Other companies are initiating lifecycle assessments, using recent innovations to measure the carbon footprint of various products (see Chapter 13). The advantages for these firms are clear: In addition to helping management understand the value chain more completely and highlighting potential CSR transgressions before managers read about them in the media, such analyses also identify waste, thus making cost savings possible. Such tools "helped companies discover that vendors consume as much as 80% of the energy, water, and other resources used by a supply chain, and that they must be a priority in the drive to create sustainable operations."[54]

A step that is essential for validity is to have an audit conducted, or at least verified, by an independent third party in the same way that an independent auditor verifies a company's financial reports.[55] Some form of objective verification lends credence to the data reported, with industry standards being the ultimate goal (e.g., see SASB, http://www.sasb.org/). In spite of companies following GRI guidelines, firms still often produce a document that conveys few metrics that can be used to compare performance with that of other firms. As a result, many CSR reports fail to explain clearly "what the company is trying to achieve with all its policies and processes, nor whether it is on track to achieve any real impact as a result."[56] According to Mallen Baker, there are really only four questions that need to be addressed in a CSR report, with everything else being relegated to the appendix:[57]

1. What will it look like for your company to be sustainable?

2. What do you need to do to get there?

3. How much progress have you made?

4. What are the big problems you still have to solve?

Producing a CSR report is one thing; ensuring it is accurate, that it enables external observers to understand the firm's CSR activities, and that performance is comparable across organizations represents another level of transparency altogether.

Ethics Code and Training

One way to encourage the desired CSR behavior throughout the firm is to record the expectations for and boundaries of acceptable behavior in an ethics code:

> By adopting its own code, a company can clarify for all parties, internal and external, the standards that govern its conduct and can thereby convey its commitment to responsible practice wherever it operates.[58]

An ethics code forms the foundation of an ethics and compliance program, something that "81 percent of companies" are now estimated to have in place.[59] In addition to having an ethics code, however, it is essential to reinforce those rules and norms via regular ethics training. Both establishing the rules and reinforcing them via training are essential to promoting a consistent culture throughout the organization:

> In 1995, [the Institute of Business ethics] estimated that six out of ten larger companies had codes of ethics (or similar). In 2010, the number is closer to 80% of the FTSE 100. . . . However, in this survey . . . only six out of ten UK companies provide training in business ethics for all their staff.[60]

Similar to a vision or mission statement for the firm, both the ethics code and ethics training program must be genuine and substantive in order to be meaningful. As seen with the collapse of Enron, it is only too easy to say one thing (the *right* thing), yet do something different:

> Enron . . . won a spot for three years on the list of the 100 Best Companies to Work for in America. In 2000 it received six environmental awards. It issued a triple bottom line report. It had great policies on climate change, human rights and (yes indeed) anti-corruption. Its CEO gave speeches at ethics conferences and put together a statement of values emphasizing "communication, respect, and integrity." The company's stock was in many social investing mutual funds when it went down. Enron fooled us.[61]

How can stakeholders trust a firm's actions if its CSR pronouncements are designed to mislead them into believing the firm is something that it is not? After all,

Kenneth Lay wrote to employees in Enron's code of ethics, "As officers and employees of Enron Corp.,... we are responsible for conducting the business affairs of the Company in accordance with all applicable laws and in a moral and honest manner."[62]

Enron's Code of Ethics

Enron stands on the foundation of its Vision and Values. Every employee is educated about the Company's Vision and Values and is expected to conduct business with other employees, partners, contractors, suppliers, vendors and customers keeping in mind respect, integrity, communication and excellence.[63]

Everything we do evolves from Enron's Vision and Values statements.... We are dedicated to conducting business according to all applicable local and international laws and regulations... and with the highest professional and ethical standards.[64]

Employees of Enron Corp., its subsidiaries, and its affiliated companies (collectively the "Company") are charged with conducting their business affairs in accordance with the highest ethical standards. An employee shall not conduct himself or herself in a manner which directly or indirectly would be detrimental to the best interests of the Company or in a manner which would bring to the employee financial gain separately derived as a direct consequence of his or her employment with the Company. Moral as well as legal obligations will be fulfilled openly, promptly, and in a manner which will reflect pride on the Company's name.[65]

In addition to having an ethics code for their own operations, firms need to be aware of what is happening throughout the value chain. The operations of suppliers, in particular, are a potential risk, especially when key elements of the production process are outsourced to low-cost environments. As discussed earlier, Nike experienced firsthand the potential danger this presents to the brand when it ignored unacceptable working conditions in its own supply chain.[66] Many other firms have also had to respond to accusations (fairly or unfairly) that they are insufficiently aware of the conditions under which their products are being made.

Firms rectify this potential risk by asking suppliers (and, where appropriate, distributors) to sign codes of conduct that adhere to the firm's ethics rules and norms as detailed in their internal ethics codes. While this is widely practiced by firms today, however, what is unclear is the extent of a firm's responsibility throughout its supply chain (as discussed in the Part IV case). Supply chain responsibility is an evolving but essential area of the CSR debate (as discussed in the Part IV case study). At present, the profile of the brand, rather than the nature of the reported offense, seems to be the best predictor of media exposure in the event of a supply chain issue, along with the firm's, industry's, or culture's CSR threshold (see Chapter 10).

Ethics Helpline

In addition to an ethics code and regular training for employees, a key component of the continuous internal reinforcement necessary for a CSR policy to remain effective is an anonymous feedback, complaint, or whistle-blowing system. This process should be available either internally or via a third party and is a requirement in the United States as a result of the Sarbanes-Oxley Act (2002),[67] which compelled firms to establish a confidential reporting procedure (e.g., a toll-free telephone number or email "helpline") for employees to report ethics transgressions.[68]

Using an independent third party to perform this job guarantees the protection of employees' identities, thus reducing the risk of retaliation. This infrastructure encourages the reporting of any breaches of policy that can affect the company's stated CSR position. Ideally, a helpline also encourages positive feedback in the form of ideas from employees, who are often best placed to evaluate the firm's CSR policies in action. The option of anonymity is essential in a committed organization because human nature indicates that retribution is a common reaction to a threat:[69]

A study carried out by Public Concern at Work, a UK whistleblowing charity, found that 50 per cent of those who had raised concerns about malpractice at work in 2014 had been fired or resigned. A further 28 per cent were bullied by colleagues or victimized or disciplined by their employers. Only 16 per cent reported that their whistleblowing had a positive outcome, such as being thanked by their superiors.[70]

Along similar lines, reports in the United States suggest that as many as one in five employees who report wrongdoing to a supervisor subsequently suffer some form of retaliation:

[Since the 2007–2008 financial crisis,] the number of tips received by the "Whistleblower Office" of America's [SEC] has risen steadily . . . to nearly 4,000 a year. . . . Though official encouragement of whistleblowers is growing, corporate retaliation remains a problem. Of those who report internally first, the number who perceive that they have suffered retribution has been steady at around 20% since 2011.[71]

It is essential that the board and senior management ensure a system is in place to collect and respond to the concerns of employees or other potential whistle-blowers. While it is in the firm's interest to learn about wrongdoing before serious damage occurs,

45% of U.K. employees still don't raise concerns about behavior in their organization. Of those who do speak up, only 39% said that they were satisfied with the outcome. . . . The numbers from employees in Germany, France, Spain and Italy weren't much better, with 54% saying they chose not to raise concerns of misconduct because they didn't believe corrective actions would be taken.[72]

While the survey data suggest employees are reluctant to come forward, they also suggest there is considerable risk to firms from wrongdoing that is currently going unreported. Moreover, if employees are pushed past a certain point and find no productive avenue to voice their concerns internally, there is the chance they will disengage, take to social media anonymously, or, in the most serious cases, leak the information to the media or the relevant regulatory office.

Unless a company is able to protect and even reward employees who are willing to come forward and report transgressions where they see them, the firm will be unable to fix the problems. Not only does such wrongdoing negatively affect the firm's performance, but it also damages employee morale and, as a result, productivity.

Organizational Design

In order for all these elements to coalesce into an effective strategic CSR framework that represents stakeholder interests within the strategic planning process of the firm, a deliberate effort is essential. CSR must have visibility to be effectively implemented.

Ideally, the day-to-day operationalization of CSR demands the direct involvement of top management, together with board oversight. It will be evident that firms are taking CSR seriously when the board puts it on the same level as other key governance issues, such as the integrity of the firm's financial information. Further, giving the CSR officer access to the CEO and a direct reporting relationship to the board suggests further operational support, along with significant organizational resources dedicated to enforcing the firm's ethics code, delivering regular ethics training to all employees, and instituting a responsive ethics helpline with protection for whistle-blowers. In well-run, ethical, and socially responsible firms, tangible visibility for CSR within the organizational structure is the most visible demonstration of genuine commitment.

MEDIUM- TO LONG-TERM IMPLEMENTATION

Beyond establishing minimum start-up conditions, the firm must institutionalize and externalize the substance of its CSR policies. Over the medium to long term, the firm should communicate its perspective, while seeking regular feedback from stakeholders. The longer the period of time that is considered, the more the *true* intentions of the firm toward CSR will become apparent.

Stakeholder Engagement

All large, publicly held corporations have well-developed investor relations departments. They have become the norm because managers, particularly in English-speaking economies, perceive shareholders to be the firm's primary stakeholders. As a company's share price has become the key indicator of corporate and management success, keeping investors happy has become central to a CEO's ability to retain their job.

As part of moving CSR to the center of a company's strategic outlook, this two-way avenue of communication should be expanded to include a firm's broader set of stakeholders. One approach would be to change the focus of the investor relations department so that it becomes the *stakeholder relations department*. The goal should be to develop close ties to all stakeholders. Rather than being caught unawares by a viral campaign, a firm that has built relationships over years with all of its stakeholders will benefit from an honest exchange of ideas and interests and hopefully avoid the worst conflicts. At the same time, the firm opens up potential avenues to work together with stakeholders— whether on product development or issues that can mitigate the worst effects of the firm's operations.

Lobbying

An important stakeholder for the firm is the government, and a useful way to interact with elected representatives is through lobbying. In order for lobbying to be considered socially responsible, however, managers should follow a set of principles:

Good	Bad
Proactive	Reactive
Work toward industry standards	Work toward individual firm exceptions
Spending to support scientific research	Paid endorsements and campaign donations
Transparent	Secretive

Following these principles should ensure that an honest and open exchange of information cannot be construed as an attempt to disrupt or distort the democratic process:

Exxon, for example, spent more than $130m in lobbying and political contributions between 2002 and 2010. The balance of these contributions was heavily tilted: the oil giant donated ten times as much money to politicians who opposed emissions reductions [as] they did to those who supported such policies. This tendency to fund advocacy groups that reject climate science contributes significantly to stalling the national climate debate.[73]

Marketing

Strategic CSR that is genuine and substantive needs to be communicated to the firm's stakeholders. As such, a firm's marketing department is an important medium through which the firm can communicate its CSR progress. But firms need to be careful as this is a sensitive area. Stakeholders soon come to interpret excessive self-promotion as merely a cynical effort of going through the CSR motions to receive public relations benefits, and they come to suspect *greenwash*.

While avoiding the impression of spin is crucial, it is also good business to convey to stakeholders that their input is valued. More importantly, firms do not want their identity defined by others in the media. The aim, therefore, is to meet stakeholder expectations by matching promises with reality. In particular, as the free flow of information shifts the balance of power in an information age, firms need to develop the skills necessary to communicate with stakeholders through the media of their choice. As one of "The 36 Rules of Social Media," firms should remember that, increasingly, "Your fans own your brand":[74]

> Social network websites account for over 22% of all time spent on the internet. . . . [Today], information on a brand's actions travel fast and brand managers must work harder to ensure consistency of the brand's values along their supply chain.[75]

Given the importance of the firm's brand today, as a driver of both marketplace success and CSR (Chapter 1), the potential exists in a progressive firm for the marketing department to take a strong role in shaping the firm's implementation of CSR. As discussed in Chapter 12, strategic CSR is about day-to-day operations, not philanthropy. Whenever the firm is seeking to shape external perceptions of its business, responsibility for that work should be placed in the marketing department, which has the media experts and knowledge of brand management.

There are many examples of companies that have failed to take the lead in shaping their reputations. It is important that firms get it right. Often the perception of a company in the public mind, once created, is difficult to shift. For example, in spite of its recent progressive work, Nike's initial failure to anticipate the backlash against its outsourcing business model has ensured that, for some stakeholders, the company will always be associated with sweatshops. Go to Nike's corporate website[76] today, however, and it soon becomes apparent that the firm has redefined the way it conducts its operations and presents its corporate message to the outside world. Due to its early transgressions, however, Nike continually finds itself having to play catch-up, with some stakeholders refusing to grant the company any concessions at all.

Corporate Governance

Corporate governance matters. It is the primary interface between the firm and its shareholders. The board of directors advises the CEO on strategy and the firm's overall direction; the board also acts in an oversight function, ensuring the firm is well managed. Effective corporate governance is central to the well-managed firm.

Transparency and *accountability* have become the watchwords of good corporate governance, which has also become a vital aspect of effective CSR. Increased legal requirements reinforce this change in sentiment for all but the most shortsighted of corporate boards. Reinforcing the dynamic legal environment and corresponding expectations of compliance are shareholder activists, who drive reform in corporate law and company policy. Ensuring a firm's procedures and practices are transparent, that its managers are accountable to external stakeholders, and that the process by which board directors are appointed is democratic are all crucial to ensuring good governance.

Corporate governance will increasingly become the target of reforms prompted by insufficient attention to CSR. Following the financial and ethical scandals early in this century, firms face significantly increased reporting requirements that require substantial investments in compliance. This is particularly true for the financial industry. The 2007–2008 financial crisis revealed market abuses that resulted in the near total collapse of the world financial system. The result in the United States was the Dodd-Frank Act of 2010, which enforced increased scrutiny of corporate finance and investments and more attention to the crucial oversight function of boards of directors.

Legislation such as this is merely backlash initiated by stakeholders whose interests were insufficiently protected by firms. It would have been less likely or less severe if boards had more effectively integrated CSR into the firms' operations. As such, these waves of resistance illustrate the *Iron Law of Social Responsibility,* and the result is greater constraints on how corporations are governed. In future, the most effective boards will form a CSR subcommittee on which both the CEO and president sit, incorporate ethics and compliance benchmarks into director (and senior executive) performance evaluation, and institute a direct reporting line from the CSR officer to remain in touch with areas of risk throughout the firm. Such structural reforms go a long way toward ensuring that the organizational design reinforces the firm's CSR commitments, minimizes risk, and maximizes performance over the medium to long term.

Social Activism

Social activism is an important way for a firm to establish an identity that attracts stakeholders and fulfills the firm's mission and vision. Both The Body Shop and Ben & Jerry's, however, found that activism alone is insufficient to remain viable in the long run. In both cases, the founders were forced to cede operational control to professional managers as their firms grew in complexity. Social activism of any sort must support an economically viable business. No firm can benefit any of its stakeholders if it is stuck in bankruptcy court. Economic viability and legal compliance are minimum conditions for survival.

Social activism does not preserve an operation if basic economical, legal, or other business fundamentals are missing. That said, a sincere activist focus helps the firm further its viability over the long term by solidifying relationships with various stakeholders. And activism need not be confrontational—advocating certain positions can help consolidate support for the firm. Working with other firms in the same industry to form industry associations, for example, can help raise standards while also protecting against potential mutual threats.

Examples include the Roundtable on Sustainable Palm Oil (RSPO; http://www .rspo.org/) or the Fair Labor Association (http://www.fairlabor.org/). Corporate advocacy like this matters because, for firms like Nike and other lifestyle brands, taking clear positions can help align the firm's actions with the values of customers. Advocacy may also serve as a potential defense—a form of brand insurance.[77] Social activism can win the support of other stakeholders—from employees, local communities, and government agencies. Such messages, however, must be consistent with the firm's mission and vision and extend from the boardroom and senior executives, via CSR professionals, throughout the firm.

THE SOCIALLY RESPONSIBLE FIRM

An overview of the different components of the implementation of CSR throughout an organization is presented in Figure 14.2.[78] Together, they represent a comprehensive plan of action for firms seeking to implement a CSR perspective. For the firm, plans are meaningless unless they are translated into action. Press releases to the media, speeches to employees or trade groups, or assertions of CSR in annual reports are not the goal. Necessary as these activities may be to raise awareness among stakeholders, both internal and external, CSR must be operationally integrated into day-to-day activities.

The ultimate test of implementation, therefore, is the firm's actions. CSR must be integrated genuinely into strategic planning. Concern must focus not only on the *ends* but also on the *means* used to achieve those ends. This focus must also be constantly recalibrated to accommodate, as much as possible, the evolving interests of the firm's broad range of stakeholders. This is achieved for each component of the implementation process via a series of steps, each of which helps further embed socially responsible practices throughout the organization:

- Risk analysis (firm-wide audit)
- Policy statement (formation and announcement)
- Risk management (monitoring the implementation and reacting to any issues)
- Reporting (transparency and stakeholder interaction)
- Review and revision via risk analysis update

Each of these steps should be adhered to vigilantly. The way the firm's actions are received by those most affected by them indicates the success of the process by which the socially responsible firm matches plans and intentions to actions and results. The goal of CSR implementation is to create a culture that is infused throughout the organization:

Creating a culture of integrity begins with tone at the top, but it has to include the mood in the middle and the buzz at the bottom. Culture is what people see as recognized and rewarded. For employees, the face of culture might be their supervisor. The voices of culture are the legendary stories told throughout an organization that reinforce the fundamental values that it stands for. As important and essential as compliance is, in the struggle between culture and compliance, culture always wins.[79]

Figure 14.2   A Firm's CSR Plan of Implementation

Time Frame	Action	Summary
Short to Medium Term	Executive Investment	The CEO must establish the necessary components of an effective CSR policy and ensure that CSR is institutionalized within the firm as a core component of day-to-day operations.
	CSR Officer	CSR needs both visibility and sponsorship within the firm. Backing by the CEO equals sponsorship, while the creation of a CSR Officer position staffed by a company executive (and with a direct reporting relationship to the board of directors) creates visibility.
	CSR Vision	A CSR vision statement allows stakeholders (internal and external) to understand the firm's CSR position and how that stance affects them.
	Performance Metrics	The creation of rewards and measures that align the firm's production and social responsibility goals, increases awareness of CSR and its profile within the firm.
	Integrated Reporting	A genuine firm-wide audit, with published results integrated with the firm's financial statements, furthers awareness among internal and external stakeholders about the firm's CSR activities.
	Ethics Code and Training	One way to encourage CSR throughout the firm and its supply chain is to record expectations and the boundaries of acceptable behavior in an Ethics Code and ethics training for all employees, and a Code of Conduct for suppliers.
	Ethics Helpline	A key component of the continuous internal reinforcement necessary for a CSR policy to remain effective is an anonymous whistle-blowing procedure that is available to all stakeholders.
	Organizational Design	In order for all these CSR elements to coalesce into an effective CSR policy, tangible support for CSR within the organizational structure demonstrates the firm's genuine commitment.
Medium to Long Term	Stakeholder Involvement	As part of moving CSR to the center of a company's strategic outlook, a two-way avenue of communication should be opened with the firm's broader set of stakeholders.
	Manage the Message	*Strategic CSR* that is genuine and substantive needs to be communicated to all stakeholders. Essential today is for the firm to establish an effective social media strategy.
	Corporate Governance	*Transparency* and *accountability* are essential for effective corporate governance, but need a committed Board of Directors with structural reforms that reinforce CSR throughout the firm.
	Activism and Advocacy	While no substitute for business fundamentals, corporate activism and advocacy help define the firm's identity by solidifying relationships with its various stakeholders.

Strategic CSR Debate

MOTION: The CEO is the *chief ethics officer.*

QUESTIONS FOR DISCUSSION AND REVIEW

1.   Why is top-management support for CSR so critical? Can CSR be delegated? If so, why and to whom?

2.   List four of the eight components of a firm's plan of action necessary to implement CSR over the short to medium term. What examples from business can you think of where firms have performed these actions successfully?

3. How does a firm avoid the perception that its CSR report is *greenwash*? Does it matter whether the reasons behind an action are genuine or cynical if the outcome is the same?

4. What do you imagine the day-to-day work of an ethics and compliance officer (ECO) entails? Do you think it is viewed as a position of importance within companies today?

5. An important component of implementing an ethical or CSR perspective firm-wide is consistency across departments. Do you feel that the important lessons you are learning in this class are supported by classes from other departments in the business school?

Chapter 15

SUSTAINABLE VALUE CREATION

As discussed in Chapter 1, "After more than half a century of research and debate, there is not a single widely accepted definition of CSR." Although there is no commonly agreed-upon definition, however, there has been a common purpose to all of the work generated in the name of CSR: "to broaden the obligations of firms to include more than financial considerations."[1] The field of CSR and business ethics has long focused on the ends of business, presenting *profit* as a corrupting influence on behavior. The result has been a lot of wasted energy and many premature pronouncements. As Howard Bowen claimed optimistically in his 1953 book *Social Responsibilities of the Businessman*:

> The day of plunder, human exploitation, and financial chicanery by private businessmen has largely passed. And the day when profit maximization was the sole criterion of business success is rapidly fading. We are entering an era when private business will be judged solely in terms of its demonstrable contribution to the general welfare.[2]

Urging firms to "include more than financial considerations" as part of their business model is *not* the purpose of strategic CSR. Instead, this textbook refocuses the CSR debate on the way business is conducted. Demanding that managers expand the goals of the firm suggests a problem with the *ends* of capitalism (i.e., profit). In contrast, the underlying principles of strategic CSR suggest that any problem with capitalism, as currently practiced, is with the *means*. The pursuit of profit (the best measure we have of long-term value added) is not the problem; it is the methods by which profit is sought that can be problematic. In short, it is not *what* firms do but *how* they do it that matters. When rules are broken, costs are externalized, and key stakeholders ignored (or worse, abused), value is broadly diminished. While some firms may benefit from such practices in the short term, the costs are borne by society as a whole.[3]

As such, strategic CSR represents an extension of the CSR debate, redefining our understanding of this complex topic. It is related to, but is fundamentally different from, concepts such as sustainability and business ethics. While *CSR* has become associated with philanthropy, *sustainability* focuses on resource utilization and ecological preservation, and *business ethics* constructs normative prescriptions of right and wrong, strategic CSR is a practical management philosophy that is grounded in the day-to-day operations of the firm.

The nature of business is changing as globalization intensifies and the room for error shrinks. Firms that fail to deliver are quickly replaced, as indicated by the average life span of a Fortune 500 company, which "has fallen from 75 years in the 1930s to perhaps just 15 years today."[4] Strategic CSR stands as an antidote to these forces. It draws on what we know about economic exchange and human psychology to explain how markets work and how value is created. Understanding these processes allows managers to build a sustainable competitive advantage for the firm. That is, in a dynamic business environment with *rules* that are defined by the collective decisions of the firm's stakeholders, value is optimized when stakeholders convey and enforce their needs. Within such an environment, it is in the firm's best interests to respond to those stimuli. These economic and social exchanges are therefore interactions that form around the collective set of values prevalent in society at any point in time. It is the degree of *fit* with these values that determines directly the success or failure of any given for-profit firm.

VALUES, MORALS, AND BUSINESS ETHICS

The purpose of this book is to build a compelling argument for firms to integrate CSR into their strategic planning and day-to-day operations. To do this, it is essential that they be open to collaborative relationships with their primary constituents. In other words, a stakeholder perspective is an integral part of a comprehensive, strategic approach to CSR. Firms will differ on which stakeholders should be prioritized, an ordering that will shift from issue to issue. What is important though, is that firms are aware of their stakeholders' interests and account for them when making decisions. To the extent that managers consider and consult with stakeholders before making decisions, the ability of the firm to create value for those groups increases.

Adopting a stakeholder perspective, however, is something that is easy to say but difficult to do. By definition, the interests and demands of stakeholders will evolve and conflict. As such, firms will not be able to please all stakeholders all the time. Adapting its strategic planning process with the goal of trying to do so, however, helps the firm make better decisions, while insulating it from potential threats. The goal should be to engage with stakeholders whenever possible and minimize the danger of stakeholder disillusionment. Not many companies do this well, but what effective firms have in common is a genuine commitment to the process. Defining characteristics of such firms include an organizational culture and set of values that are more inclusive than exclusive and a view of profit as the outcome of a process by which value is created for a broad range of stakeholders—in other words, progressive management. In short, they are businesses that are *moral* and *ethical*.

Business Ethics Versus CSR Versus *Strategic CSR*

Business ethics traditionally differs from CSR in two important ways. First, while *CSR* tends to take more of a macro perspective and evaluates the extent to which firm behavior affects society as a whole, *business ethics* focuses on more micro issues, such as individual behavior and decision making. Second, while *CSR* is often externally focused and tied more closely to functions such as marketing, *business ethics* focuses internally on creating an ethical environment and has its roots in legal compliance.[5]

Strategic CSR bridges both the macro and the micro, the external and the internal, to present a comprehensive management philosophy of the firm across all stakeholders.

Morals Versus Ethics

When we teach children not to steal, we are teaching them morality. When you have a conflict between two or more things that morality requires, that's when ethics steps up to the plate.[6]

An important question, therefore, is this: What drives a company to be *ethical* and *moral*? How should stakeholders distinguish between actions that are genuine and those that are symbolic? After all, many of the observable components of CSR (a CSR officer, code of conduct, CSR report, ethics training, etc.) ostensibly can look the same in both cases. When stakeholders see that "95% of consumer products [labels contain] at least one offense of 'greenwashing,'"[7] or that the firm's CEO has been fired for dishonesty,[8] or any number of other transgressions that create news every day, how can they tell whether the event is representative of a firm's business practices or the exception to the rule in an otherwise well-run organization? In general, should we assume that firms are *ethical* and that transgressions are rare, or that firms will try to get away with what they can unless restrained by vigilant stakeholders?

Take a look at this list of corporate values: Communication. Respect. Integrity. Excellence. They sound pretty good don't they? Strong, concise, meaningful. Maybe they even resemble your own company's values. . . . If so, you should be nervous. These are the corporate values of Enron, as stated in the company's 2000 annual report. And as events have shown, they're not meaningful; they're meaningless.[9]

At all levels, Enron's approach to CSR was ill-defined and superficially championed. But many of its flaws are present, to lesser extents, across all firms—an "obsession with profits and share prices, greed, lack of concern for others and a penchant for breaking legal rules."[10] What drives this kind of behavior, and how can this tendency in humans be countered? In general, the culture of the group is the aggregate of all the set of values held by the individuals who make up the group. As such, the ethics and morals of an organization start with the ethics and morals of the individual. Yet it is not clear how an individual's values, morals, and ethical standards translate to behavior in the workplace. Evidence suggests, for example, that many people who consider themselves to be ethical are also highly capable of unethical behavior: "As much as we would like to think that, put on the spot, we would do the right—and perhaps even heroic—thing, research has shown that that usually isn't true."[11] This applies particularly in the workplace:

> When we are busy focused on common organizational goals, like quarterly earnings or sales quotas, the ethical implications of important decisions can fade from our minds. Through the ethical fading, we end up engaging in or condoning behavior that we would condemn if we were consciously aware of it. The underlying psychology helps explain why ethical lapses in the corporate world seem so pervasive and intractable.[12]

This is important because students understand this and expect to be challenged by it throughout their careers: "Fifty-two percent of MBA students say they expect to have to make decisions [at work] that conflict with their values."[13] In response, the MBA Oath stands as a counterpoint to corporate wrongdoing and executive excess. It reflects the desire to channel the power of the market and business for good—"to foment social good and not just financial success. . . . to be a service to society."[14]

The MBA Oath

The MBA Oath was started in 2009 by a group of Harvard business school students who wanted to develop a professional oath similar to the Hippocratic Oath taken by medical professionals—"a voluntary pledge for graduating MBAs and current MBAs to 'create value responsibly and ethically.'" The Oath requires students to pledge the following:[15]

As a business leader I recognize my role in society.

- My purpose is to lead people and manage resources to create value that no single individual can create alone.
- My decisions affect the well-being of individuals inside and outside my enterprise, today and tomorrow.

Therefore, I promise that:

- I will manage my enterprise with loyalty and care, and will not advance my personal interests at the expense of my enterprise or society.
- I will understand and uphold, in letter and spirit, the laws and contracts governing my conduct and that of my enterprise.
- I will refrain from corruption, unfair competition, or business practices harmful to society.

- I will protect the human rights and dignity of all people affected by my enterprise, and I will oppose discrimination and exploitation.
- I will protect the right of future generations to advance their standard of living and enjoy a healthy planet.
- I will report the performance and risks of my enterprise accurately and honestly.
- I will invest in developing myself and others, helping the management profession continue to advance and create sustainable and inclusive prosperity.

In exercising my professional duties according to these principles, I recognize that my behavior must set an example of integrity, eliciting trust and esteem from those I serve. I will remain accountable to my peers and to society for my actions and for upholding these standards.

This oath I make freely, and upon my honor.

Companies need to understand the importance of a culture that is defined by a positive set of values. Such a culture will ultimately differentiate firms that are serious about optimizing value creation from those that adopt a narrower, short-term view of business. Increasingly, companies are being held to account by their stakeholders for all aspects of operations. Those that attempt to circumvent responsibility with superficial commitments to CSR therefore run the risk of exposure in our always-on, media-driven world. Different firms and different industries have different *CSR thresholds*, but firms that avoid crossing their threshold by adopting an effective CSR perspective stand a much better chance of long-term survival. Those firms that ignore their threshold, like Enron, eventually are held accountable for their actions. Those firms that embrace stakeholder relations and act with integrity via employees embedded in an organizational culture devoted to pro-social change, however, will be rewarded in the marketplace.

CREATING VALUE

Strategic CSR delivers an operational and strategic advantage to the firm. As such, it is central to the goal of value creation, which is the primary purpose of a firm's top management. Strategic CSR represents an enlightened approach to management that is a subtle tweak of our economic model, but with radical implications. In essence, strategic CSR retains the focus on adding value that is emphasized by a traditional bottom-line business model, but does so with a sensitivity to the needs and concerns of the firm's broad range of stakeholders. Equally important to implementing strategic CSR comprehensively, the focus of the firm has to be on optimizing value over the long term by acting in areas in which it has expertise (related to core operations).

Value Creation

The generation of a perceived benefit for an individual or group, as defined by that individual or group

This focus on long-term added value distributed across the firm's broad range of stakeholders is the principal difference between a traditional shareholder-focused business model and a strategic CSR model integrated throughout operations. This shift in perspective (from short to long term, from narrow to broad value creation) is relatively easy to envision, but much more difficult to implement firm-wide. Nevertheless, in a global, online business environment with stakeholders empowered to reward behavior they support and punish behavior they do not, strategic CSR offers the best approach to building a competitive advantage that is truly sustainable. Strategic CSR, therefore, is as simple (and as complex) as conducting all aspects of business operations in a responsible manner. It involves incorporating this perspective into the strategic planning processes of the firm in ways that optimize value.

Strategic CSR focuses on evolution, not revolution. It encapsulates the way humans behave and the way business is conducted. It does not alter the goals of the firm (profit, except to say that a short-term focus is counterproductive), and it does not alter our understanding of fundamental economic theory (actors pursuing their self-interest can optimize value, broadly defined). Instead, it alters the perspective from which operational and strategic decisions are made. For example, do a firm's managers believe they can optimize performance by paying employees a *minimum* wage (because there is sufficient unemployment that, if one person leaves, another can be hired), or do they believe performance can be optimized by paying employees a *living* wage (because it raises morale and productivity, while decreasing turnover and the costs associated with hiring replacement workers)? These two positions are substantively different approaches to business. Good arguments can be made in defense of either position, but they are fundamentally different and therefore represent a choice for managers. This is the arena in which strategic CSR operates. It is a progressive, enlightened approach to management that places the interests of a wide range of stakeholders within the firm's strategic decision matrix.[16]

The essential difference between those firms that do strategic CSR well and those that do it poorly, therefore, is a greater sensitivity to the needs and concerns of the firm's broad range of stakeholders. This provides the firm with an acute ability to understand when the (stakeholder-defined) rules that define the firm's operating environment have changed and a framework within which to apply that knowledge to the firm's strategic advantage. Those firms that can respond to (and, ideally, anticipate) change in a more genuine, authentic way will find the associated benefits are sustained because the effort is more effective and valued.

A short-term focus, driven by quarterly earnings guidance to investors with little long-term interest in the organization's survival, is of little concern (and is most likely detrimental) to firms committed to implementing strategic CSR. Similarly, while economic value and social value cover similar ground, the overlap is not perfect. Externalities and transgressions are the result. Values help fill the gap and aid the strategic CSR decision-making process.[17] To this end, the *CSR filter* is the tool the firm can use to apply its values within its strategic plan and day-to-day operations to identify both opportunities and problems before they arise. The result is that, rather than profit *maximization* with a short-term focus, profit *optimization* emphasizes the importance of meeting the needs of these stakeholders over the medium to long term.

Strategic CSR, therefore, refines the economic system in which capitalism drives social and economic progress. In short, strategic CSR equals value creation in today's complex and dynamic business environment—*sustainable* value creation. What does this mean in practice? Primarily, it means that those firms that "get" strategic CSR will be able to create more value over a longer period of time than those firms that either do not understand the strategic benefits of CSR for the firm or ignore it altogether. Firms best able to attain this level of performance do so by orienting themselves around a set of values—beliefs, practices, and norms that appeal to specific segments of society. In short, they implement a management philosophy that can be thought of as capitalism with a conscience.

Conscious Capitalism

The outcome of the implementation of strategic CSR, when extrapolated across a wide range of firms, is the *evolution*[18] of the dominant capitalist economic model. There is much to commend in the power of the market to alleviate human poverty and suffering. It is essential to remember, for example, that "the percentage of people in the world living on $1 a day has declined by 80 percent since the 1970s, adjusting for inflation. That's the greatest increase in human possibility in human history. The primary cause is globalized capitalism."[19] Strategic CSR seeks to build on this model. Rather than focus narrowly on short-term shareholder wealth, firms will exist to serve the needs and concerns of stakeholders, broadly defined, over the medium to long term—a combination of the *Most Ethical Companies*[20] and the *Most Inspiring Companies*.[21] The idea that most closely maps onto what this might look in practice is *conscious capitalism*.

> ### Conscious Capitalism
>
> An emerging economic system that "builds on the foundations of Capitalism—voluntary exchange, entrepreneurship, competition, freedom to trade and the rule of law. These are essential to a healthy functioning economy, as are other elements of Conscious Capitalism including trust, compassion, collaboration and value creation."[22]
>
> Synonymous with strategic CSR, it is based on four principles that encourage the development of values-based businesses: higher purpose, stakeholder interdependence, conscious leadership, and conscious culture.

John Mackey, founder and co-CEO of Whole Foods Market, is the leading business proponent of conscious capitalism.[23] In his view,[24] there are four main principles that define conscious capitalism: Higher Purpose ("Why does the business exist?"), Stakeholder Interdependence ("the six major stakeholders are interdependent and the business is managed . . . to optimize value creation for all of them"), Conscious Leadership ("the quality and commitment of the leadership at all levels of the organization"), and Conscious Culture ("This naturally evolves from the enterprise's commitments to higher purpose, stakeholder interdependence, and conscious leadership").[25] As such, conscious capitalism inhabits similar ground as strategic CSR. As Mackey reaffirms, "While there is nothing wrong with making money, indeed it is absolutely necessary for the enterprise to flourish; it is not by itself a very inspiring purpose for the enterprise."[26] Instead, he argues that firms exist to solve problems using capitalist principles:

> Conscious capitalism is not primarily about virtue or "doing good." . . . Ordinary business exchanges are inherently virtuous. Business creates value for all of its major stakeholders that are exchanging with it and these acts of value creation are "good." . . . I believe the argument can be successfully made that ordinary business exchanges aggregated collectively are the greatest creator of value in the entire world and that this value creation is the source of "business virtue."[27]

The goal is to build companies that are ethical and responsible—organizations that are profitable because they inspire the stakeholders with whom they interact:

> "Consumers are not only feeling inspired by certain businesses, but are acting inspired by spending more with these companies while evangelizing to others about their inspiring experience," says Terry Barber, chief inspiration officer for Performance Inspired. "We now see there is a validated set of drivers to inspiration and when these drivers are activated, it elevates employee engagement that shows up in the customer experience."[28]

Practice suggests that "companies that abide by the tenets of conscious capitalism have generated handsome returns for investors." An investor in Starbucks the day it went public (June 26, 1992), for example, would have received a return that "outperformed the S&P 500 by 1,944 percent" over the same time frame.[29] Similarly, "in recent years [Patagonia] has doubled the size of its operations and tripled its profitability." This has occurred in spite of the company launching a marketing campaign that "tells customers not to buy its clothes."[30]

Strategic CSR argues that success in today's globalized business environment is correlated highly with ethical, responsible, and inspiring behavior (to the extent that such behavior aligns with the collective values of the firm's stakeholders). Firms that respond to stakeholder needs and concerns in ways that win them over, and continue to win them over in an ongoing, virtuous cycle of positive exchange, will be the firms that define the 21st century. An important component of a conscious capitalist system, therefore, is businesses that reflect the system's core principles—in other words, values-based businesses.

VALUES-BASED BUSINESS

Values-based businesses view CSR as an "opportunity,"[31] rather than a *cost*. A genuine implementation of strategic CSR throughout operations lays the groundwork for the construction of such firms. Values-based businesses stand for something positive, something that both defines and unites the organization. Strategic CSR provides a road map to achieving this goal.

> **Values-Based Business**
>
> A for-profit firm that is founded on a vision and mission defined by a strategic CSR perspective

Values are important because they are shared beliefs that "drive an organization's culture and priorities and provide a framework in which decisions are made."[32] They therefore form the backbone of the firm. They are core to what the firm does and how it plans for the future. Based on principles similar to conscious capitalism, a values-based business seeks to build an organization that reflects its stakeholders' interests. In other words, a firm that merely layers CSR and ethics on top of business as usual in evaluating performance

> is a long way from the power of a genuinely values-led business. A genuine culture of values is based on a community of people that understand what is expected of them, what is seen to be right behaviour, and the responsibility they have to each other. As soon as you put money onto that, you remove the essence of what makes these values—and turn it simply into a group of individuals being personally rewarded to take actions that mimic those taken by those united by common values.[33]

As Peter Drucker noted, "profit for a company is like oxygen for a person. If you don't have enough of it, you're out of the game. But if you think your life is about breathing, you're really missing something." Throughout history, humans have sought a deeper meaning to life that financial success alone cannot provide.[34] That success has to reflect a sense of making a broader contribution in order to have meaning. Values-based businesses speak to these needs:

> With few exceptions . . . entrepreneurs who start successful businesses don't do so to maximize profits. Of course they want to make money, but that is not what drives most of them. They are inspired to do something that they believe needs doing. The heroic story of free-enterprise capitalism is one of entrepreneurs using their dreams and passion as fuel to create extraordinary value for [all stakeholders].[35]

In essence, a values-based business looks like Patagonia, whose goal is to "find new measures of success that do not depend on selling an ever increasing number of goods and services."[36] It is instructive to read about the business philosophy of founder Yvon Chouínard:

He vowed to create products durable enough and timeless enough that people could replace them less often, reducing waste. He put "The Footprint Chronicles" up on Patagonia's website, exhaustively cataloging the environmental damage done by his own company. He now takes responsibility for every item Patagonia has ever made—promising either to replace it if the customer is dissatisfied, repair it (for a reasonable fee), help resell it (Patagonia facilitates exchanges of used clothes on its website), or recycle it when at last it's no longer wearable.[37]

Zappos' Core Values[38]

As we grow as a company, it has become more and more important to explicitly define the core values from which we develop our culture, our brand, and our business strategies. These are the ten core values that we live by:

1. Deliver WOW Through Service

2. Embrace and Drive Change

3. Create Fun and A Little Weirdness

4. Be Adventurous, Creative, and Open-Minded

5. Pursue Growth and Learning

6. Build Open and Honest Relationships With Communication

7. Build a Positive Team and Family Spirit

8. Do More With Less

9. Be Passionate and Determined

10. Be Humble

The idea of businesses founded on values is not new. Adam Smith in the *Theory of Moral Sentiments*,[39] for example, "gave an account of morality resting on empathy and conscience" and, in the process, addressed the great challenge of "how to order a society in which competition and ethical sensibility are combined."[40] Increasingly, firms are adopting these aims and using them to reform the way they conduct business:

As Walmart grew into the world's largest retailer, its staff were subjected to a long list of dos and don'ts covering every aspect of their work. Now the firm has decided that its rules-based culture is too inflexible to cope with the challenges of globalisation and technological change, and is trying to instill a "values-based" culture, in which employees can be trusted to do the right thing because they know what the firm stands for.[41]

Unfortunately, values-based businesses remain rare. A survey conducted by the Boston Research Group aimed at learning more about the governance and leadership cultures inside firms, found that "only 3% fell into the category of 'self-governance,' in which everyone is guided by a 'set of core principles and values that inspire everyone to align around a company's mission.'"[42] Rectifying this paucity of values-based firms is central to reinvigorating public support for capitalism, which has suffered in recent years as a series of CSR transgressions have caused widespread economic harm.

Strategic CSR is about empowered stakeholders imposing their values on for-profit firms. While this occurs already via market forces, these forces alone are insufficient. Jeffrey Sachs speaks to this debate by critiquing Adam Smith's concept of the *invisible hand*. He suggests that, while the invisible hand works in principle, "the paradox of self-interest breaks down when stretched too far." More specifically, "successful capitalism has never rested on a moral base of self-interest, but rather on the practice of self-interest embedded within a larger set of values."[43] The idea that capitalism *succeeds* when it is embedded in a larger value system is central to strategic CSR. In other words, some form of individual restraint is crucial. In many societies, that value system is provided by religion. Without some form of civilizing restraint, as the 2007–2008 financial crisis reminds us, unfettered capitalism can degenerate into raw selfishness and deceit.

Joseph Nye of Harvard University addresses something similar when he talks about the CEO as the "tri-sector athlete"—a leader who is "good at private sector, public sector, social sector."[44] Such leaders are able to motivate the firm's stakeholders in terms that appeal across traditional dividing lines and draw on the multiple resources these stakeholders bring in order to collectively achieve the firm's goals. As such, the firm's employees are a core component of a values-based business. Firms such as Southwest Airlines[45] and Johnson & Johnson[46] understand this. They place valuing their employees, both intrinsically and extrinsically, at the heart of what the firm does and stands for, believing that satisfied

Figure 15.1   Strategic Decision Making in a Values-Based Business

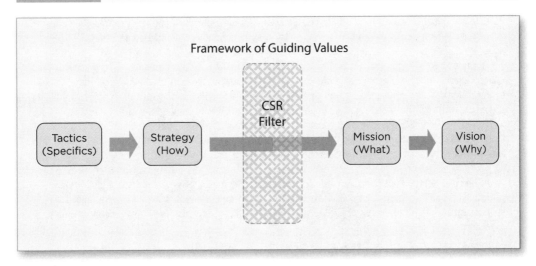

Framework of Guiding Values

CSR Filter

Tactics (Specifics) → Strategy (How) → Mission (What) → Vision (Why)

employees are the core to a successful business. As John Mackey puts it, "Happy team members results in happy customers, which results in happy investors."[47]

Figure 15.1 presents the strategic decision-making model for a values-based business. While the core strategy process remains the same (tactics inform the strategy, which serves to achieve the mission and vision), the *CSR filter* ensures that stakeholder concerns are placed at the heart of the decision-making process. Surrounding this core is a set of guiding values that define the organizational culture, structure its priorities, and provide employees with a framework that they can use in day-to-day operations. It is the decisions that employees make every day that, over time, reinforce the guiding values and redefine the firm—what it stands for, what actions it takes, and, ultimately, whether it fails or survives and prospers.[48]

The Dark Side of CSR?

The challenge of a values-based approach to CSR is apparent when a firm proudly announces support for values with which you disagree. *The Economist*[49] raises a good example of this and, in the process, summarizes an important critique of the CSR debate:

> Conservatives sceptical of the corporate social responsibility (CSR) movement have often charged that CSR is a stalking horse for liberal causes that have failed to get traction through ordinary political channels. This charge finds some support, I think, in the fact that few in the media seem to see Chick-fil-A's Christian-influenced culture and business practices as an example of CSR, though obviously it is. Doesn't the demand that corporations act responsibly in the interests of society, in ways other than profit-seeking, directly imply that corporate leaders who find same-sex marriage socially irresponsible should do something or other to discourage it?

> If we encourage a firm pledging to move to zero-waste manufacturing plants because the executives are concerned about climate change, then we must also support a firm acting to prevent the widespread acceptance of same-sex marriage. Both are issues with passionate advocates who believe the realization of their position will benefit society:

> CSR, when married to norms of ethical consumption, will inevitably incite bouts of culture-war strife. CSR with honest moral content . . . is a recipe for the politicisation of production and sales.

This textbook seeks to construct an economic argument for CSR, with a particular focus on operational relevance (applicable to the zero-waste example above; less obvious in terms of same-sex marriage). Central to this framework is the idea that a firm seeking to meet the needs and demands of its key stakeholders *should* advocate for the beliefs that are important to those stakeholders (whether or not those beliefs are supported by the majority). Assuming the action advocated is not illegal, individual values differ and, as long as there are sufficient numbers of people willing to demonstrate support for a position, then a firm can make an economic argument for advocating on behalf of that position:

> People can run their businesses according to whatever principles they prefer. It's just stupid business for owners and managers who want to sell their firm's goods and services to people who don't happen to share their morals or politics, especially in cultures in which consumers are increasingly expected to vote with their wallets.

In other words, the only danger for Chick-fil-A is that it is on the wrong side of a fast-moving social issue. Given the number of people who showed up at the firm's restaurants to support a *buycott*, however, it is clear that the company has stakeholder support today:

Matters of moral truth aside, what's the difference between buying a little social justice with your coffee and buying a little Christian traditionalism with your chicken?

Unless we allow firms equally to support all issues that are important to their key stakeholders, we are being hypocritical. Chick-fil-A's position is consistent with prior positions the firm has adopted and is important to many of the firm's customers. As such, from a strategic CSR perspective, Chick-fil-A is a values-based business.

Although managers increasingly understand the benefits of orienting their firm to a core set of values, the task is harder if they seek to do so too late. If a change in values orientation comes in response to a transgression by a firm or industry, stakeholders may dismiss the effort as superficial. In such cases, attempts to instill a values-based culture face a higher hurdle for success. As such, in the aftermath of the 2012 LIBOR interest rate–fixing scandal (in which traders from a number of banks manipulated rates for personal gain),[50] Barclays' CEO Antony Jenkins told employees:

They should uphold the company's new values or leave. . . . [He] said bonuses will now be based in part on how employees and business units uphold five values [respect, integrity, service, excellence and stewardship], rather than "just on what we deliver. . . .

"We must never again be in a position of rewarding people for making the bank money in a way which is unethical or inconsistent with our values. . . .

"There might be some who don't feel they can fully buy in to an approach which so squarely links performance to the upholding of our values. . . .

"My message to those people is simple: Barclays is not the place for you. The rules have changed."[51]

Of course, the extent to which the company is serious about this will only reveal itself over time. But as an indication of genuine intent, it is essential to know how Barclays will measure adherence to these values and how performance evaluation will translate into individual compensation.

The true test of any organizational culture, of course, is the firm's reaction in the face of adversity or criticism. One company that has proved to hold a genuine commitment to its core values is Starbucks, which in 2008 had to be rescued by its founder, Howard Schultz:

Our stock was in free fall. One day, I found myself on a phone call with one large institutional shareholder. He addressed the longstanding health coverage for our employees, which at the time cost $250 million. He said this would be the perfect time for Starbucks and me to cut health care. . . . I tried to describe to him that the essence of the brand is humanity, and our culture is steeped in two primary benefits that have defined who we are: comprehensive health-insurance coverage for our people and equity in the form of stock options, which we give to anyone who works more than 20 hours a week. I told him, "This is a nonstarter at every level because you don't understand the essence of our company. After all these years, if you believe the financial crisis should change our principles and core purpose, perhaps you should sell your stock. I'm not building a stock. I'm trying to build a great, enduring company." We are a performance-driven organization, but we have to lead the company through the lens of humanity.[52]

Ben & Jerry's

Another good example of a values-based business is Ben & Jerry's, which opened its first shop in Vermont in 1981 and went public in 1984.[53] In building Ben & Jerry's into a global brand, cofounders Ben Cohen and Jerry Greenfield set out to redefine the concept of a concerned and responsive employer. An important step in this process was codifying the firm's founding principles in its groundbreaking *Social & Environmental Assessment Report*—first commissioned in 1989. Ben & Jerry's was the first major corporation to allow an independent social audit of its business operations:

> This social auditor recommended that the report be called a "Stakeholders Report" (the concept of stakeholders existed but this was possibly the first-ever report to stakeholders) and that it be divided into the major stakeholder categories: Communities, . . . Employees, Customers, Suppliers, Investors. . . . B&J continued to issue annual social reports, rotating to different social auditors as they sought to develop the concept.[54]

Ben & Jerry's has continued to develop the concept of a firm that places its stakeholder concerns at the core of its business model, a stance that is reflected in its mission statement.

Ben & Jerry's Mission Statement[55]

Ben & Jerry's operates on a three-part mission that aims to create linked prosperity for everyone that's connected to our business: suppliers, employees, farmers, franchisees, customers, and neighbors alike:

Our Product Mission drives us to make fantastic ice cream—for its own sake.

Our Economic Mission asks us to manage our Company for sustainable financial growth.

Our Social Mission compels us to use our Company in innovative ways to make the world a better place.

A core principle for the company was embedded in its compensation policy. Specifically, no employee could earn more than seven times the salary of the lowest paid worker.[56] Similarly, other aspects of working for Ben & Jerry's, such as its benefits (e.g., on-site day care) and "no-layoff policy," ensured the commitment and loyalty of the firm's employees:

> If a position required revamping or removal, the employee holding the position would be transferred to another position, with attention given to matching responsibilities and qualifications.[57]

As Ben & Jerry's became more successful, it began to attract the attention of other firms. As people began to worry about the prospect of a merger or acquisition, calls increased to protect the firm's independence and its stakeholder-centric approach to business. The Vermont State government responded by passing legislation "allowing a company's directors to reject a bid if 'they deem it to be not in the best interests of employees, suppliers, and the economy of the state.'"[58] In Vermont, the law became known as the "Ben & Jerry's law," which gave any firm's directors the legal protection to reject a takeover offer "based on the best interests of the State of Vermont," even when that company "was offered a financial premium in a buyout situation."[59]

In spite of this legislation, Ben & Jerry's board agreed to a $326 million takeover by the corporate giant Unilever in August 2000,[60] although this occurred only after Unilever made significant concessions designed to protect Ben & Jerry's unique approach to business:

> It agreed to let Ben & Jerry's continue as a Vermont-chartered corporation, with Unilever as its sole shareholder. This allows Ben & Jerry's to retain an independent board of directors, and nine of that board's 11 members are appointed without any input from Unilever. This independent board exists in perpetuity . . . and has the primary responsibility for "preserving and enhancing the objectives of the historical social mission of the company as they may evolve." . . . Unilever has primary responsibility for the financial and operational aspects of the business. So Unilever does own Ben & Jerry's, but it does not completely control it.[61]

As such, although the takeover resulted in a short-term hit to the firm's cult status among activists (e.g., *Business Ethics* dropped Ben & Jerry's from its list of 100 Best Corporate Citizens in 2001, and the top-to-bottom compensation ratio, including benefits and bonuses, jumped to an average of 16:1 by 2001),[62] today the firm's managers continue to reaffirm a strong activist message while claiming to run Ben & Jerry's by "leading with Progressive Values across our business."[63] In addition, the following message is relayed by Ben & Jerry's CEO to visitors at "the world-famous Ben & Jerry's ice-cream factory" in Vermont:

> Our commitment to social and economic justice and the environment is as important to us as profitability. It's our heritage. . . . This isn't a short-term strategy to drive up sales. These are issues that are important for our society to address.[64]

Still, the suspicion remains that things have changed and the firm's commitment to its cofounders' original values is not as strong as it once was. This accusation is voiced by critics who say that the firm's activist message has become "just a slick Madison Avenue advertising gimmick to hike profits." [65] But, this position is becoming harder to defend as Unilever emerges as one of the most progressive voices in the CSR debate. For example, Ben & Jerry's still prominently claims, "We have a progressive, nonpartisan Social Mission that seeks to meet human needs and eliminate injustices in our local, national and international communities."[66] The firm's commitment to social justice and progressive politics appears as strong as ever:

> Capitalism and the wealth it produces do not create opportunity for everyone equally. . . . We strive to create economic opportunities for those who have been denied them and to advance new models of economic justice that are sustainable and replicable. . . .
> We strive to minimize our negative impact on the environment. . . .
> We seek and support nonviolent ways to achieve peace and justice. We believe government resources are more productively used in meeting human needs than in building and maintaining weapons systems. . . .
> We strive to show a deep respect for human beings inside and outside our company and for the communities in which they live.[67]

While today Ben & Jerry's is clearly a subsidiary of a large corporation (e.g., the emphasis immediately after the acquisition was on Ben & Jerry's being "Unilever legal"),[68] it has benefitted from the discipline Unilever has brought. Moreover, there is growing evidence to suggest that the influence is not all one way and that Unilever has also learned some lessons from Ben & Jerry's. For example, "Ben & Jerry's was the first ice-cream company in the world to use Fairtrade-certified ingredients in 2005; Unilever has a broader target of sourcing all agricultural raw materials sustainably by 2020."[69] In addition,

> the company supports marriage equality and campaign finance reform. And [in 2015] it introduced a flavor, Save Our Swirled, intended to raise awareness about climate change. The label is illustrated with cows perched atop melting icebergs, and Ben & Jerry's is urging customers to lobby government leaders to embrace clean-energy standards.[70]

Today, as part of Unilever's efforts to push the boundaries in relation to CSR,[71] it sees the value in allowing Ben & Jerry's to retain its broad stakeholder-focused, values-based business model. This is evident in Ben Cohen's involvement with the financing of Occupy Wall Street[72] and when the firm "decided to celebrate the legalization of gay marriage in the US by rechristening its Chubby Hubby ice-cream Hubby Hubby in 2009."[73] It was also evident in 2012 when Ben & Jerry's announced it had become B Corp certified:

> A quarter-century after pioneering the socially responsible business movement, Ben & Jerry's is throwing its support behind the growing B Corporation (B Corp) movement. . . . Ben & Jerry's is the first wholly-owned subsidiary to gain B Corp certification. The move was supported by Unilever . . . as consistent with Ben & Jerry's core values and mission and fully aligned with Unilever's own ambitious sustainability agenda.[74]

For Unilever and Ben & Jerry's, basing their operating principles on a strategic CSR perspective is proving to be central to their ability to survive and thrive in business today.

STRATEGIC CSR IS GOOD BUSINESS

Strategic CSR is good for the firm—*good* in that it is effective business, but *good* also in that it is ethical, moral, and values based. Strategic CSR creates value for the firm's broad range of stakeholders in a way that is sustainable.

As Howard Schultz notes, the business case for Starbucks operating along a set of clearly defined, well-advertised principles is clear, both internally ("We have successfully linked the percent of store partners in a given store who think we're living up to our values to the performance of that store") and externally ("Starbucks has found that more than a quarter of the public opinion of its brand is based not on its store experience or its coffee products, but on what customers think of Starbucks as an institution"):

> This is not altruistic; this is business. Values are a big part of both the balance sheet and the income statements of Starbucks—it's behind the performance. . . . You can't attract and retain great people if your sole purpose is to make money because people, especially young people, want a sense of belonging—to be part of an organization they really believe is doing great work.[75]

Stakeholders have always shaped the rules by which businesses operate, consciously or otherwise, and they will continue to do so. The questions that are essential for any manager to ask, therefore, are *What are the rules today?* and *What are they likely to be tomorrow?* The rules are always changing, but the aggregate effect of millions of people making millions of decisions every day determines the overall environment in which firms must act.

Corporations cannot force consumers to buy their products, as long as consumers are willing to make their purchase decisions based on something other than convenience or the lowest price. Similarly, corporations cannot prevent the enactment of legislation, as long as politicians are willing to prioritize governing over campaign contributions and lobbying pressures. And corporations cannot force employees to work for abusive pay levels, as long as workers ensure they have the skill set to demand higher pay and better conditions. Each of these decisions is a values-based judgment made by one of the firm's stakeholders. Managers, therefore, need to understand the values that underpin these decisions at any given point in time because they have operational consequences for the firm. Those managers who understand the rules most completely are best placed to help their firm succeed by aligning the firm's actions with the underlying values of its stakeholders.

While we can define and discuss CSR at an objective, idealistic level, it is more helpful to do so at a subjective, realistic level. If we talk about the social responsibility of a particular firm, for example, that literally means behavior that is deemed by society to be responsible. In other words, what is *responsible* is defined by the firm's stakeholders (society in the aggregate). So as long as the firm defines it stakeholders broadly and acts on their concerns, by definition it is being *socially responsible*. Of course, there are problems of interpretation, prioritization, and conflicting interests (as discussed in Chapter 4), but as long as the firm seeks to create value for its broad range of stakeholders, it will be meeting societal expectations. To understand whether the firm is doing this and as a way of implementing CSR, a firm instead should think in terms of *value creation*. Not only does this concept operationalize CSR in a way that is useful, but it also brings CSR to the center of everything the firm does. If CEOs set out to do anything every day, it is to create value. If strategic CSR equals value creation, then it immediately becomes central to the CEO's job.

In seeking to redefine the CSR debate, this textbook argues that how business is conducted matters. Rather than obsess about what the firm does (generate profits), strategic CSR focuses instead on how the firm does it. In other words, framing the argument is key, and policies or practices that lower costs and/or raise revenues over the medium to long term are of primary importance. In order to illustrate this, let's return to the debate between paying a living wage and a minimum wage: Does a firm pay its employees a living wage because it feels that they deserve something better, or does it pay them a living wage because it understands that the investment raises morale and loyalty, raises productivity, and decreases the recruitment and training costs that are associated with higher turnover? As Paul Polman, CEO of Unilever, frames it:

> To pay a textile worker in Pakistan 11 cents an hour doesn't make good business sense. . . . [Before I became CEO,] we had a lot of contingent labour or we outsourced it and we looked at that as a cost item but we had a tremendous amount of turnover. Now we pay more and we have greater loyalty, more energy and higher productivity.[76]

To be sure, the philosophy of strategic CSR is demanding. It requires stakeholders to act in order to shape society in their collective interests. It also requires firms to respond to these demands and, where possible, to anticipate them. But again, as long as stakeholders are willing to enforce their values and beliefs, conforming to those expectations is in the firm's economic self-interest. Strategic CSR is not a passive philosophy; therefore, it is proactive. The result is a society that is actively *shaped*, rather than one that passively *forms*. If stakeholders are motivated to change the rules in a way that promotes value, broadly defined, then for-profit firms are the best means we have of interpreting those new standards: They will respond more rapidly and efficiently than any other organizational form in any other economic system.

Strategic CSR Debate

MOTION: Business is a moral endeavor.

QUESTIONS FOR DISCUSSION AND REVIEW

1.   What makes one person more or less ethical than another? Where does that component of an individual's character come from?

2.   What does it mean for an organization to be *ethical?* What is the difference between an *unethical* and an *illegal* act?

3.   In your view, what does a values-based business look like? Think of an example that you have seen or read in the news: What do you think would be different about working for a firm like that?

4.   Look at Ben & Jerry's values (http://www.benjerry.com/values/). What do you think about the company's *Product Mission, Economic Mission,* and *Social Mission?* What about the social causes the firm adopts? Does this information make you more or less likely to buy the company's ice cream? Is this what a for-profit company should be doing?

5.   Watch this video: https://www.youtube.com/watch?v=EseNAh9UwjI. Do you agree that business is "a moral endeavor"?

Part V Case Study

EMPLOYEES

Employees are an important stakeholder of the firm.[1] To the extent that managers foster the loyalty of its workforce, the firm benefits. Employees are motivated to work for values-based businesses, a drive that translates into the quality of work that is produced:

> CSR programs provide a competitive advantage in workforce recruitment. . . . [Survey results report] that 82% of American workers said they would be willing to be paid less to work for a company with ethical business practices than receive higher pay at a company with questionable ethics.[2]

The idea that a "purpose-driven business can be profitable"[3] is no more evident than in the case of Unilever. As its CEO, Paul Polman, explained in an article laying out his vision of the for-profit corporation, a large reason for Unilever's success lies with the firm's employees:

> Business is here to serve society. . . . Business simply can't be a bystander in a system that gives it life in the first place. . . . That's very motivational for our employees. . . . Our employee engagement and motivation have gone up enormously over the past four or five years. People are proud to work on something where they actually make a difference in life, and that is obviously the hallmark of a purpose-driven business model. We're getting more energy out of the organization, and that willingness to go the extra mile often makes the difference between a good company and a great one.[4]

Herb Kelleher, founder of Southwest Airlines, is similarly a strong proponent of his firm's employees:

> If the employees come first, then they're happy. . . . A motivated employee treats the customer well. The customer is happy so they keep coming back, which pleases the shareholders. It's not one of the enduring great mysteries of all time, it is just the way it works. . . .

344

The core of our success. That's the most difficult thing for a competitor to imitate. They can buy all the physical things. The things you can't buy are dedication, devotion, loyalty—the feeling that you are participating in a crusade.[5]

The Benefits of Motivated and Loyal Employees

There are many benefits for companies that ensure their employees remain happy and healthy at work.

- Employee retention reduces turnover costs—advertising, training, and lost productivity as the new staff gain experience in their positions:

  Workers are six times more likely to stay in their jobs when they believe their company acts with integrity.... But when workers mistrust their bosses' decisions and feel ashamed of their firm's behavior, four out of five workers feel trapped at work and say they are likely to leave their jobs soon.[6]

- Employee safety leads to reduced amounts of lost time and productivity:

  [Intel's] CEO Craig Barrett insists he be sent an e-mail report within 24 hours any time one of his firm's 80,000 employees loses a single day of work to injury.... Intel's worldwide injury rate was just .27 injuries per 100 employees, compared to an industry average of 6.7.[7]

- Happy employees are productive and creative:

  [At 3M,] workers are actually pushed to take regular breaks, as time away from a problem can help spark a moment of insight.... The company also encourages its employees to take risks, not only by spending masses on research (nearly 8% of gross revenue), but also by expecting workers to spend around 15% of their time pursuing speculative ideas. Most of these efforts will fail, but some, such as masking tape, an early 3M concept, will generate real profit for the company.[8]

The opposite effect, of course, occurs when employees are disenchanted and demotivated. "Gallup estimates that actively disengaged employees cost more than $300 billion in lost productivity."[9] One likely reason is that, while good people management is essential to the success of an organization, it is something most organizations do not take seriously:

Peter Drucker once observed that, "Much of what we call management consists of making it difficult for people to work." . . . The most valuable resource that many companies have is the time of their employees. And yet they are typically far less professional about managing that time than they are at managing their financial assets.[10]

It seems clear that unmotivated or otherwise alienated employees "can wreak more damage on a company than competitors." In spite of this, many companies fail at a fundamental level to treat their employees with respect:

According to a recent survey by Accenture, a consultancy, 31% of employees don't like their boss, 32% were actively looking for a new job, and 43% felt that they received no recognition for their work. The biggest problem with trying to do more with less is that you can end up turning your . . . biggest resources into your biggest liabilities.[11]

To the extent that a firm treats its employees as a cost, something to be managed and minimized wherever possible (as encouraged by modern accounting convention), employees are likely to feel the organization deserves neither their loyalty nor 100% of their effort. To the extent that employees are valued by management and identified as the key to customer satisfaction (and, therefore, the organization's success), employees are likely to be more engaged, productive, and loyal. Unfortunately, it appears that companies are better at engendering the first reaction among their employees than the second one, so much so that "each year, the average company loses anywhere from 20% to 50% of its employee base."[12]

In failing to motivate their employees, corporations are undervaluing one of their key resources—the people who enact the firm's strategy and interact with customers on a day-to-day basis. Senior executives like to think of themselves as central to the firm's success, but the best strategy in the world is useless unless it is implemented by engaged and creative employees. When critics ask for a "bottom-line" benefit a firm can realize by implementing a comprehensive CSR perspective, employees are one of the most rewarding places to look. Creating a positive and inclusive workplace culture takes effort, but the return on investment tends to offset any corresponding risk. This is especially true of employee volunteer programs.

Timberland

In terms of loyalty and retention, volunteer programs offer a particularly effective way to invigorate employees. Such programs expose employees to a new environment away from their everyday position, allowing them to feel pride in their company and its standing within the community while also leading to the development of new skills. The value of these programs, especially when adopted by multinational firms, can be significant.

Employee Volunteer Programs

Increasingly, firms are recognizing the benefits of employee volunteer programs and are prepared to dedicate increasing amounts of resources to ensure the programs' success:

- **Bain & Co.**—"In 2012 and 2013 we volunteered 49,000 hours—over five person-years—and we helped more than 200 organizations."[13]
- **Pfizer**—"250,000 service projects per year, 30 different countries, 30 million hours of service a year, $635 million annual value of volunteer hours."[14]
- **Wells Fargo**—"In 2014, 64,350 team members volunteered a record 1.74 million hours, a 3% increase over 2013."[15]

One of the most celebrated employee volunteer programs is run by Timberland.[16] The program, inspired by company CEO Jeffrey Swartz, was launched in 1992.[17] Swartz saw the power the company possessed to evoke social change and had the foresight to see the potential benefits this activism would bring. He also saw Timberland's employees as central to that success. The firm's Path of Service[18] volunteer program was the result:

> The program has continued for almost 20 years, challenging all Timberland employees to invest of themselves with 40 hours of paid leave each year for community service during the workweek. Service sabbaticals, which provide up to six months of paid time leave for employees to serve in capacity building roles in social justice organizations is another evolution of the Path of Service™ program. Path of Service helped demonstrate that for-profit business can harness the instinct of its employees to do real good, without compromising the business mission.[19]

In response to a survey conducted by Timberland to learn more about the reception of the plan among employees, "79 percent of employees agree with the statement: 'Timberland's commitment to community is genuine and not a public relations vehicle.'" In addition, the survey "reveals that 89 percent of employees say community service is valuable to them, while 50 percent report that Timberland's volunteer programs influenced their decision to work for the company."[20]

Another company that has created an innovative volunteer program is Accenture:

> Hundreds [of employees] applied, and those accepted now must wait weeks or months for an assignment. The program makes Accenture "more attractive as an employer," says Jill Smart, senior managing director of human resources.[21]

Moreover, Accenture does not expect the program to cost it any money. The firm is essentially running a social enterprise start-up that is designed to "break even financially. The company contributes, the employees contribute (via a cut in pay when they are doing it) and the client will pay a fee—although it is a fraction of the market cost."[22] In return, Accenture benefits from greater employee loyalty, additional employee training, and improved relations with its community stakeholders.

THE GIG ECONOMY

The benefits of employee volunteer programs suggest strongly that the success of the firm and the well-being of its employees are highly correlated. To put this another way, it is very difficult to think of a successful firm that does not have the day-to-day support of its employees, who contribute the creativity and energy that constitutes the firm's value-creating activities. In spite of this, it is not clear that firms always value their employees as central to their success. In the UK, for example, CEOs now earn 183 times the average employee's wage;[23]

in the United States, the ratio is closer to 330:1, while CEOs in industries such as fast-food "make 1,000 times the pay of the average fast-food worker."[24] To put that in perspective,

> America's highest-paid CEO [in 2013], John Hammergren of McKesson Corp., received compensation of over $131 million. That is the equivalent of about $63,000 per hour, or $10,000 more than the annual median household income in the United States. Meanwhile, some of this country's lowest-paid workers—those on minimum wage—made just $15,080 annually at $7.25 per hour. Mr. Hammergren had surpassed that amount by 9:15a.m. on his first workday of the year.[25]

One of the criticisms of unfettered capitalism is that, in spite of its efficiencies and creativity, "what it's not good at is distributing the fruits, because the logic in the boardroom . . . is always cut your labor costs to improve your quarterly [numbers] and your profit margins for shareholder value."[26] Employees, in particular, are sometimes treated as a means to an end, rather than being valued as a partner in the process:

> Layoffs. Downsizing. Rightsizing. Job cuts. Separations. Terminations. Workforce reductions. Off-shoring. Outsourcing. Whatever the term, getting rid of employees can be a necessary and beneficial strategic move for companies to make.[27]

The effort to minimize the costs of production is a legitimate business strategy. But corporations must also come to terms with the fact that the employees whose wages they squeeze can also be the customers on whom they rely for sales, "So when you [sack] them . . . you slowly lose the purchasing power to empty inventories and long-term savings in the form of institutional pension funds to invest in the stocks and bonds of these companies."[28] Firms should also consider the implications of cutting jobs for their reputation, as well as the damage layoffs do to morale of the remaining employees and any effects that has on future productivity. In particular, the wages a firm pays are a strong indicator of the extent to which it values its employees.

Henry Ford[29]

Nearly a century ago, Henry Ford drew no distinction between his employees and his customers. Challenging the conventional wisdom that the best way to maximize profits was to tailor your product to the wealthiest segment of society, Ford decided to market his black Model T as the car for "America's Everyman":

> For Ford, mass production went hand in hand with mass consumption. His benchmark for worker compensation was whether his own workers could afford to buy the product they were making. He offered a $5-a-day minimum wage for *all* his workers (crashing through the race barriers of the day)—twice the prevailing automobile industry average.

In doing so, Ford created a *virtuous circle*. Workers flocked to his factory to apply for positions. If they managed to secure one of Ford's coveted jobs, then in time they too would be able to afford one of his cars. The company flourished based on the twin pillars of a desirable product and a highly motivated employee base. "By the time production ceased for the Model T in 1927, more than 15 million cars had been sold—or half the world's output."

The value of employees to the firm speaks to the evolving nature of work in a globalizing world. In essence, "What does it mean to be an employee in modern [society], with its extensive use of contractors and franchisees, and armies of temporary workers?"[30] The disenchantment of increasing numbers of Millennials with a *traditional* career has sparked the rise of the *gig economy* (or *sharing economy*), where firms like TaskRabbit (https://www.taskrabbit.com/), Amazon's Mechanical Turk (https://www.mturk.com/), Uber (https://www.uber.com/), and Airbnb (https://www.airbnb.com/) assign short-term tasks (gigs) that allow those supplying the labor to work when and where they wish to.[31] While the short-term attraction of this flexibility is apparent, it is unclear whether such positions are in the long-term interests of the individuals themselves. In essence, what does it mean for workers to participate in this new economy? What protections do they have? What protections should they have?[32] As long as they are voluntarily participating, do companies have an obligation to look out for them? Are they *employees* with rights and benefits, or are they *contractors* with only an arm's-length relationship to the firm?[33] What about the self-interest of firms—will those that safeguard the interests of these gig employees perform more effectively than those that do not?

This issue of vulnerability is heightened when we realize that "47% of today's jobs could be automated in the next two decades."[34] The consequences of this trend to substitute technology for labor will likely be profound: "The question is whether we are equipped to deal with the possibility that in future, there will be people who—despite being willing and fit to work—have no economic value as employees."[35] The contrary position is that reactionary fears have always been raised whenever revolutionary technology is invented but, in reality, new technology has always created more jobs than it has destroyed:

Be wary of those who lament the demise of jobs for checkout clerks and meter readers, as if preserving such jobs will lead to a healthier economy. This Luddite fallacy is based on a presumption that there is only a set amount of goods and services people want. If technology permits those things to be produced more efficiently, Luddites argue, there will be less work to do. In reality, technology leads to an increase in productivity and wealth. That in turn leads to increased demand for goods and services and thus more jobs, including ones in fields we can barely imagine.[36]

In a number of ways, the relationship between firms and their employees is evolving. As well as shifting patterns of work, there are threats from machines as firms are increasingly using automation and computation to replace the

Figure V.1   The Threat to Work From Automation

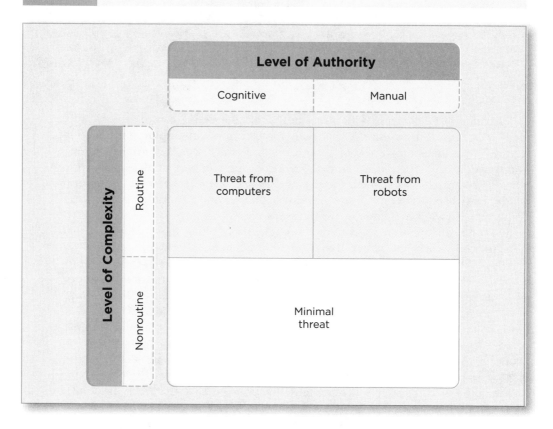

efforts of individual workers. As indicated by Figure V.1, in determining the extent of that threat, what matters is not whether the work is white-collar or blue-collar (cognitive or manual) but whether it is routine or nonroutine. While the increasing prevalence of machines in the workplace has, to date, primarily affected blue-collar workers performing repetitive manual work, as computers begin to acquire *artificial intelligence*, white-collar workers are also finding their work can be done more efficiently by computers:

> It is occupations in administration and middle management, which involve cognitive but routine tasks, that have been the most vulnerable to automation so far. By contrast, employees whose work is cognitive but not routine have largely gained from technological change. . . . Likewise, many forms of manual employment have proved difficult to computerise, and have thus been largely unaffected. This explains a pattern that has become common in the labour markets of advanced economies in recent decades, whereby there has been growth in employment at both the top and the bottom of the spectrum but a hollowing-out in the middle.[37]

This pattern will continue to evolve, however, as artificial intelligence progresses to the point where computers can tackle more intuitive tasks via extreme processing power and the elimination of all possible alternatives until only the *best* option remains. IBM's progress, initially with Deep Blue's[38] ability to master chess and more recently with Watson's[39] ability to master *Jeopardy!*, hints at the advances still to come.

From the firm's perspective, understanding this evolving situation and ensuring employees feel valued will increasingly be a source of competitive advantage. A strategic CSR perspective argues that employees should be treated as an *asset* rather than as a *cost*. In this view, employees, as with any asset, will grow and improve with investment, making a strong business case for placing employees at the core of the firm's mission. This approach has been adopted by firms such as Costco, the membership-based warehouse-style retailer, whose CFO states:

> From day one, we've run the company with the philosophy that if we pay better than average, provide a salary people can live on, have a positive environment and good benefits, we'll be able to hire better people, they'll stay longer and be more efficient.[40]

A number of other firms share Costco's willingness to invest in their employees, believing that the motivation and loyalty such policies generate outweigh the potential cost savings gained by lower wages. A step beyond a more equal sharing of the firm's resources, however, is to institutionalize employees' privileged status. Such companies demonstrate that truly valuing employees extends beyond compensation to ownership.

EMPLOYEE-CENTERED FIRMS

To ensure greater investment among employees, it is intuitive that they should feel *ownership* of the enterprise. While this is true conceptually, there is also a strong argument for making it true in reality. Firms can begin to do this via employee share-ownership schemes, such as Starbucks' Bean Stock program.[41] The principle of valuing employees in this way has a long history in the United States,[42] stretching back to George Washington's efforts "to rebuild New England's cod industry after the war of independence."[43] Moreover, it is widely practiced today:

> The National Center for Employee Ownership (NCEO) estimates that around 28 million employees—about 20% of America's non-governmental workforce—participate in some kind of employee stock ownership program. This figure includes roughly 9 million people who receive some portion of their pay in equity as well as folks who buy stock through employee-only deals or whose employers match retirement savings with company stock.[44]

The logic behind such schemes is that share ownership increases the likelihood employees will feel more committed to the firm and more motivated at work. Evidence suggests that such companies see notable improvements in job motivation and satisfaction:

> Companies that spread ownership throughout a large portion of their workforce, through any form . . . deliver total shareholder returns that are two percentage points higher than at similar companies. . . . Better stock performance isn't the only benefit. Companies with significant employee ownership do better on a wide range of performance metrics, including productivity, profit margins, and return on equity, according to the studies.[45]

Beyond encouraging share ownership (something any listed company can do), an extension of this idea is to place the actual ownership of the firm in the hands of its employees.

John Lewis

There are a number of arguments in favor of and against employee-owned firms. A particularly well-known example in the UK is John Lewis, a department store that was founded in the early 1900s but became employee owned after the founder's death in 1928:[46]

> Its ownership structure dates back to 1929, when John Spedan Lewis, son of the founder, set up a profit-sharing scheme that became the John Lewis Partnership; a second settlement, made in 1950, transferred all his remaining shares into the partnership. John Lewis now has more than [81,000] employees, who are known as partners, and the success of the company is widely attributed to their loyalty and commitment.[47]

Employee ownership represents an alternative form of for-profit organization that reprioritizes the firm's goals along the lines of a social enterprise. Ownership can come in many forms, such as "cooperatives, employee-owned firms, social enterprises, and community land trusts," with proponents arguing that these alternatives are a fundamental reform of capitalism ("a permanent shift in the underlying architecture of economic power").[48] Equally important, they are scalable to a level where meaningful change can be realized:

> Consider, for example, the John Lewis Partnership (JLP) [which is] the largest department store chain in the country, with 35 department stores and 272 Waitrose grocery stores. Revenues of this company are more than $11.5 billion. If placed into the Fortune 500 list of the largest U.S. corporations, JLP would settle in around 212—a little higher than Starbucks. It's 100 percent owned by its employees.[49]

In other words, employees feel invested *in* the company because they *are* the company. Reflecting this, John Lewis's constitution states that "the purpose of the group is to ensure 'the happiness of all its members, through their worthwhile and satisfying employment in a successful business'":[50]

> The John Lewis Partnership is built around the value of fairness. . . . Each year, after the firm sets aside a portion of profits for reinvestment in the business, the remainder—generally between 40 and 60 percent of profit—is distributed to employees. . . . Employees in this firm are not a countervailing power. They're not legally outside the firm, negotiating with it. They are the firm.[51]

The result is a firm that feels different yet performs as well, if not better, than its competitors:[52]

> The mood in [John Lewis] stores is markedly different from any other company. The staff are more attentive and professional. They own the place and it shows. . . . John Lewis was recently named Britain's favourite retailer for the third year in succession. . . . Its Christmas sales outstripped those of its rivals and Waitrose, its food arm, was the fastest-growing retailer.[53]

Although there are many components to employee satisfaction, rate of pay is one of the most important and contentious. At Whole Foods Market, for example, a firm that is consistently ranked as one of Fortune's "100 Best Companies to Work For,"[54] "the pay of every employee is known, and even senior executives receive no more than 19 times the average wage."[55] At John Lewis, the pay differential is larger, but there is still a defined ratio that limits the disparity between senior executives and junior employees:

> [The founder's son] Spedan Lewis ensured that all staff would benefit from an annual share of profits, and that pay would be regulated according to a ratio. The highest paid staff member cannot earn more than 75 times the average wage of the shop-floor salesperson.[56]

In spite of the many advantages of this organizational structure, its long history, and its favored status as "a more caring, cuddly capitalism," adoption has remained relatively narrow. This is because there are also perceived barriers to application, primary among which is that employee-ownership is no guarantee of success—"It does not prevent bad decisions: having a quarter of shares in employees' hands did not save Lehman Brothers from bankruptcy."[57] Others feel employee-owned firms are less likely to fire someone for poor performance, which "can entrench bad management and undermine a company's long-term competitiveness."[58]

Perhaps more importantly, this ownership structure poses risks to employees. While their job security is higher, a concentrated investment in their own firm can leave them exposed to shifts in the firm's share price. In the case of Enron, where employee stock options were widely used to motivate employees, for example, "many employees lost everything when [the firm] collapsed."[59] Ultimately, these disadvantages may outweigh any advantages:

> Companies that are wholly-owned by their staff may face barriers to growth. Many firms need a flexible capital base to expand—one reason the partnership model in banking declined. Employee mobility promotes innovation. At base, it is unrealistic to expect many bastions of capitalism to turn their shares over to their workforce.[60]

Similar ownership forms have been explored in other countries, such as the United States, and employee protection has long been an important part of the economies of countries such as Germany and Japan. The hybrid forms of employee ownership that are most prominent in these countries, however, still face limitations in comparison to full employee ownership:[61]

> In the US, many companies have Employee Share Ownership Plans (ESOPs) and in a few cases the ESOP controls a majority of the shares, but these arrangements are rarely linked to joint decision-making. . . . In Germany, co-determination gives extensive consultation rights to employees through works councils and supervisory board membership, but does not usually involve employee shareholdings.[62]

Nevertheless, these hybrid models are still effective in flattening the organization's hierarchy and reducing inequality among employees. As managers' and workers' interests become better aligned, productivity generally increases, "as long as it is linked to a coherent package of work practices that reduce the level of supervision and give greater responsibility to employees."[63] This idea that there is a link between enhanced employee status, reduced supervision (the elimination of layers of management), and productivity is beginning to take hold in a number of innovative firms, such as Zappos, with interesting results.

Zappos

This idea of a flatter organization, with fewer bosses to supervise workers, has been explored by the management commentator Gary Hamel.[64] In spite of the value of managers, he argues, the downside of what Alfred D. Chandler called "the visible hand"[65] is it is "inefficient and often ham-fisted." As an alternative, Hamel suggests an organizational structure in which

- no one has a boss;
- employees negotiate responsibilities with their peers;
- everyone can spend the company's money;
- each individual is responsible for acquiring the tools needed to do their work;
- there are no titles and no promotions; and
- compensation decisions are peer based.[66]

It is these characteristics that define Morning Star Company, the world's largest tomato processor and the model of best practice that Hamel describes and argues should be more widely adopted. One example of a firm that has done so is Valve, a video game maker. Like many technology firms, Valve has a lot of perks for its employees, but "one thing it doesn't have: bosses."[67] Reportedly, in the absence of hierarchical oversight, employees are motivated by the innovative structure, which seems to generate a culture that veers from anarchy to altruism:

At Valve, there are no promotions, only new projects. To help decide pay, employees rank their peers—but not themselves—voting on who they think creates the most value. . . . Firings, while relatively rare, work the same way: teams decide together if someone isn't working out. As for projects, someone typically emerges as the de facto manager, says Greg Coomer, a 16-year veteran of Valve who works on product design. When no one takes the lead, he adds, it's usually a sign that the project isn't worth doing.[68]

The goal of structures like this is to better align the interests of the employees with the firm's performance (similar to employee-owned companies), and an essential component of this alignment is a tight fit between the values of the individual and the organizational culture. This is something that Zappos (a company that takes its culture very seriously) has put a lot of thought into.[69] At Zappos, an online retailer of shoes and handbags, customer service is the number one priority. But that is not just a tag line—it is embedded at every level of the organization. To start with, the firm makes sure its employees are highly motivated and share the firm's values:

After a few weeks of intensive training, new call-center employees are offered [$2,000] on top of what they have already earned to that point if they want to quit. The theory . . . is that the people who take the money "obviously don't have the sense of commitment" Zappos requires from its employees. The company says [less than 2] percent of its trainees take the offer.[70]

To further emphasize that customer service is central to its purpose, Zappos goes out of its way to support customer service employees by locating them on the top floor of the headquarters building, real estate normally reserved for the CEO and senior executives.[71] Moreover, as an indicator of the firm's general support for the firm's 1,500 employees, in 2014 "Zappos did away with job titles" and stopped advertising open job positions. Interested applicants can no longer search for vacancies on LinkedIn or Monster.com, or even on Zappos' website:

Instead, they will have to join a social network, called Zappos Insiders, where they will network with current employees and demonstrate their passion for the company—in some cases publicly—in hopes that recruiters will tap them when jobs come open.[72]

Instead of job titles and the hierarchy that is common in most other organizations, Tony Hsieh, Zappos' founder and CEO, has introduced a management philosophy known as *holacracy* (see http://www.holacracy.org/). The term "is derived from author Arthur Koestler's term 'holon,' which means a whole that is part of a larger whole." It is intended to provide greater flexibility for the firm, while encouraging individual autonomy and responsibility, but is not a one-size-fits-all model.[73] More a general approach to management, it is adapted to suit each organization's needs. As Hsieh explains:

> Instead of a hierarchy of people that you see in a traditional corporate structure, we have a hierarchy of purpose. In holacracy jargon, there are different circles. There's a general company circle. Then each circle has roles in it, and subcircles. Each circle has its own purpose. Each role has its own purpose. Employees can fill multiple roles in multiple circles.[74]

Evidence that holacracy is a very different approach to management lies in the immediate aftermath of Zappos' conversion, when "14 percent, or 210, of its roughly 1,500 employees" decided they could not or did not want to adapt, choosing instead to leave the firm after being offered the option of receiving three months' severance pay.[75] And more recently, reports have emerged that suggest Zappos continues to have issues with its implementation of holacracy. From 2015 to 2016, for example, "29% of the staff has turned over,"[76] while 2016 was the first year for almost a decade that Zappos did not make *Fortune*'s list of the 100 Best Companies to Work For. Now, Hsieh has announced that the firm is evolving to a higher state of existence, known as "Teal":

> Hsieh was referring to a 2014 book by consultant Frederic Laloux, who argues that throughout history people have organized themselves in various ways. Laloux assigned a color to each type: orange for modern corporations such as Walmart, and green for what he views as more evolved operations, like Starbucks. Teal, he wrote, was the next stage of development, characterized by self-management, bringing one's "whole" self to work, and having a purpose beyond making money.[77]

While it is unclear exactly what that means in practice (other than that it focuses on "self-management"), what is clear is that it was not something that made everyone at Zappos comfortable. As a result of the radical nature of Hsieh's social experiment at Zappos, "in the end, 18% of the 1,500 employees took buyouts, and another 11% left without a package."[78]

Nevertheless, the idea of a flatter and more flexible hierarchy is finding support in larger and more traditional companies such as GE, which "has run some aviation-manufacturing facilities with no foremen or shop-floor bosses" for a number of years.[79] A similar structure that minimizes layers of hierarchy was built in to W. L. Gore, the successful maker of Gore-Tex, by the firm's founders. Today, the hierarchy remains "almost completely flat."[80] As a result, the firm provides perhaps the best example of how this approach to business can work in practice:

Since it was founded in 1958, W.L. Gore has operated under what it calls a "lattice" management structure, which relies on teams in place of bosses and traditional chains of command. . . . Gore's 10,000 employees, who work mainly in engineering and manufacturing, take on leadership roles based on their ability to "gain the respect of peers and to attract followers," says Ms. Kelly, the CEO. Those who choose not to take the lead also are valued, she adds, noting that the company prides itself on staff "followership."[81]

The result is a convoluted and sometimes unwieldy decision-making process that Terri Kelly, the firm's CEO, describes as "very chaotic," but also highly effective.[82] Executives believe that, what they sacrifice in terms of speed, they make up for in terms of broad buy-in to decisions that are made. As Kelly explains, "you have to sell your ideas, even if you're the CEO. You have to explain the rationale behind your decision and do a lot of internal selling." The firm is more meritocratic, with only those ideas that enjoy broad support progressing:

In Gary Hamel's book, *The Future of Management*, he quotes a Gore associate, Rich Buckingham, who sums up the company's approach. "We vote with our feet. If you call a meeting, and people show up, you're a leader."[83]

Strategic CSR Debate

Motion: Access to a job that pays a *fair* wage is a right in a civilized society.

QUESTIONS FOR DISCUSSION AND REVIEW

1. What are some of the benefits to companies of an employee volunteer program? How can companies encourage employees to participate in such a program and avoid the suspicion that "by volunteering, they are potentially derailing their chances for a promotion because of the time they'll spend out of the office"?[84]

2. What is a fair wage? What does *fair* mean?[85] What is the lowest hourly wage for which you would be willing to work? Think of some of the jobs you have done—would you have worked harder if your pay had been higher?

3. Where would you rather shop—Walmart or Costco? If you answered "Walmart" based on the price of its products, would you be willing to pay a higher price if you knew that the extra money would go directly to the firm's employees? If you answered "Costco," is it OK that the firm pays its employees above-market wages and passes those costs on to you, the customer, in the form of higher prices?

4. Is it a good idea for companies to apply a pay scale ratio to the highest and lowest wages in the organization (such as at Whole Foods Market)? If so, what do you think that ratio should be? If not, is there no limit to the amount that a person should be paid?

5. What is your impression of John Lewis and W. L. Gore? Are they good firms? Are they successful firms? Are those two things (*good* and *successful*) the same? Would you like to work at a company like these? Would you accept a lower salary to do so?

Final Thoughts

On one level, this book is about *corporate social responsibility (CSR)*. It is about redefining that term as central to the value-creating activities of the firm. On another and more important level, however, this book is about how firms operate in today's global business environment. It is about how firms conduct business—every aspect of operations—and how they can optimize performance in the wired, interconnected world in which we all live.

As such, this book addresses a question that is subtly different from the question most CSR books seek to address. Rather than ask, *What are the social responsibilities of businesses?* this book asks, *What is the role of business in society?* In other words, rather than trying to define the list of responsibilities that firms supposedly must address, the concept of strategic CSR seeks to identify how for-profit firms can create the most value for the broadest section of society.

After many years of thinking about this issue, I have found that this subtle distinction prompts a very different approach to understanding how firms work and how they contribute to societal progress. Asking the question *What is the role of business in society?* has profound implications for the way we understand business, the way we conduct business, and, therefore, the way that we teach business. Properly understood and internalized, a strategic CSR perspective infuses everything the firm does. As such, it also has implications for every subject taught in the business school. My first instinct is to teach CSR in my strategic management capstone class, but the same perspective can be incorporated into courses dedicated to marketing, operations, finance, accounting, and so on.

As a result of these shifts in perspective, the question *What is the role of business in society?* is quite simply the most important question we face. It will determine the future of humanity—the way we live, the way we interact, and whether or not we leave a habitable planet to future generations. The question *What is the role of business in society?* is existential. And it is a question that cannot be delayed. We need to address it today and start putting in place the policies and practices necessary to create a sustainable economic system. To progress, we must retain much of our current economic system. It has been responsible for the incredible rise in living standards that developed economies have experienced since the Industrial Revolution. Clearly, however, it is not sustainable. As such, we need to understand what is good about what we have and what needs to be changed.

Strategic Corporate Social Responsibility: Sustainable Value Creation provides a road map for that discussion. It builds a theory of empowered stakeholders who, as long as they are willing to hold firms to account for their actions, can create an economy that meets the needs of society, broadly defined. It understands that capitalism is merely a means of organizing society and for-profit firms are the primary tool used to implement its guiding principles. As a tool, firms must serve the interests of the majority and not the minority. Capitalism provides the system of incentives and constraints to make that possible, but it requires the active participation of all of us in order to shape the outcomes that serve our best interests.

Good luck as you join that journey and seek to implement strategic CSR.

ENDNOTES

Glossary

1. For a comprehensive review of the evolution of CSR as an academic discipline, see Archie B. Carroll, "Corporate Social Responsibility: Evolution of a Definitional Construct," *Business and Society,* Vol. 38, No. 3, September 1999, pp. 268–295. Also, William C. Frederick, *Corporation Be Good! The Story of Corporate Social Responsibility*, Dog Ear Publishing, 2006, offers a comprehensive timeline and discussion of the evolution of CSR.

2. Margaret Atwood, "A survival story," *The Economist (The World in 2016)*, December 2015, p. 110.

3. Conscious Capitalism, "An Introduction to Conscious Capitalism," http://www.conscious capitalism.org/node/3998/ (accessed February 2016).

4. See David Grayson & Adrian Hodges, *Corporate Social Opportunity! Seven Steps to Make Corporate Social Responsibility Work for Your Business*, Greenleaf Publishing, July 2004.

5. William McDonough & Michael Braungart, *Cradle to Cradle: Remaking the Way We Make Things*, North Point Press, April 2002.

6. "Making Money and Sustainable Progress with Ecopreneurship," Network for Business Sustainability, March 5, 2012, http://nbs.net/knowledge/making-money-and-sustainable-progress-with-ecopreneurship/.

7. Woody Tasch, "The Buck Slows Here—Why the Time for Slow Money Is Now," *Triple Pundit*, March 21, 2013, http://www.triple pundit.com/2013/03/buck-slows-time-slow-money/.

8. See A. J. Weberman, *My Life in Garbology*, Amazon Digital Services, 2011; and Edward Humes, *Garbology: Our Dirty Love Affair with Trash*, Avery Publishing, 2012.

9. See United Nations Global Compact, https://www.unglobalcompact.org/.

10. "Effluence of affluence," *The Economist*, January 7, 2012, p. 52.

11. Alex William, "That Buzz in Your Ear May Be Green Noise," *The New York Times*, June 15, 2008, http://www.nytimes.com/2008/06/15/fashion/15green.html.

12. UL Environment, "The Sins of Greenwashing," http://sinsofgreenwashing.com/index.html (accessed February 2016).

13. See Centre For Bhutan Studies & GNH Research, "Gross National Happiness," http://www.grossnationalhappiness.com/.

14. See the United Nations Universal Declaration of Human Rights (http://www.un.org/en/universal-declaration-human-rights/index.html), which was adopted by the UN General Assembly on December 10, 1948.

15. Mark Boleat, "Inclusive capitalism: Searching for a purpose beyond profit," *The Guardian*, May 27, 2014, http://www.theguardian.com/sustainable-business/inclusive-capitalism-purpose-beyond-profit/.

16. Investopedia, "Shariah-Compliant Funds," http://www.investopedia.com/terms/s/shariah-compliant-funds.asp (accessed February 2016).

17. Keith Davis, "The Case for and Against Business Assumption of Social Responsibilities," *Academy of Management Journal*, Vol. 16, No. 2, 1973, pp. 312–322.

18. This concept was developed by William C. Frederick to capture his belief that all business actions are products of natural evolutionary processes. See Bill's website at http://www.williamcfrederick.com/business-nature.html and his book *Natural Corporate Management: From the Big Bang to Wall Street*, Greenleaf Publishing, 2012.

19. Center for Media and Democracy, quoted in Andrew Adam Newman, "Good/Corps Aims to Help Business Meet Social Goals," *The New York Times*, May 13, 2011, p. B3.

20. See Slow Money, https://slowmoney.org/.

21. Bill Baue, "Brundtland Report Celebrates 20th Anniversary Since Coining Sustainable Development," SocialFunds.com, June 11, 2007, http://www.socialfunds.com/news/save.cgi?sfArticleId=2308. This definition was developed by the Brundtland Commission (which was chaired by Gro Harlem Brundtland, the former prime minister of Norway). The Commission was established by the United Nations in 1983 to address growing concerns about the deteriorating condition of the natural environment (see http://www.un-documents.net/wced-ocf.htm).

22. John Micklethwait & Adrian Wooldridge, "The Company: A Short History of a Revolutionary Idea," Modern Library, 2003, p. 8.

23. C. K. Prahalad & Gary Hamel, "The Core Competence of the Corporation," *Harvard Business Review*, May–June 1990, pp. 79–91; Gary Hamel & C. K. Prahalad, *Competing for the Future*, Harvard Business School Press, 1994.

24. Michael E. Porter, "The Five Competitive Forces That Shape Strategy," *Harvard Business Review*, January 2008, pp. 79–93; Michael E. Porter, *Competitive Strategy*, The Free Press, 1980.

25. See, for example, TaskRabbit (https://www.taskrabbit.com/).

26. https://en.wikipedia.org/wiki/Prosumer (accessed February 2016).

27. See, for example, Uber (https://www.uber.com/) or Airbnb (https://www.airbnb.com/).

28. Michael E. Porter, *Competitive Advantage*, The Free Press, 1985.

Preface

1. Milton Friedman, *Capitalism and Freedom*, University of Chicago Press, 1962, p. 133.

Part I

1. In his well-known September 13, 1970, *New York Times Magazine* article "The Social Responsibility of Business Is to Increase Its Profits," in which he declared CSR to be a "fundamentally subversive doctrine," Milton Friedman built part of his argument around the idea that "only people can have responsibilities. . . . 'Business' as a whole cannot be said to have responsibilities." Putting aside the idea that a for-profit firm in our society can have *rights* (which Friedman recognizes) but not *responsibilities* (which Friedman dismisses), in this textbook the organization is the actor of primary focus. As such, I will refer to firms as entities that, for example, can "act in their own best interest." While I would prefer not to anthropomorphize corporations, in order to discuss their responsibilities, it is necessary to separate the collective (the company) from the individuals who act on its behalf (executives, directors, and employees).

Chapter 1

1. For an idea of the potential for government to play a role in encouraging CSR, see the UK government's 2014 report *Good for Business & Society: Government Response to Call for Views on Corporate Responsibility* at https://www.gov.uk/government/uploads/system/uploads/attachment_data/file/300265/bis-14-651-good-for-business-and-society-government-response-to-call-for-views-on-corporate-responsibility.pdf.

2. It is interesting to speculate about where organizations founded by social entrepreneurs fit within this taxonomy. The emergence of benefit corporations (and certified B Corps) further confuses traditional definitions of organizational forms. While CSR advocates often seek to place such organizations (which describe themselves as seeking to meet social goals via business practices) as a hybrid that is best described as a "fourth type" of organization, my sense is that they are no different from a for-profit. All companies exist to solve some social problem. In this sense, a supermarket is as much a "social enterprise" as TOMS Shoes.

3. National Center for Charitable Statistics, http://nccs.urban.org/statistics/quickfacts.cfm (accessed February 2016).

4. While Ed Freeman defines a stakeholder as "any group or individual who can affect or is affected by the achievement of the organization's objectives" (R. Edward Freeman, *Strategic Management: A Stakeholder Approach*, Pitman, 1984, p. 46), others offer

subtle variations. Post, Preston, and Sachs, for example, provide a narrower definition of a firm's stakeholder that ties the group or actor more directly to the firm's operations: "The stakeholders in a firm are individuals and constituencies that contribute, either voluntarily or involuntarily, to its wealth-creating capacity and activities, and who are therefore its potential beneficiaries and/or risk bearers" ("Managing the Extended Enterprise: The New Stakeholder View," *California Management Review*, Vol. 45, No. 1, Fall 2002, p. 8).

5. Agency theory emerged out of economics. It seeks to model the relationship between the principals of a firm (the owners or shareholders) and the agents (the managers) who are appointed by the principals to manage their assets (i.e., run the firm) on their behalf. The theory defines and then attempts to solve the fundamental principal–agent problem: How can the principal ensure that the agent acts in the principal's interests, rather than in their own interests? In particular, see Michael C. Jensen & William H. Meckling, "Theory of the firm: Managerial behavior, agency costs and ownership structure," *Journal of Financial Economics*, Vol. 3, No. 4, October 1976, pp. 305–360. A fundamental pillar of strategic CSR is that, legally, shareholders do not own the firm (see Chapter 6), which therefore undermines the central premise of agency theory (that the "principals" have the right to expect their "agents" to manage the organization in the principals' interests).

6. See Dave Carroll, "United Breaks Guitars," https://www.youtube.com/watch?v=5YGc4zOqozo (July 6, 2009).

7. The phrase *fiduciary responsibility* is widely used in business but not widely understood. In its simplest form, it means a responsibility of one party that is a result of a formal relationship with another party. The responsibility is founded on trust and often involves financial transactions. While this responsibility can clearly exist as a result of a legal or contractual relationship, it can also emerge from an ethical relationship, which expands its relevance within a discussion of CSR. The *Oxford English Dictionary* reports that the origin of the term lies in the late 16th century and comes from the Latin *fiduciarius*, which means "trust."

8. Milton Friedman, "The Social Responsibility of Business Is to Increase Its Profits," *The New York Times Magazine*, September 13, 1970.

9. Charles Handy, "What's a Business For?" *Harvard Business Review,* December 2002, p. 54.

10. For a comprehensive review of the evolution of CSR as an academic discipline, see Archie B. Carroll, "Corporate Social Responsibility: Evolution of a Definitional Construct," *Business and Society,* Vol. 38, No. 3, September 1999, pp. 268–295 and Herman Aguinis & Ante Glavas, "What We Know and Don't Know About Corporate Social Responsibility: A Review and Research Agenda," *Journal of Management*, Vol. 38, No. 4, July 2012, pp. 932–968. Also, traditional textbooks elaborate on these issues; see Anne T. Lawrence & James Weber, *Business and Society: Stakeholders, Ethics, Public Policy* (14th edition), McGraw-Hill, 2013. Finally, William C. Frederick, *Corporation Be Good! The Story of Corporate Social Responsibility*, Dog Ear Publishing, 2006, offers a comprehensive timeline and discussion of the evolution of CSR.

11. Archie B. Carroll, "A Three-Dimensional Conceptual Model of Corporate Performance," *Academy of Management Review,* 1979, Vol. 4, No. 4, p. 500.

12. Archie B. Carroll, "The Pyramid of Corporate Social Responsibility: Toward the Moral Management of Organizational Stakeholders," *Business Horizons,* July–August 1991.

13. See Mark S. Schwartz & Archie B. Carroll, "Corporate Social Responsibility: A Three-domain Approach," *Business Ethics Quarterly*, Vol. 13, No. 4, 2003, pp. 503–530, for an update on Carroll's pyramid of CSR. Instead of four levels of responsibility, Schwartz and Carroll divide a firm's responsibilities into three domains—economic, legal, and ethical. These three overlapping domains result in seven "CSR categories," or firm profiles, with the appropriate category determined by the firm's orientation (i.e., its distinctive emphasis on each domain).

14. See Alexander Dahlsrud, "How Corporate Social Responsibility Is Defined: An Analysis of 37 Definitions," *Corporate*

Social Responsibility and Environmental Management, Vol. 15, No. 1, 2006. Other researchers have identified "three fundamental lines of CSR inquiry prevalent in the academic literature"—stakeholder driven, performance driven, and motivation driven. See Kunal Basu & Guido Palazzo, "Corporate Social Responsibility: A Process Model of Sensemaking," *Academy of Management Review*, Vol. 33, No. 1, 2008, p. 122.

15. Michael McComb, "Profit to Be Found in Companies That Care," *South China Morning Post*, April 14, 2002, p. 5.

16. Ruth Lea, "Corporate Social Responsibility: IoD Member Opinion Survey," *The Institute of Directors* (UK), November 2002, p. 10.

17. "A Renewed EU Strategy 2011–14 for Corporate Social Responsibility," *European Commission,* COM(2011) 681 final, Brussels, October 25, 2011, clause 3.1, p. 6.

18. "Introduction to Corporate Social Responsibility," United Nations Institute for Training and Research, 2012, http://www.unitar.org/event/introduction-corporate-social-responsibility/.

19. Christine Bader, "Why Corporations Fail to Do the Right Thing," *The Atlantic*, April 21, 2014, http://www.theatlantic.com/business/archive/2014/04/why-making-corporations-socially-responsible-is-so-darn-hard/360984/.

20. Michael Hiltzik, "Peter Drucker's revolutionary teachings decades old but still fresh," *Los Angeles Times*, December 31, 2009, http://articles.latimes.com/2009/dec/31/business/la-fi-hiltzik31-2009dec31/.

21. John Kay, "The left is still searching for a practical philosophy," *Financial Times*, May 5, 2010, p. 9.

22. It is worth reinforcing the idea that legally permissible actions may still be morally or ethically objectionable to certain stakeholders. In response, these activists can use obscure treaties and statutes (e.g., the Alien Tort Claims Act passed in 1789 by the first US Congress) to file lawsuits against firms in order to right actual or perceived wrongs.

23. "What's the alternative?" *The Economist*, August 15, 2015, p. 75.

24. For the history of CSR "from the nineteenth century through World War I in the United Kingdom, United States, Japan, India, and Germany," see Bryan W. Husted, "Corporate Social Responsibility Practice from 1800–1914: Past Initiatives and Current Debates," *Business Ethics Quarterly*, Vol. 25, No. 1, January 2015, pp. 125–141.

25. Adrian Henriques, "Ten things you always wanted to know about CSR (but were afraid to ask); Part One: A Brief History of Corporate Social Responsibility (CSR)," *Ethical Corporation,* May 26, 2003.

26. Michael Arndt, "An Ode to 'The Money-Spinner,'" *BusinessWeek,* March 24, 2003, pp. 22–23.

27. Adam Hochschild, "How the British Inspired Dr. King's Dream," *The New York Times*, January 17, 2005, p. A21.

28. For more on Interface's revolutionary approach to environmental stewardship and its commitments to zero emissions and zero waste, see http://www.interfaceglobal.com/Sustainability.aspx.

29. Nick Aster, "Ray Anderson—Excerpt from 'The Corporation,'" *Triple Pundit*, October 31, 2007, http://www.triplepundit.com/2007/10/ray-anderson-excerpt-from-the-corporation/.

30. For a comprehensive description of high-frequency trading, see Michael Lewis, *Flash Boys: A Wall Street Revolt*, W. W. Norton & Company, 2014. See Lewis interviewed on *60 Minutes*, CBS, August 17, 2014, http://www.cbsnews.com/news/michael-lewis-explains-his-book-flash-boys/.

31. For additional background information on Malden Mills, see Rebecca Leung, "The Mensch of Malden Mills," *60 Minutes*, CBS, July 6, 2003, http://www.cbsnews.com/stories/2003/07/03/60minutes/main561656.shtml. See also Gretchen Morgenson, "GE Capital vs. the Small-Town Folk Hero," *The New York Times*, October 24, 2004, p. BU5.

32. Marianne Jennings, "Seek Corporate Balance," *Miami Herald,* September 1, 2002, p11L.

33. Roger Martin, "The Virtue Matrix," *Harvard Business Review,* March 2002, Vol. 80, No. 3, pp. 68–75.

34. Marianne Jennings, "Seek Corporate Balance," *Miami Herald,* September 1, 2002, p. 11L.

35. Manuel G. Velasquez, *Business Ethics: Concepts and Cases* (5th edition), Prentice Hall, 2002, pp. 122–123.

36. Mitchell Pacelle, "Can Mr. Feuerstein Save His Business One Last Time?" *The Wall Street Journal,* May 9, 2003, pp. A1, A6.

37. In spite of emerging from bankruptcy protection in 2004, the firm continued to struggle and filed for bankruptcy again in 2007. Today, the company continues to make its clothing under the brand name Polartec (http://www.polartec.com/). For a similar story about a company that maintained its commitment to its employees throughout a period of economic hardship (maintaining a "record of not having fired an employee for economic reasons in more than 80 years"), but that emerged successfully as a result, see James Shotter, "Cutler who turned the Swiss army knife into a global gadget," *Financial Times*, June 8/9, 2013, p. 14.

38. Charles Duhigg & Keith Bradsher, "How the U.S. Lost Out on iPhone Work," *The New York Times*, January 21, 2012, http://www.nytimes.com/2012/01/22/business/apple-america-and-a-squeezed-middle-class.html.

39. Frank Worstall, "Offshoring and Onshoring: It's All a Bit More Complex Than You Think," *Forbes*, March 21, 2012, http://www.forbes.com/sites/timworstall/2012/03/21/ofshoring-and-onshoring-its-all-a-bit-more-complex-than-you-think/.

40. "The third industrial revolution," *The Economist*, April 21, 2012, p. 15.

41. "Just Good Business: A Special Report on Corporate Social Responsibility," *The Economist*, January 19, 2008, p. 3.

42. Dom Phillips, "Ambitious law seeks São Paulo transformation," *FT Special Report, Green New Deal: Regional Solutions, Financial Times*, September 21, 2009, p. 1.

43. "The Latinobarómetro poll: The discontents of progress," *The Economist*, October 29, 2011, p. 48.

44. Rushworth Kidder, "Why Corporate Social Responsibility Needs Ethics," *Ethics Newsline*, October 3, 2011.

45. Ibid.

46. For more information and debate about these different ethical approaches, see Michael Sandel's Harvard University undergraduate course Justice. A series of videos relaying a semester of classes from the course is online at http://www.justiceharvard.org/.

47. Mark S. Schwartz & Archie B. Carroll, "Corporate Social Responsibility: A Three-domain Approach," *Business Ethics Quarterly*, Vol. 13, No. 4, 2003, p. 512.

48. Ibid.

49. Ibid., pp. 511–512.

50. It is important to note that, while both *morals* and *ethics* deal with aspects of *right* and *wrong*, what distinguishes them is the level of analysis to which they apply. Specifically, "ethics refer to rules provided by an external source, e.g., codes of conduct in workplaces or principles in religion. Morals refer to an individual's own principles regarding right and wrong" ("Ethics vs. Morals," http://www.diffen.com/difference/Ethics_vs_Morals/, accessed February 2016).

51. Howard R. Bowen, *Social Responsibilities of the Businessman*, Harper & Brothers, 1953, p. 135.

52. Design Thinking, "Peter Senge's Necessary Revolution," *BusinessWeek*, June 11, 2008, http://www.businessweek.com/innovate/content/jun2008/id20080611_566195.htm.

53. Charles Handy, "What's a Business For?" *Harvard Business Review*, December 2002, pp. 51–52.

54. Will Hutton, "The Body Politic Lies Bleeding," *The Observer*, May 13, 2001, http://www.guardian.co.uk/politics/2001/may/13/election2001.uk6.

55. Michael Skapinker, "How to fill the philanthropy-shaped hole," *Financial Times*, January 27, 2009, p. 13.

56. Adam Smith published *The Wealth of Nations* in 1776, but it is his book *The Theory of Moral Sentiments* (first published in 1759), that leads many observers to describe Smith as a moral philosopher rather than an economist. For example, see James R. Otteson, "Adam Smith: Moral Philosopher," *The Freeman*, Vol. 50, No. 11, November 2000, http://www.thefreemanonline.org/features/adam-smith-moral-philosopher/.

57. Adam Smith, "An Inquiry into the Nature and Causes of the Wealth of Nations," Book V, Chapter 2, Part II (On Taxes), 1776. Quoted in Sam Fleischacker, "Adam Smith vs. George Bush on Taxes," *Los Angeles Times*, January 22, 2001, http://articles.latimes.com/2001/jan/22/local/me-15437/.

58. For an indication of how quickly public sentiment can change on even the most sensitive or culturally embedded issues (and, as a result, why it is in a firm's interests to

remain engaged with all its stakeholders), see Alex Tribou & Keith Collins, "This Is How Fast America Changes Its Mind," *Bloomberg Businessweek*, June 26, 2015, http://www.bloomberg.com/graphics/2015-pace-of-social-change/.

59. Eliot Spitzer, "Strong Law Enforcement Is Good for the Economy," *The Wall Street Journal*, April 5, 2005, p. A18.

60. Keith Davis & Robert Blomstrom, *Business and Its Environment*, McGraw-Hill, 1966. See also Keith Davis, "The Case for and Against Business Assumption of Social Responsibilities," *Academy of Management Journal*, Vol. 16, No. 2, 1973, pp. 312–322.

61. Gregory J. Millman, "HSBC Costs Illustrate New Cost of Banking," *The Wall Street Journal*, November 4, 2014, http://blogs.wsj.com/riskandcompliance/2014/11/04/the-morning-risk-report-hsbc-costs-illustrate-new-cost-of-banking/.

62. http://www.ceres.org/bicep/

63. http://www.us-cap.org/

64. Jonathan Birchall, "Business fights for tougher rules on emissions," *Financial Times*, November 20, 2008, p. 4.

65. Suzanne Charlé, "When Addressing Climate Change Is Good Business," *strategy+business*, February 20, 2007, p. 1.

66. Some of the most important research in the business management literature on the relationship between CSR and firm performance is being done by Joshua Margolis of Harvard Business School (e.g., Joshua Margolis & James Walsh, "Misery Loves Companies: Rethinking Social Initiatives by Business," *Administrative Science Quarterly*, Vol. 48, No. 2, 2003, pp. 268–305, and Joshua Margolis & Hillary Elfenbein, "Do Well by Doing Good? Don't Count on It," *Harvard Business Review*, Vol. 86, No. 1, 2008, pp. 19–20). Margolis's main conclusion from his research is that, while there is little evidence that CSR predicts firm performance, there does seem to be evidence of the reverse relationship—firm performance predicting CSR. In other words, while CSR does not increase profits, higher profits lead to greater CSR. One explanation for this failure to establish a conclusive link between CSR and firm performance is that the tools we currently use to measure CSR are not very good. While data and methods are improving all the time, we have yet to identify a sufficiently comprehensive means of measuring a firm's CSR profile, making CSR's relationship with performance a sizeable black box. In the absence of such a measure, continuing to study whether CSR activities have positive (or negative) correlations with performance seems difficult to justify.

67. The Forum for Sustainable and Responsible Investment, "SRI Basics," http://www.ussif.org/sribasics (accessed February 2016).

68. Ibid.

69. Milton Friedman, *Capitalism and Freedom*, University of Chicago Press, 1962, p. 133.

Chapter 2

1. This phenomenon was reflected in the financial crisis of 2007–2008, when issues like climate change dropped down the list of economic and social priorities in developed economies, such as the in the United States and UK: "The proportion of adults reporting that they are willing to change their behaviour to limit climate change has fallen from 77% in 2006 to 72% in 2010 and 65% in 2011" (in "Public attitudes to climate change and the impact of transport in 2011," Department for Transport (UK), January 26, 2012, p. 4, https://www.gov.uk/government/statistics/public-attitudes-to-climate-change-and-the-impact-of-transport-in-2011/).

2. Patricia Cohen, "Study Finds Global Wealth Is Flowing to the Richest," *The New York Times*, January 19, 2015, p. B6.

3. "The third great wave," *The Economist Special Report: The World Economy*, October 4, 2014, p. 4.

4. For example, see "Nike Campaign," Center for Communication & Civic Engagement, http://depts.washington.edu/ccce/polcommcampaigns/Nike.htm. For a current example of an anti-Nike campaign, see "Sweatfree Communities," Global Exchange, http://www.globalexchange.org/fairtrade/sweatfree/nike/.

5. John Parker, "The world reshaped," *The Economist: The World in 2015*, January 2015, p. 96.

6. "Shoots, greens and leaves," *The Economist*, June 16, 2012, p. 68.

7. "The emerging-world consumer is king," *The Economist*, January 5, 2013, p. 53.

8. "Shoots, greens and leaves," *The Economist*, June 16, 2012, p. 68.

9. George Will, "The Fourth Great Awakening," *The Bryan Times*, June 1, 2000, p. 4.

10. Alex Tribou & Keith Collins, "This Is How Fast America Changes Its Mind," *Bloomberg BusinessWeek*, June 26, 2015, http://www.bloomberg.com/graphics/2015-pace-of-social-change/.

11. "Global Warming Puts the Arctic on Thin Ice," Natural Resources Defense Council, November 22, 2005, http://www.nrdc.org/globalwarming/qthinice.asp.

12. "New NASA Satellite Survey Reveals Dramatic Arctic Sea Ice Thinning," Jet Propulsion Laboratory, NASA, July 7, 2009, http://www.jpl.nasa.gov/news/news.cfm?release=2009-107.

13. A good example of the planet's ecological limits came in 2014, when it was announced that the "Earth lost half its wildlife in the past four decades. . . . Overall animal populations fell 52% between 1970 and 2010" (in Gautam Naik, "Study: Half of Wildlife Lost in 40 Years," *The Wall Street Journal*, October 1, 2014, p. A3).

14. Johan Rockström, "We have three chances to change the world for the better in 2015," *The Guardian*, April 14, 2015, http://www.theguardian.com/sustainable-business/2015/apr/14/we-have-three-chances-to-change-the-world-for-the-better-in-2015/. See also the Stockholm Resilience Centre, "Research: About the research," http://www.stockholmresilience.org/21/research/research-programmes/planetary-boundaries/planetary-boundaries/about-the-research/the-nine-planetary-boundaries.html.

15. Joel E. Cohen, "7 Billion," *The New York Times*, October 24, 2011, p. A19.

16. Juliette Jowit, "Paul Ehrlich: A prophet of global population doom who is gloomier than ever," *The Guardian*, October 23, 2011, http://www.guardian.co.uk/environment/2011/oct/23/paul-ehrlich-global-collapse-warning/.

17. "The joy of crowds," *The Economist*, July 28, 2012, p. 73.

18. See Chapter 13 for a more detailed consideration of the COP21 agreement and its implications for the sustainability debate.

19. This video is also available at http://www.youtube.com/watch?v=zORv8wwiadQ.

20. For an entertaining and educational video about the resource-intensive economic system and the waste it generates, see http://www.storyofstuff.org/movies-all/story-of-stuff/. For more videos by the same authors on different aspects of our economic model, see http://www.storyofstuff.com/.

21. See the following two articles for interesting discussions about the central role of continuous growth in our economic models: Andrew Marr, "Charles: right or wrong about science?" *The Observer*, May 21, 2000, http://www.theguardian.com/theobserver/2000/may/21/focus.news, and Steven Stoll, "Fear of fallowing: The specter of a no-growth world," *Harper's Magazine*, March 2008, pp. 88–94.

22. http://www.ge.com/about-us/ecomagination/.

23. http://www.unilever.com/sustainable-living/.

24. Christina Farr & Nichola Groom, "Apple invests heavily in solar energy to cut costs," *Christian Science Monitor*, February 11, 2015, http://www.csmonitor.com/Technology/2015/0211/Apple-invests-heavily-in-solar-energy-to-cut-costs/.

25. Amy Harder, "Companies to Pledge $140 Billion in Efforts to Cut Carbon Emissions," *The Wall Street Journal*, July 26, 2015, http://www.wsj.com/articles/companies-to-pledge-140-billion-in-efforts-to-cut-carbon-emissions-1437950378/.

26. While in 1999, 19 of the top 25 S&P 500 corporations in terms of market capitalization were US firms, by 2009, this number had dropped to 14. See "New Sectors and Regions Dominate the World's Top 25 Companies," *The Wall Street Journal*, December 20, 2009, p. R4. By 2013, 95 Chinese companies were part of the Fortune Global 500 (*Fortune*, http://fortune.com/global500/2014/).

27. "How the BRICs were baked," *The Economist*, December 10, 2011, p. 86. In China alone, it is estimated that "urban private consumption will rise from $3.2 trillion today to $5.6 trillion in 2020" (in "The wild, wild east," *The Economist Special Report: Business in China*, September 12, 2015, p. 12).

28. South Africa is not the only African country with significant growth potential. Already throughout the African continent, there are

over 500 African companies with $100 million in annual revenues, while about 150 companies have $1 billion in annual revenues.

29. Irene Lacher, "In New Book, Professor Sees a 'Mania' in U.S. for Possessions and Status," *The New York Times,* March 12, 2005, p. A21.

30. For more information about Adam Smith, as well as examples of his work (in particular, *The Theory of Moral Sentiments*), see http://www.adamsmith.org/introduction/.

31. Alan Murray, "The End of Management," *The Wall Street Journal*, August 21–22, 2010, p. W3.

32. See the review of the book *All Business Is Local* by John Quelch & Katherine Jocz in "Local heroes," *The Economist*, January 14, 2012, p. 83.

33. "To fly, to fall, to fly again," *The Economist*, July 25, 2015, p. 18.

34. "Why Companies Need to Be Prepared for Online Criticism," Ethical Corporation, 2012, http://reports.ethicalcorp.com/reports/smcc/infographic.php.

35. Margaret Ackrill & Leslie Hannah, *Barclays: The Business of Banking, 1690–1996*, Cambridge University Press, 2001.

36. "Royal Dutch/Shell in Nigeria (A)," Harvard Business School Case 9-399-126, August 10, 2006.

37. Jeff Ballinger, "The New Free-Trade Heel: Nike's Profits Jump on the Backs of Asian Workers," *Harper's Magazine*, August 1992, pp. 46–47. Quote from Debora L. Spar, "Hitting the Wall: Nike and International Labor Practices," Harvard Business School Case 9-700-047, September 6, 2002, pp. 5–6.

38. Ben Quinn, "Ikea Apologises Over Removal of Women from Saudi Arabia Catalogue," *The Guardian*, October 2, 2012, http://www.guardian.co.uk/world/2012/oct/02/ikea-apologises-removing-women-saudi-arabia-catalogue/.

39. Debora L. Spar, "Hitting the Wall: Nike and International Labor Practices," *Harvard Business School Press* [9-700-047], September 6, 2002.

40. "GAP Hit by 'Sweatshop' Protests," BBC News, November 21, 2002, http://news.bbc.co.uk/2/hi/business/2497957.stm.

41. Nandlal Master, Lok Samiti, & Amit Srivastava, "India: Major Protest Demands Coca-Cola Shut Down Plant," GlobalResearch.ca, April 8, 2008, http://www.globalresearch.ca/india-major-protest-demands-coca-cola-shut-down-plant/8591/.

42. "Google censors itself for China," BBC News, January 25, 2006, http://news.bbc.co.uk/2/hi/technology/4645596.stm.

43. Don Tapscott & David Ticoll, "The Naked Corporation," *The Wall Street Journal*, October 14, 2003, p. B2.

44. Thomas L. Friedman, "A Question from Lydia," *The New York Times*, May 16, 2010, p. WK10.

45. Jon Gertner, "Nate Silver," *Fast Company Magazine*, June 2013, p. 72.

46. "Planet of the phones," *The Economist*, February 28, 2015, p. 9.

47. Thomas L. Friedman, "The Virtual Mosque," *The New York Times*, June 17, 2009, p. A21.

48. Francesco Muzzi, "The World's 50 Most Innovative Companies," *Fast Company Magazine*, March 2013, p. 144.

49. Matt Ridley, "The Myth of Basic Science," *The Wall Street Journal*, October 24–25, 2015, p. C1.

50. Michael Elliott, "Embracing the Enemy Is Good Business," *Time,* August 13, 2001, p. 29.

51. Matt Ridley, "The Myth of Basic Science," *The Wall Street Journal*, October 24–25, 2015, p. C1.

52. William Gibson, "The Road to Oceania," *The New York Times,* June 25, 2003, p. A27.

53. "The primary mandate of Grameen Telecom (GTC) is to promote development of telecommunication services in rural areas of the country with a view to reducing poverty by creating new opportunities for income generation through self-employment with access to modern information and communication based technologies. . . . The company came into existence in the year 1995 as an association not-for-profit." (http://www.grameentelecom.net.bd/, accessed February 2016).

54. Bill Clinton, "The Case for Optimism," *Time Magazine*, October 1, 2012, http://www.time.com/time/magazine/article/0,9171,2125031,00.html.

55. "It's a hit," *The Economist*, May 12, 2012, p. 57.

56. Matt Richtel, "AT&T Chief Speaks Out on Texting at the Wheel," *The New York Times*, September 20, 2012, p. B1.

57. Ben Worthen, "The Perils of Texting While Parenting," *The Wall Street Journal*, September 29–30, 2015, p. C1.

58. Matthew Garrahan & Hannah Kuchler, "The Future of News," *Financial Times*, July 2, 2015, p. 9.

59. In Africa, for example, "57% of tweets are sent from mobile phones." See "#AfricaTweets," *The Economist*, February 4, 2012, p. 52.

60. "India has more mobile phones than toilets: UN report," *The Daily Telegraph*, April 15, 2010, http://www.telegraph.co.uk/news/worldnews/asia/india/7593567/India-has-more-mobile-phones-than-toilets-UN-report.html.

61. "Schumpeter: Too much buzz," *The Economist*, December 31, 2011, p. 50.

62. Ludwig Siegele, "Welcome to the yotta world," *The Economist: The World in 2012*, p. 124.

63. See Anjali Mullany, "Social media goes global," *Fast Company Magazine,* December 2015/January 2016, p. 66.

64. Warren St. John, "Quick, After Him: Pac-Man Went Thataway," *The New York Times,* May 9, 2004, Section 9, p. 1.

65. Rushworth M. Kidder, "Protest 2011," *Ethics Newsline*, December 12, 2011.

66. Elizabeth Holmes, "Tweeting Without Fear," *The Wall Street Journal*, December 9, 2011, p. B1.

67. "Beware the angry birds," *The Economist*, October 11, 2014, p. 76.

68. "Don't shoot," *The Economist*, December 10, 2011, p. 34.

69. "Schumpeter: Too much buzz," *The Economist*, December 31, 2011, p. 50.

70. Yasmin Crowther, "Swimming in social media's fast changing tide," *Ethical Corporation*, August 22, 2012, http://www.ethicalcorp.com/communications-reporting/swimming-social-medias-fast-changing-tide/.

71. "Boom and backlash," *The Economist*, April 26, 2014, p. 61.

72. For examples of stakeholders creating websites to criticize the firms they particularly dislike, see http://walmartsucks.org/ and http://targetsucks.blogspot.com/.

73. Anya Kamenetz, "On the Internet, Everyone Knows You're a Dog," *Fast Company Magazine*, December 2008/January 2009, pp. 53–55.

74. "Schumpeter: Too much buzz," *The Economist*, December 31, 2011, p. 50.

75. Interbrand, *Best Global Brands 2015*, http://interbrand.com/best-brands/best-global-brands/2015/.

76. Ben & Jerry's, "Our Values," http://www.benjerry.com/values/.

77. William B. Werther & David Chandler, "Strategic Corporate Social Responsibility as Global Brand Insurance," *Business Horizons*, Vol. 48, No. 4, July 2005, 317–324.

78. Mallen Baker, "Johnson & Johnson and Tylenol: Companies in Crisis—What to Do When It All Goes Wrong," http://www.mallenbaker.net/csr/crisis02.php.

79. Gary Silverman, "Big businesses aim to brew the right thing," *Financial Times,* March 21–22, 2015, p. 7.

80. For some of the CSR challenges associated with big data, see Jay Stanley, "Eight Problems With 'Big Data,'" ACLU, April 25, 2012, https://www.aclu.org/blog/technology-and-liberty/eight-problems-big-data/.

Chapter 3

1. John Micklethwait & Adrian Wooldridge, "The Company: A Short History of a Revolutionary Idea," Modern Library, 2003, pp. xiv–xv.

2. Todd Stitzer, "Business must loudly proclaim what is stands for," *Financial Times*, June 1, 2006, p. 11.

3. "Wal-Mart, the most prodigious job creator in the history of the private sector in this galaxy, has almost as many employees (1.3 million) as the U.S. military has uniformed personnel. A McKinsey company study concluded that Wal-Mart accounted for 13 percent of the nation's productivity gains in the second half of the 1990s, which probably made Wal-Mart about as important as the Federal Reserve in holding down inflation. By lowering consumer prices, Wal-Mart costs about 50 retail jobs among competitors *for every 100 jobs Wal-Mart creates*. Wal-Mart and its effects save shoppers more than $200 billion a year, dwarfing such government programs as food stamps ($28.6 billion) and the earned-income tax credit ($34.6 billion)" (in George F. Will, "Democrats vs. Wal-Mart," *The Washington Post,* September 14, 2006, p. A21).

4. See, for example, http://makingchangeat walmart.org/.

5. "Peculiar people," *The Economist*, March 26, 2011, p. 78.

6. Martha C. White, "Idea of company-as-person originated in late 19th century," *The Washington Post*, January 31, 2010, http://www.washingtonpost.com/wp-dyn/content/article/2010/01/30/AR2010013000030.html.

7. Ibid.

8. See also *Cohen v. California* (403 U.S. 15, 1971).

9. "What's the most important Supreme Court case no one's ever heard of?" *The Atlantic*, May 2013, p. 96.

10. "The Rights of Corporations" [Editorial], *The New York Times*, September 22, 2009, p. 30.

11. While *The New York Times* argued that the Court's current view of corporate rights should not be expanded, for an alternative perspective on the same case, see this op-ed article in *The Wall Street Journal*: Theodore B. Olsen, "The Chance for a Free Speech Do-over," September 7, 2009, http://online.wsj.com/article/SB10001424052970 2035850045743932500083568972.html.

12. Chief Justice John Marshall, *Trustees of Dartmouth College v. Woodward* (17 U.S. 518, 1819).

13. The Conference Board, "Corporate Political Spending: A Resource," July 2015, https://www.conference-board.org/politicalspending/.

14. Vipal Monga & Maxwell Murphy, "A Stubborn Political Divide," *The Wall Street Journal*, September 15, 2015, p. B6.

15. "As the court noted, 26 states and the District of Columbia already permit independent corporate and union campaign spending. There have been no stampedes in those states' elections. Having a constitutional right is not the same as requiring one to exercise it, and there are many reasons businesses and unions may not spend much more on politics than they already do" (in Jan Witold Baran, "Stampede Toward Democracy" [Editorial], *The New York Times*, January 25, 2010, http://www.nytimes.com/2010/01/26/opinion/26baran.html). For more comment on the influence of *Citizens United* on campaign spending in the 2012 US presidential election, see

"Money trouble," *The Economist*, September 29, 2012, p. 35; Eric Lipton & Clifford Krauss, "Fossil Fuel Ads Dominate TV In Campaign," *The New York Times*, September 14, 2012, p. A1; and Eduardo Porter, "Unleashing Corporate Contributions," *The New York Times*, August 29, 2012, p. B1.

16. Adam Liptak, "Justices' Ruling Is Wrapped in an English Lesson," *The New York Times*, March 2, 2011, p. 15.

17. "Peculiar people," *The Economist*, March 26, 2011, p. 78.

18. Ibid.

19. Ibid.

20. "Corporations and the court," *The Economist*, June 25, 2011, p. 75.

21. Martha C. White, "Idea of company-as-person originated in late 19th century," *The Washington Post*, January 31, 2010, http://www.washingtonpost.com/wp-dyn/content/article/2010/01/30/AR2010013000030.html.

22. Joel Bakan, *The Corporation: The Pathological Pursuit of Profit and Power*, Free Press, 2004, p. 35.

23. *Dodge v. Ford Motor Company*, 204 Mich. 459, 170 N.W. 668 (1919).

24. Joel Bakan, *The Corporation: The Pathological Pursuit of Profit and Power*, Free Press, 2004, p. 36.

25. Lynn Stout, *The Shareholder Value Myth: How Putting Shareholders First Harms Investors, Corporations, and the Public*, Berrett-Koehler, 2012, pp. 3–4.

26. John Micklethwait & Adrian Wooldridge, *The Company: A Short History of a Revolutionary Idea*, Modern Library, 2003, pp. 43, 46.

27. Peter Kinder, "Public purpose—Corporate history's lesson for companies now," *Ethical Corporation*, October 3, 2007.

28. Ibid.

29. *The Economist* describes limited liability ("one of the greatest wealth-creating inventions of all time") as "a privilege" and "a concession—something granted by society because it has a clear purpose" (in "Light and wrong," *The Economist*, January 21, 2012, p. 16).

30. James E. Austin & James Quinn, "Ben & Jerry's: Preserving Mission and Brand within Unilever," Harvard Business School Case 9-306-037, December 8, 2005, p. 5.

See also John Tozzi, "New Legal Protections for Social Entrepreneurs," *BusinessWeek*, April 22, 2010, http://www.bloomberg.com/bw/stories/2010-04-22/new-legal-protections-for-social-entrepreneursbusinessweek-business-news-stock-market-and-financial-advice/.

31. Mallen Baker, "Remuneration—Value society, Mr President," *Ethical Corporation,* March 11, 2009.

32. Charles Handy, "The Unintended Consequences of Good Ideas," *Harvard Business Review*, October 2012, http://hbr.org/2012/10/the-unintended-consequences-of-good-ideas/.

33. Kent Greenfield, "It's Time to Federalize Corporate Charters," *Business Ethics Magazine,* Fall 2002, p. 6.

34. Ibid.

35. Leslie Wayne, "To Delaware, With Love," *The New York Times,* July 1, 2012, p. 4.

36. State of Delaware Department of State, http://corp.delaware.gov/aboutagency.shtml (accessed February 2016).

37. Kent Greenfield, "It's Time to Federalize Corporate Charters," *Business Ethics Magazine,* Fall 2002, p. 6.

38. Liz Hoffman, "Dole and Other Companies Sour on Delaware as Corporate Haven," *The Wall Street Journal*, August 2, 2015, http://www.wsj.com/articles/dole-and-other-companies-sour-on-delaware-as-corporate-haven-1438569507/.

39. Kent Greenfield, "It's Time to Federalize Corporate Charters," *Business Ethics Magazine,* Fall 2002, p. 6.

40. Alex Marshall, "How to Get Business to Pay Its Share," *The New York Times,* May 4, 2012, p. A23.

41. Of course, with federal oversight of corporate law, the risk is that firms incorporate overseas in those places with the most favorable tax treatments. Even with the current favorable regulatory environment, this is happening. See, for example, Vanessa Houlder, "The tax avoidance story as a morality tale," *Financial Times*, November 22, 2004, p. 7.

42. *Tax avoidance* refers to a reduction in tax liability via legal means, while *tax evasion* refers to a criminal nonpayment of tax that is owed.

43. "Shells and shelves," *The Economist*, April 7, 2012, p. 70.

44. Citizen Works, "The Code for Corporate Responsibility," http://www.citizenworks.org/fact%20sheet%20-%20the%20code%20for%20corporate%20responsibility.pdf.

45. Bruce Watson, "Can we create an 'Economy for the Common Good'?" *The Guardian,* January 6, 2014, http://www.theguardian.com/sustainable-business/values-led-business-morals-economy-common-good/.

46. Steven Davidoff Solomon, "Regulators Unbundle Some Attractions of Mergers," *The New York Times*, November 4, 2015, p. B4.

47. Flemmich Webb, "The new ethical supermarket that wants Sainsbury's and Tesco's customers," *The Guardian,* July 16, 2013, http://www.theguardian.com/sustainable-business/ethical-sustainable-supermarkets-compete-sainsburys/.

48. Benefit Corporation, http://benefitcorp.net/what-is-a-benefit-corporation/ (accessed February 2016).

49. Benefit Corporation, http://benefitcorp.net/policymakers/state-by-state-status (accessed February 2016).

50. Danielle Sacks, "The Miracle Worker," *Fast Company Magazine*, December 2009/January 2010, pp. 122–123.

51. Bart King, "Patagonia Is First to Register for 'Benefit Corporation' Status in California," Sustainable Brands, January 4, 2012, http://www.sustainablebrands.com/news_and_views/articles/patagonia-first-register-%E2%80%98benefit-corporation%E2%80%99-status-california/.

52. Craig Sams, "Why Kraft Must Keep Organic Cacao Farmers Sweet," *The Guardian*, January 20, 2005, http://www.guardian.co.uk/environment/2010/jan/20/kraft-green-black-cadbury-ethical/.

53. David Teather, "Roddick Nets £130m from Body Shop Sale," *The Guardian*, March 17, 2006, http://www.guardian.co.uk/business/2006/mar/18/highstreetretailers.retail/.

54. "Firms with benefits," *The Economist*, January 7, 2012, http://www.economist.com/node/21542432/.

55. Angus Loten, "With New Law, Profits Take a Back Seat," *The Wall Street Journal*, January 19, 2012, http://online.wsj.com/article/SB10001424052970203735304577168591470161630.html.

56. "Patagonia Pioneers Sustainability Legal Status," *Environmental Leader*, January 5, 2012, http://www.environmentalleader.com/2012/01/05/patagonia-pioneers-sustainability-legal-status/.

57. Benefit Corporation, "Misconception: Benefit corporations and Certified B Corps are the same thing," http://benefitcorp.net/ (accessed February 2016). To learn more about the differences between benefit corporations and B Corps, see http://benefitcorp.net/businesses/benefit-corporation-vs-certified-b-corp/.

58. B Lab, http://www.bcorporation.net/ (accessed February 2016).

59. Jo Confino, "Ben & Jerry's: Parent Companies Don't Always Know Best," *The Guardian*, October 22, 2012, http://www.guardian.co.uk/sustainable-business/ben-jerrys-b-corporation-social-responsibilities/.

60. "Firms with benefits," *The Economist*, January 7, 2012, http://www.economist.com/node/21542432/.

61. UNEP Finance Initiative, "A legal framework for the integration of environmental, social, and governance issues into institutional investment," October 2005, http://www.unepfi.org/fileadmin/documents/freshfields_legal_resp_20051123.pdf.

62. Toby Webb, "Alternative capitalism: What's the big idea?" *Ethical Corporation*, June 4, 2012, http://www.ethicalcorp.com/business-strategy/alternative-capitalism-whats-big-idea/.

63. Critiquing the need for benefit corporations should not detract from the fundamental value of the B-Corp certification. It is essential for all firms to analyze their operations as a test of CSR. The B Impact Assessment is a valuable tool by which they can do this. A close reading of corporate law, however, suggests that altering the firm's legal form to become a benefit corporation is at best symbolic. At worst, promoting this entity as a cure for capitalism relieves *regular* corporations from the responsibility of creating value for all their stakeholders.

64. https://movetoamend.org/.

Part I Case Study

1. https://ask.census.gov/faq.php?id=5000&faqId=29 (accessed February 2016).

2. Carl Bialik, "Estimates of Religious Populations Require a Bit of Faith," *The Wall Street Journal*, August 14–15, 2010, p. A2.

3. The most recent US Census data is from 2010. The next scheduled Census is in 2020. The 2012 Statistical Abstract is the most recent national estimate by the Census Bureau regarding religious affiliation.

4. Frank Newport, "Three-Quarters of Americans Identify as Christian," *Gallup*, December 24, 2014, http://www.gallup.com/poll/180347/three-quarters-americans-identify-christian.aspx.

5. Jon Meacham, "The End of Christian America," *Newsweek*, April 4, 2009, http://www.newsweek.com/meacham-end-christian-america-77125/.

6. "Lift every voice," *The Economist*, May 4, 2012, p. 29.

7. Daniel Stone, "One Nation Under God," *Newsweek*, 2009, http://www.newsweek.com/newsweek-poll-americans-religious-beliefs-77349/.

8. "While shepherds watched," *The Economist*, December 22, 2012, p. 100.

9. Daniel Stone, "One Nation Under God," *Newsweek*, 2009, http://www.newsweek.com/newsweek-poll-americans-religious-beliefs-77349/.

10. "Speak low if you speak God," *The Economist*, August 4, 2012, p. 59. See also Hanna Rosin, "Religious Revival," *The New York Times Book Review*, April 26, 2009, p. 14; Laurie Goodstein, "More Atheists Are Shouting It From Rooftops," *The New York Times*, April 27, 2009, p. A1; and Charles M. Blow, "Defecting to Faith," *The New York Times*, May 2, 2009, p. A14.

11. Chick-fil-A's founder, Truett Cathy, died in 2014. See Julie Jargon & Michael Calia, "Chicken, With a Helping of Religion," *The Wall Street Journal*, September 9, 2014, p. B2.

12. For more information on Dan Cathy's controversial statements about his operating principles at Chick-fil-A, see "In Chick-fil-A, Parties Feast on Fast Feud," *The Wall Street Journal*, August 4–5, 2012, p. A4; and William McGurn, "The Chick-fil-A War Is Back On," *The Wall Street Journal*, September 25, 2012, p. A17.

13. Dan Cathy quoted in K. Allan Blume, "'Guilty as charged,' Cathy says of Chick-fil-A's stand on biblical & family values,"

Baptist Press, July 16, 2012, http://www
.bpnews.net/38271/.

14. While there is growing evidence of disillusionment with organized religion in the
United States (e.g., Tamara Audi,
"Unaffiliated Americans Outrank Catholics,
Study Says," *The Wall Street Journal*, May
12, 2015, p. A4), this is different from a
willingness to label oneself an atheist,
which is still culturally unacceptable in
many parts of the country.

15. See "High office, low church," *The Economist*,
April 13, 2013, p. 59.

16. "Growing disbelief," *The Economist*, August
25, 2012, p. 23.

17. See "The Hobby Lobby hubbub," *The
Economist*, March 29, 2014, p. 28; "Believe it
or not," *The Economist*, July 5, 2014, p. 25;
and "The Hobby Lobby Case: Religious
Freedom, Corporations and Individual
Rights," *Knowledge@Wharton*, March 31,
2014, http://knowledge.wharton.upenn
.edu/article/hobby-lobby-case-religious-
freedom-corporations-individual-rights/.

18. Michael Corkery & Jessica Silver-Greenberg,
"When Scripture Is the Rule of Law," *The
New York Times*, November 3, 2015, p. B6.

19. James Blitz, "BA under fire over ban on
employee's crucifix," *Financial Times*,
October 16, 2006, p. 3.

20. The increasing number of Muslims living in
the West is leading to cultural conflict as conservative elements in society consider their
way of life to be threatened. As such, firms
must ensure religious discrimination is absent
from operational practices and policies (e.g.,
see Jess Bravin, "Justices Hear Abercrombie
Case Involving Religious Garb," *The Wall
Street Journal*, February 26, 2015, p. B3, and
"Supreme Court Sides With Muslim
Abercrombie Job Applicant over Head Scarf,"
The Wall Street Journal, June 1, 2015, http://
www.wsj.com/articles/supreme-court-sides-
with-muslim-abercrombie-job-applicant-over-
head-scarf-1433170999/).

21. James Blitz, "BA under fire over ban on
employee's crucifix," *Financial Times*,
October 16, 2006, p. 3.

22. "Veils harm equal rights – Harman," BBC
News, October 11, 2006, http://news.bbc
.co.uk/2/hi/uk_news/politics/6040016.stm.

23. "When is a crucifix not religious?" *The
Economist*, September 14, 2013, p. 46.

24. Ellen Barry, "Local Russian Hijab Ban Puts
Muslims in Squeeze," *The New York Times*,
March 19, 2013, p. A8.

25. Marta Falconi & John Letzing, "Swiss Region
Bans Wearing of Burqas," *The Wall Street
Journal*, September 23, 2013, p. A13.

26. "Faith in the workplace," *The Economist*,
April 12, 2014, p. 66, and Melanie Trottman,
"Religious-Discrimination Claims on the
Rise," *The Wall Street Journal*, October 27,
2013, http://www.wsj.com/articles/SB10001
4240527023046825045791534629213 46076/.

27. Richard Dawkins, *The God Delusion*,
Houghton Mifflin Harcourt, 2006.

28. See https://humanism.org.uk/about/atheist-
bus-campaign/.

29. Bill Symonds, "The Media Hears the
Sermon," *BusinessWeek*, December 14, 2005,
http://www.businessweek.com/bwdaily/
dnflash/dec2005/nf20051214_8338_db016
.htm.

30. James C. McKinley Jr., "For Atheist Ads on
Buses, Equally Mobile Reaction," *The New
York Times*, December 14, 2010, p. A19.

31. http://w2.vatican.va/content/francesco/en/
apost_exhortations/documents/papa-fran
cesco_esortazione-ap_20131124_evangelii-
gaudium.html.

32. http://w2.vatican.va/content/francesco/en/
encyclicals/documents/papa-francesco_
20150524_enciclica-laudato-si.html.

33. http://w2.vatican.va/content/leo-xiii/en/
encyclicals/documents/hf_l-xiii_enc_
15051891_rerum-novarum.html.

34. "Faith, hope—and how much change?" *The
Economist*, March 8, 2014, p. 60.

35. David Brooks, "Fracking and the Franciscans,"
The New York Times, June 23, 2015, p. A23.

36. Craig Sams, "Sweet industry," *Financial
Times*, November 13–14, 2010, Life & Arts
p. 16.

37. Janet Adamy, "Are Businesses Entitled to
Same Religious Protections as People?" *The
Wall Street Journal*, March 22–23, 2014,
pp. A1, A10.

38. Rob Moll, "Outer Office, Inner Life," *The
Wall Street Journal*, January 20, 2010,
p. A15.

39. For additional advice on how to accommodate the religious interests of stakeholders,
both internally and externally, see Simon
Webley, "Multiculturalism: Is your workplace
faith-friendly?" *Ethical Corporation*, April 4,

2011, and "Speak low if you speak God," *The Economist*, August 4, 2012, p. 59.

40. Linda Tischler, "God and Mammon at Harvard," *Fast Company*, May 2005, p. 81.

41. Ken Costa, *God at Work: Living Every Day with Purpose*, Continuum Books, 2007.

42. Stefan Stern, "In the market for a messiah," *Financial Times*, September 6, 2007, p. 10.

43. Max Colchester, "British Banks Face Heat From on High," *The Wall Street Journal*, October 1, 2012, p. C1.

44. Stefan Stern, "In the market for a messiah," *Financial Times*, September 6, 2007, p. 10.

45. Rob Moll, "Doing God's Work—At the Office," *The Wall Street Journal*, February 11, 2011, p. A11.

46. Lindsay Gellman, "Investing as a Religious Practice," *The Wall Street Journal*, November 3, 2013, http://www.wsj.com/articles/SB10001424052702304106704579135321491814430.

47. Aryeh Spero, "What the Bible Teaches about Capitalism," *The Wall Street Journal*, January 30, 2012, p. A15.

48. "Prayers and playthings," *The Economist*, July 14, 2012, p. 54.

49. As a result of this ban, Christians turned to Jews for moneylending services "since they were presumed to be already excommunicated" (Gillian Tett, "Make money, not war," *Financial Times*, September 23–24, 2006, p. WK2).

50. See *Dante's Inferno*, "Circle 7, cantos 12–17," University of Texas at Austin, http://danteworlds.laits.utexas.edu/circle7.html.

51. "Gold, God and forgiveness," *The Economist*, December 17, 2011, p. 147.

52. *Dante's Inferno*, "Circle 7, cantos 12–17," University of Texas at Austin, http://danteworlds.laits.utexas.edu/circle7.html.

53. "Cap and tirade," *The Economist*, November 30, 2013, p. 70.

54. "On the origin of specie," *The Economist*, August 18, 2012, p. 68.

55. Ibid.

56. "The dangers of demonology," *The Economist*, January 7, 2012, p. 60.

57. *Dante's Inferno*, "Circle 7, cantos 12–17," University of Texas at Austin, http://danteworlds.laits.utexas.edu/circle7.html.

58. John Micklethwait & Adrian Wooldridge, *The Company: A Short History of a Revolutionary Idea*, Modern Library, 2003, p. 8.

59. Niall Ferguson, *The Ascent of Money*, BBC, 2008.

60. Online Etymology Dictionary, January 2013, http://www.etymonline.com/index.php?term=money.

61. "Gold, God and forgiveness," *The Economist*, December 17, 2011, p. 147.

62. Robyn Blumner, "Road to ruin: Usury, greed and the paper economy," *Chicago Tribune*, in *The Daily Yomiuri*, March 31, 2009, p. 16.

63. US Supreme Court, *Marquette National Bank of Minneapolis v. First of Omaha Service Corp.*, 439 U.S. 299 (1978).

64. Amy Goodman, "Thomas Geoghegan on 'Infinite Debt: How Unlimited Interest Rates Destroyed the Economy,'" Democracy Now!, March 24, 2009, http://www.democracynow.org/2009/3/24/thomas_geoghegan_on_infinite_debt_how/. See also Thomas Geoghegan, "Infinite debt," *Harper's Magazine*, April 2009, http://harpers.org/archive/2009/04/infinite-debt/.

65. http://www.investopedia.com/terms/s/shariah.asp (accessed February 2016).

66. For a commentary of the relevance of CSR for Islam, see Asyraf Wajdi Dusuki, "What Does Islam Say about Corporate Social Responsibility?" *Review of Islamic Economics*, Vol. 12, No. 1, 2008, pp. 5–28.

67. Frederik Balfour, "Islamic Finance May Be On to Something," *BusinessWeek*, November 24, 2008, p. 88.

68. Department of Halal Certification (Ireland), http://halalcertification.ie/halal/halal-market-size/ (accessed February 2016).

69. Liz Gooch, "Malaysia Seeks to Gain Bigger Role in Halal Food," *The New York Times*, January 1, 2011, p. B6.

70. Yaroslav Trofimov, "Malaysia Transforms Rules for Finance Under Islam," *The Wall Street Journal*, April 4, 2007, p. A1.

71. For examples of the range of issues covered under the umbrella term *Islamic finance* and to get a sense of how the industry has evolved, see the *Financial Times'* special report *Islamic Finance*, December 15, 2011, http://im.ft-static.com/content/images/d1924118-2521-11e1-8bf9-00144feabdc0.pdf.

72. Yaroslav Trofimov, "Malaysia Transforms Rules for Finance Under Islam," *The Wall Street Journal*, April 4, 2007, p. A1.

73. Gillian Tett, "Banks seek Islamic scholars versed in world of finance," *Financial Times*, May 20–21, 2006, p. 1.

74. Joanna Slater, "When Hedge Funds Meet Islamic Finance," *The Wall Street Journal*, August 9, 2007, p. A1.

75. For a detailed explanation of *sukuk*, see Usman Hayat, "Islamic finance's sukuk explained," *Financial Times: FT Monthly Review of the Fund Management Industry*, April 12, 2010, http://www.ft.com/cms/s/0/cec38bf2-440b-11df-9235-00144feab49a.html.

76. Gillian Tett, "Secondary trading in Islamic bonds promises earthly riches," *Financial Times*, July 14, 2006, p. 20.

77. Frederik Balfour, "Islamic Finance May Be On to Something," *BusinessWeek*, November 24, 2008, p. 88.

78. "Contemporary Islamic finance began with an initial experiment in Egypt in the early 1960s, then moved slowly into the Persian Gulf countries in the 1970s and Pakistan in the 1980s, before retreating and then emerging in today's globalized form in the late 1990s and early 2000s" (in Jon Fasman, "The Profits," *The New York Times Book Review*, March 22, 2015, p. 15).

79. "Big interest, no interest," *The Economist*, September 13, 2014, p. 79.

80. David Oakley, "Growth survives the storms," *Financial Times Special Report: The Future of Islamic Finance*, December 14, 2010, p. 2.

81. Farhan Bokhari, Roula Khalaf, & Gillian Tett, "Booming Gulf gives fillip to Islamic bonds," *Financial Times*, July 11, 2006, p. 17.

82. Gillian Tett, "Make money, not war," *Financial Times*, September 23–24, 2006, p. WK2.

83. Chris Prystay, "Malaysia Seeks Role as Global Player after Nurturing Islamic Bond Market," *The Wall Street Journal*, August 9, 2006, p. C1.

84. Yaroslav Trofimov, "Malaysia Transforms Rules for Finance under Islam," *The Wall Street Journal*, April 4, 2007, p. A1.

85. "Banking on the ummah," *The Economist*, January 5, 2013, p. 60.

86. Manu Mair & Mehreen Khan, "Britain to lead the world in Islamic finance," *The Telegraph*, February 26, 2015, http://www.telegraph.co.uk/finance/newsbysector/banksandfinance/11435465/Britain-to-lead-the-world-in-Islamic-finance.html.

87. "Finding a Home for Islamic Finance in France," *Knowledge@Wharton*, November 2, 2010, http://knowledge.wharton.upenn.edu/arabic/article.cfm?articleId=2557.

88. See Harry Wilson, "Britain to become first non-Muslim country to launch sharia bond," *The Telegraph*, October 29, 2013, http://www.telegraph.co.uk/finance/newsbysector/banksandfinance/10410467/Britain-to-become-first-non-Muslim-country-to-launch-sharia-bond.html.

89. Hugh Pope, "Islamic Banking Grows, With All Sorts of Rules," *The Wall Street Journal*, May 3, 2005, p. C1.

90. FTSE Shariah Global Equity Index Series, http://www.ftse.com/products/indices/Global-Shariah/ (accessed February 2016).

91. See Faiza Saleh Ambah, "Islamic Banking: Steady in Shaky Times," *The Washington Post*, October 31, 2008, p. A16, and John Aglionby, "Islamic banks urged to show west the sharia was forward," *Financial Times*, March 3, 2009, p. 3.

92. Robin Wigglesworth, "Islamic banks caught between two worlds," *Financial Times*, April 20, 2010, p. 15.

93. For an example of how Islamic finance seeks to extend the range of sharia-compliant instruments, see Sophia Grene, "Moves afoot to plug gap in Islamic finance," *Financial Times FTfm*, August 3, 2009, p. 3.

94. Tarek El Diwany, "How the banks are subverting Islam's ban on usury," *Financial Times*, July 14, 2006, p. 11.

95. Andrew Ross Sorkin, "A Financial Mirage in the Desert," *The New York Times*, December 1, 2009, p. B1.

96. Harris Irfan, "Could Islamic finance save capitalism?" *The Guardian*, December 4, 2014, http://www.theguardian.com/sustainable-business/2014/dec/04/could-islamic-finance-solution-capitalism/.

97. Tarek El Diwany, "How the banks are subverting Islam's ban on usury," *Financial Times*, July 14, 2006, p. 11.

Part II

1. Many commentators present a *stakeholder* perspective as an alternative to a *shareholder* perspective. I believe that the shareholder value versus stakeholder value

debate is a red herring. Since shareholders are also stakeholders, a shareholder perspective is actually the same thing as a stakeholder perspective, with the line concerning which stakeholders the firm will concern itself with drawn in a different place. (Do you draw the line at shareholders or also include other stakeholders?) The primacy of shareholders emerged out of a belief that US law compelled a fiduciary duty among executives to the shareholder. For an excellent argument debunking this myth, see Lynn Stout, *The Shareholder Value Myth: How Putting Shareholders First Harms Investors, Corporations, and the Public*, Berrett-Koehler Publishers, 2012.

Chapter 4

1. For a more complete discussion of the importance of approaching CSR using a strategic lens, see Part IV.
2. Eric Rhenman, *Foeretagsdemokrati och foeretagsorganisation*, S.A.F. Norstedt: Företagsekonomiska Forsknings Institutet, Thule, Stockholm, 1964.
3. R. Edward Freeman, *Strategic Management: A Stakeholder Approach*, Pitman, 1984, p. 46.
4. James E. Post, Lee E. Preston, & Sybille Sachs, "Managing the Extended Enterprise: The New Stakeholder View," *California Management Review*, Vol. 45, No. 1, Fall 2002, p. 8.
5. The earliest reference to the term *stakeholder* that I have been able to find in the academic management literature is to "an internal memorandum at the Stanford Research Institute in 1963" (quoted in R. Edward Freeman & David L. Reed, "Stockholders and Stakeholders: A New Perspective on Corporate Governance," *California Management Review*, 1983, p. 89). In addition, Klaus Schwab claims to have "developed the 'stakeholder' theory for business" around 1970 (quoted in Klaus Schwab, "A breakdown in our values," *The Guardian*, January 6, 2010, http://www.guardian.co.uk/commentisfree/2010/jan/06/bankers-bonuses-crisis-social-risk/).
6. Frank W. Pierce, "Developing Tomorrow's Business Leaders," an address to the Cincinnati Chapter of the Society for the Advancement of Management, December 6, 1945, quoted in Howard R. Bowen, *Social Responsibilities of the Businessman*, Harper & Brothers, 1953, p. 51.
7. Frank W. Abrams, "Management's Responsibilities in a Complex World," *Harvard Business Review*, Vol. 29, No. 3, 1951, pp. 29, 30.
8. Howard R. Bowen, *Social Responsibilities of the Businessman*, Harper & Brothers, 1953, pp. 41–42.
9. Eric Rhenman, *Foeretagsdemokrati och foeretagsorganisation*, S.A.F. Norstedt: Företagsekonomiska Forsknings Institutet, Thule, Stockholm, 1964. See also R. Edward Freeman, Jeffrey S. Harrison, Andrew C. Wicks, Bidhan L. Parmar, & Simone de Colle, *Stakeholder Theory: The State of the Art*, Cambridge University Press, 2010, p. 48.
10. It is important to note that, while anyone who considers themselves a stakeholder can be thought of as such, the firm also plays an important role in identifying those stakeholders it considers important (as implied by the Freeman definition). In other words, it is conceivable that there are stakeholders who might not consider themselves as such, but the company treats them as a stakeholder as a result of its operations or strategic interests.
11. Samantha Miles, "Stakeholder: Essentially Contested or Just Confused?" *Journal of Business Ethics*, 2012, p. 295.
12. R. Edward Freeman, Jeffrey S. Harrison, Andrew C. Wicks, Bidhan L. Parmar, & Simone de Colle, *Stakeholder Theory: The State of the Art*, Cambridge University Press, 2010, p. 208.
13. See Rebecca Tuhus-Dubrow, "US: Sued by the forest," *The Boston Globe,* July 19, 2009, reprinted by CorpWatch, http://www.corpwatch.org/article.php?id=15413, and Mark Starik, "Should Trees Have Managerial Standing? Toward Stakeholder Status for Non-human Nature," *Journal of Business Ethics*, Vol. 14, No. 3, 1995, pp. 207–217.
14. See the United Nations' 1989/1990 Convention on the Rights of the Child, http://www.ohchr.org/en/professionalinterest/pages/crc.aspx, and Bo Viktor Nylund, "Can businesses offer children a public voice?" *The Guardian,* November 25, 2013,

http://www.theguardian.com/sustainable-business/businesses-offer-children-public-voice/.

15. Eduardo Porter, "Electing to Ignore the Poorest of the Poor," *The New York Times*, November 18, 2015, p. B1.

16. For a network-based stakeholder perspective, see James E. Post, Lee E. Preston, & Sybille Sachs, "Managing the Extended Enterprise: The New Stakeholder View," *California Management Review*, Vol. 45, No. 1, 2002, pp. 6–28.

17. Howard R. Bowen, *Social Responsibilities of the Businessman*, Harper & Brothers, 1953, p. 102.

18. John Mackey, quoted in April Fulton, "Whole Foods Founder John Mackey on Fascism and 'Conscious Capitalism,'" National Public Radio, January 17, 2013, http://www.npr.org/blogs/thesalt/2013/01/16/169413848/whole-foods-founder-john-mackey-on-fascism-and-conscious-capitalism/.

19. John Mackey, quoted in John Bussey, "Are Companies Responsible for Creating Jobs?" *The Wall Street Journal*, October 28, 2011, p. B1.

20. Andrew Likierman, "Stakeholder dreams and shareholder realities," *Financial Times*, June 16, 2006, p. 10.

21. Hedrick Smith, "When Capitalists Cared," *The New York Times*, September 2, 2012, http://www.nytimes.com/2012/09/03/opinion/henry-ford-when-capitalists-cared.html.

22. See the discussion around "A Rational Argument for CSR" in Chapter 1 of this textbook.

23. http://www.accountability.org/.

24. Simon Zadek, "The Path to Corporate Responsibility," *Harvard Business Review*, December 2004, pp. 125–132.

25. Ibid., p. 127.

26. Ibid., p. 128.

27. Stephanie Strom, "Social Media as a Megaphone to Push Food Makers to Change," *The New York Times*, December 31, 2013, p. B1.

28. Anne Lawrence suggests that there are four strategies managers can employ to engage stakeholders: "Wage a fight," "Withdraw," "Wait," and "Work it out." See Anne T. Lawrence, "Managing Disputes with Nonmarket Stakeholders," *California Management Review*, Vol. 53, No. 1, Fall 2010, pp. 90–113.

29. The model in Figure 4.4 was developed with the assistance of Richard E. Wokutch, professor of management, and his class of PhD students at the Pamplin College of Business at Virginia Polytechnic Institute and State University.

Chapter 5

1. Deborah Doane, "The Myth of CSR: The problem with assuming that companies can do well while also doing good is that markets don't really work that way," *Stanford Social Innovation Review*, Fall 2005, p. 26.

2. "The money trap," *The Economist*, August 22, 2015, p. 69.

3. For example, see Stephen Gandel, "Jamie Dimon calls regulation un-American, once again," *Fortune*, January 14, 2015, http://fortune.com/2015/01/14/jamie-dimon-financial-regulation/.

4. Milton Friedman, "The Social Responsibility of Business Is to Increase Its Profits," *The New York Times Magazine*, September 13, 1970, p. SM17.

5. Ibid.

6. Charles Handy, "What's a Business For?" *Harvard Business Review*, December 2002, pp. 49–55.

7. Ibid.

8. Milton Friedman, "The Social Responsibility of Business Is to Increase Its Profits," *The New York Times Magazine*, September 13, 1970, p. SM17.

9. Ibid.

10. Archie B. Carroll, "The Pyramid of Corporate Social Responsibility: Toward the Moral Management of Organizational Stakeholders," *Business Horizons,* July–August 1991, p. 43.

11. Ian Davis, "The biggest contract," *The Economist*, May 28, 2005, p. 73.

12. For example, see Claire Zillman, "Here's what a $15 per hour wage means for fast food prices," *Fortune,* July 30, 2015, http://fortune.com/2015/07/30/15-per-hour-fast-food-prices/.

13. EarthShare, "We Live in the House We All Build" [Advertisement], Summer 2008,

http://www.earthshare.org/psa/earthshare_printpsa_2008.pdf.

14. Ibid.

15. What is the nature of a *responsibility*? The notion of a firm's *responsibility* or *obligation* toward its stakeholders only carries weight if there are significant consequences for those firms that fail to fulfill such responsibilities and obligations. If such consequences do not arise, then those actions, in fact, are likely not valued by stakeholders and, as such, are more likely to be ill-advised expenditures of the firm's capital. In those instances where such consequences do arise, then the firm's executives can be said to have failed in their *responsibility* to protect the firm's long-term interests. For stakeholders to support firms means for them collectively to bestow the legitimacy the organization needs to continue conducting business. Those firms that no longer perform a valued service or produce a valued product will not remain viable (in a market system). Such value is determined by the collective consensus of all stakeholders. Thus, it can be argued, that it is in the best interests of the executives of a firm to strive to meet the needs and demands of stakeholders, while it is in the best interests of stakeholders to maintain a clear idea of the value they expect from a firm and hold these organizations to account to ensure they deliver it.

16. For an ethics perspective on the responsibilities of stakeholders, see Jerry D. Goodstein & Andrew C. Wicks, "Corporate and Stakeholder Responsibility: Making Business Ethics a Two-way Conversation," *Business Ethics Quarterly*, Vol. 17, No. 3, 2007, pp. 375–398.

17. For additional discussion of these ideas, see Duane Windsor, "Stakeholder Responsibilities: Lessons for Managers," *Journal of Corporate Citizenship*, April 2002, pp. 19–35, and Mike Barnett, "Business & Society Version 3.0: Attending to What Stakeholders Attend To," Network for Business Sustainability, February 22, 2012, http://nbs.net/business-society-version-3-0-attending-to-what-stakeholders-attend-to/. See also David Chandler, "Why Aren't We Stressing Stakeholder Responsibility?" *HBR Blog Network*, April 29, 2010, http://blogs.hbr.org/what-business-owes-the-world/2010/04/why-arent-we-stressing-stakeho.html.

18. The concept of corporate stakeholder responsibility presented here is different from the idea of "company stakeholder responsibility" advocated by Ed Freeman and colleagues, which is more similar to the concept of strategic CSR. See R. Edward Freeman, S. Ramakrishna Velamuri, & Brian Moriarty, "Company Stakeholder Responsibility: A New Approach to CSR," Business Roundtable Institute for Corporate Ethics, 2006, http://www.corporate-ethics.org/pdf/csr.pdf.

19. Arthur C. Brooks, "The Trick to Being More Virtuous," *The New York Times*, November 27, 2014, http://www.nytimes.com/2014/11/28/opinion/the-trick-to-being-more-virtuous.html.

20. "Lumber Liquidators," *60 Minutes*, CBS, August 16, 2015, http://www.cbsnews.com/news/lumber-liquidators-linked-to-health-and-safety-violations-2/, and Myles Udland, "*60 Minutes* airs troubling report detailing major problems at Lumber Liquidators factories in China," *Business Insider*, March 1, 2015, http://www.businessinsider.com/lumber-liquidators-60-minutes-report-2015-3/.

21. Joann Muller, "VW's $7 Billion Screwup: A Lesson in How to Destroy a Brand," *Forbes*, September 22, 2015, http://www.forbes.com/sites/joannmuller/2015/09/22/vws-7-billion-screw-up-a-lesson-in-how-to-destroy-a-brand/.

22. Bill Vlasic & Aaron M. Kessler, "It Took E.P.A. to Pressure VW to Admit Fault," *The New York Times*, September 22, 2015, p. A1.

23. For an understanding of this concept as originally constructed, see Jean Jacques Rousseau, *Of the Social Contract, or Principles of Political Right*, 1762 (translated in 1782 by G. D. H. Cole).

24. For an argument that humans are innately focused on the short term, see Peter Wilby, "Humanity must recognize our entire way of life is chronically short termist," *The Guardian*, June 1, 2007, p. 33.

25. Rob Walker, "Sex vs. Ethics," *Fast Company Magazine*, No. 124, April 2008, pp. 54–56.

26. Chandran Nair, "Ethical consumers—cop-out at the checkout," Global Institute for Tomorrow, September 10, 2008, http://www.global-inst.com/ideas-for-tomorrow/2008/the-ethical-corporation-column-september.html.

27. Andrew Bounds, "Ethical goods prove popular despite downturn," *Financial Times*, December 14, 2011, http://www.ft.com/cms/s/0/759e0b12-2666-11e1-85fb-00144feabdc0.html.

28. Christine Bader, "Why Corporations Fail to Do the Right Thing," *The Atlantic*, April 21, 2014, http://www.theatlantic.com/business/archive/2014/04/why-making-corporations-socially-responsible-is-so-darn-hard/360984/.

29. I define *value* in its broadest sense to encapsulate both economic and social contributions to the common good. This includes the idea that financial profit already incorporates much of the value to society added by the pursuit of profit (at a minimum jobs, taxes, a product consumers demand, etc., but much more subtle and far-reaching value added as well). It is inaccurate to say that firms that pursue profit do not also add social value. *Economic value* and *social value* are closer to being synonymous than being mutually exclusive. Defining value more broadly, however, also recognizes that there are large numbers of externalities currently excluded from the market pricing mechanism that affect total value added and are better encapsulated within the term *social value*.

30. Thomas L. Friedman, "Advice From Grandma," *The New York Times*, November 22, 2009, p. WK10.

31. Adam Bluestein, "You Sign, Companies Listen," *Fast Company Magazine*, September 2013, pp. 34, 36.

32. Valeriya Safronova, "Millennials Get a Cyber Voice," *The New York Times*, December 21, 2014, p. 12.

33. Interbrand, "Best Global Brands 2015," http://interbrand.com/best-brands/best-global-brands/2015/.

34. Warren Bass, "A Brave New World in 9/11 Aftermath" [Review of *The World Is Flat: A Brief History of the Twenty-First Century*, by Thomas L. Friedman, Farrar Straus Giroux, 2005], *Miami Herald,* April 10, 2005, p. 7M.

35. Kathleen Parker, "Attention, Wal-Mart shoppers: You have a say," *Orlando Sentinel* (reprinted in the *Austin American Statesman*), January 30, 2006, p. A9.

36. Moisés Naim, "Corporate Power Is Decaying. Get Used to It," *Bloomberg Businessweek*, February 21, 2013, http://www.bloomberg.com/bw/articles/2013-02-21/corporate-power-is-decaying-dot-get-used-to-it/.

37. Figure 5.3 is adapted from a figure presented by Mark Newton, environmental policy manager, DELL Inc.'s Corporate Sustainability Team, at "Sustainability as a global business imperative—What do facts show?" Center for Customer Insight and Marketing Solutions, The University of Texas at Austin, September 27, 2007.

38. For a more detailed discussion about the CSR threshold, see Chapter 10.

39. An interesting thought experiment is to imagine how a firm could move the CSR threshold line to the left. It is important that this be done in a productive way (creating value for stakeholders), rather than as a cynical effort to delay a day of reckoning. Perhaps a dramatic and genuine move to accommodate stakeholder(s) concerns would generate sufficient goodwill to delay the timing of any stakeholder retribution.

40. See Gallup for the raw data: http://www.gallup.com/poll/1654/honesty-ethics-professions.aspx.

41. "Capitalism and its discontents," *The Economist*, October 3, 2015, p. 71.

42. "Getting it right," *The Economist*, October 10, 2015, p. 86.

43. "Capitalism and its discontents," *The Economist*, October 3, 2015, p. 71.

44. For an analysis of the awareness and importance of CSR to the public and other corporate stakeholders, see Jenny Dawkins & Stewart Lewis, "CSR in Stakeholder Expectations: And Their Implication for Company Strategy," *Journal of Business Ethics,* May 2003, Vol. 44, pp. 185–193: "Over ten years of research at MORI has shown the increasing prominence of corporate responsibility for a wide range of stakeholders, from consumers and employees to legislators and investors. . . . Traditionally, the factors that mattered most to consumers when forming an opinion of a company were product quality, value for money and financial performance. Now, across a worldwide sample of the public, the most commonly mentioned factors relate to corporate responsibility (e.g., treatment of employees, community involvement, ethical and environmental issues)."

45. David Ogilvy, quoted in Dara O'Rourke, "Behavioral tracking and neuroscience are tools for sustainable innovation," *The Guardian*, July 25, 2014, http://www.theguardian.com/sustainable-business/behavioural-insights/behavioural-tracking-neuroscience-tools-sustainable-innovation-advertising-marketing-consumers/.

46. Dara O'Rourke, "Behavioral tracking and neuroscience are tools for sustainable innovation," *The Guardian*, July 25, 2014, http://www.theguardian.com/sustainable-business/behavioural-insights/behavioural-tracking-neuroscience-tools-sustainable-innovation-advertising-marketing-consumers/.

47. Ibid.

48. Sally Blount, "Yes, the World Needs More MBAs. Here's Why," *Bloomberg Businessweek*, May 13, 2014, http://www.bloomberg.com/bw/articles/2014-05-13/yes-the-world-needs-more-mbas-dot-heres-why/

49. Ibid.

50. Daniel Akst, "Ethics' Afternoon Swoon," *The Wall Street Journal*, November 9–10, 2013, p. C4.

51. Aspen Institute, http://www.beyondgreypinstripes.org/. The MBA ranking was suspended by The Aspen Institute in the spring of 2012.

52. The Aspen Institute Business & Society Program, "Beyond Grey Pinstripes 2011–2012: Preparing MBAs for Social and Environmental Stewardship," 2012, p. 1, http://www.aspeninstitute.org/publications/beyond-grey-pinstripes-2011-2012-top-100-mba-programs/.

53. "From Fringe to Mainstream: Companies Integrate CSR Initiatives into Everyday Business," *Knowledge@Wharton*, May 23, 2012, http://knowledge.wharton.upenn.edu/article/from-fringe-to-mainstream-companies-integrate-csr-initiatives-into-everyday-business/.

54. Ibid.

55. https://www.netimpact.org/about (accessed February 2016).

56. See also 50+20, Management Education for the World, http://50plus20.org/.

57. http://www.unprme.org/participants/index.php (accessed February 2016).

58. http://www.unprme.org/about-prme/the-six-principles.php (accessed February 2016).

59. Ibid.

60. "You are not special," *The Economist*, May 23, 2015, p. 73.

61. Jon Alexander, "The 'just go shopping' message from advertisers has a dangerous effect," *The Guardian*, January 10, 2014, http://www.theguardian.com/sustainable-business/behavioural-insights/just-go-shopping-message-advertisers-dangerous-effect/.

62. The table in Figure 5.6 was developed with Tim Hart of the University of Tulsa.

Chapter 6

1. The ideas presented and expanded upon in this chapter were first published in David Chandler, *Corporate Social Responsibility: A Strategic Perspective*, Business Expert Press, 2014.

2. It is commonly understood that the original purpose of incorporation (by crown charter) was to accomplish continuity of life (beyond that of the original mix of an organization's investors). Limited liability was achieved over time by a legal sleight of hand, redrafting investor obligations in relation to calls for additional capital. If a bankrupt company had an enforceable right to call in capital from investors, for example to shore up the continued viability of an enterprise, creditors could claim that right as an asset of the firm and pursue the call (by right of subrogation). Gradually, lawyers began excluding these obligations, with the result that there was no legal claim for creditors to use, thus, by definition, limiting the investors' liability. Once established and accepted, limited liability gained its own legitimacy as an inducement to investors to support entrepreneurs in the value creation process.

3. Subhabrata Bobby Banerjee, "Corporate Social Responsibility: The Good, the Bad and the Ugly," *Critical Sociology*, Vol. 34, No. 1, 2008, p. 53.

4. For a thorough discussion of the founding of the modern-day corporation and, in particular, the construction of the concept of limited liability, see John Micklethwait & Adrian Wooldridge, *The Company: A Short History of a Revolutionary Idea*, Modern Library, 2003.

5. John Micklethwait & Adrian Wooldridge, *The Company: A Short History of a Revolutionary Idea*, Modern Library, 2003, pp. 43, 46.

6. It is important to note that this discussion relates primarily to the ownership and purpose of publicly traded corporations in the United States. Although there are similarities, corporate law naturally varies across countries and cultures. And even in the United States, legal precedent governing firms differs among states and based on whether the firms are private or closely held. This can be seen in *Revlon Inc. v. MacAndrews & Forbes Holdings, Inc.*, 506 A.2d 173 (Del. 1986), a case of limited application in which the Delaware Supreme Court announced, "Where the company was being 'broken up' and shareholders were being forced to sell their interests in the firm to a private buyer, the board had a duty to maximize shareholder wealth by getting the highest possible price for the shares." See Lynn A. Stout, "Why We Should Stop Teaching *Dodge v. Ford*," *Virginia Law & Business Review*, Vol. 3, No. 1, 2008, p. 172.

7. Martin Lipton & William Savitt, "The Many Myths of Lucian Bebchuk," *Virginia Law Review*, Vol. 93, No. 3, 2007, p. 754.

8. Adolph A. Berle & Gardiner C. Means, *The Modern Corporation and Private Property*, Macmillan, 1932.

9. "Rise of the distorporation," *The Economist*, October 26, 2013, p. 30.

10. Steven M. Davidoff, "S.E.C.'s Review of Trading Will See Some of Its Own Work," *The New York Times*, February 14, 2014, p. B5.

11. Jonathan Rosenthal, "Rise of the robotraders," *The Economist: The World in 2014*, January 2014, p. 130.

12. "Fast times," *The Economist*, April 5, 2014, p. 73.

13. For a detailed exposition of how high-frequency traders utilize technology to exploit arbitrage opportunities in the market and trade on the intentions of other investors, see Michael Lewis, *Flash Boys: A Wall Street Revolt*, W. W. Norton, 2014. In essence, "high-frequency trading firms would post the 'best price' for every stock and then when hit with a trade, knowing there was a buyer in the market, take advantage of the fragmentation of exchanges and dark pools and latency (high-frequency traders can get to an exchange faster than you) to buy up shares from other HFTs or from Wall Street dark pools, and then nudge the price up and sell those shares. In other words, front run the customer. . . . It's sleazy and maybe even illegal, akin to nanosecond-scale insider trading" (in Andy Kessler, "High-Frequency Trading Needs One Quick Fix," *The Wall Street Journal*, June 16, 2014, p. A15. See also Michael Lewis, "The Wolf Hunters of Wall Street," *The New York Times Magazine*, March 31, 2014, pp. 27–35, 42–44, 50–51.

14. "Fast times," *The Economist*, April 5, 2014, p. 73.

15. "The monolith and the markets," *The Economist*, December 7, 2013, p. 25.

16. Ibid., p. 26.

17. John Maynard Keynes, *The General Theory of Employment, Interest and Money*, Harcourt Brace and Co., 1936, p. 156.

18. Paul Krugman, "Now That's Rich," *The New York Times*, May 9, 2014, p. A25.

19. Howard R. Bowen, *Social Responsibilities of the Businessman*, Harper & Brothers, 1953, p. 34.

20. http://www.merriam-webster.com/ and http://www.oed.com/ (accessed February 2016).

21. While a number of US state corporate codes contain language that defines *shareholders* as the owners of *shares*, which are "the units into which the proprietary interests in a corporation are divided" (e.g., Colorado Corporation Code, Section 7-101-401, http://tornado.state.co.us/gov_dir/leg_dir/olls/sl1993/sl_191.pdf), Delaware, "the single most important [US] state for corporate law purposes . . . does not define the term *stock* or otherwise say what it represents. . . . The Delaware statute is simply silent on the issue of ownership" (in Julian Velasco, "Shareholder Ownership and Primacy," *University of Illinois Law Review*, Vol. 2010, No. 3, 2010, pp. 929–930). Equally silent are the company laws of the next four most important states for US corporate law: New York, California, Illinois, and Pennsylvania. It is instructive

that the law in each of these five states fails to define the shareholders of the corporation as its owners. Nevertheless, it is also correct to note that there is inconsistency among all 50 states. As such, it seems fair to conclude that the essence of *ownership* lies more in how corporate law is enforced and, in particular, how it is enforced in Delaware. In other words, I argue it is how courts interpret the relationship between the corporation and its shareholders in reality that is the ultimate determinant of who legally *owns* the corporation.

22. Luh Luh Lan & Loizos Heracleous, "Rethinking Agency Theory: The View from Law," *Academy of Management Review*, Vol. 35, No. 2, 2010, p. 301.

23. For related work that builds on the argument that the firm has obligations to its stakeholders, broadly defined, see James E. Post, Lee E. Preston, & Sybille Sachs, *Redefining the Corporation: Stakeholder Management and Organizational Wealth*, Stanford Business Books, 2002, and Sybille Sachs & Edwin Ruhli, *Stakeholders Matter: A New Paradigm for Strategy in Society*, Cambridge University Press, 2012.

24. Martin Wolf, "AstraZeneca is more than investors' call," *Financial Times*, May 8, 2014, http://www.ft.com/cms/s/0/6fe31054-d691-11e3-b251-00144feabdc0.html.

25. In December 2015, Apple announced that its board of directors had approved bylaws that "allow a shareholder, or a group of up to 20 shareholders, holding 3% of its shares continuously for three years to include board nominees in the company's annual proxy statement." What is interesting about this announcement is that, even this incremental advance in favor of shareholder democracy was treated as *good news* for governance activists. In reality, the firm gave up very little, since owning 3% of Apple's shares would constitute an investment of $18 billion. Moreover, "the bylaw allows shareholders to nominate up to 20% of Apple's directors. Apple's board currently has eight members, so shareholders could nominate one director." That such a minor concession by Apple should be heralded as a major advance indicates the sorry state of shareholder democracy in the United States.

See Scott Thurm, "Apple Offers Proxy Access," *The Wall Street Journal*, December 22, 2015, http://www.wsj.com/articles/apple-inc-offers-proxy-access-1450824690/.

26. Dennis K. Berman, "Boardroom Defenestration," *The Wall Street Journal*, March 16, 2006, p. B1.

27. Joann S. Lublin & Theo Francis, "Where Majority Doesn't Rule," *The Wall Street Journal*, May 12, 2014, p. B8.

28. Eugene F. Fama, "Agency Problems and the Theory of the Firm," *Journal of Political Economy*, Vol. 88, 1980, p. 290.

29. Luh Luh Lan & Loizos Heracleous, "Rethinking Agency Theory: The View from Law," *Academy of Management Review*, Vol. 35, No. 2, 2010, p. 301.

30. "And what was particularly grotesque about this was that the 14th amendment was passed to protect newly-freed slaves. So, for instance, between 1890 and 1910, there were 307 cases brought before the Court under the 14th amendment—288 of these brought by corporations; 19 by African-Americans. [As a result of the Civil War,] 600,000 people were killed to get rights for people and then, with strokes of the pen over the next 30 years, judges applied those rights to capital and property, while stripping them from people." See *The Corporation* documentary, 2003, http://www.thecorporation.com/.

31. In reality, the detail of which rights and responsibilities should be legally ascribed to corporations and which should be reserved for humans alone is an ongoing constitutional debate (see Chapter 3). As a result, corporations are neither fully fledged individuals, nor are they artificial entities devoid of rights—legal precedent has determined they fall somewhere in between: "In the past, Supreme Court opinions have recognized the need for differing approaches to the recognition (or not) of constitutional rights of business corporations in various settings. For example, the Court has decided that the constitutional protection against 'double jeopardy' for an alleged crime covers organizational persons (such as a corporation), but the right protecting against forcible 'self-incrimination' does not. Similarly, the Court has recognized a right of political free

speech for organizations in *Citizens United*, but not 'rights to privacy' which have been reserved for individual human beings. In other words, the Court finds some constitutional rights make sense to extend to organizational persons, and it leaves others to cover only individual people" (in Eric W. Orts, "The 'Hobby Lobby' Case: Religious Freedom, Corporations and Individual Rights," *Knowledge@Wharton*, March 31, 2014, https://knowledge.wharton.upenn.edu/article/hobby-lobby-case-religious-freedom-corporations-individual-rights/).

32. "The business of business," *The Economist*, March 21, 2015, p. 62.

33. Jonathan R. Macey, "A Close Read of an Excellent Commentary on *Dodge v. Ford*," *Virginia Law & Business Review*, Vol. 3, No. 1, 2008, p. 180.

34. Ibid., p. 190.

35. Joann S. Lublin & Theo Francis, "Where Majority Doesn't Rule," *The Wall Street Journal*, May 12, 2014, p. B8.

36. Ibid.

37. *HL Bolton (Engineering) v. TJ Graham and Sons Ltd*. [1957] 1 QB 159 (Court of Appeal), Denning LJ (p. 172).

38. Shareholders also have a claim to the residual of the firm when it enters bankruptcy. As with many other so-called shareholder *rights*, however, this claim reveals the nature of the legal relationship between the firm and its investors, who must line up behind the firm's bondholders and all other creditors.

39. *Dodge v. Ford Motor Co.*, 204 Mich. 459, 170 N.W. 668 (1919).

40. For additional insight into this case and why it has historically been misinterpreted as support for the idea the directors of a firm have a fiduciary responsibility to maximize shareholder value, see Lynn A. Stout, "Why We Should Stop Teaching *Dodge v. Ford*," UCLA School of Law, Law-Econ Research Paper No. 07-11, 2008.

41. Moreover, because investors are not one homogenous group with similar goals, investment time frames, or values (they include pension funds, day traders, and high-frequency computer algorithms), they cannot approximate the legal or actual influence of a sole proprietor who owns 100% of a firm's shares (or even a majority owner).

42. See The Modern Corporation, "Fundamental rules of corporate law," http://themoderncorporation.wordpress.com/company-law-memo/ (accessed February 2016).

43. John Kay, "Shareholders think they own the company—they are wrong," *Financial Times*, November 11, 2015, p. 9.

44. Ibid.

45. For example, see Jacob M. Rose, "Corporate Directors and Social Responsibility: Ethics versus Shareholder Value," *Journal of Business Ethics*, Vol. 73, No. 3, July 2007, pp. 319–331. This study reports that "directors . . . sometimes make decisions that emphasize legal defensibility at the expense of personal ethics and social responsibility. Directors recognize the ethical and social implications of their decisions, but they believe that current corporate law requires them to pursue legal courses of action that maximize shareholder value" (p. 319).

46. In the business school, we are largely oblivious to this debate, which is occurring in the academic corporate law community. For more information, see http://themoderncorporation.wordpress.com/company-law-memo/.

47. Julian Velasco, "Shareholder Ownership and Primacy," *University of Illinois Law Review*, Vol. 2010, No. 3, 2010, p. 899.

48. The corporate legal scholars at The Modern Corporation who authored the statement "Fundamental rules of corporate law" (http://themoderncorporation.wordpress.com/company-law-memo/, accessed February 2016) argue that this absence of a fiduciary responsibility of directors is "applicable in almost all jurisdictions."

49. For a detailed examination of the legal foundation (or lack thereof) for the idea that the primary fiduciary responsibility of the firm's executives and directors is to serve the interests of the firm's shareholders, see Lynn A. Stout, *The Shareholder Value Myth: How Putting Shareholders First Harms Investors, Corporations, and the Public*, Berrett-Koehler, 2002.

50. See The Modern Corporation, "Fundamental rules of corporate law," http://themoderncorporation.wordpress.com/company-law-memo/ (accessed February 2016).

51. Luh Luh Lan & Loizos Heracleous, "Rethinking Agency Theory: The View from

Law," *Academy of Management Review*, Vol. 35, No. 2, 2010, p. 300.

52. *Dodge v. Ford Motor Company*, 204 Mich. 459, 170 N.W. 668 (1919).

53. Lynn A. Stout, "Why We Should Stop Teaching *Dodge v. Ford*," *Virginia Law & Business Review*, Vol. 3, No. 1, 2008, p. 166.

54. "*Dodge v. Ford* is best viewed as a case that deals not with directors' duties to maximize shareholder wealth, but with controlling shareholders' duties not to oppress minority shareholders. The one Delaware opinion that has cited *Dodge v. Ford* in the last thirty years, *Blackwell v. Nixon*, cites it for just this proposition" (in Lynn A. Stout, "Why We Should Stop Teaching *Dodge v. Ford*," *Virginia Law & Business Review*, Vol. 3, No. 1, 2008, p. 168.

55. Lynn A. Stout, "Why We Should Stop Teaching *Dodge v. Ford*," *Virginia Law & Business Review*, Vol. 3, No. 1, 2008, pp. 163–176.

56. Lynn A. Stout, *The Shareholder Value Myth: How Putting Shareholders First Harms Investors, Corporations, and the Public*, Berrett-Koehler, 2012, pp. 3–4.

57. An indirect attempt to rebut Stout's arguments was made by Leo E. Strine Jr., chief justice of the Delaware Supreme Court, in an essay in the *Columbia Law Review* ("Can We Do Better by Ordinary Investors? A Pragmatic Reaction to the Dueling Ideological Mythologists of Corporate Law," Vol. 114, No. 2, pp. 449–502). The essay is primarily a response to the idea of the firm as a "shareholder-driven direct democracy" (p. 449), which advocates for wider shareholder powers and more frequent shareholder votes to govern firm policy. In arguing against this model, Strine also addresses the "skeptics [who] go so far as to deny that boards of directors must, within the constraints of the law, make the best interests of stockholders the end goal of the governance of a for-profit corporation" (p. 452). Unfortunately, however, Strine fails to acknowledge the near impossible task of defining what those "interests" might be (given that the firm's stockholders include high-frequency traders holding positions for microseconds, day traders, and pension funds). He also bases his case on facts such as "only stockholders

get to elect directors" (p. 453), as if that depicts ownership, without acknowledging that, in reality, shareholders vote on the candidates nominated by management and that additional *legal rights* are constrained because many votes (e.g., shareholder resolutions) are nonbinding. Most damagingly, by undermining the idea of the direct democracy model (which would at least be more consistent with the idea of shareholders as owners) by arguing that "the best way to ensure that corporations generate wealth for diversified stockholders is to give the managers of corporations a strong hand to take risks and implement business strategies without constant disruption by shifting stock market sentiment," Strine essentially reinforces Stout's case that the courts tend to favor management over stockholders in any dispute.

58. Jonathan R. Macey, "A Close Read of an Excellent Commentary on *Dodge v. Ford*," *Virginia Law & Business Review*, Vol. 3, No. 1, 2008, p. 180.

59. Floyd Norris, "Companies That Lie Increasingly Win in Court," *The New York Times*, March 21, 2014, p. B1.

60. Loizos Heracleous & Luh Luh Lan, "The Myth of Shareholder Capitalism," *Harvard Business Review*, April 2010, p. 24. See also Luh Luh Lan & Loizos Heracleous, "Rethinking Agency Theory: The View from Law," *Academy of Management Review*, Vol. 35, No. 2, 2010, pp. 294–314.

61. Jessica Shankleman, "Tim Cook tells climate change sceptics to ditch Apple shares," *The Guardian*, March 3, 2014, http://www.theguardian.com/environment/2014/mar/03/tim-cook-climate-change-sceptics-ditch-apple-shares/.

62. Michael Skapinker, "Long-term corporate plans may be lost in translation," *Financial Times*, November 23, 2010, p. 13.

63. Francesco Guerrera, "Welch condemns share price focus," *Financial Times*, March 12, 2009, http://www.ft.com/cms/s/0/294ff1f2-0f27-11de-ba10-0000779fd2ac.html.

64. "Jack Welch Elaborates: Shareholder Value," *Bloomberg Businessweek*, March 16, 2009, http://www.businessweek.com/bwdaily/dnflash/content/mar2009/db20090316_630496.htm.

65. Although most of us are shareholders, in that we are invested in pension funds that hold shares, in reality this relationship is indirect since these assets are managed by others on our behalf. Most people would not describe themselves primarily as a shareholder and, often, have a greater proportion of their total wealth invested in other assets, such as property.

66. It is important to draw a distinction between *rights* and *influence*. If executives believe shareholders own the firm, they will respond to shareholder demands. This is true whether or not shareholders actually own the firm. However, it is interesting to ask: If shareholders have no legal power, how is this pressure manifested or felt, especially if the firm is not seeking additional capital? One answer highlights the extent to which executive compensation is increasingly tied to firm performance, which is often measured by share price. While this effect helps align the interests of executives and shareholders, it is not clear that the results benefit the long-term interests of the firm. See Justin Fox & Jay W. Lorsch, "What Good Are Shareholders?" *Harvard Business Review*, July–August 2012, pp. 49–57.

67. Danielle Chesebrough & Rory Sullivan, "What can companies do about investor short-termism?" *Ethical Corporation*, November 26, 2013, http://www.ethicalcorp.com/stakeholder-engagement/what-can-companies-do-about-investor-short-termism/.

68. Andrew Ross Sorkin, "A CEO Urges Others to Stop Being So Nice to Investors," *The New York Times*, April 14, 2015, p. B1.

69. Buttonwood, "Losing a tailwind," *The Economist*, July 18, 2015, p. 61. See also Steven Russolillo, "Companies Binge on Share Buybacks," *The Wall Street Journal*, December 24, 2013, p. C1.

70. There are two ways that a firm can redistribute profits to its shareholders—share buybacks or dividends. While both methods ultimately raise the firm's share price, buybacks raise it directly (by decreasing the number of shares outstanding), while dividends do it indirectly (by making the shares a more attractive investment). The ratio of share buybacks to dividends among US firms is approximately 1:0.62. This figure is calculated using third-quarter figures for 2013, during which "U.S. companies in the S&P 500-stock index bought back $128.2 billion of their own shares. . . . Combined, stock buybacks and dividends totaled $207 billion" (in Steven Russolillo, "Companies Binge on Share Buybacks," *The Wall Street Journal*, December 24, 2013, p. C1).

71. "Capitalism and its discontents," *The Economist*, October 3, 2015, p. 71.

72. "Reform school for bankers," *The Economist*, October 5, 2013, p. 73.

73. It is worth emphasizing here that shareholder pressure is not the only reason that firms focus on the short term. Executive compensation packages that rely disproportionately on share price as an indicator of firm performance (or contain large amounts in stock options) also have the same effect. As noted by Robert Pozen of Harvard Business School, "At present, most firms distribute case bonuses and stock grants on the basis of the prior year's results. This approach does encourage top executives to favor short-term results over long-term growth" (in Robert C. Pozen, "The Misdirected War on Corporate Short-Termism," *The Wall Street Journal*, May 19, 2014, http://online.wsj.com/news/articles/SB10001424052702304547704579564390935661048/).

74. Gregory J. Millman, "Firms See Value Opportunity in Shareholder Base," *The Wall Street Journal*, May 22, 2014, http://blogs.wsj.com/riskandcompliance/2014/05/22/the-morning-risk-report-companies-see-value-opportunity-in-shareholder-base/.

75. Julian Velasco, "Shareholder Ownership and Primacy," *University of Illinois Law Review*, Vol. 2010, No. 3, 2010, pp. 901, 902.

76. In game theory, this concept of the likelihood of repeat or future interactions has been termed the "shadow of the future." See Robert Axelrod, *The Evolution of Cooperation*, Basic Books, 1984.

77. See Elizabeth Rigby & Jenny Wiggins, "Unilever Chief Executive Rules Out Return to Issuing Financial Targets," *Financial Times*, May 7, 2009, http://www.ft.com/cms/s/0/c49d164c-3a9e-11de-8a2d-00144feabdc0.html. As Unilever's CEO stated, "At Unilever, . . . we have moved away from quarterly profit reporting; since we don't operate on a 90-day cycle for advertising,

marketing, or investment, why do so for reporting?" (in Paul Polman, "The remedies for capitalism," McKinsey & Company, http://www.mckinsey.com/features/capitalism/paul_polman/ (no longer available online)).

78. See Unilever's Sustainable Living campaign, http://www.unilever.com/sustainable-living/.

79. "How far can Amazon go?" *The Economist*, June 21, 2014, p. 11.

80. An important step in the transition from shareholder focus to stakeholder focus is for the firm to prioritize its stakeholders (see Chapter 4). In the process, firms should understand that a shareholder perspective and a stakeholder perspective are not alternatives but are different shades of the same perspective. Although many commentators talk in terms of a choice between independent constructs, in reality, this is a forced dichotomy. Since shareholders are also stakeholders, a shareholder perspective is actually just a stakeholder perspective with a narrow focus on one stakeholder (shareholders) instead of many.

81. Although in management theory, these ideas are best captured by stakeholder theory, in corporate law and economics, a similar effect is described using the concept of *team production*. Team production theory applies in the case of team production problems, which "are said to arise in situations where a productive activity requires the combined investment and coordinated effort of two or more individuals or groups." Team production theory is applied to corporations as a result of "the observation—generally accepted even by corporate scholars who adhere to the principal-agent model—that shareholders are not the only group that may provide specialized inputs into corporate production" (in Margaret M. Blair & Lynn A. Stout, "A Team Production Theory of Corporate Law," *Virginia Law Review*, Vol. 85, No. 2, March 1999, pp. 249, 250.

Part II Case Study

1. For more information about impact investing, see the Global Impact Investing Network (GIIN), which exists to increase "the scale and effectiveness of impact investing" (http://www.thegiin.org/about/, accessed February 2016). Also, for a general discussion of the different components of impact investing, together with example projects, see "Happy returns," *The Economist*, September 10, 2011, p. 84.

2. Lauren Gensler, "Double Duty Dollars: Behind the Crazy Idea That Investors Can Make Money and Change the World at the Same Time," *Forbes*, June 17, 2015, http://www.forbes.com/sites/laurengensler/2015/06/17/impact-investing/.

3. For example, see Kate Burgess, "Investors are taking a share in revolution," *Financial Times*, May 6, 2009, p. 15.

4. Caitlin Kauffman, "Proxy Preview 2015 Examines Record-Breaking Number of Sustainability-Related Shareholder Resolutions," Sustainable Brands, March 11, 2015, http://www.sustainablebrands.com/news_and_views/marketing_comms/caitlin_kauffman/proxy_preview_2015_examines_record-breaking_number_s/.

5. See Myles Udland, "Carl Icahn: Apple is worth $240 a share," *Business Insider*, May 18, 2015, http://www.businessinsider.com/carl-icahn-on-apple-share-price-2015-5/, and Dawn C. Chmielewski, "Carl Icahn calls Netflix's poison pill measures 'poor governance,'" *Los Angeles Times*, November 5, 2012, http://articles.latimes.com/2012/nov/05/entertainment/la-et-ct-icahn-questions-netflix-poison-pill-20121105/.

6. Bill Baue, "Investing in . . . Genocide?" CSRwire, March 31, 2009, http://www.csrwire.com/press_releases/15577-The-Latest-Corporate-Social-Responsible-News-Investing-in-Genocide-/.

7. Ed Crooks, "Shareholders lead eco-crusade," *Financial Times*, March 8, 2011, p. 15.

8. "An investor calls," *The Economist*, February 7, 2015, p. 23.

9. Ben Protess & Katherine Reynolds Lewis, "Changing Face of Investor Activism," *The New York Times*, June 8, 2012, p. B1.

10. Sheila McNulty, "Shareholder Activists Hijack Exxon's AGM," *Financial Times*, May 9, 2003, p. 17.

11. Ben Protess & Katherine Reynolds Lewis, "Changing Face of Investor Activism," *The New York Times*, June 8, 2012, p. B1.

12. Quoted by an officer from the Investor Responsibility Research Center on *The NewsHour with Jim Lehrer*, PBS, June 10, 2003.

13. As You Sow, *Proxy Preview 2012: Helping Shareholders Vote Their Values*, November 2012, p. 6, http://www.missioninvestors.org/system/files/tools/proxypreview-2012-helping-shareholders-vote-their-values-heidi-welsh-and-michael-passoff-as-you-sow-and-sustainable-investments-institute.pdf (accessed 2012).

14. For example, see David Enrich, "Barclays Shareholders Vent on Pay," *The Wall Street Journal*, April 28–29, 2012, p. B2, and Julia Werdigier, "Amid Shouts of Hecklers, Barclays' Board Apologizes to Shareholders," *The New York Times*, April 28, 2012, p. B2.

15. Investopedia, "Socially Responsible Investment—SRI," November 2012, http://www.investopedia.com/terms/s/sri.asp.

16. David Bogoslaw, "Social Investing Gathers Momentum," *BusinessWeek*, February 3, 2010, http://www.businessweek.com/investor/content/feb2010/pi2010023_247094.htm.

17. Anna Prior, "Investing with a Mission," *The Wall Street Journal*, July 18–19, 2015, p. B7.

18. Chris Gay, "Are Bank Stocks 'Responsible'?" *The Wall Street Journal*, February 6, 2012, p. R6.

19. "SRI Basics," US SIF, http://www.ussif.org/sribasics (accessed February 2016).

20. Ibid.

21. Kevin Mahn, "Modern Sustainable Responsible Impact Investing Versus Traditional Socially Responsible Investing," *Forbes*, April 16, 2015, http://www.forbes.com/sites/advisor/2015/04/16/modern-sustainable-responsible-impact-investing-versus-traditional-socially-responsible-investing/.

22. Simon Howard & Charlene Cranny, "SRI in the United Kingdom," *GreenMoney*, July 2015, http://www.greenmoneyjournal.com/july-2015/uk/.

23. Dimitrios Mavridis, "The State of SRI in Europe—Past, Present and Future," *GreenMoney*, July 2015, http://www.greenmoneyjournal.com/july-2015/europe/.

24. Jessica Robinson, "The State of Sustainable and Responsible Investment in Asia," *GreenMoney*, July 2015, http://www.greenmoneyjournal.com/july-2015/asia/.

25. Kevin Mahn, "Modern Sustainable Responsible Impact Investing Versus Traditional Socially Responsible Investing," *Forbes*, April 16, 2015, http://www.forbes.com/sites/advisor/2015/04/16/modern-sustainable-responsible-impact-investing-versus-traditional-socially-responsible-investing/.

26. David Bogoslaw, "Social Investing Gathers Momentum," *BusinessWeek*, February 3, 2010, http://www.businessweek.com/investor/content/feb2010/pi2010023_247094.htm.

27. Barbara Kiviat, "Heart on One's Sleeve, Eye on Bottom Line," *Miami Herald*, January 19, 2003, p. 3E.

28. Joe Nocera, "Well-Meaning but Misguided Stock Screens," *The New York Times*, April 7, 2007, p. B1.

29. Chris Flood, "Standards for socially responsible investment too sloppy," *Financial Times*, December 7, 2015, p. 2.

30. See Pilita Clark, "Investors turn up heat on fossil fuels," *Financial Times*, January 6, 2015, p. 13.

31. Russ Blinch, "Urge to purge: Millennial movement to dump coal and oil investments," *The Guardian*, May 23, 2014, http://www.theguardian.com/sustainable-business/stanford-millennial-coal-oil-dump-investment-endowmen/.

32. For a timeline of the evolution of sustainable investing, see "UBS Research Focus: Sustainable Investing," UBS Financial Services Inc., July 2013, pp. 4–5, https://www.ubs.com/content/dam/WealthManagementAmericas/documents/UBS-Research-Focus-Sustainable-Investing-July2013.pdf.

33. Ibid., p. 6.

34. "A dull shade of green," *The Economist*, October 29, 2012, p. 87.

35. Mike Cherney, "'Green Bond' Sales Struggle," *The Wall Street Journal*, June 25, 2015, p. C4.

36. Alex Davidson, "Water: The New Screen for Investment Risk," *The Wall Street Journal Report: Investing in Funds & ETFs*, September 9, 2015, p. R8.

37. Chana R. Schoenberger, "The Bond Crowd Seems to Care About Other Kinds of Green, Too," *The Wall Street Journal Report: Investing in Funds & ETFs*, September 9, 2015, p. R8.

38. Paul Sullivan, "With an Eye to Impact, Investing Through a 'Gender Lens,'" *The New York Times*, August 15, 2015, p. B5.

39. Daisy Maxey, "Men Had Their Chance; New Funds Bet on Women," *The Wall Street Journal*, August 4, 2014, p. R1.

40. Chris Newlands & Sophia Grene, "Boards with more women do 36% better," *Financial Times FTfm*, December 7, 2015, p. 1.

41. David Oakley, "Vatican-backed index aims to meet demand for ethical stocks," *Financial Times,* April 27, 2010, p. 13.

42. http://christianinvestmentforum.org/bri/ (accessed February 2016).

43. John Siverling, "Bridging a Great Divide: The Evolving Evangelical Relationship with SRI," *GreenMoney,* February 2015, http://www.greenmoneyjournal.com/february-2015/bridging/.

44. Daisy Maxey, "Men Had Their Chance; New Funds Bet on Women," *The Wall Street Journal*, August 4, 2014, p. R1.

45. See also Andrew Ross Sorkin, "The Women of the S&P 500 and Investor Activism," *The New York Times*, February 10, 2015, p. B1.

46. Robert Goldsborough, a fund analyst at investment research firm Morningstar Inc., quoted in Daisy Maxey, "Men Had Their Chance; New Funds Bet on Women," *The Wall Street Journal*, August 4, 2014, p. R1.

47. For additional explanation, see Meir Statman, "Our Unconscious Investing Motives—And How They Get Us in Trouble," *The Wall Street Journal (Journal Report: Wealth Management)*, June 15, 2015, p. R1.

48. Jem Bendell, "Have you seen my business case?" *Ethical Corporation,* November 2, 2002.

49. USA Mutuals, "Barrier Fund," June 30, 2015, http://www.usamutuals.com/i/u/6149817/f/BarrierFund/Fact_Sheet_-_Barrier_Fund-2015-Q2.pdf.

50. Ed Crooks, "US group bucks trend for social responsibility," *Financial Times*, October 12, 2015, p. 14.

51. Sam Stovall, "Tobacco Stocks: A Classic Defensive Play," *BusinessWeek,* January 29, 2008, http://www.bloomberg.com/bw/stories/2008-01-29/tobacco-stocks-a-classic-defensive-playbusinessweek-business-news-stock-market-and-financial-advice/.

52. James Mackintosh & John Authers, "Sin pays as tobacco and alcohol stocks outpace their sober rivals since 1900," *Financial Times,* February 11, 2015, p. 1.

53. USA Mutuals, "Barrier Fund," June 30, 2015, http://www.usamutuals.com/i/u/6149817/f/BarrierFund/Fact_Sheet_-_Barrier_Fund-2015-Q2.pdf.

54. Luther Ragin Jr. & Tracy Palandjian, "Social Impact Bonds: Using Impact Investment to Expand Effective Social Programs," Federal Reserve Bank of San Francisco, pp. 63–67, http://www.frbsf.org/community-development/files/social-impact-bonds-impact-investment-expand-effective-social-programs.pdf.

55. David Leonhardt, "What Are Social-Impact Bonds?" *The New York Times*, February 8, 2011, http://economix.blogs.nytimes.com/2011/02/08/what-are-social-impact-bonds/.

56. Caroline Preston, "Getting Back More Than a Warm Feeling," *The New York Times*, "Giving Special" section, November 9, 2012, p. F1.

57. Investopedia, "Social Impact Bond—SIB," http://www.investopedia.com/terms/s/social-impact-bond.asp (accessed February 2016).

58. "Commerce and conscience," *The Economist*, February 23, 2013, p. 71.

59. See "Social Impact Bonds: Can This New Asset Class Create More Than a Win-Win?" *BusinessThink*, March 11, 2011, https://www.businessthink.unsw.edu.au/Pages/Social-Impact-Bonds-Can-This-New-Asset-Class-Create-More-Than-a-Win-Win.aspx.

60. "Social Finance's Tracy Palandjian on the Next Generation of Responsible Investing," *Knowledge@Wharton*, March 14, 2012, http://knowledge.wharton.upenn.edu/article.cfm?articleid=2956.

61. "Social Impact Bonds: Can a Market Prescription Cure Social Ills?" *Knowledge@Wharton*, September 12, 2012, http://knowledge.wharton.upenn.edu/article.cfm?articleid=3078.

62. David W. Chen, "Goldman to Invest in City Prison Program, Reaping Profit If Recidivism Drops," *The New York Times*, August 2, 2012, p. A14.

63. "Being good pays," *The Economist*, August 18, 2012, p. 28.

64. Eduardo Porter, "Wall St. Cash Meets Social Policy in City Jail," *The New York Times*, July 29, 2015, p. B1.

65. Ibid.

66. Nathaniel Popper, "For Goldman, Success in Social Impact Bond That Aids Schoolchildren," *The New York Times*, October 8, 2015, p. B7.

67. Nathaniel Popper, "Did Goldman Make the Grade?" *The New York Times*, November 4, 2015, p. B1.

68. "Social Impact Bonds: Can a Market Prescription Cure Social Ills?" *Knowledge@*

Wharton, September 12, 2012, http://knowl edge.wharton.upenn.edu/article.cfm?article id=3078.

69. Stephanie Strom, "Philanthropists Take On Big Problems by Enlisting Capitalists," *The New York Times*, December 12, 2012, p. F19.

70. Joseph Daniel Anson, "Adding Profit Incentives to Nonprofit Work," *The Wall Street Journal*, November 6, 2015, p. A11.

Chapter 7

1. John Mackey, "To Increase Jobs, Increase Economic Freedom," *The Wall Street Journal*, November 16, 2011, p. A17.

2. The ideas presented and expanded upon in the first two sections of this chapter were first published in David Chandler, *Corporate Social Responsibility: A Strategic Perspective*, Business Expert Press, 2014.

3. Forest Reinhardt, Ramon Casadesus-Masanell, & Hyun Jin Kim, "Patagonia" [Harvard Business School case study 9-711-020], October 19, 2010, p. 8.

4. For examples of the range of prices of different T-shirts, see Christina Passariello, Tripti Lahiri, & Sean McLain, "Bangladesh's Tale of the T-Shirts," *The Wall Street Journal*, July 1, 2013, pp. B1, B8.

5. Esha Chhabra, "H&M's $1m recycling prize is clever but no solution to fast fashion," *The Guardian*, August 25, 2015, http://www .theguardian.com/sustainable-business/ 2015/aug/25/hms-1m-recycling-prize-clever- overproduction-fast-fashion/.

6. While a reasonable response to this statement is that the relationship between company and consumer is iterative with no clear starting point, given that firms are less able to predict market trends than they are able to respond to those trends, it seems the pre-eminent direction of influence is from consumer to company (and not the other way around).

7. Howard R. Bowen, *Social Responsibilities of the Businessman*, Harper & Brothers, 1953, p. 111.

8. Ibid., p. 48.

9. Ibid., p. 146.

10. Michael C. Jensen, "Value Maximization, Stakeholder Theory, and the Corporate Objective Function," *Business Ethics Quarterly*, Vol. 12, No. 2, 2002, p. 239.

11. Driving our materialism to new depths is the concept of *conspicuous virtue*—the idea that it is the perception of a good, rather than its functional value, that drives the consumption of that good. A good example is a consumer who drives a Prius primarily because they want to convey to others their concern for the environment. This idea has parallels with what economists call a *Veblen good*—"a product that is valued and desirable simply for being more expensive" (in Eric Felten, "Fake Authenticity for Sale," *The Wall Street Journal*, January 28, 2011, http://www.wsj .com/articles/SB1000142405274870426810457 6108200922251310/). This concept of con-spicuous consumption can be recast to high-light the idea of *conspicuous virtue*, actions by consumers who "are not seeking an out-right demonstration of wealth. Instead, they consume to demonstrate their innate good-ness. They spend not to suggest the deepness of their pockets but the deepness of their hearts" (in Joseph Rago, "Conspicuous Virtue and the Sustainable Sofa," *The Wall Street Journal*, March 23, 2007, p. W13.)

12. Jennifer M. George, "Compassion and Capitalism: Implications for Organizational Studies," *Journal of Management*, Vol. 40, No. 1, January 2014, p. 5.

13. Edward Wyatt, "U.S. Struggles to Keep Pace in Delivering Broadband Service," *The New York Times*, December 30, 2013, p. B1.

14. The "paradox of value," for example, is a concept used by economists to demonstrate our distorted sense of value whereby "a glass of water costs very little; a diamond costs a lot. Yet there is nothing more useful than water; while the most priced uses of diamonds are decorative" (Tim Harford, "When diamonds aren't on tap," *Financial Times*, March 21/22, 2015, p. 20).

15. Howard R. Bowen, *Social Responsibilities of the Businessman*, Harper & Brothers, 1953, p. 146.

16. Ibid., pp. 89–90.

17. Ibid., p. 114.

18. Michael C. Jensen, "Value Maximization, Stakeholder Theory, and the Corporate Objective Function," *Business Ethics Quarterly*, Vol. 12, No. 2, 2002, p. 245.

19. Charles Handy, "What's a Business For?" *Harvard Business Review,* December 2002, p. 55.

20. Larry Elliott & Ed Pilkington, "New Oxfam report says half of global wealth held by the 1%," *The Guardian,* January 19, 2015, http://www.theguardian.com/business/2015/jan/19/global-wealth-oxfam-inequality-davos-economic-summit-switzerland/.

21. C. K. Prahalad & Allen Hammond, "Serving the World's Poor, Profitably," *Harvard Business Review,* September 2002, Vol. 80, No. 9, pp. 48–58.

22. "Face Value: Profits and Poverty," *The Economist,* August 21, 2004, p. 54.

23. While the BOP market overseas is potentially lucrative for firms, there is also a sizeable market of poor people at home who can benefit from the skills in marketing, product design and packaging, and distribution that the firms develop overseas: "The same [BOP] logic is now being applied to the poorest Westerners (there are 46m Americans living in poverty and almost 50m still without health-care insurance)" (in "Gold-hunting in a frugal age," *The Economist,* December 15, 2012, p. 70). See also "The bottom of the pyramid," *The Economist,* June 25, 2011, p. 80.

24. "A market of 4 billion people," *The Daily Yomiuri,* October 22, 2012, p. 5.

25. Stephanie Strom, "Multinational Companies Court Lower-Income Consumers," *The New York Times,* September 18, 2014, p. B1.

26. Michael Schuman, "Emerging Markets Are Still the Future," *Bloomberg Businessweek,* September 3, 2015, http://www.bloomberg.com/news/articles/2015-09-03/emerging-markets-are-still-the-future.

27. Cait Murphy, "The Hunt for Globalization That Works," *Fortune,* October 28, 2002, http://archive.fortune.com/magazines/fortune/fortune_archive/2002/10/28/330941/index.htm.

28. C. K. Prahalad outlines his work and ideas in this area in a *Wall Street Journal* article, "Aid Is Not the Answer," August 31, 2005, p. A8, and in his book *The Fortune at the Bottom of the Pyramid: Eradicating Poverty Through Profits,* Wharton School, 2004.

29. C. K. Prahalad, quoted in "Face Value: Profits and Poverty," *The Economist,* August 21, 2004, p. 54.

30. Sonya Misquitta, "Cadbury Redefines Cheap Luxury—Marketing to India's Poor, Candy Maker Sells Small Bites for Pennies," *The Wall Street Journal,* June 8, 2009, p. B4.

31. See "Will Corporations Really Help the World's Poor?" [Lifeworth press release], CSRwire, January 31, 2005, http://www.csrwire.com/press_releases/19946-Will-Corporations-Really-Help-the-World-s-Poor-/, and Mallen Baker, "Is there REALLY a fortune at the Bottom of the Pyramid," Mallenbaker.net, September 3, 2006, http://mallenbaker.net/article/category/is-there-really-a-fortune-at-the-bottom-of-the-pyramid/.

32. Lifeworth, "2004 Lifeworth Annual Review of Corporate Responsibility," 2005, p. 2.

33. "Business Prophet," *BusinessWeek Special Report,* January 23, 2006.

34. Vince Besier, "Save the Poor. Sell Them Stuff. Cheap!" *Miller-McCune,* May/June 2011, pp. 48–50.

35. "Vital for the poor," *The Economist,* November 10, 2012, p. 52.

36. Howard Sharman, "Markets can work for development gain," *Ethical Corporation,* May 25, 2012, http://www.ethicalcorp.com/stakeholder-engagement/view-middle-markets-can-work-development-gain/.

37. Cait Murphy, "The Hunt for Globalization That Works," *Fortune,* October 28, 2002, http://archive.fortune.com/magazines/fortune/fortune_archive/2002/10/28/330941/index.htm.

38. Barney Jopson, "Unilever looks to clean up in Africa," *Financial Times,* November 15, 2007, p. 20.

39. "In search of good business," *The Economist,* August 9, 2014, p. 56.

40. Unilever, "Sustainable Living," https://www.unilever.com/sustainable-living/. Unilever provides regular updates on its performance in relation to these goals; see "Sustainable Living News: Latest News," https://www.unilever.com/sustainable-living/sustainable-living-news/news/.

41. Michael Skapinker, "Long-term corporate plans may be lost in translation," *Financial Times,* November 23, 2010, p. 13.

42. "In search of good business," *The Economist,* August 9, 2014, p. 56.

43. Geoff Colvin, "From High-Minded to High Value," *Fortune,* December 22, 2014, p. 38.

44. "After dominating our corporate sustainability leadership ranking for more than five years, Unilever has further improved its position and is now ahead of competitors by 27 percentage points. Patagonia, the only other company to be mentioned by more than 10 percent of experts, remains in second place" (in "The 2015 Sustainability Leaders," GlobeScan/SustainAbility, May 28, 2015, slide 13 of 24, http://www.globescan.com/component/edocman/?view=document&id=179&Itemid=591).

45. Ellen Byron, "Emerging Ambitions," *The Wall Street Journal*, July 16, 2007, p. A1.

46. Henny Sender, "Unilever learns how to tap Pakistan's consumption boom," *Financial Times,* December 27, 2013, p. 14.

47. "Good business; nice beaches," *The Economist*, May 19, 2012, p. 76.

48. See Jennifer Reingold, "Can P&G Make Money in Places Where People Earn $2 a Day?" *Fortune*, January 17, 2011, pp. 86–91; Erik Simanis, "At the Base of the Pyramid," *The Wall Street Journal*, October 26, 2009, p. R7; and V. Kasturi Rangan, Michael Chu, & Djordjija Petkoski, "The Globe: Segmenting the Base of the Pyramid," *Harvard Business Review*, June 2011, http://hbr.org/2011/06/the-globe-segmenting-the-base-of-the-pyramid/.

49. "Fighting for the next billion shoppers," *The Economist*, June 30, 2012, p. 65.

50. Marc Gunther, "The base of the pyramid: Will selling to the poor pay off?" *The Guardian,* May 22, 2014, http://www.theguardian.com/sustainable-business/prahalad-base-bottom-pyramid-profit-poor/.

51. John Micklethwait & Adrian Wooldridge, *The Company: A Short History of a Revolutionary Idea*, Modern Library, 2003, p. xv.

Chapter 8

1. Sharon Begley, "Green Shopping Won't Save the Planet," *Newsweek,* April 20, 2010, http://www.newsweek.com/green-shopping-wont-save-planet-70373/.

2. "Stopping slurping," *The Economist,* November 28, 2015, pp. 67–68.

3. Joe Nocera, "How to Prevent Oil Spills," *The New York Times,* April 14, 2012, p. A17.

4. "Over-regulated America," *The Economist,* February 18, 2012, p. 9. In the current US healthcare coding system, there are also "21 separate categories for 'spacecraft accidents' and 12 for bee stings. There are over 140 million words of binding federal statutes and regulations, and states and municipalities add several billion more" (in Philip K. Howard, "Starting Over with Regulation," *The Wall Street Journal*, December 3–4, 2011, p. C2.

5. Robert Pear, "One Symptom in New Codes: Doctor Anxiety," *The New York Times,* September 14, 2015, p. A1.

6. Charles Murray, "Fifty Shades of Red," *The Wall Street Journal,* May 9–10, 2015, p. C2.

7. Peter S. Goodman, "Rule No. 1: Make Money by Avoiding Rules," *The New York Times*, May 23, 2010, p. WK3.

8. Mallen Baker, "Time to move on from the endless regulation debate," *Ethical Corporation,* March 27, 2006.

9. Milton Friedman, quoted in "The Chicago question," *The Economist*, July 28, 2012, p. 68.

10. Greg Ip, "A Less-Visible Role for the Fed Chief: Freeing Up Markets," *The Wall Street Journal,* November 19, 2004, pp. A1 & A8 (this version of the printed article available at https://gregip.files.wordpress.com/2009/02/greenspan-the-deregulator-11-19-05-a-less2.pdf).

11. Greg Ip, "A Less-Visible Role for the Fed Chief: Freeing Up Markets," *The Wall Street Journal*, November 19, 2004, pp. A1 & A8, http://www.wsj.com/articles/SB11008 1981338978661.

12. Chris Lester, "Alan, like Atlas, shrugged," *The Kansas City Star*, November 4, 2008.

13. Alex Blyth, "EU Multi-Stakeholder Forum Presents Final Report," *Ethical Corporation,* July 5, 2004.

14. Will Hutton, "Capitalism must put its house in order," *The Observer,* November 24, 2002, http://www.theguardian.com/politics/2002/nov/24/politicalcolumnists.guardiancolumnists/.

15. Deborah Doane, "Mandated Risk Reporting Begins in UK," *Business Ethics Magazine,* Spring 2005, p. 13.

16. Lorenzo Fioramonti et al., "Say goodbye to capitalism: Welcome to the Republic of Wellbeing," *The Guardian,* September 2, 2015, http://www.theguardian.com/sustainable-business/2015/sep/02/say-goodbye-to-capitalism-welcome-to-the-republic-of-wellbeing/.

17. Margot Sanger-Katz, "Yes, Soda Taxes Do Seem to Discourage Soda Drinking," *The New York Times,* October 13, 2015, p. A3.

18. "The endangered public company," *The Economist,* May 19, 2012, p. 13.

19. Anheuser-Busch, "Our Responsibility: Environment: Reduce, Reuse and Recycle," http://anheuser-busch.com/index.php/our-responsibility/environment-our-earth-our-natural-resources/reduce-reuse-and-recycle/ (accessed February 2016).

20. Mike Esterl, "Plastic Recycling Falls Short as Too Few Do It," *The Wall Street Journal,* August 19, 2011, p. B1.

21. Susan Freinkel, "Plastic: Too Good to Throw Away," *The New York Times,* March 18, 2011, p. A27.

22. Elizabeth Royte, "Moneybags: Citywide plastic-bag bans are gaining momentum. But will companies be the ones that force us to change?" *Fast Company,* October 2007, p. 64.

23. Ibid.

24. "The Results are in . . . Over 92% of IKEA Customers Bagged the Plastic Bag! As of October 2008, IKEA will no longer offer plastic or paper bags" [IKEA press release], CSRwire, April 2, 2008, http://www.csrwire.com/press_releases/16626-The-Results-are-in-Over-92-of-IKEA-Customers-Bagged-the-Plastic-Bag-/.

25. Ibid. For additional results, see "The 'No More Plastic Bag' Movement Continues" [IKEA press release], CSRwire, April 28, 2009, http://www.csrwire.com/press_releases/16628-The-No-More-Plastic-Bag-Movement-Continues-/.

26. "In 2002, Bangladesh became the first country to introduce a ban on thin plastic bags" (in Dan Bilefsky, "British Begin Attack Aimed at a Scourge of the Realm," *The New York Times,* October 7, 2015, p. A4.

27. Elisabeth Rosenthal, "Motivated by a Tax, Irish Spurn Plastic Bags," *The New York Times,* February 2, 2008, http://www.nytimes.com/2008/02/02/world/europe/02bags.html.

28. Ibid.

29. Dan Bilefsky, "British Begin Attack Aimed at a Scourge of the Realm," *The New York Times,* October 7, 2015, p. A4.

30. Ibid.

31. Elisabeth Rosenthal, "Motivated by a Tax, Irish Spurn Plastic Bags," *The New York Times*, February 2, 2008, http://www.nytimes.com/2008/02/02/world/europe/02bags.html. See also Elisabeth Rosenthal, "Carbon Taxes Make Ireland Even Greener," *The New York Times*, December 28, 2012, http://www.nytimes.com/2012/12/28/science/earth/in-ireland-carbon-taxes-pay-off.html.

32. Greg Davies, "Is it rational to listen to the Sirens?" *The Daily Telegraph*, June 2, 2012, p. R25.

33. James S. Duesenberry, "Comment on 'An Economic Analysis of Fertility,'" in *Demographic and Economic Change in Developed Countries*, Princeton University Press, 1960, p. 233.

34. Jason Zweig, "The Anti-Poverty Experiment," *The Wall Street Journal*, June 6–7, 2015, p. C2.

35. Doug Steiner, "Honesty That Benefits All," *The New York Times*, November 12, 2013, p. F10.

36. "Nudge, nudge, think, think," *The Economist*, March 24, 2012, p. 78.

37. Similar experiments in the United States have reported similar results. See Binyamin Appelbaum, "Behaviorists Show the U.S. How to Nudge," *The New York Times*, September 30, 2015, p. B1.

38. "Nudge, nudge, think, think," *The Economist*, March 24, 2012, p. 78.

39. "Fiscal blackmail," *The Economist*, May 24, 2014, p. 71.

40. Beth Terry, "Will a NYC Ban on Large Sugary Sodas Decrease Obesity or Increase Plastic Waste?" *My Plastic-Free Life*, June 19, 2012, http://myplasticfreelife.com/2012/06/will-a-nyc-ban-on-large-sugary-sodas-decrease-obesity-or-increase-plastic-waste/.

41. Daniel E. Lieberman, "Evolution's Sweet Tooth," *The New York Times*, June 6, 2012, p. A23.

42. Betsy McKay, "Dramatic Drop in Trans Fat in U.S. Adults," *The Wall Street Journal*, February 14, 2012, p. D5.

43. Brian Wansink, David R. Just, & Joe McKendry, "Lunch Line Redesign," *The New York Times*, October 22, 2010, p. A25.

44. Shankar Vedantam, "How Partitioned Grocery Carts Can Help Shoppers Buy Healthier Foods," National Public Radio,

May 26, 2015, http://www.npr.org/2015/05/26/409671975/how-partitioned-grocery-carts-can-help-shoppers-buy-healthier-foods/.

45. Sean Poulter & Rosie Taylor, "Supermarkets are still tempting us with sweets at the checkouts as they claim to be helping shoppers make healthy choices," *The Daily Mail*, October 24, 2012, http://www.dailymail.co.uk/news/article-2222785/Supermarkets-tempting-sweets-checkouts.html.

46. David Brooks, "The Unexamined Society," *The New York Times*, July 8, 2011, p. A21.

47. "Learning from failure," *The Economist*, October 10, 2015, p. 88.

48. Richard H. Thaler, "The Power of Nudges, for Good and Bad," *The New York Times*, November 1, 2015, p. BU6.

49. Dina Spector, "18 Facts About Walmart That Will Blow Your Mind," *Business Insider*, November 15, 2012, http://www.businessinsider.com/crazy-facts-about-walmart-2012-11/.

50. Dan Myers, "10 Things You Didn't Know About the Food at Walmart," *The Daily Meal*, December 19, 2014, http://www.thedailymeal.com/eat/10-things-you-didnt-know-about-food-walmart/.

51. Steven Greenhouse, "At Wal-Mart, Choosing Sides Over $9.68 an Hour," *The New York Times*, May 4, 2005, http://www.nytimes.com/2005/05/04/business/at-walmart-choosing-sides-over-968-an-hour.html.

52. Walmart, "Our Locations," http://corporate.walmart.com/our-story/locations/ (accessed February 2016).

53. Anthony Bianco & Wendy Zellner, "Is Wal-Mart Too Powerful?" *BusinessWeek,* October 6, 2003, pp. 100–110.

54. Farhad Manjoo, "Dot Convert," *Fast Company Magazine*, December 2012/January 2013, p. 131.

55. "Each week, Walmart serves more than 200 million customers at more than 9,600 retail outlets in 28 countries" (in Dina Spector & Ujala Sehgal, "16 Facts About Walmart That Will Blow Your Mind," *Business Insider*, November 14, 2011, http://www.businessinsider.com/walmart-facts-earnings-2011-11/).

56. Anthony Bianco & Wendy Zellner, "Is Wal-Mart Too Powerful?" *BusinessWeek,* October 6, 2003, pp. 100–110.

57. Charles Fishman, "The Wal-Mart You Don't Know," *Fast Company Magazine*, November 15, 2008, http://www.fastcompany.com/magazine/77/walmart.html.

58. Constance L. Hays, "When Wages Are Low, Discounters Have Pull," *The New York Times,* December 23, 2003, pp. C1, C4.

59. For example, see, John M. Broder, "Stymied by Politicians, Wal-Mart Turns to Voters," *The New York Times,* April 5, 2004, p. A12; Steven Malanga, "The War on Wal-Mart," *The Wall Street Journal,* April 7, 2004, p. A18; Ann Zimmerman, "Wal-Mart Loses Supercenter Vote," *The Wall Street Journal,* April 8, 2004, p. B7; and, for a different viewpoint, George F. Will, "Waging War on Wal-Mart," *Newsweek,* July 5, 2004, p. 64.

60. The Fortune 500 ranks firms according to their revenues.

61. In 2006, Exxon was named number one; Walmart returned to the top spot in 2007 and 2008. Exxon and Walmart have shared the top two spots, occasionally changing places, ever since.

62. "Wal-Mart tops most admired list," February 24, 2004, CNN Money, http://money.cnn.com/2004/02/23/news/companies/fortune_best/.

63. *Fortune*, "World's Most Admired Companies," http://fortune.com/worlds-most-admired-companies/ (accessed February 2016).

64. Jonathan Birchall, "Duke faces test of his political aptitude," *Financial Times*, November 22–23, 2008, p. 9.

65. Stacy Mitchell, "Walmart's greenwash: Why the retail giant is still unsustainable," *grist*, November 7, 2011, http://grist.org/series/2011-11-07-walmart-greenwash-retail-giant-still-unsustainable/.

66. For example, Erica L. Plambeck & Lyn Denend, "The greening of Wal-Mart," *Stanford Social Innovation Review*, Spring 2008, pp. 53–59; "Wal-Mart Celebrates Thanksgiving by Sourcing Local Food, Supporting Hunger-Relief, and Buying Wind Power," CSRwire, November 26, 2008, http://www.csrwire.com/press_releases/15548-The-Latest-Corporate-Social-Responsibility-News-Wal-Mart-Celebrates-Thanksgiving-by-Sourcing-Local-Food-Supporting-Hunger-Relief-and-Buying-Wind-Power/; and Danielle Sacks, "Working with the Enemy,"

Fast Company Magazine, September 2007, http://www.fastcompany.com/magazine/118/node/60374/.

67. Ryan Chittum, "Wal-Mart to Give $35 Million for Wildlife Areas," *The Wall Street Journal,* April 13, 2005, p. B4; and Stephanie Strom, "Wal-Mart Donates $35 Million for Conservation and Will Be Partner With Wildlife Group," *The New York Times,* April 13, 2005, p. A16.

68. Lee Scott, "Wal-Mart: Twenty First Century Leadership," October 23, 2005, http://corporate.walmart.com/_news_/executive-viewpoints/twenty-first-century-leadership/.

69. Ann Zimmerman & Valerie Bauerlein, "At Wal-Mart, Emergency Plan Has Big Payoff," *The Wall Street Journal*, September 12, 2005, http://www.wsj.com/articles/SB112648681539237605/; and Michael Barbaro & Justin Gillis, "Wal-Mart at Forefront of Hurricane Relief," *The Washington Post*, September 6, 2005, p. D1.

70. Lisa Roner, "Wal-Mart—An environmental epiphany?" Climate Change Corp, December 7, 2005.

71. For more background on the origination of Walmart's commitment to sustainability, see Daniel Diermeier, "The case study: A disaster can improve reputation," *Financial Times*, March 24, 2011, p. 12.

72. Lee Scott, "Wal-Mart: Twenty First Century Leadership," October 23, 2005, http://corporate.walmart.com/_news_/executive-viewpoints/twenty-first-century-leadership/.

73. Ibid.

74. Ibid.

75. Ibid.

76. Ibid.

77. Jonathan Birchall, "Big Box looks to small packages," *Financial Times*, November 4, 2008, p. 16.

78. "Walmart turns on the lights," *Fast Company Magazine*, December 2015/January 2016, p. 58.

79. See Orville Schell, "How Walmart Is Changing China," *The Atlantic*, December 2011, http://www.theatlantic.com/magazine/archive/2011/12/how-walmart-is-changing-china/308709/.

80. Rajesh Chhabara, "Wal-Mart—Thinking outside the big box," *Ethical Corporation*, September 7, 2009.

81. "No. 9: Walmart," *Fast Company Magazine*, March 2010, p. 66.

82. See Walmart, http://corporate.walmart.com/global-responsibility/environment-sustainability/sustainability-index, and The Sustainability Consortium, http://www.sustainabilityconsortium.org/.

83. Kate Rockwood, "Will Walmart's 'Sustainability Index' Actually Work?" *Fast Company Magazine*, February 1, 2010, http://www.fastcompany.com/1518194/will-walmarts-sustainability-index-actually-work/.

84. The Sustainability Consortium, "What We Do," http://www.sustainabilityconsortium.org/what-we-do/.

85. For more detail on Walmart's sustainability program, see Lyn Denend & Erica Plambeck, "Walmart's Sustainability Strategy (B): 2010 Update," Stanford Graduate School of Business case OIT-71B, October 15, 2010.

86. Joel Makower, "How Walmart Became a Sustainability Leader," LinkedIn, November 18, 2015, https://www.linkedin.com/pulse/how-walmart-became-sustainability-leader-joel-makower/.

87. Marc Gunther, "Walmart is slapping itself on the back for sustainability but it still has a way to go," *The Guardian*, November 18, 2015, http://www.theguardian.com/sustainable-business/2015/nov/18/walmart-climate-change-carbon-emissions-renewabe-energy-environment/.

88. Christopher Helman, "Everyday Renewable Energy," *Forbes*, November 23, 2015, pp. 66–67.

89. Ibid., p. 67.

90. Marc Gunther, "Walmart is slapping itself on the back for sustainability but it still has a way to go," *The Guardian*, November 18, 2015, http://www.theguardian.com/sustainable-business/2015/nov/18/walmart-climate-change-carbon-emissions-renewabe-energy-environment/.

91. See Walmart, "Global Responsibility Report," http://corporate.walmart.com/global-responsibility/global-responsibility-report/.

92. See Pratap Chatterjee, "Greenwashing Walmart," *CorpWatch Blog*, April 18, 2012, http://www.corpwatch.org/article.php?id=15707; and Stacy Mitchell, "Walmart's greenwash: Why the retail giant is still

unsustainable," *grist*, November 7, 2011, http://grist.org/series/2011-11-07-walmart-greenwash-retail-giant-still-unsustainable/.

93. Facts quoted from Stacy Mitchell, "Walmart's Greenwash," Institute for Local Self-Reliance, March 2012, p. 4.

94. Terrachoice, http://sinsofgreenwashing.org/. For another definition of *greenwashing* and related information, see http://www.triplepundit.com/topic/greenwashing/.

95. Michael Skapinker, "Virtue's reward?" *Financial Times*, April 28, 2008, p. 8.

96. Steven Greenhouse & Reed Abelson, "Wal-Mart Cuts Some Health Care Benefits," *The New York Times*, October 21, 2011, p. B1.

97. Michael Skapinker, "Virtue's reward?" *Financial Times*, April 28, 2008, p. 8.

98. See David Barstow, "Vast Mexico Bribery Case Hushed Up by Wal-Mart After Top-Level Struggle," *The New York Times*, April 22, 2012, p. A1; and David Barstow & Alejandra Xanic von Bertrab, "The Bribery Aisle: How Wal-Mart Used Payoffs to Get Its Way in Mexico," *The New York Times*, December 18, 2012, p. A1.

99. Even when Walmart reported to the Justice Department that it had begun an internal investigation into the bribery allegations, *The New York Times* claimed in its initial story that the firm did so only because it had learned of the newspaper's investigation.

100. David Barstow, "Vast Mexico Bribery Case Hushed Up by Wal-Mart after Top-Level Struggle," *The New York Times*, April 22, 2012, p. A12.

101. Ibid.

102. Stephanie Clifford, "Pension Plan Sues Wal-Mart Official over Failures," *The New York Times*, May 4, 2012, p. B1.

103. Gretchen Morgenson, "New York Pension Funds to Challenge Wal-Mart," *The New York Times*, May 1, 2012, p. B1.

104. "Walmart's Mexican morass," *The Economist*, April 28, 2012, p. 71.

105. Ben DiPietro, "Wal-Mart Records $157 Million Charge for Mexican Bribery Probe," *The Wall Street Journal*, February 21, 2013, http://blogs.wsj.com/corruption-currents/2013/02/21/wal-mart-records-157-million-charge-for-mexican-bribery-probe/.

106. Mallen Baker, "Bhopal—25 years later the echoes are still loud," Business Respect, August 18, 2009, http://businessrespect.net/page.php?Story_ID=2529.

107. Tom Huddleston Jr., "Walmart is giving these workers a raise," *Fortune*, June 2, 2015, http://fortune.com/2015/06/02/walmart-workers-raise/.

108. Corby Kummer, "The Great Grocery Smackdown," *The Atlantic*, March 2010, http://www.theatlantic.com/magazine/archive/2010/03/the-great-grocery-smack-down/307904/. See also Stephanie Clifford, "Unexpected Ally Helps Wal-Mart Cut Waste," *The New York Times*, April 14, 2012, p. B1.

109. Richard Milne, "Skirting the boards," *Financial Times*, June 15, 2009, p. 2.

110. Aaron A. Dhir, "What Norway Can Teach the U.S. About Getting More Women Into Boardrooms," *The Atlantic*, May 4, 2015, http://www.theatlantic.com/business/archive/2015/05/what-norway-can-teach-the-us-about-getting-more-women-into-boardrooms/392195/.

Chapter 9

1. Christine Bader, "Why Corporations Fail to Do the Right Thing," *The Atlantic*, April 21, 2014, http://www.theatlantic.com/business/archive/2014/04/why-making-corporations-socially-responsible-is-so-darn-hard/360984/.

2. Alexander Dahlsrud, "How Corporate Social Responsibility Is Defined: An Analysis of 37 Definitions," *Corporate Social Responsibility and Environmental Management*, Vol. 15, 2008, p. 1.

3. Herman Aguinis & Ante Glavas, "What We Know and Don't Know about Corporate Social Responsibility: A Review and Research Agenda," *Journal of Management*, Vol. 38, No. 4, 2012, p. 933.

4. Timothy M. Devinney, "Is the Socially Responsible Corporation a Myth? The Good, the Bad, and the Ugly of Corporate Social Responsibility," *Academy of Management Perspectives*, Vol. 23, 2009, p. 44.

5. See Alexander Dahlsrud, "How Corporate Social Responsibility Is Defined: An Analysis of 37 Definitions," *Corporate Social Responsibility and Environmental Management*, Vol. 15, 2008, pp. 1–13.

6. Mallen Baker, "PUMA plucks numbers out of the CO_2," May 17, 2011, http://www.mallen baker.net/csr/post.php?id=394 (no longer available online).

7. "Scientists already talk of the dawning of a new geological age, the Anthropocene, named because humans, or rather, the industrial civilization they have created, have become the main factor driving the evolution of Earth" (in "Stopping a scorcher," *The Economist*, November 23, 2013, p. 81).

8. Fleming and Jones refer to CSR as the "opium of the people" for the intoxicating, but in their eyes misleading, prospect this idea holds for meaningful change within the current economic system. See Peter Fleming & Marc T. Jones, *The End of Corporate Social Responsibility: Crisis & Critique*, SAGE, 2013, p. 67.

9. Timothy M. Devinney, "Is the Socially Responsible Corporation a Myth? The Good, the Bad, and the Ugly of Corporate Social Responsibility," *Academy of Management Perspectives*, Vol. 23, 2009, pp. 51, 52.

10. In December 2013, the American Customer Satisfaction Index released data correlating firms' customer service scores with their subsequent stock market performance, "suggesting that the most-hated companies perform better than their beloved peers. . . . There's no statistical relationship between customer-service scores and stock-market returns. . . . If anything, it might hurt company profits to spend money making customers happy" (quoted in Eric Chemi, "Proof That It Pays to Be America's Most-Hated Companies," *Bloomberg Businessweek*, December 17, 2013, http://www.bloomberg.com/bw/articles/2013-12-17/proof-that-it-pays-to-be-americas-most-hated-companies/).

11. For details on studies analyzing the relationship between CSR and firm performance, see Joshua D. Margolis & James P. Walsh, "Misery Loves Companies: Rethinking Social Initiatives by Business," *Administrative Science Quarterly*, Vol. 48, No. 2, 2003, pp. 268–305; Marc Orlitzky, Frank L. Schmidt, & Sara L. Rynes, "Corporate Social and Financial Performance: A Meta-analysis," *Organization Studies*, Vol. 24, No. 3, 2003, pp. 403–441; and Herman Aguinis & Ante Glavas, "What We Know and Don't Know About Corporate Social Responsibility: A Review and Research Agenda," *Journal of Management*, Vol. 38, No. 4, 2012, pp. 932–968.

12. Rich McEachran, "Ethical awards: Green wash or genuinely recognising sustainability," *The Guardian*, September 3, 2013, http://www.theguardian.com/sustainable-business/blog/ethical-awards-green-wash-sustainability/.

13. Mallen Baker, "Ethics and financial performance: The big question—Is there really a business case?" Ethical Corporation, May 2, 2008, http://www.ethicalcorp.com/communications-reporting/ethics-and-financial-performance-big-question-there-really-business-case/.

14. The work that Walmart (and other retailers) is doing to create a "sustainability index" that would allow comparisons of the ecological footprint across all its products carries the potential to revolutionize the way that we measure CSR. For more information, visit The Sustainability Consortium's website at http://www.sustainabilityconsortium.org/.

15. See Timothy M. Devinney, "Is the Socially Responsible Corporation a Myth? The Good, the Bad, and the Ugly of Corporate Social Responsibility," *Academy of Management Perspectives*, Vol. 23, 2009, pp. 44–56.

16. Heather Mak, "Eco-labels: Radical rethink required," *Ethical Corporation*, January 17, 2012, http://www.ethicalcorp.com/environment/eco-labels-radical-rethink-required/.

17. "Patagonia Takes Next Step in Corporate Transparency and Accountability," CSRwire, March 25, 2008, http://www.csrwire.com/press_releases/15514-The-Latest-Corporate-Social-Responsibility-News-Patagonia-Takes-Next-Step-in-Corporate-Transparency-and-Accountability/.

18. Paul Hohnen, "What sustainability reports say about the state of business," *Ethical Corporation*, July 12, 2011, http://www.ethicalcorp.com/communications-reporting/what-sustainability-reports-say-about-state-business/.

19. Ernst Ligteringen, "Global Reporting Initiative: The sustainability reporting revolution," *The Guardian*, May 22, 2013, http://www.theguardian.com/sustainable-business/blog/global-reporting-initiative-sustainability-revolution/.

20. Paul Hohnen, "What sustainability reports say about the state of business," *Ethical Corporation*, July 12, 2011, http://www.ethicalcorp.com/communications-reporting/what-sustainability-reports-say-about-state-business/.

21. B Lab, "What are B Corps?" http://www.bcorporation.net/what-are-b-corps/ (accessed February 2016). For a timeline of B Lab's development, see https://www.bcorporation.net/what-are-b-corps/the-non-profit-behind-b-corps/our-history/.

22. The Carbon Disclosure Project (CDP Worldwide), https://www.cdp.net/en-US/Pages/About-Us.aspx (accessed February 2016).

23. Ceres, "The Ceres Principles," http://www.ceres.org/about-us/our-history/ceres-principles/ (accessed February 2016).

24. See Beth Richardson, "Sparking Impact Investing through GIIRS," *Stanford Social Innovation Review*, October 24, 2012, http://ssir.org/articles/entry/sparking_impact_investing_through_giirs/.

25. GRI, "About GRI," https://www.globalreporting.org/information/about-gri/ (accessed February 2016).

26. Greenhouse Gas Protocol, "About the GHG Protocol," http://www.ghgprotocol.org/about-ghgp/ (accessed February 2016).

27. International Labour Organization, "Introduction to International Labour Standards," http://www.ilo.org/global/standards/introduction-to-international-labour-standards/lang--en/index.htm (accessed February 2016).

28. International Labour Organization, "Labour Standards," http://www.ilo.org/global/standards/lang--en/index.htm (accessed February 2016).

29. Jason Perks, "Reporting—Ensuring true assurance," *Ethical Corporation*, August 31, 2011, http://www.ethicalcorp.com/communications-reporting/invitation-reporting-ensuring-true-assurance/.

30. Paul Hohnen, "ISO moves towards a social responsibility standard," *Ethical Corporation,* October 5, 2005, http://www.hohnen.net/articles/20051005_EthicalCorp.html.

31. Organisation for Economic Co-operation and Development (OECD), "About the OECD Guidelines for Multinational Enterprises," http://mneguidelines.oecd.org/about/ (accessed February 2016).

32. Deborah Leipziger, "Codes of conduct and standards: The pick of the bunch," *Ethical Corporation*, February 21, 2011, http://www.ethicalcorp.com/business-strategy/codes-conduct-and-standards-pick-bunch/.

33. Sustainability Accounting Standards Board (SASB), http://www.sasb.org/ (accessed February 2016).

34. United Nations, "Transforming our world: The 2030 Agenda for Sustainable Development," September 25, 2015, https://sustainabledevelopment.un.org/post2015/transformingourworld/. The list of all 17 sustainable development goals (SDGs) and their corresponding targets can be found at https://sustainabledevelopment.un.org/topics/. For more commentary on the SDGs, see "Beyond handouts," *The Economist*, September 19, 2015, pp. 55–56; and Tim Smedley, "Sustainable development goals: What business needs to know," *The Guardian*, September 24, 2015, http://www.theguardian.com/sustainable-business/2015/sep/24/sustainable-development-goals-business-sdg-targets/.

35. See United Nations Global Compact, "The Ten Principles of the UN Global Compact," http://www.unglobalcompact.org/AboutTheGC/TheTenPrinciples/index.html.

36. United Nations Global Compact, "What Is UN Global Compact?" https://www.unglobalcompact.org/what-is-gc/ (accessed February 2016).

37. UN Human Rights Council, "New Guiding Principles on Business and Human Rights endorsed by the UN Human Rights Council," June 2011, http://www.ohchr.org/en/NewsEvents/Pages/DisplayNews.aspx?NewsID=11164.

38. Deborah Leipziger, "Codes of conduct and standards: The top ten, part II," *Ethical Corporation*, February 21, 2011, http://www.ethicalcorp.com/communications-reporting/codes-conduct-and-standards-top-ten-part-ii/.

39. Mallen Baker, "The Global Reporting Initiative (GRI)," January 2013, http://www.mallenbaker.net/csr/gri.php (no longer available online).

40. Michael Skapinker, "Responsible companies need more than words," *Financial Times*, May 26, 2011, p. 14.

41. For a full consideration of the GRI, as well as detailed insight into the G4 consultation document, see Mallen Baker, "The Global Reporting Initiative is growing up," Mallenbaker.net, July 25, 2012, http://www.mallenbaker.net/csr/page.php?Story_ID=2739.

42. Mallen Baker, "Is the GRI's new focus really a positive change in direction?" Mallenbaker.net, June 10, 2015, http://www.mallenbaker.net/csr/post.php?id=497 (no longer available online). See also Tobias Webb, "Five reasons why you won't be using GRI's new G4 guidelines any time soon," *Sustainability = Smart Business*, November 7, 2013, http://sustainablesmartbusiness.com/2013/11/five-reasons-you-wont-be-using-gris-new/.

43. Mallen Baker, "Is the GRI's new focus really a positive change in direction?" Mallenbaker.net, June 10, 2015, http://www.mallenbaker.net/csr/post.php?id=497 (no longer available online.

44. Peter Knight, "Letter from the mid-Atlantic—SASB, GRI and IIRC—A reporting standards shootout," *Ethical Corporation*, July 11, 2013, http://www.ethicalcorp.com/business-strategy/letter-mid-atlantic-sasb-gri-and-iirc-reporting-standards-shootout/.

45. We have also recently discovered that the Exxon CEO's environmental skepticism was not necessarily shared by the firm's many scientists, in spite of the firm's willingness to fund NGOs campaigning against efforts to reverse climate change. See David Chandler, "Strategic CSR—Exxon," November 9, 2015, http://strategiccsr-sage.blogspot.jp/2015/11/strategic-csr-exxon.html and Suzanne Goldenberg, "Exxon knew of climate change in 1981, email says—but it funded deniers for 27 more years," *The Guardian*, July 8, 2015, http://www.theguardian.com/environment/2015/jul/08/exxon-climate-change-1981-climate-denier-funding/.

46. Natalya Sverjensky, "Beyond petroleum: Why the CSR community collaborated in creating the BP oil disaster," *Ethical Corporation*, August 2, 2010, http://www.ethicalcorp.com/stakeholder-engagement/beyond-petroleum-why-csr-community-collaborated-creating-bp-oil-disaster/.

47. See the discussion around integrated reporting in Chapter 14.

48. Other certifications include the Social Progress Index (http://www.socialprogressimperative.org/data/spi/, accessed February 2016), a "framework for measuring the multiple dimensions of social progress, benchmarking success, and catalyzing greater human wellbeing," and the Social Stock Exchange (http://socialstockexchange.com/), "the world's first regulated exchange dedicated to businesses and investors seeking to achieve a positive social and environmental impact through their activities" (http://socialstockexchange.com/about-ssx/us/, accessed February 2016).

49. David Jolly, "An Ecolabel for McDonald's Fish Fare," *The New York Times*, January 27, 2013, http://green.blogs.nytimes.com/2013/01/27/an-ecolabel-for-mcdonalds-fish-fare/.

50. Rebecca Smithers, "Britons want to buy sustainable fish but labels leave us baffled," *The Guardian*, May 24, 2010, http://www.guardian.co.uk/environment/2010/may/24/sustainable-fish-seafood-supermarkets-labels/.

51. Additional detail about the ISO 26000 can be found at http://www.iso.org/iso/iso26000/.

52. Mallen Baker, "Labelling the good company," GreenBiz, August 31, 2005, http://www.greenbiz.com/blog/2005/08/31/labeling-good-company/.

53. Jon Entine, "ISO 26000: Sustainability as standard?" *Ethical Corporation*, July 11, 2012, http://www.ethicalcorp.com/business-strategy/iso-26000-sustainability-standard/.

54. Mallen Baker, "Why CSR reporting is broken—and how it should be fixed," *Ethical Corporation,* November 28, 2008.

55. Sarah Skidmore, "Whole Foods to label seafood's sustainability," MSNBC, September 17, 2010, http://www.nbcnews.com/id/39156472/ns/business-consumer_news#.VnvZm6Pn-M8.

56. Heather Mak, "Eco-labels: Radical rethink required," *Ethical Corporation*, January 17, 2012, http://www.ethicalcorp.com/environment/eco-labels-radical-rethink-required/.

57. Tanzina Vega, "Agency Seeks to Tighten Rules for 'Green' Labeling," *The New York Times*, October 7, 2010, p. B4.

58. Jon Entine, "Ecolabels: Chemical reactions," *Ethical Corporation*, June 4, 2013, http://www.ethicalcorp.com/environment/ecolabels-chemical-reactions/; and Jon Entine, "Organic

food—What is an 'organic' label really worth?" *Ethical Corporation*, July 12, 2013, http://www.ethicalcorp.com/supply-chains/organic-food-what-organic-label-really-worth/.

59. Peter Marko, "Facing an epidemic of mislabeled seafood," *Los Angeles Times*, December 8, 2014, http://www.latimes.com/opinion/op-ed/la-oe-marko-fish-mislabeling-20141209-story.html, and Nicholas St. Fleur, "Though Labeled 'Wild,' That Serving of Salmon May Be Farmed of 'Faux,'" *The New York Times*, October 29, 2015, p. A24.

60. Tim Smedley, "If the palm oil industry waited for consumers to care, sustainability would get nowhere," *The Guardian*, October 26, 2015, http://www.theguardian.com/sustainable-business/2015/oct/26/palm-oil-industry-consumer-understanding-sustainability-cspo-packaging-marks-spencer-boots-ecover/.

61. Tanzina Vega, "Agency Seeks to Tighten Rules for 'Green' Labeling," *The New York Times*, October 7, 2010, p. B4.

62. Peter Marsh, "Clothing companies in push for eco-impact labelling," *Financial Times*, March 1, 2011, p. 15.

63. Alison Neumer Lara, "Nike, Walmart, Target, Other Brands Launch Eco Clothing Index," *Earth911*, March 1, 2011, http://earth911.com/news/2011/03/01/nike-walmart-target-other-brands-launch-eco-clothing-index/.

64. Kate Rockwood, "Attention, Walmart Shoppers: Clean-up in Aisle Nine," *Fast Company Magazine*, February 2010, p. 30.

65. Jeni Bauser, "Eco Index: How green are your clothes?" *Ethical Corporation*, October 15, 2010, http://www.ethicalcorp.com/stakeholder-engagement/eco-index-how-green-are-your-clothes/.

66. Tom Zeller Jr., "Clothes Makers Join to Set 'Green Score,'" *The New York Times*, March 1, 2011, p. B1.

67. Ibid., p. B4.

68. Marc Gunther, "Behind the scenes at the Sustainable Apparel Coalition," GreenBiz, July 26, 2012, https://www.greenbiz.com/blog/2012/07/26/behind-scenes-sustainable-apparel-coalition/.

69. *Oxford English Dictionary*, http://www.oed.com/view/Entry/66996 (accessed July 2015).

70. Usman Hayat, "Future challenges for sustainable investing," *Financial Times (FTfm)*, February 7, 2011, p. 12.

71. David Leonhardt, "The Battle over Taxing Soda," *The New York Times*, May 19, 2010, p. B1. For more information about Pigovian taxes, see R. H. Coase, "The Problem of Social Cost," *The Journal of Law & Economics*, Vol. III, October 1960, pp. 1–44; and William J. Baumol, "On Taxation and the Control of Externalities," *The American Economic Review*, Vol. 62, June 1972, pp. 307–322.

72. Robert H. Frank, "Of Individual Liberty and Cap and Trade," *The New York Times*, January 10, 2010, p. BU7.

73. See Walkers (http://www.walkerscarbonfootprint.co.uk/) and PepsiCo (Andrew Martin, "How Green Is My Orange?" *The New York Times*, January 21, 2009, http://www.nytimes.com/2009/01/22/business/22pepsi.html).

74. For more about the circular economy, see "Driving the circular economy infographic," *The Guardian*, May 13, 2013, http://www.theguardian.com/sustainable-business/driving-circular-economy-infographic/. See also the EU's action plan: European Commission, "Closing the loop—An EU action plan for the Circular Economy" [COM (2015) 614/2], December 2, 2015, http://ec.europa.eu/priorities/jobs-growth-and-investment/towards-circular-economy_en/; for commentary, see Edward Robinson, "'Hollow words': Why there'll be a fight over EU's plan to deal with our waste," *The Guardian*, December 8, 2015, http://www.theguardian.com/sustainable-business/2015/dec/08/hollow-words-fight-over-eu-waste-plans-circular-economy/.

75. See Nike, "NIKE, Inc. & Creative Commons Create a System for Sharing Innovation," http://www.nikebiz.com/crreport/content/environment/4-4-0-case-study-greenxchange.php.

76. Natalya Sverjensky, "A sustainable future: Why Al Gore is wrong," *Ethical Corporation*, August 24, 2011, http://www.ethicalcorp.com/environment/sustainable-future-why-al-gore-wrong/.

77. See http://www.youtube.com/watch?v=l_P_V0jk3Ig.

78. Ray Anderson, "The business logic of sustainability," presentation at TED 2009, February 2009, http://www.ted.com/talks/ray_anderson_on_the_business_logic_of_sustainability.html.

79. Dieter Helm, "Nature gives us everything free—Let's put it at the heart of everyday economic life," *The Guardian*, June 9, 2015, http://www.theguardian.com/sustainable-business/2015/jun/09/nature-free-put-heart-economic-compensate/.

80. Marc Gunther, "Natural capital: Breakthrough or buzzword?" *The Guardian*, March 6, 2014, http://www.theguardian.com/sustainable-business/natural-capital-nature-conservancy-trucost-dow/.

81. Duncan Jefferies, "Can business learn to speak the language of natural capital?" *The Guardian*, January 29, 2015, http://www.theguardian.com/sustainable-business/2015/jan/29/businesses-learn-language-of-natural-capital-2015/.

82. Beth Macy, "The World Buys a Coke," *The New York Times Book Review*, January 4, 2015, p. 11.

83. World Wildlife Fund, "The Impact of a Cotton T-Shirt," January 16, 2013, http://www.worldwildlife.org/stories/the-impact-of-a-cotton-t-shirt/.

84. Eduardo Porter, "Invisible Hand Is Kept Off Carbon," *The New York Times*, July 1, 2015, p. B7.

85. Paul Glimcher & Michael A. Livermore, "What Is Nature Worth to You?" *The New York Times*, August 9, 2015, p. SR10. "Contingent valuation" involves asking people what they are willing to pay for an item (clean air, for example). While this is a start, the process relies on a survey, which presents a distorted picture of true intentions.

86. Calculated by Gil Friend, founder of Natural Logic and Chief Sustainability Officer of the City of Palo Alto, California, and presented at The Alliance for Sustainable Colorado, Denver, November 2, 2015.

87. Gillian Tett, "As values shift bookkeepers need a new perspective—anthropology," *Financial Times*, February 28/March 1, 2015, p. 8.

88. For a discussion about the limits of our current economic model based on growth and consumption, see Tim Jackson, "New economic model needed not relentless consumer demand," *The Guardian*, January 17, 2013, http://www.guardian.co.uk/sustainable-business/blog/new-economic-model-not-consumer-demand-capitalism/.

89. Rob Walker, "Wasted Data," *The New York Times Magazine*, December 5, 2010, p. 20.

90. Joe Flower, "Sustainable Goes Strategic," *strategy+business*, No. 54, Spring 2009, pp. 7–8.

91. Michael J. Ybarra, "Free to Choose, and Conserve," *The Wall Street Journal*, June 11, 2012, p. A11.

92. Adam Smith, *The Wealth of Nations*, 1776, Book IV, Chapter II, Paragraph 9.

93. Adam Gopnik, "Market Man," *New Yorker*, October 18, 2010, http://www.newyorker.com/magazine/2010/10/18/market-man/.

94. "Hare-grained," *The Economist*, November 14, 2015, p. 18.

95. "Seize the day," *The Economist*, January 17, 2015, p. 9.

96. "The deepest cuts," *The Economist*, September 20, 2014, p. 21.

97. Eric Roston, "The 'Shocking' Cost of Letting Companies Pollute for Free," *Bloomberg Businessweek*, May 19, 2015, http://www.bloomberg.com/news/articles/2015-05-19/here-s-how-much-cheap-energy-really-costs.

98. Mark Thoma, "The Problem with Completely Free Markets," *The Fiscal Times*, June 30, 2015, http://www.thefiscaltimes.com/Columns/2015/06/30/Problem-Completely-Free-Markets/.

99. N. Gregory Mankiw, "Shifting the Tax Burden to Cut Carbon," *The New York Times*, September 6, 2015, p. BU6.

100. Gernot Wagner, "Going Green but Getting Nowhere," *The New York Times*, September 8, 2011, p. A25.

Part III Case Study

1. Some commentators have identified "June 12, 2007, when news broke that two Bear Stearns hedge funds speculating in mortgage-backed securities were melting down" as the starting point of the 2007–2009 economic crisis (in Allan Sloan, "Unhappy Anniversary," *Fortune*, June 8, 2009, p. 14).

2. Lionel Barber, "How gamblers broker the banks," *Financial Times Special Report: The FT Year in Finance*, December 16, 2008, p. 1.

3. David Leonhardt, "We're Spent," *The New York Times*, July 17, 2011, p. SR1.

4. Thomas L. Friedman, "The Great Unraveling," *The New York Times*, December 17, 2008, p. A29.

5. See George A. Akerlof & Robert J. Shiller, *Animal Spirits: How Human Psychology Drives the Economy, and Why It Matters for Global Capitalism*, Princeton University Press, 2009, for an excellent description of the varied motivations driving human behavior with respect to the economy and financial markets.

6. David Brooks, "An Economy of Faith and Trust," *The New York Times*, January 16, 2009, p. A27.

7. Luke Johnson, "A tragedy for champions of free markets," *Financial Times*, February 4, 2009, p. 10.

8. John Kay, "What a carve up," *Financial Times*, August 1, 2009, Life & Arts, p. 12.

9. Thomas L. Friedman, "All Fall Down," *The New York Times*, November 26, 2008, p. A31.

10. "When the music stops" [Editorial], *The Guardian*, November 6, 2007, http://www.guardian.co.uk/commentisfree/2007/nov/06/comment.business/.

11. Liar loans were mortgages that were approved "without verifying people's finances" (in Matt Scully & Jody Shenn, "Liar Loans Redux: They're Back and Sneaking Into AAA Rated Bonds," *Bloomberg Businessweek*, September 8, 2015, http://www.bloomberg.com/news/articles/2015-09-08/liar-loans-redux-they-re-back-and-sneaking-into-aaa-rated-bonds/.

12. George Soros, "The worst market crisis in 60 years," *Financial Times*, January 23, 2008, p. 9.

13. Ibid.

14. Martin Wolf, "Why the financial turmoil is an elephant in a dark room," *Financial Times*, January 23, 2008, p. 9.

15. While "from 1980 to 2006, the finance sector of the American economy grew to 8.6% of GDP from 4.9%," John Kay of the *Financial Times* suggests this growth "contributes little, if anything, to the betterment of lives and the efficiency of business." Rather, highly paid investors spend their time and creativity developing "algorithms for computer trading in securities that exploit the weaknesses of other algorithms for computerized trading in securities" (in Burton G. Malkiel, "Trading

Places," *The Wall Street Journal*, September 24, 2015, p. A15).

16. Martin Wolf, "Why the financial turmoil is an elephant in a dark room," *Financial Times*, January 23, 2008, p. 9.

17. David Ignatius, "Obama's vision of new foundation should reassure summiteers," *The Washington Post*, reprinted in *The Daily Yomiuri*, April 3, 2009, p. 17.

18. See Martin Wolf's excellent discussion of the causes of and solutions to the economic crisis in the *Financial Times* at http://blogs.ft.com/economistsforum/. Here is a typical post: Martin Wolf, "Choices made in 2009 will shape the globe's destiny," *Financial Times*, January 7, 2009, p. 9.

19. Seumas Milne, "Leaders still aren't facing up to scale of crisis," *The Guardian*, reprinted in *The Daily Yomiuri*, April 3, 2009, p. 17.

20. "Bashing the rich counterproductive," *The Economist*, April 4, 2009, reprinted in *The Daily Yomiuri*, April 5, 2009, p. 8.

21. Joe Nocera, "Two Days in September," *The New York Times*, September 15, 2012, p. A23.

22. Ibid.

23. Thomas L. Friedman, "The Inflection Is Near?" *The New York Times*, March 8, 2009, p. WK12.

24. "A Question Revisited: Is Capitalism Working?" *Knowledge@Wharton*, March 4, 2009, http://knowledge.wharton.upenn.edu/article/a-question-revisited-is-capitalism-working/.

25. Michael Lewis, "The End: How Wall Street did itself in," *Portfolio.com*, November 11, 2008 (updated December 11, 2015), http://upstart.bizjournals.com/news-markets/national-news/portfolio/2008/11/11/the-end-of-wall-streets-boom.html.

26. Michael Lewis & David Einhorn, "The End of the Financial World As We Know It," *The New York Times*, January 4, 2009, p. WK9.

27. Martin Wolf, "Seeds of its own destruction," *Financial Times*, March 9, 2009, p. 7.

28. Bill Gates, *Creative Capitalism: A Conversation with Bill Gates, Warren Buffett, and Other Economic Leaders*, Simon & Schuster, 2008. See also the text of Gates's speech at the 2008 World Economic Forum at Davos, Switzerland, http://www.gatesfoundation.org/media-center/speeches/2008/01/bill-gates-2008-world-economic-forum/.

29. Muhammad Yunus, *Creating a World Without Poverty: Social Business and the Future of Capitalism*, Public Affairs, 2009.

30. Thomas L. Friedman, "The Inflection Is Near?" *The New York Times*, March 8, 2009, p. WK12.

31. Skeptics, on the other hand, advise caution and suggest that talk of reform is premature: "'Capitalism with a conscience' promised on the sickbed may be quickly forgotten in recovery. Don't imagine the stake is through the neoliberal heart yet" (in Polly Toynbee, "Brown should spend more to save young people," *The Times*, reprinted in *The Daily Yomiuri*, April 6, 2009, p. 8).

32. William Yardley, "The Branding of the Occupy Movement," *The New York Times*, November 28, 2011, p. B1.

33. Donald Cohen, "The Education of Alan Greenspan," *The Huffington Post*, October 30, 2008, http://www.alternet.org/workplace/105414/the_education_of_alan_greenspan/.

34. See Justin Fox, *The Myth of the Rational Market*, Harper Business, 2009, and Richard Thaler, "The price is not always right and markets can be wrong," *Financial Times*, August 5, 2009, p. 7.

35. "A survival plan for capitalism" [Editorial], *Financial Times*, March 9, 2009, p. 8.

36. Sheelah Kolhatkar, "Billions in Fines, but No Jail Time for Bank of America," *Bloomberg Businessweek*, March 27, 2014, http://www.bloomberg.com/bw/articles/2014-03-27/billions-in-fines-but-no-jail-time-for-bank-of-america/. In response to the criticism it received for its failure to hold any individuals to account for the Financial Crisis, in 2015 the US Department of Justice announced that, in the future when it prosecutes corporate crime, "it plans to focus on prosecuting the actual individuals who commit corporate crime, no matter how senior they may be within a company, rather than focusing only on civil cases against the companies themselves" (in Sheelah Kolhatkar, "The DOJ Is Finally Conceding It Prosecutes Corporate Crime All Wrong," *Bloomberg BusinessWeek*, September 10, 2015, http://www.bloomberg.com/news/articles/2015-09-10/the-doj-is-finally-conceding-it-prosecutes-corporate-crime-all-wrong. The Department of Justice memo is available at http://www.nytimes.com/interactive/2015/09/09/us/politics/document-justice-dept-memo-on-corporate-wrongdoing.html.

37. Donal Griffin & Dakin Campbell, "U.S. Bank Legal Bills Exceed $100 Billion," *Bloomberg BusinessWeek*, August 28, 2013, http://www.bloomberg.com/news/2013-08-28/u-s-bank-legal-bills-exceed-100-billion.html. The total figure of $103 billion was later revised upward to $107 billion just for settlements alone (i.e., excluding legal fees).

38. Ben McLannahan, "Banks' post-crisis legal costs hit $300bn," *Financial Times*, June 8, 2015, http://www.ft.com/cms/s/0/debe3f58-0bd8-11e5-a06e-00144feabdc0.html.

39. Eric Lipton, "Ex-lenders Profit from Home Loans Gone Bad," *The New York Times*, March 4, 2009, p. A1.

40. For more background information on the rise and fall of Countrywide, see Gretchen Morgenson, "How Countrywide Covered the Cracks," *The New York Times*, October 17, 2010, p. BU1.

41. James R. Hagerty, "Marketing Into a Meltdown," *The Wall Street Journal*, January 7, 2009, p. A11.

42. Angelo Mozilo in a deposition to a congressional inquiry, September 2010 (in Ben Protess, "From Ex-Chief, a Staunch Defense of Countrywide's Legacy," *The New York Times*, February 18, 2011, p. B5.

43. James R. Hagerty, "Marketing Into a Meltdown," *The Wall Street Journal*, January 7, 2009, p. A11.

44. Michael Lewis, in Thomas L. Friedman, "All Fall Down," *The New York Times*, November 26, 2008, p. A31.

45. Edward Luce, "Subprime explosion: Who isn't guilty?" *Financial Times*, May 6, 2009, p. 3.

46. David Hechler, "Risky Business," *Corporate Counsel*, April 1, 2009, http://www.law.com/corporatecounsel/PubArticleCC.jsp?id=1202429141994.

47. James R. Hagerty, "Marketing Into a Meltdown," *The Wall Street Journal*, January 7, 2009, p. A11.

48. Karl Rove, "President Bush Tried to Rein in Fan and Fred," *The Wall Street Journal*, January 8, 2009, p. A13.

49. Ibid.

50. Petter S. Goodman & Gretchen Morgenson, "Saying Yes to Anyone, WaMu Built Empire

on Shaky Loans," *The New York Times*, December 28, 2008, p. A1.

51. "Northern Rock to be nationalized," *BBC News*, February 17, 2008, http://news.bbc.co.uk/1/hi/business/7249575.stm.

52. John Cassidy, "Lessons from the collapse of Bear Stearns," *Financial Times*, March 15, 2010, p. 11.

53. Bill Baue, "CSRwire Reports Top Corporate Social Responsibility News of 2008," CSR wire.com, January 12, 2009, http://www.csrwire.com/press/press_release/22696/.

54. Mara Der Hovanesian, "Sex, Lies, and Mortgage Deals," *BusinessWeek*, November 24, 2008, p. 71.

55. State of California Department of Justice, Office of the Attorney General, "Brown Sues Countrywide For Mortgage Deception" [Press release], June 25, 2008, https://oag.ca.gov/news/press-releases/brown-sues-countrywide-mortgage-deception. See also *People v. Countrywide*, Los Angeles Superior Court case number LC081846.

56. State of California Department of Justice, Office of the Attorney General, "Atty. Gen. Brown Discloses New Evidence Of Countrywide's Deceptive Practices" [Press release], July 17, 2008, https://oag.ca.gov/news/press-releases/atty-gen-brown-discloses-new-evidence-countrywides-deceptive-practices/.

57. Angelo Mozilo, in deposition to a congressional inquiry, September 2010 (in Ben Protess, "From Ex-Chief, a Staunch Defense of Countrywide's Legacy," *The New York Times*, February 18, 2011, p. B5).

58. *Marketplace*, National Public Radio, January 16, 2009.

59. William Cohen, "The tattered strategy of the banker of the year," *Financial Times*, January 20, 2009, p. 13.

60. Saskia Scholtes, "BofA lays Countrywide brand to rest," *Financial Times*, April 27, 2009, p. 17.

61. Greg Farrell, "Mortgage executives charged by SEC," *Financial Times*, June 5, 2009, p. 1.

62. Angelo Mozilo, in deposition to a congressional inquiry, September 2010 (in Ben Protess, "From Ex-Chief, a Staunch Defense of Countrywide's Legacy," *The New York Times*, February 18, 2011, p. B5).

63. Jessica Silver-Greenberg & Peter Eavis, "In Deal, Bib Bank Extends Retreat from Mortgages," *The New York Times*, January 8, 2013, p. A1.

64. William D. Cohen, "The Wrecking Crew," *Vanity Fair*, April 2015, p. 150.

65. Ibid.

66. Dan Fitzpatrick, "Banks Haunted by Houses," *The Wall Street Journal*, June 30, 2011, p. C2.

67. Ben Protess, "From Ex-Chief, a Staunch Defense of Countrywide's Legacy," *The New York Times*, February 18, 2011, p. B5.

68. William Alden, "Dow Index Replaces 3 of Its 30 Stocks," *The New York Times*, September 11, 2013, p. B7.

Chapter 10

1. Bruce D. Henderson, "The Origin of Strategy," *Harvard Business Review*, November–December 1989, pp. 134–143.

2. An alternative tool to analyze a firm's strategy that emphasizes the importance of a comprehensive approach is the "strategy diamond." This approach is detailed in an article by Donald C. Hambrick & James W. Fredrickson: "Are you sure you have a strategy?" *Academy of Management Executive*, Vol. 19, No. 4, 2005, pp. 51–62. The strategy diamond contains five elements that cover the range of actions taken by firms to achieve their goals: *arenas* (the areas in which the firm will compete), *vehicles* (the ways in which the firm will achieve its goals), *differentiators* (the means by which the firm will differentiate itself from its competitors), *staging* (the speed and order of implementation), and *economic logic* (the route to profitability). While the strategy diamond draws on existing knowledge, its value lies in combining this knowledge into a comprehensive tool to analyze a firm's strategy—"an integrated overarching concept of how the business will achieve its objectives" (p. 51).

3. C. K. Prahalad & Gary Hamel, "The Core Competence of the Corporation," *Harvard Business Review*, May–June 1990, pp. 79–91.

4. Gary Hamel & C. K. Prahalad, *Competing for the Future*, Harvard Business School Press, 1994.

5. "Google's mission is to organize the world's information and make it universally accessible and useful," http://www.google.com/about/company/ (accessed February 2016).

6. C. K. Prahalad & Gary Hamel, "The Core Competence of the Corporation," *Harvard Business Review*, May–June 1990, p. 81.

7. James L. Heskett, "Southwest Airlines—2002: An Industry under Siege," Harvard Business School case study 9-803-133, March 11, 2003, p. 4.

8. Barney's framework was first published in a 1991 article (Jay B. Barney, "Firm Resources and Sustained Competitive Advantage," *Journal of Management*, Vol. 17, No. 1, pp. 99–120) as VRIN (value, rareness, imperfect imitability, and non-substitutability). This framework was subsequently refined in 1995 (Jay B. Barney, "Looking Inside for Competitive Advantage," *Academy of Management Executive*, Vol. 9, No. 4, pp. 49–61) as VRIO (valuable, rare, costly to imitate, firm organized to capture value).

9. Jay B. Barney & William S. Hesterly, *Strategic Management and Competitive Advantage* (5th ed.), Prentice-Hall, 2015, p. 112.

10. James L. Heskett, "Southwest Airlines—2002: An Industry Under Siege," Harvard Business School case study 9-803-133, March 11, 2003, p. 4.

11. Michael E. Porter, "How Competitive Forces Shape Strategy," *Harvard Business Review*, March/April 1979, pp. 137–145.

12. Michael E. Porter, *Competitive Strategy*, The Free Press, 1980.

13. Michael E. Porter, *Competitive Advantage*, The Free Press, 1985.

14. Michael E. Porter, "The Five Competitive Forces That Shape Strategy," *Harvard Business Review*, January 2008, pp. 79–93.

15. The other two airlines that might be considered competitors, Bombardier (Canada) and Embraer (Brazil), each have less than 10% market share.

16. "New IATA Passenger Forecast Reveals Fast-growing Markets of the Future" [Press Release No. 57], International Air Travel Association, October 16, 2014, http://www.iata.org/pressroom/pr/Pages/2014-10-16-01.aspx.

17. James L. Heskett & W. Earl Sasser Jr., "Southwest Airlines: In a Different World," Harvard Business School case study 910419, April 22, 2010. See also James L. Heskett, "Southwest Airlines—2002: An Industry Under Siege," Harvard Business School case study 9-803-133, March 11, 2003.

18. "After breaking even less than two years after its founding in 1971, the airline . . . enjoyed 30 consecutive years of profit beginning in 1973, a record unmatched by any airline in the world" (from James L. Heskett, "Southwest Airlines—2002: An Industry Under Siege," Harvard Business School case study 9-803-133, 2003, p. 4).

19. To some extent, this issue is addressed in Porter's 2008 update of his original paper ("The Five Competitive Forces That Shape Strategy," *Harvard Business Review*, January 2008, pp. 79–93.) The original five forces structure remains intact, however, to the exclusion of all other stakeholder relationships.

20. C. K. Prahalad & Allen Hammond, "Serving the World's Poor, Profitably," *Harvard Business Review,* September 2002, pp. 48–58; and C. K. Prahalad, *The Fortune at the Bottom of the Pyramid: Eradicating Poverty Through Profits*, Wharton School Publishing, 2006.

21. The person most closely associated with continuing Prahalad's work on the bottom of the pyramid is Stuart L. Hart of Cornell University. For an overview of his ideas and a list of publications, see http://www.stuartlhart.com/.

22. C. K. Prahalad & Allen Hammond, "Serving the World's Poor, Profitably," *Harvard Business Review,* September 2002, pp. 48–58.

23. Michael E. Porter & Mark R. Kramer, "The Competitive Advantage of Corporate Philanthropy," *Harvard Business Review*, December 2002, pp. 57–68.

24. Michael E. Porter & Mark R. Kramer, "Strategy & Society," *Harvard Business Review*, December 2006, pp. 78–92.

25. Michael E. Porter & Mark R. Kramer, "Creating Shared Value," *Harvard Business Review*, February 2011, pp. 62–77.

26. Michael E. Porter & Mark R. Kramer, "Strategy & Society," *Harvard Business Review*, December 2006, p. 88.

27. Ibid., p. 84.

28. Ibid., p. 92.

29. For a detailed explanation of the characteristics of valuable, rare, imperfectly imitable,

and non-substitutable resources that lead to a "sustained competitive advantage" for the firm, see Jay Barney, "Firm Resources and Sustained Competitive Advantage," *Journal of Management*, Vol. 17, No. 1, 1991, pp. 99–120.

30. I would like to thank Marta White of Georgia State University for introducing this idea and allowing me to build on it for inclusion in this chapter of *Strategic CSR*.

31. David Grayson & Adrian Hodges, *Corporate Social Opportunity! Seven Steps to Make Corporate Social Responsibility Work for Your Business*, Greenleaf Publications, 2004.

32. William B. Werther & David Chandler, "Strategic Corporate Social Responsibility as Global Brand Insurance," *Business Horizons*, Vol. 48, No. 4, July 2005, pp. 317–324.

33. http://www.nike.com/us/en_us/c/innovation/flyknit/.

34. Anheuser-Busch claims that "we recycle 99.8 percent of the solid waste generated in the brewing and packaging process, including beechwood chips, aluminum, glass, brewers' grain, scrap metal, cardboard and many other items" (http://anheuser-busch.com/index.php/our-responsibility/environment-our-earth-our-natural-resources/reduce-reuse-and-recycle/, accessed February 2016).

35. "The soda giant announced it will replenish all the water used in making its beverages by the end of 2015" (in Alison Moodie, "Coca-Cola to reach water goal five years early," *The Guardian*, August 25, 2015, http://www.theguardian.com/sustainable-business/2015/aug/25/coca-cola-replenish-water-goals-early-watersheds/).

36. Timberland, "Timberland Responsibility," http://responsibility.timberland.com/service/living-our-values/.

37. Jonathan Birchall, "Business fights for tougher rules on emissions," *Financial Times*, November 20, 2008, p. 4. See also Meridian Institute, "United States Climate Action Partnership," http://www.merid.org/en/Content/Projects/United_States_Climate_Action_Partnership.aspx.

38. William Werther & David Chandler, "Strategic Corporate Social Responsibility as Global Brand Insurance," *Business Horizons,* Vol. 48, No. 4, 2005, p. 322.

39. Stephanie Clifford & Stephanie Strom, "Wal-Mart to Announce Women-Friendly Plans," *The New York Times*, September 14, 2011, p. B3.

40. Ibid.

41. Although there are disagreements as to which categorization best fits different business models, what all these firms have in common is that their strategies seek to provide customers with superior value.

42. A firm's business-level strategy stands in contrast to its corporate-level strategy, which is the strategy of the firm as a whole. Strategy at this level involves decisions about which businesses the firm will compete in and whether to enter into partnerships with other firms via joint ventures, mergers, or acquisitions.

43. Michael Porter, "What Is Strategy?" *Harvard Business Review*, November–December 1996, p. 62.

44. Mallen Baker, "Financial services: Will banks ever treat customers fairly?" *Ethical Corporation*, April 1, 2008, http://www.ethicalcorp.com/content/financial-services-will-banks-ever-treat-customers-fairly/.

45. Ibid.

46. Richard Gibson, "McDonald's Seeks Ways to Pitch Healthy Living," *The Wall Street Journal,* May 27, 2004, p. D7.

47. Altria, "Smoking & Health Issues," http://www.altria.com/our-companies/philipmorrisusa/smoking-and-health-issues/Pages/default.aspx (accessed February 2016).

48. "The price of oil: Shell in the Niger Delta," Greenpeace, October 7, 2011, http://www.greenpeace.org.uk/blog/climate/price-oil-shell-niger-delta-20111007/.

49. Friends of the Earth, *Who Benefits from GM Crops? An Analysis of the Global Performance of GM Crops (1996–2006)*, January 2007, http://www.foeeurope.org/publications/2007/whobenefits_gmcrops2007full.pdf; and Friends of the Earth, "Monsanto Moves to Force-Feed Europe Genetically Engineered Corn," January 10, 2006, http://www.organicconsumers.org/ge/europecorn011106.cfm.

50. Lisa Roner, "Starbucks and Oxfam Team Up on Ethiopian Development Programme," *Ethical Corporation,* October 18, 2004; and Alison Maitland, "Starbucks Tastes Oxfam's Brew," *Financial Times* (US edition), October 14, 2004, p. 9.

51. C. K. Prahalad, *The Fortune at the Bottom of the Pyramid: Eradicating Poverty Through Profits*, Wharton School Publishing, 2006; and C. K. Prahalad & Allen Hammond, "Serving the World's Poor, Profitably," *Harvard Business Review,* September 2002, pp. 48–58.

52. Also see Michael Hopkins, *Corporate Social Responsibility and International Development: Is Business the Solution?* Earthscan, 2007.

53. "2015 Green Rankings," *Newsweek,* http://www.newsweek.com/green-2015/top-green-companies-world-2015/ (accessed February 2016).

54. Heather Lang, "Newsweek Green Rankings 2011: How Do Global Companies Compare?" *Newsweek,* October 16, 2011, http://www.newsweek.com/newsweek-green-rankings-2011-how-do-global-companies-compare-68275/.

55. Ibid.

56. Ibid.

57. Transparency International, "Corruption Perceptions Index," http://www.transparency.org/research/cpi/overview/ (accessed February 2016).

58. Transparency Internation, "Corruption Perceptions Index 2014: Results," http://www.transparency.org/cpi2014/results/.

Chapter 11

1. The flip side of each of these "constraints" is opportunities for the firm to build a sustainable competitive advantage.

2. Nike, "How We Work," http://www.nikeresponsibility.com/; Nike, "CR Report," http://www.nikeresponsibility.com/report/.

3. In one of the field's most highly regarded strategy textbooks, firm capabilities are described as "the organizational and managerial skills necessary to orchestrate a diverse set of resources and to deploy them strategically" (in Frank Rothaermel, *Strategic Management: Concepts*, McGraw-Hill/Irwin, 2013, p. 87).

4. See Archie B. Carroll, "A Three-Dimensional Conceptual Model of Corporate Performance," *Academy of Management Review,* 1979, Vol. 4, No. 4, pp. 497–505.

5. Same-sex partner employee benefits will likely be the next form of discrimination to be corrected by legal mandate. Many progressive firms today are proactively implementing such policies so as to avoid being forcefully sanctioned by litigation as the tide of social acceptability turns. See Kathryn Kranhold, "Groups for Gay Employees Are Gaining Traction," *The Wall Street Journal*, April 3, 2006, p. B3.

6. Dan Myers, "9 Things You Didn't Know About the Food at Walmart," *The Daily Meal*, December 19, 2014, http://www.thedailymeal.com/eat/10-things-you-didnt-know-about-food-walmart/.

7. Wal-Mart reports "our average, full-time hourly wage for Walmart stores is $11.24 and is even higher in urban areas. The average full-time hourly wage is $11.66 in Atlanta, $12.55 in Boston, $11.61 in Chicago, $11.25 in Dallas, $11.43 in San Francisco and $11.50 in New York City" (in Walmart, "Corporate Facts: Walmart By the Numbers" [corporate fact sheet], September 2009, http://walmartstores.com/FactsNews/FactSheets/ (no longer available online).

8. Miguel Bustillo & Ann Zimmerman, "In Cities That Battle Wal-Mart, Target Gets a Welcome," *The Wall Street Journal*, October 15, 2010, p. B1.

9. Walmart, "Sustainability Progress to Date 2007–2008," http://walmartstores.com/sites/sustainabilityreport/2007/communityJobs.html (no longer available online).

10. Kathleen Parker, "Attention, Wal-Mart shoppers: You have a say," *Orlando Sentinel* (reprinted in the *Austin American Statesman*), January 30, 2006, p. A9.

11. Cathryn Creno, "Wal-Mart's Sustainability Efforts Draw Praise," *The Arizona Republic*, May 26, 2008, http://www.azcentral.com/business/articles/2008/05/26/20080526biz-greenretailers0526-ON.html.

12. "Harris Poll: Young Adults Willing to Pay Extra for Green Products," *Green Retail Decisions*, May 31, 2012, http://www.greenretaildecisions.com/news/2012/05/31/harris-poll-young-adults-willing-to-pay-extra-for-green-products/.

13. "Only 22 percent of consumers willing to pay more for green," *The Independent*, September 4, 2011, http://www.solarworld4u.net/alg_artikel.asp?Bericht=841&Title=Only-22-percent-of-consumers-willing-to-pay-more-for-green/.

14. Gregory Unruh, "No, Consumers Will Not Pay More for Green," *Forbes*, July 28, 2011, http://www.forbes.com/sites/csr/2011/07/28/no-consumers-will-not-pay-more-for-green/.

15. David Grayson & Adrian Hodges, *Corporate Social Opportunity!*, Greenleaf Publications, 2004.

16. Karen K. Nathan, "Behind the Label: The case for eco-disclosure," *Barron's*, August 3, 2009, p. 32 (review of the book by Daniel Goleman, *Ecological Intelligence: How Knowing the Hidden Impacts of What We Buy Can Change Everything*, Broadway Business, 2009).

17. Alina Tugend, "Too Many Choices: A Problem That Can Paralyze," *The New York Times*, February 27, 2010, p. B5.

18. For ideas about the determinants of greenwashing, see Magali A. Delmas & Vanessa Cuerel Burbano, "The Drivers of Greenwashing," *California Management Review*, 2011, Vol. 54, No. 1, pp. 64–87.

19. Terrachoice, "The Sins of Greenwashing," http://sinsofgreenwashing.org/findings/greenwashing-report-2010/index.html.

20. Terrachoice, "The Sins of Greenwashing: Home and Family Edition," 2010, p. 10, http://sinsofgreenwashing.com/index35c6.pdf. See also Elizabeth Wasserman, "7 Sins of Greenwashing (And 5 Ways to Keep It Out of Your Life)," *EcoWatch*, April 23, 2014, http://ecowatch.com/2014/04/23/7-sins-of-greenwashing/.

21. Dan Mitchell, "Being Skeptical of Green," *The New York Times*, November 24, 2007, p. 5.

22. Sarah Nassauer, "To Scream Green, Dyeing Paper a Light Brown," *The Wall Street Journal*, January 25, 2012, p. D3.

23. Nick Bunkley, "Payoff for Efficient Cars Takes Years," *The New York Times*, April 5, 2012, p. B1.

24. Daniel Nelson, "Greenwashing the Olympics," CorpWatch, July 4, 2012, http://www.corpwatch.org/article.php?id=15748.

25. Joe Nocera, "The Paradoxes of Businesses as Do-Gooders," *The New York Times*, November 11, 2006, p. B1.

26. Alex William, "That Buzz in Your Ear May Be Green Noise," *The New York Times*, June 15, 2008, http://www.nytimes.com/2008/06/15/fashion/15green.html. The idea of "green noise" adds value to the debate. While terms like *greenwashing* describe the conduct of firms, *green noise* presents a consumer perspective on the exponential growth in information related to the environment and climate change that is often contradictory.

27. Mallen Baker, "Marketing and marketers: Use the dark arts for good," *Ethical Corporation*, December 11, 2011, http://www.ethicalcorp.com/communications-reporting/marketing-and-marketers-use-dark-arts-good/.

28. Mallen Baker, "Four emerging trends in corporate social responsibility," Business Respect, October 8, 2012, http://www.businessrespect.net/page.php?Story_ID=2747.

Chapter 12

1. "Just Good Business: A Special Report on Corporate Social Responsibility," *The Economist*, January 19, 2008.

2. See *Standard Oil Co. of New Jersey v. United States* (221 U.S. 1, 1911). Ironically, it was the proceeds from stock sales as a result of the breakup of Standard Oil that gave John D. Rockefeller "a cash windfall of unprecedented magnitude," which he then used to begin the Rockefeller Foundation. See Jonathan Lopez, "The Splendid Spoils of Standard Oil," *The Wall Street Journal*, November 20–21, 2010, p. C7.

3. See David Grayson & Adrian Hodges, "Corporate Social Opportunity! Seven Steps to Make Corporate Social Responsibility Work for Your Business," Greenleaf Publishing, July 2004.

4. Marc Gunther, "The Mosquito in the Tent: A Pesky Environmental Group Called the Rainforest Action Network Is Getting Under the Skin of Corporate America," *Fortune*, May 31, 2004, http://money.cnn.com/magazines/fortune/fortune_archive/2004/05/31/370717/index.htm. The Equator Principles is "a risk management framework, adopted by financial institutions, for determining, assessing and managing environmental and social risk in [financial] projects" (Equator Principles, "About the Equator Principles," http://www.equator-principles.com/index.php/about-ep/, accessed February 2016).

5. See http://www.unilever.com/sustainable-living/. For more comment on Unilever's

approach to CSR, see http://strategiccsr-sage.blogspot.com/2011/03/strategic-csr-unilever.html.

6. See GE, "Ecomagination," http://www.ge.com/about-us/ecomagination/. For commentary on the 10th anniversary of Ecoimagination, see Mallen Baker, "Ecoimagination's 10th birthday marks GE's progress from polluter to pioneer," *Business Respect*, May 12, 2015, http://www.mallenbaker.net/csr/page.php?Story_ID=2819.

7. Michael Porter & Mark Kramer, "The Competitive Advantage of Corporate Philanthropy," *Harvard Business Review,* December 2002, p. 67.

8. The work of John Mackey (Whole Foods Market) on conscious capitalism (http://consciouscapitalism.org/) is, in many ways, complementary to the argument underlying strategic CSR.

9. Michael E. Porter & Mark R. Kramer, "Strategy & Society," *Harvard Business Review*, December 2006, p. 85.

10. Michael E. Porter & Mark R. Kramer, "The Competitive Advantage of Corporate Philanthropy," *Harvard Business Review*, December 2002, pp. 57–68.

11. Dell, "Dell Trade-In & Recycling Program," http://www.dell.com/learn/us/en/19/campaigns/trade-in-program/. See also "Dell Will Offer Free Recycling for Its Computer Equipment," *The Wall Street Journal*, June 29, 2006, p. D3.

12. Dell, "Reducing Your Footprint," http://www.dell.com/learn/us/en/uscorp1/corp-comm/plantatreeforme/. See also "Dell unveils 'plant a tree for me,'" *Financial Times*, January 10, 2007, p. 17.

13. Jack Welch, former CEO of GE, condemned firms' primary focus on shareholder value, even though he was closely associated with such a focus during his time at GE, in a series of articles: first, in the *Financial Times* (Francesco Guerrera, "Welch condemns share price focus," March 12, 2009) and, second, in *BusinessWeek* ("Jack Welch Elaborates: Shareholder Value," March 16, 2009). In the *Financial Times* article, Welch said, "On the face of it, shareholder value is the dumbest idea in the world. . . . Your main constituencies are your employees, your customers and your products." In the *BusinessWeek* follow-up article, Welch confirmed, "I was asked what I thought of

'shareholder value as a strategy.' My response was that the question on its face was a dumb idea. Shareholder value is an outcome—not a strategy."

14. Martin Wolf, "Britain's strategic chocolate dilemma," *Financial Times*, January 29, 2010, p. 9.

15. Sumantra Ghoshal, "Bad Management Theories Are Destroying Good Management Practices," *Academy of Management Learning & Education*, Vol. 4, No. 1, March 2005, pp. 79–80.

16. Johnson & Johnson, "Our Credo Values," http://www.jnj.com/connect/about-jnj/jnj-credo/.

17. Although Johnson & Johnson's response to the Tylenol crisis remains a best-practice model for crisis management, there is evidence to suggest that the firm has strayed from its core principles in recent years. See "Patients versus Profits at Johnson & Johnson: Has the Company Lost Its Way?" *Knowledge@Wharton*, February 15, 2012, http://knowledge.wharton.upenn.edu/article.cfm?articleid=2943; and Alex Nussbaum, David Voreacos, & Greg Farrell, "Johnson & Johnson's Quality Catastrophe," *Bloomberg Businessweek*, March 31, 2011, http://www.bloomberg.com/bw/magazine/content/11_15/b4223064555570.htm.

18. James L. Heskett, "Southwest Airlines—2002: An Industry under Siege," Harvard Business School case study 9-803-133, March 11, 2003.

19. "Starbucks Corporation: Building a Sustainable Supply Chain," Stanford Graduate School of Business case study GS-54, May 2007.

20. Stephen P. Bradley & Pankaj Ghemwat, "Wal-Mart Stores, Inc.," Harvard Business School case study 9-794-024, November 6, 2002.

21. Yvon Chouinard, *Let My People Go Surfing: The Education of a Reluctant Businessman*, Penguin Press, 2005.

22. Joe Nocera, "Putting Customers First? What an Amazonian Concept," *The New York Times*, January 5, 2008, p. B1.

23. See "Strategic CSR—Blackrock," http://strategiccsr-sage.blogspot.jp/2015/09/strategic-csr-blackrock.html. See also Andrew Ross Sorkin, "A CEO Urges Others to Stop Being So Nice to Investors," *The New York Times*, April 14, 2015, p. B1.

24. "A new contract for growth," *The Economist*, August 15, 2015, p. 65.

25. Quoted in Jeff Sommer, "A Mutual Fund Master, Too Worried to Rest," *The New York Times*, August 12, 2012, p. BU1.

26. Michael Powell & Danny Hakim, "The Lonely Redemption of a Wall Street Critic," *The New York Times*, September 16, 2012, p. 27.

27. Jeff Sommer, "A Mutual Fund Master, Too Worried to Rest," *The New York Times*, August 12, 2012, p. BU1.

28. "Wait a second," *The Economist* [Editorial], August 11, 2012, p. 10.

29. It is important not to overstate this case. This a complex issue with many contributing factors, not least of which is executive compensation packages crammed with stock options that reinforce a disproportionate focus on share price. Moreover, it is undoubtedly true that shareholders play an important management oversight function (in many cases, more effectively than directors). Short-sellers, in particular, focus on identifying ineffective top management teams. See "The story and the numbers," *The Economist,* October 31, 2015, p. 66.

30. For alternative ideas on how to incentivize longer term perspectives among shareholders, see Julia Werdigier, "A Call for Corporations to Focus on the Long Term," *The New York Times*, May 15, 2012, p. B9; and Richard Lambert, "Sir Ralph's lessons on how to end short-term capitalism," *Financial Times*, May 23, 2011, p. 11.

31. James Grant, "Magical thinking divorces markets from reality," *Financial Times*, July 21, 2015, p. 11.

32. Nathaniel Popper, "Short-Termism," *The New York Times Deal Book*, November 5, 2015, p. F4.

33. Ibid.

34. John Kay, "Beauty in markets is best judged by the beholder," *Financial Times*, June 10, 2009, p. 9.

35. John Maynard Keynes, *The General Theory of Employment, Interest and Money*, Harcourt Brace, 1936, p. 156.

36. Richard Milne, "The jovial locust killer," *Financial Times*, November 1–2, 2008, p. 7.

37. "Shooting the Messenger: Quarterly Earnings and Short-term Pressure to Perform," *Knowledge@Wharton*, July 21, 2010, http:// knowledge.wharton.upenn.edu/article.cfm?articleid=2550.

38. Paul Ziobro & Serena Ng, "P&G Looks Into Its Own Guidance," *The Wall Street Journal*, June 12, 2013, http://www.wsj.com/articles/SB100014241278873240495045785418908944496194.

39. Robert C. Pozen & Mark J. Roe, "Those Short-sighted Attacks on Quarterly Earnings," *The Wall Street Journal*, October 8, 2015, p. A17.

40. Peter Eavis, "Privately Public," *The New York Times Deal Book,* November 5, 2015, p. F19.

41. For examples, see Andrew Hill, "Real value looks past quarterly reporting," *Financial Times*, April 19, 2011, p. 10; Michael Skapinker, "Banks will be judged by actions not words," *Financial Times*, October 5, 2010, p. 13; and Andrew Ross Sorkin, "Do Stockholders Really Know Best?" *The New York Times*, November 17, 2009, p. B1.

42. Paul C. Godfrey, "The Relationship between Corporate Philanthropy and Shareholder Wealth: A Risk Management Perspective," *Academy of Management Review*, Vol. 30, No. 4, 2005, pp. 777–798.

43. This is why the India government's CSR law (which was passed in 2013 and is designed to compel all businesses to "give 2 per cent of their net profits to corporate social responsibility projects") is misguided (in James Crabtree, "Take a closer look at the hand that gives," *Financial Times*, August 15, 2013, p. 8.

44. Graham McLaughlin, "Why brands should focus on social change, not philanthropy," *The Guardian*, January 17, 2014, http://www.theguardian.com/sustainable-business/responsibility-good-business-long-term/.

45. Ibid.

46. Ibid.

47. Mark Boleat, "Inclusive capitalism: Searching for a purpose beyond profit," *The Guardian*, May 27, 2014, http://www.theguardian.com/sustainable-business/inclusive-capitalism-purpose-beyond-profit/.

48. In this sense, the work of C. K. Prahalad and Stuart Hart on delivering goods and services to consumers at the bottom of the pyramid is much closer to the idea of strategic CSR because the conceptualization of the developing world as an underserved market

(rather than a charitable cause) speaks to the power of business to deliver market-based solutions that address some of society's most intractable problems. See C. K. Prahalad, *The Fortune at the Bottom of the Pyramid: Eradicating Poverty Through Profits*, Wharton School Publishing, 2004; and Stuart L. Hart, *Capitalism at the Crossroads: The Unlimited Business Opportunities in Solving the World's Most Difficult Problems*, Wharton School Publishing, 2005.

49. A transcript of Gates's remarks, with a link to a video of his January 24, 2008, speech, can be found at http://www.gatesfoundation .org/media-center/speeches/2008/01/bill-gates-2008-world-economic-forum/.

50. Ibid.

51. Michael Kanellos, "On 'creative capitalism,' Gates gets it," CNET, January 25, 2008, http://www.cnet.com/news/on-creative-capitalism-gates-gets-it/.

52. Declan McCullagh, "Gates misses the point on 'creative capitalism,'" CNET, January 25, 2008, http://www.cnet.com/news/gates-misses-the-point-on-creative-capitalism/.

53. William R. Easterly, "Why Bill Gates Hates My Book," *The Wall Street Journal*, February 7, 2008, p. A18.

54. See Muhammad Yunus, *Creating a World Without Poverty: Social Business and the Future of Capitalism*, Public Affairs, 2008.

55. Alan Beattie, "Poor returns," *Financial Times*, February 2, 2008, p. 33.

56. Ibid.

57. Michael E. Porter & Mark R. Kramer, "Creating Shared Value," *Harvard Business Review*, January–February 2011, p. 64.

58. For additional commentary on Porter and Kramer's ideas, see Tobias Webb, "Does Michael Porter understand sustainable business?" *Sustainability = Smart Business*, January 21, 2011, http://tobiaswebb.blogs pot.com/2011/01/does-michael-porter-understand.html.

59. Andrew Hill, "Society and the right kind of capitalism," *Financial Times*, February 22, 2011, p. 14.

60. See William B. Werther & David Chandler, "Strategic Corporate Social Responsibility as Global Brand Insurance," *Business Horizons*, Vol. 48, No. 4, 2005, pp. 317–324.

Part IV Case Study

1. Toby Webb, "Supply chain stats," *Sustainability = Smart Business*, October 1, 2012, http://sustainablesmartbusiness.com/ 2012/10/supply-chain-stats/.

2. Jathon Sapsford & Norihiko Shirouzu, "Mom, Apple Pie and . . . Toyota?" *The Wall Street Journal*, May 11, 2006, p. B1.

3. Glenn Hubbard, "Offshoring can benefit workers of all skill levels," *Financial Times*, September 28, 2006, p. 19.

4. Thomas L. Friedman, "How Did the Robot End Up With My Job?" *The New York Times*, October 2, 2011, p. SR11.

5. Thomas L. Friedman, "Average Is Over," *The New York Times*, January 25, 2012, p. A25.

6. The Hackett Group, "750,000 Jobs Lost to Outsourcing by 2016," *Product, Design & Development*, March 29, 2012, http://www .pddnet.com/news/2012/03/750000-jobs-lost-outsourcing-2016/.

7. For example, see Declan Walsh, "Anger Rolls across Pakistani City in Aftermath of Factory Fire," *The New York Times*, September 14, 2012, p. A6.

8. Jo Johnson, "India extends prohibitions on employing children," *Financial Times*, August 3, 2006, p. 4.

9. Andrea Tunarosa, "What Do NGOs Have Against Poor Guatemalans?" *The Wall Street Journal*, July 21, 2006, p. A15; and Glenn Hubbard, "Offshoring can benefit workers of all skill levels," *Financial Times*, September 28, 2006, p. 19.

10. See Sam Chambers, "China's factories— Exploitation ain't what is used to be," *Ethical Corporation*, August 30, 2006, http://www.ethicalcorp.com/content .asp?ContentID=4458 (no longer available online); "Secrets, Lies, and Sweatshops," *BusinessWeek*, November 26, 2006, http:// www.bloomberg.com/bw/stories/ 2006-11-26/secrets-lies-and-sweatshops; and Richard McGregor, "We must count the true cost of cheap China," *Financial Times*, August 2, 2007, p. 7.

11. Pia Catton, "Beware False Thrift," *The Wall Street Journal*, June 23–24, 2012, p. C10.

12. For an interesting example of firms being caught in the middle of a cultural clash, see the scandal that erupted in 2012 following

IKEA's decision to delete photos of women from its catalogs in Saudi Arabia (Reuters, "IKEA slammed for female-free Saudi catalog," *The Daily Yomiuri*, October 4, 2012, p. 1)—a decision for which the firm apologized (Anna Molin, "IKEA Regrets Cutting Women From Saudi Ad," *The Wall Street Journal*, October 1, 2012, http://online.wsj.com/article/SB1000087239639044459240457803027420038713G.html).

13. Dale Neef, "Supply chain ethics: The devil is in the details," *Ethical Corporation*, April 14, 2005.

14. For example, see Kris Hudson & Wilawan Watcharasakwet, "The New Wal-Mart Effect: Cleaner Thai Shrimp Farms," *The Wall Street Journal*, July 24, 2007, p. B1.

15. For example, see the controversy that surrounds the use of forced child labor to harvest cotton: Toby Webb, "Special Report Cotton: Corporate action on Uzbeki white gold," *Ethical Corporation*, March 6, 2008, http://www.ethicalcorp.com/supply-chains/special-report-cotton-supply-chains-corporate-action-uzbeki-white-gold/.

16. See the discussion in Chapter 8 of the cost savings Walmart is able to secure by operating more sustainably.

17. The 2009 *Conscious Consumer Report* from the branding consultancy BBMG, for example, notes that 67% of Americans agree that "even in tough economic times, it is important to purchase products with social and environmental benefits," and also that 71% of consumers agree that they "avoid purchasing from companies whose practices they disagree with" (in Jack Loechner, "Consumers Want Proof It's Green," Center for Media Research, April 9, 2009, http://www.mediapost.com/publications/article/103504/consumers-want-proof-its-green.html).

18. For information about sustainable certification schemes that rival fair trade (e.g., Rainforest Alliance and Utz Certified), see John Russell, "Coffee sourcing: Nespresso points Nestlé towards sustainability," *Ethical Corporation*, June 29, 2009, http://www.ethicalcorp.com/business-strategy/coffee-sourcing-nespresso-points-nestle-towards-sustainability/.

19. James E. Austin & Cate Reavis, "Starbucks and Conservation International," Harvard Business School Case 9-303-055, May 1, 2004, p. 14.

20. Fairtrade Foundation, "What Is Fairtrade?" http://www.fairtrade.org.uk/what_is_fairtrade/faqs.aspx (accessed January 2013).

21. Katy McLaughlin, "Is Your Grocery List Politically Correct?" *The Wall Street Journal*, February 17, 2004, pp. D1, D2.

22. Tim Hunt, "Drinking an ethical cup of coffee: How easy is it?" *The Guardian*, May 29, 2015, http://www.theguardian.com/sustainable-business/2015/may/29/drinking-an-ethical-cup-of-coffee-how-easy-is-it/.

23. Andrew Stark, "The Price of Moral Purity," *The Wall Street Journal*, February 4, 2011, p. A13.

24. Ibid.

25. Rebecca Smithers, "Global Fairtrade sales reach £4.4bn following 15% growth during 2013," *The Guardian*, September 3, 2014, http://www.theguardian.com/global-development/2014/sep/03/global-fair-trade-sales-reach-4-billion-following-15-per-cent-growth-2013/.

26. Ibid.

27. Quote from the 2005 *Green and Ethical Consumer Report* (in Poulomi Mrinal Saha, "Ethics Still Not Influencing UK Consumers," *Ethical Corporation*, March 15, 2005).

28. Michael Skapinker, "No markets were hurt in making this coffee," *Financial Times*, November 9, 2010, p. 11.

29. Alan Beattie, "Follow the thread," *Financial Times*, July 22–23, 2006, p. WK1.

30. "Good thing, or bad?" *The Economist*, July 5, 2014, p. 72.

31. Katy McLaughlin, "Is Your Grocery List Politically Correct?" *The Wall Street Journal*, February 17, 2004, pp. D1, D2.

32. Parminder Bahra, "Tea workers still waiting to reap Fairtrade benefits," *The Times*, January 2, 2009, http://www.timesonline.co.uk/tol/news/uk/article5429888.ece.

33. Michael Skapinker, "No markets were hurt in making this coffee," *Financial Times*, November 9, 2010, p. 11.

34. John Vidal, "New choc on the bloc," *The Guardian*, June 3, 2005, http://www.theguardian.com/world/2005/jun/03/outlook.development/.

35. Alan Beattie, "Follow the thread," *Financial Times*, July 22–23, 2006, p. WK1.

36. Peter Heslam, "George and the Chocolate Factory," The London Institute for Contemporary Christianity, September 2005.

37. James E. McWilliams, "Food That Travels Well," *The New York Times*, August 6, 2007, http://www.nytimes.com/2007/08/06/opinion/06mcwilliams.html; and Claudia H. Deutsch, "For Suppliers, the Pressure Is On," *The New York Times*, Special Section: Business of Green, November 7, 2007, p. 1.

38. "Cadbury Dairy Milk Commits to Going Fairtrade" [Cadbury press release], CSRwire, March 3, 2009, http://www.csrwire.com/press_releases/13812-Cadbury-Dairy-Milk-commits-to-Going-Fairtrade-/. See also Michael Skapinker, "Fairtrade and a new ingredient for business," *Financial Times*, March 10, 2009, p. 11.

39. "Hershey to Source 100% Certified Cocoa by 2020," *Environmental Leader*, October 8, 2012, http://www.environmentalleader.com/2012/10/08/hershey-to-source-100-certified-cocoa-by-2020/.

40. Nicholas D. Kristof, "In Praise of the Maligned Sweatshop," *The New York Times*, June 6, 2006, p. A21.

41. Nicholas D. Kristof, "Where Sweatshops Are a Dream," *The New York Times*, January 15, 2009, p. A27.

42. Roger Martin, "The Virtue Matrix," *Harvard Business Review,* March 2002, Vol. 80, No. 3, pp. 68–75.

43. For example, see Bob Herbert, "In America: Nike's Boot Camps," *The New York Times,* March 31, 1997, p. A15.

44. Paul S. Adler, "The Environmental Crisis and Its Capitalist Roots: Reading Naomi Klein with Karl Polanyi," *Administrative Science Quarterly*, Vol. 60, No. 2, 2015, p. NP19.

45. Frank Wijen, "Banning child labour imposes naïve western ideals on complex problems," *The Guardian*, August 26, 2015, http://www.theguardian.com/sustainable-business/2015/aug/26/ban-child-labour-developing-countries-imposes-naive-western-ideals-complex-problems/.

46. Annie Kelly, "The UK's new slavery laws explained: What do they mean for business?" *The Guardian*, December 15, 2015, http://www.theguardian.com/sustainable-business/2015/dec/14/modern-slavery-act-explained-business-responsibility-supply-chain/.

47. "Faster, cheaper fashion," *The Economist*, September 5, 2015, p. 66.

48. See Shelly Banjo, "Inside Nike's Struggle to Balance Cost and Worker Safety," *The Wall Street Journal*, April 22, 2014, pp. A1, A12.

49. Global Exchange, "Nike Campaign," http://www.globalexchange.org/campaigns/sweatshops/nike/; "Don't Do It Foundation," http://dontdoitfoundation.org/.

50. Derrick Daye & Brad VanAuken, "Social Responsibility: The Nike Story," *Branding Strategy Insider*, July 25, 2008, http://www.brandingstrategyinsider.com/2008/07/social-responsi.html.

51. Jane L. Levere, "New Balance Celebrates Its Homemade Footprint," *The New York Times*, April 5, 2012, p. B2.

52. Jonathan Birchall, "Nike to strengthen efforts to combat worker abuse," *Financial Times*, May 31, 2007, p. 9.

53. Network for Business Sustainability, "Just Do It: How Nike Turned Disclosure into an Opportunity," January 23, 2012, http://nbs.net/knowledge/just-do-it-how-nike-turned-disclosure-into-an-opportunity/.

54. "The boomerang effect," *The Economist Special Report: Manufacturing and Innovation*, April 21, 2012, p. 8.

55. Chad Brooks, "What's Bringing US Jobs Back from Overseas?" Yahoo! News, October 2, 2012, http://news.yahoo.com/whats-bringing-us-jobs-back-overseas-154734351.html.

56. Securities and Exchange Commission, Conflict Minerals Final Rule, November 13, 2012, http://www.sec.gov/rules/final/2012/34-67716.pdf.

57. Steven Davidoff Solomon, "Humanitarian Effort in Congo Puts S.E.C. in Unintended Role," *The New York Times,* August 28, 2012, http://dealbook.nytimes.com/2012/08/28/humanitarian-effort-in-congo-puts-wall-st-regulator-in-unintended-role/.

58. Emily Chasan & Maxwell Murphey, "The Big Number: 743," *The Wall Street Journal*, September 16, 2014, p. B10.

59. Ibid. See also Lynnley Browning, "Complex Law on Conflict Metal," *The New York Times*, September 8, 2015, p. B1; and Emily Chasan, "'Conflict Minerals' Prove Hard to Trace," *The Wall Street Journal*, August 4, 2015, p. B4.

60. Don Clark, "Apple Reports on Its Sources of 'Conflict Minerals,'" *The Wall Street Journal*,

May 29, 2014, http://www.wsj.com/articles/apple-reports-on-its-sources-of-conflict-minerals-1401405074/.

61. "When workers dream of a life beyond the factory gates," *The Economist*, December 15, 2012, p. 63.

62. Charles Isherwood, "Moral Issues Behind iPhone and Its Makers," *The New York Times*, October 18, 2012, p. C1.

63. Charles Duhigg & Keith Bradsher, "How the U.S. Lost Out on iPhone Work," *The New York Times*, January 21, 2012, http://www.nytimes.com/2012/01/22/business/apple-america-and-a-squeezed-middle-class.html.

64. Charles Duhigg & David Barboza, "In China, the Human Costs That Are Built Into an iPad," *The New York Times*, January 26, 2012, pp. A1, B10–B11.

65. Associated Press, "Chinese iPhone workers strike at Foxconn plant," *The Daily Yomiuri*, October 8, 2012, p. 5.

66. Paul Mozur, "New Labor Attitudes Fed into China Riot," *The Wall Street Journal*, September 27, 2012, p. B1.

67. Rob Cooper, "Inside Apple's Chinese 'sweatshop' factory where workers are paid just £1.12 per hour to produce iPhones and iPads for the West," *The Daily Mail*, January 25, 2013, http://www.dailymail.co.uk/news/article-2103798/Revealed-Inside-Apples-Chinese-sweatshop-factory-workers-paid-just-1-12-hour.html.

68. David Barboza & Charles Duhigg, "Apple Supplier Accused of Using Forced Student Labor," *The Salt Lake Tribune*, September 11, 2012, http://www.sltrib.com/sltrib/money/54873765-79/foxconn-students-apple-labor.html.csp.

69. David Barboza, "Workers Poisoned at Chinese Factory Wait for Apple to Fulfill a Pledge," *The New York Times*, February 23, 2011, p. B1.

70. David Barboza & Charles Duhigg, "Pressure, Chinese and Foreign, Drives Changes at Foxconn," *The New York Times*, February 20, 2012, p. B1.

71. Charles Duhigg & Nick Wingfield, "Apple, in Shift, Pushes an Audit of Sites in China," *The New York Times*, February 14, 2012, p. B6.

72. Loretta Chao, James T. Areddy, & Aries Poon, "Apple Pact to Ripple across China," *The Wall Street Journal*, March 31–April 1, 2012, p. B3.

73. Mallen Baker, "The tricky task of measuring a reputation," *Business Respect*, February 21, 2012, http://www.mallenbaker.net/csr/page.php?Story_ID=2723.

74. Paul Mozur, "Foxconn Workers: Keep Our Overtime," *The Wall Street Journal*, December 18, 2012, p. B1.

75. Eduardo Porter, "Dividends in Pressing Apple over Labor," *The New York Times*, March 7, 2012, p. B5.

76. See also "When the job inspector calls," *The Economist*, March 31, 2012, p. 73.

77. James Hyatt, "China Checkup," *CRO Magazine*, May 2008, http://www.thecro.com/topics/politics-legislation/china-checkup/.

78. For example, see Sean Ansett & Jeffrey Hantover, "Bangladesh factory fires—The hidden dangers of subcontracting," *Ethical Corporation*, February 5, 2013, http://www.ethicalcorp.com/supply-chains/bangladesh-factory-fires-hidden-dangers-subcontracting/; and Stephanie Kang, "Nike Cuts Ties With Pakistani Firm," *The Wall Street Journal*, November 21, 2006, p. B5.

79. While we have done a better job within the CSR community of holding firms responsible for their supply chain, we seem less willing to apply the same standards to firms further up the distribution chain. Why are extraction firms, for example, not held accountable for subsequent uses of the raw materials they take out of the ground? While there has been some discussion of *conflict diamonds/minerals*, responsibility for the supply chain appears to rest with the firm that sells the finished product, rather than with the firm that sells the component parts. This is an issue that has yet to emerge for distributors, but it is not difficult to imagine a day when that will happen. If we want to hold GAP, Nike, and Walmart responsible for the actions of other firms far removed from them, closer to source, we will one day surely hold extraction firms responsible for the actions of other firms and consumers closer to consumption.

80. "Walmart Announces Sustainable Product Index" [Walmart press release], July 16, 2009, http://news.walmart.com/news-archive/2009/07/16/walmart-announces-sustainable-product-index.

81. Amelia Gentleman, "Gap Vows to Combat Child Labor at Suppliers," *The New York Times*, November 16, 2007, p. 6.

82. Ibid.

83. Jo Confino, "Interview: Unilever's Paul Polman on diversity, purpose and profits," *The Guardian*, October 2, 2013, http://www.theguardian.com/sustainable-business/unilver-ceo-paul-polman-purpose-profits/.

84. David A. Kaplan, "Strong Coffee," *Fortune*, December 12, 2011, p. 114.

85. Schultz bought Starbucks in 1987 "when it had just six shops." From that point, he has built "a global empire of 20,000 stores in 63 countries that now employs 200,000 people and serves 70 million customers a week" (in Leslie Helm, "Caffeinating the World," *Delta Sky Magazine*, March 2014, p. 70).

86. Stanley Homes & Geri Smith, "For Coffee Growers, Not Even a Whiff of Profits," *BusinessWeek,* September 9, 2002, p. 110.

87. Fairtrade Foundation, "Farmers and Workers: Coffee," http://www.fairtrade.org.uk/en/farmers-and-workers/coffee/ (accessed September 2015).

88. Michael Skapinker, "No markets were hurt in making this coffee," *Financial Times,* November 9, 2010, p. 11.

89. Jon Entine, "Ethical branding: Fairtrade laid bare," *Ethical Corporation,* February 2, 2012, http://www.ethicalcorp.com/supply-chains/ethical-branding-fairtrade-laid-bare/.

90. Starbuck's policies regarding fair trade and ethical sourcing can be found at http://www.starbucks.com/responsibility/sourcing/coffee/.

91. "Starbucks Coffee Agronomy Company Opens in Costa Rica to Help Farmers Improve Their Coffee Quality" [Starbucks financial release], January 28, 2004, http://investor.starbucks.com/phoenix.zhtml?c=99518&p=irol-newsArticle&ID=489261.

92. Oliver Balch, "Peter Torrebiarte, Starbucks Coffee Agronomy Company," *Ethical Corporation,* June 24, 2004.

93. List that follows quoted from Starbucks, http://www.starbucks.com/responsibility/sourcing/coffee/ (accessed February 2016). For more information about Starbucks' work with Conservation International, see its *Global Responsibility Report 2014*, http://www.starbucks.com/responsibility/global-report/.

94. For more detailed information on Starbucks' C.A.F.E. Practices scorecard, see *C.A.F.E. Practices Generic Scorecard*, November 2012, http://www.scsglobalservices.com/files/CAFE_SCR_Genericv3.0_101812.pdf.

95. Oliver Balch, "Peter Torrebiarte, Starbucks Coffee Agronomy Company," *Ethical Corporation,* June 24, 2004.

96. To see how Starbucks' efforts have influenced the coffee industry, see Tim Hortons Coffee Partnership, http://www.timhortons.com/us/en/social/coffee-partnership.php.

97. "Starbucks Corporate: Building a Sustainable Supply Chain," Stanford Graduate School of Business case GS-54, May 2007, p. 2.

98. Javier Blas & Jenny Wiggins, "Coffee and sugar prices stirred by shortages," *Financial Times*, May 11, 2009, p. 13.

99. See Brad Stone, "The Empire of Excess," *The New York Times*, July 4, 2008, p. C1; and Jenny Wiggins, "McDonald's lays the ground to mug Starbucks in Europe," *Financial Times*, May 27, 2009, p. 13.

100. McDonald's, which serves 69 million people daily, has formed a partnership with the Rainforest Alliance to certify its coffee (see Marc Gunther, "Coffee and the consumer: Can McDonald's mainstream sustainability?" *The Guardian*, September 24, 2013, http://www.theguardian.com/sustainable-business/mcdonalds-coffee-sustainability/). On the firm's sales targets for fair trade coffee, see Andrew Downie, "Fair Trade In Bloom," *The New York Times*, October 2, 2007, p. C1; and "McDonald's to Sell Fair Trade Certified Coffee" [Oxfam America press release], CSRwire, October 27, 2005, http://www.csrwire.com/press/press_release/21423/.

101. "Starbucks Serves Up Its First Fairtrade Lattes and Cappuccinos Across the UK and Ireland," Fairtrade Foundation, September 2, 2009, http://www.fairtrade.org.uk/press_office/press_releases_and_statements/september_2009/starbucks_serves_up_its_first_fairtrade_lattes_and_cappuccinos.aspx.

102. Hanna Thomas, "Starbucks and palm oil, wake up and smell the coffee," *The Guardian*, August 25, 2015, http://www.theguardian.com/sustainable-business/2015/aug/25/starbucks-palm-oil-campaign-2015-sumofus-consumers-deforestation-commitments/.

Chapter 13

1. Due to political intransigence at the national and international level, provinces and cities hold greater potential for more immediate and radical action. For example,

the Canadian province British Columbia implemented a carbon tax in 2008: "At C$30 ($24) a tonne it is high relative to others that have been adopted. Relatively few sources of carbon ... are exempted from the tax. Emissions are down 5–15% since its adoption" (in "The best is the enemy of the green," *The Economist*, December 5, 2015, p. 75). See also "Alberta to introduce carbon tax," *The Guardian*, November 23, 2015, http://www.theguardian .com/environment/2015/nov/23/alberta-to-introduce-carbon-tax/. And for a view of what is happening at the city level, see Michael R. Bloomberg, "What Paris Talks Have Accomplished So Far," *BloombergView*, December 6, 2015, http://www.bloom bergview.com/articles/2015-12-06/what-paris-talks-have-accomplished-so-far/.

2. See "The compelling case for global carbon pricing," *Financial Times*, June 2, 2015, p. 10; and Henry M. Paulson Jr., "The Coming Climate Crash," *The New York Times*, June 22, 2014, p. SR1.

3. United Nations, *Our Common Future*, 1987, http://www.un-documents.net/our-common-future.pdf.

4. For other highlights of the report, see Nigel Roome, "Looking Backward to Move Forward: Revisiting the Brundtland Report," Network for Business Sustainability, January 17, 2014, http://nbs.net/looking-backward-to-move-forward-revisiting-the-brundtland-report/.

5. "Goal difference," *The Economist*, December 5, 2015, p. 76.

6. Bill Baue, "Brundtland Report Celebrates 20th Anniversary Since Coining Sustainable Development," SocialFunds, June 11, 2007, http://www.socialfunds.com/news/article .cgi/article2308.html.

7. Michael Hopkins, "Sustainable development: From word to policy," *openDemocracy*, April 11, 2007, http://www.opendemocracy .net/globalization-institutions_government/ sustainable_word_4515.jsp.

8. United Nations, "Our Common Future, Chapter 2: Towards Sustainable Development," http://www.un-documents.net/ocf-02.htm.

9. Gabriele Steinhauser, "Big Divisions Haunt Climate Talks," *The Wall Street Journal*, November 24, 2015, p. A8.

10. Hiroko Kono, "COP21 framework offers a glimmer of hope," *The Japan News*, December 17, 2015, p. 5.

11. Bjorn Lomborg, "Gambling the World Economy on Climate," *The Wall Street Journal*, November 17, 2015, p. A19.

12. Associated Press, "Nearly 200 nations adopt global climate pact at COP21 in Paris," *The Japan News*, December 15, 2015, p. 1.

13. This will not be easy given that the Paris commitments, to be implemented by 2030, are estimated to "cost the global economy at least $1 trillion a year"—and this assumes efficient decision making and execution (in Bjorn Lomborg, "A climate agreement powered by hypocrisy," *The Japan News*, December 20, 2015, p. 5). Another impediment will be public opinion: "People in highly developed countries view climate change as the tenth most important issue out of a list of 16. . . . In poor countries— and indeed in the world as a whole—climate change comes 16th out of 16" (in "Groupthink," *The Economist Special Report: Climate Change*, November 28, 2015, p. 6).

14. Pilita Clark, "High pressure in Paris," *Financial Times*, November 13, 2015, p. 6.

15. Ibid.

16. It is worth noting that the 2-degree limit is "a somewhat arbitrary threshold ... [that represents] the observable range of temperature over the last several hundred thousand years." The thinking behind the target is that it is safer for humanity to avoid venturing beyond these known parameters. For a discussion of this issue, see Gautam Naik, "Climate Experts Question Temperature Benchmark," *The Wall Street Journal*, November 30, 2015, pp. A1, A12.

17. Chris Mooney, "Historic, yes. But the climate pact alone won't solve the problem," *The Washington Post*, reprinted in *The Japan News*, December 15, 2015, p. 10.

18. Oliver Geden, "The Dubious Carbon Budget," *The New York Times*, December 1, 2015, p. A25.

19. Thomas L. Friedman, "The Earth Is Full," *The New York Times*, June 8, 2011, p. A21.

20. Nathaniel Rich, "Earth Control," *The New York Times Book Review*, October 13, 2013, p. 18.

21. Charles Eisenstein, "Concern about overpopulation is a red herring; consumption's the

problem," *The Guardian*, March 28, 2014, http://www.theguardian.com/sustainable-business/blog/concern-overpopulation-red-herring-consumption-problem-sustainability/.

22. James Hansen, "Game Over for the Climate," *The New York Times*, May 9, 2013, p. A25.

23. "No sweat," *The Economist*, January 5, 2013, p. 45.

24. Electricity sources in 2015: coal (37.7%), natural gas (28%), nuclear (19.6%), hydroelectric (6.6%), other (including wind and solar, 8.1%) (in Marcelo Prince & Joseph Shoulak, "What Is the Future of Nuclear Power?" *The Wall Street Journal*, June 3, 2015, http://blogs.wsj.com/corporate-intelligence/2015/06/03/what-is-the-future-of-nuclear-power/).

25. Adam Frank, "Is a Climate Disaster Inevitable?" *The New York Times*, January 18, 2015, p. SR6.

26. "Clear thinking needed," *The Economist*, November 28, 2015, p. 11.

27. Justin Gillis, "Paris climate pact a step, if not a cure," *International New York Times*, December 14, 2015, p. 7.

28. Justin Gillis, "Short Answers to Hard Climate Questions," *The New York Times*, December 1, 2015, p. D1.

29. "Boundary conditions," *The Economist*, June 16, 2012, p. 87.

30. For background information about this report, see *Stern Review on the Economics of Climate Change*, HM Treasury, 2006, http://webarchive.nationalarchives.gov.uk/+/http:/www.hm-treasury.gov.uk/sternreview_index.htm.

31. John Kay, "Climate change: the (Groucho) Marxist approach," *Financial Times*, November 28, 2007, p. 11.

32. Ibid.

33. "Raise the green lanterns," *The Economist*, December 5, 2015, p. 43.

34. *BizEthics Buzz*, December 2002. *BizEthics Buzz* is an online news report from *Business Ethics Magazine*.

35. Andrew Zolli, "Learning to Bounce Back," *The New York Times*, November 2, 2012, http://www.nytimes.com/2012/11/03/opinion/forget-sustainability-its-about-resilience.html.

36. While it is important for firms to adapt to climate change, the rise of *resilience* feels a little too much like giving up—letting for-profit firms off the hook when, in reality, they are best placed to prevent (or at least mitigate) the worst excesses of our changing environment. In other words, resilience encourages an approach of "this is happening, so we need to adapt," rather than "we need to be doing all we can to prevent this from becoming as bad as it can be." As such, rather than resilience, focusing on radically incorporating an understanding of carbon reduction into current business models is closer to a strategic CSR perspective.

37. Steven E. Koonin, "Tough Realities of the Climate Talks," *The New York Times*, November 4, 2015, p. A27.

38. Franklyn Cater, "'Chief Resilience Officers' Could Help Cities Cope with Calamity," *The Two-Way*, National Public Radio, November 7, 2014, http://www.npr.org/sections/thetwo-way/2014/11/07/362393636/chief-resilience-officers-could-help-cities-cope-with-calamity/. See also 100 Resilient Cities, http://www.100resilientcities.org/.

39. See City of Boulder, Colorado, "Resilient Boulder," https://bouldercolorado.gov/resilience/.

40. Sissel Waage, "How can the value of nature be embedded in the world of business?" *The Guardian*, March 31, 2014, http://www.theguardian.com/sustainable-business/finance-nature-no-value-natural-capital/.

41. Usman Hayat, "Future challenges for sustainable investing," *Financial Times (FTfm)*, February 7, 2011, p. 12.

42. Marc Gunther, "Natural capital: Breakthrough or buzzword?" *The Guardian*, March 6, 2014, http://www.theguardian.com/sustainable-business/natural-capital-nature-conservancy-trucost-dow/.

43. "PUMA Completes First Environmental Profit and Loss Account Which Values Impacts at €145 Million," PUMA, November 16, 2011, http://about.puma.com/en/newsroom/corporate-news/2011/november/puma-completes-first-environmental-profit-and-loss-account-which-values-impacts-at-145-million-euro/. See also Richard Anderson, "Puma first to publish environmental impact," BBC News, May 16, 2011, http://www.bbc.co.uk/news/business-13410397/.

44. For an in-depth discussion of this issue, see Oliver Balch, "Carbon accounting—Emissions disclosure stacking up," *Ethical Corporation*, July 21, 2009, http://www

.ethicalcorp.com/business-strategy/carbon-accounting-emissions-disclosure-stacking/.

45. David Gelles, "A Carbon Tax Imposed by the Head Office," *The New York Times*, September 27, 2015, p. BU3.

46. Marc Gunther, "Natural capital: Breakthrough or buzzword?" *The Guardian*, March 6, 2014, http://www.theguardian.com/sustainable-business/natural-capital-nature-conservancy-trucost-dow/.

47. "PepsiCo and Carbon Trust Announce Groundbreaking Agreement and Certify Carbon Footprint of Tropicana" [PepsiCo press release], CSRwire, January 22, 2009, http://www.csrwire.com/press_releases/15992-PepsiCo-and-Carbon-Trust-Announce-Groundbreaking-Agreement-and-Certify-Carbon-Footprint-of-Tropicana/.

48. Andrew Martin, "How Green Is My Orange?" *The New York Times*, January 22, 2009, p. B1.

49. Fiona Harvey, "Food footprints coming soon to a label near you," *Financial Times, Special Report: Sustainable Business*, October 12, 2007, p. 4.

50. "Environmental Leaders: Green beacons burning bright," *Ethical Corporation*, September 3, 2009, http://www.ethicalcorp.com/business-strategy/environmental-leaders-green-beacons-burning-bright/.

51. In contrast, some industries (such as food, beverage, and tobacco) have been accused of "ignoring their largest climate impacts by failing to disclose emissions from agricultural production" (in Frances Way, "Food and drink companies found to be ignoring biggest impact on climate," *The Guardian*, September 3, 2015, http://www.theguardian.com/sustainable-business/2015/sep/03/biggest-food-drink-companies-ignoring-climate-impacts-supply-chain/).

52. David K. Woodyard, "Goodyear's Commitment to Sustainability," Suppliers Partnership for the Environment, January 11, 2012, http://www.supplierspartnership.org/members_only/Supplier%20Partnership%20GDYR%20Sustainability%20Overview%201-11-12.pdf.

53. See Unilever, "Sustainable Living," https://www.unilever.com/sustainable-living/.

54. "In search of good business," *The Economist*, August 9, 2014, p. 56.

55. Marc Gunther, "Money and Morals at GE," *Fortune*, November 15, 2004, p. 178.

56. Alan G. Robinson & Dean M. Schroeder, "Greener and Cheaper," *The Wall Street Journal*, March 23, 2009, p. R4.

57. Daniel Vermeer & Robert Clemen, "Why sustainability is still going strong," *Financial Times, Managing in a Downturn: Part IV, Sustainable Business*, February 13, 2009, p. 4.

58. John Bradburn, "10 things General Motors learned about going landfill-free," *GreenBiz.com*, November 16, 2012, http://www.greenbiz.com/blog/2012/11/16/10-things-general-motors-learned-about-going-landfill-free/.

59. "The next big bet," *The Economist*, October 1, 2011, p. 75.

60. Ram Nidumolu, C. K. Prahalad, & M. R. Rangaswami, "Why Sustainability Is Now the Key Driver of Innovation," *Harvard Business Review*, September, 2009, p. 57.

61. David Gelles, "Unilever Finds That Shrinking Its Footprint Is a Giant Task," *The New York Times*, November 22, 2015, p. BU1.

62. Padma Nagappan, "Carpet giant Interface shares pointers on being a green innovator," GreenBiz, September 6, 2012, http://www.greenbiz.com/blog/2012/09/06/interface-shares-pointers-green-innovator/.

63. "Interface Pioneers Plant-Based Carpeting," *SustainableBusiness.com*, September 18, 2012, http://www.sustainablebusiness.com/index.cfm/go/news.display/id/24088/.

64. "Ray Anderson," *The Economist*, September 10, 2011, p. 99.

65. Paul Hawken, *The Ecology of Commerce*, Harper Collins, 1993.

66. Paul Vitello, "Ray Anderson, a Carpet Innovator, Dies at 77," *The New York Times*, August 11, 2011, p. B17.

67. For more detail about Marks & Spencer's Plan A and its value for the firm, see David E. Bell, Nitin Sanghavi, & Laura Winig, "Marks and Spencer: Plan A" [Harvard Business School case study #9-509-029], January 5, 2009.

68. Marks and Spencer, "About Plan A," http://corporate.marksandspencer.com/plan-a/our-stories/about-plan-a/.

69. Simon Bowers, "M&S promises radical change with £200m environmental action plan," *The Guardian*, January 15, 2007, http://www.guardian.co.uk/business/2007/jan/15/marksspencer.retail.

70. Ibid.

71. Michael Skapinker, "Why corporate responsibility is a survivor," *Financial Times*, April 21, 2009, p. 11.

72. EC Newsdesk, "Marks and Spencer—A-grade progress," *Ethical Corporation,* March 2, 2009, http://www.ethicalcorp .com/business-strategy/marks-spencer-grade-progress/.

73. Rob Bailes, "Sustainability commercialized: Marks & Spencer—Helping suppliers get with the plan," *Ethical Corporation,* September 5, 2012, http://www.ethicalcorp .com/business-strategy/sustainability-commercialised-marks-spencer-helping-suppliers-get-plan/.

74. Marks and Spencer, "About Plan A," http:// corporate.marksandspencer.com/plan-a/ our-stories/about-plan-a/ (accessed February 2016).

75. Knut Haanaes, David Michael, Jeremy Jurgens, & Subramanian Rangan, "Making Sustainability Profitable," *Harvard Business Review*, March 2013, p. 115.

76. Starbucks, "Goals & Progress: Cup Recycling," http://www.starbucks.com/responsibility/ global-report/environmental-stewardship/ cup-recycling/ (accessed February 2016).

77. "Talking trash," *The Economist Technology Quarterly*, June 2, 2012, p. 12.

78. Julie Makinen, "Moooncakes' unwelcome hangover," *Los Angeles Times*, reprinted in *The Daily Yomiuri*, October 16, 2012, p. 12.

79. Edward Humes, "Grappling With a Garbage Glut," *The Wall Street Journal*, April 14–15, 2012, p. C3.

80. Ibid.

81. Ibid. See also Jodie Allen, "America's Biggest Trade Export to China? Trash," *U.S. News*, March 3, 2010, http://www.usnews.com/ opinion/blogs/jodie-allen/2010/03/03/amer icas-biggest-trade-export-to-china-trash/.

82. See "A cadmium lining," *The Economist*, January 26, 2013, p. 56.

83. See Greenpeace, "Greener Electronics," http://www.greenpeace.org/international/ en/campaigns/detox/electronics/.

84. For an example of the consequences of e-waste disposal, see Lorraine Chow, "Stunning Photos Capture Devastation Caused by Electronic Waste Across the Globe," *Alternet*, April 15, 2015, http://www .alternet.org/environment/stunning-photos-capture-devastation-caused-electronic-waste-across-globe/.

85. Alex Scott, "Innovations in mobile phone recycling: Biomining to dissolving circuit boards," *The Guardian*, September 30, 2014, http://www.theguardian.com/sustainable-business/2014/sep/30/innovations-mobile-phone-recycling-biomining-dissolving-circuit-boards/.

86. Marc Gunther, "Amazon, Best Buy and the free rider problem," *The Guardian*, August 5, 2015, http://www.theguardian.com/sustain able-business/2015/aug/05/amazon-best-buy-electronic-waste-walmart-recyling/.

87. Sarah Finnie Robinson, "Got iPhone 5 Fever? Here's how to recycle your old phone," *practicallygreen*, September 13, 2012.

88. Many of these obsolete models are first stored, rather than thrown away. In fact, it is estimated that "the average American has at least three expired cellphones stockpiled at home" (in Sarah Finnie Robinson, "Got iPhone 5 Fever? Here's how to recycle your old phone," *practicallygreen*, September 13, 2012) and that "99 million television sets sit unused in closets and basements across the [United States])" (in Leslie Kaufman, "New Laws Offer a Green Way to Dump Low-Tech Electronics," *The New York Times*, June 30, 2009, p. A1).

89. EPA data, quoted in "Fact and Figures on E-Waste and Recycling," Electronics TakeBack Coalition, February 21, 2012, pp. 2–3.

90. The amount of e-waste generated every year is difficult to measure accurately, but "by some estimates, consumers threw away 92 billion pounds of used electronics [in 2014], up from 87.7 billion pounds the previous year" (in Brian X. Chen, "How to Sell or Recycle Old Electronics," *The New York Times*, December 3, 2015, p. B6).

91. For a comprehensive look at the consequences of our electronics industry, see The Story of Stuff Project, "Story of Electronics," http://storyofstuff.org/movies/story-of-electronics/.

92. Verne Kopytoff, "The Complex Business of Recycling E-waste," *Bloomberg Businessweek*, January 8, 2013, http://www.bloomberg .com/bw/articles/2013-01-08/the-complex-business-of-recycling-e-waste/.

93. Laurie J. Flynn, "A State Says Makers Must Pay for Recycling PCs and TVs," *The New York Times*, March 25, 2006, p. B2.

94. Melanie Warner, "Green Business: Plastic Potion No. 9," *Fast Company*, September 2008, p. 103.

95. "The Wasteland," *60 Minutes*, CBS News, August 30, 2009.

96. David Murphy, "Toxic town," *South China Morning Post*, June 7, 2005, p. A16.

97. "Where gadgets go to die," *The Economist Technology Quarterly*, September 6, 2014, p. 9.

98. "A cadmium lining," *The Economist*, January 26, 2013, p. 56.

99. David Murphy, "Toxic town," *South China Morning Post*, June 7, 2005, p. A16.

100. Electronics TakeBack Coalition, "State Legislation," http://www.electronicstakeback.com/promote-good-laws/state-legislation/ (accessed February 2016).

101. For an overview of the scope of TerraCycle's work and an indication of why its business model is successful, see founder and CEO of TerraCycle Tom Szaky, "Eliminating the Idea of Waste," March 7, 2013, https://www.youtube.com/watch?v=LHqwd-LBp5c.

102. Alex Scott, "Innovations in mobile phone recycling: Biomining to dissolving circuit boards," *The Guardian*, September 30, 2014, http://www.theguardian.com/sustainable-business/2014/sep/30/innovations-mobile-phone-recycling-biomining-dissolving-circuit-boards/.

103. Marc Gunther, "Sustainability at McDonald's. Really," September 24, 2013, http://www.marcgunther.com/sustainability-at-mcdonalds-really/.

104. "Back on top," *The Economist*, September 21, 2013, pp. 24–25.

105. Jason Clay, *How big brands can help save biodiversity*, TedGlobal, July 2010, http://www.ted.com/talks/jason_clay_how_big_brands_can_save_biodiversity.html.

Chapter 14

1. Kerry Capell, "Zara's Fast Track to Fashion," *BusinessWeek*, June 2008, http://www.bloomberg.com/ss/06/08/zara/source/1.htm.

2. Ibid.

3. Andrew McAfee, Anders Sjoman, & Vincent Dessain, "Zara: IT for Fast Fashion" [Harvard Business School case study 9-604-081], September 6, 2007; "Store Wars: Fast Fashion," BBC News, June 9, 2004, http://news.bbc.co.uk/2/hi/business/3086669.stm.

4. The Ethics and Compliance Initiative (https://www.ethics.org/; previously the Ethics and Compliance Officer Association) has stated that the CEO acronym should also stand for "chief ethics officer."

5. John Kay, "Weasel words have the teeth to kill great ventures," *Financial Times*, January 14, 2009, p. 9.

6. Quote from Mark Goyder, "Redefining CSR: From the Rhetoric of Accountability to the Reality of Earning Trust," in Mallen Baker, "Redefining CSR as a process that starts at the heart of the company," *mallenbaker.net*, July 27, 2003, http://www.mallenbaker.net/csr/page.php?Story_ID=1020.

7. Nick Wingfield, "Fixing Apple's Supply Lines," *The New York Times*, April 2, 2012, p. B1.

8. Jeffrey Hollender, "Walmart's Sustainability Efforts Stall Under New Leadership," *Triple Pundit*, March 28, 2012, http://www.triplepundit.com/2012/03/walmarts-sustainability-efforts-stall-new-leadership/.

9. See also Oliver Balch, "How a new boss can breathe fresh life into sustainability," *The Guardian*, May 18, 2015, http://www.theguardian.com/sustainable-business/2015/may/18/how-a-new-boss-can-breathe-fresh-life-into-sustainability/.

10. Brendan May, "Government: If only the political species faced extinction," *Ethical Corporation*, January 31, 2012, http://www.ethicalcorp.com/stakeholder-engagement/government-if-only-political-species-faced-extinction/.

11. Jane Perdue, "Should executives take an oath of office?" *The Guardian*, March 20, 2014, http://smartblogs.com/leadership/2014/03/20/should-executives-take-an-oath-of-office/.

12. Ben DiPietro, "Difference Between Compliance, Ethics," *The Wall Street Journal*, June 30, 2014, http://blogs.wsj.com/riskandcompliance/2014/06/30/the-difference-between-compliance-and-ethics/.

13. Daniel Franklin, "The year of unsustainability," *The World in 2009, The Economist*, November 19, 2008, p. 20.

14. The title of this position varies considerably across firms and includes corporate responsibility officer, sustainability officer, ethics and compliance officer, or even chief customer officer ("The magic of good service," *The Economist*, September 22, 2012, p. 78). The important point is that a position is created to focus on CSR-related issues and that it has the substantive support of the CEO.

15. "What Does It Mean to Be VP of CSR? A Conversation with Sandra Taylor of Starbucks," *Business Ethics Magazine,* Summer 2004, p. 4.

16. "Nike Names New VP of Corporate Responsibility" [Nike press release], CSRwire, October 20, 2004, http://www.csrwire.com/press_releases/24945-Nike-Names-New-VP-of-Corporate-Responsibility-Maria-Eitel-Becomes-President-of-the-Nike-Foundation/.

17. Gregory J. Millman & Samuel Rubenfeld, "For Corporate America, Risk Is Big Business," *The Wall Street Journal*, January 16, 2014, p. B1.

18. Ibid., p. B7.

19. Shelly Banjo, "After public outrage over worker treatment, Amazon's hiring a director of social responsibility," *Quartz*, September 9, 2015, http://qz.com/498320/after-public-outrage-over-worker-treatment-amazons-hiring-a-director-of-social-responsibility/.

20. ISO 26000—Social responsibility, http://www.iso.org/sr/.

21. Aaron Chatterji & David Levine, "Breaking Down the Wall of Codes: Evaluating Non-financial Performance Measurement," *California Management Review*, Vol. 48, No. 2, 2006, p. 35.

22. Charles J. Fombrun, "List of Lists: A Compilation of International Corporate Reputation Ratings," *Corporate Reputation Review*, Vol. 10, No. 2, 2007, pp. 144–153.

23. Aaron Chatterji & David Levine, "Breaking Down the Wall of Codes: Evaluating Non-financial Performance Measurement," *California Management Review*, Vol. 48, No. 2, 2006, p. 29.

24. "America's Most Admired Companies," 2008, http://archive.fortune.com/magazines/fortune/mostadmired/2008/index.html.

25. Toby A. A. Heaps & Michael Yow, 2015 *Newsweek* Green Rankings: FAQ and Advisory Council, June 4, 2015, http://www.newsweek.com/2015-newsweek-green-rankings-faq-338193/.

26. Global Strategic Alliances, http://www.globalreporting.org/.

27. MSCI, https://www.msci.com/esg-integration/.

28. Allen White, "New rigorous ratings tool help investors and companies," *Ethical Corporation*, August 10, 2012, http://www.ethicalcorp.com/business-strategy/new-rigorous-ratings-tools-help-investors-and-companies/.

29. See Toby Webb, "Podcast: Hannah Jones, VP sustainable business and innovation at Nike, on targets, performance, outlook and ambition," *Ethical Corporation*, September 27, 2011.

30. Here, it is important for the CSR officer to balance the role of "CSR crusader" (passionate believer) with the important role of "CSR diplomat" (grounded in economic and business realities) so as to win supporters within the firm. See Aman Singh, "Changing Business from the Inside Out: How to Pursue a Career in CSR and Sustainability," CSRwire, August 16, 2012, http://www.csrwire.com/blog/posts/503-changing-business-from-the-inside-out-how-to-pursue-a-career-in-csr-and-sustainability/.

31. "For Employee Buy-In, Supervisors Trump the CEO," Network for Business Sustainability, March 3, 2013, http://nbs.net/knowledge/for-employee-buy-in-supervisors-trump-the-ceo/.

32. Cadbury Schweppes, *Corporate Social Responsibility Report 2006*, https://www.unglobalcompact.org/system/attachments/971/original/COP.pdf?1262614234.

33. Toby Webb, "Vision and mission: A barrier to sustainability strategy," *Smarter Business Blog*, September 10, 2012, http://sustainablesmartbusiness.com/2012/09/vision-and-mission-barrier-to/.

34. "A new green wave," *The Economist*, August 30, 2014, p. 61.

35. Ben DiPietro, "Tech Use Raises Many Compliance Issues," *The Wall Street Journal*, March 5, 2015, http://blogs.wsj.com/riskandcompliance/2015/03/05/the-morning-risk-report-tech-use-raises-many-compliance-issues/.

36. "Green growth," *The Economist*, September 17, 2011, p. 72.

37. David Kestenbaum, "Pop Quiz: How Do You Stop Sea Captains From Killing Their Passengers?" National Public Radio, September 10, 2010, http://www.npr.org/

blogs/money/2010/09/09/129757852/pop-quiz-how-do-you-stop-sea-captains-from-killing-their-passengers/.

38. Tomasz Obloj, "Financial incentives and bonus schemes can spell disaster for business," *The Guardian*, December 11, 2013, http://www.theguardian.com/sustainable-business/financial-incentives-bonus-schemes-lloyds-fine/.

39. David Chandler, *Organizations and Ethics: Antecedents and Consequences of the Adoption and Implementation of the Ethics and Compliance Officer Position*, The University of Texas at Austin, 2011.

40. Skewed performance incentives are a common problem for organizations. Take the issue of CEO pay, where best practice supposes that an individual's incentives are most effective when tied to performance. Rather than the performance of the CEO, however, it is the performance of the firm that is usually measured. That is, the CEO is paid according to the performance of the firm rather than the performance of the CEO. The assumption, of course, is that these two things are correlated. This is dubious, to say the least. At a minimum, there are many factors (both internal and external to the firm), in addition to the CEO's contribution, that determine the firm's success or failure in the market. This explains why CEOs can be paid handsomely while they themselves are poor managers; similarly, the CEO can perform excellently while the firm performs badly relative to competitors. The reason this compensation structure continues, of course, is that CEO performance is very difficult to measure. It is far easier to measure an assumed proxy for that performance, such as firm-level outcomes, which are already measured due to accounting rules. The problem is that the chosen proxy may not reflect the behavior the firm seeks to incentivize.

41. See Simon Zadek, "The Path to Corporate Responsibility," *Harvard Business Review*, December 2004, pp. 125–132, for a detailed discussion of how Nike aligned its incentive scheme for subcontractors with its corporate responsibility goals.

42. Mark Cohen, "SEC Recognizes Climate Change as Material Business Risk," *Resources for the Future*, February 5, 2010, http://common-resources.org/2010/sec-recognizes-climate-change-as-material-business-risk/.

43. Elaine Moore, "Enthusiasm may wane as companies pursue growth," *Financial Times Responsible Business*, July 8, 2014, p. 2.

44. Rikki Stancich, "Recession Ethics: CSR in a Downturn—Recession-proof Ethics Can Weather the Storm," *Ethical Corporation*, March 5, 2008, http://www.ethicalcorp.com/communications-reporting/recession-ethics-csr-downturn-recession-proof-ethics-can-weather-storm/.

45. Emily Chasan, "Sustainability Reports Gain Traction," *The Wall Street Journal*, June 10, 2014, http://blogs.wsj.com/cfo/2014/06/10/sustainability-reports-gain-traction/.

46. "UK ranks top in biggest global CR reporting survey ever published," *Green Business News*, November 7, 2011, http://www.greenwisebusiness.co.uk/news/uk-ranks-top-in-biggest-global-cr-reporting-survey-ever-published-2770.aspx.

47. "A green light," *The Economist*, March 29, 2014, p. 74.

48. Jerome Chaplier, "EU to force large companies to report on environmental and social impacts," *The Guardian*, February 28, 2014, http://www.theguardian.com/sustainable-business/eu-reform-listed-companies-report-environmental-social-impact/.

49. "A green light," *The Economist*, March 29, 2014, p. 74.

50. Jo Confino, "97% of companies fail to provide data on key sustainability indicators," *The Guardian*, October 13, 2014, http://www.theguardian.com/sustainable-business/2014/oct/13/97-companies-fail-to-provide-data-key-sustainability-indicators-stoc ck-exchange-report/.

51. The phrase *triple bottom line* was first introduced in 1994 by John Elkington of SustainAbility (http://www.sustainability.com/) "to describe social, environmental, and financial accounting." The term was used in conjunction with the launch of SustainAbility's "first survey benchmarking non-financial reporting" (in William Baue, "Sustainability Reporting Improves, but Falls Short on Linking to Financial Performance," *Social Funds*, November 5, 2004, http://www.socialfunds.com/news/article.cgi/article1565.html.

52. Elizabeth Becker, "At Shell, Grades for Citizenship," *The New York Times,* November 30, 2003, Section 3, p. 2.

53. Ibid.

54. Ram Nidumolu, C. K. Prahalad, & M. R. Rangaswami, "Why Sustainability Is Now the Key Driver of Innovation," *Harvard Business Review*, September 2009, p. 59.

55. Verité (http://www.verite.org/) is a good example of a firm that provides this verification service: "Verité aims to ensure that globalization is made to work for poor and vulnerable people around the world. We ensure that powerful institutions, and particularly the private sector, take responsibility for solving human rights problems where goods are made and crops are grown." (Verité, "About Us," http://www.verite.org/About-Us/, accessed February 2016).

56. Mallen Baker, "Urgently for your attention! We have nothing to report," *Respectful Business Blog*, August 12, 2015, http://mallenbaker.net/article/clear-reflection/urgently-for-your-attention-we-have-nothing-to-report/.

57. Ibid.

58. Lynn Paine, Rohit Deshpandé, Joshua D. Margolis, & Kim Eric Bettcher, "Up to Code: Does Your Company's Conduct Meet World-Class Standards?" *Harvard Business Review*, December 2005, p. 123.

59. Elizabeth Barber, "Fewer are behaving badly at work, survey finds. What changed?" *The Christian Science Monitor*, February 25, 2014, http://www.csmonitor.com/USA/Society/2014/0225/Fewer-are-behaving-badly-at-work-survey-finds.-What-changed/.

60. Simon Webley, "Are corporate ethics programmes really 'alive'?" *Ethical Corporation*, June 28, 2011.

61. "The Next Step for CSR: Economic Democracy," *Business Ethics Magazine,* Summer 2002, p. 10.

62. Memorandum from Kenneth Lay to all employees, Subject: Code of Ethics, July 1, 2000.

63. Enron Corporation, "Code of Ethics," p. 5.

64. Ibid.

65. Ibid., p. 12.

66. Debora L. Spar, "Hitting the Wall: Nike and International Labor Practices" [Harvard Business School case study 9-700-047], September 6, 2002.

67. Also in 2002, both the NYSE and NASDAQ altered their listing requirements, compelling firms listed on the exchange to adopt and disclose both corporate governance guidelines and a code of business conduct and ethics for all employees, following SEC approval of standards for such reports.

68. Sarbanes-Oxley Act, 2002, § 301(4)(B), https://www.sec.gov/about/laws/soa2002.pdf.

69. For example, see Stephen Dockery, "New U.K. Rules Encourage Banking Whistleblowers," *The Wall Street Journal*, October 6, 2015, http://blogs.wsj.com/riskandcompliance/2015/10/06/new-u-k-rules-encourage-banking-whistleblowers/.

70. Michael Skapinker, "What to do if you discover your company is corrupt," *Financial Times*, October 15, 2015, p. 12.

71. "The age of the whistleblower," *The Economist*, December 5, 2015, pp. 61–62.

72. Ben DiPietro, "HBOS Report Shows Whistleblower Importance," *The Wall Street Journal*, November 20, 2015, http://blogs.wsj.com/riskandcompliance/2015/11/20/the-morning-risk-report-hbos-report-shows-whistleblower-importance/.

73. Gretchen Goldman, "An unwilling leader: The potential impact of Exxon Mobil's climate report," *The Guardian*, April 11, 2014, http://www.theguardian.com/sustainable-business/unwilling-leader-exxon-mobil-climate-report/.

74. Anjali Mullany, "What Your Social Media Consultant Should Tell You," *Fast Company Magazine*, September 2012, p. 73.

75. Paloma Lopez, "Marketing: New sustainable skills for leading marketers," *Ethical Corporation*, July 29, 2011, http://www.ethicalcorp.com/supply-chains/marketing-new-sustainable-skills-leading-marketers/.

76. http://news.nike.com/.

77. William B. Werther & David Chandler, "Strategic Corporate Social Responsibility as Global Brand Insurance," *Business Horizons*, Vol. 48, No. 4, July 2005, pp. 317–324.

78. For additional ideas regarding a comprehensive implementation plan, it might also be helpful to read Susan Graff, "Six Steps to Sustainability," *CRO Magazine*, June 2007, http://www.thecro.com/topics/environment/six-steps-to-sustainability/.

79. Keith Darcy, "How Boards Can Raise the Bar on Ethics and Compliance," *The Wall Street*

Journal, April 22, 2014, http://deloitte.wsj
.com/riskandcompliance/2014/04/22/keith-
darcy-how-boards-can-raise-the-bar-on-
ethics-and-compliance/.

Chapter 15

1. R. Edward Freeman, Jeffrey S. Harrison, Andrew C. Wicks, Bidhan L. Parmar, & Simone de Colle, *Stakeholder Theory: The State of the Art*, Cambridge University Press, 2010, p. 235.

2. Howard R. Bowen, *Social Responsibilities of the Businessman*, Harper & Brothers, 1953, p. 52.

3. For a discussion on this issue, see R. H. Coase, "The Problem of Social Cost," *Journal of Law and Economics*, Vol. 3, No. 1, 1960, pp. 1–44.

4. "When workers are owners," *The Economist*, August 22, 2015, p. 56.

5. See also "Strategic CSR—CSR vs. ethics," *Strategic Corporate Social Responsibility* [Newsletter], January 18, 2012, http://strate giccsr-sage.blogspot.com/2012/01/strategic-csr-csr-vs-ethics.html.

6. Ken Goodman, "The ethics of right and wrong," *The Miami Herald,* March 14, 2004, p. 3L.

7. Gwendolyn Bounds, "Misleading Claims on 'Green' Labeling," *The Wall Street Journal*, October 26, 2010, p. D4.

8. Michael J. de la Merced & Evelyn M. Rusli, "Again Yahoo Loses Chief, This Time in a Scandal," *The New York Times*, May 14, 2012, p. B1; and Amir Efrati & Joann S. Lublin, "Resume Trips Up Yahoo's Chief," *The Wall Street Journal*, May 5–6, 2012, p. A1.

9. Patrick M. Lencioni, "Make Your Values Mean Something," *Harvard Business Review,* Vol. 80, No. 7, July 2002, pp. 113–117.

10. Joel Bakan, *The Corporation: The Pathological Pursuit of Profit and Power*, Free Press, 2004, quoted in *Business Ethics Magazine,* Spring 2004, p. 6.

11. Alina Tugend, "Doing the Ethical Thing May Be Right, but It Isn't Automatic," *The New York Times*, November 19, 2011, p. B5.

12. Max H. Bazerman & Ann E. Tenbrunsel, "Stumbling Into Bad Behavior," *The New York Times*, April 21, 2011, p. A21.

13. Judith Samuelson & Bill Birchard, "The Voice of the Stakeholder," *strategy+business*, No. 32, p. 8.

14. Melissa Korn, "B-School Mixes Faith, Finance," *The Wall Street Journal*, January 8, 2013, p. B9.

15. MBA Oath, "About the Oath: Read and Download the MBA Oath," http://mba oath.org/about/the-mba-oath/ (accessed February 2016).

16. For additional discussion around the idea that strategic CSR represents progressive management, see Thomas E. Graedel & Braden R. Allenby, *Industrial Ecology and Sustainable Engineering*, Prentice Hall, 2009. The authors are industrial ecologists who argue that there is no such thing as *green management*, only *good management*.

17. Firms that understand the powerful motivating force of a values-based business include Zappos, Nike, Whole Foods, and Patagonia. Inspiring people, however, is difficult and expensive. As such, many firms employ a thin veil of values to bolster their compliance (a neutral approach), rather than building their firms around values that inspire their stakeholders (a positive approach). The result demonstrates the difference between those firms that understand the powerful and radical consequences of implementing strategic CSR and those that do not.

18. An important note of concern relates to the issue of unintended consequences, which is one of the most important issues within the CSR debate. When we try to subvert centuries of economic development, attempting to substitute social or altruistic motivation for economic incentives, we should tread carefully. That is why strategic CSR advocates for evolutionary, rather than revolutionary, reform. It happens again and again—whether it is government subsidies or tax breaks for a particular kind of alternative energy or a new technical innovation that interacts with some other factor (or is applied inappropriately) to generate some unexpected outcome. In short, there is much that we do not understand about the social and economic forces that drive human behavior and the relationship between these forces and societal-level outcomes. By definition, we can only base future projections on past experience, and are constrained when we do so. When we propose solutions, we envisage the benefits and fail (or

are unable) to fully understand all the risks. That does not mean that we should not try to implement change, but it does imply we should be humble in attempts to temper these highly evolved forces.

19. David Brooks, "Capitalism for the Masses," *The New York Times*, February 21, 2014, p. A23.

20. Jacquelyn Smith, "The World's Most Ethical Companies," *Forbes*, March 15, 2012, http://www.forbes.com/sites/jacquelyn smith/2012/03/15/the-worlds-most-ethical-companies/.

21. Jacquelyn Smith, "America's 25 Most Inspiring Companies," *Forbes*, September 25, 2012, http://www.forbes.com/sites/jacquelyn smith/2012/09/25/americas-25-most-inspiring-companies/.

22. Conscious Capitalism, "An Introduction to Conscious Capitalism," http://www.con sciouscapitalism.org/node/3998/ (accessed February 2016).

23. See John Mackey & Raj Sisodia, *Conscious Capitalism: Liberating the Heroic Spirit of Business*, Harvard Business Review Press, 2013.

24. There are other perspectives; see, for example, James O'Toole & David Vogel, "Two and a Half Cheers for Conscious Capitalism," *California Management Review*, Vol. 53, No. 3, pp. 60–82.

25. John Mackey, "What Conscious Capitalism Really Is," *California Management Review*, Vol. 53, No. 3, pp. 83–85. Note: On Conscious Capitalism's website, the "Stakeholder Interdependence" principle is labeled "Stakeholder Orientation" (http://consciouscapital ism.org/learnmore/, accessed February 2016), bringing conscious capitalism even closer to strategic CSR.

26. John Mackey, "What Conscious Capitalism Really Is," *California Management Review*, Vol. 53, No. 3, p. 83.

27. Ibid., pp. 85–86.

28. Jacquelyn Smith, "America's 25 Most Inspiring Companies," *Forbes*, September 25, 2012, http://www.forbes.com/sites/jacquelyn smith/2012/09/25/americas-25-most-inspiring-companies/.

29. Susan Berfield, "Will Investors Put the Lid on the Container Store's Generous Wages?" *Bloomberg Businessweek*, February 19, 2015, http://www.bloomberg.com/news/arti cles/2015-02-19/container-store-conscious-capitalism-and-the-perils-of-going-public/.

30. Danielle Sacks, "Patagonia CEO Rose Marcario Fights the Fights Worth Fighting," *Fast Company Magazine*, February 2015, pp. 34–36. For an example advertisement in its "Don't Buy This Jacket" campaign, see http://www .patagonia.com/email/11/112811.html (accessed February 2016).

31. David Grayson & Adrian Hodges, *Corporate Social Opportunity!*, Greenleaf Publications, 2004.

32. Toby Webb, "The case for re-evaluating values," *Sustainability = Smart Business*, March 5, 2012, http://sustainablesmartbusiness .com/2012/03/case-for-re-evaluating-values/.

33. Mallen Baker, "Paying the market rate for morality?" September 18, 2012, in *Business Respect—CSR Dispatches*, No. 185, October 8, 2012, http://www.mallenbaker.net/csr/post .php?id=451 (no longer available online).

34. Michael Skapinker, "Why do business titans need to 'give back'?" *Financial Times*, November 30, 2010, p. 13.

35. Alan Murray, "Chicken Soup for a Davos Soul," *The Wall Street Journal*, January 17, 2013, p. A15.

36. Jo Confino, "Patagonia plans global campaign for responsible capitalism," *The Guardian*, February 11, 2013, http://www.theguardian .com/sustainable-business/blog/patagonia-campaign-responsible-capitalism/.

37. Seth Stevenson, "America's Most Unlikely Corporate Guru," *The WSJ Magazine*, April 26, 2012, p. 88. See also Patt Morrison, "Yvon Chouínard: Capitalist cat," *The Los Angeles Times*, March 12, 2011, http:// articles.latimes.com/2011/mar/12/opinion/ la-oe-morrison-chouinard-031111/.

38. See Zappos, "About Zappos Cultures," http:// www.zappos.com/d/about-zappos-culture/ (accessed February 2016).

39. Adam Smith published *The Wealth of Nations* in 1776, but it is his book *The Theory of Moral Sentiments* (1759) that leads many observers to describe Smith as a moral philosopher, rather than an economist. For example, see James R. Otteson, "Adam Smith: Moral Philosopher," *The Freeman Ideas on Liberty,* Vol. 50, No. 11, November 2000, http://www.thefreemanon

line.org/features/adam-smith-moral-philo sopher/; and Adam Gopnik, "Market Man," *New Yorker*, October 18, 2010, http://www .newyorker.com/magazine/2010/10/18/ market-man/.

40. David Willetts, "The invisible hand that binds us all," *Financial Times*, April 25, 2011, p. 8.

41. "The view from the top, and bottom," *The Economist*, September 24, 2011, p. 76.

42. Ibid.

43. Jeffrey Sachs, "Self-interest, without morals, leads to capitalism's self-destruction," *Financial Times*, January 18, 2012, reprinted by *The Philosophy Blog,* http://theoligarch .com/capitalism_justice.htm.

44. Dominic Barton, CEO of McKinsey & Co., in Stefan Stern, "A strategy for staying sacred," *Financial Times*, August 16, 2010, p. 10.

45. See Herb Kelleher, *The business of business is people*, 2008, http://www.youtube.com/ watch?v=oxTFA1kh1m8.

46. Johnson & Johnson, "Our Credo Values," http://www.jnj.com/about-jnj/jnj-credo/.

47. "Mackey Speaks on the Business of Conscious Capitalism," McCombs School of Business, March 28, 2011, http://www.today.mccombs .utexas.edu/2011/03/mackey-speaks-on-the- business-of-conscious-capitalism/.

48. This framework, within the overriding con- cept of strategic CSR, mirrors Mark Schwartz's three-component VBA (value, bal- ance, accountability) model, where value = net social benefit; balance = the inclusion of interests, values, and standards; and accountability = transparency to all stake- holders. Thus, "Value + Balance + Accountability = Proper Role of Business in Society." See Mark S. Schwartz, *Corporate Social Responsibility: An Ethical Approach*, Broadview Press, 2011, as reviewed by William C. Frederick, "A Conceptual Toolkit for All Seasons," October 2012, http:// williamcfrederick.com/articles%20archive/ SwartzReview.pdf.

49. "Feathers flying," *The Economist*, August 7, 2012, http://www.economist.com/blogs/ democracyinamerica/2012/08/conscien- tious-consumption-and-culture-war/.

50. James McBride, Christopher Alessi, & Mohammed Aly Sergie, "Understanding the Libor Scandal," Council on Foreign Relations,

May 21, 2015, http://www.cfr.org/united- kingdom/understanding-libor-scandal/ p28729/.

51. Margot Patrick, "Barclays Tells Staff to Uphold New Values or Leave," *The Wall Street Journal*, January 17, 2013, http:// online.wsj.com/article/SB100014241278873 23468604578247461697635932.html.

52. In "10 Conversations That Changed Our World: Starbucks Saves the Modern Organization," *Fast Company Magazine,* February 2013, p. 7. In addition to health- care and stock-based compensation, Starbucks partially pays for its employees' education ("From baristas to BA-ristas," *The Economist,* June 21, 2014, p. 63).

53. For a detailed history of Ben & Jerry's, see James E. Austin & James Quinn, "Ben & Jerry's: Preserving Mission and Brand within Unilever" [Harvard Business School case study 9-306-037], December 8, 2005.

54. Alice Marlin & John Tepper Marlin, "A Brief History of Social Reporting," *Business Respect,* March 9, 2003, http://business respect.net/print.php?Story_ID=857.

55. Ben & Jerry's, "Our Values," http://www .benjerry.com/values/ (accessed February 2016).

56. Kris Axtman & Ron Scherer, "Enron lapses and corporate ethics," *The Christian Science Monitor*, February 4, 2002, http://www .csmonitor.com/2002/0204/p01s01-ussc .html.

57. James E. Austin & James Quinn, "Ben & Jerry's: Preserving Mission and Brand within Unilever," [Harvard Business School case study 9-306-037], December 8, 2005, p. 2.

58. "Ben & Jerry's takes a licking," *Eurofood*, February 3, 2000.

59. James E. Austin & James Quinn, "Ben & Jerry's: Preserving Mission and Brand within Unilever" [Harvard Business School case study 9-306-037], December 8, 2005, p. 5.

60. "Unilever Scoops Up Ben & Jerry's," BBC News, April 12, 2000, http://news.bbc.co. uk/1/hi/business/710694.stm.

61. Brad Edmondson, "How Ben & Jerry's brought maverick ideas to mainstream busi- ness," *The Guardian*, March 18, 2014, http:// www.theguardian.com/sustainable-business/ ben-jerrys-maverick-ideas-mainstream- business-values/.

62. Today, other firms have similar total compensation ratio limits in place. An example is Whole Foods Market, which has a 19:1 ratio between its *highest* and *average* paid employees (Leslie Kwoh, "Firms Resist New Pay-Equity Rules," *The Wall Street Journal*, June 27, 2012, p. B8) and the Swiss knife company, Victorinox, which has a ratio of 5:1 between its *highest* and *average* paid employees ("How to cope with a slump in demand," *Financial Times*, December 23, 2010, p. 10). For more background on Whole Foods's decision to introduce this pay ratio, see Alison Griswold, "Here's Why Whole Foods Lets Employees Look Up Each Other's Salaries," *Business Insider*, May 3, 2014, http://www.businessinsider.com/whole-foods-employees-have-open-salaries-2014-3/.

63. Ben & Jerry's, "Our Values," http://www.benjerry.com/values/ (accessed February 2016).

64. Stephen Moore, "Ice Cream Hangover," *The Wall Street Journal*, October 20, 2005, p. A15.

65. Ibid.

66. Ben & Jerry's, *2014 Social & Environmental Assessment Report*, "Leading with Progressive Values Across Our Business," http://www.benjerry.com/about-us/sear-reports/2014-sear-report/.

67. Ibid.

68. James E. Austin & James Quinn, "Ben & Jerry's: Preserving Mission and Brand within Unilever" [Harvard Business School case study 9-306-037], December 8, 2005, p. 9.

69. Louise Lucas, "Preserve your unique flavor," *Financial Times*, February 8, 2011, p. 12.

70. David Gelles, "Gobbled Up, but Still Doing Good for the World," *The New York Times*, August 23, 2015, p. BU3.

71. See "Strategic CSR—Unilever," *Strategic Corporate Social Responsibility* [Newsletter], March 23, 2011, http://strategiccsr-sage.blogspot.com/2011/03/strategic-csr-unilever.html.

72. Venessa Wong, "Ben & Jerry's Cohen Repos Occupy Wall Street's 'Batmobile,'" *Bloomberg Businessweek*, October 2, 2012, http://www.bloomberg.com/bw/articles/2012-10-02/ben-and-jerry-repo-their-occupy-wall-street-batmobile/.

73. Louise Lucas, "Preserve your unique flavor," *Financial Times*, February 8, 2011, p. 12.

74. "Ben & Jerry's Joins the Growing B Corporation Movement" [Ben & Jerry's press release], CSRwire, October 22, 2012, http://www.csrwire.com/press_releases/34773-Ben-Jerry-s-Joins-the-Growing-B-Corporation-Movement-/.

75. Susan Berfield, "Will Investors Put the Lid on the Container Store's Generous Wages?" *Bloomberg Businessweek*, February 19, 2015, http://www.bloomberg.com/news/articles/2015-02-19/container-store-conscious-capitalism-and-the-perils-of-going-public.

76. Jo Confino, "Interview: Unilever's Paul Polman on diversity, purpose and profits," *The Guardian*, October 2, 2013, http://www.theguardian.com/sustainable-business/unilver-ceo-paul-polman-purpose-profits/.

Part V Case Study

1. A firm like Walmart, for example, currently has a total of 2.2 million employees, second in organizational size worldwide only to the Chinese People's Liberations Army, which has 2.33 million members ("Bigger for now," *The Economist*, September 19, 2015, p. 41).

2. "Does the Good Outweigh the Bad? Sizing up 'Selective' Corporate Social Responsibility," *Knowledge@Wharton* June 5, 2013, http://knowledge.wharton.upenn.edu/article/does-the-good-outweigh-the-bad-sizing-up-selective-corporate-social-responsibility/.

3. Scheherazade Daneshkhu and David Oakley, "Unilever under pressure to step up growth rate," *Financial Times*, February 10, 2015, p. 13.

4. Paul Polman, "Business, society, and the future of capitalism," McKinsey & Company, May 2014, http://www.mckinsey.com/insights/sustainability/business_society_and_the_future_of_capitalism/.

5. Rob Marsh, "9 Inspirational Quotes on Business by Herb Kelleher," LogoMaker, May 21, 2012, http://www.logomaker.com/blog/2012/05/21/9-inspirational-quotes-on-business-by-herb-kelleher/.

6. David Batstone, "Saving the Corporate Soul—and (Who Knows?) Maybe Your Own," Jossey-Bass, 2003, p. 3.

7. Peter Asmus, "100 Best Corporate Citizens of 2003," *Business Ethics Magazine,* Spring 2003, pp. 6–10.

8. "Throwing muses," *The Economist*, March 17, 2012, p. 93.

9. Bushra Tobah, "Help Employees Help You: Five Research-based Ways to Boost Engagement," Network for Business Sustainability, March 19, 2012, http://nbs.net/help-employees-help-you-five-research-based-ways-to-boost-engagement/.

10. "Decluttering the company," *The Economist*, August 2, 2014, p. 53.

11. "The enemy within," *The Economist*, July 25, 2015, p. 53.

12. "Declining Employee Loyalty: A Casualty of the New Workplace," *Knowledge@Wharton*, May 9, 2012, http://knowledge.wharton.upenn.edu/article.cfm?articleid=2995.

13. Bain Social Impact, "Community engagement," http://www.socialimpactatbain.com/pursue-your-passions/community-engagement/index.aspx (accessed February 2016).

14. Points of Light, "Pfizer," http://www.pointsoflight.org/tag/pfizer/ (accessed February 2016).

15. Wells Fargo, "Wells Fargo Volunteers," https://www.wellsfargo.com/about/csr/team/volunteerism/ (accessed February 2016).

16. Timberland, "Timberland Responsibility," http://responsibility.timberland.com/service/.

17. For a detailed history of Timberland's volunteer program, see Avery Yale Kamila, "Timberland Goes Beyond Philanthropy: Building Value for Community & Brand with Volunteers," *SustainableBusiness.com*, June 3, 2004, http://www.sustainablebusiness.com/index.cfm/go/news.feature/id/1110/.

18. Timberland was acquired by VF Corporation in 2011. Path of Service celebrated its 20th anniversary in 2012. Details of the program are reported at http://responsibility.timberland.com/service/living-our-values/.

19. City Year, "Jeffery Swartz," http://www.cityyear.org/node/6885/ (accessed February 2016).

20. Avery Yale Kamila, "Timberland Goes Beyond Philanthropy: Building Value for Community and Brand with Volunteers," *SustainableBusiness.com*, June 3, 2004, http://www.sustainablebusiness.com/index.cfm/go/news.feature/id/1110/.

21. Loretta Chao, "Theory & Practice: Sabbaticals Can Offer Dividends for Employers," *The Wall Street Journal*, July 17, 2006, p. B5.

22. Rhymer Rigby, "Time out to help less fortunate is its own reward," *Financial Times*, July 21, 2009, p. 10.

23. "Chief executives earn '183 times more than workers,'" BBC News, August 17, 2015, http://www.bbc.com/news/business-33952393/.

24. Susan Bertfield, "Fast-Food CEOs Make 1,000 Times the Pay of the Average Fast-Food Worker," *Bloomberg Businessweek*, April 22, 2014, http://www.bloomberg.com/bw/articles/2014-04-22/fast-food-ceos-make-1-000-times-the-average-fast-food-worker/.

25. Ralph Nader, "America's Miserly Minimum Wage Needs an Upgrade," *The Wall Street Journal*, April 16, 2013, p. A15.

26. Interview of Jeremy Rifkin by David Batstone, "The Future of Work," first published in *Business 2.0 Magazine,* reprinted by Right Reality Inc., February 10, 2004.

27. "Short-Circuited: Cutting Jobs as Corporate Strategy," *Knowledge@Wharton*, April 4, 2007, http://knowledge.wharton.upenn.edu/article/short-circuited-cutting-jobs-as-corporate-strategy/.

28. Interview of Jeremy Rifkin by David Batstone, "The Future of Work," first published in *Business 2.0 Magazine,* reprinted by Right Reality Inc., February 10, 2004.

29. Quoted from David Batstone & David Chandler, "Ford's Success Formula Not Followed to a T," *Atlanta Journal-Constitution,* December 17, 2004. See also Lee Iacocca, "Driving Force: Henry Ford," *Time,* December 7, 1998, http://content.time.com/time/magazine/article/0,9171,989769,00.html.

30. "Work to rule," *The Economist*, September 5, 2015, p. 66.

31. See also "The workforce in the cloud," *The Economist*, June 1, 2013, p. 63; "There's an app for that," *The Economist*, January 3, 2015, pp. 9, 17–20; and "McJobs and UberJobs," *The Economist*, July 4, 2015, p. 58.

32. This issue is related to the level of union membership, which in the United States is around 11% of the total workforce, including 36% in the public sector and 7% in the private sector ("Who's the boss?" *The Economist*,

August 22, 2015, p. 27). In Europe, union membership is significantly higher, ranging from 8% in France, to 26% in the UK, to as high as 70% in the Scandinavian countries ("Our turn to eat," *The Economist*, September 5, 2015, p. 58; and Worker-participation.eu, "Trade Unions: Union Density," http://www .worker-participation.eu/National-Industrial-Relations/Across-Europe/Trade-Unions2/, accessed February 2016).

33. This is a complex legal issue that is currently working its way through the courts. The rulings will have dramatic consequences, both for the new-gig companies but also for more established companies, such as McDonald's and FedEx, that have traditionally treated the many people who work in their franchised outlets or drive their trucks as *contractors*. Being forced to treat them as *employees* will revolutionize these firms' fundamental business model.

34. "Coming to an office near you," *The Economist*, January 18, 2014, p. 9.

35. Tim Hartford, "The robots are coming and will terminate your jobs," *Financial Times*, December 28/29, 2013, p. 7.

36. Walter Isaacson, "Luddites fear humanity will make short work of finite wants," *Financial Times*, March 4, 2015, p. 7.

37. "Automation angst," *The Economist*, August 15, 2015, p. 68.

38. Michele McPhee, K. C. Baker, and Corky Siemaszko, "Deep Blue, IBM's supercomputer, defeats chess champion Garry Kasparov in 1997," *New York Daily News*, May 10, 2015, http://www.nydailynews .com/news/world/kasparov-deep-blues-losingchess-champ-rooke-article-1.762264/.

39. See "Elementary," *The Economist*, October 3, 2015, pp. 81–82.

40. Richard Galanti, Costco's CFO (quoted in Ann Zimmerman, "Costco's Dilemma: Be Kind to Its Workers, or Wall Street?" *The Wall Street Journal,* March 26, 2004, p. B1.

41. See Starbucks, "Bean Stock," http://star bucksbeanstock.com/.

42. Although owned by its consumers rather than its employees, the outdoor clothing retailer REI "is now the nation's largest consumer co-op, continuing to return the majority of profits to our members through annual member refunds based on their purchases" ("REI Celebrates 75 Years" [REI press release], January 16, 2013, http:// newsroom.chainstoreguide.com/2013/01/ rei-celebrates-75-years/.

43. "George Washington signed a law in 1792 giving shipowners 'allowances' (i.e., subsidies) to offset the tariffs they had to pay on their inputs. Two conditions were attached to the support: Shipowners had to sign a profit-sharing agreement with their crew, with whom they also had to split the allowance. Thus one of America's first tax breaks was designed to encourage owners to share profits with their workers" (in "Turning workers into capitalists," *The Economist,* November 23, 2013, p. 75).

44. Samantha Sharf, "Why Starbucks Pays Its Baristas with Stock: A Beginners' Guide to Company Stock," *Forbes,* March 18, 2015, http://www.forbes.com/sites/samantha sharf/2015/03/18/why-starbucks-pays-its-baristas-with-stock-a-beginners-guide-to-company-stock/.

45. Nanette Byrnes et al., "Beyond Options," *BusinessWeek,* July 28, 2003, pp. 36–37.

46. For a complete history of the firm, see http://www.johnlewispartnership.co.uk/ about/our-founder.html.

47. Geoffrey Owen, "When the workers take over," *Financial Times*, April 28, 2011, p. 10.

48. Marjorie Kelly, "Can There Be 'Good' Corporations?" *Yes! Magazine*, April 16, 2012, http://www.yesmagazine.org/issues/ 9-strategies-to-end-corporate-rule/can-there-be-201cgood201d-corporations/.

49. Ibid.

50. Andrew Hill, "A rather civil partnership," *Financial Times*, January 20, 2012, http:// www.ft.com/intl/cms/s/0/30ca497e-438a-11e1-9f28-00144feab49a.html.

51. Marjorie Kelly, "Can There Be 'Good' Corporations?" *Yes! Magazine*, April 16, 2012, http://www.yesmagazine.org/issues/ 9-strategies-to-end-corporate-rule/can-there-be-201cgood201d-corporations/.

52. For example, "Enterprises like Spain's Mondragon Co-operative Group, the UK's Co-op Group and John Lewis, with revenues of £14bn, £12bn and £11bn respectively, have been shown to be more efficient than most private companies" (in Jules Peck, "The future of business: What are the

alternatives to capitalism?" *The Guardian*, April 29, 2013, http://www.theguardian .com/sustainable-business/future-business-alternatives-capitalism/).

53. Michael Skapinker, "Staff ownership can save a company's soul," *Financial Times*, February 9, 2010, p. 13.

54. *Fortune*, "100 Best Companies to Work For 2006," http://money.cnn.com/magazines/ fortune/bestcompanies/.

55. Stefan Stern, "Authoritarian boss belongs in the past," *Financial Times*, September 13, 2007, p. 12.

56. Andrew Hill, "A rather civil partnership," *Financial Times*, January 20, 2012, http:// www.ft.com/intl/cms/s/0/30ca497e-438a-11e1-9f28-00144feab49a.html.

57. "The feeling is mutual," *The Economist*, January 21, 2012, p. 62.

58. "When workers are owners," *The Economist*, August 22, 2015, p. 56.

59. "The feeling is mutual," *The Economist*, January 21, 2012, p. 62.

60. Ibid.

61. For detailed case studies of the processes by which two firms (Tullis Russell, a papermaking firm in Fife, Scotland, and Trace, a business software company in London) became employee owned, see Geoffrey Owen, "When the workers take over," *Financial Times*, April 28, 2011, p. 10; and Richard Tomkins, "Sold to the lowest bidder," *Financial Times: Life & Arts*, December 8/9, 2007, p. 1. For a comprehensive comparison of employee-owned organizations across different countries and cultures, see Henry Hansmann, *The Ownership of Enterprise*, Harvard University Press, 2000.

62. Geoffrey Owen, "When the workers take over," *Financial Times*, April 28, 2011, p. 10.

63. Ibid.

64. Gary Hamel, "The Big Idea: First, Let's Fire All the Managers," *Harvard Business Review*, December 2011, pp. 4–13. See also "Going Boss-free: Utopia or 'Lord of the Flies'?" *Knowledge@Wharton*, August 1, 2012, http:// knowledge.wharton.upenn.edu/article .cfm?articleid=3059.

65. Alfred D. Chandler Jr., *The Visible Hand: The Managerial Revolution in American Business*, Harvard University Press, 1977.

66. Gary Hamel, "The Big Idea: First, Let's Fire All the Managers," *Harvard Business Review*, December 2011, pp. 4–13.

67. Rachel Emma Silverman, "Who's the Boss? There Isn't One," *The Wall Street Journal*, June 20, 2012, p. B1.

68. Ibid.

69. For example, see this case study about Zappos: Winter Nie & Beverley Lennox, "Creating a distinct corporate culture: How to embed a sense of passion," *Financial Times*, February 17, 2011, p. 10.

70. This quote has been updated using more current information from Zappos' website (http://about.zappos.com/it-true-zappos-offers-new-hires-2000-quit/). The original quote was from Dan Mitchell, "Shoe Seller's Secret of Success," *The New York Times*, May 24, 2008, p. B5.

71. Noted by Zappos CEO and founder Tony Hseih in an interview with *The New York Times*, "Welcome to My Rain Forest," December 29, 2013, p. BU3.

72. Adam Auriemma, "Zappos Zaps Job Postings, Seeks Hires on Social Media," *The Wall Street Journal*, May 27, 2014, p. B5.

73. For additional detail on how holacracy is implemented in practice, see Rebecca Greenfield, "How Zappos Converts New Hires to Its Bizarre Office Culture," *Bloomberg Businessweek*, June 30, 2015, http://www.bloomberg.com/news/articles/2015-06-30/how-zappos-converts-new-hires-to-its-bizarre-office-culture.

74. Noted by Zappos CEO and founder Tony Hseih in an interview with *The Wall Street Journal*, "The No-Boss Company," *The Wall Street Journal*, October 27, 2015, p. R3. See also Justin Fox, "Running a Company Without Bosses," *Bloomberg Businessweek*, June 24, 2015, http://www.bloombergview.com/ articles/2015-06-24/q-a-with-a-manager-who-wants-to-get-rid-of-managers/.

75. Rachel Emma Silverman, "At Zappos, Banishing the Bosses Brings Confusion," *The Wall Street Journal*, May 20, 2015, http:// www.wsj.com/articles/at-zappos-banishing-the-bosses-brings-confusion-1432175402/.

76. Jennifer Reingold, "How a Radical Shift Left Zappos Reeling," *Fortune*, March 2016, http:// fortune.com/zappos-tony-hsieh-holacracy/.

77. Ibid.

78. Ibid.

79. Rachel Emma Silverman, "Who's the Boss? There Isn't One," *The Wall Street Journal*, June 20, 2012, p. B1.

80. Peter Marsh & Stefan Stern, "The chaos theory of leadership," *Financial Times*, December 2, 2008, http://www.ft.com/intl/cms/s/0/4f20ec38-c012-11dd-9222-0000779fd18c.html.

81. Rachel Emma Silverman, "Who's the Boss? There Isn't One," *The Wall Street Journal*, June 20, 2012, p. B1.

82. Peter Marsh & Stefan Stern, "The chaos theory of leadership," *Financial Times*, December 2, 2008, http://www.ft.com/intl/cms/s/0/4f20ec38-c012-11dd-9222-0000779fd18c.html.

83. Ibid.

84. Karl Moore & Richard Pound, "Volunteering—A Great Way to Learn Real Executive Leadership," *Forbes*, December 21, 2011, http://www.forbes.com/sites/karlmoore/2011/12/21/volunteering-a-great-way-to-learn-real-executive-leadership/.

85. For a detailed discussion of "What does it mean to be *fairly* compensated?" see "Balancing the Pay Scale: 'Fair' vs. 'Unfair,'" *Knowledge@Wharton*, May 22, 2013, http://knowledge.wharton.upenn.edu/article/balancing-the-pay-scale-fair-vs-unfair/.

Company Index

Subject Index

ABOUT THE AUTHOR

David Chandler (david.chandler@ucdenver.edu) is Assistant Professor of Management and Co-Director of the Managing for Sustainability Program at the University of Colorado Denver Business School. His research focuses on the dynamic interface between the organization and its institutional environment, which he operationalizes within the context of corporate social responsibility, business ethics, and firm/stakeholder relations. His research has been published in *Organization Science*, *Academy of Management Review*, *Journal of Management*, and *Strategic Organization*. Additional related publications include the book *Corporate Social Responsibility: A Strategic Perspective* (Business Expert Press, 2014). He received his PhD in Management from The University of Texas at Austin.